T0180819

Communications in Computer and Information Science   1798

Rationale

The CCIS series is devoted to the publication of proceedings of computer science conferences. Its aim is to efficiently disseminate original research results in informatics in printed and electronic form. While the focus is on publication of peer-reviewed full papers presenting mature work, inclusion of reviewed short papers reporting on work in progress is welcome, too. Besides globally relevant meetings with internationally representative program committees guaranteeing a strict peer-reviewing and paper selection process, conferences run by societies or of high regional or national relevance are also considered for publication.

Topics

The topical scope of CCIS spans the entire spectrum of informatics ranging from foundational topics in the theory of computing to information and communications science and technology and a broad variety of interdisciplinary application fields.

Information for Volume Editors and Authors

Publication in CCIS is free of charge. No royalties are paid, however, we offer registered conference participants temporary free access to the online version of the conference proceedings on SpringerLink (http://link.springer.com) by means of an http referrer from the conference website and/or a number of complimentary printed copies, as specified in the official acceptance email of the event.

CCIS proceedings can be published in time for distribution at conferences or as post-proceedings, and delivered in the form of printed books and/or electronically as USBs and/or e-content licenses for accessing proceedings at SpringerLink. Furthermore, CCIS proceedings are included in the CCIS electronic book series hosted in the SpringerLink digital library at http://link.springer.com/bookseries/7899. Conferences publishing in CCIS are allowed to use Online Conference Service (OCS) for managing the whole proceedings lifecycle (from submission and reviewing to preparing for publication) free of charge.

Publication process

The language of publication is exclusively English. Authors publishing in CCIS have to sign the Springer CCIS copyright transfer form, however, they are free to use their material published in CCIS for substantially changed, more elaborate subsequent publications elsewhere. For the preparation of the camera-ready papers/files, authors have to strictly adhere to the Springer CCIS Authors' Instructions and are strongly encouraged to use the CCIS LaTeX style files or templates.

Abstracting/Indexing

CCIS is abstracted/indexed in DBLP, Google Scholar, EI-Compendex, Mathematical Reviews, SCImago, Scopus. CCIS volumes are also submitted for the inclusion in ISI Proceedings.

How to start

To start the evaluation of your proposal for inclusion in the CCIS series, please send an e-mail to ccis@springer.com.

Isaac Woungang · Sanjay Kumar Dhurandher ·
Kiran Kumar Pattanaik · Anshul Verma ·
Pradeepika Verma
Editors

Advanced Network Technologies and Intelligent Computing

Second International Conference, ANTIC 2022
Varanasi, India, December 22–24, 2022
Proceedings, Part II

Springer

Editors
Isaac Woungang
Ryerson University
Toronto, ON, Canada

Sanjay Kumar Dhurandher
Netaji Subhas University of Technology
New Delhi, India

Kiran Kumar Pattanaik
ABV-Indian Institute of Information
Technology and Management
Gwalior, India

Anshul Verma
Banaras Hindu University
Varanasi, India

Pradeepika Verma
Indian Institute of Technology
Patna, India

ISSN 1865-0929   ISSN 1865-0937 (electronic)
Communications in Computer and Information Science
ISBN 978-3-031-28182-2   ISBN 978-3-031-28183-9 (eBook)
https://doi.org/10.1007/978-3-031-28183-9

This Springer imprint is published by the registered company Springer Nature Switzerland AG
The registered company address is: Gewerbestrasse 11, 6330 Cham, Switzerland

Preface

The 2nd International Conference on Advanced Network Technologies and Intelligent Computing (ANTIC-2022) was organized by Department of Computer Science, Institute of Science, Banaras Hindu University, Varanasi, India in hybrid mode from 22nd to 24th December 2022. ANTIC-2022 aimed to bring together leading academicians, scientists, research scholars, and UG/PG students across the globe to exchange and share their research outcomes. It provided a state-of-the-art platform to discuss all aspects (current and future) of Advanced Network Technologies and Intelligent Computing. This enabled the participating researchers to exchange ideas about applying existing methods in these areas to solve real-world problems.

ANTIC-2022 solicited two types of submissions: full research papers (equal to or more than 12 pages) and short research papers (between 8 and 11 pages). These papers identify and justify a principled advance to the theoretical and practical foundations for the construction and analysis of systems, where applicable supported by experimental validation. A total 443 research papers were received through the EquinOCS portal of Springer and 79 papers (17.83%) were accepted after the rigorous review process. Out of 79 accepted papers, 68 papers (86.07%) are full papers and 11 papers (13.92%) are short papers. All 79 accepted papers have been selected for publication in the Communications in Computer and Information Science (CCIS) series of Springer. These are grouped into two thematic categories: Advanced Network Technologies and Intelligent Computing.

We would like to thank everyone who helped to make ANTIC-2022 successful. In particular, we would like to thank the authors for submitting their papers to ANTIC-2022. We are thankful to our excellent team of reviewers from all over the globe who deserve full credit for the hard work put in to review the high-quality submissions with rich technical content. We would also like to thank the members of the Advisory Committee and the Program Committee for their guidance and suggestions in making ANTIC-2022 a success. We would also like to thank all the Track Chairs, Organizing Committee and Technical Program Committee members for their support and co-operation.

December 2022

Isaac Woungang
Sanjay Kumar Dhurandher
Kiran Kumar Pattanaik
Anshul Verma
Pradeepika Verma

Organization

Chief Patron

Sudhir K. Jain (Vice-chancellor)   Banaras Hindu University, India

Patron

V. K. Shukla (Rector)   Banaras Hindu University, India

Co-patrons

A. K. Tripathi (Director)   Institute of Science, Banaras Hindu University, India

Madhoolika Agrawal (Dean)   Institute of Science, Banaras Hindu University, India

Advisory Board

Anil Kumar Tripathi   Indian Institute of Technology (BHU), Varanasi, India

Jagannathan Sarangpani   Missouri University of Science and Technology, USA

Jawar Singh   Indian Institute of Technology, Patna, India

Manish Gaur   Institute of Engineering & Technology, Lucknow, India

Pradip Kr. Das   Indian Institute of Technology, Guwahati, India

Rajeev Srivastava   Indian Institute of Technology (BHU), Varanasi, India

Rajkumar Buyya   University of Melbourne, Australia

Sanjay Kumar Madria   Missouri University of Science & Technology, USA

Sundaraja Sitharama Iyengar   Florida International University, USA

General Chairs

Isaac Woungang	Toronto Metropolitan University, Canada
Sanjay Kumar Dhurandher	Netaji Subhas University of Technology, India
K. K. Pattanaik	ABV-Indian Institute of Information Technology and Management, Gwalior, India

Conference Chair

Vivek Kumar Singh	Banaras Hindu University, India

Program Chairs

S. Karthikeyan	Banaras Hindu University, India
Pramod Kumar Mishra	Banaras Hindu University, India
Anshul Verma	Banaras Hindu University, India

Convener

Anshul Verma	Banaras Hindu University, India

Organizing Secretaries

Gaurav Baranwal	Banaras Hindu University, India
Ankita Vaish	Banaras Hindu University, India
S. Suresh	Banaras Hindu University, India
Pradeepika Verma	Indian Institute of Technology Patna, India

Track Chairs

Himanshu	Punjabi University, Patiala, India
Karm Veer Arya	ABV-Indian Institute of Information Technology and Management, Gwalior, India
P. K. Singh	ABV-Indian Institute of Information Technology and Management, Gwalior, India
Rajiv Ranjan Tewari (Retd.)	University of Allahabad, India
Sanjay Kumar	Pt. Ravishankar Shukla University, Raipur, India

Udai Shanker	Madan Mohan Malaviya University of Technology, Gorakhpur, India
Alireza Izaddoost	California State University, Dominguez Hills, USA
Binod Kumar Singh	National Institute of Technology, Jamshedpur, India
Divakar Singh Yadav	National Institute of Technology, Hamirpur, India
Huy Trung Nguyễn	People's Security Academy, Vietnam Ministry of Public Security, Vietnam
Joshua D. Reichard	Omega Graduate School, American Centre for Religion/Society Studies, USA
Lalit Garg	University of Malta, Malta
Pradeepika Verma	Indian Institute of Technology Patna, India
Shensheng Tang	St. Cloud State University, USA
Yousef Farhaoui	Moulay Ismail University, Morocco
Jatinderkumar R. Saini	Symbiosis Institute of Computer Studies and Research, India
Priyanka Sharma	Rashtriya Raksha University, India

Organizing Committee

Achintya Singhal	Banaras Hindu University, India
Manoj Kumar Singh	Banaras Hindu University, India
Rakhi Garg	Banaras Hindu University, India
Manjari Gupta	Banaras Hindu University, India
Vandana Kushwaha	Banaras Hindu University, India
Awadhesh Kumar	Banaras Hindu University, India
Manoj Mishra	Banaras Hindu University, India
S. N. Chaurasia	Banaras Hindu University, India
Sarvesh Pandey	Banaras Hindu University, India
Vibhor Kant	Banaras Hindu University, India
Jyoti Singh Kirar	Banaras Hindu University, India

Publication Committee

Sanjeev Sharma	Indian Institute of Information Technology, Pune, India
Vibhav Prakash Singh	Motilal Nehru National Institute of Technology, Allahabad, India
Dharmendra Prasad Mahato	National Institute of Technology, Hamirpur, India

Vijay Bhaskar Semwal   Maulana Azad National Institute of Technology,
                                  Bhopal, India
Bhawana Rudra   National Institute of Technology, Karnataka, India

Publicity Committee

Prashant Singh Rana   Thapar Institute of Engineering & Technology,
                                  India
Harish Sharma   Rajasthan Technical University, India
Puneet Misra   University of Lucknow, India
Sachi Nandan Mohanty   College of Engineering, Pune, India
Koushlendra Kumar Singh   National Institute of Technology, Jamshedpur,
                                  India

Finance Committee

Praveen Kumar Singh   Banaras Hindu University, India
Kishna Murari   Banaras Hindu University, India
Sunil Kumar   Banaras Hindu University, India
Shashi Shukla   Banaras Hindu University, India
Santosh Kumar   Banaras Hindu University, India
Saurabh Srivastava   Banaras Hindu University, India

Technical Program Committee

A. Senthil Thilak   National Institute of Technology, Surathkal, India
Abdus Samad   Aligarh Muslim University, India
Abhay Kumar Rai   Banasthali Vidyapith, India
Abhilasha Sharma   Delhi Technological University, India
Ade Romadhony   Telkom University, Indonesia
Afifa Ghenai   Constantine 2 University, Algeria
Ajay   Shree Guru Gobind Singh Tricentenary
                                  University, India
Ajay Kumar   Chandigarh University, India
Ajay Kumar   Central University of Himanchal Pradesh, India
Ajay Kumar Gupta   Madan Mohan Malaviya University of
                                  Technology, Gorakhpur, India
Ajay Kumar Yadav   Banasthali Vidyapith, India

Ajay Pratap	Indian Institute of Technology (BHU), Varanasi, India
Akande Noah Oluwatobi	Landmark University, Nigeria
Akash Kumar Bhoi	KIET Group of Institutions & Sikkim Manipal University, India
Alberto Rossi	University of Florence, Italy
Aleena Swetapadma	Kalinga Institute of Industrial Technology, India
Ali El Alami	Moulay Ismail University, Morocco
Amit Kumar	BMS Institute of Technology and Management, India
Amit Kumar	Jaypee University of Engineering and Technology, Guna, India
Amit Rathee	Government College Barota, India
Angel D.	Sathyabama Institute of Science and Technology, India
Anil Kumar	London Metropolitan University, UK
Anirban Sengupta	Jadavpur University, India
Anita Chaware	SNDT Women's University, India
Anjali Shrikant Yeole	VES Institute of Technology, Mumbai, India
Anjula Mehto	Thapar Institute of Engineering and Technology, India
Ankur Jain	IGDTUW, India
Ansuman Mahapatra	National Institute of Technology, Puducherry, India
Antriksh Goswami	Indian Institute of Information Technology, Vadodara, India
Anupam Biswas	National Institute of Technology, Silchar, India
Anuradha Yarlagadda	Gayatri Vidhya Parishad College of Engineering, India
Anurag Sewak	Rajkiya Engineering College, Sonbhadra, India
Arun Kumar	ABV-Indian Institute of Information Technology and Management, Gwalior, India
Arun Pandian J.	Vel Tech Rangarajan Dr. Sagunthala R&D Institute of Science and Technology, India
Ashish Kumar Mishra	Rajkiya Engineering College, Ambedkar Nagar, India
Ashutosh Kumar Singh	United College of Engineering and Research, India
Aymen Jaber Salman	Al-Nahrain University, Iraq
B. Surendiran	National Institute of Technology, Puducherry, India
B. Arthi	SRM Institute of Science and Technology, India
B. S. Charulatha	Rajalakshmi Engineering College, India

Balbir Singh Awana	Vanderbilt University, USA
Baranidharan B.	SRM Institute of Science and Technology, India
Benyamin Ahmadnia	Harvard University, USA
Bharat Garg	Thapar Institute of Engineering & Technology, India
Bharti	University of Delhi, India
Bhaskar Mondal	National Institute of Technology, Patna, India
Binod Prasad	ABV-Indian Institute of Information Technology and Management, Gwalior, India
Boddepalli Santhi Bhushan	Indian Institute of Information Technology, Allahabad, India
Brijendra Singh	VIT Vellore, India
Chanda Thapliyal Nautiyal	DU Govt. Degree College, Narendra Nagar, India
Chandrashekhar Azad	National Institute of Technology, Jamshedpur, India
Chetan Vyas	United University, Prayagraj, India
Chittaranjan Pradhan	Kalinga Institute of Industrial Technology, India
D. Senthilkumar	Anna University, India
Dahmouni Abdellatif	Chouaib Doukkali University, Faculty of Sciences of El Jadida, Morocco
Darpan Anand	Chandigarh University, India
Deepak Kumar	Banasthali Vidyapith, India
Dharmveer Kumar Yadav	Katihar Engineering College, India
Dhirendra Kumar	Delhi Technological University, India
Dinesh Kumar	Motilal Nehru National Institute of Technology Allahabad, India
Divya Saxena	The Hong Kong Polytechnic University, China
Ezil Sam Leni A.	KCG College of Technology, India
Gargi Srivastava	Rajiv Gandhi Institute of Petroleum Technology, India
Gaurav Gupta	Shoolini University, India
Gyanendra K. Verma	National Institute of Technology, Kurukshetra, India
Hardeo Kumar Thakur	Manav Rachna University, India
Hasmat Malik	Netaji Subhas University of Technology, India
Inder Chaudhary	Delhi Technological University, India
Itu Snigdh	Birla Institute of Technology, Mesra, India
J. K. Rai	Defence Research and Development Organisation, India
J. Jerald Inico	Loyola College, India
Jagadeeswara Rao Annam	Gudlavalleru Engineering College, India
Jagannath Singh	Kalinga Institute of Industrial Technology, India

Jagdeep Singh	Sant Longowal Institute of Engineering and Technology, India
Jainath Yadav	Central University of South Bihar, India
Jay Prakash	National Institute of Technology, Calicut, India
Jaya Gera	Shyama Prasad Mukherji College for Women, India
Jeevaraj S.	ABV- Indian Institute of Information Technology & Management, Gwalior, India
Jolly Parikh	Bharati Vidyapeeth's College of Engineering, New Delhi, India
Jyoti Singh	Banaras Hindu University, India
K. T. V. Reddy	Pravara Rural Education Society, India
Kanu Goel	Amity University, Punjab, India
Koushlendra Kumar Singh	National Institute of Technology, Jamshedpur, India
Kunwar Pal	National Institute of Technology, Jalandhar, India
Lakshmi Priya G.	VIT University, India
Lalatendu Behera	National Institute of Technology, Jalandhar, India
Lokesh Chauhan	National Institute of Technology, Hamirpur, India
M. Joseph	Michael Research Foundation, Thanjavur, India
M. Nazma B. J. Naskar	Kalinga Institute of Industrial Technology, India
M. Deva Priya	Sri Krishna College of Technology, India
Mahendra Shukla	The LNM Institute of Information Technology, India
Mainejar Yadav	Rajkiya Engineering College, Sonbhadra, India
Manish Gupta	Amity University, Gwalior, India
Manish K. Pandey	Birla Institute of Technology, Mesra, India
Manish Kumar	M S Ramaiah Institute of Technology, India
Manpreet Kaur	Manav Rachna University, India
Mariya Ouaissa	Moulay Ismail University, Morocco
Mariyam Ouaissa	Moulay Ismail University, Morocco
Meriem Houmer	Ibn Zohr University, Morocco
Minakhi Rout	Kalinga Institute of Industrial Technology, India
Mohd Yaseen Mir	National Central University, Taiwan
Mohit Kumar	National Institute of Technology, Jalandhar, India
Monica Chauhan Bhadoriya	Madhav Institute of Technology & Science, India
Muhammad Abulaish	South Asian University, India
Mukesh Mishra	Indian Institute of Information Technology, Dharwad, India
Mukesh Rawat	Meerut Institute of Engineering and Technology, India
Mukta Sharma	Michigan State University, USA

Nagarajan G.	Sathyabama Institute of Science and Technology, India
Nagendra Pratap Singh	National Institute of Technology, Hamirpur, India
Nandakishor Yadav	Fraunhofer Institute for Photonic Microsystems, Germany
Narendran Rajagopalan	National Institute of Technology, Puducherry, India
Neetesh Kumar	IIT Roorkee, India
Nisha Chaurasia	National Institute of Technology, Jalandhar, India
Nisheeth Joshi	Banasthali Vidyapith, India
Nitesh K. Bharadwaj	OP Jindal University, India
Om Jee Pandey	SRM University, Andhra Pradesh, India
P. Manikandaprabhu	Sri Ramakrishna College of Arts and Science, India
Partha Pratim Sarangi	KIIT Deemed to be University, India
Pavithra G.	Dayananda Sagar College of Engg., India
Pinar Kirci	Bursa Uludag University, Turkey
Piyush Kumar Singh	Central University of South Bihar, Gaya, India
Pooja	University of Allahabad, India
Prabhat Ranjan	Central University of South Bihar, Gaya, India
Pradeeba Sridar	Sydney Medical School, Australia
Pradeep Kumar	University of KwaZulu-Natal, South Africa
Prakash Kumar Singh	Rajkiya Engineering College, Mainpuri, India
Prakash Srivastava	KIET Group of Institutions, India
Prasenjit Chanak	Indian Institute of Technology (BHU), Varanasi, India
Prateek Agrawal	Lovely Professional University, India
Praveen Pawar	Indian Institute of Information Technology, Bhopal, India
Preeth R.	Indian Institute of Information Technology, Design and Manufacturing, Kurnool, India
Preeti Sharma	Chitkara University Institute of Engineering and Technology, Punjab, India
Priya Gupta	ABVSME, Jawaharlal Nehru University, India
Priyanka Verma	University of Galway, Ireland
Pushpalatha S. Nikkam	SDM College of Engineering and Technology, Dharwad, India
R. Rathi	VIT, India
Raenu Kolandaisamy	UCSI University, Malaysia
Rahul Kumar Verma	Indian Institute of Information Technology, Lucknow, India
Rahul Kumar Vijay	Banasthali Vidyapith, India

Ramesh Chand Pandey	Rajkiya Engineering College, Ambedkar Nagar, India
Rashmi Chaudhry	Netaji Subhas University of Technology, India
Rashmi Gupta	Atal Bihari Vajpayee University, India
Ravilla Dilli	Manipal Institute of Technology, India
Revathy G.	Sastra University, India
Richa Mishra	University of Allahabad, India
Rohit Kumar Tiwari	Madan Mohan Malaviya University of Technology, Gorakhpur, India
Rohit Singh	International Management Institute, Kolkata, India
S. Gandhiya Vendhan	Bharathiar University, India
Sadhana Mishra	ITM University, India
Sanjeev Patel	NIT Rourkela, India
Santosh Kumar Satapathy	Pandit Deendayal Energy University, India
Saumya Bhadauria	ABV-Indian Institute of Information Technology and Management, Gwalior, India
Saurabh Bilgaiyan	Kalinga Institute of Industrial Technology, India
Saurabh Kumar	The LNM Institute of Information Technology, India
Seera Dileep Raju	Dr. Reddy's Laboratories, India
Shailesh Kumar	Jaypee Institute of Information Technology, Noida, India
Shantanu Agnihotri	Bennett University, India
Shiv Prakash	University of Allahabad, India
Shivam Sakshi	Indian Institute of Management, Bangalore, India
Shivani Sharma	Thapar Institute of Engineering & Technology, India
Shubhra Jain	Thapar Institute of Engineering & Technology, India
Shyam Singh Rajput	National Institute of Technology, Patna, India
Siva Shankar Ramasamy	International College of Digital Innovation - Chiang Mai University, Thailand
Sonali Gupta	J.C. Bose University of Science and Technology, YMCA, India
Sonu Lamba	Thapar Institute of Engineering & Technology, India
Sri Vallabha Deevi	Tiger Analytics, India
Srinidhi N. N.	Sri Krishna Institute of Technology, India
Sudhakar Singh	University of Allahabad, India
Sudhanshu Kumar Jha	University of Allahabad, India
Suneel Yadav	Indian Institute of Information Technology, Allahabad, India

Sunil	Jamia Millia Islamia, New Delhi, India
Sunil Kumar Chawla	Chandigarh University, India
Suparna Biswas	Maulana Abul Kalam Azad University of Technology, India
Suresh Raikwar	Thapar Institute of Engineering & Technology, India
Sushopti Gawade	Pillai College of Engineering, India
Syed Mutahar Aaqib	Government Degree College, Baramulla, India
U. Anitha	Sathyabama Institute of Science and Technology, India
V. D. Ambeth Kumar	Panimalar Engineering College, Anna University, India
Venkanna U.	National Institute of Technology, Trichy, India
Vijay Kumar Dwivedi	United College of Engineering and Research, India
Vikas Mohar	Madhav Institute of Technology & Science, India
Vinay Kumar Jain	SSTC-SSGI, India
Vinay Singh	ABV-Indian Institute of Information Technology and Management, Gwalior, India
Vinita Jindal	Keshav Mahavidyalaya, University of Delhi, India
Vinod Kumar	University of Allahabad, India
Vishal Pradhan	KIIT University, India
Vishal Shrivastava	Arya College of Engineering and IT, India
Vivek Kumar	PSIT Kanpur, India
Yadunath Pathak	Visvesvaraya National Institute of Technology, Nagpur, India
Yogish H. K.	M. S. Ramaiah Institute of Technology, India
Vijay Kumar Sharma	Shri Mata Vaishno Devi University, India
Muhammad Sajjadur Rahim	University of Rajshahi, Bangladesh
Anjana Jain	Shri G. S. Institute of Tech. and Sc., India
K. Ramachandra Rao	Shri Vishnu Engineering College for Women, India
Mamta Dahiya	SGT University, India
Satyadhyan Chickerur	KLE Technological University, India

Contents – Part II

Contents – Part I

Intelligent Computing

ADASEML: Hospitalization Period Prediction of COVID-19 Patients Using ADASYN and Stacking Based Ensemble Learning

Ferdib-Al-Islam[1]([⊠]) [iD], Rayhan Robbani[1], Md Magfur Alam[2],
Mostofa Shariar Sanim[1], and Khan Mehedi Hasan[1]

[1] Northern University of Business and Technology, Khulna, Bangladesh
ferdib.bsmrstu@gmail.com
[2] Tiller, Bangladesh

Abstract. The COVID-19 pandemic places additional constraints on hospitals and medical services. Understanding the period for support requirements for COVID-19 infected admitted to hospitals is critical for resource distribution planning in hospitals, particularly in resource-reserved settings. Machine Learning techniques are being used to approximate a patient's duration of stay in the hospital. This research uses Decision Tree, Random Forest and K-Nearest Neighbors, Voting classifiers, and Stacking classifiers to predict patients' length of stay in the hospital. Due to the imbalance in the dataset, Adaptive Synthetic (ADASYN) was used to resolve the issue, and the permutation feature importance method was employed to find the feature importance scores in identifying important features during the models' development process. The proposed "ADASEML" has shown superior performance to the earlier works, with an accuracy of 80%, precision of 78%, and recall of 80%.

Keywords: COVID-19 · Length of stay · Imbalanced dataset · ADASYN · Voting classifier · Stacking classifier

1 Introduction

COVID-19 is still doing havoc, even though immunizations established globally in recent years do not guarantee 100% protection against infection. COVID-19 is caused by the virus, which mutates over time. Numerous changes affect how the virus should be detected [1]. As of February 2022, there have been 350 million verified COVID-19 cases globally, with over 6 million reported fatalities [2]. Meanwhile, governments are attempting to resolve the matter. As a result of the massive outburst of COVID-19 infection, health care centres have been turned into "COVID-19-only" treatment facilities, ignoring the bulk of regular patients. The scarcity of healthcare facilities is a crucial element in COVID-19 recovery instances. Daily news reports on COVID-19 difficulties are so serious that even industrialized governments are unable to prevent the virus from spreading, much alone in undeveloped and underprivileged countries [3].

© The Author(s), under exclusive license to Springer Nature Switzerland AG 2023
I. Woungang et al. (Eds.): ANTIC 2022, CCIS 1798, pp. 3–15, 2023.
https://doi.org/10.1007/978-3-031-28183-9_1

Globally, the COVID-19 outbreak has engaged healthcare organisms under unprecedented strain, with the demand for treatment in hospitals and critical care units quickly increasing (ICUs). As the epidemic spreads, estimating the accompanying healthcare commodities needs (beds, employees, and apparatus) has become a precedence for a number of countries [3]. Forecasting upcoming demand entails estimating the length of stay necessary for patients at different treatment levels. While there are several ML approaches in healthcare administration, the patient hospitalization period is a critical measure to screen and predict to enhance hospital administration effectiveness [4, 5]. The challenge is how to operate hospitals in the most professional and efficient manner possible. This trait supports hospitals in recognizing persons at increased risk of an extended stay at the time of admission [4]. Once identified, patients at increased risk may change their treatment regimens to shorten their hospital stay and minimize infection risk from staff/visitors. Furthermore, prior knowledge of the duration of the stay may aid with practical considerations such as empty spaces and bed allocation.

In this work, stacking-based ensemble learning using ML classifiers – Decision Tree (DT), Random Forest (RF), and K-Nearest Neighbors (KNN) was utilized to estimate the hospitalization period of COVID-19 infected for comforting optimum hospital administration. The stacked-based ensemble of classifiers outperformed both the base classifiers and voting classifiers. Before feeding the features into the ML classifiers, the ADASYN algorithm was used to eliminate the imbalance of the dataset. Feature importance scores have been figured using the permutation feature importance method from the trained models to recognize the influence of features on the creation of the models.

The arrangement of the paper is as follows: The section "Literature Review" summarizes current findings and shortcomings on the prediction of hospitalization period for patients, the "Proposed Methodology" section describes the methodology used in this study, the section "Result and Discussion" summarizes the findings of the study, and the section "Conclusion" describes conclusion and the recommendations based on the findings.

2 Literature Review

This segment discusses recent research on estimating the duration of hospital stays for COVID-19 infected by exploiting data mining, machine learning, and other homogeneous techniques.

Three different ML algorithms were implemented to predict the "Length of Stay" (LoS) of more than 8 days by Ebinger et al. [6]. A total of 350 variables were considered in the models. Data obtained on or near those dates had been used to generate the three models for hospitalizations. The model's capability to forecast in respect of the AUC was about 0.819. There are also some imperfections in this research, such as the predicated classifications of "Short Stay will be 3 days" and "Long Stay will be more than 8 days" and the limited sample size, which should be more accurate. Weissman et al. [7] anticipated the length of medical service disruption and the different case circumstances for demand on hospital assets in a community setting caused by COVID-19. They used the SIR and CHIME models to estimate the short period of hospital capability challenges through the early periods of an eruption. The model parameters had been accumulated or constructed directly from historical health system data; therefore, that approach constituted a shortcoming of the research.

A machine learning-based forecasting model could be exploited to classify patients needing to be shifted to the intensive care unit (ICU) within 24 h, as Cheng et al. [8] illustrated. They trained the RF model by employing 10-fold-CV and assessed its effectiveness. The estimator unveiled a sensitivity of 72.8% and an AUC of 79.9% compared to actual admission. Roimi et al. [9] pioneered predicting every medical consequence and hospital utilization. Cox regression technique was applied to develop the model for examining several-phases survival. The model anticipated the patient's complaint progression during serious, severe, or moderate clinical phases. The model also forecasts clinical exploitation at the functional magnitude of the hospital or healthcare system, and the AUC was 0.88 with a sample size of 2703 for the model. Using the instance of COVID-19-affected individuals, Vekaria et al. [10] issued a set of openly viewable models and approaches for estimating "LoS". They employed an AFT concept and a TC technique based on Weibull distributions. All operations would be computed during the patient's stay in the hospital.

Machine learning was implemented by Dan et al. [11] to check if COVID-19 patients needed to be admitted to the ICU and how long patients would need to stay there. Their recommended method had an AUC of 0.8429 after being built with 10 attributes and the SVM "poly" kernel. Pei et al. [12] implemented KNN, SVM, and RF algorithms to classify the "LoS" of COVID-19 patients in hospitals. To classify the length of stay in the hospital, the classification was divided into eleven categories. KNN, SVM, and RF algorithms were inadequate for categorization tasks, and these algorithms' accuracy was around 34.42%, 35.24% and 35.41% individually. Ferdib-Al-Islam et al. [23] analyzed the same dataset [12] and used four machine learning models – DT, RF, KNN, and GB – to estimate the hospitalization length to provide effective hospital management. The shortcoming of that study was the poor performance of ML models.

This study introduces a stacking-based ensemble model to estimate the hospitalization period with satisfactory prediction performance.

3 Proposed Methodology

The designed methodology of "ADASEML" involves data preprocessing, analysis, the implication of ADASYN, and classification using the base, voting, and stacking classifiers. The proposed work's approach has been divided into the subsequent steps:

3.1 Dataset Details and Preprocessing

The dataset utilized in this investigation is downloadable from Kaggle [13]. Pei et al. [12] also utilized the same dataset in their analysis. This dataset comprises 318438 occurrences of 18 columns [23].

Several attributes were not necessary to consider in this investigation, so those have been removed [23]. In this dataset, the missing values were expressed as "NaN." Because the dataset had a sufficient number of cases, the rows having "NaN" values were discarded. Following that, the dataset had 313793 occurrences. Due to the inability of computing machines to cope with categorical variables, the majority of ML algorithms require algebraic values as input. Thus, before categorical attributes can be fed into ML classifiers, those must be transformed into an algebraic illustration. Label encoding is a method that may be used to achieve this task. This investigation transformed categorical attributes into numeric inputs, applying label encoding. The goal of feature scaling is to equalize the size of all variables. This research used the min-max scaling approach to each feature was normalized. It is a technique for rescaling values between zero and one. Equation (1) outlines the principle of normalization:

$$Feat' = \frac{Feat - Feat_{\min}}{Feat_{\max} - Feat_{\min}} \tag{1}$$

where $Feat_{max}$ and $Feat_{min}$ are the peaks and the lowest feature values.

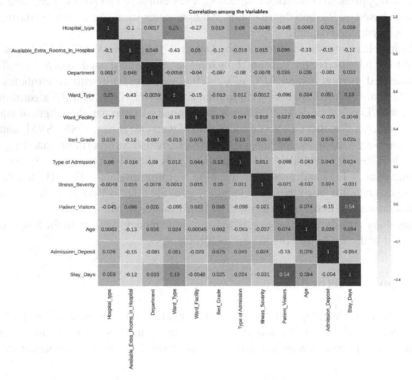

Fig. 1. Correlation among the variables

3.2 Exploratory Data Analysis

EDA is a technique for interpreting data to gain new insights or find key traits. This step included the calculation of correlations between variables. Correlation affects the relevance of characteristics when two traits/variables are closely related. As a consequence, they are not required to be retained separately. Figure 1 illustrates the correlations between factors. However, "Patient Visitors" significantly influences the "Stay Days" (output variable) more than other attributes.

3.3 Class Balancing Using ADASYN

ADASYN (Adaptive Synthetic) is a method for adaptively oversampling skewed datasets. This approach is similar to SMOTE, except it creates a variable number of samples based on an approximation of the class's local distribution [14, 15]. The primary principle of ADASYN is to produce more artificial data for minority class examples that are more complex to learn than for minority class examples that are easier to learn. ADASYN may adaptively add artificial data samples for the minority class based on the accurate data distribution, reducing the bias imposed by the unbalanced data distribution. Additionally, ADASYN may adjust the classifier's decision boundary autonomously to focus more on difficult-to-learn cases, enhancing learning performance. These two aims are realized by dynamic weight modification and an adaptive learning technique that adapts to data distribution. The mathematical operation behind the ADASYN algorithm has been demonstrated in (2) to (8).

$$d = \frac{m_s}{m_l} \tag{2}$$

where m_l and m_s denote the number of samples from the minority and majority classes, respectively. If d is less than a specified value, start the algorithm.

$$G = (m_l - m_s) \times \beta \tag{3}$$

Here, G denotes the total number of minorities for whom data must be generated. β is the ideal minority:majority data fraction after ADASYN. $\beta = 1$ indicates that the data set is adequately balanced using ADASYN.

$$r_i = \frac{\#majority}{k} \tag{4}$$

The r_i value represents the majority class's dominance in a particular neighborhood. Neighborhoods with a higher r_i include more instances of the dominant class and are thus more challenging to learn.

Normalize the r_i values such that their total equals one.

$$\hat{r}_i = \frac{r_i}{\sum r_i} \tag{5}$$

$$\sum r_i = 1 \tag{6}$$

Determine the number of artificial samples that should be generated for each neighborhood.

$$G_i = G\hat{r}_i \tag{7}$$

Because r_i is more significant in neighborhoods influenced by majority class instances, such neighborhoods will create a more significant number of artificial minority class examples. As a result, the ADASYN method is adaptable; more data is created for "difficult-to-learn" areas.

$$s_i = x_i + (x_{zi} - x_i) \times \lambda \tag{8}$$

According to the above equation, λ denotes a random integer between 0 and 1, si denotes a new synthetic example, and x_i and x_{zi} denote two minority cases inside the same neighborhood.

Figure 2 represents the data distribution before and after the implication of ADASYN. The total number of instances before and after using ADASYN were 313793 and 949537, respectively.

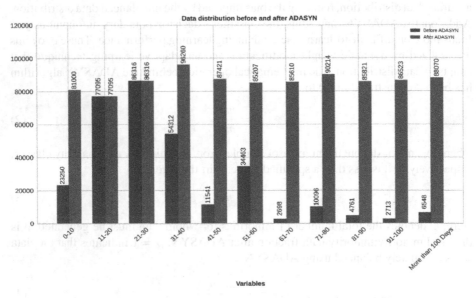

Fig. 2. Class-wise data distribution before and after using ADASYN

3.4 ML Classifiers for Classification

In this work, DT, RF, and KNN were used as the base classifiers, and after that, voting and stacking classifiers were produced using these base classifiers. The optimal parameters of the classifiers have been found using the "GridSearchCV" algorithm [16].

Decision Tree. A tree-like form simulates likely consequences, resource and utility costs, and possible implications [17]. Decision trees present the algorithms via the use of conditional control expressions. They are one of the most effective learning algorithms since they include various learning approaches. Table 1 illustrates the optimal values of the parameters of the DT classifier.

Table 1. Optimal parameters of DT model

Parameter	Optimal Value
Criterion	Entropy
Splitter	Random
Max_Features	Sqrt

Random Forest. A random forest is a meta-algorithm based on decision tree classifiers to different subsamples of the dataset and then utilizes averaging to increase predicted accuracy [17]. When the current tree's training set is constructed using sampling with replacement, about one-third of the instances are omitted from the sample. This out-of-bag data is utilized to provide an approximate solution to the classification error when new trees are added to the forest. Table 2 illustrates the optimal values of the parameters of the RF classifier.

Table 2. Optimal parameters of RF model

Parameter	Value
n_estimators	100
Criterion	Gini
Max_features	Sqrt

K-Nearest Neighbor. The k-nearest neighbor method maintains all existing data and classifies new data points according to their similarity (e.g., distance functions) [18]. This refers to when new data becomes available. Then, the K-NN method is readily sorted into a suitable category. KNN is a simple classifier often used as a baseline for more complicated classifiers such as SVM and ANN. Table 3 illustrates the optimal values of the parameters of the KNN classifier.

Table 3. Optimal parameters of KNN model

Parameter	Value
n_neighbors	3
Metric	'minkowski'
p	1

Voting Classifier. A voting classifier is a model trained on an ensemble of multiple models and estimates an output (class) based on the class with the greatest likelihood of being picked as the output [19]. The voting classifier is capable of two distinct voting forms – hard and soft voting. The probable output class in hard voting is the most significant majority of votes, i.e., the class with the highest chance of being predicted by every classifier. The forecast class in soft voting is the average probability assigned to that class. The voting classifier was formed in this work using the soft voting technique with DT, RF, and KNN classifiers.

Stacking Classifier. Stacking is a technique for ensemble classification models that use two-layer estimators [20]. The first layer (called level-0 models or base models) contains all of the baseline models used to forecast the outcomes on the test datasets. The second layer (called level-1 model or meta-model) comprises a meta-classifier that utilizes all of the baseline models' predictions as input and generates new predictions. In this research, DT, RF, and KNN model have been used as level-0 models, and logistic regression has been used as the level-1 model.

3.5 Feature Importance Scores Calculation

Permutation feature importance decreases a definitive score when a solitary feature value is arbitrarily rearranged [21]. This methodology breaks the association between the feature and the objective. Permutation importance can be calculated on the training set or held-out testing. The method benefits by being a model sceptic and can be determined commonly with the permutation of the feature.

4 Result and Discussion

Classification techniques were employed to forecast the duration of hospitalization for COVID-19 infected. Following the principles mentioned in (9), (10), and (11), the performance of the created system was evaluated using three single performance methods: accuracy, precision, and recall.

$$Acc. = \frac{TP + TN}{TP + FP + FN + TN} \tag{9}$$

$$\Pr ec. = \frac{TP}{TP + FP} \tag{10}$$

$$Rec. = \frac{TP}{TP + FN} \tag{11}$$

Each classification model's classification report is shown in Table 4. After using ADASYN, each performance indicator shows a considerable improvement. The stacking model ranked the best in terms of accuracy, precision, and recall among the machine learning models utilized in this study. It obtained 78% precision, 80% recall, and 80% accuracy.

The AUC is a metric to indicate a classifier's ability to categorize between classes (ROC characteristics). The highest AUC score is 0.96; from both RF and Voting models,

Table 4. Classification Report of ML Models

Model	Without SMOTE			With SMOTE		
	Acc. (%)	Prec. (%)	Rec. (%)	Acc. (%)	Prec. (%)	Rec. (%)
DT	29	29	29	69	68	69
RF	35	34	35	75	75	75
KNN	32	30	32	79	77	79
Voting	35	35	35	77	77	77
Stacking	36	35	36	80	78	80

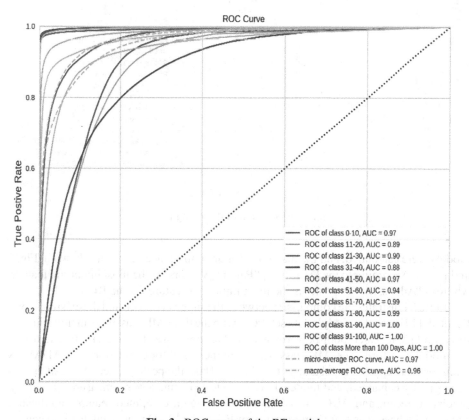

Fig. 3. ROC curve of the RF model

which are represented in Fig. 3 and Fig. 4 correspondingly. The AUC score of the DT, KNN and Stacking models are 0.82, 0.88, and 0.95, respectively.

The phrase "feature importance" states the approach that quantifies the value of input features for predicting a target variable. The KNN classifier cannot generate a feature significance score [22]. In this study, the feature important scores from the DT and RF

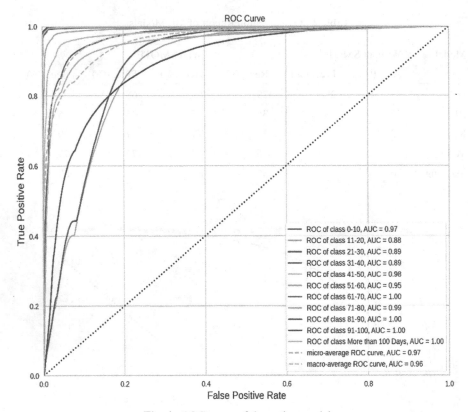

Fig. 4. ROC curve of the voting model

models were calculated, and the matching feature importance scores are shown in Fig. 5 and Fig. 6. According to the DT model, "Patient_Visitors" is the most important feature, whereas "Admission_Deposit" is the most important feature for the RF model.

Table 5 illustrates the comparison between the suggested work and the existing work. Pei et al. [12] used this study's data set. PCA with the three ML classifiers included in that research [12] revealed poor performance, and accuracy was the sole criterion to assess the model's performance. ML classifiers were then used for estimation after ADASYN methods were applied to rebalance the classes. Thus, the performance of classifiers has been greatly enhanced, and models have been tested using several measures (accuracy, precision, recall, and AUC). In addition, this research computed feature significance scores, which were absent from the work of Pei et al. [12]. On the hand, the imbalanced class problem and the poor prediction performance found in [12] were also eradicated by Ferdib-Al-Islam et al. [23]. The introduction of SMOTE and ML classifiers removed those problems. But, that work also lacks satisfactory performance in classification. As SMOTE created the synthetic data, it sometimes causes a problem in model generalization (underfitting) and sometimes overfitting. But, the proposed strategy uses

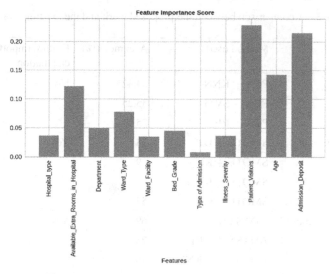

Fig. 5. Feature importance score of the DT model

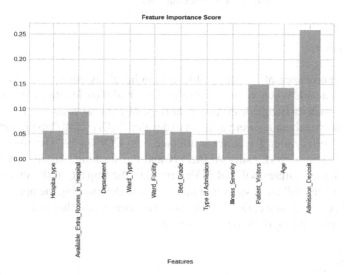

Fig. 6. Feature importance score of the RF model

ADASYN for synthetic data generation, which prevents the previously mentioned problem. The proposed work performs better in classification than the techniques presented by Ferdib-Al-Islam et al. [23].

Table 5. A comparison between the proposed work and the existing works

Author	Method used	Accuracy (%)	Feature importance score calculation
Pei et al. [12]	PCA + KNN	34.42	No
	PCA + SVM	35.25	
	PCA + RF	35.41	
Ferdib-Al-Islam et al. [23]	SMOTE + DT	58	Yes
	SMOTE + RF	69	
	SMOTE + KNN	73	
	SMOTE + GB	57	
"ADASEML" (Proposed work)	ADASYN + DT	69	Yes
	ADASYN + RF	75	
	ADASYN + KNN	79	
	ADASYN + Voting	77	
	ADASYN + Stacking	80	

5 Conclusion

The critical significance of resource allocation in hospitals during the COVID-19 era cannot be overstated. When the number of patients and their length of stay rise, developing nations such as Bangladesh face a shortage of medical equipment. In this study, machine learning techniques were utilized to develop "ADASEML" to predict the likely duration of hospitalization for patients infected with COVID-19. The suggested study outperforms previous work using ADASYN and the stacking classifier. Additionally, feature significance ratings will aid in determining the impact on the creation of ML models. This study will aid responsible authorities in determining the appropriate level of hospital care based on a patient's hospitalization period. Further analysis using deep learning may improve prediction performance.

References

1. Tracking SARS-CoV-2 variants: https://www.who.int/en/activities/tracking-SARS-CoV-2-variants
2. February 2020 Coronavirus News Updates – Worldometer, https://www.worldometers.info/coronavirus/feb-2020-news-updates-covid19/
3. Rees, E., et al.: COVID-19 length of hospital stay: a systematic review and data synthesis. BMC Med. **18**(1), 270 (2020)
4. Wu, S., et al.: Understanding factors influencing the length of hospital stay among non-severe COVID-19 patients: a retrospective cohort study in a Fangcang shelter hospital. PLOS ONE **15**(10), e0240959 (2020)
5. Pianykh, O., et al.: Improving healthcare operations management with machine learning. Nat. Mach. Intell. **2**(5), 266–273 (2020)

6. Ebinger, J., et al.: A machine learning algorithm predicts duration of hospitalization in COVID-19 patients. Intell.-Based Med. **5**, 100035 (2021)
7. Weissman, G., et al.: Locally informed simulation to predict hospital capacity needs during the COVID-19 pandemic. Ann. Intern. Med. **173**(1), 21–28 (2020)
8. Cheng, F., et al.: Using machine learning to predict ICU transfer in hospitalized COVID-19 patients. J. Clin. Med. **9**(6), 1668 (2020)
9. Roimi, M., et al.: Development and validation of a machine learning model predicting illness trajectory and hospital utilization of COVID-19 patients: a nationwide study. J. Am. Med. Inform. Assoc. **28**(6), 1188–1196 (2021)
10. Vekaria, B., et al.: Hospital length of stay for COVID-19 patients: data-driven methods for forward planning. BMC Infect. Dis. **21**(1), 700 (2021)
11. Dan, T. et al.: Machine learning to predict ICU admission, ICU mortality and survivors' length of stay among COVID-19 patients: toward optimal allocation of ICU resources. In: 2020 IEEE International Conference on Bioinformatics and Biomedicine (BIBM), pp. 555–561 (2020)
12. Pei, J., et al.: Prediction of patients' length of stay at hospital during COVID-19 pandemic. J. Phys.: Conf. Ser. **1802**(3), 032038 (2021)
13. COVID-19 Hospitals Treatment Plan: https://www.kaggle.com/arashnic/covid19-hospital-treatment
14. Ferdib-Al-Islam et al.: Hepatocellular carcinoma patient's survival prediction using oversampling and machine learning techniques. In: 2021 2nd International Conference on Robotics, Electrical and Signal Processing Techniques (ICREST), pp. 445–450 (2021)
15. Haibo, H., et al.: ADASYN: adaptive synthetic sampling approach for imbalanced learning. In: 2008 IEEE International Joint Conference on Neural Networks (IEEE World Congress on Computational Intelligence), pp. 1322–1328 (2008)
16. Olatunji, S., et al.: Machine learning based preemptive diagnosis of lung cancer using clinical data. In: 2022 7th International Conference on Data Science and Machine Learning Applications (CDMA), pp. 115–120 (2022)
17. Brunda, S., et al.: Crop price prediction using random forest and decision tree regression. Int. Res. J. Eng. Technol. **7**(9), 235–237 (2022)
18. Shokrzade, A., et al.: A novel extreme learning machine based kNN classification method for dealing with big data. Expert Syst. Appl. **183**, 115293 (2021)
19. Kumari, S., et al.: An ensemble approach for classification and prediction of diabetes mellitus using soft voting classifier. Int. J. Cogn. Comput. Eng. **2**, 40–46 (2021)
20. El-Rashidy, N., et al.: Intensive care unit mortality prediction: an improved patient-specific stacking ensemble model. IEEE Access **8**, 133541–133564 (2020)
21. Altmann, A., et al.: Permutation importance: a corrected feature importance measure. Bioinformatics **26**(10), 1340–1347 (2010)
22. KNNClassifier(), H., Phillips, M.: How to find 'feature importance' or variable importance graph for KNNClassifier(), https://stackoverflow.com/a/55315400
23. Ferdib-Al-Islam et al.: COV-HM: prediction of COVID-19 patient's hospitalization period for hospital management using SMOTE and machine learning techniques. In: 2nd International Conference on Computing Advancements (ICCA 2022), pp. 25–33. ACM (2022)

A Novel Weighted Visibility Graph Approach for Alcoholism Detection Through the Analysis of EEG Signals

Parnika N. Paranjape(✉), Meera M. Dhabu, and Parag S. Deshpande

Department of Computer Science and Engineering,
Visvesvaraya National Institute of Technology (VNIT),
Nagpur, Maharashtra, India
parnika.paranjape@students.vnit.ac.in

Abstract. Detection of neurological disorders such as Alzheimer, Epilepsy, etc. through electroencephalogram (EEG) signal analysis has become increasingly popular in recent years. Alcoholism is one of the severe brain disorders that not only affects the nervous system but also leads to behavioural issues. This work presents a weighted visibility graph (WVG) approach for the detection of alcoholism, which consists of three phases. The first phase maps the EEG signals to WVG. Then, the second phase extracts important network features, viz., modularity, average weighted degree, weighted clustering coefficient, and average degree. It further identifies the most significant channels and combines their discriminative features to form feature vectors. Then, these feature vectors are trained by different machine learning classifiers in the third phase, achieving 98.91% classification accuracy. The visibility graph (VG) is not only robust to noise, but it also inherits many dynamical properties of EEG time series. Moreover, preserving weight on the links in VG aids in detecting sudden changes in the EEG signal. Experimental analysis of the alcoholic EEG signals indicates that the average accuracy of the proposed approach is higher or comparable to other reported studies.

Keywords: Alcoholism detection · EEG signals · Weighted visibility graph · Complex network features

1 Introduction

Excessive consumption of alcohol not only affects the neurological system but also leads to several other issues such as high blood pressure, liver disorder, cognitive and physical problems, etc. As per the global status report on alcohol use, released by WHO, almost 1 in 20 deaths are due to excessive consumption of alcohol and leads to more than 5% of total global diseases [14]. Taking into account the hazardous effects of alcoholism, it is essential to develop a way to distinguish alcoholic people from normal subjects and recognize the symptoms at an early stage. This will help us to take necessary measures to prevent severe brain disorders and other alcohol disorders.

I. Woungang et al. (Eds.): ANTIC 2022, CCIS 1798, pp. 16–34, 2023.
https://doi.org/10.1007/978-3-031-28183-9_2

The most commonly used diagnostic methods are questionnaire-based tools, blood test, stress assessment, etc. However, these conventional approaches require manual intervention and they cannot analyze the changes occurring in human brain caused due to alcohol consumption. Therefore, a reliable, accurate, automated, and non-invasive method is needed to detect alcoholism. Alcohol consumption causes neurological changes and such changes can be recorded using different techniques like MRI, fMRI, and EEG. EEG signal is best suited to record the changes in brain activities because it is non-invasive and reflects the complex dynamics of brain activities.

Researchers have widely used the frequency and time domain methods to distinguish alcoholics from controlled drinkers. This includes both linear and non-linear methods. Linear methods include Fourier transform (FFT) and wavelet transform. EEG signals are non-stationary, non-linear, and chaotic in nature. Therefore, linear methods have limited capabilities for EEG signal analysis [20]. Non-linear features like Lyapunov exponent, sample entropy, approximate entropy, Hjorth mobility, Hjorth complexity, kurtosis, median frequency (MDF), etc. have also been extracted by several researchers to detect alcoholism [1,6,11,15]. However, these methods cannot capture all properties of EEG signals such as chaotic and non-stationary nature [19]. Therefore, we need a visibility graph approach which can capture many dynamic properties of time series and helps to detect alcoholism.

Zhang and Small [24] proposed to model time series as complex network and demonstrated that multiple behaviour of time series can be discriminated by different network features. Lacasa et al. [10] introduced the concept of visibility graph (VG) algorithm to map time series data to complex network. They demonstrated that VG can capture several dynamical properties of time series. VG is also robust to noise and several researchers got promising results using VG [21]. Owing to these properties, visibility graph and complex network features gained popularity in the detection of brain disorders like Epilepsy [20] and Alzheimer [9] and analysis of EEG sleep stages [21]. Zhu et al. [25] applied the visibility graph approach to distinguish the EEG signals of alcoholics and controlled drinkers. However, they utilized horizontal visibility graph (HVG) which is a subgraph of VG and they did not consider weights on the links of the graph. Weight information clearly indicates the strong and weak connections in the network and plays an important role in detecting sudden changes in EEG signals.

Taking into account these limitations of existing approaches, we introduce a novel three-phase approach to detect alcoholism by modeling EEG signals as weighted visibility graphs and extracting complex network features from these graphs. The goal of this work is to analyze how the weights on the links in visibility graph help to distinguish EEG signals of alcoholic and controlled drinkers.

Contributions

- **Data transformation:** The proposed work maps each EEG signal to a weighted visibility graph (WVG) by employing a visibility graph algorithm and an edge-strength technique.

- **Complex network feature extraction:** Once the EEG signals are mapped to WVG, graph properties are analysed and important network features, viz. average weighted degree, modularity, weighted clustering coefficient, and average degree are extracted. Further, the discriminative network features extracted from the most significant channels are combined to achieve higher classification accuracy.
- **Classification:** Finally, the network feature set is forwarded to different machine learning classifiers. Experimental study suggests that the performance of the proposed approach is higher or comparable to other reported results.

The remaining contents of the paper are organized as follows. A detailed literature survey related to the analysis of alcoholic EEG signals is given in Sect. 2. Section 3 presents the details of the methodology of the proposed approach. Description of the dataset used in experiments, results and discussion are provided in Sect. 4. Section 5 concludes the paper.

2   Related Work

This section presents a brief review of the studies that performed alcoholism detection through EEG signal analysis. Both frequency and time domain features have been widely used in literature to detect alcoholism. Acharya et al. [1] extracted certain non-linear features, viz. largest lyapunov exponent, approximate entropy, sample entropy and higher order spectral features from each EEG signal. Further, they computed statistical significance of these features and trained SVM classifier using significant features. However, they could achieve only 91.7% accuracy. Shri et al. [18] extracted a non-linear feature, viz. approximate entropy (ApEn) from the EEG signals of significant channels to detect alcoholism. They ranked ApEn features extracted from all the channels and forwarded the top 32 features from the significant channels to SVM and BPNN classifiers, reporting an accuracy of 90%. Zhu et al. [25] mapped EEG signals to horizontal visibility graph (HVG) to detect alcoholism. However, HVG is a subgraph of visibility graph (VG) and they constructed unweighted HVGs, whereas the proposed approach maps each EEG signal to a weighted visibility graph because weight plays an important role in differentiating dynamic properties of EEG signals. Further they extracted graph entropy as a feature from 13 optimal channels and reported 95.8% classification accuracy. In recent years, several researchers have utilized the features extracted from different frequency sub-bands of EEG signals for alcoholism detection. In [3], Ahmadi et al. decomposed the EEG signals into five frequency sub-bands using wavelet transform and extracted various non-linear features from these sub-bands. Further, the most discriminative features were forwarded to different classifiers, achieving 99% classification accuracy. However, they have not reported the version of the dataset used in their experiments. Therefore, their results cannot be directly compared with our proposed approach. EEG rythm-based approach was proposed by Taran and Bajaj [22] to distinguish alcoholics from controlled drinkers. They decomposed the EEG signals into intrinsic mode functions (IMFs) and extracted the features, viz. inter quartile range, mean absolute deviation, entropy, coefficient of variation, and neg-entropy. These features were classified by ELM method, producing 97.92% classification accuracy. Sharma et al. [17] decomposed the alcoholic and normal EEG signals into 9 sub-bands using dual-tree complex wavelet transform and extracted two features, viz. log-energy entropies (LEEs) and l2 norms (L2Ns) from each sub-band. Further, the most significant features were forwarded to fuzzy sugeno (FSC) classifiers, SMO-SVM, and LS-SVM, reporting an accuracy of 97.91%. To overcome the limitations of wavelet transform, Anuragi and Sisodia [4] proposed to decompose the EEG signals into different sub-bands using flexible analytical wavelets transform (FAWT) and extracted approximate and detailed wavelet coefficients. Further, they extracted statistical features from these coefficients for each sub-band, followed by classification of feature vectors using different machine learning classifiers. They achieved 99.17% classification accuracy. However, they experimented with a subset of 120 recordings each for the alcoholics and controlled drinkers. On the other hand, the proposed work experimented with the whole large dataset having 600 recordings each in the training and test data files. Therefore, the results obtained by Anuragi and Sisodia are not comparable with our approach. In [6], Bavkar et al. separated the EEG signals into five EEG rhythms using Butterworth narrow band pass filter and extracted linear, non-linear and statistical features from these rhythms. Finally, the significant features were classified by ensemble subspace KNN classifier, achieving 98.25% classification accuracy. However, this approach utilized total 800 EEG recordings which is a subset of the large dataset containing 600 recordings each in the training and test set.

Anuragi and Sisodia [5] applied the empirical wavelet transform (EWT) to decompose the alcoholic and normal EEG signals and extracted statistical and entropy-based features from each sub-band of the decomposed signal. Further, the significant features were employed to train various machine learning models achieving an accuracy of 98.75% with the LS-SVM classifier. However, they experimented on the small version of the EEG dataset containing only 30 EEG recordings for both the normal and alcoholic class. Mehla et al. [11] decomposed the EEG signals using Fourier decomposition method (FDM) and then, they extracted the time-domain features from the orthogonal components called Fourier intrinsic band functions (FIBFs). Their approach achieved an accuracy of 99.98% using the SVM classifier however, this result was obtained using a small version of the dataset containing only 30 EEG recordings for each of the two classes. Prabhakar and Rajaguru [15] proposed an approach to cluster the alcoholic EEG signals using Correlation Dimension (CD) and then the suitable features were extracted from these signals by employing different distance metrics. Further, different classifiers were trained with the selected features and an accuracy of 98.99% was reported. However, this method utilized a full version of the dataset that is incomplete. Also, a few recordings contain empty files or are labeled 'err'. Recently, Mukhtar et al. [12] proposed a deep neural network approach for alcoholism detection that applied convolutional neural network (CNN) model to the raw EEG data and reported 98% accuracy. However, they experimented with a subset of the original dataset containing only 60 EEG recordings for both classes. Agarwal and Zubair [2] proposed another EEG signal decomposition-based approach to decompose the EEG signals using Sliding Singular Spectrum Analysis (S-SSA) method and applied the independent component analysis (ICA) to identify the significant alcoholic and non-alcoholic features from the EEG signals. Then, these features were forwarded to various machine learning classifiers achieving an accuracy of 98.97%. However, this approach utilized the full version of the dataset, which is incomplete, and some EEG recordings are either empty or labeled as "err". Buriro et al. [8] investigated the strength of the EEG features extracted using wavelet scattering transform (WST) to detect alcoholism. They experimented with only a subset of the full dataset and correctly classified all records of the subset. Therefore, their results are not comparable with our results obtained using a whole large dataset. Recently, Salankar et al. [16] devised an approach to decompose the EEG signals using hybridization of the oscillatory modes decomposition and extracted features of the Second Order Difference Plots (SODPs) of these oscillatory modes. Further, the most significant features were selected to train different machine learning classifiers and an accuracy of 99.89% was reported. However, they experimented with a small version of the dataset containing only 30 EEG records for each of the two classes.

The above-mentioned frequency or time domain features cannot capture all properties of EEG signals such as chaotic and non-stationary nature [19]. As opposed to this, a visibility graph can preserve several dynamic properties of the time series which makes it suitable for the detection of alcoholism. In [25], Zhu et al. proposed a horizontal visibility graph (HVG) approach. However, they constructed unweighted HVGs. The links of the graph carry different strengths i.e. weights and preserving this weight information in the visibility graph gives promising results [9,20,21]. Therefore, the proposed work presents a novel weighted visibility graph (WVG) approach and employs complex network features for alcoholism detection. To the best of our knowledge, the proposed work is the first of its kind to analyze the EEG signals for alcoholism detection using WVG and complex network features.

3   Methodology

A visibility graph (VG) can inherit dynamic properties of the time series, it is robust to noise and more promising results can be obtained by preserving weights on the links in VG instead of binary networks. Therefore, we present a novel three-phase approach based on the weighted visibility graph to classify the EEG signals of alcoholics and controlled drinkers. The first phase obtains the weighted visibility graph (WVG) representation of the EEG signals by employing visibility graph algorithm and edge weight function. Further, the second phase extracts the important and widely used network features, viz. average weighted degree, modularity, weighted clustering coefficient, and average degree. This phase also combines the discriminative network features of the most significant channels. Finally, these feature vectors are inputted into different ML classifiers like SVM and KNN for model building and decision-making in the third phase. The steps involved in the proposed work are depicted in Fig. 1 and described in detail as follows.

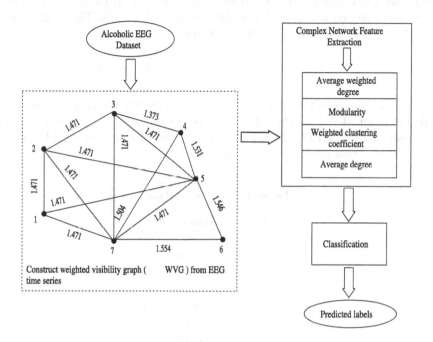

Fig. 1. Flow diagram of the proposed approach

3.1 Phase I: EEG Signal to Weighted Visibility Graph (WVG)

The proposed work employs Lacasa visibility graph [10] algorithm to map EEG time series to visibility graph as it is a non-parametric approach unlike other methods such as TSCN [23] and recurrence network which are parametric. Weighted visibility graph construction involves the following steps.

1. Node assignment: Let $\{y_t\}$; $t = 1, 2, ..., N$ denotes a time series. To transform y_t to a graph $G(N, E)$, each data point in y_t is represented by a unique node in N_i.
2. Determination of edge between two nodes: An edge exists between any two nodes of the VG if they satisfy the following condition [10].

$$y(t_k) < y(t_i) + (y(t_j) - y(t_i)) * \left(\frac{t_k - t_i}{t_j - t_i}\right), \quad t_i < t_k < t_j \tag{1}$$

where, t_i, t_j, and t_k represent the time points such that $t_i < t_k < t_j$ and $y(t_k)$, $y(t_i)$, and $y(t_j)$ denote the nodes of the visibility graph (VG).

3. Computing weights on the links of VG: Preserving weights on the links of visibility graph gives more promising results [9,20,21]. Moreover, weight information clearly denotes the strong and weak connections in the network and helps to discriminate different dynamical structures in EEG signals. Therefore, we construct a weighted visibility graph in this work. The weight on the link between two nodes is calculated as follows.

$$w_{ij} = \left| arctan \left(\frac{y\left(t_j\right) - y\left(t_i\right)}{t_j - t_i} \right) \right|, \quad i < j \tag{2}$$

Here, w_{ij} represents the absolute weight between two nodes $y\left(t_j\right)$ and $y\left(t_i\right)$. We have considered all the edge weights in radian. Table 1 shows a sample time series data and Fig. 2 shows its corresponding weighted visibility graph. The edges of this graph are given in Table 2.

Table 1. Time series data

Time point	Data point
t_1	−8.575
t_2	10.468
t_3	−16.876
t_4	−7.111
t_5	0.702
t_6	−3.204
t_7	22.186
t_8	−24.2

Table 2. Edges along with weights of the weighted visibility graph

Edge	Weight	Edge	Weight
e_{12}	1.518332	e_{27}	1.167492
e_{14}	0.454002	e_{28}	1.399424
e_{15}	1.163708	e_{34}	1.468746
e_{16}	0.821156	e_{37}	1.468751
e_{17}	1.378163	e_{45}	1.443497
e_{18}	1.149607	e_{47}	1.468752
e_{23}	1.534242	e_{56}	1.320163
e_{24}	1.457511	e_{57}	1.477971
e_{25}	1.272758	e_{67}	1.531431
e_{26}	1.286171	e_{78}	1.549241

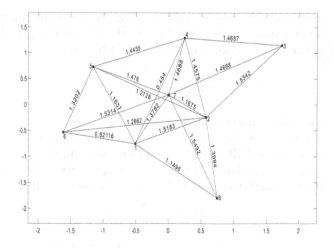

Fig. 2. Weighted visibility graph for the time series in Table 1

Consider an EEG time series data $y = \{40, 50, 60, 55, 80, 40, 100, 90, 95, 120\}$. Here, $y(t_1) = 40$, $y(t_6) = 40$, and $y(t_7) = 100$. Weights for the pair of nodes $(y(t_1), y(t_7))$ and $(y(t_6), y(t_7))$ are calculated as follows.

$$w_{17} = arctan\left(\frac{100 - 40}{7 - 1}\right) = 1.471$$

$$w_{67} = arctan\left(\frac{100 - 40}{7 - 6}\right) = 1.554$$

As it can be seen, both $y(t_1)$ and $y(t_6)$ have the same value but the strengths with which they will connect to the node $y(t_7)$ are different. Therefore, fluctuations in the EEG signals will be captured through edge weights and this will help to distinguish different dynamic properties of EEG signals.

3.2   Phase II: Complex Network Feature Extraction

Feature extraction is an important step for classification because the performance of any classifier mainly depends on the strength of the features extracted from the original input data. The proposed work extracts four important and widely used complex network features, viz. modularity, average weighted degree, weighted clustering coefficient, and average degree from the weighted visibility graph (WVG).

1. **Weighted clustering coefficient:** Clustering coefficient of a node represents the degree to which neighboring vertices of the node are connected with each other. The weighted clustering coefficient of a node will also consider the weights of the links attached to the given node. It is defined as follows.

$$C_u = \frac{1}{k_u(k_u - 1)} * \sum_{v,z} (\tilde{w}_{uv} * \tilde{w}_{vz} * \tilde{w}_{zu})^{\frac{1}{3}}$$

where $\tilde{w}_{uv}$ represents the edge weight between the nodes 'u' and 'v' which is scaled by the maximum edge weight in the network. The weighted clustering coefficient of the entire network is computed as follows.

$$CC_{Net} = \frac{\sum\limits_{u \in N} C_u}{|N|} \tag{3}$$

2. **Average weighted degree:** Node degree is an important characteristic of the complex network. As discussed earlier, edge weight varies with respect to the fluctuations in the EEG signals. Therefore, we compute weighted degree of the network. Let $w_{u,v}$ be the weight of the edge between two nodes 'u' and 'v'. Then, the weighted degree of a node 'u' is defined as follows.

$$WD_u = \sum_{v \in NB_u} w_{u,v}$$

where, NB_u denote the set of neighboring nodes of 'u'. The average weighted degree of the entire network is defined as follows.

$$AWD_{Net} = \frac{\sum\limits_{u \in N} WD_u}{|N|} \tag{4}$$

where N represents a set of the nodes of the complex network and $|N|$ represents the cardinality of the set 'N'.

3. **Modularity:** Modularity measures the strength of partitioning a network into smaller modules or clusters and it was proposed by Newman [13]. The modularity 'Q' is computed as follows.

$$Q = \frac{1}{2p} * \sum_{u,v} \left(A_{u,v} - \frac{k_u k_v}{2p} \right) * \delta\left(C_u, C_v \right) \tag{5}$$

where
$A_{u,v} =$ Weight of the edge between two nodes 'u' and 'v'.
$p = \frac{1}{2} * \sum_{u,v} A_{u,v}$ denote the total number of edges in the network.
$k_u = \sum_v A_{u,v}$ denote weighted degree of vertex 'u'.
C_u is the cluster to which node 'u' belongs.
$\delta\left(C_u, C_v \right) = 1$ if 'u' and 'v' belong to same cluster otherwise, $\delta\left(C_u, C_v \right) = 0$.

In this work, we have employed Louvain [7] algorithm for finding modularity because it is efficient for large networks. It comprises of two stages. In the first stage, smaller modules are locally determined using the optimization of modularity. Then, in the second stage, vertices belonging to the same module are combined to form a new network with modules being the new vertices. Steps 1 and 2 are repeated until there is no further gain in modularity. The gain in modularity is defined as follows.

$$\Delta Q_{lm} = \left[\frac{\sum_{mn} + k_{l,mn}}{2p} - \left(\frac{\sum_{total} + k_l}{2p} \right)^2 \right] - \left[\frac{\sum_{mn}}{2p} - \left(\frac{\sum_{total}}{2p} \right)^2 - \left(\frac{k_l}{2p} \right)^2 \right] \tag{6}$$

where,
$\sum_{mn}$ = Total weights of the links that belong to cluster 'm'.
$\sum_{total}$ = Total weights of the links that are attached to the nodes in the cluster.
$k_{l,mn}$ = Total weights of the links from the cluster 'l' to 'm'.
k_l = Total weights of the links attached to node 'l'.
p = Total weight of all the links in the complex network.

4. **Average degree:** Average degree of a network with 'N' as a set of nodes and 'E' as a set of edges is defined as follows.

$$AD_{Net} = \frac{2 * |E|}{|N|} \tag{7}$$

After extracting these four network features from all the channels, we further identify the most significant channels and combine the discriminative network features from these channels. It is observed from the experimental analysis that combining the features from the significant channels provides better classification performance.

3.3 Classification

The classifiers such as SVM, KNN, naive Bayes (NB), ensemble methods, etc. are the popular choices among researchers for the classification of EEG signals. Among these methods, SVM and KNN have been the most widely used classifiers for the detection of alcoholism. Therefore, the proposed work forwards the combined feature set to these two classifiers for separating the EEG signals of alcoholics and controlled drinkers. We estimate the optimal hyperparameters (C, σ) required by the SVM-RBF kernel using the grid search method. The parameter 'C' can take values from the set $\{10^{-2}, 10^{-1}, ..., 10^5, 10^6\}$ and the set of values for parameter 'σ' is $\{10^{-5}, 10^{-4}, ..., 10^2, 10^3\}$. The KNN classifier requires the parameter 'k' whose optimal value is determined by cross-validating the model with different 'k' values and choosing the one which yields the best accuracy.

4   Experimental Study and Discussion

This section presents the details of the dataset used in this work and the experimental analysis of the proposed approach for the detection of alcoholism. Experimental study includes: 1) performance analysis of individual channels using different complex network features; and 2) performance analysis of the group of significant channels using channel-wise discriminative network features. These experiments are carried out on an Intel(R) Core i7 machine having 1.8 GHz CPU, 8 GB RAM, and 64 bit Windows platform. The proposed work is implemented using Matlab R2018a. The performance metric considered in the proposed work is the classification accuracy.

4.1   Dataset

The experimental dataset used in this work corresponds to the EEG signals of alcoholic and controlled drinkers. This dataset is obtained from UCI[1] machine learning repository. EEG signals were recorded from 122 subjects and each subject underwent 120 trials, where three different stimuli were presented. Each recording consists of 64 channels, where 61 channels correspond to EEG signals, two are EOG channels and one is reference channel. EEG signals of all the channels were sampled 256 Hz for a duration of 1 s. The full version of this dataset is incomplete where some EEG recordings are either empty or labelled as "err". Hence, we have conducted experiments using large version of the dataset which contains training and test files as: 'SMNI_CMI_TRAIN' and 'SMNI_CMI_TEST'. Both training and test data contains 600 recordings having EEG signals from 64 channels. The reference channel 'nd' has been ignored from the analysis in this work. The baseline EEG signals were already cleaned to remove the artifacts like eye blinks and other noises added during recording [4].

4.2   Analysis of Individual Channels

The proposed work extracts four important and widely used complex network features, viz. weighted clustering coefficient, average weighted degree, modularity, and average degree from the complex networks of EEG signals of individual channels belonging to alcoholic dataset. Then, the effectiveness of individual features of each channel is assessed using SVM and KNN classifiers. The alcoholic EEG dataset available at UCI repository contains the training and test data files, viz. 'SMNI_CMI_TRAIN' and 'SMNI_CMI_TEST'. Therefore, we have used the samples in training file for training the classifiers and the samples in test file for evaluating the performance of classifiers on the unknown samples. Figures 3, 4, 5, and 6 depict the classification accuracy of different channels using individual network features. From these figures, it can be seen that the SVM classifier performs better than the KNN classifier. Another observation is that the effectiveness of each feature in achieving class separation varies across the channels and a single feature is not sufficient to achieve better class separation for individual channels. Therefore, we analyze the performance of individual channels using different groups of discriminative network features.

For each channel, features are selected based on their classification accuracy and then the top two, top three, and all four network features are forwarded to SVM classifier. The KNN classifier is not effective here because it produced poor results as compared to SVM classifier for individual features. Figure 7 shows the performance comparison for each individual channel obtained using top two, top three, and all four network features. It is evident that the SVM classifier with top two discriminative features produced poor results as compared to other combinations of features for all the channels. Moreover, the results obtained with

---

[1] http://archive.ics.uci.edu/ml.

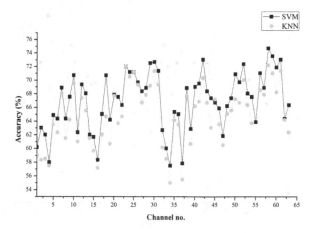

Fig. 3. Classification accuracy of different channels using weighted clustering coefficient

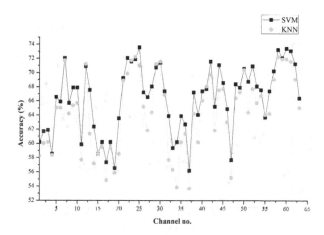

Fig. 4. Classification accuracy of individual channels using average weighted degree

all four network features are slightly higher or comparable to the results obtained with top three discriminative features. Another observation is that combining the discriminative features for each channel improved the classification performance of individual channels in most of the cases. It can be seen that as the channels, viz. 32 and 63 are EOG channels, they are not useful in the classification of EEG signals in all the experiments.

To further enhance the classification accuracy, the proposed approach combines the discriminative features from different significant channels. Results for the groups of significant channels are presented in Sect. 4.3.

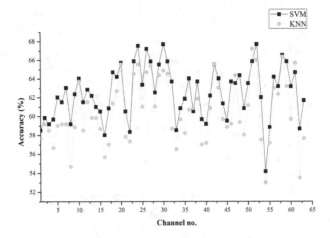

Fig. 5. Classification accuracy of individual channels using modularity

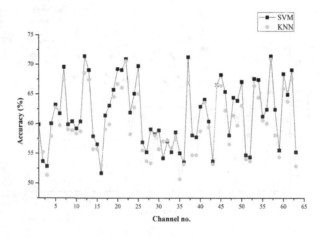

Fig. 6. Classification accuracy of individual channels using average degree

4.3 Analysis of the Group of Significant Channels

In this section, we analyze the behaviour of combined feature set formed using discriminative complex network features extracted from the different groups of significant channels. We first conduct the experiments with 'SMNI_CMI_TRAIN' as the training data and 'SMNI_CMI_TEST' as the test data. As discussed in Sect. 4.2, SVM classifier always performed better than KNN classifier for all the channels. The same behaviour is also seen for the combined feature set, see the Tables 3, 4, and 5. Again, the result obtained by combining top two features from the different groups of significant channels is poor than that

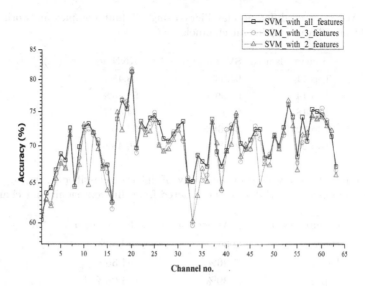

Fig. 7. Comparison of classification accuracies obtained using different combinations of network features for each channel

Table 3. Accuracy of different classifiers using top two discriminative complex network features extracted from different significant channels

# channels used	SVM accuracy (%)	KNN accuracy (%)
Top 11	93.81%	90.80%
Top 18	96.49%	93.48%
Top 27	96.66%	94.31%
Top 32	**96.66%**	92.98%
Top 39	95.65%	92.31%

Table 4. Accuracy of different classifiers using top three discriminative complex network features extracted from different significant channels

# channels used	SVM accuracy (%)	KNN accuracy (%)
Top 11	95.82%	94.48%
Top 16	95.65%	94.31%
Top 20	96.15%	94.65%
Top 28	**96.82%**	94.48%
Top 32	95.98%	95.15%

Table 5. Accuracy of different classifiers using all four complex network features extracted from different significant channels

# channels used	SVM accuracy (%)	KNN accuracy (%)
Top 11	94.98%	93.48%
Top 14	96.99%	94.15%
Top 18	97.16%	94.82%
Top 22	**98.66%**	94.65%
Top 28	97.99%	96.48%

Table 6. Ten-fold cross-validation accuracy of different classifiers using top two discriminative complex network features extracted from different significant channels

# channels used	SVM accuracy (%)	KNN accuracy (%)
Top 8	92.34%	90.82%
Top 15	95.96%	94.36%
Top 22	97.39%	95.96%
Top 27	97.31%	95.37%
Top 35	**97.56%**	95.20%

Table 7. Ten-fold cross-validation accuracy of different classifiers using top three discriminative complex network features extracted from different significant channels

# channels used	SVM accuracy (%)	KNN accuracy (%)
Top 12	94.53%	94.02%
Top 18	96.63%	95.45%
Top 28	**98.06%**	95.03%
Top 33	97.81%	95.37%

obtained using other feature combinations. The maximum accuracy with two features is 96.66%. It is evident from the Tables 4 and 5 that the combination of all four complex network features extracted from the top 22 significant channels produced the best result which is 98.66%. The 22 significant channels are $\{20, 18, 53, 19, 58, 59, 60, 25, 42, 54, 56, 24, 17, 37, 22, 31, 26, 61, 11, 30, 10, 52\}$.

In literature, certain studies for alcoholism detection have validated the results of their proposed approach using 10-fold cross-validation [6, 22, 25]. Therefore, we also validate the result of the proposed approach using 10-fold cross-validation. The original datasets, viz. 'SMNI_CMI_TRAIN' and 'SMNI_CMI_TEST' are merged to perform 10-fold cross-validation on the entire dataset. The results of the 10-fold cross-validation for top two, top three, and all four complex network features extracted from the different groups of optimal channels are listed in Tables 6, 7, and 8 respectively. As it can be seen from these tables, the results obtained using top two features are not better than that obtained

Table 8. Ten-fold cross-validation accuracy of different classifiers using all four complex network features extracted from different significant channels

# channels used	SVM accuracy (%)	KNN accuracy (%)
Top 11	94.61%	94.44%
Top 15	96.04%	94.61%
Top 22	96.97%	94.78%
Top 28	98.23%	94.87%
Top 35	**98.91%**	95.03%
Top 38	98.57%	96.04%
Top 40	98.23%	94.95%

Table 9. Performance comparison of the proposed approach and other state-of-the-art approaches

Method	Features used	Classifier	Accuracy (%)
Acharya et al. [1]	Largest lyapunov exponent, approximate entropy, sample entropy, 4 higher order spectral features	SVM (polynomial kernel)	91.7%
Shri et al. [18]	Approximate entropy (ApEn)	SVM (polynomial kernel), BPNN	90%
Zhu et al. [25]	Horizontal visibility graph entropy (HVGE)	SVM (RBF kernel), KNN	95.8%
Taran and Bajaj [22]	Inter quartile range, mean absolute deviation, entropy, coefficient of variation, and neg-entropy	ELM, LS-SVM	97.92%
Sharma et al. [17]	Log-energy entropies (LEEs), l2 norms (L2Ns)	FSC, SMO-SVM, LS-SVM	97.91%
Bavkar et al. [6]	Linear, non-linear, and statistical features from EEG rhythms	Ensemble subspace KNN	98.25%
Proposed approach	Complex network features (average weighted degree, modularity, weighted clustering coefficient, average degree)	SVM (RBF kernel), KNN	**98.91%**

using top three and all four network features. The highest classification accuracy is 98.91% which is achieved by harnessing 35 optimal channels and all four complex network features. The optimal channels are: $\{20, 18, 54, 53, 19, 42, 24, 60, 22, 25, 10, 59, 7, 61, 17, 62, 56, 58, 23, 30, 41, 51, 37, 57, 43, 52, 45, 12, 46, 47, 50, 26, 31, 11, 13\}$.

In literature, many researchers studied the problem of alcoholism detection and developed different state-of-the-art methods. A comparison of the results of the proposed approach and other state-of-the-art reported results is presented in Table 9. Some state-of-the-art approaches are not listed in this comparison because of the different dataset versions used in their work. In the study by Ahmadi et al. [3], the dataset size is not mentioned and in other works either the small version of the dataset or only a subset of the full version of the dataset has been used [2, 4, 5, 8, 11, 12, 15, 16]. These approaches have been discussed in detail in Sect. 2. Experimental results in Table 9 confirm the ascendancy of the

Table 10. Performance metrics for the highest accuracy of the proposed approach

Accuracy	Sensitivity	Specificity	F-score	Kappa
98.91%	98.66%	99.1%	0.9891	0.9781

proposed method compared to other state-of-the-art methods. The results also suggest that the weighted visibility graph along with the network features produce promising results and the proposed approach is useful in detecting alcoholism.

Table 10 shows the other performance metrics for the best result achieved using 10-fold cross-validation and all four network features.

5   Conclusion

Alcoholism is a brain disorder caused due to excessive consumption of alcohol. It not only affects the neurological system but also leads to several physical and behavioural problems. Considering the severity of these problems, an automated and feasible approach is required to classify the EEG signals of alcoholics and controlled drinkers. Therefore, a novel three-phase approach has been proposed in this work to detect alcoholism. The first phase modeled the EEG signals as weighted visibility graphs (WVGs) because VG can inherit many dynamic properties of the time series and it is also robust to noise. Moreover, the weights on the links in the visibility graph help to differentiate the strong and weak connections in the network and to recognize the fluctuations in EEG signals. Then, the second phase extracted complex network features, viz. weighted clustering coefficient, average weighted degree, modularity, and average degree from the corresponding WVGs. Further, the optimal channels were identified and their discriminative network features were combined to form feature vectors. These feature vectors were trained using machine learning classifiers for predicting unknown samples in the third phase. In all experiments, the SVM-RBF classifier outperformed the KNN classifier. Experimental analysis of the alcoholic dataset suggests that the results obtained by the proposed method are higher or comparable to other state-of-the-art approaches. It is also evident that combining all four network features extracted from the 35 optimal channels produced the best classification accuracy of 98.91%. This result shows that the notion of weights in the visibility graph and the complex network features are effective and useful for the detection of alcoholism.

In future, the EEG signals can be decomposed into different frequency sub-bands. Then, the EEG signal of each sub-band can be mapped to the weighted visibility graph (WVG) and the complex network features are extracted from the corresponding WVG. This may help to further boost the classification performance as the WVG is applied to individual EEG rhythms. The effectiveness of WVG and complex network features can also be examined for other EEG applications such as BCI-oriented EEG study.

References

1. Acharya, U.R., Sree, S.V., Chattopadhyay, S., Suri, J.S.: Automated diagnosis of normal and alcoholic EEG signals. Int. J. Neural Syst. **22**(03), 1250011 (2012)
2. Agarwal, S., Zubair, M.: Classification of alcoholic and non-alcoholic EEG signals based on sliding-SSA and independent component analysis. IEEE Sens. J. **21**(23), 26198–26206 (2021)
3. Ahmadi, N., Pei, Y., Pechenizkiy, M.: Detection of alcoholism based on EEG signals and functional brain network features extraction. In: 2017 IEEE 30th International Symposium on Computer-Based Medical Systems (CBMS), pp. 179–184. IEEE (2017)
4. Anuragi, A., Sisodia, D.S.: Alcohol use disorder detection using EEG signal features and flexible analytical wavelet transform. Biomed. Sig. Process. Control **52**, 384–93 (2018)
5. Anuragi, A., Sisodia, D.S.: Empirical wavelet transform based automated alcoholism detecting using EEG signal features. Biomed. Sig. Process. Control **57**, 101777 (2020)
6. Bavkar, S., Iyer, B., Deosarkar, S.: Detection of alcoholism: an EEG hybrid features and ensemble subspace K-NN based approach. In: Fahrnberger, G., Gopinathan, S., Parida, L. (eds.) ICDCIT 2019. LNCS, vol. 11319, pp. 161–168. Springer, Cham (2019). https://doi.org/10.1007/978-3-030-05366-6_13
7. Blondel, V.D., Guillaume, J.L., Lambiotte, R., Lefebvre, E.: Fast unfolding of communities in large networks. J. Stat. Mech: Theory Exp. **2008**(10), P10008 (2008)
8. Buriro, A.B., et al.: Classification of alcoholic EEG signals using wavelet scattering transform-based features. Comput. Biol. Med. **139**, 104969 (2021)
9. Cai, L., Deng, B., Wei, X., Wang, R., Wang, J.: Analysis of spontaneous EEG activity in Alzheimer's disease using weighted visibility graph. In: 2018 40th Annual International Conference of the IEEE Engineering in Medicine and Biology Society (EMBC), pp. 3100–3103. IEEE (2018)
10. Lacasa, L., Luque, B., Ballesteros, F., Luque, J., Nuno, J.C.: From time series to complex networks: the visibility graph. Proc. Natl. Acad. Sci. **105**(13), 4972–4975 (2008)
11. Mehla, V.K., Singhal, A., Singh, P.: A novel approach for automated alcoholism detection using Fourier decomposition method. J. Neurosci. Methods **346**, 108945 (2020)
12. Mukhtar, H., Qaisar, S.M., Zaguia, A.: Deep convolutional neural network regularization for alcoholism detection using EEG signals. Sensors **21**(16), 5456 (2021)
13. Newman, M.E.: Analysis of weighted networks. Phys. Rev. E **70**(5), 056131 (2004)
14. Organization., W.H.: Global status report on alcohol and health, In: World Health Organization: Geneva, Switzerland (2018)
15. Prabhakar, S.K., Rajaguru, H.: Alcoholic EEG signal classification with correlation dimension based distance metrics approach and modified AdaBoost classification. Heliyon **6**(12), e05689 (2020)
16. Salankar, N., Qaisar, S.M., Pławiak, P., Tadeusiewicz, R., Hammad, M.: EEG based alcoholism detection by oscillatory modes decomposition second order difference plots and machine learning. Biocybern. Biomed. Eng. **42**(1), 173–86 (2022)
17. Sharma, M., Sharma, P., Pachori, R.B., Acharya, U.R.: Dual-tree complex wavelet transform-based features for automated alcoholism identification. Int. J. Fuzzy Syst. **20**(4), 1297–1308 (2018)

18. Shri, T.P., Sriraam, N., Bhat, V.: Characterization of EEG signals for identification of alcoholics using ANOVA ranked approximate entropy and classifiers. In: International Conference on Circuits, Communication, Control and Computing, pp. 109–112. IEEE (2014)
19. Siuly, S., Li, Y.: Designing a robust feature extraction method based on optimum allocation and principal component analysis for epileptic EEG signal classification. Comput. Methods Programs Biomed. **119**(1), 29–42 (2015)
20. Supriya, S., Siuly, S., Wang, H., Cao, J., Zhang, Y.: Weighted visibility graph with complex network features in the detection of epilepsy. IEEE Access **4**, 6554–6566 (2016)
21. Supriya, S., Siuly, S., Wang, H., Zhang, Y.: EEG sleep stages analysis and classification based on weighed complex network features. IEEE Trans. Emerg. Top. Comput. Intell. **5**(2), 236–46 (2018)
22. Taran, S., Bajaj, V.: Rhythm-based identification of alcohol EEG signals. IET Sci. Meas. Technol. **12**(3), 343–349 (2017)
23. Wang, F., Meng, Q., Chen, Y.: A novel feature extraction method for epileptic EEG based on degree distribution of complex network. WSEAS Trans. Inf. Sci. Appl. **12**, 10 (2015)
24. Zhang, J., Small, M.: Complex network from pseudoperiodic time series: topology versus dynamics. Phys. Rev. Lett. **96**(23), 238701 (2006)
25. Zhu, G., Li, Y., Wen, P.P., Wang, S.: Analysis of alcoholic EEG signals based on horizontal visibility graph entropy. Brain inform. **1**(1–4), 19–25 (2014)

A Dehusked Areca Nut Classification Algorithm Based on 10-Fold Cross-Validation of Convolutional Neural Network

Sameer Patil[1], Aparajita Naik[4(✉)], Marlon Sequeira[2], and Jivan Parab[3(✉)]

[1] Department of Electronics, Dnyanprassarak Mandal's College and Research Centre, Goa, India
[2] Electronics Programme, Goa University, Goa, India
marlon@unigoa.ac.in
[3] Research Supervisor, Electronics Programme, Goa University, Goa, India
jsparab@unigoa.ac.in
[4] Electrical Engineering, Cambridge University, Cambridge, UK
an656@cam.ac.uk

Abstract. In the process of production of Areca nut, segregation is one of the important stages. As of now, most commercial retailers use skilled workers for quality segregation, which means a lot of time is required for finalising the product costing. In this paper, Convolutional Neural Network (CNN) and MobileNet based methodology was proposed to identify the healthy and diseased Areca nut. The dataset containing images of healthy and diseased nuts was created. Furthermore, the augmentation method was applied to enhance the dataset. The confusion matrix was applied to check the performance of the models and the same was cross-validated using the 10-fold method. The CNN and MobileNet achieved accuracy, precision, recall, and an F1-score of 100%. After applying the 10-fold method, the CNN achieved average accuracy, precision, recall, and F1-score of 95%, 97%, 96%, and 94%, respectively. Whereas, MobileNet outperforms CNN by 100% for all metrics.

Keywords: Areca nut · Segregation · Convolutional neural networks (CNN) · MobileNet

1 Introduction

Areca palm (*Areca catechu L.*) is grown for its kernel which is popularly known as Areca nut (or Betel nut or Supari) in India. It is grown on a commercial scale along the western coast of India (Maharashtra, Goa, Karnataka), Kerala, Tamil Nadu, West Bengal, and Assam [1]. It is a tropical crop grown commercially in Southeast and South Asian countries, parts of east Africa, and some of the tropical pacific nations [2, 3]. Since ancient times, it is used as a masticator wherein, a slice of Areca nut along with slaked lime (aqueous Calcium hydroxide paste) and some aromatics (clove, cardamom, saffron) for extra flavour, is wrapped in a betel leaf [4]. In ancient Indian scripts, it is mentioned that Areca nut can be used as a therapeutic agent for leucoderma, leprosy, anemia, and

© The Author(s), under exclusive license to Springer Nature Switzerland AG 2023
I. Woungang et al. (Eds.): ANTIC 2022, CCIS 1798, pp. 35–45, 2023.
https://doi.org/10.1007/978-3-031-28183-9_3

obesity and also has de-worming properties due to which it is used in gastrointestinal disorders [5]. Areca nut has many pharmacological properties and hence is widely used in Medicine. It has anti-allergic, anti-parasitic, anti-microbial, and anti-aging properties. Areca nuts are also used in the production of adhesives, non-woven fabrics, textile dyes, and building materials. Hence, due to its high economic significance, the Areca nut has become an important cash crop.

As per the latest studies, India tops at the global level, contributing to approximately 904 thousand metric tons in 2020 [6]. The top 10 Areca nut producing countries in the world are shown in Fig. 1.

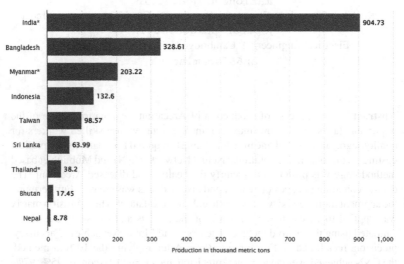

Fig. 1. Areca nut production in Asia Pacific in 2020 by country (in 1000 metric tons) [6]

The Areca nut kernel is hard from the outside with the inner endosperm marbled in dark brown and white [7]. Following are the important stages involved in the production of Areca nut.

1. Harvesting
2. Drying
3. De-husking
4. Nut segregation is based on its quality.

Of the above stages involved in the production process, nut segregation is hectic and consumes a lot of time. In the state of Goa (India), Goa Bagayatdar, a cooperative organisation is a leading Areca nut collector. At their collection centres, nuts are classified based on texture, colour, and quality. Nuts are segregated into seven different categories (Supari, Safed, Laal, Vench, Kharad, Tukda, and Baad) [8]. But, due to the shortage of skilled laborers for the above said work, there is a necessity to develop a unit of segregation based on its quality. This will not only solve the issue of scarcity of laborers but also will save the time of farmers.

2   Literature Review

A lot of research is ongoing in the area of image processing and Machine learning for the identification, classification, and grading of agricultural produce. S. Siddesha et al., in their study of the texture-based classification of Areca nut, extracted different texture features using Wavelet, Gabor, Local Binary Pattern, Gray Level Difference Matrix, and Gray Level Co-Occurrence Matrix features. They used the Nearest Neighbor classifier for the classification of Areca nuts. A classification rate of 91.43% is achieved with Gabor wavelet features [9]. Mallaiah Suresha et al., have proposed the classification of diseased and undiseased Areca nuts using texture features of Local Binary Pattern (LBP), Haar Wavelets, GLCM, and Gabor. They achieved a success rate of 92.00% [10]. T. Liu et.al have tried to achieve automatic classification by extracting the colour, shape, and texture features of de-husked Areca nut [11]. Huang K.Y., used Neural Networks and Image processing techniques for quality detection and classification of areca nuts. Six geometric features, 3 color features, and defects were used for the classification process. This method of classification achieved an accuracy of 90.9% [12]. A. Rajendra et. al have done work on areca nut disease detection using image processing wherein, Neural Networks and image processing techniques were used for classification. They used back propagation cellular network classifier [13]. H. Chandrashekhara et. al have proposed a Classification of Healthy and Diseased Arecanuts using an SVM Classifier, in which they used the Structured Matrix Decomposition model (SMD) for image segmentation and the SVM classifier is used for extracting LBP features. An accuracy of 98% is achieved [14].

The use of Deep Learning (DL) techniques in machine learning due to high levels of abstraction and the ability to learn patterns present in images automatically makes it more vital [15]. Among the various architectures used, Convolutional Neural Network (CNN) is the most popular DL architecture used for image processing [16–18]. CNN is a type of Artificial Neural Network (ANN) that uses convolution operations in at least one of its layers [16].

As regards to Areca nut, researchers have worked in the area of husked areca nut classification. But, to the best of our knowledge, there is very little work done in the area of classification of de-husked Areca nuts using CNN.

In this work, authors created a dataset containing a total of 120 images of healthy (60 images) and diseased (60 images) Areca nuts. Two DL methods such as customized CNN and MobileNet were devised for the classification of Areca nuts. The augmentation method was applied to enhance the performance of the models due to the small size of the dataset. First, the originally captured images were applied to train and validate the models, and later, augmented images were applied. The outcome of these two methods was compared and the best suitable method is suggested to identify the healthy and diseased Areca nut.

3 Dataset Description

This paper deals with the quality classification of Areca nut from the Konkan belt of India, in particular from the state of Goa. Since there is no publicly available database of de-husked Areca nut images, a special setup was designed for the creation of a preliminary database. Figure 2, shows the captured images of healthy and diseased Areca nuts.

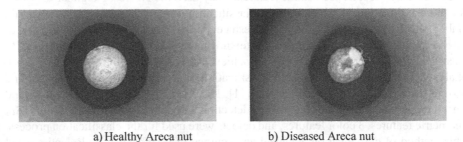

a) Healthy Areca nut   b) Diseased Areca nut

Fig. 2. Captured images of Areca nuts

4 Methodology

Figure 3 shows the framework of the proposed method for the identification of healthy and diseased Areca nuts. First, the dataset of healthy and diseased Areca nut images was captured. The augmentation method was applied to increase the dataset. The CNN and MobileNet models were trained and tested on augmented and un-augmented images. Finally, the confusion matrix and 10-fold method were applied for model performance evaluation.

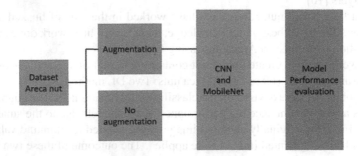

Fig. 3. The framework of the proposed method

4.1 Data Augmentation

Data augmentation is a technique in CNN and is normally applicable when the training samples are limited. Thus, for training a network, we can generate more training samples using existing images. This is done by using image processing functions such as scaling, rotation about an axis, translation, and reflection about an axis. This generates a much larger training sample size from the existing data [19].

To evaluate our CNN, we use 10-fold cross-validation. In 10-fold cross-validation, the database is split into 10 distinct folds of which 9 folds will be used in training and the 10th fold is used for testing. This means that every sample which was used for testing is now included in the training set and one from the training set is used for testing. Thus, the procedure is repeated 10 times, with each iteration having a new fold from one of the 10 folds for testing [20].

4.2 Convolutional Neural Network

Convolutional Neural Networks (CNN) are being extensively studied in recent literature [21, 22]. CNN is a class of deep learning algorithms that is especially efficient in the classification of data by recognizing patterns in an image. A CNN is a feed-forward network and consists of basic building blocks like a convolutional layer, pooling layer, and activation layer, which are stacked together with varying permutations and combinations. This varying arrangement of the convolutional layer, pooling layer, and activation layer together form the feature extraction segment of a CNN [23]. The extracted features are then given to a fully connected layer and the classification layer, which are part of the classification segment [24].

In the proposed work, activation function ReLU, average pooling, dropout, batch normalization (BN), flatten, and dense layer are utilised. The pooling layer consists of a down-sampling operation which decreases the dimension of the feature map. To avoid over-fitting by randomly selected neurons, a dropout was used. BN is used for speeding up the training process which intern makes learning easier. FC layer input is attached to every one of the outputs hence, the term "fully connected" and also called a dense layer.

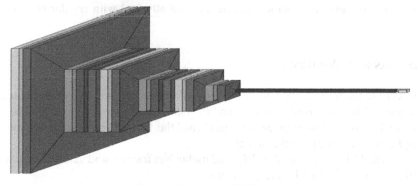

Fig. 4. The custom CNN model

Below mentioned are the various layers used in the custom CNN model shown in Fig. 4.

1) Conv2d, 128 kernel with relu
2) Batch normalisation (BN) layer
3) Average pooling layer with 2x2 pool size
4) Dropout with 0.1
5) Batch normalisation (BN) layer
6) Conv2d, 64 kernel with relu
7) Batch normalisation (BN) layer
8) Average pooling layer with 2x2 pool size
9) Dropout with 0.1
10) Batch normalisation (BN) layer
11) Conv2d, 32 kernel with relu
12) Batch normalisation (BN) layer
13) Average pooling layer with 2x2 pool size
14) Dropout with 0.1
15) Batch normalisation (BN) layer
16) Flatten layer
17) Dense layer with 2 neurons with softmax function

4.3 MobileNet model

MobileNet was employed to satisfy the applications involving restricted resources such as low power, and low latency models [25]. MobileNet comprises a depth-separable convolution that allows a regular convolution into a depth-wise convolution and a point-wise convolution (1×1). In the deep convolution layer of each input channel in the MobileNet architecture, a single filter is used. In pointwise convolution, the outputs are combined by a convolution size of 1×1 into a penetration-wise convolution. Inputs joint with newly generated outputs in one step are attached with regular convolution filters.

5   Results and Analysis

In this section, the performance of the CNN and MobileNet models was evaluated on augmented and non-augmented images and then the outcome was compared. The confusion matrix was used to evaluate the models and the 10-fold cross-validation method was applied to cross-validate the models.

Figure 5 and Fig. 6 indicate the CNN and mobileNet training and validation accuracy and training and validation loss respectively.

In this section, we have presented the classification accuracy for all four databases. We train a CNN model with 10-fold cross-validation with and without data augmentation for each database.

Figure 7 shows that using the 10-fold method for CNN without augmentation, an average accuracy, precision, recall, and F1-score of 95%, 97%, 96%, and 94%, respectively were achieved.

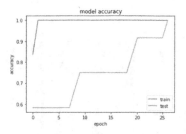
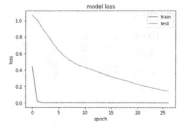

a) CNN Training and validation accuracy   b) CNN Training and validation loss

Fig. 5. CNN training and validation accuracy and training and validation loss

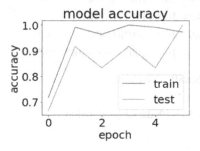
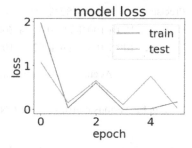

a)   MobileNet Training and validation accuracy b) MobileNet Training and validation loss

Fig. 6. MobileNet training and validation accuracy and training and validation loss

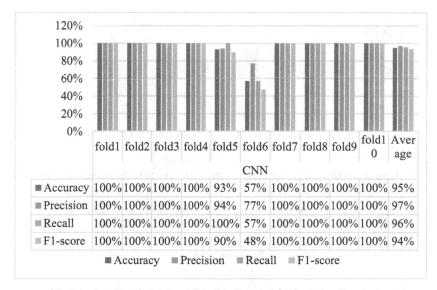

	fold1	fold2	fold3	fold4	fold5	fold6	fold7	fold8	fold9	fold10	Average
■ Accuracy	100%	100%	100%	100%	93%	57%	100%	100%	100%	100%	95%
■ Precision	100%	100%	100%	100%	94%	77%	100%	100%	100%	100%	97%
■ Recall	100%	100%	100%	100%	100%	57%	100%	100%	100%	100%	96%
■ F1-score	100%	100%	100%	100%	90%	48%	100%	100%	100%	100%	94%

■ Accuracy   ■ Precision   ■ Recall   ■ F1-score

Fig. 7. Various metrics for the CNN model without data augmentation

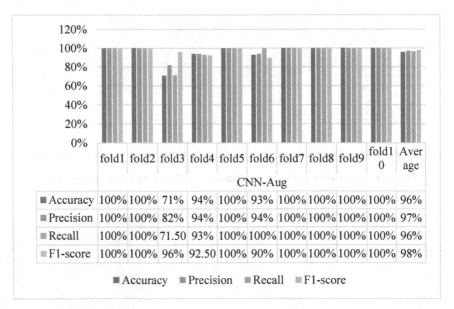

Fig. 8. Various metrics for the CNN model with data augmentation

Figure 8 shows that using the 10-fold method for CNN with augmentation technique, an average accuracy, precision, recall, and F1-score of 96%, 97%, 96%, and 98%, respectively were achieved.

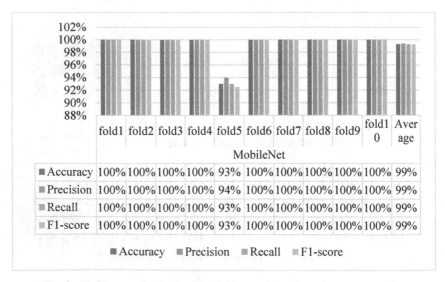

Fig. 9. Various metrics for the MobileNet model without data augmentation

Figure 9 shows that using the 10-fold method for the MobileNet network without augmentation technique, an average accuracy, precision, recall, and F1-score of 100% respectively were achieved.

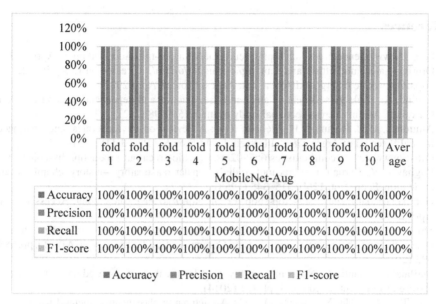

Fig. 10. Various metrics for the MobileNet model with data augmentation

Figure 10 shows that using the 10-fold method for the MobileNet network with augmentation technique, an average accuracy, precision, recall, and F1-score of 100% respectively were achieved.

6 Conclusion

The identification of the Areca nut types is a very difficult task. The authors proposed an efficient method using two different DL methods (CNN and MobileNet). The augmentation method was also applied to enhance the dataset due to which the performance of the models increased. The models were also cross-validated using the 10-fold method and obtained an average 100% F1-score for MobileNet and 98% for CNN. MobileNet outperforms the CNN model as well as the literature reported work.

The authors tried to develop a customized CNN model and achieved a good performance. The benefit of the proposed method is that it identifies healthy and diseased Areca nuts with 100% accuracy. This method can be of great help for farmers to identify healthy and diseased Areca nuts easily.

The limitation of the work is that the dataset has only healthy and diseased Areca nut images. In future work, more types of Areca nuts will be included in the dataset. The author will also try to implement other DL models such as DenseNet201, VGG16, etc., to develop the system.

Acknowledgment. The authors acknowledge the help extended by the skilled segregators for classification, and officials of Goa Bagayatdar, for providing a large number of samples of Areca nut used for this work.

References

1. https://www.sciencedirect.com/topics/neuroscience/areca-nut. Accessed on 28 April 2022
2. Origin — areca nut. https://arecanut.org/arecanut-1/origin/. Accessed on 15 April 2022
3. https://en.wikipedia.org/wiki/Areca_nut. Accessed on 28 April 2022
4. Arvind, K., et al.: Assessment of areca nut use, practice and dependency among people in Guwahati, Assam: a cross-sectional study ecancer **15**, 1198 (2021)
5. Amudhan, M.S., Begum, V.H., Hebbar, K.B.: A Review on Phytochemical and Pharmacological Potential of Areca catechu L Seed. Int J Pharm Sci Res. **3**(11), 4151–4157
6. https://www.statista.com/statistics/657902/asia-pacific-areca-nut-production-by-country/
7. Raghavan, V., Baruah, H.: Arecanut: India's popular masticatory—history, chemistry, and utilization. Econ. Bot. **12**(4), 315–345 (1958)
8. Goa bagayatdar bazar – one-stop-shop for all. https://goabagayatdar.com/. Accessed on 13 April 2022
9. Siddesha, S., et al.: Texture based classification of areca nut. In: 2015 International Conference on Applied and Theoretical Computing and Communication Technology (iCATccT), pp. 688–692 (2015)
10. Mallaiah, S., Danti, A., Narasimhamurthy, S.: Classification of diseased arecanut based on texture features. Int. J. Comp. Appl. **1**, 1 (2014)
11. Liu, T., Xie, J., He, Y., Xu, M., Qin, C.: An automatic classification method for betel nut based on computer vision. IEEE Int. Conf. Roboti. Biomim. (ROBIO) **2009**, 1264–1267 (2009). https://doi.org/10.1109/ROBIO.2009.5420823
12. Huang, K.Y.: Detection and classification of areca nuts with machine vision. Computers, and Mathematics with Applications **64**(5), 739–746 (2012). https://doi.org/10.1016/j.camwa.2011.11.041
13. Rajendra, A.B., Rajkumar, N., Shetty, P.D.: Area Nut Disease Detection Using Image Processing. In: Pant, M., Kumar Sharma, T., Arya, R., Sahana, B.C., Zolfagharinia, H. (eds.) Soft Computing: Theories and Applications. AISC, vol. 1154, pp. 925–931. Springer, Singapore (2020). https://doi.org/10.1007/978-981-15-4032-5_83
14. Chandrashekhara, H., Mallaiah, S.: Classification of healthy and diseased arecanuts using SVM classifier. Int. J. Comp. Sci. Eng. **7**, 544–548 (2019). https://doi.org/10.26438/ijcse/v7i2.544548
15. Naranjo-Torres, J., Mora, M., Hernández-García, R., Barrientos, R.J., Fredes, C., Valenzuela, A.: A review of convolutional neural network applied to fruit image processing. Appl. Sci. **10**, 3443 (2020). https://doi.org/10.3390/app10103443
16. Goodfellow, I., Bengio, Y., Courville, A.: Deep Learning; MIT Press: Cambridge. MA, USA (2016)
17. Wick, C.: Deep Learning. Informatik-Spektrum **40**(1), 103–107 (2016). https://doi.org/10.1007/s00287-016-1013-2
18. Zeiler, M.D., Fergus, R.: Visualizing and Understanding Convolutional Networks. In: Fleet, D., Pajdla, T., Schiele, B., Tuytelaars, T. (eds.) ECCV 2014. LNCS, vol. 8689, pp. 818–833. Springer, Cham (2014). https://doi.org/10.1007/978-3-319-10590-1_53
19. Zhong, Z., Zheng, L., Kang, G., Li, S., Yang, Y.: Random erasing data augmentation. In: Proceedings of the AAAI Conference on Artificial Intelligence, vol. 34, no. 07, pp. 13001–13008 (2020 April)

20. Wong, T.T., Yeh, P.Y.: Reliable accuracy estimates from k-fold cross-validation. IEEE Trans. Knowl. Data Eng. **32**(8), 1586–1594 (2019)
21. Jia, W., Tian, Y., Luo, R., Zhang, Z., Lian, J., Zheng, Y.: Detection and segmentation of overlapped fruits based on optimized mask R-CNN application in apple harvesting robot. Comput. Electron. Agric. **172**, 105380 (2020)
22. Mai, X., Zhang, H., Jia, X., Meng, M.Q.H.: Faster R-CNN with classifier fusion for automatic detection of small fruits. IEEE Trans. Autom. Sci. Eng. **17**(3), 1555–1569 (2020)
23. Detection of Nuclei in H&E-Stained Sections Using Convolutional Neural Networks Mina Khoshdeli Richard Cong Bahram Parvin
24. Imagenet classification with deep convolutional neural networks Krizhevsky, Alex and Sutskever, Ilya and Hinton, Geoffrey E
25. Lanjewar, M.G., Morajkar, P.P., Parab, J.: Detection of tartrazine colored rice flour adulteration in turmeric from multi-spectral images on smartphone using convolutional neural network deployed on PaaS cloud. Multimed Tools Appl **81**, 16537–16562 (2022). https://doi.org/10.1007/s11042-022-12392-3

Customer Segmentation Based on RFM Analysis and Unsupervised Machine Learning Technique

Lourth Hallishma$^{(\boxtimes)}$

Department of Computer Science and Engineering, R. N. G. Patel Institute of Technology, Isroli,
Gujarat, India
hallishmalourth1@gmail.com

Abstract. Customers should be one of the main focal points of any profitable business. Loyal customers who develop a relationship with the organization raise multitudes of business prospects. An organization looking to reap benefits from such opportunities must find a way to first of all, identify such customers and secondly, market their products to them in an individualized way to develop a lucrative business. This would require the organization to spot such customers and then differentiate their personal needs, preferences and behaviours. The aim of this paper is to tackle this problem using RFM analysis and Unsupervised Machine Learning technique called K-Means Clustering. RFM (Recency, Frequency, Monetary) analysis helps determine the behaviour of the customer with the organisation. The RFM values for each customer are calculated first following with the RFM Scores. Then, K-Means Clustering is implemented on the basis of the RFM Scores and in the end, we get clusters of customers. At this point, we will be able to analyze each cluster and accurately identify the characteristics of the customers. This will make it easy for the organization to customize their marketing strategies according to the customer behaviour, which will result in raised profits.

Keywords: Unsupervised Machine Learning · Clustering · RFM Analysis · Customer Relationship Management(CRM)

1 Introduction

The concept of Customer Relationship Management(CRM) entails improving customer-business connections and relationships. There are many existing ways of doing that but through the lens of technology and Machine Learning, we can apply various techniques that have enormous potential in increasing the profitability of an organization through CRM. Customer Segmentation is one such profit-producing part of CRM which is what we'll look at in this paper. Through customer segmentation, we will be able to divide the plethora of customer data in segments that can help us differentiate the most profitable customers from the least profitable ones. This can be very useful for the organization as they will further be able to strategize various marketing ideas to personalize their selling points to different segments of the customers. This will assuredly lead to more sales and profit. Generally, customer segmentation methods mostly include experience description

I. Woungang et al. (Eds.): ANTIC 2022, CCIS 1798, pp. 46–55, 2023.
https://doi.org/10.1007/978-3-031-28183-9_4

method, traditional statistical methods and non- statistical methods [1]. A study shows that customer relationship management has significant effect on the customer satisfaction and both variables have positive relation. Company makes its CRM as strong and reliable the customer will be more satisfied and retain with the company. The increase in the satisfaction level will lead the customer to use the company's products again and again and that will increase the sales level of the company which causes the increase in organizational profit [2]. Based on these positive effects, we propose an efficient system for customer segmentation using an Unsupervised Machine Learning technique.

This paper is organized as follows: Section 2 describes some existing approaches in tackling this particular problem. Section 3 explains the various step involved in the proposed system. Section 4 contains the results and analysis of the implementation process.

2 Existing Approaches

The concept of Customer Relationship Management was actually developed in the 1970s when customer satisfaction was manually recorded in the form of surveys. The pioneers of CRM were actually Dr. Robert and Kate Kestnbaum who introduced the concept of Database Marketing, namely applying statistical methods to analyse and gather customer data and after that it was started to use commercially as customer relationship management through using various contact tools and software [3]. Sukrun Ozan applied supervised machine learning techniques of normal equation method, linear regression model and logistic regression model to classify customers into a standard or a premium customer [4]. Zhang xiao-bin et al. implemented the Fuzzy C- means clustering algorithm to segment customers and conclude high value customer group characteristics from a data-set in telecom industry [5]. HUANG Jianwei et al. executed Analytic Hierarchy Process based research on segmentation method of customer's value in aviation cargo transportation [6]. Minghua Han uses Principal Component Analysis as a statistical tool to help with customer segmentation of a retail business [7].

A lot of such approaches have been proposed to solve the problem of customer segmentation but there a few roadblocks that get in the way of efficient analysis. It is a daunting task to undertake because of the sheer magnitude of the customer database. It is important for the system to give accurate results while not diminishing any of the important variables required for the analysis. The proposed system does excellent performance in that.

2.1 The Proposed System

The implementation is carried out mainly in a two-stage process. First, we conduct RFM (Recency, Frequency, Monetary Value) analysis on each and every customer in the database. We collect the individual R, F and M values for each and every customer. This process is conducted in a speedy manner. Moving along, we calculate RFM Scores by assigning weights to each feature of RFM using quantiles. Then, we perform k-means clustering to cluster them into groups based on the RFM scores through which we can identify the groups of customers based on their potential profitability to the organization.

2.2 Data Pre-processing

The first and vital process before analysing data is to pre-process it. First, we check to see if there are any negative values under the 'Price' and 'Quantity' columns of the data and then we remove them. Then we find and eliminate all the null values in the data. Then, we check for outliers in the data and remove them. We perform these operations with the help of a python library called Pandas.

2.3 RFM Analysis

The RFM model measures when people buy, how often they buy and how much they buy. It is a technique for grouping the existing customers into segments which can give us useful insights into their past behaviour through which we can predict future sales and increase profits by marketing to them individually. The characteristics of three variables are:

- **Recency:** The time since the last purchase transaction of the customer.
- **Frequency:** It denotes the number and rate of purchase transactions of the customer.
- **Monetary:** It indicates the value of the purchases done by the customer.

We calculated these indicators at CustomerID level individually for each customer in the database so that we get information from the personal transactional data. We perform two tasks:

1) We calculate Recency, Frequency and Monetary value individually for each customer based on the data.
2) We then use quantiles to sub-divide the data base into segments on the basis of RFM. We will get individual RFM scores like this which we will add up to get the final RFM_Score.

2.4 Selecting Optimum Number of Clusters

We will be using the k-means clustering algorithm to get our clusters. The 'K' in K-means stands for the number of clusters that the algorithm will divide the data into. The first step would be find out the optimal number of clusters (K) that we want. We use two methods to calculate K. These are:

1) **Elbow Method:** It is one of the popular ways to find out the optimal number of clusters for k-means clustering. The idea behind the Elbow method is to calculate the Within- Cluster-Sum of Squared Errors (WSS) for different number of clusters (k) and select the K for which this value starts to decrease. We look for an elbow formation in the curve which will indicate the number of clusters that will be optimal choice for our clustering.

2) **The Silhouette Coefficient:** It is defined for a point i as follows: where $b(i)$ is the smallest average distance of point i to all points in any other cluster and $a(i)$ is the average distance of i from all other points in its cluster.

$$S(i) = \frac{b(i) - a(i)}{\max\{a(i), b(i)\}}$$

The silhouette coefficient is the average value of all silhouette coefficients of the points in the database. It tells us if each point is mapped perfectly according to the cluster or not.

2.5 K Means Clustering

Now that we have K, we will cluster the data using the unsupervised K-means clustering machine learning algorithm. In K-Means clustering, we have dataset, D, which has n data points and k, is the number of cluster. K-Means is a partitioning algorithm that segments data points into partitions (clusters), where k ≤ n.

1) The steps of K-means clustering are: 1. Calculate the number of cluster (k).
2) Calculate the distance between each object with each center point object. Euclidean distance space is measured using the formula:

$$D(x_2, x_1) = \sqrt{\sum_{j-1}^{p} |x_{2j} - x_{1j}}$$

where X2 is the 2nd data point, X1 is the centroid of the 1st cluster data.
3) Map each data point into a nearest cluster (most similar to centroid).
4) Update mean value (centroid) of each cluster using the formula:

$$C_1 = \frac{1}{M} \sum \frac{M}{j=1} X_j$$

5) Repeat step 3–4 until all centroids are not changed.

Now our data is divided into clusters according to the RFM Scores.

2.6 Data Visualisation and Analysis

Proper Visualisation leads to accurate understanding of the results. We plot the clusters in a 3D scatter plot to observe the behaviour of each cluster. Then we calculate the mean of each Recency, Frequency and Monetary factors grouped by each cluster to extract results. The best customers will have the lowest Recency as they should have shopped recently. They should have the highest Frequency and Monetary values as they should have shopped frequently and spent a lot of money on the organization. Applying this, we calculate the results and conclude (Fig. 1).

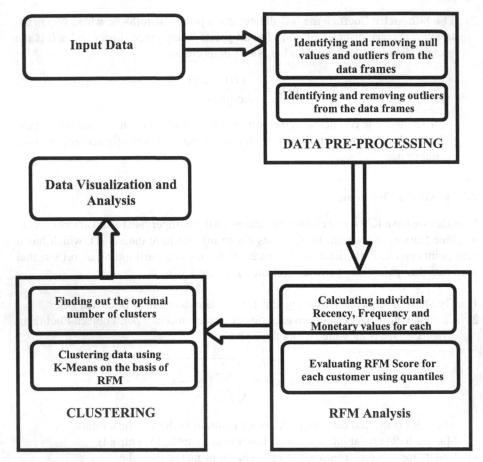

Fig. 1. Flowchart of the proposed system.

3 Results and Analysis

The proposed system is simulated in python using the dataset that is described in the further sentences. In this paper, we use the data-set from the UCI Machine Learning Repository. It contains customer details of a UK-based store that sells unique gift items. Here, is the attribute information of the data-set (Table 1):

After data-cleaning, we calculate the individual Recency, Frequency and Monetary score of the customer and group it by the CustomerID so that we can track each customer's spending habits and behaviours individually to get personalized results. The image below shows the data-frame at this point (Table 2).

So, we assign the values of RFM individually for each customer in the range of 1 to 4. We do this by comparing the values of RFM obtained with the quantiles and segmentation according to that. Then we add a column that shows the combined concatenated score of RFM in three digits. We add another column that gives us the sum of these three digits

Table 1. Attributes of the database

Attribute Name
Invoice
StockCode
Description
Quantity
InvoiceDate
Price
CustomerID
Country
Total Price
Date

Table 2. Calculated Recency, Frequency and Monetary_Value along-with CustomerID

	CustomerID	Recency	Frequency	Monetary_Value
0	12346.0	325	1	77183.60
1	12747.0	2	103	4196.01
2	12748.0	0	4595	33719.73
3	12749.0	3	199	4090.88
4	12820.0	3	59	942.34

and we consider that as our RFM Score. The image below shows us the data frame table at this point (Table 3).

Table 3. Calculated individual R_quantile, F_quantile, M_quantile. Alongwith concatenated score of RFM in three digits labelled as RFM_Segment. Finally, the RFM_Score which is the sum of those three digits.

	Customer ID	Recency	Frequency	Monetary_Value	R_quantile	F_quantile	M_quantile	RFM_Segment	RFM_Score
0	12346.0	529	33	372.86	4	3	3	433	10
1	12347.0	367	71	1323.32	1	2	2	122	5
2	12348.0	438	20	222.16	3	3	4	334	10
3	12349.0	407	102	2671.14	2	2	1	221	5
4	12351.0	375	21	300.93	1	3	4	134	8

Now, we select the number of clusters. Before we start clustering, we need to choose optimal number of clusters. The elbow method plots the value of the cost function that is acquired by different values of k. Using the Elbow Method we got the optimal number of clusters to be k=4. The image below illustrates that (Figs. 2, 3 and 4).

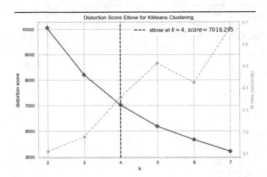

Fig. 2. Elbow method to find out the optimal number of clusters to choose.

Using the Silhouette Score method, we get optimal number of clusters as k=4.

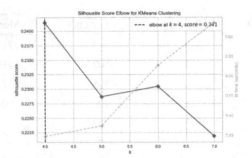

Fig. 3. Elbow method to find out the optimal number of clusters to choose

We perform K-means clustering on the data having k=4. Visualizing the clusters in a 3-D scatter plot (Table 4).

Now we analyse the data. We calculate the mean of the three factors R,F and M and finally we'll count the number of data points in each cluster also. The below image shows this representation (Table 5).

Now, we analyse the clusters. To find the cluster contaning the best customers, we must remember that the recency must be as low as possible and Frequency and Monetary factors both must be as high as possible. We conclude the following:

- **Cluster number '0'** has 'Profitable Customers' as the Recency is the lowest. Alongwith that, the cluster's frequency and monetary is highest.
- **Cluster number '1'** has 'Least Profitable Customers' as the Recency is high and they purchased very few items and spent little.
- **Cluster number '2'** has 'Almost forgotten Customers' as their Recency is high, which means they haven't purchased in a while but they used to purchase a lot in the past so

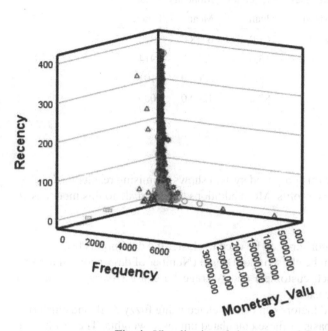

Fig. 4. Visualization of clusters on a 3-D scatter plot

Table 4. Final data frame with the clusters.

	Recency	Frequency	Monetary_Value	Cluster
0	325	1	77183.60	2
1	2	103	4196.01	0
2	0	4595	33719.73	6
3	3	199	4090.88	0
4	3	59	942.34	3

the organisation should strategize to get these customers back as their Monetary_Value and Frequency was high in the past.

- **Cluster number '3'** has 'Loyal Customers' as they spend a lot and have reasonable Recency and Frequency values.
- The quantitative measures are indicated in Table 5. It shows the mean and count of Monetary value, the mean of Recency and Frequency clusters.

Table 5. The calculated mean of Recency, Frequency and Monetary_Value, along-with the count of data-points in each cluster.

Cluster	Recency	Frequency	Monetary_Value	
	Mean	Mean	Mean	Count
0	16.0	261.0	6018.0	816
1	179.0	15.0	281.0	914
2	115.0	33.0	709.0	1101
3	53	83.0	1249.0	1089

4   Future Work

The preliminary results of this proposed system shows promising results for Customer segmentation to raise profits. More additions can be made to this model as follows:

- An Improved K-Means algorithm can be used to cluster the data-points [8].
- More factors like RFM can be chosen like Length (Number of days between the first and last transaction of each customer) and Average Purchase (Average number of items purchased by each customer).
- The weights of these added factors can be calculated using fuzzy AHP and clustering can be performed on the basis of these calculated unbiased weights. The results will be even more precise this way.

5   Conclusion

The proposed method used K-means clustering to effectively organise customers into segments according to their engagement towards the organisation. Using this, the organisation can maximise profits by looking at each segment and studying the behaviour of customers in that segment and following it up with marketing and sales strategies that are designed to attract such customers. The data analysed will provide numerous information on the customers that can be in turn used to build a "customer-centric" strategy system deployed to raise profits and sales.

References

1. Cao, S., Zhu, Q., Hou, Z.: Customer segmentation based on a novel hierarchical clustering algorithm. In: 2009 Chinese Conference on Pattern Recognition (6 November 2009)
2. Hassan,R.S., Maryam, A.N., Lashari, M.N., Zafar, F.: Effect of customer relationship management on customer satisfaction. Procedia Economics and Finance **23**, 563-567 (2015)
3. Hasan, Md.T.: Customer Relationship Management in Business: A Study on Bangladesh. IOSR Journal of Business and Management (IOSR-JBM) **20**(12). Ver. IV, 16–20 (December 2018). e-ISSN: 2278-487X, p-ISSN: 2319-7668

4. Ozan, S.: A Case Study on Customer Segmentation by using Machine Learning Methods. In: 2018 International Conference on Artificial Intelligence and Data Processing (IDAP) (2018)
5. Zhang, X., Feng, G., Hui, H.: Customer-Churn Research Based on Customer Segmentation. In: 2009 International Conference on Electronic Commerce and Business Intelligence, pp. 443–446 (2009)
6. Jianwei, H., Li, C.: AHP based research on segmentation method of customer's value in aviation cargo transportation. In: 2006 IEEE International Conference on Service Operations and Logistics, and Informatics, pp. 696- 698 (2006)
7. Han, M.: Customer segmentation model based on retail consumer Behavior Analysis. In: 2008 International Symposium on Intelligent Information Technology Application Workshops, pp. 914–917 (2008)
8. Qin, X., Zheng, S., Huang, Y., Deng, G.: Improved K-Means algorithm and application in customer segmentation. In: 2010 Asia-Pacific Conference on Wearable Computing Systems, pp. 224–227 (2010)

Manifold D-CNN Architecture for Contrastive Disease Classification Based on Respiratory Sounds

Bam Bahadur Sinha[1]($\boxtimes$)(iD), R. Dhanalakshmi[2], and K. Balakrishnan[2]

[1] Indian Institute of Information Technology Ranchi, Ranchi, Jharkhand, India
bahadurbam@iiitranchi.ac.in
[2] Indian Institute of Information Technology Tiruchirappalli, Tiruchirappalli, Tamil Nadu, India

Abstract. Several medical specialists today use X-ray and CT scan pictures of the lungs to classify respiratory disorders for specific diagnosis. Respiratory illness categorization based on inhaling and gasping sounds is still a work in progress in the scientific area. Respiratory illnesses have a high fatality rate among some of the chronic diseases. Early identification of respiratory disorders is critical for lowering death rates and curing illness. The automated categorization of respiratory sounds seems to have the capability to identify irregularities in the early phases of a respiratory disorder and, as a result, boost the efficacy of decision-making process. In this paper, a novel approach for classifying respiratory diseases using manifold D-CNN (Deep Convolutional Neural Network) is proposed to contrast different respiratory diseases accurately. Audio features are extracted using LibROSA (Mel-frequency Cepstral Coefficients, Spectrogram, and Chromagram). The performance of the model is tested using Respiratory Sound database and an accuracy of 96.23% is obtained, thus ensuring its supremacy over numerous state-of-art comparative models.

Keywords: Respiratory diseases · Convolutional Neural Network · Automated classification · Breathing sounds · Deep learning

Abbreviations:

MFCC:	Mel Frequency Cepstral Coefficients
LRTI:	Lower respiratory tract infection
URTI:	Upper respiratory tract infection
HMM:	Hidden Markov Model
COPD:	Chronic obstructive pulmonary disease
D-CNN:	Deep Convolutional Neural Network

1 Introduction

Respiratory disorders impose a tremendous physical, economic, and social cost on society and are also the third highest cause of mortality globally. They also place

I. Woungang et al. (Eds.): ANTIC 2022, CCIS 1798, pp. 56–70, 2023.
https://doi.org/10.1007/978-3-031-28183-9_5

a significant financial and administrative strain on health services. A substantial amount of work has been committed to strengthening the early diagnosis and monitoring of patients with respiratory disorders in order to facilitate prompt therapies [1]. The sounds made by the lungs are an important sign of lung health. In comparison to X-rays and laboratory testing for the identification of respiratory disorders, auscultation is a more straightforward, quicker, and simpler screening procedure. Throughout the globe, respiratory disorders are among the primary causes of mortality and deformity. To lower the fatality rate, it is necessary to detect and eradicate disease at an early stage. People of all ages are affected by various types of respiratory diseases, including LRTI [2], Pneumonia, Asthma, URTI [3], Bronchitis, and COPD [4]. LRTI is the most common type of respiratory infection. The filthy air we breathe will impair the functioning of our lungs, resulting in the development of several respiratory ailments. Some respiratory illnesses may be passed down from generation to generation. Seasonal respiratory disorders are caused by harsh weather conditions and unexpected climatic shifts in the environment. Respiratory disorders affect the lives of even children. The classification of respiratory disorders is based on the pictures of the lungs obtained by X-ray and CT scan. The recording of respiratory sounds using stethoscopes may also be utilised for the categorization of respiratory diseases. In the long run, it is a non-invasive procedure that has no negative consequences for the patients. Patients who are exposed to X-ray and CT scan equipment on a regular basis may suffer long-term consequences. Respiratory sound recordings are accomplished by placing the stethoscope at different chest spots, capturing inhaling and gasping sounds, and then indexing, labelling, and storing the data files.

The analysis of respiratory sounds has lately gained a lot of attention since it can be done using sophisticated machine learning and deep learning algorithms. In both techniques, the systems presented usually consist of two basic processes, which are referred to as the front-end that deals with performing extracting features and the back-end model, respectively. Past developments have witnessed the widespread usage of machine learning techniques in the medical domain, like diagnostic screening and auxiliary investigations. The categorization of respiratory sounds has been the subject of several applications of machine learning. In order to classify respiratory sounds, they are processed as features and afterwards passed to the model. The MFCC (Mel Frequency Cepstral Coefficients) [5], the harmonicity [5], the short-term temporal characteristics [6] and others are common factors of respiratory sounds. Prior to this study, researchers employed techniques such as: BP neural network [7], HMM [8], and decision tree [9] to categorise the aforementioned traits. From the background study, it is observed that most of the machine learning and deep learning models have achieved good accuracy but they also leave an open end for further improvising the prediction accuracy with faster convergence. In this paper, a manifold D-CNN (Deep Convolutional Neural Network) is proposed to identify respiratory sound diseases with high accuracy. The proposed model is compared with two baseline models: *i.)* Traditional Convolutional Neural Network model, and *ii.)* Convolutional

Neural Network with MFCC. The following are the major contributions of the paper:

- A novel architecture for classifying respiratory disease using manifold D-CNN architecture is proposed.
- Extraction of audio features using LibROSA (Mel-frequency Cepstral Coefficients, Spectrogram, and Chromagram)
- Tested the proposed model using different optimizers: Adam, nadam, Stochastic Gradient Descent (SGD), and RMSprop for choosing the optimal configuration of manifold D-CNN.
- Handled the imbalanced dataset by appropriate train/test division in a stratified manner.

The remaining section of the paper is structured as follows: Sect. 2 discusses the related work, followed by the proposed framework in Sect. 3. The dataset description and experimental setup are also provided in Sect. 3. Section 4 discusses the obtained results at each stage of the proposed model through comparative analysis with other baseline models. The closing Sect. 5 highlights the key conclusive points and future direction.

2   Related Background

The classification models based on machine learning make use of handcrafted features such as MFCC, or a combination of four features namely: range, variance, moving average, and spectrum mean). These combined features are fed into the machine learning models of HMM [17], SVM [18], DT [19] to perform classification tasks. Deep learning algorithms, on the other hand, employ spectrograms that include both spectral and temporal data. Following the formation of these spectrograms, CNNs [11] or RNNs [20] are used to examine the data. There is a clear advantage to deep learning over other techniques, as shown by Pham et al. [21] comparison to other traditional strategies.

In [10,11] Respiratory Sound has been used to categorise asthma and COPD, both of which are chronic respiratory disorders, using a linear classifier. Using deep residual networks, [12] it is possible to classify normal, crackle, and wheeze sounds. SVM and extreme learning classifiers are used to compute morphological embedding complexity [13], which are expressed in terms of entropy, skewness, lacunarity, and kurtosis, as well as to classify people with respiratory illnesses and healthy ones. Using wheezing sounds, integrated power and spectral characteristics, as well as KNN, SVM, and ensemble classifiers [14], are used to assess asthma severity in patients. In pulmonary diagnostics, the ability to record and analyse acoustic signals from the lungs might be helpful. The diagnosis of asthma in individuals [15] is accomplished by the use of the MFCC as a characteristic and an SVM classification algorithm. SVM is used to classify asthmatic breathing sounds [16], with parameters such as the spectral envelope and the tonality index being used. Breathing sounds are used to distinguish between asthma and COPD using wavelet higher-order spectral characteristics [15]. The following points summarize the key findings about sound feature extraction and respiratory sound classification:

- *Feature Extraction:* Respiratory sounds may be classified based on a variety of factors, including the qualities of the sounds themselves. Classification was done by extracting MFCC, BPM, inharmoniousness, tuning frequency and chord strength using the boosting tree. [8] used HMM in conjunction with Gaussian mixture to perform the classification after extracting MFCC as input feature. In this paper, Librosa's feature extraction method has been used. The features are extracted one by one, for testing them in order to see the performance.
- *Respiratory Sound classification using deep learning:* Deep learning has gotten a lot of attention lately because of its success in medical image diagnosis. Because of this, the use of deep learning systems to classify respiratory sounds is a potential research strategy. According to [22], respiratory sounds may be classified into four distinct groups using a Noise Marking RNN framework. The breathing cycles are divided into two categories by the attention network: noisy and quiet (no noise). In order to train CNN-RNN model [23] transformed the respiratory sounds into spectrograms (Mel frequency) and designed a patient-specific model. This model classifies the patients into two categories: healthy & unhealthy. In this paper, a novel manifold D-CNN model has been applied to classify respiratory sounds in order to diagnose the respiratory disease.
- *Augmentation of sound data:* The amount of respiratory sound data available in the dataset is very small and thus is not sufficient enough to reach optimal performance while performing classification using any deep learning approach. Several researchers proposed different approaches such as signal estimation algorithm, voice synthesis, Griffin-Lim, WORLD Vocoder, [24] etc. to augment the sound data. In this paper, augmentation of dataset hasn't been performed. The augmentation part has been kept as future work for the proposed framework in our paper.

3   Proposed Framework

In this section, the proposed framework has been discussed by highlighting the key stages of the model. The dataset being used by the proposed model is also discussed in this section. The description of the respiratory sound data used for training and testing the proposed model is as follows:

The Respiratory Sound Database [25] originally developed by two research groups based in Portugal and Greece, respectively. It contains 920 annotated recordings ranging in duration from 10 s to 90 s. A total of 126 patients provided recordings for this work. There seem to be a maximum of 5.5 h of recordings including 6898 respiratory cycles. Out of this 6898 cycle, 1864 includes crackles, 886 contain wheezes, and 506 have both crackles and wheezes. The data set contains both clean respiratory sounds and noisy recordings that are meant to imitate real-world circumstances. Infants, adults, and the elderly are all represented among the patients' age categories. The audio files stored in the dataset are pre-processed prior to its usage in the proposed framework. Figure 1 illustrates the working flow of the proposed manifold D-CNN architecture. The proposed model is tested against two baseline models namely: traditional CNN, and CNN with MFCC.

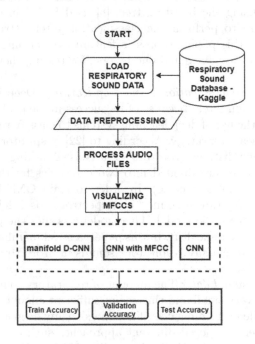

Fig. 1. Proposed framework

The complete working flow of the problem can be categorised into 4 stages. The first stage deals with loading and pre-processing the dataset. After pre-processing the data, the audio files are processed to select the part that contains the respiratory cycles in stage 2 of the proposed framework. Stage 3 illustrates MFCC visualization and model training. Three different models are trained to accurately classify the respiratory disease. Finally, in stage 4, the performance of the model is measured in terms of accuracy. The experimental results and observations obtained at each block of the proposed model is discussed in the upcoming Sect. 4 of the paper.

4   Results and Discussion

Before discussing the result obtained by the manifold D-CNN model. Let's discuss about the data available to us in different files of the respiratory sound database. The respiratory sound database consist of 920 sound files with .wav

	start	end	crackles	weezels	pid	mode	filename	disease
0	0.036	2.436	0	0	168	sc	168_1b1_Al_sc_Meditron	Bronchiectasis
1	2.436	5.250	0	0	168	sc	168_1b1_Al_sc_Meditron	Bronchiectasis
2	5.250	8.422	0	0	168	sc	168_1b1_Al_sc_Meditron	Bronchiectasis
3	8.422	11.222	0	0	168	sc	168_1b1_Al_sc_Meditron	Bronchiectasis
4	11.222	13.807	0	0	168	sc	168_1b1_Al_sc_Meditron	Bronchiectasis

Fig. 2. Pre-processed data (respiratory sound database)

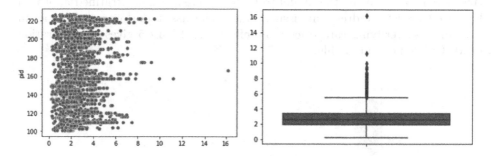

Fig. 3. Processing audio files for deciding best length

extension, 920 annotations with .txt extension, 4 text files where text_file:1 comprise of patient diagnosis details, text_file:2 consist of file naming format, text_file:3 consist of list of 91 names, and the fourth text file consist of demographic information of the patient. The referred dataset is transformed into suitable format before pre-processing the audio files. Figure 2 illustrates the pre-processed data format used in our work. The main objective behind processing the audio file is to trim the part of audio file that contains the respiratory cycle. This can be done by utilizing the start and end time for these cycles from our constructed pre-processed dataframe. Now the input images to our cnn is required to be of same size, and for that audio files must be of same length i.e. (start - end). The best length that can be obtained is illustrated by Fig. 3. The pre-processing of audio files helps in filtering out the irrelevant information from the audio files. By trimming the respiratory cycle, the audio processing time is reduced to be used for further classification. From Fig. 3 plots it can concluded that best length is 6. Also if difference is <6 we must Zero Pad it to get it to required length. Zero Padding means silent. The processed audio file is stored in a directory for performing classification in further stages. Librosa module to load the audio files and Soundfile module to write the audio file to output path has been used. In total, 6898 audio files are processed in the pre-processing stage of the proposed framework. The diagnosis information available in the dataset is imbalanced, that's why the model has tried to extract Id of each processed audio file and then merge them with their respective class label such that the model can split files in to train and validation folder in stratified manner. The imbalanced diagnostic information is illustrated via Fig. 4a and the stratified train-validate split is shown via Fig. 4b, and Fig. 4c. The imbalanced information available in the disease diagnosis data clearly indicates the need of any class balancing approach. Due to the presence of imbalanced information, even if the model achieves very high accuracy, it might not be a reliable solution for classification as most of the class belongs to one specific class. For example: in this dataset, most of the disease belongs to COPD class, if the model predicts all disease as COPD, still the model will yield very high accuracy value. Therefore, it is not viable solution to use direct models on imbalanced class information. In this paper, before using the model to perform classification, stratified approach has been used to address this issue. This would assist the proposed model in learning and verifying categories more effectively. Figure 5 gives an illustration of MFCCS on one audio file.

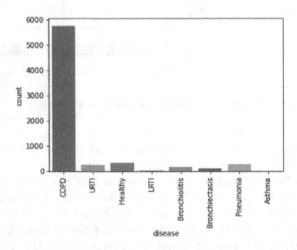

(a) Imbalanced Disease Diagnosis Information

COPD	0.832910	COPD	0.833333
Healthy	0.046756	Healthy	0.046377
Pneumonia	0.041319	Pneumonia	0.041304
URTI	0.035158	URTI	0.035507
Bronchiolitis	0.023197	Bronchiolitis	0.023188
Bronchiectasis	0.015042	Bronchiectasis	0.015217
LRTI	0.004712	LRTI	0.004348
Asthma	0.000906	Asthma	0.000725

(b) Train (Stratified)   (c) Validate (Stratified)

Fig. 4. Handling imbalanced diagnosis information

MFCC is one of the most commonly used feature extraction technique while working with audio files. In the proposed model, Librosa's feature extraction methods are used. Firstly the characteristics are extracted one by one and then tested to analyse how well they performed, but the majority of them provided high accuracy, so ultimately the model opted to utilise them all.

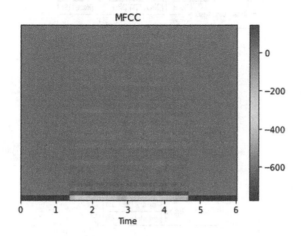

Fig. 5. Mel Frequency Cepstral Coefficients (MFCC)

Once the feature extraction process is complete, the next stage targets to train the proposed manifold D-CNN model. The processed audio data is also tested using CNN with MFCC and traditional CNN approach. The architecture of proposed manifold D-CNN and CNN is illustrated via Figs. 6 and 7 [20] respectively. Total parameters of D-CNN is: 221533, out of which trainable parameters are 219997, and non-trainable parameters are 1536. The model is tested using different optimizers namely: Adam, nadam, RMSprop, and SGD. Table 1 highlights the obtained accuracy using different configurations.

The manifold D-CNN model and baseline models are trained for 500 epochs with a learning rate of 0.001. The model is tested on different configurations, the model yielded best results on optimizer: RMSprop, learning rate: 0.001, and epochs: 500. The maximum test accuracy obtained by the proposed manifold D-CNN model is 97.32%. The proposed model also possess an additional advantage of faster convergence with high accurate classification results. Figure 8a, 8b, 8c, and 8d illustrates the convergence of proposed model while using different optimizer in the D-CNN architecture.

Although the proposed D-CNN performed better than baseline models, traditional CNN architecture also demonstrated promising results in terms of training accuracy. The accuracy of our proposed model can be further improvised by

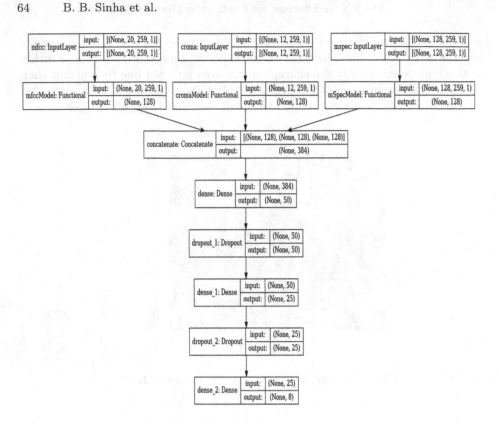

Fig. 6. Manifold D-CNN architecture

Table 1. Performance comparison with baseline models

Optimizer	Model	Train accuracy	Test accuracy
SGD	CNN with MFCC	86.41%	83.08%
Adam		46.19%	38.28%
nadam		36.96%	32.01%
RMSprop		86.41%	83.08%
SGD	CNN	90.17%	85.86%
Adam		98.77%	91.30%
nadam		98.36%	91.84%
RMSprop		99.59%	91.84%
SGD	manifold D-CNN	95.4%	94.8%
Adam		93.48%	91.63%
nadam		92.97%	94.022%
RMSprop		96.23%	**97.32%**

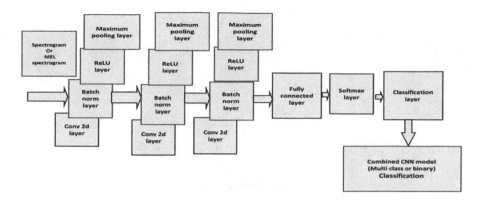

Fig. 7. CNN architecture [20]

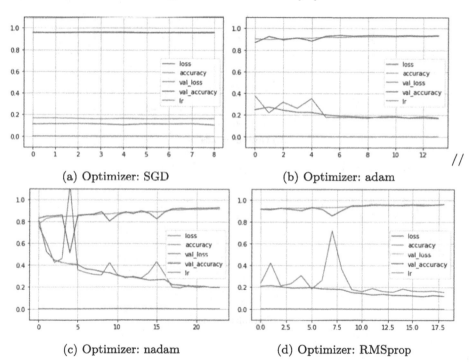

(a) Optimizer: SGD

(b) Optimizer: adam

(c) Optimizer: nadam

(d) Optimizer: RMSprop

Fig. 8. Convergence of manifold D-CNN architecture

increasing the size of the respiratory sound datasets through augmentation. The ROC curve generated by the traditional CNN along with classification report for different optimizers are illustrated via Fig. 9a, 10a, 9b, 10b, 9c, 10c, 9d, and 10d respectively.

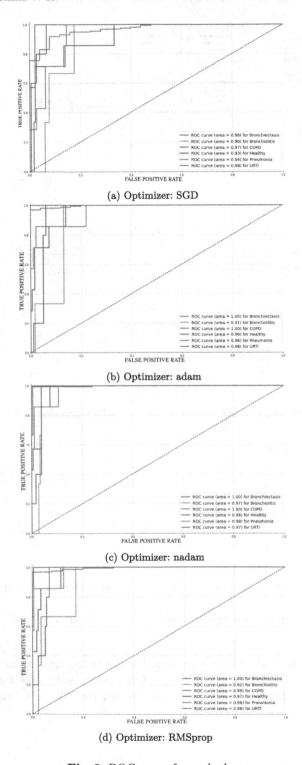

(a) Optimizer: SGD

(b) Optimizer: adam

(c) Optimizer: nadam

(d) Optimizer: RMSprop

Fig. 9. ROC curve for each class

	precision	recall	f1-score	support
Bronchiectasis	0.00	0.00	0.00	3
Bronchiolitis	0.00	0.00	0.00	3
COPD	0.96	0.95	0.95	159
Healthy	0.28	0.71	0.40	7
Pneumonia	0.40	0.29	0.33	7
URTI	0.00	0.00	0.00	5
accuracy			0.86	184
macro avg	0.27	0.32	0.28	184
weighted avg	0.85	0.86	0.85	184

(a) Classification Report: SGD

	precision	recall	f1-score	support
Bronchiectasis	0.60	1.00	0.75	3
Bronchiolitis	0.00	0.00	0.00	3
COPD	0.98	0.99	0.98	159
Healthy	0.50	0.43	0.46	7
Pneumonia	0.67	0.57	0.62	7
URTI	0.20	0.20	0.20	5
accuracy			0.91	184
macro avg	0.49	0.53	0.50	184
weighted avg	0.90	0.91	0.91	184

(b) Classification Report: adam

	precision	recall	f1-score	support
Bronchiectasis	0.67	0.67	0.67	3
Bronchiolitis	0.00	0.00	0.00	3
COPD	0.96	0.99	0.98	159
Healthy	0.75	0.43	0.55	7
Pneumonia	0.80	0.57	0.67	7
URTI	0.33	0.40	0.36	5
accuracy			0.92	184
macro avg	0.59	0.51	0.54	184
weighted avg	0.91	0.92	0.91	184

(c) Classification Report: nadam

	precision	recall	f1-score	support
Bronchiectasis	0.75	1.00	0.86	3
Bronchiolitis	0.00	0.00	0.00	3
COPD	0.98	0.99	0.98	159
Healthy	0.75	0.43	0.55	7
Pneumonia	0.80	0.57	0.67	7
URTI	0.29	0.40	0.33	5
accuracy			0.92	184
macro avg	0.59	0.56	0.56	184
weighted avg	0.93	0.92	0.92	184

(d) Classification Report: RMSprop

Fig. 10. Classification report

5   Conclusion and Future Work

This study has given an investigation of multiple deep learning models for identifying respiratory abnormality from audio recordings, as well as the results of that investigation. Using a large number of tests on the respiratory sound dataset, it is discovered that the proposed manifold D-CNN model, which incorporates three distinct CNN architectures, surpasses the current state-of-the-art systems in terms of accuracy. The suggested model exhibits promising results when it comes to accurate diagnosis of respiratory diseases, establishing its superiority over the baseline CNN models. The proposed model achieves an accuracy of 97.32%. In future, the model can be further strengthened by training it with augmented data. The current size of the audio data is small and thus restricting its accuracy. Using different augmentation methods in future can help in efficient training of the CNN models, which can further improvise the results obtained by manifold D-CNN architecture.

References

1. Johnson, R.A., Brunson, D.B.: Respiratory disease. In: Canine and Feline Anesthesia and Co-existing Disease, pp. 86–109 (2022)
2. Lewnard, J.A., et al.: Effectiveness of 13-valent pneumococcal conjugate vaccine against medically attended lower respiratory tract infection and pneumonia among older adults. Clin. Infect. Diseases **75**(5), 832–841 (2022)
3. Christian, M.T.,et al.: Evaluation of daily low-dose prednisolone during upper respiratory tract infection to prevent relapse in children with relapsing steroid-sensitive nephrotic syndrome: the PREDNOS 2 randomized clinical trial. JAMA Pediatr. **176**(3), 236–243 (2022)
4. Faustini, A., et al.: Air pollution and multiple acute respiratory outcomes. Eur. Respir. J. **42**(2), 304–313 (2013)
5. Sreeram, A.S.K., Ravishankar, U., Sripada, N.R., Mamidgi, B.: Investigating the potential of MFCC features in classifying respiratory diseases. In: 2020 7th International Conference on Internet of Things: Systems, Management and Security (IOTSMS), pp. 1–7. IEEE, December 2020
6. Ren, M., et al.: The short-term effects of air pollutants on respiratory disease mortality in Wuhan, China: comparison of time-series and case-crossover analyses. Sci. Rep. **7**(1), 1–9 (2017)
7. Fan, D., et al.: Effectively measuring respiratory flow with portable pressure data using back propagation neural network. IEEE J. Transl. Eng. Health Med. **6**, 1–12 (2018)
8. Jakovljević, N., Lončar-Turukalo, T.: Hidden Markov model based respiratory sound classification. In: Maglaveras, N., Chouvarda, I., de Carvalho, P. (eds.) Precision Medicine Powered by pHealth and Connected Health. IP, vol. 66, pp. 39–43. Springer, Singapore (2018). https://doi.org/10.1007/978-981-10-7419-6_7
9. Ma, F., Yu, L., Ye, L., Yao, D.D., Zhuang, W.: Length-of-stay prediction for pediatric patients with respiratory diseases using decision tree methods. IEEE J. Biomed. Health Inform. **24**(9), 2651–2662 (2020)

10. De La Torre Cruz, J., Cañadas Quesada, F.J., Ruiz Reyes, N., García Galán, S., Carabias Orti, J.J., Peréz Chica, G.: Monophonic and polyphonic wheezing classification based on constrained low-rank non-negative matrix factorization. Sensors **21**(5), 1661 (2021)
11. Albuquerque, R.Q., Mello, C.A.B.: Automatic no-reference speech quality assessment with convolutional neural networks. Neural Comput. Appl. **33**(16), 9993–10003 (2021). https://doi.org/10.1007/s00521-021-05767-4
12. Chen, H., Yuan, X., Pei, Z., Li, M., Li, J.: Triple-classification of respiratory sounds using optimized s-transform and deep residual networks. IEEE Access **7**, 32845–32852 (2019)
13. Chen, Q., Zhang, W., Tian, X., Zhang, X., Chen, S., Lei, W.: Automatic heart and lung sounds classification using convolutional neural networks. In: 2016 Asia-Pacific Signal and Information Processing Association Annual Summit and Conference (APSIPA), pp. 1–4. IEEE, December 2016
14. Nabi, F.G., Sundaraj, K., Lam, C.K.: Identification of asthma severity levels through wheeze sound characterization and classification using integrated power features. Biomed. Sig. Process. Control **52**, 302–311 (2019)
15. Milicevic, M., Mazic, I., Bonkovic, M.: Asthmatic wheezes detection-what contributes the most to the role of MFCC in classifiers accuracy? Int. J. Biol. Biomed. Eng. **10**, 176–182 (2016)
16. Wiśniewski, M., Zieliński, T.P.: Joint application of audio spectral envelope and tonality index in an e-asthma monitoring system. IEEE J. Biomed. Health Inform. **19**(3), 1009–1018 (2014)
17. Ma, Y., et al.: LungBRN: a smart digital stethoscope for detecting respiratory disease using bi-resnet deep learning algorithm. In: 2019 IEEE Biomedical Circuits and Systems Conference (BioCAS), pp. 1–4. IEEE, October 2019
18. Palaniappan, R., Sundaraj, K.: Respiratory sound classification using cepstral features and support vector machine. In: 2013 IEEE Recent Advances in Intelligent Computational Systems (RAICS), pp. 132–136. IEEE, December 2013
19. Esteban, C., et al.: Development of a decision tree to assess the severity and prognosis of stable COPD. Eur. Respir. J. **38**(6), 1294–1300 (2011)
20. Revathi, A., Sasikaladevi, N., Arunprasanth, D., Amirtharajan, R.: Robust respiratory disease classification using breathing sounds (RRDCBS) multiple features and models. Neural Comput. Appl. 1–18 (2022)
21. Pham, L., McLoughlin, I., Phan, H., Tran, M., Nguyen, T., Palaniappan, R.: Robust deep learning framework for predicting respiratory anomalies and diseases. In: 2020 42nd Annual International Conference of the IEEE Engineering in Medicine and Biology Society (EMBC), pp. 164–167. IEEE, July 2020
22. Kochetov, K., Putin, E., Balashov, M., Filchenkov, A., Shalyto, A.: Noise masking recurrent neural network for respiratory sound classification. In: Kůrková, V., Manolopoulos, Y., Hammer, B., Iliadis, L., Maglogiannis, I. (eds.) ICANN 2018. LNCS, vol. 11141, pp. 208–217. Springer, Cham (2018). https://doi.org/10.1007/978-3-030-01424-7_21
23. Acharya, J., Basu, A.: Deep neural network for respiratory sound classification in wearable devices enabled by patient specific model tuning. IEEE Trans. Biomed. Circuits Syst. **14**(3), 535–544 (2020)

24. Zhao, X., Shao, Y., Mai, J., Yin, A., Xu, S.: Respiratory sound classification based on BiGRU-attention network with XGBoost. In: 2020 IEEE International Conference on Bioinformatics and Biomedicine (BIBM), pp. 915–920. IEEE, December 2020
25. Maglaveras, N., Chouvarda, I., de Carvalho, P.: Precision Medicine Powered by pHealth and Connected Health, vol. 66, pp. 18–21 (2018)

A Pipelined Framework for the Prediction of Cardiac Disease with Dimensionality Reduction

G. Shobana[1]([✉]) and Nalini Subramanian[2]

[1] Department of Computer Applications, Madras Christian College, Chennai, India
gmshobana@gmail.com
[2] Department of Information Technology, Rajalakshmi Engineering College, Thandalam, India

Abstract. Cardiac diseases are diseases that affect people across the globe, and cardiac failure occurs without any warning. Identification of cardiac diseases at an early stage becomes a challenge for researchers in the health domain. Machine learning frameworks and algorithms are effectively used in the current medical field to predict and classify various diseases accurately. In this paper, we explore the traditional supervised machine learning techniques and algorithms and their cardiac disease classification accuracy. We further investigate the feature extraction technique Kernel Principal Component Analysis with a pipelined framework. The proposed framework overcomes the issue of overfitting and increases the prediction accuracy most effectively. Random Forest produced the most perfect result and Extreme Gradient Boost technique achieved an accuracy of 99.02%. Other Boosting classifiers, Gradient Boosting and Light Gradient Boosted Machine produced an accuracy of 94.16% and 98.38% respectively.

Keywords: Supervised machine learning algorithms · Kernel principal component analysis · Cardiac disease · Light gradient boosting · Random forest

1 Introduction

Heart disease is a non-contiguous health problem that disturbs enormous humans around the world without exhibiting any initial symptoms. There are numerous types of heart diseases. Congestive cardiac failure is commonly called Heart Failure. Due to heart failure, the body's requirement for oxygen is not sufficiently met. Atherosclerosis occurs when there is a block in the arteries. Sometimes, blood clots formation occurs that interrupts the normal flow of the heart blood. Cardiac stroke may be the result of this condition. When there is irregular rhythm of the heart, then the condition is termed as Arrhythmia. Heart beat rate less than 60 beats per minute, which is slow, is known as Bradycardia while 100 beats per minute, which is fast, is known as Tachycardia. Stenosis is a condition that rises due to improper functioning of the valves of the heart. Other heart diseases occur due to genetic and birth deformities [1]. 8,05000 US people were found to have a heart attack every year. Unhealthy diet and an inactive life-style are the main reasons for a heart attack [2]. Various examinations are conducted on the affected patients to

I. Woungang et al. (Eds.): ANTIC 2022, CCIS 1798, pp. 71–81, 2023.
https://doi.org/10.1007/978-3-031-28183-9_6

determine the cause of occurrence of the disease. Diagnostic tests and advanced procedures accurately identify and classify the disease. Manual analysis of a large population of affected patients becomes a major challenge for physicians. Machine learning is the perfect technique to be employed to classify healthy and unhealthy patients. In this paper, all the conventional and ensemble machine learning algorithms were applied to the heart disease related dataset, obtained from the UCI open repository with 1025 observations and 14 attributes, using Scikit learn [3]. The training and the testing data was taken in the ratio 70:30. 308 samples were used for the testing. By implementing the proposed methodology, the Random forest achieved a high and perfect prediction accuracy of 100% and Extreme Gradient Boosting achieved an accuracy of 99.02%. Another significant advantage of this methodology is that it efficiently manages the overfitting problem.

2 Related Work

World Health Organization (WHO) reports states that approximately 17.9 million humans across the earth die due to heart ailments or Cardiovascular diseases (CVDs) [4]. High cholesterol levels, lack of exercise, diabetes, smoking and obesity are some of the factors that contribute to the development of this disease. In the past several decades there has been a significant rise of cardiac diseases among the Indian urban population. The annual death rate due to cardiovascular diseases is around 4.77 million in 2020 and is expected to rise in the coming years [5]. The major factors that cause CVDs in India are consumption of alcohol and excessive use of tobacco products. The other factors include hypertension and diabetes. 80% of CVDs related deaths occur in developing countries [6].

Savita et al. analysed the performance of Six machine learning methods like Support vector machine, Decision Tree, Multilayer Perceptron, Linear Regression, Naïve Bayes and K-Nearest Neighbor. They performed K-fold Cross Validation with 5 and 10. They investigated Switzerland, Hungarian and Cleveland datasets from the UCI repository. They concluded that SVM and KNN performed better than other models [7].

Saumendra et al. classified cardiac disease using Support Vector Machines. They drew Cleveland heart disease dataset from the UCI repository. They took 303 observations with 13 attributes for the experiment and the training-testing ratio was 90:10.They investigated the performance of four types of SVM Kernels like Polynomial, RBF, Linear and Sigmoid with the dataset. They found that SVM with Polynomial kernel achieved a higher accuracy of 87.5% [8].

Deepak Kumar et al. identified non-contagious Heart Disease using three supervised machine learning techniques SVM, RF and K-NN with 10 fold cross-validation. They used a South African dataset for heart diseases and found that RF achieved high accuracy of 95% [9].

Hiteshwar et al. compared the performance of Naïve Bayes, K-Nearest Neighbor and Random Forest on the Cleveland and Statlog dataset obtained from the open UCI repository. Random forest achieved higher accuracy than the other two models with 93.02%, while KNN and Naïve Bayes achieved 90.69% and 83.72% of prediction accuracy [10].

Muhammad Saqib Nawaz et al. have predicted Cardiovascular diseases using Gradient Descent optimization technique (GDO).This method has achieved an accuracy of

99.43%. They performed a detailed study and found that Random Forest achieved accuracy of 90.16%. Boosting algorithms and Extreme Machine Learning technique obtained 92.45%. Kernel based support vector obtained 93.33%. Fuzzy Systems achieved 94.50% while advanced Neural Networks produced 83.67% and Gradient Descent Optimization method obtained 98.54% [11].

Sibo et al. proposed a novel optimized algorithm to predict cardiac disease. They utilized the heart disease dataset from the UCI repository. They explored ML models like Naïve Bayes, KNN, Bayesian Optimized SVM (BO-SVM) and Salp Swarm Optimized Neural Network (SSA-NN). BO-SVM achieved higher accuracy of 93.3% while SSA-NN produced and accuracy of 86.7% [12].

Dengqing zhang et al. predicted Cardiac disease using their proposed model which achieved an accuracy of 98.56% [13]. They proposed a methodology that incorporated Linear SVM with feature selection technique and they obtained the dataset from kaggle [14].

Rohit et al. predicted heart disease by exploring various machine learning algorithms like Random Forest, conventional Decision Tree, (LR) Logistic Regression, boosting algorithm like XGBoost, kernel-based Support Vector Machine and optimized deep learning techniques. They used the heart disease dataset with 14 attributes from the UCI open repository. They achieved 94.2% accuracy by implementing deep learning technique [15].

Women in post menopausal stage are also likely to have a heart failure. Machine learning approaches can be efficiently used to diagnose the occurrence of heart failure [16]. Chayakrit et al. predicted cardiovascular diseases and investigated various ML models. They concluded that SVM and Boosting algorithms performed well with more than 92% prediction accuracy [17].

3   The Proposed Methodology

3.1   Attributes Description and Dataset

The Cardiac or heart disease dataset was obtained from the UCI open and vast repository with 1025 instances and 14 features. There were 499 samples with class 0 in the target feature and 526 samples with class 1 in the target feature. The binary classification classifies the patients in to with and without heart disease. The features define the age, sex (Male-1,Female-0), the type of chest pain, blood pressure, blood sugar while fasting, level of serum cholesterol, other cardiac parameters during exercise and information of major vessels.

3.2   Proposed Framework

Several researchers have employed varieties of procedures to classify heart disease. Both data and images were used in the medical field for the classification and prediction purpose. The proposed methodology has four major phases namely the acquisition of the dataset from the repository, pre-processing, designing an efficient pipeline and selecting the best model as shown in Fig. 1.

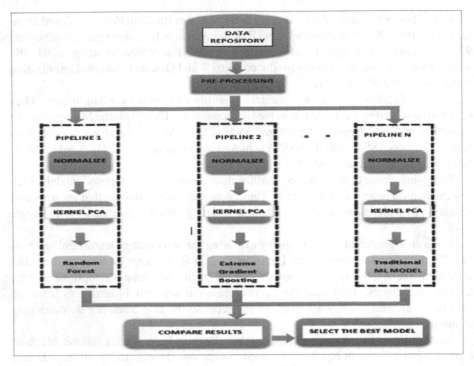

Fig. 1. Proposed methodology

Procedure:

Step 1: Acquire the Cardiac disease dataset from the UCI repository.
Step 2: Pre-processing involves identifying missing values and filling them.
Step 3: Create a pipeline that performs three different steps.

- Normalize the data, since the data might fall into different ranges.
- Apply feature extraction technique Kernel PCA and select the important features.
- Apply both conventional, ensemble and Boosting algorithms to the dataset.

Step 4: Compare and observe the result of all the pipelines.
Step 5: Select the best performing machine learning model.

The structured pipeline helps to overcome data leakage. The pipeline with ensemble technique, Random Forest produces 100% prediction accuracy while comparing to other machine learning models. Among the Boosting algorithms, Extreme Gradient Boosting achieved the highest accuracy of 99.02%.

4   Results

With the proposed methodology, Random forest obtained the perfect prediction accuracy of 100%. The dataset was split in to 70% for training and 30% for testing respectively. Figure 2 shows the output generated by the Random Forest Classifier.

```
Test Accuracy: 1.000
                   precision    recall  f1-score   support

              0        1.00      1.00      1.00       145
              1        1.00      1.00      1.00       163

       accuracy                            1.00       308
      macro avg        1.00      1.00      1.00       308
   weighted avg        1.00      1.00      1.00       308

[[145   0]
 [  0 163]]
accuracy is 1.0
Accuracy on training set: 1.000
Accuracy on test set: 1.000
```

Fig. 2. Output generated by Random Forest

The parameters used for the Kernel PCA was n_components $= 2$, Kernel $=$ 'rbf' and gamma $= 0.01$. The ideal accuracy score of 100% was attained when a pipeline was set up with a scaling of the data, followed by the feature extraction process of Kernel PCA, and then applying Random Forest. Figure 3 shows the confusion matrix where the diagonal elements were the correctly identified elements 145 and 163 respectively while there were no misclassified elements. Figure 4 shows the training and testing accuracy. Figure 5 show the ROC generated by the Random Forest.

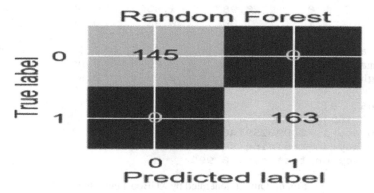

Fig. 3. Confusion matrix generated by Random Forest

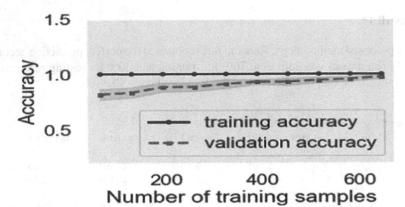

Fig. 4. Training and testing accuracy by Random Forest

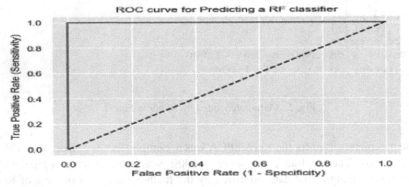

Fig. 5. ROC curve by Random Forest

```
Test Accuracy: 0.990
                precision    recall  f1-score   support

            0       0.98      1.00      0.99       145
            1       1.00      0.98      0.99       163

     accuracy                          0.99       308
    macro avg       0.99      0.99      0.99       308
 weighted avg       0.99      0.99      0.99       308

[[145   0]
 [  3 160]]
accuracy is 0.9902597402597403
Accuracy on training set: 1.000
Accuracy on test set: 0.990
```

Fig. 6. Output generated by XGBoost classifier

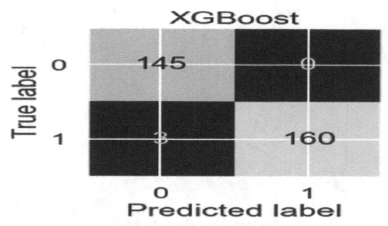

Fig. 7. Confusion matrix generated by XGBoost classifier

The boosing algorithms also produced high prediction accuracy above 94% with XGBoost classifier achieving 99.02% accuracy as shown in Fig. 6. Figure 7 shows the confusion matrix of XGBoost classifier where 145 and 160 are correctly classified elements while 3 elements were misclassified. Light Gradient Boosted Machine Classifier obtained 98% accuracy.

Figure 8 shows the training and testing accuracy generated by the XGBoost Classifier. The curve clearly shows that the proposed methodology has overcome the issue of overfitting. Figure 9 shows the ROC generated by the XGBoost Classifier.

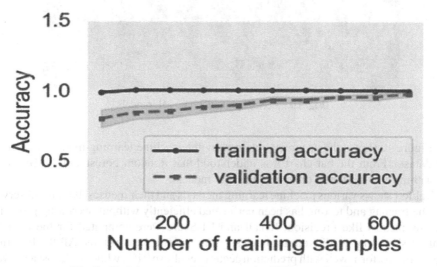

Fig. 8. Training and testing accuracy by XGBoost classifier

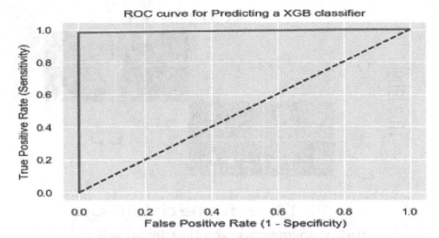

Fig. 9. ROC curve by XGBoost classifier

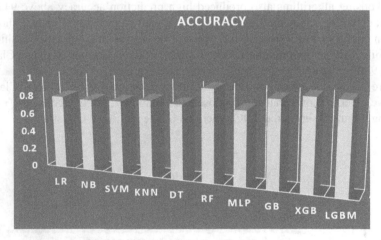

Fig. 10. Accuracy obtained by ML models

Figure 10 shows the accuracy obtained by the machine learning models applied to the dataset. From the bar chart it is understood that Random Forest and the Boosting algorithms perform better compared to other models.

Table 1 shows various machine learning methods and their metrics. It is also observed that the training and testing has been performed efficiently without overfitting problem. Various metrics like Precision, Recall and F1-Score were computed for the models. Table 2 shows the prediction accuracies of the Boosting algorithms. All the boosting algorithms perform well with prediction accuracies above 94%, while XGBoost achieved the highest with over 99%.

Table 1. Machine learning models and their metrices

ML-models	Precision	Recall	F1-score	Training	Testing
LR	0.80	0.80	0.80	0.810	0.795
NB	0.79	0.78	0.78	0.806	0.782
SVM	0.81	0.80	0.79	0.824	0.795
KNN	0.83	0.83	0.83	0.907	0.828
DT	0.82	0.81	0.81	0.838	0.812
RF	1.00	1.00	1.00	1.000	1.000
MLP	0.81	0.80	0.80	0.808	0.802

Table 2. Boosting ML models and their prediction accuracies

Boosting Models	Training	Testing
Gradient boost	0.974	0.942
XGBoost	1.000	0.990
LGBM	0.997	0.984

4.1 Comparative Study

Several researchers have explored different datasets of heart diseases from the vast and open UCI repository. Cleveland, Long Beach VA, Statlog, Switzerland and Hungarian are the popular datasets. In this paper, we have drawn the Heart disease dataset from the UCI repository with 1025 observations and 14 features. Figure 11 compares the result produced by other researchers and our proposed methodology.

The researchers have incorporated several techniques like Reduction Feature Elimination, Principal Component Analysis, Pearson Correlation, Gradient Descent Optimization and Lasso regularization to enhance the prediction accuracy. They explored the efficient computation of machine learning algorithms like Support Vector machines, Random Forest, M5P, Neural Networks, Reduced Error Pruning, other traditional and Boosting classifiers. They achieved a maximum prediction accuracy of 99% [18]. The proposed methodology has produced higher prediction accuracy of 100% as shown in Fig. 11. Random Forest obtained the accurate result while Extreme Boosting Machine (XGBoost) achieved an accuracy of 90.06%. For agroinformatic data, the proposed methodology would also produce significantly high accuracy rate [19].

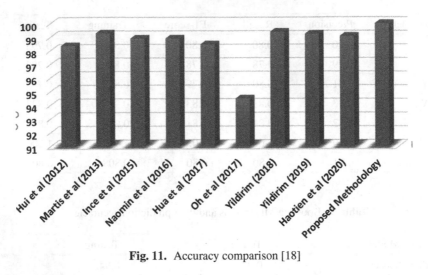

Fig. 11. Accuracy comparison [18]

5   Conclusion

Cardiovascular diseases affect enormous people across the world regardless of age. Sedentary lifestyle with high calorie based food intake is one of the main causes or reasons for this disease. Identification of this disease at an early stage is most challenging and manual examination of patient history is very tedious and might not produce accurate prediction results. Researchers have explored several machine learning techniques and optimization methodologies to enhance the prediction accuracy. In this paper, we have proposed an efficient methodology that accurately classified the cardiac dataset, while other methodologies produced a maximum accuracy of 99%. This technique has proved efficient with a comprehensive dataset. Future work might involve large datasets and other novel ensemble and hybrid methodologies. The performance of this methodology with other similar types of diseases dataset may be investigated.

References

1. www.heart.org/en/health-topics/consumer-healthcare.
2. www.cdc.gov/heartdisease.
3. https://scikit-learn.org.
4. www.who.int/health-topics.
5. Huffman, M.D., et al.: Incidence of cardiovascular risk factors in an Indian urban cohort results from the New Delhi birth cohort. J. Am. Coll. Cardiol. **57**(17), 1765–1774 (2011). https://doi.org/10.1016/j.jacc.2010.09.083
6. https://world-heart-federation.org/wp-content.
7. Wadhawan, S., Maini, R.: Performance analysis of machine learning techniques for predicting cardiac disease. In: 2021 6th International Conference on Communication and Electronics Systems (ICCES), pp. 1625–1630 (2021). https://doi.org/10.1109/ICCES51350.2021.9489197

8. Mohapatra, S.K., Behera, S., Mohanty, M.N.: A comparative analysis of cardiac data classification using support vector machine with various kernels. In: 2020 International Conference on Communication and Signal Processing (ICCSP), pp. 515–519 (2020). https://doi.org/10.1109/ICCSP48568.2020.9182189

9. Kumar, D., Verma, C., Gupta, A., Raboaca, M.S., Bakariya, B.: Detection of cardiac disease and association with family history using machine learning. In: 2021 10th International Conference on System Modeling and Advancement in Research Trends (SMART), pp. 670–675 (2021). https://doi.org/10.1109/SMART52563.2021.9676234

10. Singh, H., Gupta, T., Sidhu, J.: Prediction of heart disease using machine learning techniques. In: 2021 Sixth International Conference on Image Information Processing (ICIIP), pp. 164–169 (2021). https://doi.org/10.1109/ICIIP53038.2021.9702625

11. Nawaz, M.S., Shoaib, B., Ashraf, M.A.: Intelligent Cardiovascular Disease Prediction Empowered with Gradient Descent Optimization. Heliyon (2021)

12. Prasad Patro, S., Gouri, S.N., Padhy, N.: Heart disease prediction by using novel optimization algorithm: a supervised learning prospective. Inform. Med. Unlock. 26,100696 (2021). ISSN: 2352-9148

13. Zhang, D., et al.: Heart disease prediction based on the embedded feature selection method and deep neural network. J. Healthc. Eng. 2040–2295 (2021)

14. https://www.kaggle.com/johnsmith88/heart-disease-dataset

15. Rohit, B., Aditya, K., Mohammad, S., Gaurav, D., Sagar, P., Parneet, S.: Prediction of heart disease using a combination of machine learning and deep learning. Comput. Intell. Neurosci. 1687–5265. https://doi.org/10.1155/2021/8387680

16. Tison, G.H., et al.: Predicting incident heart failure in women with machine learning: the Women's Health Initiative Cohort. Can. J. Cardiol. 37(11), 1708–1714 (2021)

17. Krittanawong, C., et al.: Machine learning prediction in cardiovascular diseases: a meta-analysis. Sci. Rep. 10, 16057 (2020). https://doi.org/10.1038/s41598-020-72685-1

18. Yadav, D., Pal, S.: Prediction of heart disease using feature selection and random forest ensemble method. Int. J. Pharm. Res. Scholars. 12, 56–66 (2020). https://doi.org/10.31838/ijpr/2020.12.04.013

19. Shobana, G., Bushra, S.N., Maheswari, K.U., Subramanian, N.: Multivariate classification of dry beans using pipelined dimensionality reduction technique. In: 2022 International Conference on Innovative Computing, Intelligent Communication and Smart Electrical Systems (ICSES), pp. 1–6 (2022). https://doi.org/10.1109/ICSES55317.2022.9914079

Prediction of Air Quality Index of Delhi Using Higher Order Regression Modeling

Bibek Upadhyaya, Udita Goswami, and Jyoti Singh Kirar[✉]

DST-CIMS, Banaras Hindu University, Varanasi, UP 221005, India
kirarjyoti@gmail.com

Abstract. Air Quality Index is an index that measures air quality on a daily basis. Poor quality of air is very harmful to human health. The study of the Air Quality Index is very necessary to know the air quality of a particular city or country. It creates awareness amongst the citizens about the air quality of a particular city or country. It thus, compels the authority to bring certain remedial measures to control air pollution and develop a proper system that works for the betterment of the air quality of a particular city or country. The main objective is to analyze the air quality index of Delhi, to study the pattern and to study the major factors contributing to the higher Air Quality Index. In this literature, a sturdy and robust framework for AQI prediction is proposed, where first done Data Collection is done, then Data Pre-processing, after that KNN Imputation, Exploratory Data Analysis (EDA), Outliers Detection, Comparison of AQI distribution year wise, quarter wise, month wise, and week wise, Feature Selection are implemented, followed by Data Standardization, Data Splitting, then different Machine Learning (ML) regressors are applied on the data set, finally 10-fold Cross-validation is implemented. Here, Random Forest Regressor has the highest 10-fold Cross-validation score of 88.27% and this regressor is used for building the best predictive model.

Keywords: AQI · KNN · EDA · XGBoost

1 Introduction

Air Quality Index (AQI) is a scheme that transforms weighted values of individual air pollution-related parameters into a single number. It provides legal framework for air pollution control. Air Quality of India is controlled by Indian National Air Quality Standards (INAQS) and is monitored by National Air Monitoring Program (NAMP).

Basically, AQI is divided into six categories,

Viz. Good (0–50), Satisfactory (51–100), Moderately Polluted (101–200), Poor Unhealthy (201–300), Very Poor Very Unhealthy (301–400) and Severe Hazardous (401–500).

The basic approach would be to study the detailed patterns followed by the Air Quality Index with the help of Statistical and Machine Learning techniques. The AQI of Delhi will be predicted with maximum accuracy. The major factors contributing to the higher AQI will be identified so as to bring the focus on reducing these contributing factors.

I. Woungang et al. (Eds.): ANTIC 2022, CCIS 1798, pp. 82–100, 2023.
https://doi.org/10.1007/978-3-031-28183-9_7

2 Literature Review

Analyzing and Forecasting AQI is nowadays done by many researchers. Several Machine Learning and Statistical approaches are being used for this pur-pose.Several research papers published in this field have employed various ma-chine learning techniques to predict AQI of India and find some patterns in the data [1]. Sanjeev (2021) examined a dataset that included pollutant concentrations as well as meteorological factors. The author examined and predicted air quality, claiming that the Random Forest (RF) classifier performed best because it is less prone to over-fitting [2]. Castelli et al. (2020) used the Support Vector Regression (SVR) ML algorithm to forecast air quality in California in terms of pollutants and particulate levels. The researchers claimed to have created a novel method for modeling hourly atmospheric pollution [3]. Madan et al. (2020) compared the performance of ML algorithms and discovered that many works used meteorological data such as humidity, wind speed, and temperature to more accurately predict pollution levels. They discovered that the Neural Network (NN) and boosting models outperformed the other leading machine learn-ing (ML) algorithms [4]. Patil et al. (2020) presented some research papers on vari-ous machine learning techniques for AQI modeling and forecasting. The authors discovered that most scholars used Artificial Neural Network (ANN), Linear Re-gression and Logistic regression for AQI prediction [5]. Kujawska et al. (2022) compared machine learning models for forecasting PM10 levels in the air in the city of Lublin using linear regression (LR), K-nearest neighbors regression (KNNR), support vector machines (SVM), regression trees (RT), Gaussian process regression models (GPR), artificial neural networks (ANN), and long short-term memory networks (LSTM) [6]. Gopalakrishnan (2021) used machine learning to fore-cast air quality at various locations in Oakland, California using Google Street View data. She concentrated on the locations where the data were missing. In order to forecast air quality for every area in city neighborhoods, the author created a web application [7]. The concentration of SO2 in the air in Maharashtra, India, was predicted using the ML approach by Bhalgat et al. (2019). The writers came to the conclusion that certain of the cities in this Indian region need urgent care because they are so heavily polluted. The authors noted that their model was unable to get the desired results [8]. The AQI prediction problem was further developed by Zhu et al. (2018) as a multi-task learning problem. The authors made an effort to minimise the number of parameters by using largescale optimization approaches. They asserted, based on their empiri-cal findings, which the proposed model performed better than other regression models [9]. Monisri et al. (2020) attempted to create a mixed model for forecasting air quali-ty by gathering data on air pollution from multiple sources. According to the authors, the suggested app-roach seeks to assist residents of small towns in analysing and forecast-ing air quality [10]. To anticipate India's AQI, Soundari et al. (2019) created a model based on NNs. When historical data on pollutant concentrations were available, the au-thors claimed that their suggested model could forecast the AQI for the entire county, for any province, or for any geographic area. It has been noted that academics paid less attention to research studies on AQI analysis and forecasting for Indian cities. Few academics have looked into AQI prediction from the Indian perspective, despite the fact that nine of the 10 most polluted cities in the world are Indian (Deshpande 2021). The current work aims to close this gap by analysing five years' worth of significant air pollution data of New

Delhi. The current work is a sincere endeavour to add to the literature by exploring fresh data visualisation techniques, using exploratory data analysis, outliers detection, features selec-tion, and evaluating the performance of five major machine learning models.

3   Methodology

In this paper, a Regression Analysis approach has been employed to predict the AQI of India. The whole analysis is based on the flow chart (Fig. 1) shown below:

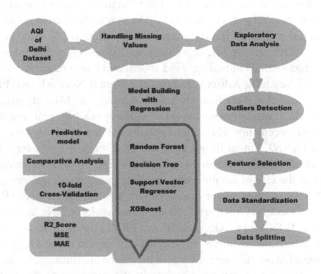

Fig. 1. Flow-chart showing the proposed methodology

3.1   Dataset Description

The data have been scrapped for the analysis from Kaggle (https://www.kaggle.com/datasets/rohanrao/air-quality-data-in-india) that has been made publicly available by the Central Pollution Control Board: https://cpcb.nic.in/ which is the official portal of Government of India. The aim of the dataset is to monitor and understand the quality of air is of immense importance to our well-being.

The dataset contains AQI (Air Quality Index) at hourly and daily level of New Delhi. It has 15 columns viz. NO2, NOx, NH3, CO, SO2, O3, Benzene, Toluene, Xylene, AQI. Here, AQI or Air Quality Index is the target variable.

3.2   Handling Missing Values

Then it is checked if there are any null values in the data. The missing values have been dealt with by imputing K Nearest Neighbors, where K = 5 is considered. The K parameter, commonly known as the distance from the missing data, is specified in this method. The missing value will be predicted using the mean of the neighbors.

From Fig. 2, it can be inferred that Xylene has the highest proportion of missing values.

	Proportion
Xylene	0.388751
SO2	0.054754
O3	0.041812
PM10	0.038328
AQI	0.004978
NH3	0.004480
PM2.5	0.000996
NO	0.000996
NO2	0.000996

Fig. 2. Proportion of the missing values in different features

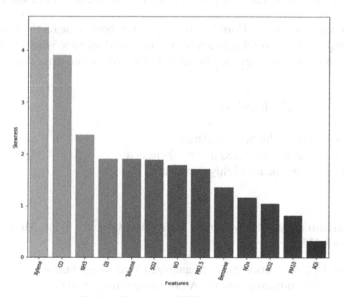

Fig. 3. Skewness of different features

3.3 Exploratory Data Analysis

Then, Exploratory Data Analysis is applied on the dataset. Exploratory data analysis is the crucial process of doing preliminary analyses on data in order to find patterns, identify anomalies, test hypotheses, and double-check assumptions with the aid of descriptive statistics and graphical illustrations.

Distribution and Skewness of variables. Histograms of all the features have been plotted to find their distributions. Further, their skewness is analyzed and it is found that the dataset is heavily skewed. In Fig. 3, it can be seen that Xylene has the highest skewness, followed by CO, NH3, and O3.

Outlier Detection. With the help of Box plot diagram, it can be found that the concerned data have many outliers present in it. The outliers have been removed with the help of Inter-Quartile Range. The box plot, often known as a box and whisker diagram, is a common approach to show how data are distributed using the five number summary.

- Minimum
- First quartile
- Median
- Third quartile
- Maximum

The central rectangle of the simplest box plot crosses the first quartile and the third quartile (the inter-quartile range or IQR). Now, the data is reduced to 1461 rows.

Correlation Analysis. Next, Correlation analysis has been done on the dataset. A statistical technique called Correlation analysis is used to determine whether or if there is a relationship between two variables or datasets and how strong that relationship might be.

From Fig. 4, it can be found out that

i) PM2.5 & PM10 are highly correlated.
ii) NO, NOx, NO2 are correlated among themselves.
iii) Toluene and Benzene are highly correlated.

3.4 Comparison of AQI Distribution Year Wise, Quarter Wise, Month Wise, and Week Wise

After that, the AQI distribution has been analyzed Year wise, Quarter wise, Month wise, and Week wise and compared how the AQIs changed during all these phases. In Fig. 5, the average AQI over the years having AQI greater than 400 has been plotted.

In Fig. 6, the average AQI over the quarters having AQI greater than 400 has been plotted.

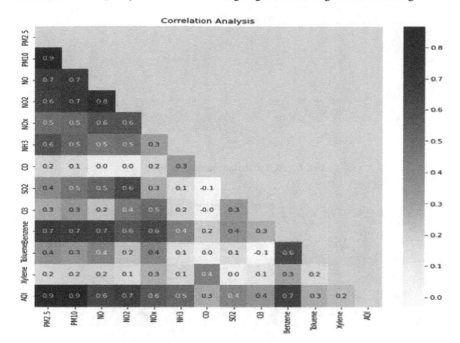

Fig. 4. Correlation matrix

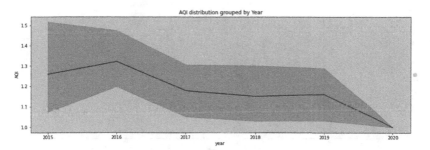

Fig. 5. AQI distribution year wise

In Fig. 7, the average AQI over the months having AQI greater than 400 has been plotted.

In Fig. 8, the average AQI over the months having AQI greater than 400 has been plotted.

3.5 Feature Selection

In machine learning, the goal of feature selection is to find the best set of features that will allow one to build useful models of studied phenomena. Here, Mutual Information for feature selection has been used. Mutual information is calculated between two variables and measures the reduction in uncertainty for one variable when the other variable's value

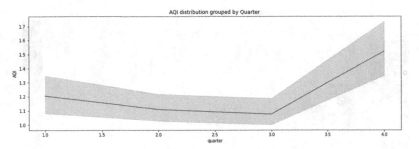

Fig. 6. AQI distribution quarter wise

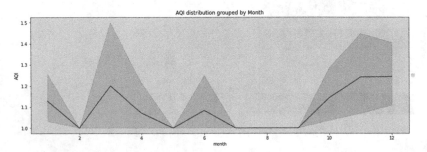

Fig. 7. AQI distribution month wise

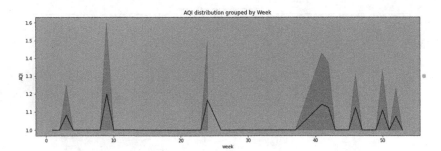

Fig. 8. AQI distribution week wise

is known. In this research, unique theoretical findings are presented that demonstrate the emergence of conditional mutual information when limiting the optimal regression errors attained by various subsets of features.

The mutual information between two random variables X and Y is as follows:

$$H(X) - H(X|Y) = I(X; Y) \tag{1}$$

Where I(X; Y) represents the mutual information for X and Y, H(X) represents the entropy for X, and H(X|Y) represents the conditional entropy for X given Y. Based on the information from Correlation matrix and Mutual Information, the following features have been selected:

- PM2.5
- NOx
- Benzene
- CO
- O3
- NH3
- SO2

Figure 9 shows the bar plot of Mutual Information gain of variables.

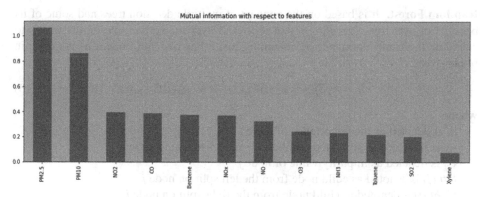

Fig. 9. Bar plot showing the Mutual Information gain of variables

3.6 Data Standardization

Standardization, commonly referred to as Z-score normalization, is a method for rescaling the values similar to normalizing while maintaining the characteristics of the standard normal distribution. Consequently, the dataset's mean value after normalization would be zero, and its standard deviation would be 1. Here, the data have been scaled with the help of Standard Scalar function.

The value of Standard Normal variable is

$$Z_i = \frac{X_i - \mu}{\sigma} \tag{2}$$

where, X_i is a random variable with mean μ and standard deviation σ.

3.7 Data Splitting

Here, the train-test split is used for splitting the dataset into training set and testing set. The train set is used to fit the model. The test set is used to evaluate the fit machine learning model. 20% of the available data have been used for testing and the remaining data for training.

3.8 Regression Techniques

Regression is a method of machine learning in which the model forecasts the result as a continuous numerical value. The following regression techniques have been implemented in this research work-

- Random Forest Regressor
- Decision Tree Regressor
- Support Vector Regressor
- XGBoost Regressor

Random Forest. It is based on the concept of multiple decision trees and some of its benefits of over tree algorithm is that it doesn't over fit. Further, the motto here is to calculate the Gini importance by assuming that it has two child nodes as it's done in binary trees:

$$ni_j = w_j C_j - w_{left}(j)C_{left}(j) - w_{right}(j)C_{right}(j) \tag{3}$$

where,

n_i is denoted as the importance of node j
w_j is indicated as weighted number of samples reaching node j
C_j is denoted as impurity value of node j
left (j) is denoted as child node from the left split on node j
right (j) is denoted as child node from the right split on node j

Now, each feature's importance will be evaluated as –

$$fi_i = \frac{\sum_{j:node\ j\ splits\ on\ feature\ i} i_j}{\sum_{k\ \in\ all\ nodes} ni_k} \tag{4}$$

here, fi_i = importance of feature
The values will be normalized now using:

$$Norm\ fi_i = \frac{fi_i}{\sum_{j\in all\ features} fi_j} \tag{5}$$

At the Random Forest level, the final feature importance is given as the average of over all the trees.

$$RF\ fi_i = \frac{\sum_{j\in all\ trees} norm\ fi_j}{T} \tag{6}$$

here,

$RF\ fi_i$ is denoted as the importance of feature i calculated from all trees.
$norm\ fi_j$ is denoted as the normalized feature importance for feature i in tree j
T = total number of trees
We have used the default parameters like n_estimators, criterion, max_depth, max_features, bootstrap, and max_samples of the RandomForestRegressor function.
Figure 10 shows the Predicted vs. Actual values of AQI in case of Random Forest Regressor.

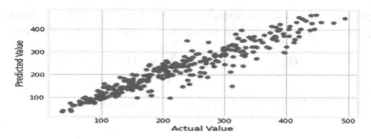

Fig. 10. Predicted vs. actuals in case of random forest Regressor

Decision Tree. Decision tree regression trains a model in the form of a tree to predict data in the future and generate useful continuous output by observing the properties of an item.

Let the training vectors be denoted as $x_i \in R^n$, $i = 1, ..., l$ along with a label vector as $y \in R^l$. The motto here is to do a partition in such a manner that the samples from the feature space with the same labels/same target values should get grouped together.

Let the data at node m be represented by S_m with N_m samples. Let the candidate split $\theta = (j, t_m)$ consist of a feature j and threshold t_m, such that we partition the data into and subsets.

$$S_m^{right}(\theta) S_m^{left}(\theta) = \{(x, y) | x_j \leq t_m\} \tag{7}$$

$$S_m^{right}(\theta) = \frac{S_m}{S_m^{left}(\theta)} \tag{8}$$

Now, the impurity function or the loss function, denoted here by $H()$ will be computed, so as to evaluate the quality of our candidate split of node,

$$G(S_m, \theta) = \frac{N_m^{left}}{N_m} H\left(S_m^{left}(\theta)\right) + \frac{N_m^{right}}{N_m} H\left(S_m^{right}(\theta)\right) \tag{9}$$

Now, the aim is to pick those bunches of parameters that are minimizing the impurity.

$$\theta^* = \underset{\theta}{argmin}\, G(S_m, \theta) \tag{10}$$

We will now recourse for the subsets $S_m^{left}(\theta)$ and $S_m^{right}(\theta)$ till we have the attained the maximum allowable depth, i.e. $N_m < min.samples$ or $N_m = 1$.

Classification Criteria. Here the target variable is an outcome of classification, which in turn is taking on the values 0, 1, 2, ..., K−1, for the node m, let pmk

$$P_{mk} = \frac{1}{N_m \sum_{y \in S_m} I(y=k)} \tag{11}$$

be the proportion of class k observations in node m. If m is a terminal node, *predict_proba* for this region is set to p_{mk}. Common measures of impurity are the following:

$$Gini: \qquad H(S_m) = \sum_k p_{mk}(1 - p_{mk}) \qquad (12)$$

$$Entropy: \qquad H(S_m) = -\sum_k p_{mk} \log p_{mk} \qquad (13)$$

$$Misclassification: \quad H(S_m) = 1 - \max_k p_{mk} \qquad (14)$$

We have used the default parameters like criterion, splitter, max_depth, min_samples_split, min_samples_leaf, and max_features of the DecisionTreeRegressor function.

Figure 11 shows the Predicted vs. Actual values of AQI in case of Decision Tree Regressor.

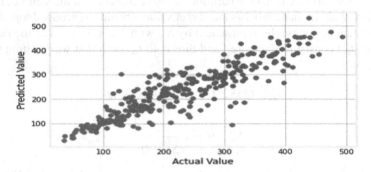

Fig. 11. Predicted vs. actuals in case of decision tree Regressor

Support Vector. An approach for supervised learning called support vector regression is used to forecast discrete values. Finding the optimum fit line is the fundamental tenet of SVR. The hyperplane with the most points is the best-fitting line in SVR. The concept on which we make separating plane or decision boundary is based on equation which is of the form –

$$y = mx + c \qquad (13)$$

Let us consider the mathematical equation:

$$g(x) = w^T x + b \qquad (14)$$

$$Maximize\ k\ such\ that: \ -w^T x + b- \geq k\ for\ d_i == 1.$$
$$-w^T x + b \leq k\ for\ d_i == -1.$$

Value of (x) depends upon $\|w\|$, so we have to keep a look at the following:

- Keep $\|w\| = 1$ and maximize (x)
- Keep $(x) \geq 1$ and minimize $\|w\|$

The default parameters like kernel, degree, gamma, coef0, tol, C, epsilon, and max_iter of the SVR function have been used.

Figure 12 shows the Predicted vs. Actual values of AQI in case of Support Vector Regressor.

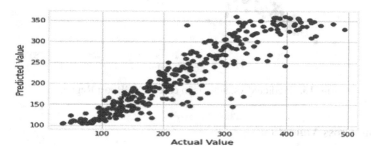

Fig. 12. Predicted vs. actuals in case of support vector Regressor

XGBoost. Extreme Gradient Boosting (XGBoost) is an open-source library that implements the gradient boosting algorithm in an efficient and effective way. It is generally used for regression predictive modeling. It employs a more regularized model formulation to control over fitting, resulting in improved performance for which it is also known as "Regularized Boosting".

$$Obj^{(t)} = \sum_{i=1}^{n} L(y_i, F_t(x_i)) + \sum_{t=1}^{T} \Omega(h_t) \tag{15}$$

where, $L(y_i, F_t(x_i))$ is the Loss function and $\Omega(h_t)$ is the regularization term.

XGBoost solves this minimization of loss function problem by Newton's Method. The default parameters like n_estimators, max_depth, eta, subsample, and colsample_bytree of the XGBRegressor function have been used. Figure 13 shows the Predicted vs. Actual values of AQI in case of XGBoost Regressor.

4   Results

The accuracies of Regression techniques have been checked with the help of K-fold Cross-validation, R2_score, Mean Squared Error (MSE), and Mean Absolute Error (MAE).

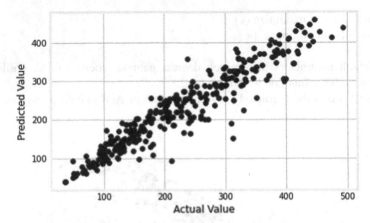

Fig. 13. Predicted vs. actuals in case of XGBoost Regressor

4.1 K-fold Cross-Validation

It is a procedure used to estimate the skill of the model on the dataset and to avoid over fitting or under fitting. Generally, the K-fold Cross-validation is conducted where the value for k is chosen such that each of the train set or test set is large enough to be statistically representative of the broader dataset. The value of k is chosen as 10.

From Fig. 14, it can be inferred that Random Forest Regressor gives the highest 10-fold Cross-validation score of 88.27.

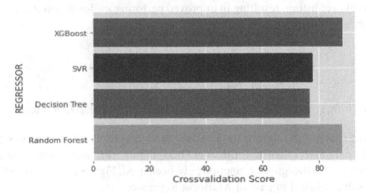

Fig. 14. 10-fold cross-validation score of different Regressors

4.2 R2_score

R2_score is a statistical measure that represents the goodness of fit of a regression model. The ideal value for the R2 score is 1. The closer the value of r-square to 1, the better is the model fitted. It is a comparison of the residual sum of squares (SS_{res}) with the total sum of squares (SS_{tot}).

Total sum of squares is calculated by summation of squares of perpendicular distance between actual data points and the average line.

$$SS_{tot} = \sum_{t=1}^{n} (z_t - \bar{z})^2 \tag{16}$$

where z_t is the actual value at t^{th} point of time & $\bar{z}$ is the mean of all the actual values.

Residual sum of squares is calculated by the summation of squares of perpendicular distance between actual data points and the best-fitted line.

$$SS_{res} = \sum_{t=1}^{n} \left(z_t - \hat{z_t}\right)^2 \tag{17}$$

where z_t is the actual value at t^{th} point of time & $\hat{z_t}$ is the forecasted value corresponding to z_t.

R2 Score is calculated by using the following formula:

$$R^2 = 1 - \frac{SS_{res}}{SS_{tot}} \tag{18}$$

It is pronounced as R squared and is also known as the coefficient of determination. It works by measuring the amount of variance in the predictions explained by the dataset.

From Fig. 15, it can be inferred that Random Forest Regressor has the highest R2_ score of 0.903.

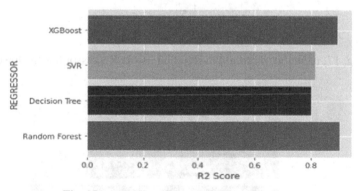

Fig. 15. AAAR2_ scores of different Regressors

4.3 Mean Squared Error

MSE or Mean Squared Error is the average squared difference between the forecasted values and the actual values. MSE is almost always strictly positive (and not zero). The formula for MSE is given by:

$$MSE = \frac{1}{n} \sum_{t=1}^{n} \left(z_t - \hat{z_t}\right)^2 \tag{19}$$

From Fig. 16, it can be inferred that Random Forest Regressor has the lowest MSE of 1071.79.

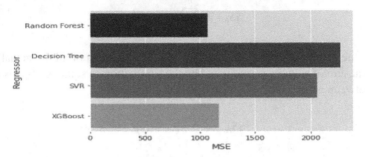

Fig. 16. MSE of different Regressors

4.4 Mean Absolute Error

MAE or Mean Absolute Error calculates the absolute value average difference between the forecasted values and actual values. It is also known as scale-dependent accuracy as it calculates errors in observations taken on the same scale. The formula for MAE is given by:

$$MAE = \frac{1}{n} \sum_{t=1}^{n} |z_t - \hat{z}_t| \qquad (20)$$

From Fig. 17, it can be inferred that Random Forest Regressor has the lowest MAE of 23.86.

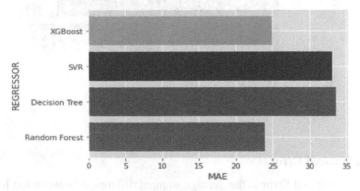

Fig. 17. MAE of different Regressors

4.5 Final Prediction

Random Forest Regressor is the best technique for predicting the Air quality Index (AQI) of Delhi, having the highest R2_score, 10-fold Cross-validation score and lowest MSE and MAE. So, the predictive model will be saved with this regressor.

4.6 Comparative Analysis

Table 1. Comparative analysis of the proposed framework against the state-of-the-art works.

Author's name	Description	Outcomes	Research Gap	Contrast
Dyuthi Sanjeev (2021)	The use of the machine learning techniques Random Forest (RF), Support Vector Machine (SVM), and Artificial Neural Networks (ANN) is being explored in this article	The accuracy scores of the Random Forest-based model, Support Vector Machine-based model, and Artificial Neural Network-based model are 99.4%, 93.5%, and 90.4%, respectively	The model is over-fitted, data pre-processing has not been done properly, for which there are ample loopholes in the data itself	Missing values can be handled by KNN Imputation technique, outliers should be detected by IQR, and proper features should be selected in order to build a user-friendly model
Castelli, Clemente (2020)	In this project work, Support Vector Regressor with RBF kernel is used to predict AQI in California	SVR with RBF kernel correctly predicted hourly pollutant concentrations for the state of California, including those for carbon monoxide, sulphur dioxide, nitrogen dioxide, ground-level ozone, and particulate matter 2.5	More regressors can be implemented with different parameters. Data from other cities can be used	Parameters like kernel, degree, gamma, coef0, tol, C, epsilon, and max_iter of the SVR function are used to increase the accuracy of the model

(continued)

Table 1. (*continued*)

Author's name	Description	Outcomes	Research Gap	Contrast
Kujawska, Kulisz, Oleszczuk (2022)	The study's goal was to compare machine learning models for predicting PM10 levels in the air in the city of Lublin using various techniques, including linear regression, K-nearest neighbours regression, support vector machines, regresssion trees, Gaussian process regression models, artificial neural networks, and long short-term memory net-works (LSTM)	The models were trained using data from the Lublin-Radawiec meteorological station for the years 2017 through 2019. There were 18 meteorological and chemical input variables utilised in the models, but the seasons were not taken into account. The ANN model had the highest quality (R2_Score = 0.904, MSE = 68.09), and the RT model had the lowest quality (R2_Score = 0.77, MSE = 156.57)	More variables affecting the air quality should be considered in order to build a real-time model. Train data do not have values greater than 300. This has to be addressed	Random forest regressor with default parameters like n_estimators, criterion, max_depth, max_features, bootstrap, and max_samples can solve the problem

In Table 1, a comparative analysis of the proposed framework has been done against the state-of-the-art works. Here, the overall comparison is made on project description, outcomes of the respective projects, followed by gaps in research methodologies and finally contrasting changes have been incorporated in the proposed framework to make it more refine and user-friendly.

Table 2. Comparative performance of our proposed framework against the state-of-the-art works.

Regressors	Accuracy (%)			
	Our Project	Dyuthi Sanjeev (2021)	Castelli, Clemente (2020)	Kujawska, Kulisz, Oleszczuk (2022)
RF	88.31	90.40	94.10	68.55
DT	76.67	78.91	75.23	71.15
SVR	77.83	93.50	76.32	74.75
XGBoost	88.45	85.20	82.36	77.64

In Table 2, a comparison of the proposed framework has been made against the state-of-the-art works based on the accuracies of the selected ML techniques like Random Forest, Decision Trees, Support Vector, and XGBoost.

5 Conclusion and Future Enhancement

As contaminants and particulate matters are highly volatile, dynamic, and variable in both place and time, predicting the quality of air is a difficult undertaking. Simultaneously, due to the essential effects of air pollution on human health and the environment, it is becoming more and more crucial to model, predict, and monitor air quality, particularly in urban areas.

In order to predict the levels of pollutants and particles and to correctly identify the AQI, this work presented a study of Random Forest, Decision Tree, Support Vector, and XGBoost Regressors. It was possible to acquire, typically, good accuracy in modelling pollutant concentrations including PM2.5, NOx, Benzene, CO, O3, NH3, and SO2 because the researched method provided a reasonable model of the yearly, quarterly, monthly, and weekly air pollution.

The following issues will be improved and examined as part of this continuing research to see how ML regressors may be used to forecast air quality:

Consider choosing a large dataset with more measurements and parameters to help the development of more precise predictive models for air pollutants and particulates, in particular PM2.5 and NOx. The default parameters of each regressor's model have a significant impact on how well it performs; therefore, it would be fascinating to examine and in-clude additional parameters as well as tune the hyperparameters.

References

1. Sanjeev, D.: Implementation of machine learning algorithms for analysis and prediction of air quality. Int. J. Eng. Res. Technol. **10**(3), 533–538 (2021)
2. Madan, T., Sagar, S., Virmani, D.: Air quality prediction using machine learning algorithms–a review. In: 2nd International Conference on Advances in Computing, Communication Control and Networking (ICACCCN), pp. 140–145 (2020).https://doi.org/10.1109/ICACCCN51052.2020.9362912
3. Deshpande, T.: India has 9 of world's 10 most-polluted cities, but few air quality monitors. Indiaspend. https://www.indiaspend.com/pollution/india-has-9-of-worlds-10-most-polluted-cities-but-few-air-quality-monitors-792521. (2021)
4. Gopalakrishnan, V.: Hyperlocal air quality prediction using machine learning. Towards Data Science.https://towardsdatascience.com/hyperlocal-air-quality-prediction-using-machine-learning-ed3a661b9a71. (2021)
5. Castelli, M., Clemente, F.M., Popovič, A., Silva, S., Vanneschi, L.: A machine learning approach to predict air quality in California. Complexity 2020 (8049504), 1–23. https://doi.org/10.1155/2020/8049504. (2020)
6. Doreswamy, H.K.S., Yogesh, K.M., Gad, I.: Forecasting Air pollution particulate matter (PM2.5) using machine learning regression models. Procedia Comput. Sci. **171**, 2057–2066 (2020). https://doi.org/10.1016/j.procs.2020.04.221

7. Mahalingam, U., Elangovan, K., Dobhal, H., Valliappa, C., Shrestha, S., Kedam, G.: A machine learning model for air quality prediction for smart cities. In: 2019 International Conference on Wireless Communications Signal Processing and Networking (WiSPNET) , pp. 452–457. IEEE. https://doi.org/10.1109/WiSPNET45539.2019.9032734. (2019)

8. Kujawska, J., Kulisz, M., Oleszczuk, P., Cel, W.: Machine learning methods to forecast the concentration of PM10 in Lublin. Poland Energies **15**(17), 6428 (2022). https://doi.org/10.3390/en15176428

9. Bhalgat, P., Bhoite, S., Pitare, S.: air quality prediction using machine learning algorithms. Int. J. Comput. Appl. Technol. Res. **8**(9), 367–370 (2019). https://doi.org/10.7753/IJCATR0809.1006

10. Zhu, D., Cai, C., Yang, T., Zhou, X.: A machine learning approach for air quality prediction: model regularization and optimization. Big Data Cogn. Comput. (2018). https://doi.org/10.3390/bdcc2010005

11. Goyal, P.:Flexibililty in estimating air quality index; a case study of Delhi. Global Journal of Flexible Systems Management July–Sept, 2001 (2001)

12. Sharma, M., Maheswari, M., Pandey, R.: Development of Air Quality Index for Data Interpr. Department of civil Engineering, IIT Kanpur, Report submitted to CPCB, Delhi (2001)

13. Sharma, M., Maheswari, M., Sengupta, B., Shukla, B.P.: Design of a website for dissemination of an air quality index in India. Environ. Model. Softw. **18**, 405–411 (2003)

14. Sharma, M., Pandey, R., Maheswari, M., Sengupta, B., Shukla, B.P., Mishra, A.: Air quality Index and its interpretation for the city of Delhi. Clean Air International Journal on Energy for a Clean Environment **4**, 83–98 (2003)

15. Environmental Protection Agency: National Air Quality and Emission Trends Report 1997. EPA 454: R-98-016. EPA, Office of Air Quality Planning and Standards, Research Triangle Park (1998)

16. Parivesh News Letter: 4, CPCB, New Delhi

17. CPCB (Central pollution Control Board):Air quality in Delhi (1989-IJAET/Vol. I/Issue II/July-Sept., 2010/106–114 2000). NAAQMS/17/2000–2001.CPCB, New Delhi (2001)

18. Soundari, A.G., Jeslin, J.G., Akshaya, A.C.: Indian air quality prediction and analysis using machine learning. Int. J. Appl. Eng. Res. **14**(11), 181–186 (2019)

19. Monisri, P.R., Vikas, R.K., Rohit, N.K., Varma, M.C., Chaithanya, B.N.: Prediction and analysis of air quality using machine learning. Int. J. Adv. Sci. Technol. **29**(5), 6934–6943 (2020)

Deep Learning for the Classification of Cassava Leaf Diseases in Unbalanced Field Data Set

Ernesto Paiva-Peredo$^{(\boxtimes)}$ (iD)

Universidad Tecnológica del Perú, Lima, Peru
epaiva@utp.edu.pe

Abstract. Cassava is one of the main sources of carbohydrates in the world. However, the diagnosis of diseases in cassava crops is laborious, time-consuming and requires specialised personnel. In addition, very little research is available on images of cassava leaves taken with mobile phones and under field conditions. Therefore, the study designs deep learning models for the detection of diseases in cassava leaves from photos taken with mobile phones in the field. This study used a dataset of 21'397 images of cassava bacterial blight, cassava brown streak disease, cassava green mottle and cassava mosaic disease from a Kaggle competition. Twelve CNN models have been evaluated by applying transfer learning and data augmentation. Each of the models was trained with uniform samples and class-weighted samples. The results showed that the use of weighted samples reduced F1 score and accuracy in all cases. Furthermore, the DenseNet169 model was outstanding with an accuracy and F1 score of 74.77% and 0.59 respectively. Finally, the causes that hinder correct classification have been identified. The results reveal that it is still necessary to work on creating a balanced and refined database.

Keywords: Deep learning · Plant disease · Convolutional neural networks · Leaf disease · Classification

1 Introduction

Manihot esculenta, commonly called cassava, is an ancient crop, which is native to South America [1–3]. However, it is found all over the world, with the greatest popularity in the Americas and Africa. Cassava is a food rich in carbohydrate content, which makes it one of the most important sources of energy in the world [4,5]. Nevertheless, cassava is reputed to be a crop often produced in the poorest and most remote areas [6]. Additionally, yields in central and west Africa compared to other cassava producing regions such as Asia or Latin America are generally lower [7].

Since 2011, Food and Agriculture Organization (FAO) and other studies have warned about the epidemic effects of the cassava brown streak that attacks in Africa [8]. In addition, studies have also indicated that climate change is expected to increase the incidence of diseases [9].

I. Woungang et al. (Eds.): ANTIC 2022, CCIS 1798, pp. 101–114, 2023.
https://doi.org/10.1007/978-3-031-28183-9_8

Examination or inspection by the naked eye for plant diseases usually based on colour changes or the existence of spots or rotten areas on the leaves is the most commonly used mechanism to detect and classify diseases [10]. However, farmers and inexperienced people have difficulties in identifying diseases based on the symptoms shown as the same diseases may show different symptoms or different diseases may show similar symptoms [11]. Even determining or evaluating a disease by symptoms is difficult if done manually by one or more specialists [12]. In addition, inspection by experts is often costly, time-consuming, slow, subjective and in some cases impractical [13,14,16].

Crops can be affected by two types of diseases; biotic and abiotic diseases [17]. Biotic diseases are caused by living organisms, such as batteries, viruses and fungi. These diseases are contagious and, depending on the case, can be dangerous. On the other hand, abiotic diseases are caused by ecological circumstances, such as climatic conditions, use of chemicals, hail, etc. These diseases are neither infectious nor transmissible and are usually preventable [18].

Disease symptoms in plants can show up in the whole plant structure, e.g. in leaves, stems or roots. However, leaf analysis is more commonly used for disease detection [18].

[14] reviewed the state of the art in plant leaf disease classification, in which it is mentioned that most of the Machine Learning (ML) studies implemented Support Vector Machines (SVM), K-Nearest Neighbours (KNN) and Random Forest. While the main disadvantages of these methods include: low performance, necessity of manual feature extraction [15] and use of segmentation algorithms.

In a real environment, classification of plant leaf diseases is a very complex activity. Different diseases may present the same symptoms and different degrees of disease severity have to be analysed. In addition, we have to deal with a variety of scenarios, different natural lighting conditions, noises in the image, changes in the size of the lesions, etc. [19]. Thus, studies based on deep learning algorithms for the detection of diseases in leaves are of interest to the academic field and with prospects for market applications [16,19,20].

Several surveys have shown that Deep Learning (DL), essentially Convolutional Neural Networks (CNN), have had outstanding performances with respect to traditional Machine Learning algorithms in the task of leaf disease detection and classification [14,16,21,22].

Several state-of-the-art DL models have already been implemented for leaf disease detection. For example in [23], ResNet obtained the best results in the identification of apple leaf diseases compared to AlexNet and GoogleNet. In [24], 8 types of leaf diseases were identified. Three feature classifiers, SVM, Extreme Learning Machine (ELM) and KNN, were used. Six DL models such as GoogLeNet, ResNet-50, ResNet-101, Inception-v3, InceptionResNetv2 and SqueezeNet were used as feature extractor. This study concluded that Resnet-50 and SVM obtained the best results in performance metrics such as sensitivity, specificity and F1 score. In [16] a comparative study was conducted with 14 crop species and 26 diseases. They concluded that the ResNet-101, Dense-Net201 and Inceptionv3 CNN architectures were the most suitable models for using in standard computing environments, while ShuffleNet and SqueezeNet were the most suitable architectures for mobile and embedded applications.

VGG has also shown outstanding results versus other architectures. Five CNN architectures for plant disease detection and diagnosis, AlexNet, AlexNetOWTbn, GoogLeNet, Overfeat and VGG, were used in [25], where VGG outperformed all other models. Additionally, AlexNet and VGG are the most widely used models in the recent literature on leaf disease detection. Then, they are followed by ResNet [22].

In [21] a review on detection and classification of plant diseases by DL was conducted. About 40 researches were analysed, and it was found that most of the researches used the PlantVillage dataset to evaluate the accuracy and performance of DL models. This, PlanVillage is still used in various researches because, as mentioned in [14,26–28], it is currently difficult to access a dataset with adequate size and diversity. In other cases, as in [29], the datasets used contained plant images that were difficult to obtain in real life. Finally, a relevant fact is that, according to [18], no studies have been found on disease identification with acceptable accuracy in the real-world scenario.

Some studies have analysed models trained with data generated in controlled environments [16,30]. The results showed a significant deterioration in detection accuracy when the model is tested with data taken in real conditions. For example, [31] tested AlexNet and GoogLeNet models with a public database of 54306 images collected under controlled conditions to identify 14 crop species and 26 diseases. They obtained a maximum accuracy of 99.35%. However, the accuracy of the model was considerably reduced when tested under different conditions because the training was performed under ideal conditions, such as single leaves, face up, on a homogeneous background.

The scientific community has revealed the need to create models that are robust to different lighting conditions, i.e. the datasets must contain images at different times of the day. Furthermore, the models must be efficient for different real working environments [21,32]. Other authors also mention that to avoid biases, data acquisition should occur in several farms to gain robustness to different field maintenance conditions and should be captured with different devices but with similar specifications to those used during the implementation phase [33].

Variability in a data set must also be ensured by capturing various plant disease symptoms. Symptoms are known to be the result of the interaction of planting, disease, and environment [34]. Symptoms due to a plant disease depend on the stage of disease development [32], the presence of other diseases at the same time and presence of similar symptoms due to other diseases. Whereas symptoms due to the environment depend on other factors such as temperature, humidity, wind, soil conditions and sunlight [14].

The use of mobile phones has become widespread even in marginalised sectors, thanks to their easy accessibility, low cost and usefulness. Moreover, some research has already been conducted in which the mobile phone camera is used as an image capturing device [35]. This makes it feasible to use plant disease classification models through apps as proposed in [20].

However, the quality of a classification model to work in real environments is not assured with the use of mobile cameras. The model may present weaknesses if it is trained only with images taken with the optical axis perpendicular to the leaf plane or by extracting leaves for picture taking [18]. Both factors would bring us closer to experiments under controlled conditions.

In [18] analysed about a hundred researches on identification and classification of plant diseases through leaf images, in which it was reported that less than 10% of the papers have used large databases ranging in thousands. It is therefore evident that future research efforts should aim at collecting large and diverse datasets. Similarly in [22], a review of the literature concerning plant disease recognition in images using CNN was carried out, in which 130 manuscripts were reviewed, however only 2 of them had cassava as the crop analysed.

In [36] solved a multi-class classifier problem and tested the Inception V3 model with a maximum overall accuracy of 93%. Two datasets were formed: an "original cassava dataset" with only 2756 images of whole cassava leaves, and a "leaflet cassava dataset" where 15000 leaflets were manually cropped from the first dataset. The accuracy obtained were slightly higher for only three of the five diseases studied with the second dataset. Data were collected with a Sony Cybershot 20.2-megapixel digital camera under uncontrolled conditions. While in [37] a detection problem was solved and the MobileNet & SSD was tested. In addition to the 6 classes of images implemented in [36], an additional nutrient deficiency class of 336 images were included in this work. A 32% drop in F-1 score was reported for pronounced symptoms in real-world images.

It is noted that disease detection using plant leaf images is a popular field of research. Moreover, there is a clear tendency to use DL techniques because of their better performance compared to ML techniques. However, few investigations have cassava as a subject of study. In addition, most of them have a limited amount of images or were performed under controlled conditions.

The importance of this study lies in addressing the problem of disease detection in cassava leaves using the most extensive database of images taken by mobile phones in the fields and under field conditions. The paper evaluates twelve of the most popular DL models in disease detection. Additionally, the effect of using class weights during training for unbalanced data is studied. Finally, we highlight the analysis of prediction error which is not detailed in any of the papers analysed.

2   Methods

2.1   Dataset

This study used a dataset of 21'397 images labelled by experts from the National Crops Resources Research Institute (NaCRRI) in collaboration with the AI lab at Makerere University [38]. In addition, the images were collected by farmers in their own crop fields in Uganda using smartphones [39]. Therefore, the collected images faithfully represent the actual conditions of the application.

The dataset consisted of four disease categories or a fifth category corresponding to healthy leaves. The diseases under study were: cassava bacterial blight (CBB), cassava brown streak disease (CBSD), cassava green mottle (CGM) and cassava mosaic disease (CMD). However, the data was unbalanced as shown in Fig. 1.

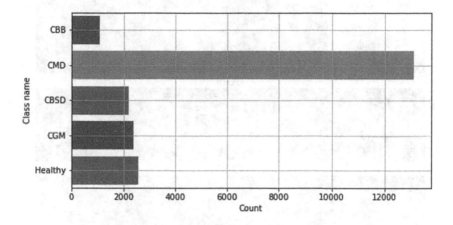

Fig. 1. Data distribution.

CMD was the class with the highest representation (61.5%), while significantly lower were the classes: Healthy (12.0%), CGM (11.2%), CBSD (10.2%) and finally CBB (5.1%). Additionally, Fig. 2 shows some samples of each class.

2.2 Pre-processing

The images were resized from 800 by 600 to 224 by 224 pixels in order to reduce the number of model parameters, thus avoiding falling into over-fitting. In addition, data augmentation techniques [40] were used to overcome the class imbalance. Therefore, random rotations from 0° to 45°, random brightness changes between 75–100%, random zooming from 0.8 to 1.2, random horizontal flipping, and random vertical flipping were applied. Finally, points outside the image boundaries were filled to the nearest value.

Transfer Learning is a methodology that uses models trained on data that is easier to obtain from a domain other than the final application and can even be applied to big data environments [41]. Transfer Learning has been shown to improve accuracy in leaf disease classification problems [14]. Therefore, this technique was used in this research on each of the 15 CNN models. Thus, a pre-processing layer was applied for each model according to the TensorFlow libraries.

CBB

Fig. 2. CBB: cassava bacterial blight. CBSD: cassava brown streak disease. CGM: cassava green mottle. CMD: cassava mosaic disease (Color figure online)

2.3   Model Architecture

The models' bases were formed by convolutional layers and the weights of the pre-trained models from the ImageNet database. In addition, the convolutional layers were followed by a flattening layer for the VGG models, see Fig. 3 A).

In contrast, the rest of the models were followed by a 2D global average pooling layer, see Fig. 3 B). Subsequently, all models used a Dropout layer with a probability of 0.25. Finally, the models end with a dense output layer with five neurons and a softmax activation function.

Table 1 shows the shape of the feature extractor, the number of trainable parameters, and the total parameters of each model. The trainable parameters are at the base of the models, while the total parameters correspond to those included in the full model.

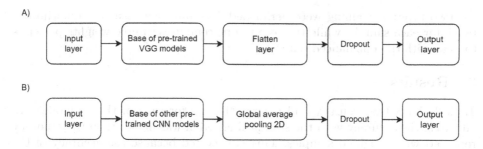

Fig. 3. A) Architecture for VGG models. B) Architecture for other CNN models

Table 1. Base shape, parameters and learning rate

Model	Total parameters	Base output shape	Trainable parameters	Learning rate
VGG16	14'840'133	(7, 7, 512)	125'445	0.0001
VGG19	20'149'829	(7, 7, 512)	125'445	0.0001
ResNet50	23'597'957	(7, 7, 2048)	10'245	0.0005
ResNet50 V2	23'575'045	(7, 7, 2048)	10'245	0.0005
ResNet101 V2	42'636'805	(7, 7, 2048)	10'245	0.0007
ResNet152 V2	58'341'893	(7, 7, 2048)	10'245	0.0008
Inception V3	21'813'029	(5, 5, 2048)	10'245	0.0002
InceptionResNetV2	54'344'421	(5, 5, 1536)	7'685	0.0007
MobileNet V2	2'264'389	(7, 7, 1280)	6'405	0.0007
DenseNet121	7'042'629	(7, 7, 1024)	5'125	0.0006
DenseNet169	12'651'205	(7, 7, 1664)	8'325	0.0006
DenseNet201	18'331'589	(7, 7, 1920)	9'605	0.0006

2.4 Training

The dataset was randomly split into training, validation, and test sets. The training set, which subsequently underwent data augmentation, consisted of 17117 images (80%), the validation set of 2140 images (10%), and the test set of 2140 images (10%). Finally, the data were batched into 32 samples.

The learning rate was found with Adam optimizer by each model following the method of [42]. The method is to start with a very small learning rate and increase it gradually. We started from 0.00001 to 0.1 following $1e-5*10^{(epoch/5)}$ where the epoch went from 0 to 20. Finally, you take as large a learning rate as possible that shows a stable decrease in losses. The learning rates found are shown in Table 1.

The training phase uses an early stopping technique, which stops training before convergence to avoid overfitting [43], that is triggered when no improvement in the validation set losses is obtained after seven epochs. Additionally, the training had a maximum duration of 20 epochs for all cases.

Two types of training were performed. The first one assumes equal importance for each sample, while the second one computes sample weights per class to deal with the unbalanced dataset.

3 Results

Table 2 shows the accuracy and macro F1 score for each of the 12 models. In all cases, the accuracy with the standard criterion was higher than the accuracy reported with weighted samples. This is expected because the accuracy of the largest class is generally reduced by having the lowest sample weight. While only the ResNet152 V2 model showed an improvement in F1 score using weighted samples.

Table 2. Comparison of test set metrics for each model with standard and weighted samples.

Model	Standard samples		Weighted samples	
	Accuracy	F1-score	Accuracy	F1-score
VGG16	60.63%	0.40	48.88%	0.40
VGG19	62.90%	0.43	48.36%	0.40
ResNet50	73.46%	0.55	61.36%	0.50
ResNet50 V2	72.34%	0.53	62.57%	0.50
ResNet101 V2	71.64%	0.52	60.56%	0.49
ResNet152 V2	70.14%	0.45	59.07%	0.47
Inception V3	69.91%	0.47	55.75%	0.45
InceptionResNetV2	69.67%	0.46	52.24%	0.45
MobileNet V2	71.17%	0.55	49.53%	0.46
DenseNet121	73.27%	0.53	58.83%	0.51
DenseNet169	74.77%	0.59	55.93%	0.50
DenseNet201	70.84%	0.52	60.09%	0.52

The model accuracy with weighted samples ranged from 48.36% to 62.57%, with the ResNet50 V2 model being the best performer. While the F1 score ranged from 0.4 to 0.52, with the DenseNet201 model being the best performer. On the other hand, the accuracy of the models with standard weights ranged from 60.03% to 74.77%, with the DenseNet169 model being the best performer. Finally, the F1 score ranged from 0.4 to 0.59, and the DenseNet169 model was again the best performer.

Therefore, the DenseNet169 model with standard sample weights obtained the best results. Thus, Fig. 4 shows its confusion matrix. The CMD class is the one with the highest accuracy, as most of the samples belong to this class. However, the other classes presented serious difficulties in classification. Most of the errors were due to incorrect classification of the samples as CMD or Healthy.

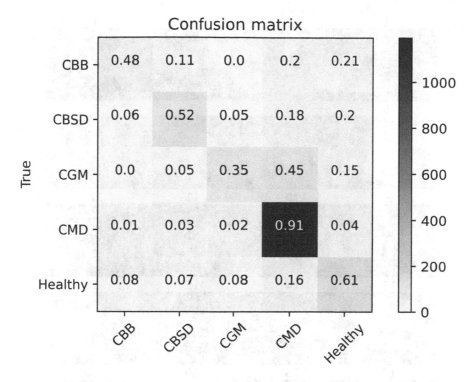

Fig. 4. Confusion matrix of the DenseNet169 model, standard samples for test set

4   Discussion

Possible causes of mistakes are analysed below. The Healthy class has been selected for its ease of inspection. Therefore, Fig. 5 shows 20 samples of the Healthy class predicted wrongly. The following sources of mistakes have been observed: the presence of another plant (sample 1), possible presence of disease (samples 2, 3, 6, 8, 9, 12, 14, 15 and 19), soil occupies a large part of the image (samples 5, 7, 10 and 14), apparently diseased leaf in the foreground (11 and 13), grass occupies a large part of the image (sample 15), yellow leaves (sample 13, and 19), blurred or out of focus photo (sample 4, 16 and 20).

[37] evaluated the performance of a Single Shot Multibox (SSD) model with the MobileNet Deep Learning model. Transfer Learning was also applied based on the Common Objects in Context (COCO) dataset. This model was trained with 2415 top view images of cassava leaves for 7 classes: healthy, CBSD, CMD, CGM, red mite damage, brown leaf spot and nutrient deficiency. [37] has a fairly good F1 score of 0.79 under controlled conditions.

However, in a second test for 120 real-world images of CBSD, CMD, CGM, the F1-score dropped to 0.54 for leaves with pronounced severity disease and dropped to 0.26 for leaves with mild severity disease. The F1-score in this research is higher than that shown by [36] for real conditions. Although [36]

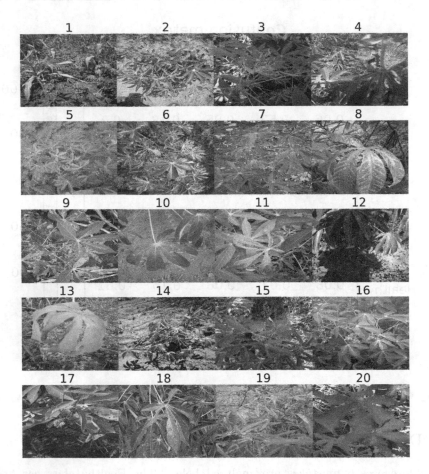

Fig. 5. Misclassified samples belonging to the Healthy class

does not use real-world images of healthy leaves, a tendency to misclassify the images as healthy was reported, as in this research.

Obviously, the accuracy in this research is lower than recent works on leaf disease detection such as [44,45], with an accuracy within the range of 99%. However, all of them have in common the use of the PlantVillage dataset to evaluate the DL. Thus, PlantVillage dataset is popular because it has many images of various plant species with their diseases, however, its images have a simple background, a single image contains only one plant leaf and the acquisition is not influenced by the real environment. Therefore, they are not suitable for practical modelling.

5 Conclusions

The results are better than other surveys that have used real-world images taken by mobile phones. This bodes well for future work that obtains balanced data or applies new techniques to combat imbalance. Thus, the positive impact of the use of DL in ecological applications is reaffirmed. On the other hand, sample weights per class for the training algorithm in the 12 CNN models showed no improvement in accuracy and F1 score compared to the versions trained with uniform sample weights. Thus, DenseNet169 model with uniform sample weights showed the best metrics with accuracy and F1 score of 74.77% and 0.59, respectively. Due to a large class imbalance, a tendency to misclassify samples as CMD or Healthy has been observed. In addition, 9/20 samples belonging to the Healthy class have been identified with visual signs of any disease. Other causes of misclassification have also been detected such as soil or grass in a large part of the image, diseased leaf in the foreground of the image, the presence of another type of plant, yellow leaves and blurred images. Therefore, there is a need for further work by the scientific community to obtain databases in real environments and correctly labelled by experts.

Acknowledgment. Thanks to the Universidad Tecnológica del Perú for its support throughout the project. The authors declare no conflict of interest related to this work. Ernesto Paiva gave the idea, did the experiments, interpreted the results and wrote the paper.

References

1. Olsen, K.M., Schaal, B.A.: Microsatellite variation in cassava (Manihot esculenta, Euphorbiaceae) and its wild relatives: further evidence for a southern Amazonian origin of domestication. Am. J. Botany **88**(1), 131–42 (2001). https://doi.org/10.2307/2657133
2. Gibbons, A.: New view of early amazonia: Recent findings suggest complex culture was indigenous to the Amazon basin-upsetting some received opinions about environment and culture. Science **248**(4962), 1488–90 (1990). https://doi.org/10.1126/science.248.4962.1488
3. Patiño, V.M.: Plantas cultivadas y animales domésticos en América Equinoccial, Imprenta Departamental (1963) (in Spanish)
4. Wanapat, M., Kang, S.: Cassava chip (Manihot esculenta Crantz) as an energy source for ruminant feeding. Animal Nutrition. **1**(4), 266–270 (2015). https://doi.org/10.1016/j.aninu.2015.12.001
5. Howeler, R., Lutaladio, N., Thomas, G.: Save and Grow: Cassava. A Guide to Sustainable Production Intensification. FAO (2013)
6. Nassar, N.M., Ortiz, R.: Cassava improvement: Challenges and impacts. J. Agricult. Sci. **145**(2), 163–171 (2007). https://doi.org/10.1017/S0021859606006575
7. Ekeleme, F., et al.: Increasing cassava root yield on farmers' fields in Nigeria through appropriate weed management. Crop Protection **150**, 105810 (2021). https://doi.org/10.1016/j.cropro.2021.105810

8. Patil, B.L., Legg, J.P., Kanju, E., Fauquet, C.M.: Cassava brown streak disease: a threat to food security in Africa. J. Gen. Virol. **96**(5), 956–68 (2015). https://doi.org/10.1099/jgv.0.000014

9. Haggag, W.M., Saber, M., Abouziena, H.F., Hoballah, E.M., Zaghloul, A.M.: Climate change potential impacts on plant diseases and their management. Der Pharm. Lettre **8**(5), 17–24 (2016)

10. Ranjan, M., Weginwar, M.R., Joshi, N., Ingole, A.B.: Detection and classification of leaf disease using artificial neural network. Int. J. Tech. Res. Appl. **3**(3), 331–3 (2015)

11. Kusumo, B.S., Heryana, A., Mahendra, O., Pardede, H.F.: Machine learning-based for automatic detection of corn-plant diseases using image processing. In: 2018 International Conference on Computer, Control, Informatics and Its Applications (IC3INA), pp. 93–97 (2018). https://doi.org/10.1109/IC3INA.2018.8629507

12. Barbedo, A., Garcia, J.: Digital image processing techniques for detecting, quantifying and classifying plant diseases. SpringerPlus **2**(1), 1–12 (2013). https://doi.org/10.1186/2193-1801-2-660

13. Sankaran, S., Mishra, A., Ehsani, R., Davis, C.: A review of advanced techniques for detecting plant diseases. Comput. Electron. Agricult. **72**(1), 1–3 (2010). https://doi.org/10.1016/j.compag.2010.02.007

14. Lu, J., Tan, L., Jiang, H.: Review on convolutional neural network (CNN) applied to plant leaf disease classification. Agriculture **11**(8), 707 (2021). https://doi.org/10.3390/agriculture11080707

15. Sharma, V.K.: Designing of face recognition system. In: 2019 International Conference on Intelligent Computing and Control Systems (ICCS), 15 May 2019, pp. 459–461. IEEE (2019)

16. Ngugi, L.C., Abelwahab, M., Abo-Zahhad, M.: Recent advances in image processing techniques for automated leaf pest and disease recognition-A review. Inf. Process. Agricult. **8**(1), 27–51 (2021). https://doi.org/10.1016/j.inpa.2020.04.004

17. Husin, Z.B., Shakaff, A.Y., Aziz, A.H., Farook, R.B.: Feasibility study on plant chili disease detection using image processing techniques. In: 2012 Third International Conference on Intelligent Systems Modelling and Simulation, pp. 291–296 (2012). https://doi.org/10.1109/ISMS.2012.33

18. Kaur, S., Pandey, S., Goel, S.: Plants disease identification and classification through leaf images: A survey. Archiv. Comput. Methods Eng. **26**(2), 507–530 (2018). https://doi.org/10.1007/s11831-018-9255-6

19. Liu, J., Wang, X.: Plant diseases and pests detection based on deep learning: a review. Plant Methods **17**(1), 1–8 (2021). https://doi.org/10.1186/s13007-021-00722-9

20. He, Y., Zhou, Z., Tian, L., Liu, Y., Luo, X.: Brown rice planthopper (*Nilaparvata lugens* Stal) detection based on deep learning. Precis. Agricult. **21**(6), 1385–1402 (2020). https://doi.org/10.1007/s11119-020-09726-2

21. Saleem, M.H., Potgieter, J., Arif, K.M.: Plant disease detection and classification by deep learning. Plants **8**(11), 468 (2019). https://doi.org/10.3390/plants8110468

22. Abade, A., Ferreira, P.A., de Barros, V.F.: Plant diseases recognition on images using convolutional neural networks: A systematic review. Comput. Electron. Agricult. **185**, 106–125 (2021). https://doi.org/10.1016/j.compag.2021.106125

23. Zhang, K., Wu, Q., Liu, A., Meng, X.: Can deep learning identify tomato leaf disease? Adv. Multim. (2018). https://doi.org/10.1155/2018/6710865

24. Türkoğlu, M., Hanbay, D.: Plant disease and pest detection using deep learning-based features. Turkish J. Electric. Eng. Comput. Sci. 27(3): 1636–1651 (2019). https://doi.org/10.3906/elk-1809-181

25. Ferentinos, K.P.: Deep learning models for plant disease detection and diagnosis. Comput. Electron. Agricult. **145**, 311–318 (2018). https://doi.org/10.1016/j.compag.2018.01.009

26. Hassan, S.M., Maji, A.K.: Plant disease identification using a novel convolutional neural network. IEEE Access **7**(10), 5390–401 (2022). https://doi.org/10.1109/ACCESS.2022.3141371

27. Ye, Y., et al.: An improved efficientNetV2 model based on visual attention mechanism: Application to identification of cassava disease. Comput. Intell. Neurosci. **8**(5) (2022). https://doi.org/10.1155/2022/1569911

28. Ravi, V., Acharya, V., Pham, T.D.: Attention deep learning-based large-scale learning classifier for Cassava leaf disease classification. Exp. Syst. **39**(2), e12862 (2022). https://doi.org/10.1111/exsy.12862

29. Arivazhagan, S., Shebiah, R.N., Ananthi, S., Varthini, S.V.: Detection of unhealthy region of plant leaves and classification of plant leaf diseases using texture features. Agricult. Eng. Int.: CIGR J. **15**(1), 211–7 (2013)

30. Thangaraj, R., Anandamurugan, S., Pandiyan, P., Kaliappan, V.K.: Artificial intelligence in tomato leaf disease detection: A comprehensive review and discussion. J. Plant Diseases Protect. 1–20 (2021). https://doi.org/10.1007/s41348-021-00500-8

31. Mohanty, S.P., Hughes, D.P., Salathé, M.: Using deep learning for image-based plant disease detection. Front. Plant Sci. **7**, 1419 (2016). https://doi.org/10.3389/fpls.2016.01419

32. Barbedo, J.G.: Factors influencing the use of deep learning for plant disease recognition. Biosyst. Eng. **172**, 84–91 (2018). https://doi.org/10.1016/j.biosystemseng.2018.05.013

33. Boulent, J., Foucher, S., Théau, J., St-Charles, P.L.: Convolutional neural networks for the automatic identification of plant diseases. Front. Plant Sci. **10**, 941 (2019). https://doi.org/10.3389/fpls.2019.00941

34. Barbedo, J.G.: A review on the main challenges in automatic plant disease identification based on visible range images. Biosyst. Eng. **144**, 52–60 (2016). https://doi.org/10.1016/j.biosystemseng.2016.01.017

35. Shrivastava, S., Hooda, D.S.: Automatic brown spot and frog eye detection from the image captured in the field. Am. J. Intell. Syst. **4**(4), 131–4 (2014). https://doi.org/10.5923/j.ajis.20140404.01

36. Ramcharan, A., Baranowski, K., McCloskey, P., Ahmed, B., Legg, J., Hughes, D.P.: Deep learning for image-based cassava disease detection. Front. Plant Sci. **8**, 1852 (2017). https://doi.org/10.3389/fpls.2017.01852

37. Ramcharan, A., et al.: A mobile-based deep learning model for cassava disease diagnosis. Front. Plant Sci. **272** (2019). https://doi.org/10.3389/fpls.2019.00272

38. Kaggle. Cassava leaf disease classification. identify the type of disease present on a cassava leaf image (2021). https://www.kaggle.com/353competitions/cassava-leaf-disease-classification

39. Mwebaze, E., Gebru, T., Frome, A., Nsumba, S., Tusubira, J.: iCassava 2019 fine-grained visual categorization challenge. arXiv preprint arXiv:1908.02900 (2019).

40. Shorten, C., Khoshgoftaar, T.M.: A survey on image data augmentation for deep learning. J. Big Data **6**(1), 1–48 (2019). https://doi.org/10.1186/s40537-019-0197-0

41. Weiss, K., Khoshgoftaar, T.M., Wang, D.D.: A survey of transfer learning. J. Big Data **3**(1), 1–40 (2016). https://doi.org/10.1186/s40537-016-0043-6

42. Smith, L.N.: Cyclical learning rates for training neural networks. In: 2017 IEEE Winter Conference on Applications of Computer Vision (WACV), pp. 464–472 (2017). https://doi.org/10.1109/WACV.2017.58

43. Prechelt, L.: Automatic early stopping using cross validation: Quantifying the criteria. Neural Netw. **11**(4), 761–7 (1998). https://doi.org/10.1016/S0893-6080(98)00010-0

44. Atila, Ü., Uçar, M., Akyol, K., Uçar, E.: Plant leaf disease classification using EfficientNet deep learning model. Ecol. Inf. **61**, 101182 (2021). https://doi.org/10.1016/j.ecoinf.2020.101182

45. Tiwari, V., Joshi, R.C., Dutta, M.K.: Dense convolutional neural networks based multiclass plant disease detection and classification using leaf images. Ecol. Inf. **63**, 101289 (2021). https://doi.org/10.1016/j.ecoinf.2021.101289

Image Classification with Information Extraction by Evaluating the Text Patterns in Bilingual Documents

Shalini Puri$^{(\boxtimes)}$ (iD)

Manipal University Jaipur, Jaipur, Rajasthan, India
eng.shalinipuri30@gmail.com

Abstract. The rapid development of digital data in today's world needs highly efficient and automatic N-lingual image document classification and information extraction systems. Several text-based image processing systems have been introduced to date for different applications. However, they are limited to character recognition, word extraction, profiling, and script and language recognition. The proposed document classification and information extraction system categorizes the bilingual English-Hindi images into mutually exclusive categories by using SVM and random forest classifiers at the character-level and document-level recognitions, respectively. It used two pseudo-thesaurus, first to store the pre-defined English and Romanized Hindi characters and second to store the keywords of the pre-defined categories. It discriminates between the languages by determining the absence or presence of the shirorekha for the English or Hindi word images, respectively, and applies the minimum distance computing method to obtain the constructed words from the mapped English and Romanized Hindi characters. This system achieved promising results in extracting the information and classifying the bi-lingual image documents. It illustrates a case study to explain the working of the system.

Keywords: Information extraction · Bilingual system · Hindi-English image documents · Language pair · Text pattern analysis

1 Introduction

With the advent of efficient and automatic document classification systems [1, 2], there is a growing preference to categorize online and offline documents of text, printed, and handwritten modes into pre-defined categories. Due to the high digitalization of the world, numerous multi-mode, multi-script, multi-font, multi-colored, and multi-type documents are produced daily and further processed using the concepts of machine learning, Natural Language Processing (NLP), and image processing [3] paradigms. The text in the N-lingual (multi-lingual) documents includes several text combinations of multiple languages, so the processing of such documents becomes very critical and requires a great deal of space and time.

Many lingual-based works have contributed to the recognition of characters and scripts, word and line segmentation, language discrimination, and feature analysis and extraction to date. Very few contributions exist for classifying the embedded contents

I. Woungang et al. (Eds.): ANTIC 2022, CCIS 1798, pp. 115–137, 2023.
https://doi.org/10.1007/978-3-031-28183-9_9

of the image document into different categories. Although such works processes the text of an image efficiently, they do not provide any type of information from the images. As we know that the words, sentences, and text present in a document lose their meanings when they become parts of an image, so the NLP standards and procedures cannot directly be applied to them as the image contents do not sustain the natural form of the text.

Bilingual document processing is one of the threads of the N-lingual document analytical systems, which analyze the text contents of two different languages. In the present scenario, such documents either contain the non-scanned, non-image pure text or contain scanned images of the text contents. The text extraction, recognition, and processing in the latter case require a great level of effort. Additionally, the scanned text form in printed (or/and) handwritten document image in the latter case also makes the text processing a challenging task.

Looking into the existing bi-lingual image recognition and identification methods, these methods first determine the lines, words, and characters from an image and then process them for character and script recognition. However many times, the processing of the intermixed words of two different languages in an image becomes critical, for example, the processing of an image of a dictionary page. Furthermore, the processing of handwritten image text is found comparatively more difficult than printed ones. Therefore, the text processing level on these documents becomes more challenging when these embedded contents are handwritten. In addition to this, the use of multiple languages and scripts and their writing patterns in a document make the document analysis and processing task a very critical one. Some other challenges are related to line and character segmentation, identification of the presence of punctuation marks, partial word image processing, and inefficiency in pattern-matching techniques. Therefore, the classification of printed and handwritten documents is very important and critical in the present scenario.

Today, many national and international languages are used across the world for reading and writing purposes. English, a Latin-scripted language, is the most common and popular language among all the languages which is used for verbal and written communication in most countries. Hindi, a Devanagari scripted language, is also getting the attention of research contributors. Devanagari script has 33 consonants and 13 vowels. Its basic consonants are क, ख, ग, घ, ङ, च, छ, ज, झ, ञ, ट, ठ, ड, ढ, ण, त, थ, द, ध, न, प, फ, ब, भ, म, य, र, ल, व, श, ष, स, and ह, and the vowels are अ, आ (ा), इ (ि), ई (ी), उ (ु), ऊ (ू), ए (े), ऐ (ै), ओ (ो), औ (ौ), ऋ, अं (ं), and अः (ः). The numerals from 0 to 9 are written as ०, १, २, ३, ४, ५, ६, ७, ८, and ९, respectively in Devanagari. Their respective Hindi forms are शून्य, एक, दो, तीन, चार, पांच, छह, सात, आठ, and नौ. Hindi words are constructed using the combination of several letters, modifiers, and shirorekha, and are therefore formed using complex modified characters and consonants. The primary modifiers in Devanagari are ौ, ि, ौ, ं, ा, ी, ु, ूो, ं, ृ, ं, ृ, ाँ, ृ, ृर, ं, ः, ं, and ं रृ. In India, a large set of Hindi text documents and other data sets are available in the form of news articles, novels, etc. Some other documents are also available in the unstructured form. A few Indian states follow the concept of the 3 (±) language rule.

Several text classification systems, analyzers, and information extractors exist that process the pure text of non-image English documents. Most of today's work primarily exists in English in single-, bi-lingual and N-lingual documents. The research paradigm on Indic languages is taking a slow but steady pace in various fields of document analysis. This research is taking place for processing the underlying text of the printed, hand-written, or both forms for many applications, say, the text extraction and processing of application forms, bills, etc. Hindi document classification through text information extraction is a very rare case.

Some research questions are given below which are related to the information extraction and classification of the bi-lingual image documents.

1. How can the information be extracted from the bi-lingual documents, especially from Indic scripted documents?
2. Will the bi-lingual or bi-script system be able to identify the extracted words from a document with high accuracy?
3. How will the system separate two scripts and two languages efficiently?
4. Will the system work properly for a large set of image documents?
5. How will the system be noise insensitive?

Therefore, all these reasons increase the need of extracting useful information from bi- or N-lingual documents. It creates a requirement to propose an efficient bilingual document classification and information extraction system that can work on the embedded language of a particular image document. This paper is designed to present the concepts of bi-lingual processing and the case scenarios of how to extract information from bilingual Hindi-English image documents.

The paper is structured as follows. Section 2 illustrates the concepts related to the processing of text patterns in a document. Furthermore, it presents a structure of document categorical schemes along with their applications. Section 3 discusses the related work of recent algorithms in detail. Section 4 proposes the concept of a bilingual document image classification system with Hindi-English language pair for information extraction. Section 5 explains the working principle of the bi-lingual English-Hindi image document classification and information extraction through a case study. Finally, Sect. 6 provides the conclusion and future recommendations.

2   Text Patterns in Bi-lingual Document Processing Paradigms

An image document text is a combination of several types of text patterns, con-tents, scripts, languages, and a variety of styles and arrangements. Its processing is done through multiple stages such as character recognition, segmentation procedures, and recognition methods. The bi-lingual English-Hindi document processing includes the processing of complex contents for identifying the characters, words, and lines and recognizing the scripts of languages.

2.1 Text Processing in Bilingual Documents

Several methods of feature extraction and text recognition have been implemented by recent research contributors to date while processing image text. The geometric and the structural feature extraction play a vital role in recognition. These features aid in analyzing the shape of the characters, connected components, jambs, diacritical points, and the hamps closely. The vertical and horizontal histograms are used to segment the lines and characters of the image. The features are extracted from profiles and contour tracing. The second set of features of the characters includes edge curvature, run length, regularity, and text-line alignment features. Along with these features, some additional features are character width, the number of characters, position of the diacritical dots, cursive, white hole, centroid, sphericity, aspect ratio features, presence and absence of features for each character, height, loops, width, lines, density, stems in the characters, upward concavities, optical densities, mean height of symbols and characteristic shapes or symbols.

These features must be extracted well for handwritten images too where the characters vary in their static and dynamic properties. The static properties of these characters are related to the character size and form, whereas dynamic properties are related to the number of diacritic segments. Such images are generally very sensitive to noise and edge thickness. Their structures depend on the characters heavily in the way that the characters should not have much overlapping, and should not have touching characters.

Template matching is one of the character recognition techniques that is used for characters and standard font recognition. However, it does not always produce good results as it is sensitive to size and style. That's why, it gives a somewhat poor performance with handwritten, noisy, and destructive characters. Some other matching approaches are word-based, text-line, image-based, and texture-based approaches.

2.2 Document Mining with Images and Non-Images

Figure 1 depicts a data mining categorization scheme that processes the image and non-image documents. This scheme has two major techniques called classification and clustering. The classification technique classifies the given text of the image or non-image document using pre-defined labels, whereas the clustering technique categorizes the data using feature processing-based methods. Although several research works do exist for the classification of pure text documents, however, the classification of image documents further needs attention.

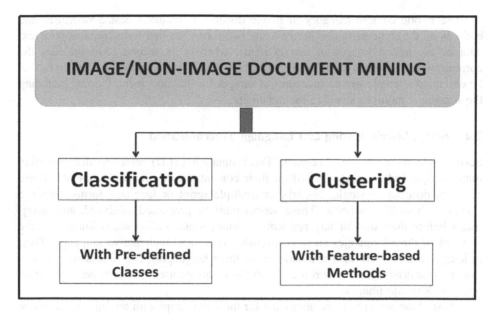

Fig. 1. Data mining categorization scheme for images and non-images.

2.3   Content Embedding and Structuring

The Content Embedding and Structuring (CES) scheme in bi-lingual image documents frames the text contents as the pure text, the non-text, and the hybrid form of both text and non-text contents. Figure 2 shows this scheme in the form of three CES types. Simple non-image documents consist of pure text contents and do not include any type of images, whereas non-image documents contain drawings, diagrams, scenes, and pictures without having any text data.

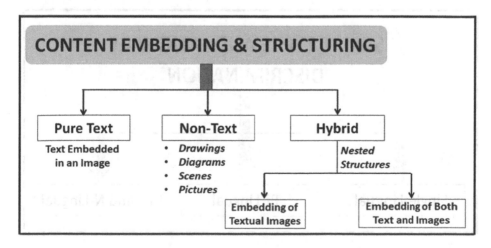

Fig. 2. A scheme for content embedding and structuring.

The hybrid content category of image documents includes nested structures and embeds all the contents in one image using two forms. Its first form contains pure text data or the nested images of text contents, whereas its second form includes the combination of text data along with pictorial images. These document forms can further be extended to create nested structures of images for one document, thereby including the images at multiple levels in the documents.

2.4   Script Discrimination and Language Discrimination

Script Discrimination and Language Discrimination (SLD) refers to differentiating many scripts and languages based on their contents in the image documents. These contents do exist in single, bi-, tri-, or multiple script or language forms. Figure 3 shows such an SLD scheme. These scripts must be processed, analyzed, and recognized before their use for any application. Many south Indian states implement the concept of three languages such as English, Hindi, and their native language. Their official documents are also available in all three languages. The processing of such images first determines the script and (or) the language used and then performs other operations on the images.

Most of the research work does exist for the Latin script with the English language for single-, bi-, tri, and N-lingual documents. In such types of documents, English is considered the first and foremost language. A few research works exist for various Indian scripts and languages as compared to English to date. Therefore, a gap is observed in the research works contributed to the Latin script and the Indic scripts. Figures 4 and 5 show pure text-based single-lingual image documents written in Sanskrit and Marathi languages, respectively. Figure 4 shows the lines of the 'Shaanti' (peace) mantra written in Sanskrit, and Fig. 5 shows a few lines of a poem written by the Marathi poet 'Vinda Karandikar'. It can be seen that both the languages use Devanagari script for writing purposes.

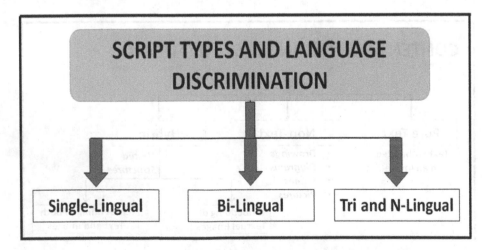

Fig. 3. Showing lingual types - discriminating different languages and scripts.

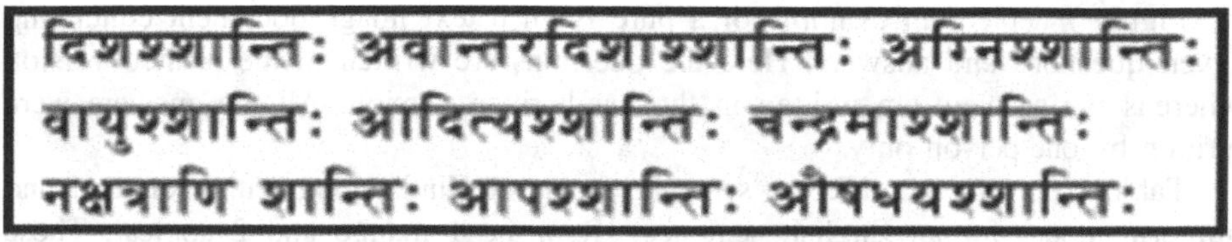

दिशश्शान्तिः अवान्तरदिशाश्शान्तिः अग्निश्शान्तिः
वायुश्शान्तिः आदित्यश्शान्तिः चन्द्रमाश्शान्तिः
नक्षत्राणि शान्तिः आपश्शान्तिः औषधयश्शान्तिः

Fig. 4. Pure text-based single-lingual image document in Sanskrit.

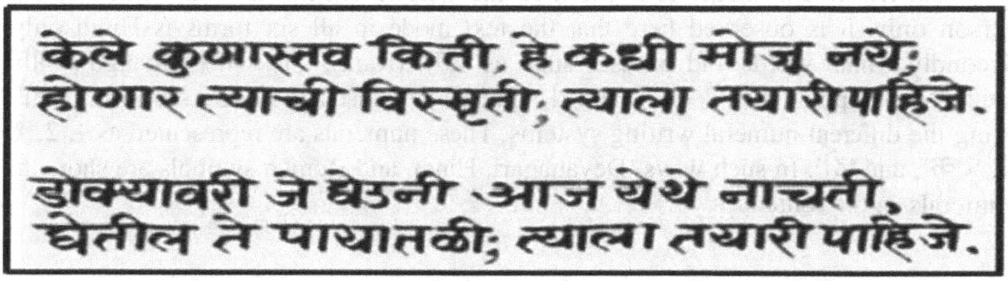

केले कुणासव किती, हे कधी मोजु नये;
होणार त्याची विस्मृती, त्याला तयारी पाहिजे.

डोक्यावरी जे घेउनी आज येथे नाचती,
घेतील ते पायातळी; त्याला तयारी पाहिजे.

Fig. 5. Pure text-based single-lingual image document in Marathi.

2.5   Text Presentation and Style in Image Documents

The Text Presentation and Style (TPS) used in the bi-lingual image document is another important criterion for text processing. Figure 6 depicts two types of TPS modes such as printed and handwritten. These modes are further extended for different types of content. The text present in the scanned image document of any language can either be in the printed or handwritten form or the combined form of printed and handwritten contents.

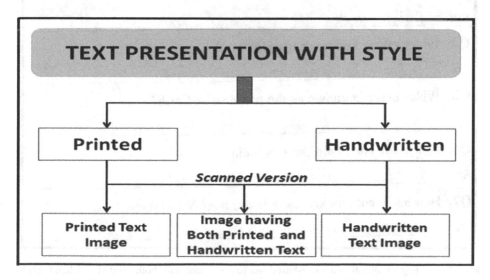

Fig. 6. Text presentation and style used in different types of image documents.

Figure 7 depicts an example of a pure English text image document containing seven questions and answers. Here the questions are written in the printed version whereas the answers are written in the handwritten version. All the answers were written by one person only.

Table 1 depicts six different sentence forms in Hindi along with their text and numeric modes for an English sentence, 'Ram ate 1 mango and 2 apples'. These sentence forms use the numerals either as English or Hindi digits or as Hindi words. In each case, the sentence is written in three forms, namely simple text, printed text image, and handwritten text image. The text of all the handwritten images was written by one person only. It is observed here that the text mode in all six forms is Hindi only. Secondly, Hindi words and phrases such as 'राम' (Ram), 'ने', 'आम' (mango), 'और' (and), 'सेब' (apple), 'खाये' (ate), and '।' (full stop) is used in all the six forms while using the different numeral writing systems. These numerals are represented as 1, 2, १, २, 'एक', and 'दो'. In such ways, Devanagari, Hindi, and Roman symbols are show the numerals in the sentences.

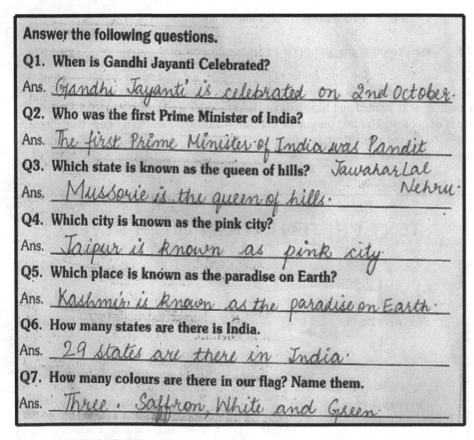

Fig. 7. An English question-answer-based image document with both printed and handwritten text contents.

Table 1. Hindi sentence forms in the text, printed and handwritten modes with Devanagari and Roman numerics.

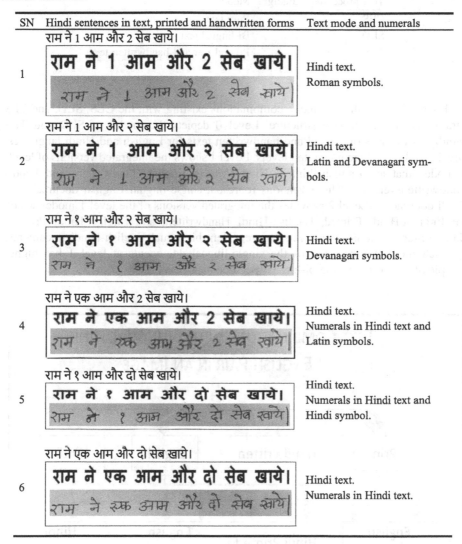

SN	Hindi sentences in text, printed and handwritten forms	Text mode and numerals
1	राम ने 1 आम और 2 सेब खाये।	Hindi text. Roman symbols.
2	राम ने 1 आम और २ सेब खाये।	Hindi text. Latin and Devanagari symbols.
3	राम ने १ आम और २ सेब खाये।	Hindi text. Devanagari symbols.
4	राम ने एक आम और 2 सेब खाये।	Hindi text. Numerals in Hindi text and Latin symbols.
5	राम ने १ आम और दो सेब खाये।	Hindi text. Numerals in Hindi text and Hindi symbol.
6	राम ने एक आम और दो सेब खाये।	Hindi text. Numerals in Hindi text.

2.6   A Case Scenario: Text Combinations with English-Hindi Pair

Sections 2.3, 2.4 and 2.5 explained CES, SLD, and TPS text processing paradigms, respectively. Table 2 depicts these paradigms along with their respective modes. The CES paradigm refers to the pure text contents in printed or handwritten form for a bi-lingual document. The SLD paradigm in a bi-lingual image document is concerned with the use of any two languages belonging to either one or two scripts. The TPS paradigm refers to the inclusion of printed or/and handwritten text forms in bi-lingual image documents.

Table 2. Text processing paradigms and modes for bi-lingual image documents.

Text processing paradigm	Mode
CES	Pure text
SLD	Bi-lingual text
TPS	Printed text and handwritten text

Figure 8 shows the text mode combinations existing with the CES, SLD, and TPS paradigms in a level-wise structure. Level 0 depicts the modes of SLD and TPS paradigms in terms of printed and handwritten texts for English and Hindi languages. Level 1 and level 2 are integrated levels. Level 1 shows the integrated versions of level-0 modes that are English-Printed, Hindi-Printed, English-Handwritten, and Hindi-Handwritten versions. These versions represent single-lingual English documents or Hindi documents. Level 2 provides the integrated versions of the level-1 modes which are English-Hindi Printed, English-Hindi Handwritten, and English-Hindi Printed-Handwritten versions. These versions represent bi-lingual English-Hindi documents. As such the text processing of the single-lingual documents at level 1 has higher complexity than that of the bi-lingual documents at level 2.

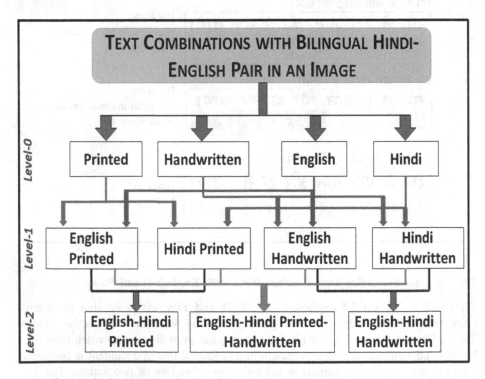

Fig. 8. Level-wise structure showing the mode combinations for the English-Hindi pair.

Consider a level-2 example of the English noun word 'dump' and its two adjective forms called 'dumpish' and 'dumpishness'. Figure 9 shows the Hindi meanings of all three English words. It represent the bi-lingual English-Hindi printed category for an English-to-Hindi dictionary. It can be seen that the word 'dump' has many Hindi meanings or translations such as बुद्धिमंदता (unintelligent), बदमिज़ाजी (bad-tempered person), निरुत्साह (discourage), धीमा नृत्य (slow dance), उदासी (sadness), दुःख (sorrow), and धुन (tune). The Hindi meanings of its adjective form 'dumpish' are निरुत्साहित (discouraged) and उदास (depressed), whereas Hindi meanings of the word 'dumpish-ness' are उत्साहहीनता (lack of enthusiasm) and उदासी (sadness). Other Hindi meanings of the word 'dump' are मंदी का गड्ढा (recession pit), दरिया का गड्ढा (river bed), नाटा आदमी (short man), नाटी वस्तु (flimsy object), and संगमरमर (marble). Many such examples do exist in the dictionary and government documents to represent bi-lingual English-Hindi integrated levels.

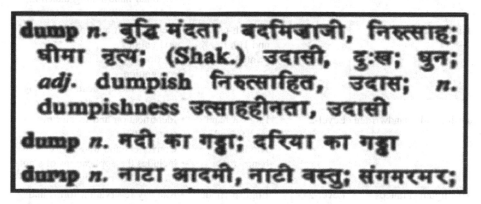

Fig. 9. An example of an English word, 'dump', with its several Hindi meanings – a case of bilingual English-Hindi document image.

2.7   Application Categories for SLD and TPS Paradigms

The SLD and TPS paradigms apply to many applications and sectors of the real world. Table 3 shows various application areas concerning these paradigms. Its criteria are paradigms at level 0, integrated levels and versions, and applications. Here the level-0 paradigms are the SLD and TPS paradigms, where the SLD paradigm can be single-lingual or bi-lingual, and the TPS paradigm can have the values of printed, handwritten, and printed-handwritten. Each level-0 entry has its integrated level and version number which applies to many applications. Table 3 lists several applications for these text-based image and non-image contents in single- and bi-lingual paradigms. A few applications such as translators, converters, web page classification, information retrieval, mail sorting, text summarization, spam detection, and Short Messaging Services (SMS) are applied especially to pure-text non-image documents.

Table 3. Depicting different paradigms along with their levels, versions, and applications.

Level-0 paradigms		Integrated level and version		Applications
SLD paradigm	TPS paradigm	Level number	Version name	
Single lingual	Printed	Level-1	English-printed or Hindi-printed	• Language identification • Text recognition in magazines, newspapers, technical reports, novels, and children's books • Official and Government documents. Demand drafts • Artistic documents
Single lingual	Handwritten	Level-1	English hand-written or Hindi handwritten	• Recognizing postal address • Signature verification and writer recognition • Criminal handwriting matching and verification
Bi-lingual	Printed	Level-2	English-printed and Hindi printed	• Identification and localization of text entities • Dictionary-based word recognition • Includes the applications of single lingual SLD paradigms as well
Bi-lingual	Handwritten	Level-2	English hand-written and Hindi handwritten	• Identification and localization of text entities • Converters and translators • Includes the applications of single lingual SLD paradigms as well
Bi-lingual	Printed-hand-written	Level-2	English-Hindi printed-handwritten	• Railway reservation forms and examination papers • Postal address identification and automated reading of postal address with phone number and ZIP code • Petition files and bank cheques • Includes applications of the last two bi-lingual SLD paradigms as well

3 Thematic Background on Bi-lingual Processing Systems

Several research contributions have been contributed to the bi-lingual document processing, recognition, and analysis systems using English-Hindi pairs to date. This is observed that a few bi-lingual English-Hindi contributions worked on the pure text processing of the non-image simple documents for implementing different applications. They generally follow the steps of pre-processing, feature analysis, and categorization.

On the other side, text-based image processing systems implement the steps of pre-processing, segmentation, feature extraction, and document classification for recognizing characters, scripts, and languages. This section discusses various pre-existing bilingual processing systems using image and non-image documents. They are discussed below.

The design of the hybrid text mining approach for Chinese and English documents discovered the concept-based feature map containing word clusters and document clusters from multilingual text collections [4]. The next approach implemented a cross-lingual, question-answering system [5] using Hindi and English languages. It first extracted the answers for a given English question from Hindi newspapers, then translated those answers along with the context surrounding each answer into English. The bilingual English - Spanish news clustering approach [6] employed the feature selection and fuzzy rule system similarity measures. It represented the news documents as named entities.

In [7], Chinese-English web pages were classified into specific domains with hierarchical topic structures based on the dictionary. This method recognized and integrated the web page encodings by using an automatic encoding detection and integration method. Another work [8] introduced the concepts of document analysis and recognition for the automatic extraction of information. A segmentation approach [9] first applied text and non-text segmentation on different image documents and then classified them into various categories. In the query system design [10], the users put queries to a Frequently-Asked-Questions (FAQ) database built in Hindi using noisy SMS English queries. This system constructed a query similarity design over FAQ questions as a combinatorial search problem where the search space contained the combinations of dictionary variations of the noisy query and its top-N translations. The affinity propagation clustering algorithm [11] first categorized the bilingual English-Chinese documents and then generated bilingual topic taxonomy using clustering before or after text feature reconstruction.

The textual entities of bilingual documents written in Chinese and English were classified by first identifying Chinese components before merging them into intact characters and sending the latter characters to a Chinese recognizer [12]. The script recognizer [13] first extracted the structural, Gabor, and discrete cosine transform features from the isolated English and Gurmukhi words. It then compared their performance and accuracy using the Support Vector Machine (SVM), K-Nearest Neighbor (KNN), and Parzen Probabilistic Neural Network (PNN). The concept-based mining model [14] used fuzzy similarity measures for English text classification. Another such system [15] implemented the N-grams technique to identify the Hindi and Sanskrit languages in the documents. The text simplification system [16] compared the baseline approach with the classifier-based approach. It was designed to improve the quality and the results of the English-Hindi machine translation system. The design of the bilingual word prediction system [17] first predicted both English and Hindi words and phrases. It then compared which model was better employed to produce better results as compared to other models.

In the same way, another method [18] identified Hinglish Tweets from the Twitter website. These tweets were considered a representation of the sentiments of the users. It created the Hindi dictionaries for the system that was provided having no spelling ambiguities. Another research work [19] compared two text categorization systems called a fuzzy similarity-based concept mining model with feature clustering (FSCMM-FC) and a concept-based mining model with a threshold (CMMT). Both system designs classified the English text documents into predefined, mutually exclusive groups. They first pre-processed the documents at the sentence, document, and integrated corpora levels; then performed feature extraction and feature reduction; then trained the classifier, and finally categorized the documents using SVM. The FSCMM-FC system had an additional layer of fuzzy similarity for feature reduction. The CMMT and FSCMM-FC systems achieved 95.8% and 94.695% feature reductions, respectively as well as 85.41% and 93.43% classification accuracies. It was found that the FSCMM-FC significantly outperformed CMMT in terms of memory usage and classification accuracy.

The document analysis review [20] provided a summary of various methodologies, feature extraction approaches, document sets, classifiers, and accuracies for English-Hindi and other language pairs used by existing N-lingual systems. It introduced the concept of a generic bilingual English-Hindi document classification system using heterogeneous documents, a dual class feeder, and two character-based corpora. Its non-image and image modules comprised pre- and post-processing phases as well as pre-segmentation and post-segmentation stages to categorize the documents into predefined classes. Furthermore, it demonstrated numerous real-world applications on societal and real-world issues. Lastly, it presented important discoveries and analytical results for both the existing and proposed systems.

Another study [21] implemented two methods for sentiment analysis and classification for the Hindi-English language pair. The study suggested an Ensemble-based methodology by fusing the Naive Bayes, SVM, linear regression, and stochastic gradient descent classifiers. Additionally, it also used the bidirectional LSTM technique for the classification. Another work [22] translated the words between Sanskrit and Hindi without using any parallel corpus. It employed a quasi-bilingual dictionary and singular value decomposition to align the text word embedding of Sanskrit and Hindi quickly in the same vector space. It assessed the dictionary's translations using the nearest neighbor, inverted Sofmax, and cross-domain similarity local scaling methods. It compared its results with other unsupervised techniques at 1, 10, and 20 neighbors. It created a test dictionary using Wikipedia's Sanskrit and Hindi Shabdkosh to evaluate the system's accuracy.

The approach in [23] classified the Hindi image documents into several categories. Another approach [24] classified the 1033 English text documents using the SVM classifier. It found that the Rocchio classifier outperformed other classifiers for the small feature set only, whereas the SVM classifier outperformed the other classifiers for all the datasets. It achieved a classification rate above 90% for more than 4000 features. The next approach [25] implemented the local binary convolutional neural networks for both Arabic and English digit recognition. It improved the accuracies by 0.04% and 0.08% for MNIST and MADBase datasets, respectively.

The Hindi summarizer [26] implemented the steps of input data acquisition, tokenization, feature extraction, score generation, and sentence extraction using a deep recurrent neural network. It achieved results of 80.89%, 95.7%, 95.051%, and 95.37% for recall-oriented understudy for gisting evaluation, recall, precision, and f-measure parameters, respectively. The character recognition system [27] implemented the linear discriminant analysis using 3877 handwritten Devanagari characters. It extracted the discrete cosine transform zigzag features, geometric features, and hue moments features. It achieved 93.6% accuracy using a combination of all the features.

This detailed background provided an overview of various bi-lingual documents. Many research contributions worked on the image documents as shown in Fig. 10. Figure 10 (a) depicts a comparison between the usage of bi-lingual non-image and the usage of image documents by the existing systems. Figure 10 (b) depicts another comparative chart between the usage of non-image and image documents for the English-Hindi pair. It is also seen here that all these image-based existing works are primarily related to character recognition, word and line segmentation, script and language discrimination, and recognition. They do not extract useful information from the embedded text contents of the bi-lingual image documents.

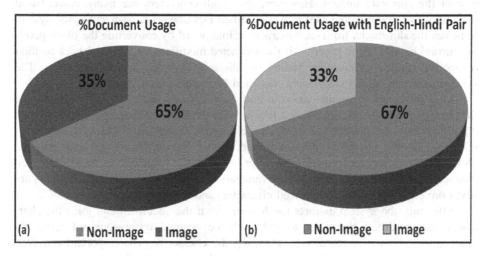

Fig. 10. (a) % Usage of non-image and image documents. (b) % Usage of non-image and image documents for English-Hindi pair.

4 Proposed Bilingual Image Classification with Information Extraction

Bilingual image document classification is a significant and demanded sector that categorizes English and Hindi images into different categories by extracting the information from the textual images [20, 23]. The idea behind this proposed bi-lingual classification system is first to accept and process the English and Hindi image documents and then to categorize them into pre-defined mutually exclusive categories by extracting the information from them with high efficiency and accuracy.

The document training processor of the proposed system pre-processes the training image documents to get the page layout and makes them noise-free. These input documents can be printed or handwritten or printed-handwritten images. After pre-processing, the system performs the steps of word-based segmentation, shirorekha-based script recognition, word construction, image classification [20, 23], and information extraction. It uses the projection profile methods to segment each image first horizontally to extract the sentence images, and then vertically to extract the word images. These gaps between two sentences and two words have a high density of white pixels, which are used to separate the two adjacent lines and adjacent words. This step is followed by the script and language recognition by determining the presence or absence of the shirorekha.

The system extracts the important features of the word images and discards the non–important ones. Next, the English and Hindi word images are segmented to get the characters. The English words are constituted using small and capital characters. As they do not have the concept of shirorekha and modifiers, so the system segments the words to extract the word images from the sentences which are further segmented to extract the character images. However, the Hindi characters use many vowel-based modifiers to convert a character into a modified Devanagari character. So, the system removes the shirorakha from each extracted Hindi word by converting the black pixels of shirorekha into white pixels. All the extracted modifiers are attached back to their respective Hindi characters by finding the distance from the nearest characters. The system then gets all the simple and modified Devanagari characters.

After the character segmentation in both languages, all the extracted characters are first mapped to their character-based labels using the Pseudo-Thesaurus-I and are then classified into the pre-defined character categories using the SVM classifier. This pseudo-thesaurus stores all the small and capital Roman characters and also the Devanagari consonants, vowels, modifiers, and half characters in the Romanized character forms. Here the extracted Devanagari characters and modified characters are first converted into small Romanized characters and are then classified.

After this, the system extracts the features from the document and joins the characters and modified characters to get back the original retrieved word forms by determining the minimum distances among the characters. The important retrieved words are kept for the classification of the image documents and the unimportant words are discarded. These retrieved words are compared with the pre-defined keywords of the Pseudo-Thesaurus-II. The Pseudo-Thesaurus-II stores a few keywords in Hindi and English both of which are related to the different pre-defined categories such as cricket, education, agriculture, etc.

If the retrieved words get matched with the pre-defined keywords of a particular category, say, 'category1' and the matching frequency of such retrieved words is higher than the pre-defined threshold of 0.7, then that image document is classified into the 'category1'. In this way, the system classifies the image documents into mutually exclusive categories using a random forest classifier. Such classification results in a specific category, say, 'category1' of the image document, and thus extracts the relevant information from the image. The accuracy of both classifiers is estimated against a set of new test documents. The algorithm of the proposed bi-lingual image classification is given below.

Bi-lingual Image Classification Algorithm ()

STEP 1: Acquire and read the textual image documents.

STEP 2: Perform preprocessing and remove noise. Convert the grayscale image into the binary image using adaptive threshold and image complement methods.

STEP 3: Perform the projection profile methods for horizontal segmentation to get the sentence images and for vertical segmentation to get the word images.

STEP 4: Determine the script from the word images using the concept of the presence or absence of the shirorekha.

STEP 5: Remove the shirorekha from the Hindi word images.

STEP 6: Get the character images from the English words, and character and modified images from Hindi word images.

STEP 7: Map all the English character images into the pre-defined labels stored in the Pseudo-Thesaurus-I.

STEP 8: Map all the Devanagari characters and modified character images into the Romanized character labels.

STEP 9: Classify all the character labels into the pre-defined set of characters using the SVM classifier.

STEP 10: Associate these extracted English character labels and Romanized Hindi character labels to construct their respective original words by determining the distance among these character labels.

STEP 11: Match these constructed words with the pre-defined keywords of the Pseudo-Thesaurus-II.

STEP 12: Classify the constructed words into the pre-defined categories using the random forest classifier and thereby classify the image documents into mutually exclusive categories.

STEP 13: Retrieve the information from the categorized documents.

This work puts a step ahead to provide a new way of bilingual document classification and information extraction. This system was implemented on a set of ten pure text bi-lingual English-Hindi image documents using MATLAB. The training and testing images were divided into a ratio of 70:30. These image documents were of two categories such as cloth (कपड़ा) and education (शिक्षा). Each image document had the contents of any one category in both languages. These bi-lingual documents were self-constructed in printed form and their scanned image versions were used for the implementation.

5 A Case Study on Image Classification with Information Extraction

Consider a pure text bi-lingual English-Hindi image document of the 'cloth' (कपड़ा) category as shown in Fig. 11. This document follows the concepts of CES, SLD, and TPS paradigms. It contains four and six text lines of text in English and Hindi languages, respectively. The document goes through the steps of pre-processing, binary image conversion, projection profiling, script determination, word image extraction, segmentation, information extraction and classification. The pseudo-thesaurus-2 stores the seven cloth-related pre-defined keywords in English such as 'charkha', 'cloth', 'cotton', 'fabric', 'fibre', 'khadi', and 'woven', and the seven कपड़ा-related pre-defined keywords in Hindi such as 'कपड़ा', 'सूत', वस्त्र, 'हथकरघा', 'खादी', 'बुन', and 'चरखा'. These pre-defined keywords of Hindi are stored in the Romanized Hindi forms in the pseudo-thesaurus-2.

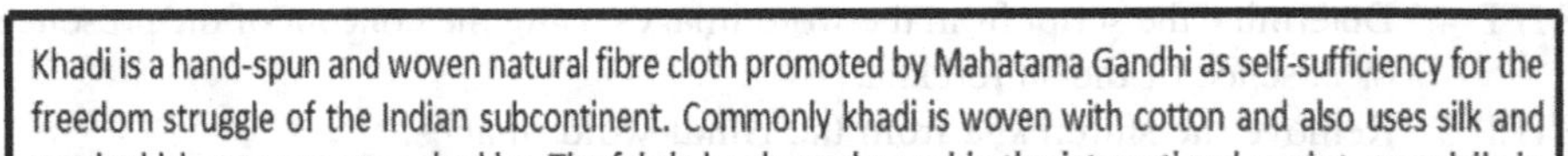

> Khadi is a hand-spun and woven natural fibre cloth promoted by Mahatama Gandhi as self-sufficiency for the freedom struggle of the Indian subcontinent. Commonly khadi is woven with cotton and also uses silk and wool which are spun on a charkha. The fabric has huge demand in the international market, especially in western countries.
>
> सफलता में कहां चूक हुई? स्वतंत्रता संग्राम से ही कुटीर उद्योग खादी व ग्रामीण हस्तशिल्पियों का महत्व समझने के बावजूद स्वतंत्रता के पांच दशक से अधिक समय बीतने के बाद भी उन्हें उचित स्थान क्यों नहीं दे पाये है? इस ज्वलंत प्रश्न की तह में देखेंगे तो स्थितियों की सच्चाई को समझने के लिए देश के सबसे महत्वपूर्ण कपड़ा उद्योग की स्थिति को जानना होगा। सरकारी आंकड़ों के अनुसार लगभग 20 प्रतिशत कपड़े का उत्पादन हथकरघा क्षेत्र में होता है, शेष 80 प्रतिशत कपड़े का उत्पादन मिल व पावरलूम क्षेत्र में होता है। जो 20 प्रतिशत उत्पादन हथकरघा क्षेत्र में होता है, उस पर संकट के बादल घिरे रहते है। गांधी जी का कहना था कि हथकरघे के लिए सूत की उपलब्धि हाथ की कताई या चरखे से होनी चाहिए। अगर गांधी के इस सुझाव पर अमल किया जाता तो हाथ से बुने कपड़े का उत्पादन एक प्रतिशत से भी कम के स्थान पर 20 प्रतिशत या उससे अधिक हो जाएं।

Fig. 11. A bi-lingual image document of category 'cloth' – 'कपड़ा'.

5.1   Word Image Extraction and Character Segmentation

The system initially pre-processes the image document to remove the noise. It then applies adaptive thresholding to segment the pre-processed image horizontally and extracts the line images from the image. It then segments the line images vertically to obtain the word images. The system obtains 54, 158, and 4 images of English, Hindi, and numerals, respectively. It obtains a total of 216 images, wherein it discards the four images of numerals.

Furthermore, the system segments the English word images and obtains the English character images. The English character images are also mapped with the English characters stored in the pseudo-thesaurus-1. Instead, the system first removes the shirorekha from the Hindi images and converts the words into shirorekha-less words. The shirorekha-less words separate the Devanagari characters and modified characters from each other. This process disconnects the upper modifiers such as ीी, िी, ोी, and ोी from many Devanagari characters. However, their Romanized Devanagari image forms are mapped with the stored Romaninzed Devanagari (Hindi) characters of the pseudo-thesaurus-1. The Romanized Hindi conversions of the ीी, िी, ोी, and ोी modifiers are 'ee', 'i', 'o', and 'ae', respectively. After mapping the character images into the labels, these character images are recognized and classified into different character-based categories.

5.2   Word Association and Image Recognition

The character images are joined together to make the English and Romanized Hindi word labels for the corresponding word images. Table 4 and Table 5 depict such labeling for Hindi and English words, respectively. Their frequencies show the number of occurrences of the word images in the image document. The primary mapping refers to the actual mapping of the word image. However, there may be some other mappings that can also be equally applicable in recognizing the word images. The 'others' category includes the additional Romanized labels for the same Hindi words. However, the word images must show the matching with the primary mappings of the words. The mismatched mappings drastically increase the chances of word image misclassification, and therefore, the image document misclassification too. The remaining English and Hindi word images are also processed but as they do not show any matching with the pre-defined keywords, so they are discarded.

Table 4. Depicting Hindi words, frequencies and Romanized Hindi mappings for the document image of 'कपड़ा' category.

Hindi word images	Hindi word frequencies	Romanized Hindi word mappings	
		Primary	Others
कुटीर	1	Kuteer	Kutir
खादी	1	Khaadee	Khaadi
हस्तशिल्पियो	1	Hastashilpiyo	Hasatashilpiyo
कपड़ा	1	Kapra	Kapara
कपड़े	3	Kapre	Kapare
हथकरघा	2	Hathkargha	Hathakaragha
पावरलूम	1	Pavarloom	Pawaraloom
हथकरघे	2	Hathkarghe	Hathakarghe
सूत	1	Soot	Soota
कताई	1	Kataaee	Kataai
चरखे	1	Charkhe	Charakhe
बुने	1	Bune	Bunae

Table 5. Depicting English words and their frequencies for the document image of the 'cloth' category.

English word images	English word frequencies	English word images	English word frequencies
Khadi	2	Cotton	1
Spun	2	Silk	1
Woven	2	Wool	1
Fibre	1	Charkha	1
Cloth	1	Fabric	1

The observations from Table 4 state that the Hindi word image 'कपड़े' had got a maximum frequency of three amon all the twenty-three word images. It was followed by the word images 'हथकरघा', 'हथकरघे', 'khadi', 'spun', and 'woven' with frequency two. Another observation states that two words have their variations such as हथकरघा-हथकरघे, and कपड़ा-कपड़े, however, their Romanized Hindi mappings are different. Each of them had a total frequency of four which is the highest frequency among all others. There are no such varying pairs in Table 5. Figure 12 depicts the recognized Hindi and English words after the word association step. Figure 13 depicts the usage of different single, double, and multiple matras (modifiers) along with half letters in the recognized Hindi words.

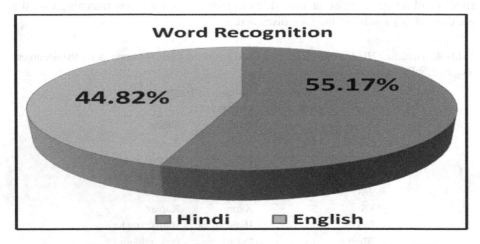

Fig. 12. % Recognition of Hindi and English words of category 'cloth' – 'कपड़ा'.

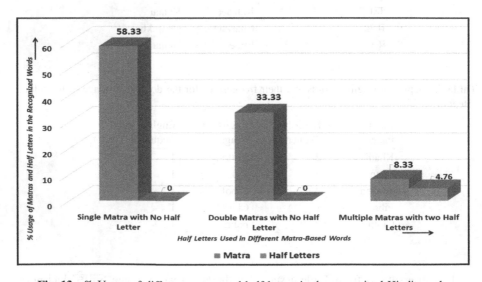

Fig. 13. % Usage of different matras and half letters in the recognized Hindi words.

5.3 Classification Findings and Information Extraction

The constructed words are matched with the pre-defined keywords and are then used to classify the image document in the predefined category, say, 'cloth' in this case scenario. After knowing the category of the document, the information is also extracted from the remaining document. In such a way, the system extracted the information from the bilingual image documents and then classified them into the 'cloth' and 'education' classes using the random forest classifier. The proposed system performed well with all testing image documents and achieved 87.5% accuracy.

The proposed system faced a lot of challenges. During segmentation, the system misclassified a few English word images as Hindi word images. These English word images had a good number of black pixels on their top area, which led them to misclassifications. The second challenge was to have an overhead to convert the shirorekha-less characters and shirorekha-less modified characters into Romanized Hindi mappings. The third challenge was to construct the words from the labeling of the character images. Additionally, this work is limited only to the processing and classification of English and Hindi languages.

The proposed bi-lingual classification system with information extraction achieved promising results. The existing bi-lingual systems discussed in Sect. 3 are limited to character recognition, language discrimination, and other such types of applications. They did not extract any type of information from the documents. Therefore, the proposed system provides an efficient and effective solution for bi-lingual image document categorization.

6 Conclusion and Future Recommendations

This study demonstrated various text processing concepts with CES, SLD, and TPS paradigms for image and non-image documents and stated many applications for them. Although many systems and algorithms have contributed to the text processing of bilingual images to date, however, they were limited to the recognition of the characters, scripts, and languages.

This paper proposed the design of a bilingual document classification and information extraction system which categorized the English-Hindi image documents into pre-defined categories. It used two pseudo-thesauruses at the character-level and document-level recognition stages, respectively. It implemented the SVM and random forest classifiers for character recognition and document classification, respectively. Furthermore, it illustrated a case study to explain the text processing of the bi-lingual image document, thereby showing the working of the proposed system. This research work can further be extended with other Indic and non-Indic languages and N-lingual documents. It can also be extended with handwritten and degraded image documents.

References

1. Dunham, M.H.: Data Mining: Introductory and Advanced Topics, 1st edn. Pearson Education India (2006)
2. Han, J., Kamber, M., Pei, J.: Data Mining: Concepts and Techniques, 3rd edn. Morgan Kaufmann Publishers Inc., USA (2011)
3. Gonzalez, R.C., Woods, R.E.: Digital Image Processing, 3rd edn. Prentice Hall, New york (2007)
4. Lee, C.H., Yang, H.C.: Text mining of bilingual parallel corpora with a measure of semantic similarity. In: IEEE International Conference on Systems, Man, and Cybernetics, vol. 1, pp. 470–475. IEEE Press (2001)
5. Sekine, S., Grishman, R.: Hindi-English cross-lingual question-answering system. ACM Trans. Asian Lang. Inf. Process. 2(3), 181–192 (2003)
6. Montalvo, S., Martínez, R., Casillas, A., Fresno, V.: Bilingual news clustering using named entities and fuzzy similarity. In: Matoušek, V., Mautner, P. (eds.) Text, Speech and Dialogue. Lecture Notes in Computer Science, vol. 4629, pp. 107–114. Springer, Berlin, Heidelberg (2007)
7. Liu, J., Liang, C., Qi, J.: Dictionary-based bilingual web page classification. In: IEEE 4th International Conference on Wireless Communications, Networking and Mobile Computing, pp. 1–4. IEEE Press (2008)
8. Marinai, S.: Introduction to document analysis and recognition. Machine Learning in Document Analysis and Recognition, Studies in Computational Intelligence 90, 1–20 (2008)
9. Ibrahim, Z., Isa, D., Rajkumar, R.: Text and non-text segmentation and classification from document images. In: IEEE International Conference on Computer Science and Software Engineering, vol. 1, pp. 973–976. IEEE Press (2008)
10. Contractor, D., Kothari, G., Faruquie, T.A., Subramaniam, L.V., Negi, S.: Handling noisy queries in cross language FAQ retrieval. In: Proceedings of ACM Conference on Empirical Methods in Natural Language Processing, pp. 87–96. ACM (2010)
11. Zhang, C.Z.: Bilingual topic taxonomy generation based on bilingual documents clustering. In: IEEE International Conference on Machine Learning and Cybernetics, vol. 4, pp. 1889–1895. IEEE Press (2011)
12. Lin, X.R., Guo, C.Y., Chang, F.: Classifying textual components of bilingual documents with decision-tree support vector machines. In: IEEE International Conference on Document Analysis and Recognition, pp. 498–502. IEEE Press (2011)
13. Rani, R., Dhir, R., Lehal, G.S.: Performance analysis of feature extractors and classifiers for script recognition of English and Gurmukhi words. In: Proceeding of the ACM workshop on Document Analysis and Recognition, pp. 30–36. ACM (2012)
14. Puri, S., Kaushik, S.: An enhanced fuzzy similarity based concept mining model for text classification using feature clustering. In: IEEE Students' Conference on Engineering and Systems, pp. 1–6. IEEE Press (2012)
15. Sreejith, C., Indu, M., Reghu, P.C.R.: N-gram based algorithm for distinguishing between Hindi and Sanskrit texts. In: Fourth IEEE International Conference on Computing, Communications and Networking Technologies, pp. 1–4. IEEE Press (2013)
16. Tyagi, S., Chopra, D., Mathur, I., Joshi, N.: Comparison of classifier based approach with baseline approach for English-Hindi text simplification. In: IEEE International Conference on Computing, Communication & Automation, pp. 290–293. IEEE Press (2015)
17. Singh, S.P., Kumar, A., Mandad, D.C., Jadwani, Y.: Word and phrase prediction tool for English and Hindi language. In: International Conference on Electrical, Electronics, and Optimization Techniques, pp. 1485–1488. IEEE Press (2016)

18. Malgaonkar, S., Khan, A., Vichare, A.: Mixed bilingual social media analytics: case study: live twitter data. In: International Conference on Advances in Computing, Communications and Informatics, pp. 1407–1412. IEEE Press (2017)
19. Puri, S.: Efficient fuzzy similarity-based text classification with SVM and feature reduction. In: Sharma, H., Saraswat, M., Yadav, A., Kim, J.H., Bansal, J.C. (eds.) CIS 2020. AISC, vol. 1335, pp. 341–356. Springer, Singapore (2021). https://doi.org/10.1007/978-981-33-6984-9_28
20. Puri, S., Singh, S.P.: Advanced applications on bilingual document analysis and processing systems. Int. J. Appl. Metaheuristic Comput., IGI Global 11(4), 149–193 (2020)
21. Yadav, K., Lamba, A., Gupta, D., Gupta, A., Karmakar, P., Saini, S.: Bi-LSTM and ensemble based bilingual sentiment analysis for a code-mixed Hindi-English social media text. In: IEEE 17th India Council International Conference, pp. 1–6. IEEE Press (2020)
22. Kumar, R., Sahula, V.: Word translation using cross-lingual word embedding: Case of Sanskrit to Hindi translation. In: 2nd International Conference on Artificial Intelligence and Signal Processing, pp. 1–7. IEEE Press (2022)
23. Puri, S., Singh, S.P.: A hybrid Hindi printed document classification system using SVM and fuzzy: an advancement. J. Inf. Technol. Res. 12(4), 107–131 (2019)
24. Luo, X.: Efficient English text classification using selected machine learning techniques. Alex. Eng. J. 60(3), 3401–3409 (2021)
25. Al-Wajih, E., Ghazali, R.: Improving the performance of local binary convolutional neural networks for bilingual digit recognition. In: International Conference on Data Analytics for Business and Industry, pp. 587–591. IEEE Press (2021)
26. Bandari, S., Bulusu, V.V.: BERT tokenization and hybrid-optimized deep recurrent neural network for Hindi document summarization. Int. J. Fuzzy Syst. Appl. 11(1), 1–28 (2022)
27. Gaikwad, S.S., Nalbalwar, S.L., Nandgaonkar, A.B.: Devanagari handwritten characters recognition using DCT, geometric and hue moments feature extraction techniques. Sādhanā 47(112), 1–20 (2022)

Probabilistic Forecasting of the Winning IPL Team Using Supervised Machine Learning

S. Krishnan[(✉)], R. Vishnu Vasan, Pranay Varma, and T. Mala

Department of Information Science and Technology, College of Engineering, Guindy,
Anna University, Chennai, Tamil Nadu, India
skrishnan2001@gmail.com, mala@auist.net

Abstract. The Indian Premier League (IPL) is one of the world's most well-known league competitions that takes place in India during the summer, with people from the cricket fraternity competing for the coveted silverware. Using the concepts of machine learning, this research intends to help viewers gain good insight into how a team is placed in a particular scenario in a match and whether they have a good chance of winning or not. It will also assist investors and franchisees in determining which team to invest in to maximize profits. Coaches, sports analysts, and technicians also gain game facts and ideas about opposing teams, which aids them in making decisions and changing plans as needed. In this study, we have used three different ML algorithms to predict the percentage chances of winning of the competing teams: Logistic Regression, Decision Tree, and Random Forest. For this purpose, two datasets have been used, one containing the match result data and the other containing ball-wise data of the IPL matches played between 2008 and 2022. Our results show that the Random Forest algorithm achieves the highest accuracy score when compared to the other two algorithms. Also, an interactive web application has been developed and hosted using Streamlit so that users can use it as a service from any convenient device.

Keywords: Machine learning · Forecasting · IPL · Logistic regression · Random forest · Decision tree

1 Introduction

The Indian Premier League, established in 2008 has become a summer staple of many Indian households. Besides the obvious commercial success and the glamour associated, it has given many talented young Indians a platform to announce themselves to the national selectors, and eventually the world. The viewership numbers in India for 2021 were estimated to be a staggering 405 million people, cementing its status as the most popular t20 league around. Research on cricket result predictions and team performance analysis has become a domain full of innovation and opportunities. From a business perspective, predictive analysis and going beyond surface level statistics could be a way for potential investors and commercial parties to decide which team would be worth championing.

© The Author(s), under exclusive license to Springer Nature Switzerland AG 2023
I. Woungang et al. (Eds.): ANTIC 2022, CCIS 1798, pp. 138–152, 2023.
https://doi.org/10.1007/978-3-031-28183-9_10

There are a lot of variables to be considered when looking at and analysing past match results in order to develop an accurate predictive model. Some aspects that have historically been influential in determining how the end result looks are the target for the chasing team, wickets in hand, overs left, the current score, and other game state variables. Besides this, there is also the complication of certain teams having niche strengths that would tilt the balance of games in their favour while other teams would tend to fail. For instance, a team with a strong bowling attack and a history of defending low scores would be more likely to win despite setting a low target than a team whose strength lies in its batting. The reverse would also hold true. Another point for consideration would be the nature of the pitch and past match trends on that particular surface, which would imply that a particular target score set there wouldn't be as easy or difficult to chase as one set on another pitch.

For predicting the winner of a match, three machine learning algorithms have been used: Logistic Regression, Random Forest and Decision Tree. One can configure details like the batting team, the bowling team, the venue of the match, the target score, the current score, overs completed, and wickets lost. These parameters are used by the three ML models selected by the user to predict the winner by probability. The project also generates certain statistics specific to the team's performance or a particular season of the IPL, presented in the form of histograms, bar charts, etc. The data presented can be used to gain valuable insights and better understand the trends seen in the biggest cricket league in the world. The dataset for this research was obtained from Kaggle [1], which has all information pertaining to a match right from the first season in 2008. The application is finally deployed using Streamlit, a cloud service provider, to leverage the benefits of cloud computing like Scalability, Reliability, Zero Downtime, etc.

The objectives of this research are to:

- Predict the probability of a team's chances of winning a match by simulating a match situation
- Visualize and analyze various statistical metrics of a given IPL team
- Compare the three models and their accuracies
- Deploy the application successfully using a cloud platform.

1.1 Motivation

Cricket, India's unofficial national game has always been a source of joy, excitement and sometimes heartbreak for the general public. The Indian Premier League is the most popular version of the shortest format of the game today, with spectators across the globe tuning in for this annual extravaganza of light, sound and above all, cricket in its most chaotic form.

Among the advancements in technology and revolutionary ideas that have shaped cricket over the years, the increasing importance placed on analytics cannot be ignored. The time when cricket players were assessed based on aesthetic criteria like natural elegance and the 'eye test' is long past. In this sense, a television broadcast would be intriguing to watch due to how diverse and in-depth the data visualizations are.

This is where the utility of analytics really shines through. Franchises, having recognized the value of data analytics, now have dedicated teams that collaborate with the rest of the think tank in order to optimize the decision-making process and maximize the likelihood of their success.

1.2 Organization of the Report

Section 2 looks at the various papers and literature that were studied in order to gain familiarity with and exposure to the different approaches and techniques involved in win prediction.

Section 3 contains the system design of the solution, split into various modules with their functionalities included. Some of the primary algorithms used in the implementation have also been discussed.

Section 4 summarizes the results of this study and illustrates the features of the web application that has been developed. A few graphs and visualizations have also been included. The performance of the models used has been compared and contrasted with a reference paper's performance metrics.

The final section concludes the paper and looks at possible future steps to improve the model's accuracy.

2 Related Works

This section deals with the existing work that has been carried out to determine the win prediction using different algorithms. It gives an overview of the challenges involved in developing this application.

Vistro in [2] proposes an application that can predict the winning team of an IPL match before the start of the match. The application predicts a team by training machine learning models on the desired features. Machine learning algorithms like Random Forest, SVM, Naive Bayes, Logistic Regression and Decision Tree were used in training and testing data to determine the accuracy of the model. Kapadia, et al. adopt machine learning techniques like Naïve Bayes, Random Forest, K-Nearest Neighbor (KNN) and Model Trees to generate predictive models from distinctive feature sets derived by the filter-based methods in [3]. One featured subset was based on home team advantage, while the other was based on Toss' decision. To create a prediction model, selected machine learning algorithms were used for both feature sets. When compared to probabilistic and statistical models, tree-based models, notably Random Forest, fared better in terms of accuracy, precision, and recall metrics.

A. Sinha in [4] proposes a method that uses a regression model with the added strength of the Naive Bayes network and Euler's strength calculation formula. The regression model was developed by considering factors like Toss, Home Ground, Captains, Favorite Players, Opposition Battle, Previous Stats etc. A. Kaluarachchi and S. V. Aparna proposed a classification-based tool to predict the outcome of cricket matches in the ODI format in [5]. They use Bayesian classifiers to predict how important factors like a home game advantage, day/night effect, winning the toss and batting first affect the outcome of the match. [6] uses popular ML algorithms like Random Forest, Extra trees and Decision Tree to predict the winner of the 2020 T20 Cricket World Cup. The ML model uses the ESPN Cricinfo dataset to make its prediction.

Kalpdrum Passi in [7] uses a variety of classifiers like Naive Bayes, Random Forest, Multiclass SVM and Decision Tree to generate the prediction models. He found Random Forest to be the most accurate in predictions for his problem. Passi measures the player's performance by using the individual player's attributes such as strike rate, average, etc. and calculating these attributes from the innings-by-innings list using aggregation functions and mathematical formulae.

A model for prospective analysis of T20 match results using machine learning approaches was reported by Gagana S in [8]. By learning from seen data, this model can predict how many runs a batsman will score on each ball. Data was gathered for previously played T20 matches, and this issue was classified as such. For this forecast, various machine learning and data mining methods were applied. With 90% as the training dataset and 10% testing dataset, the Naive Bayes algorithm has an accuracy of 42.50%. The Random Forest algorithm scored 90.88%, whereas decision trees scored 82.52%. But the Recurrent Neural Network (RNN) and Hidden Markov Model could enhance these findings (HMM).

Support Vector Machine (SVM), CTree, and Naive Bayes classifiers with accuracy rates of 95.96%, 97.7%, and 98.98%, respectively, were employed by Agrawal et al. [9] to estimate the likelihood that the matches would be won. Based on the toss and the venue, Barot et al. in [10] projected the game's result.

[11] seeks to examine the datasets, determine the IPL match winner, and evaluate the various classification methods in terms of accuracy, confusion matrix, precision, and recall. Several classification machine learning techniques such as SVM (Support Vector Machine), Decision Tree Classifier, Random Forest Classifier, and KNN were utilized to create prediction models.

Md. Aktaruzzaman Pramanik, et al. have shown a comparative analysis of different non-ensemble and ensemble machine learning classifiers [12]. Five base classifiers and five ensemble classifiers were applied for the analysis. This research claims that KNN performs better when compared to other algorithms while predicting the results before starting the game. The study also revealed that Gradient Boosting classifier is more robust than other classifiers when the match outcomes are predicted considering all the features.

3 System Design

The overall architecture of the propose model is shown in Fig. 1. The raw data is fetched from Kaggle and converted into the required format for training the ML model. The raw data is then cleaned to standardize the dataset. The model is trained to predict the probability of winning of the team entered by the user. The user can select any one model from the three models available for training and predicting. The win probability is visualized in the form of a pie chart. Finally, the ML application has been hosted as a Web App using Streamlit to provide GUI for users. Streamlit uses the code from the linked GitHub repository and updates the web app automatically after each commit or change in the repository, following the principles of continuous integration and continuous deployment. The final output can be seen in the URL generated by Streamlit.

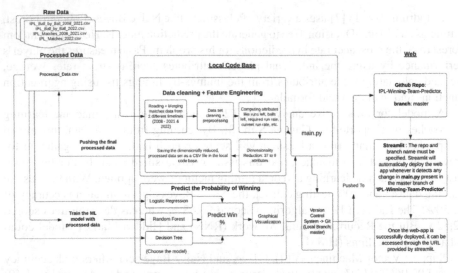

Fig. 1. Architecture diagram of the proposed model

3.1 Data Preprocessing, Aggregation and Feature Extraction-I

3.1.1 Matches Data

The matches dataset is spread across two CSV files: *IPL_Matches_2008_2021.csv* and *IPL_Matches_2022.csv*. These contain information about all the matches from 2008–2021 and 2022, respectively. Since both the data sets have the same attributes, they are aggregated together in reverse chronological order, starting with the most recent matches, so that there is a combined data set for all the matches from 2008 to 2022. The year column is then standardized, and hence certain values like 07/08, 09/10 etc. (MM/YY format) are converted to 2008 and 2010 respectively (YYYY format). The dataset has 20 attributes now (Table 1):

Table 1. Matches dataset attributes

Attribute (s)	Description
ID	Unique ID for each match
City	City where the match was held
Date	Date of play
Season	Year of the IPL season (YYYY -format)
MatchNumber	Match no. in the respective IPL season
Team1, Team2	Names of the 2 playing teams

(continued)

Table 1. (*continued*)

Attribute (s)	Description
Venue	Stadium where the match was played
TossWinner	Name of the team who won the toss
TossDecision	Toss winner's decision - bat or field
SuperOver	Was there a super over to break the tie?
WinningTeam	Name of the winning team
Margin & WonBy	Margin by which the team won (w.r.t the wickets or runs)
Player_of_the_match	Best performer of the match (Cricketer's name)
Team1Players & Team2Players	Names of the cricketers in the 2 playing teams
Umpire1, Umpire2	On-field umpire names

3.1.2 Ball by Ball Data

This dataset contains ball-by-ball data for all the IPL matches played between 2008 and 2022. Two CSV files are combined here as well: *IPL_Ball_by_Ball_2008_2021.csv* and *IPL_Ball_by_Ball_2022.csv* which have information about the seasons 2008–21 and 2022, respectively. The two datasets are converted into data frames and merged using the concatenate function. The ball-by-ball dataset has 17 columns initially. The attributes are (Table 2):

Table 2. Ball by ball dataset attributes

Attribute (s)	Description
ID	Unique ID for each match
Innings	1st or 2nd innings of the game
Ballnumber	Ball number in the innings (0 to 120)
Batter	Name of the batsman on strike
Bowler	Name of the bowler for the over
Non-strike	Name of the batsman not on strike
Extra-type	Type of extras - like wide, no-ball, leg-by, etc. if any
Batsman-run	Runs scored by the batsman in that ball
Extras-run	Runs due to extras in that ball if any
Total_run	batsman-run + extras-run for the particular ball
isWicketDelivery	1 indicates batsman was out, 0 indicates not out in that delivery
Player_out	The batsman who got out in that delivery (if isWicketDelivery)
Kind	How was the batsman out? (Bowled, caught out, run-out, lbw, hit-wicket)
Fielders-involved	Names of the fielders involved if the batsman was out caught

3.1.3   Bowling Team Addition

From the matches dataset the *id, team1 and team2* attributes are taken and a mini data frame is formed. Ball-by-ball is now updated to be a combination of its initial attributes and this reduced data frame from matches as well as another column called bowling team (which is initially blank). Inner joining is performed using id.

3.1.4   Dimensionality Reduction

Reduction from 37 attributes (20 attributes in Matches Data and 17 attributes in ball-by-ball data) to just 9 attributes (Table 3).

Table 3. Features considered for predicting the outcome

Attribute (s)	Description
Batting team	The name of the team batting in the 2nd innings
Bowling team	The name of the team fielding in the 2nd innings
City	The city where the match is taking place
Runs_left	The remaining runs to be scored by the team batting in the 2nd innings to win the game
Balls_left	Denotes the balls remaining in 2nd innings
Wickets_left	Wickets remaining for the team batting in innings 2
Total_runs_x	Total runs scored by the team batting in innings 1
Current_run_rate (CRR)	Denotes the CRR of the batting team in innings 2
Required_run_rate (RRR)	Denotes the run rate required by the batting team in innings 2 to win the match

3.1.5   Feature to be Predicted

- **Result** (Whether the team batting 2nd wins or not)

Grouping features for total score:
The ball-by-ball dataset is now grouped by *id* and then *inning* before the *total_score* column is summed up thus returning the total runs scored in each inning of a match.

3.2   Preprocessing and Feature Extraction-II

3.2.1   Computing the Derived Attributes

i)   **Total_runs** = (Score of batting team in innings 1) + 1
ii) **Runs_left** = Total_runs - (current score of batting team in innings 2)
iii) **Balls_left** = (6 * 20) - (6 * overs_completed)

iv) **Current_run_rate (CRR)** = (current score of batting team in innings 2)/overs_completed

v) **Required_run_rate (RRR)** = (Runs_left * 6)/(Balls_left)

3.2.2 Further Data Cleaning

As certain teams have gone defunct or undergone name changes, appropriate modifications must be made to the matches dataset. Teams like the Kochi Tuskers and Pune Supergiants have been removed, while the Delhi, Hyderabad, Gujarat, and Punjab franchises have been modified so that all records have the latest name(s). The matches dataset now contains only 10 unique names, i.e., the 10 active teams remain. The dataset can be further refined by removing irrelevant attributes, and hence only the id, city, target, and winning team are left in the condensed data frame.

This processed dataset will be given as input to the different machine-learning models.

3.3 Algorithm

3.3.1 Dataset Preprocessing and Feature Engineering

Input: *IPL_Matches_2008_2021.csv,* *IPL_Matches_2022.csv,* *IPL_Ball_by_Ball_2008_2021.csv and IPL_Ball_by_Ball_2022.csv*
Output: Merged, Preprocessed and feature-engineered dataset as a CSV file

1. START
2. Merge *IPL_Matches_2008_2021.csv* and *IPL_Matches_2022.csv* files into a data frame (df1) to get all match data from 2008 to 2022.
3. Sort the records of the merged data frame in reverse chronological order.
4. Standardize the *year* column to YYYY format.
5. Merge *IPL_Ball_by_Ball_2008_2021.csv and IPL_Ball_by_Ball_2022.csv* files into another data frame (df2) to get ball-wise data from 2008 to 2022.
6. *df2 = Inner Join(df1, df2)* on the attribute '*match_id*'
7. Computing derived attributes- '*total_runs*', '*runs_left*', '*ball_left*', '*CRR*' and '*RRR*' and appending to *df2.*
8. Dimensionality reduction from **37** to **9** attributes.
9. Further data cleaning - Standardizing team names that have been changed and eliminating the records of teams that have not been active in recent years.
10. Persisting *df2* as a CSV file, which will be used by the ML model.
11. STOP

3.3.2 Model Training and Prediction

Input: Merged, Preprocessed and feature-engineered dataset as a CSV file.
Output: Probability of winning (%) of the 2 playing teams.

1. START
2. Read input CSV and store in a pandas data frame (*df*).
3. Split *df* into testing & training data in the ratio **80:20**.
4. Perform column transformation on *'Batting_Team', 'Bowling_team' and 'City'* attributes
5. Set up 3 different pipelines for the 3 machine learning models - *Logistic Regression, Decision Tree and Random Forest* with the following stages:
   i) Stage 1: The outcome of the column transformation step is passed.
   ii) Stage 2: The choice of the ML model.
6. Persisting the 3 trained ML models as **pickle files**.
7. Predict the probability of winning for each playing team using the test instances.
8. STOP

3.4 Implementing the Models in a Real-Time Scenario

The winning probability is predicted using ML models. The model is trained using the datasets, and pickle files are generated to ensure that the data is persistent. Relevant features such as season, team, batting and bowling teams, venue, target, current score, overs completed, and the number of wickets down are obtained as input. On obtaining relevant inputs, additional features such as runs left, balls left, wickets in hand, the current run rate, and the required run rate, are calculated, and the model is chosen by the user. Finally, a data frame is created with the input features as well as calculated features being represented. This data frame is then fed into one of the three models, and the probability of the selected team winning or losing is displayed in the form of a pie chart after predictions have been made by the model.

3.5 Web Application

A web application using Streamlit has been hosted, and this application has a user interface that allows one to enter the input features and displays the results in a very sleek manner.

4   Result and Discussion

This section contains the final output screenshots of this research: "Probabilistic Forecasting of the Winning IPL Team using Supervised Machine Learning".

The result snapshots can be gone through in a cumulative manner. Figure 2 is the web application hosted using Streamlit where the user lands. In Fig. 3, the classifier can be toggled to be logistic regression, decision tree, or random forest. The season and team names present in the left sidebar are used for generating statistical information for a given season. The input parameters for prediction are loaded with some default values

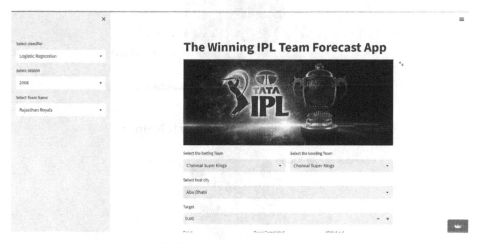

Fig. 2. Home page of the web-application

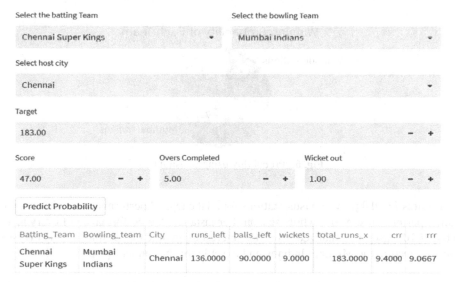

Fig. 3. Input data for the model to predict

and can be changed as per one's requirements. In this particular scenario, the Chennai Super Kings have a target of 183 against the Mumbai Indians in Chennai. The score after five overs is 47/1, and the win probability is to be calculated with this scenario in mind.

The figures - Fig. 4, Fig. 5, and Fig. 6 represent the probabilities obtained by using different algorithms for the above scenario.

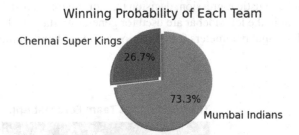

Fig. 4. Probability using logistic regression

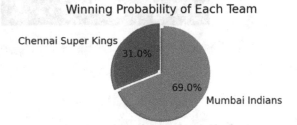

Fig. 5. Probability using random forest

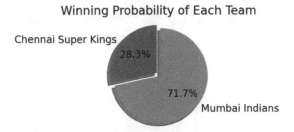

Fig. 6. Probability using decision tree

Figures 7 and 8 provide visualizations for all the teams' performances and a specific team's performance over a whole season. For instance, the performance of every team in the 2010 season is visualized here. It is interesting to note that despite having the best win-loss record, the Mumbai Indians had to settle for the runner-up spot.

Fig. 7. MI win-loss stats in 2010

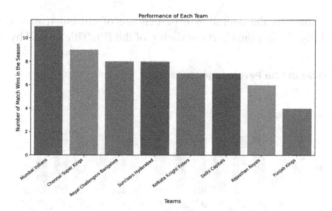

Fig. 8. Team-wise performance in 2010

Figure 9 shows us the plot of the league position of a team, and Fig. 10 presents us with the best win percentage of teams across seasons.

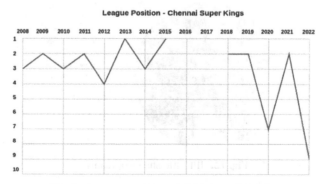

Fig. 9. League position of CSK from 2008–22

Best Win Percentage by Season

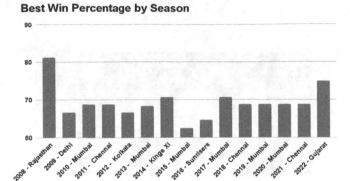

Fig. 10. Best win percentage of teams across season

Figure 11 shows us the overall win percentage of current teams across seasons (2008–22), and Fig. 12 is a pie chart consisting of the IPL Title shared by each team.

Overall Win Percentage (2008-22)

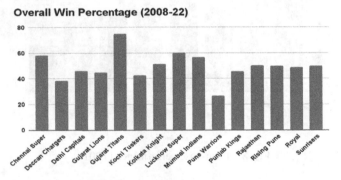

Fig. 11. Teams win % across seasons

IPL Titles Share

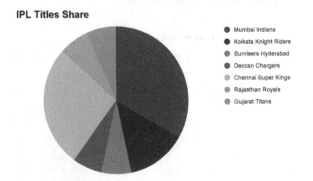

Fig. 12. IPL title shares of teams

Finally, Fig. 13 shows us the Accuracy, Precision, and Recall of the ML models used. It can be noted from the figure that Random Forest Classifier has the best Accuracy, Precision, and Recall (Table 4).

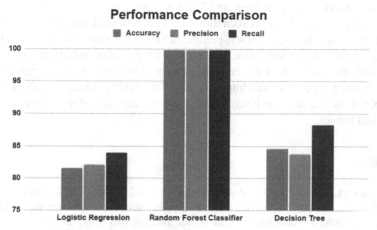

Fig. 13. Performance comparison of ML models

Table 4. Performance metrics

Model	Accuracy	Precision	Recall
Logistic Regression	81.61%	82.09%	83.91%
Random Forest	*99.83%*	*99.86%*	*99.82%*
Decision Tree	84.58%	83.73%	88.31%

[11] S. Priya, A. K. Gupta, et al. proposed a method for predicting the winner of a T20 Cricket match using only the overall match history dataset between the participating teams. The attributes used for predicting the results are team1, team2, toss_winner, toss_decision, city and venue.

The accuracy results of this research work:

Logistic Regression Classifier: **63%**
Random Forest Classifier: **74%**
Decision Tree Classifier: **73%**

Thus through our research, it has been determined that by including the ball-by-ball data to train the ML model, the results get more accurate. Also, it was determined that specific dynamic attributes like the current run rate, the required run rate, the number of balls and the wickets left for the team batting in the second innings play a key role in predicting the winner of the match by probability.

5 Conclusion and Future Work

The predictor was developed using the Python programming language and Jupyter Notebook and finally deployed as a web application using Streamlit. Three ML algorithms—Logistic Regression, Decision Tree, and Random Forest—were used, and model accuracy was compared for different scenarios. It was determined that the Random Forest Classifier gives the highest accuracy, precision, and recall score. With sports analytics garnering attention across the globe, this app can keep cricket enthusiasts engaged.

Currently, the model does not consider features like player rating, a player's form, pitch condition, temperature and humidity, etc. When sufficient data for those features is available, those features can be considered and the accuracy of the current model can be improved further.

References

1. https://www.kaggle.com/datasets/vora1011/ipl-2008-to-2021-all-match-dataset
2. Vistro, D.M., Rasheed, F., David, L.G.: The cricket winner prediction with application of machine learning and data analytics. Int. J. Sci. Technol. Res. **8**(09) (2019)
3. Kapadia, K., Abdel-Jaber, H., Thabtah, F., Hadi, W.: Sports analytics for cricket game results using machine learning: an experimental study. Appl. Comput. Inform. (2020)
4. Sinha, A.: Application of machine learning in cricket and predictive analytics of IPL 2020 (Oct 2020)
5. Kaluarachchi, A., Aparna, S.V.: CricAI: a classification based tool to predict the outcome in ODI cricket. In: 2010 Fifth International Conference on Information and Automation for Sustainability, pp. 250–255 (2010). https://doi.org/10.1109/ICIAFS.2010.5715668
6. Basit, A., Alvi, M.B., Jaskani, F.H., Alvi, M., Memon, K.H., Shah, R.A.: ICC T20 cricket world cup 2020 winner prediction using machine learning techniques. In: 2020 IEEE 23rd International Multitopic Conference (INMIC), pp. 1–6 (2020). https://doi.org/10.1109/INMIC50486.2020.9318077
7. Passi, K., Pandey, N.: Increased prediction accuracy in the game of cricket using machine learning. Int J. Data Min. Knowl. Manag. Process **8**(2), 19–36 (2018). https://doi.org/10.5121/ijdkp.2018.8203
8. Paramesha, G.S.K.: A perspective on analyzing IPL match results using machine learning. **7**(03), 1476–1479 (2019)
9. Agrawal, S., Singh, S.P., Sharma, J.K.: Predicting results of IPL T-20 match using machine learning. In: 2018 8th International Conference on Communication Systems and Network Technologies (CSNT), 24–26 Nov. 2018
10. Barot, H., Kothari, A., Bide, P., Ahir, B., Kankaria, R.: Analysis and prediction of Indian premier league. In: 2020 International Conference for Emerging Technology (INCET), 5–7 June 2020
11. Priya, S., Gupta, A.K., Dwivedi, A., Prabhakar, A.: Analysis and winning prediction in T20 cricket using machine learning. In: 2022 Second International Conference on Advances in Electrical, Computing, Communication and Sustainable Technologies (ICAECT), pp. 1–4 (2022). https://doi.org/10.1109/ICAECT54875.2022.9807929
12. Pramanik, M.A. , Hasan Suzan, M.M., Biswas, A.A., Rahman, M.Z., Kalaiarasi, A.: Performance analysis of classification algorithms for outcome prediction of T20 cricket tournament matches. In: 2022 International Conference on Computer Communication and Informatics (ICCCI), pp. 01–07 (2022), https://doi.org/10.1109/ICCCI54379.2022.9740867

Diversified Licence Plate Character Recognition Using Fuzzy Image Enhancement and LPRNet: An Experimental Approach

C. M. Sowmya(iD) and S. Anbuchelian(✉)(iD)

Ramanujan Computing Centre, College of Engineering Guindy, Anna University, Chennai, India
anbuchelianrcc@gmail.com

Abstract. The exponentially thriving vehicle population in India, accelerated by the country's growing population and economic growth, puts an extensive burden on traffic management in the country's major cities and towns. As a result, Automatic Vehicle licence Plate Recognition (AVLPR) is an interesting and crucial area of research in the Intelligent Transportation System (ITS), particularly because it may need to operate in real time. To address this challenge and concern, an efficient multi-style Indian vehicle licence plate recognition system is proposed. In this methodology, we consider three phases: Image pre−processing, licence plate object detection and character recognition. In image pre−processing, a fuzzy based image contrast enhancement algorithm is used to enhance the quality of the image. Then, for object detection, You Look Only Once Version 5 (YOLOv5) is used. Finally, the characters in the licence plate are recognized using Licence Plate Recognition Network (LPRNet), an end-to-end deep Convolutional Neural Network (CNN) with Connectionist Temporal Classification (CTC) Loss. The experiment result determines that the proposed technique is efficient and accomplishes better character recognition accuracy for English language, Tamil languages and multi-style licence plates.

Keywords: Licence plate detection · Character recognition · Fuzzy image enhancement · Deep convolutional neural network · YOLOv5

1 Introduction

The AVLPR is a relatively new concept in highway research, and ITS has attracted a lot of attention [12]. With a population of more than one billion people, India has a special set of requirements for AVLPR. The key applications of AVLPR are highway monitoring, traffic control, parking management, and law enforcement protection in neighborhoods [1]. The AVLPR accuracy levels often surpass 90% in countries like Italy, Vietnam, and Australia, which have generic vehicle licence plate, but the need for AVLPR in India is high and really quite different. The low-cost cameras have reduced visual range, have less sensitive

© The Author(s), under exclusive license to Springer Nature Switzerland AG 2023
I. Woungang et al. (Eds.): ANTIC 2022, CCIS 1798, pp. 153–168, 2023.
https://doi.org/10.1007/978-3-031-28183-9_11

motion and object detection sensors, and seem to have poor night vision abilities. These three factors contribute to a rise in the number of weak spots and the prevalence of blurred images. Furthermore, the licence plates have non-identical formats like variety of colors, sizes, fonts, hand-painted, and licence plate positioning [2]. Many research works have been carried out on multi-style licence plate detection and multi-national licence plates especially for Indian regional languages. Over the last decade, ITS has evolved, and yet many approaches and methodologies have been examined at various stages of the vehicle licence plate recognition process. Each process at every stage has its own algorithm for achieving the desired result.

This section includes a brief description about previous research findings. A typical licence plate recognition system consists of four important phases and they are data pre-processing, licence plate detection, character segmentation and character recognition [10]. An image enhancement techniques is incorporated to convert the low resolution images into high resolution images, this helps the character recognition model to perform efficiently [4]. Joshua et al. [10] introduced an AVLPR device that would identify and record plate numbers. The ResNet model achieves about 80% accuracy from the validation data, but when tested in the device, it can sometimes misclassify licence plate numbers, owing to noises that affect the segmentation process, as well as some non-standard or damaged plates. The authors have discussed various image pre−processing techniques like Histogram equalization, CLAHE and gamma correction for Clinical X-Ray images (CXR) which has been tested individually and along with adaptive median filter, median filter, total variation filter and gaussian denoising filters [13,14,17]. As part of the proposed study, eleven combinations were compared in order to find the most coherent approach which can be utilized for licence plate image processing. Though the above mentioned techniques performs well, there is a certain amount of uncertainty associated with image analysis concepts. A well-known example is that border pixels are difficult to define. The Pixels at edges of objects are sometimes uncertain, making it difficult to determine if they belong to the background or the object edges. By using fuzzy logic, uncertainty and subject concepts can be better modeled than by using crisp logic. The fuzzy theory uses linguistic rules to perform numerical computations in membership functions [6] and show improvement in object detection and character recognition according to author Fernandes et al. A fuzzy image contrast algorithm which uses neighborhood metrics is proposed by Shree Devi et al. [5]. The model uses Gaussian membership function to initiate contrast enhancement and all the neighboring pixels of each individual pixel is then processed using fuzzy C-means Clustering algorithm for grouping of similar membership values.

The licence plate localization is an arduous phase, hence algorithms like Scale Invariant Feature Transform (SIFT), YOLO are used for object candidate extraction [1]. A global licence plate recognition system based on a generic character sequence system was proposed by Chris Henry et al. [2]. The YOLOv3 object detector is used to create the model, which includes a spatial pyramid pooling block. The model has been adopted in 17 different countries. From the image, the algorithm successfully extracts the correct sequence of licence plate numbers.

The CNN for Optical Character Recognition (OCR) yields promising results, but they are inefficient and complex depending on the application scenario [3]. The authors Sergey and Alexey [11] suggested a licence plate recognition system based on deep neural networks, which had recently made significant advances in AVLPR. In languages with complex character sets, the model produced very promising results. Due to their difficulty and large character sets, the model can also be used for Indian regional languages, with results showing more than 95% accuracy on several different languages licence plates. The authors discussed five pre-trained deep neural networks architectures i.e. DenseNet169, InceptionResNetV2, MobileNet, Vgg19 and NASNetMobile as a baseline to achieve transfer learning for CXR data, which is a backbone for the Deep CNN [15,16].

The novelty of this research is the trail combination of the fuzzy image enhancement algorithm, YOLOv5 and LPRNet, an end to end Deep CNN for multi-lingual and multi-style vehicle licence plate detection. The fuzzy logic is applied for the enhancement of the images in-terms of contrast [8]. A single-stage object detector YOLOv5 is used to detect the objects which uses regression technique. In the first step, the significant and informative features from an input image are extracted based on the Cross Stage Partial Network (CSPNet) because it has betterment in processing time with deeper networks. Then in the next step, a feature pyramid is generated which helps the model to generalize well on object scaling. So the same object with different sizes and scales can be effectively identified. Finally at the last stage, the detection part is performed where the final output vectors with bounding boxes, class probabilities and object score are generated [9]. After the object detection in the input image, the next step is actual character recognition.

The following is a breakdown of our paper contribution. The introduction, related works regarding previous findings, as well as its benefits and drawbacks, are presented in Sect. 1. The working model of the proposed algorithm is described in Sect. 2. The result and discussion about experimental setup, system training model, test cases and performance evaluation are discussed in Sect. 3. Finally, Sect. 4 concludes the paper with its betterment and future enhancement.

2   System Model

The automated vehicle licence plate recognition field has emerged rapidly in the recent decades. The proposed model consists of three phases as shown in Fig. 1 in the block diagram. A Fuzzy based Image Contrast Enhancement is a technique used to sharpen and improve the resolution of the images, which are extremely helpful for further observation and recognition process. The Object Detection is the next phase, for which there are many models, in this research work, the YOLOv5 have been used to localize and detect the licence plate from the enhanced image. Finally, LPRNet, an end-to-end Deep Convolutional Neural Network with CTC Loss is used for character recognition. To be mentioned, in our research work, we ignored the character segmentation procedure in the character recognition phase.

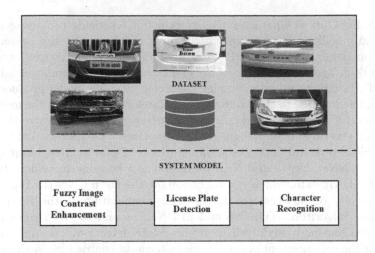

Fig. 1. Represent the block diagram of the system model.

2.1   Fuzzy Image Contrast Enhancement

The fuzzy image contrast enhancement process adjusts the relative brightness and darkness of objects in a scene in order to make them more visible. The Mamdani's method based fuzzy model approach is used to define the fuzzy rule sets as shown in the Fig. 2. The Fuzzy image contrast enhancement technique consists of Fuzzification of pixel intensity, defining Fuzzy inference rule set and Defuzzification of inference results [4].

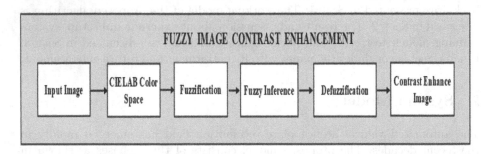

Fig. 2. Illustrate the sequence of the modules in fuzzy image contrast enhancement phase.

Fuzzification of Pixel Intensity. Consider a fuzzy set where IP_l^p is the input vector and OP_l^q is the output vector, such that l is the size of the fuzzy vector, p is the length of the input vector, where $p = 1, 2, ..., m_i$ and q is the length of the output vector, where $q = 1, 2, ..., n_j$. Let $X = x_1, x_2, ..., x_n$ is the initial set of elements. The fuzzy membership of X is defined as $\mu_G(x_i, x_j) \in \{0, 1\}, \forall\ x_i, x_j \in X$. Here, $T : X * X \rightarrow [0, 1]$.

For each pixel value, membership value is calculated based on the class defined for pixel intensity. The intensity of a pixel value ranges between 0 and 255. Figure 3 represents the membership distributions of each class of pixels. We have discussed 8 input membership functions each based on specific pixel intensity values representing the brightness of pixels such as Extremely Bright (EB), Very Bright (VB), Bright (B), Slightly Bright (SB), Slightly Dark (SD), Dark (D), Very Dark (VD), Extremely Dark (ED).

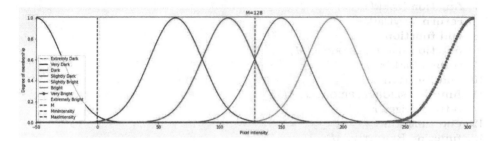

Fig. 3. Is the graph which highlights the membership function distribution for the mean value=128.

A Gaussian Membership function is defined in case of trap functions as shown in Eq. 1 and the sigmoid membership function is given by the Eq. 2. As mentioned above, the maximum and minimum intensities are 0 and 255, with respect to that the membership values of slightly bright and slightly dark classes lie nearer to M = 128. By transforming the membership functions of slightly dark to dark and slightly bright to bright, the licence plates are enhanced effectively.

$$\mu_G(A) = e^{-\frac{1}{2}\frac{(X-M)^2}{\sigma^2}} \tag{1}$$

$$f(t) = \frac{1}{1 + e^{-\sigma(X-M)}} \tag{2}$$

Fuzzy Inference Rule Set. The fuzzy inference rule set is a set of rules which maps fuzzy input values into fuzzy output values using membership function rules. The proposed algorithm consists of six rules as mentioned in the Algorithm 1, Fuzzy image contrast enhancement. These rules are analyzed and designed to get a better enhanced image for further process.

Algorithm 1. Fuzzy image contrast enhancement

1: Inputs: x, M, f, t
2: $x \leftarrow input\ pixels$
3: $M \leftarrow average\ pixel\ intensity\ value$
4: $f, t \leftarrow VeryDark,\ Dark,\ SlightlyDark, SlightlyBright,\ Bright,\ VeryBright$
5: **function** VERYDARK(x, M)
   return ExtremelyDark x
6: **end function**
7: **function** DARK(x, M)
   return VeryDark x
8: **end function**
9: **function** SLIGHTLYDARK(x, M)
   return Dark x
10: **end function**
11: **function** SLIGHTLYBRIGHT(x, M)
    return Bright x
12: **end function**
13: **function** BRIGHT(x, M)
    return VeryBright x
14: **end function**
15: **function** VERYBRIGHT(x, M)
    return ExtremelyBright x
16: **end function**
17: **function** OUTPUTFUZZYSET(x, M, f, t)
18:    result $= f(x, M)$
19:    **if** $result \geq t$ **then**
20:       $result[1] \leftarrow t$
21:    **else**
22:       $result[0] \leftarrow t$
23:    **end if**
    return result
24: **end function**
25: **for** pixel in image **do**
26:    **for** i in inferenceset **do**
27:       FuzzyTransform (i)
28:    **end for**
29: **end for**

30: **for** pixel in image **do**
31:     calculate pixel degree of membership (t)
32:     calculate all the inference ($OutputFuzzySet$)
33:     FuzzyOutput = AggregatedFuzzySet (inference)
    return FuzzyOutput
34: **end for**

Defuzzification of Inference Result. The defuzzification is the process of transferring fuzzy output values into output pixel images. We utilized Mamdani's methodology for defuzzification and it is executed by ascertaining the crisp value of centroid utilizing a weighted normal method. The graphs in Fig. 4 explains the transfer curve obtained using the fuzzy inference system. The transfer curve for different mean values 'M' are analyzed at the points 64, 128 and 192.

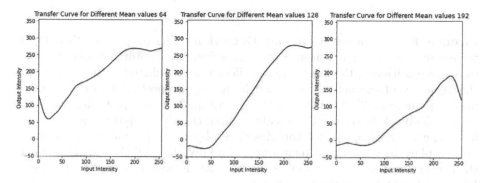

Fig. 4. Is the graph which exhibits the transfer curve for different mean (M) values M = 64, M = 128 and M = 192 respectively.

In the first graph, where M = 64 and the pixel range between (0, 10), their output intensities are increasing but based on our enhancement properties the extremely light pixels will not be transformed. Similarly, in the third graph, where M = 192 and the pixel range is between (240, 250), their output intensities are decreasing and according to our enhancement rules, extremely dark intensities remain unchanged. Consider the second graph, where M = 128 and the pixel range between (50, 210), their model attains a perfect transfer curve and satisfies our enhancement rules as the extremely light and dark pixels are unchanged.

2.2   Licence Plate Object Detection

The licence plate from the fuzzy enhanced image is identified in the second phase, which is called licence plate object detection. Here we use YOLOv5 CSP-Net architecture for object detection, because it achieves better accuracy in object detection and also less time consuming and memory usage. Though the older versions of YOLO perform well [11] they are complex and time consuming when compared to CSPNet based YOLOv5. Figure 5 shows the two major steps involved in YOLOv5 algorithm: First is, licence Plate Localization and Detection and the other is licence Plate Extraction.

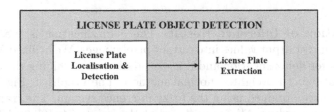

Fig. 5. Shows the modules in the licence plate object detection phase.

Licence Plate Localisation and Detection. The purpose of this step is to restrict and detect the licence plate area from the captured image. In order to achieve efficiency, the localization of licence plates should be more accurate, the accuracy of character recognition is directly proportional to the localized licence plate area [7]. As shown in the Algorithm 2, licence plate detection, the YOLOv5 object detector creates features from the given input images and then feeds the features to predict the classes of objects and draw box around the licence plate to show the detected area. Initially the YOLOv5 model predicts the center coordinates (a_c, b_c) of the licence plate as well as it predicts the width (W) and height (H) of the bounding box.

$$a_0 = a_c - \frac{W}{2} \ , \ b_0 = b_c - \frac{H}{2} \tag{3}$$

$$a_1 = a_0 + w \ , \ b_1 = b_0 + H \tag{4}$$

Further the YOLOv5 requires a ground truth about the starting coordinates (a_0, b_0) and ending coordinates (a_1, b_1) which can be calculated using the Eq. 3 and 4, then the coordinates will be normalized in order to fit them into the YOLOv5 format (a, b, w, h) using the Eqs. 5, 6 respectively.

$$a = \frac{(a_0 + a_1)}{2 * W} \ , \ b = \frac{(b_0 + b_1)}{2 * H} \tag{5}$$

$$w = \frac{(a_1 - a_0)}{W} \ , \ h = \frac{(b_1 - b_0)}{H} \tag{6}$$

Algorithm 2. licence plate detection and extraction

1: $x \leftarrow$ fuzzy contrast enhanced image
2: $t \leftarrow$ test images
3: set up YOLOv5 configuration
4: train the model
5: validate the model
6: **for all** images in t **do**
7:     *run* YOLOv5(image)
8:     *store* licence plate detected image I
9:     *store* $(top, left)$ & $(bottom, right)$ coordinates for bounding box
10:     **if** *coordinates* $== TRUE$ **then**
11:         crop I using coordinates
12:     **end if**
13: **end for**

Licence Plate Extraction. The main characteristic of YOLOv5 is the training procedure. As most of the previous versions struggled to detect small objects, the YOLOv5 used an attention network, as it extracts the critical regions of the object. The detected object coordinates are then processed into a custom built image cropping function that crops the detected object and saves it as a separate image as shown in Fig. 6. The YOLOv5 achieves maximum performance among all previous versions and other state of the art techniques. It shows improvement in terms of speed, size and predictive accuracy, and also functions better for subtle and simple tasks such as licence plate detection. The betterness of YOLOv5 object detection can be determined using the Eq. 7 and Eq. 8 which is used to calculate the Average Precision (AP) and mean Average Precision (mAP).

$$AP = \sum_{x=0}^{n-1} Recall(x) - Recall(x+1) * Precision(x) \tag{7}$$

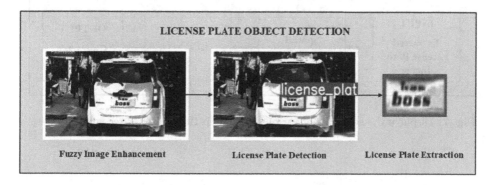

Fig. 6. Shows the modules in the licence plate object detection phase.

where, Recall(x) = 0, Precision(x) = 1 & n = Number of thresholds

$$mAP = \frac{1}{n} \sum_{x=1}^{n} AP_x \tag{8}$$

where, AP_x = Average Precision of class (x) & n = Number of classes

2.3   Character Recognition

The character recognition is the final phase, which recognizes the characters from the licence plate detected by the YOLOv5 model. The proposed LPRNet architecture is designed based on several state of the art networks such as VGGNet and ResNet called 'backbone' architecture [3]. In order to make the model adapt for our case, we redesigned the model to perform well for fast and lightweight networks. The sequence of steps has been showed in the Algorithm 3, licence plate recognition and the output of each CNN can be calculated using the Eq. 9. If the licence plate is not at the right angle, we use a spatial transformer to rotate it. Tilting the licence plate may improve character recognition, but it is not essential because the YOLOv5 model detects the plates as straight images most of the time.

The licence plate dimensions are converted into 94 X 24 and processed to the backbone architecture. The LPRNet backbone architecture takes RGB (Red Green Blue) images as input and calculates its features. The backbone consists of several small basic blocks which are useful for better training as shown in Fig. 7.

$$F_{ab}^{k} = \sigma \left(\sum_{i=0}^{m-1} \sum_{j=0}^{m-1} W_{ij} x_{(a+i)(b+j)}^{k-1} \right) + bias \tag{9}$$

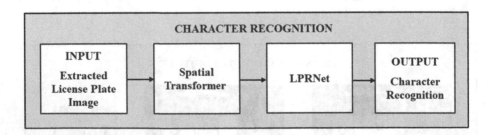

Fig. 7. Displays the sequence of various module in the character recognition phase.

A small basic block consists of four consecutive convolutional layers with single strides on the first and last. The padding heights and widths are added to the second and third convolutional layer. The extensive convolutional layer at the end of the backbone architecture with 1×13 format studies the characteristics of the character on the number plate. The model also utilizes the structure of memory based neural architecture. The output of backbone network is a set of probabilities for the sequence of characters.

Algorithm 3. licence plate character recognition

1: $x \leftarrow$ extracted licence plate image
2: $t \leftarrow$ test images
3: set up spatial transform layer
4: set up LPRNet architecture
5: train the model
6: validate the model
7: **for all** images in t **do**
8:     *run* LPRNet(image)
9:     *store* licence plate detected image I
10:     *store* recognized characters c
11: **end for**

The probability values are then processed to decoder output and the target characters are identified. Since both the target characters and decoder output length are not the same, the CTC loss method is applied as an alternative for the traditional segmentation methods. The CTC loss is one of the highly impactful approaches for different sized character sequences. It also fastens the probability calculation from going each character to each sequence of characters output.

3   Results and Discussion

3.1   Experimental Setup

To conduct the experiment, we collected datasets from Kaggle website and narrowed down around 800 images for English language based licence plates which consists of images with varied lighting conditions like day, night, varied distances, view points and so on. For the Tamil language based vehicle licence plate, there is no specific or publicly accessible dataset available. Hence we collected around 100 images from the google source as well as used the synthetic data generators to generate various combinations of Tamil font images for training. We have used 70% of the images for training the system, 20% of images for validation and 10% of the images for testing the trained system. The research experiments are developed in Python language and executed on the Google Colab platform, which has a variety of hardware requirements.

3.2　System Training Model

The first phase, Fuzzy image contrast enhancement technique based on Mamdani's approach is used to intensify the contrast of the images. The transfer curve was computed for different Mean values, and the better solution is shown in Fig. 4 and discussed in detail in Sect. 2.1 under the subsection Defuzzification of inference result. Then the next phase, licence plate object detection uses the enhanced image from the fuzzy image contrast technique as input. The YOLOv5 object detection system achieves an overall licence plate detection accuracy of 98.17%. Finally, the detected licence plate is fed into the LPRNet, end-to-end Deep CNN with CTC Loss, which was trained on a variety of hardware platforms such as Central Processing Unit, Graphics Processing Unit and Tensor Processing Unit.

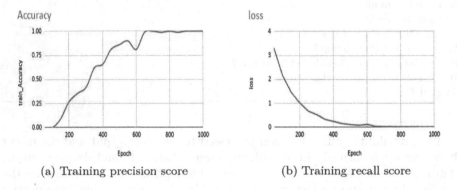

(a) Training precision score　　　　　(b) Training recall score

Fig. 8. Is the graph which illustrates the precision score and recall score

The licence plate recognition system performs admirably well when trained on varieties of English language dataset. But when considering multi-lingual datasets, especially for Tamil language, it's worth noting that the performance appears to drop at times, but then rebound on subsequent iterations. After sufficient training and testing, the proposed system model achieves an overall training precision score of 0.9916 and a recall score of 0.04 as shown in the Fig. 8. The training precision score is calculated as shown in Eq. 10 and training recall score is calculated using the Eq. 11

$$Precision = \frac{\Sigma TP}{\Sigma TP + \Sigma FP} \tag{10}$$

$$Recall = \frac{\Sigma TP}{\Sigma TP + \Sigma FN} \tag{11}$$

3.3   Test Case

In our research, we have used various types of licence plate images for training and testing. Here, seven varieties of licence plate images and the output of each phase has been shown in the Fig. 9.

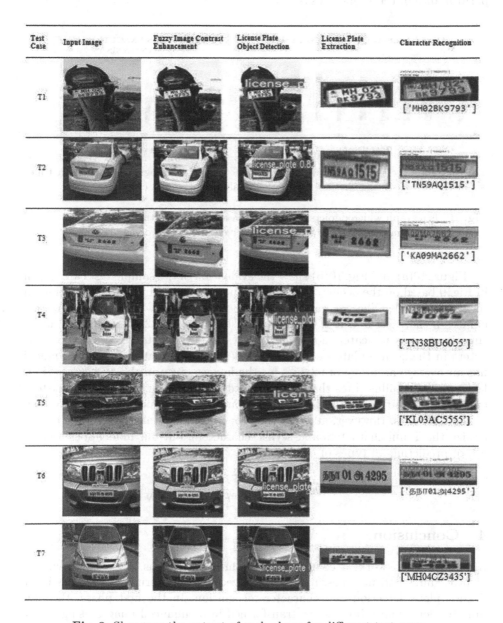

Fig. 9. Showcase the output of each phase for different test cases.

3.4 Performance Analysis

The seven different test case images shown in Fig. 9, includes an English licence plate T1, T3 & T7, a Tamil licence plate T6, an Alpha-numeric licence plate T4, and a low quality licence plate T2 & T5 to analyze and understand the performance of the proposed system.

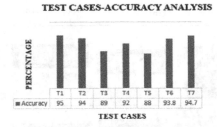

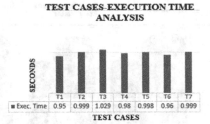

(a) Character recognition accuracy analysis of the test cases

(b) Character recognition execution time analysis of the test cases

Fig. 10. Is a graph which depicts the prediction accuracy and the execution time taken to predict the characters in the licence plate given in the test cases

Figure 10(a) and Fig. 10(b) show the evaluation of the sample test cases given in Fig. 9 based on the accuracy in terms of percentage and the execution time in terms of seconds. The accuracy percentage indicates, how well the system recognizes a character and it is calculated as shown in Eq. 12, while the execution time in seconds indicates, how long it takes the system to recognize the characters in the licence plate image. Figure 10(a) depicts that the proposed model has an average accuracy of 92.35% for the images given in the test cases. Similarly, Fig. 10(b) illustrates that the proposed system takes constantly consistent amount of time to recognize characters from various licence plate styles shown in the test cases. However, at times the proposed model takes extra time to recognize the Tamil characters and stylish characters, but our model does a great job of predicting all types of characters.

$$Accuracy = \frac{\Sigma(TP + TN)}{\Sigma(TP + FP + TN + FN)} \tag{12}$$

4 Conclusion

In this research work, a combination of three algorithms, with their own set of procedures and modules, has been utilized as an experimental approach for licence plate detection and character recognition. In the first phase, the illuminated low quality images are transformed into enhanced images using Fuzzy Image Contrast Enhancement technique. As a result, the efficiency of the character recognition phase is improved. The enhanced image is then fed into the

YOLOv5 object detector, which accurately detects and extracts the licence plates to a degree of 98.17%. Finally, in the character recognition phase, an effective technique known as LPRNet, an end-to-end Deep CNN with CTC Loss, is used to detect various licence plates with varying font styles, sizes, and positions. Our system has been well-trained to recognize English, Tamil, and Alpha-numeric fonts. We have trained a few characters in Tamil language that are commonly used in licence plates because Tamil characters are rich in context. An AVLPR must be developed and optimized to meet the hardware specifications while still being suitable for complex and real-time environments, and our proposed model ultimately satisfies the requirement. In the future, a comparative study will be conducted on image enhancement and character recognition techniques, and the model will be enhanced to distinguish duplicate licence plates.

References

1. Lin, C.H., Lin, Y.S. and Liu, W.C.: An efficient licence plate recognition system using convolution neural networks. In: 2018 IEEE International Conference on Applied System Invention (ICASI), IEEE (2018)
2. Henry, C., Ahn, S.Y., Lee, S.W.: Multinational licence plate recognition using generalized character sequence detection. IEEE Access **8**, 35185–35199 (2020)
3. Chekol, B., Celebi, N., TAŞCI, T.: Segmented character recognition using curvature-based global image feature. Turkish J. Electr. Eng. Comput. Sci. **27**(5), 3804–3814 (2019)
4. Joshi, S., Kumar, S.: Image contrast enhancement using fuzzy logic. arXiv preprint arXiv:1809.04529 (2018)
5. Devi, G.S., Rabbani, M.M.A.: Image contrast enhancement using Histogram equalization with Fuzzy Approach on the Neighbourhood Metrics (FANMHE). In: 2016 International Conference on Wireless Communications, Signal Processing and Networking (WiSPNET), IEEE (2016)
6. Fernandes, S., et al.: Adaptive contrast enhancement using fuzzy logic. In: 2019 International Conference on Advances in Computing, Communication and Control (ICAC3), IEEE (2019)
7. Tourani, A., et al.: A robust deep learning approach for automatic Iranian vehicle licence plate detection and recognition for surveillance systems. IEEE Access **8**, 201317–201330 (2020)
8. Hamdy, A., Elnagahy, F., Helmy, I.: Application of fuzzy logic on astronomical images focus measure. In: 2019 International Conference on Innovative Trends in Computer Engineering (ITCE), IEEE (2019)
9. Wang, W., et al.: A light CNN for end-to-end car licence plates detection and recognition. IEEE Access **7**, 173875–173883 (2019)
10. Hendryli, J., Herwindiati, D.E.: Automatic licence plate recognition for parking system using convolutional neural networks. In: 2020 International Conference on Information Management and Technology (ICIMTech), IEEE (2020)
11. Zherzdev, S., Alexey, G.: Lprnet: licence plate recognition via deep neural networks. arXiv preprint arXiv:1806.10447 (2018)
12. Gengec, N., et al.: Visual object detection for autonomous transport vehicles in smart factories. Turkish J. Electr. Eng. Comput. Sci. **29**(4), 2101–2115 (2021)

13. Sharma, A., Pramod Kumar, M.: Image enhancement techniques on deep learning approaches for automated diagnosis of COVID-19 features using CXR images. Multimedia Tools Appl. **81**(29), 42649–42690 (2022)
14. Sharma, A., Pramod Kumar, M.: Covid-MANet: multi-task attention network for explainable diagnosis and severity assessment of COVID-19 from CXR images. Pattern Recogn. **131**, 108826 (2022)
15. Sharma, A., Mishra, P.K.: Deep learning approaches for automated diagnosis of COVID-19 using imbalanced training CXR data. In: Woungang, I., Dhurandher, S.K., Pattanaik, K.K., Verma, A., Verma, P. (eds.) Advanced Network Technologies and Intelligent Computing. ANTIC 2021. Communications in Computer and Information Science, vol. 1534, pp. 453–472. Springer, Cham (2022). https://doi.org/10.1007/978-3-030-96040-7_36
16. Sharma, A., Pramod, K.M.: Performance analysis of machine learning based optimized feature selection approaches for breast cancer diagnosis. Int. J. Inf. Technol. **14**(4), 1949–1960 (2022)
17. Sharma, A., Promad Kumar, M.: State-of-the-art in performance metrics and future directions for data science algorithms. J. Sci. Res. **64**(2), 221–238 (2020)

High Blood Pressure Classification Using Meta-heuristic Based Data-Centric Hybrid Machine Learning Model

Satyanarayana Nimmala$^{(\boxtimes)}$ (ID), Rella Usha Rani (ID), and P. Sanakara Rao (ID)

CSE Department, CVRCE, GITAM Institute of Technology, Hyderabad,
Rangareddy 501510, India
satyauce234@gmail.com

Abstract. Blood Pressure (BP) is created when the heart pumps the blood into blood vessels. If this pressure is more than 140/90 mmHg, it is diagnosed as high blood pressure (HBP). If HBP is not noticed and treated at an early level, it may lead to life-threatening issues. The design and development of machine learning models (MLM), to predict HBP in advance based on bio-psychological factors is gaining the attention of people. MLM is assisting medical doctors in diagnosing diseases more accurately, though MLM is exceptionally doing great in this domain, they are data-dependent. Conventional MLM is evaluated for the considered dataset. The major pitfall of such a model is a dependency on the dataset. If the same model is exposed to different datasets of the same type, the performance of the model may not be consistent. This paper proposed a heuristic-based dynamic data-drive, Age, Anger level (AA)-anxiety level, cholesterol level, obesity level (ACO) based hybrid MLM to predict HBP. The proposed model initially calculates the degree of dependency in terms of Pearson correlation between the attributes and class label attributes. The model is said to be hybrid as it uses the correlation-driven apriori-based fuzzy association rule miner to predict HBP. The proposed approach is data-centric and dynamic, as it calculates the Pearson correlation value for the given dataset at runtime and also assigns the priority value to the attribute at run time. The experimental setup is done on 1100 data records; the proposed model has got 91.168% accuracy, precision of 0.946, and recall of 0.933. The output of the model is a fuzzy inference engine consisting of the top 10 meta-heuristic-based fuzzy association rules, these rules can be used by a person as a knowledge base to manage and treat HBP.

Keywords: Hypertension · Age · Obesity · Anger · Anxiety · Smoking · Alcohol consumption · Cholesterol · Sodium intake

1 Introduction

High blood pressure (HBP) is now one of the most common diseases afflicting people worldwide [1]. If a person's systolic blood pressure (SBP) is > 140 mmHg or diastolic blood pressure (DBP) is >90 mmHg, they are considered hypertensive [1]. It is therefore preferable to identify the specific causes of blood pressure (BP) elevation so that the

© The Author(s), under exclusive license to Springer Nature Switzerland AG 2023
I. Woungang et al. (Eds.): ANTIC 2022, CCIS 1798, pp. 169–188, 2023.
https://doi.org/10.1007/978-3-031-28183-9_12

underlying problem can be addressed rather than using blood pressure (BP) medications [2]. For instance, if a person has HBP, due to a higher level of obesity, his or her BP may return to normal if he or she loses weight through various means such as physical exercise or following a proper diet. The existing literature review unfolds, that Obesity, cholesterol, age, and stress levels are also linked to high blood pressure, but the quantitative relationship between these factors and HBP is not yet addressed. Furthermore, their overall influence on HBP has to be investigated. This study used heuristic-based optimized fuzzy association rules to describe the quantitative relationships between each attribute of AA-ACO and HBP, and also the overall effect of AA-ACO on HBP. The output of the study is a fuzzy inference system consisting of a set of fuzzy rules. The outcomes of the experimental results demonstrated that these rules can be applied to manage and treat HBP in everyday life. The remainder section of this paper provides an overview of meta-heuristic-based optimization problems.

Optimization is a well-known buzzword in many fields across the globe. Everyone is looking for an optimized solution for a selected problem in terms of many parameters such as time, cost, distance, selection, search, etc. [3]. The application of conventional methods to optimization problems present days is no more acceptable because either they fail to give optimized solutions or they take more time to solve [4]. Optimization problems can be solved using heuristic and meta-heuristic methods. The trade-off between heuristic and meta-heuristic methods is unlike heuristic, meta-heuristic may not start the search process from a single point, it could be from randomly selected multiple points, attempts to investigate and exploit the entire search space, and also avoids getting trapped in local optima [5]. The meta-heuristic algorithms mimic the biological behaviour of animals or birds or fish or insects or bees and they are exceptional in optimization problems [6]. HBP is the most prevalent concern of the world today [7], which cause many diseases directly and indirectly, and is also one of the silent killer of humankind at present days [8]. This study proposed a meta-heuristic-based machine learning (ML) model to predict HBP in advance so that it can be managed and avoided. The remainder section of the paper focuses on the literature review, methodology used, results obtained, limitations of work carried out, and future direction.

2 Literature Review

The BP of a person is affected by biological, psychological, and social factors. Sometimes the weather conditions in which the person lives may also raise his/her BP. This section briefly discusses the various factors affecting BP and their relationship with BP as represented in Fig. 1. The heuristic and meta-heuristic-based optimization techniques are also summarized in this section. Equation 1 and Eq. 2, show the relationship between BP and total peripheral resistance (TPR), heartbeats per minute (HBM), and cardiac output (CO). Equation 3 represents mean arterial pressure (MAP).

$$BP = CO * TPR \tag{1}$$

$$CO = HBM * BV \tag{2}$$

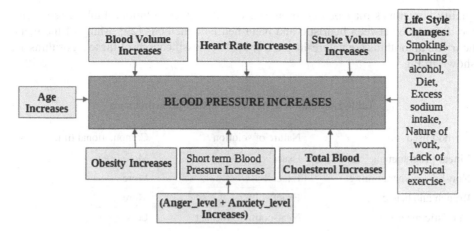

Fig. 1. Factors affecting blood pressure

$$MAP = (SBP + 2 * DBP)/3 \tag{3}$$

Aging is one of the default factors for elevated BP [9], as the person ages the arteries become thin and stiff [10]. In obese people, in many cases, it is found that they gather extra fat in various parts of the body, which raises their BP of a person [11, 12]. Although the body needs cholesterol for the function of various parts of the body [13], having high levels of low-density lipoproteins (LDL) may raise the BP of a person [14]. The most bothering factor in everybody's life today is stress, the consequence of the same would be a raise in his anger levels and anxiety levels. The existing literature unfolds that anger and anxiety levels play a significant role in raising a person's BP [15, 16].

The literature says apart from AA-ACO, there are other factors such as salt, smoking, and drinking that may elevate the BP of a person [17]. Salt (Sodium) is an essential mineral required for the smooth functioning of the human body [18], but excessive intake of salt may elevate blood pressure [19]. Apart from the factors such as age, obesity, cholesterol levels, and stress levels [20], alcohol consumption may also affect blood pressure [21]. Alcohol in the bloodstream decreases the vasodilators, which makes the blood vessels, squeeze, thus elevating the BP [22]. The habit of smoking in people is increasing day by day [23]. The nicotine in a cigarette or tobacco is absorbed by the bloodstream when a person smokes. Nicotine plays its part in hardening the arteries' walls, increasing the heart rate, and thus increasing BP [24]. Apart from blood pressure the habit of smoking for a longer period also decreases the performance of the lungs.

Nowadays we find almost in all fields, optimization is a major concern when solving real-world problems. The optimization problems are day by day becoming more complex [25]. Conventional methods used to solve such problems as airline scheduling, financial portfolio models, supply chain design in multiple industries, etc., consume too much time and the solution is not effective [26]. The methods used to solve such problems are given in Table 1. The heuristic and meta-heuristics are sorts of search techniques that are inexact but able to output near-optimal or optimal solutions in less time [27]. The solution quality and computational time differentiate these two methods [28]. Solution quality sometimes may be compromised to get a quick solution. Table 2 represents the difference between heuristic and meta-heuristic methods [29]. Many of the meta-heuristic algorithms are nature-inspired [30]. The classifications of these algorithms are shown in Fig. 4.

Table 1. Solution strategies for optimization problems

Method used	Nature of solution	Computational time
Linear programming	Exact	More
Non-linear programming	Exact	More
Branch and bound	Exact	More
Heuristic methods	Near-optimal, Inexact	Less
Metaheuristic methods	Near-optimal, Inexact	Less

Nature-inspired meta-heuristic approach to get optimized solutions for various problems using machine learning (ML) techniques is a more generic approach [30]. More precisely bio-inspired optimization approach is been common practice in the design and development of ML models. These kinds of models assist humans to obtain the optimized and desired solutions for complex problems. Nature is always a source of inspiration for various technological and scientific developments [31]. Bio-inspired meta-heuristic algorithms are iterative, problem independent, and use randomized approaches to generate populations of solutions or single solutions [32]. In present days, technological advancements are trying to mimic nature in developing optimized solutions for complex problems. Bio-inspired computing has become the most used approach in computer science to solve problems in different fields such as biomedical engineering, computer networks, security, artificial intelligence, neural networks (NN), parallel processing, and machine learning (Fig. 2).

Table 2. Heuristic vs. meta-heuristic methods

	Heuristic methods	Metaheuristic methods
Nature	Deterministic	Randomization + Heuristic
Type	Algorithmic, problem-dependent, Iterative	Nature-inspired, problem independent, Iterative
Example	Finding the Nearest neighbourhood in travelling salesman problem	Applying the Ant Colony – Optimization to solve a specific problem
Nature of solution	Inexact, Near-optimal	Inexact, Near-optimal

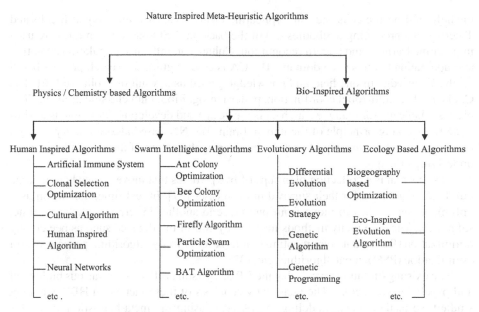

Fig. 2. Classification of bio-inspired algorithms

Bio-inspired computing or bio-inspired algorithms (BIA) are the fields of study to develop computational models based on the principle and inspiration of the biological behaviour of nature [33].

It borrows concepts from artificial intelligence, and machine learning and it strongly relies on biology, mathematics, and computer science. The BIA is further divided into swarm intelligence algorithms (SIA), human-inspired algorithms (HIA), evolutionary algorithms (EA), and ecology-based algorithms (EBA) [34].

Human Inspired Algorithms: These kinds of models mimic the working principle of different systems of the human body or nature of humans, such as artificial immune system (AIS), clonal selection optimization (CSO), cultural algorithms (CA), neural networks (NN), etc. AIS-based algorithms follow the principle of how the immune system of the human body protects humans from external threats such as viral infection, bacterial infection, and fungal infection [35]. These kinds of techniques are used exclusively in networks to find and attack, intruders to protect computer systems within the network. The CSO uses the concept of the clonal selection principle of the human immune system that responds against antigens. If the lymphocytes in the body travel through bone marrow they form B cells. The outer layer of each B cell has specific antigen receptors. If the lymphocytes travel through the thymus they form T cells. The outer layer of each T cell has also specific antigen receptors. The moment they get matured they migrate to lymph nodes through the bloodstream. The lymph nodes become their residential house. If the body gets infected with bacteria the B cell receptors bind the bacteria through its receptor and start replicating themselves. The T cells bind the bacteria with the help of dendritic cells and start replicating themselves. Now the army of B cells and T cells starts producing antibodies to kill the bacteria. CSO-based techniques are used in machine learning and pattern recognition. Culture can influence population evolution and adaptation to the search domain. The CA is used to guide the search process based on the knowledge in one field and knowledge gained as a result of evolution [36]. The CA is used in multi-robot coordination, pattern recognition, fault classification, etc. The biggest challenge for many researchers is the design and development of models to simulate the working principle of the human brain. The NN-based algorithms try to build the models in decision support systems by keeping the nature of the human brain as an underlying principle.

SIA: Swarm is a collection of groups of live particles that move somewhere in large numbers, to get food for their survival in most cases [37]. In real-time, the swarm uses optimized approaches to move from one place to another in terms of distance, time, safety, etc. They are many methods inspired by swarm intelligence such as bee colony optimization (BCO), ant colony optimization (ACO), Firefly Algorithm, particle swarm optimization (PSO), a bat algorithm, etc. [37].

The existing literature reveals that the BP of a person is affected by various biological and psychological factors. The quantitative analysis of these factors on HBP is not yet studied, so mathematical modeling of AA-ACO using the meta-heuristic method for predicting a person's HBP is gaining the attention of many research scholars.

3   Methods

Heuristic and meta-heuristic approach is used to get the categorical and fuzzified form of the attributes in AA-ACO. The experiments are being carried out using a medical database collected from the diagnosis center, doctor C, located at banjara hills in Hyderabad, India. An individual's anxiety and anger levels are calculated using a person's responses to a series of predefined standard questionnaires. The questionnaire used to collect the values of anxiety and anger levels of a person is mentioned in Fig. 3, and Fig. 4. The individual is asked to complete a questionnaire, and their responses are graded on a scale of 0 to 3. The answer could be no, never (considers as 0), yes often (considered as 1), yes very often (considered as 2), or yes always (considered as 3). The attribute value is determined by taking the mean of all the answers. The results demonstrated that the proposed model outperforms existing ML models. The meta-heuristic approach is used to get the categorical values of AA-ACO as shown in Table 3.

1. Is there constant fear about anything?
2. Is there often breathing difficulty.
3. Feeling of not having desired thing in life.
4. Always compares with others.
5. Feeling of no interest in life.
6. Always expecting right things from dear ones according to your perception.
7. Often scared without clear reason.
8. Aware of heart beat in the absence of physical exercise
9. Feeling of not doing worth noted.
10. Feeling of not confident of doing something.
11. Sense of dryness in the mouth.
12. Feeling of not getting relaxed.
13. Feeling of sleeplessness.
14. Feeling of loss of energy levels without doing any physical exercise.
15. Feeling of shaking in hands.
16. Thinking about situations which are not in your hand.
17. Thinking about the worst result of ambiguous situation.
18. Tended to over-react to the situations.
19. Executing same pattern of thought repeatedly.
20. Intolerant of people criticism.

Fig. 3. Anxiety questionnaire

3.1 Data Set Details

The experimental setup is done on a dataset consisting of 1200 records. 1100 records are used to train and test the model, in which 827 have class label no and 273 have class label yes, and 100 records collected without a class label, are used to validate the proposed model (Table 4).

3.2 Methodology Used to Extract the Rules

The model initially calculates the pearson correlation coefficient (PCC) value [38]. The PCC value is calculated between MAP and AA-AOC and tabulated in Table 5, based on the PCC value each attribute in AA-AOC is given a priority number as shown in Table 6. The proposed model works in 4 stages. Stage1. The data set is converted into a categorical form using the Meta-heuristic approach, then no class records and the yes class recodes, are separated. Stage2. The model is extracting priority-based apriori association rules from training data. Stage3. Each attribute in the antecedent part of the

Table 3. Qualitative values of AA-ACO using a meta-heuristic approach

Attribute	Continuous value of an attribute	Qualitative values
A (Age)	0 to 30	Young
	31 to 50	Middle-aged
	50 above	Old
A (Anger level)	Zero to one	Low
	One to two	Medium
	Two to three	High
A (Anxiety level)	Zero to one	Low
	One to two	Medium
	Two to three	High
C (Cholesterol level)	0 to 200	Low
	200 to 240	Medium
	240 above	High
O (Obesity level)	0 to 25	Low
	25 to 30	Medium
	30 above	High

1. Waiting for anything annoys me.
2. I get angry for the delay in completion of any Assignment.
3. I get angry if people hurt me.
4. I get angry if things won't go on my path.
5. I get angry if people won't agree with me in arguments.
6. I get angry when I remember about bad things people did to me.
7. I find it difficult to forgive people who did wrong to me.
8. I get angry if the attitude of others is wrong as per my perception.
9. I get angry if others won't respect me.
10. I am insensitive towards the feeling of others.

Fig. 4. Anger questionnaire

Table 4. Data set sample copy

A	A	A	C	O	SBP	DBP	MAP	Victim of HBP
41	2.4	2.3	135	28.8	162	87	112	No
39	2.3	2.4	159	25.5	187	111	137	Yes
31	1.1	1.1	172	22.2	111	73	86	Yes
59	1	0.9	200	25.1	122	83	96	Yes
34	0.6	0.5	139	15.6	96	57	70	No
36	0.8	0.5	169	25.4	117	82	94	No
27	0.4	0.1	159	19.5	109	69	83	Yes
24	0.5	0.1	108	18.5	102	68	80	Yes
31	0.4	0.5	132	31.6	125	81	96	No
19	0.7	0.4	119	16.7	107	69	82	Yes
35	0.9	1.2	172	23.9	111	67	82	No
44	2.4	2.1	237	24.3	134	86	102	Yes
44	2	1.6	177	30.4	146	95	112	Yes
61	1.2	1.9	217	21.9	113	77	89	No
53	2	2	177	21.8	134	88	104	YES
38	0.9	0.8	190	23.5	115	78	91	No
41	0.6	0.5	144	22.2	120	68	86	No
24	1	0.4	186	25.7	103	67	79	No
29	1.3	0.7	147	20.3	118	79	92	No
49	2.2	2.2	149	20.6	139	84	103	No
39	1.6	1.1	225	23.5	124	84	98	No
24	0.1	0.1	108	18.5	102	68	80	No
46	1.3	0.7	168	25.5	125	79	95	Yes
38	1.1	0.6	188	25.8	120	87	98	Yes
33	0.9	0.3	184	19.9	105	63	77	No
41	1.1	0.4	137	25	104	59	74	No
63	2.1	2.2	137	19.2	146	89	108	No
21	0.3	0.1	142	19.4	92	61	72	No
56	2	1.9	168	21.9	131	93	106	No
30	0.7	0.6	142	17.2	122	68	86	No

association rule is fuzzified using Eq. 5 shown below. Stage4. Then top 10 fuzzy rules are extracted to build the model. Figure 5 shows the architecture of the proposed model.

$$PC = \frac{N \sum XY - \sum X \sum Y}{\left[N \sum X^2 - (\sum X)^2\right]\left[N \sum Y^2 - (\sum Y)^2\right]} \quad (4)$$

$$\mu_A(x) = \begin{cases} 0, & x \leq a \\ \frac{x-a}{m-a}, & a < x \leq m \\ \frac{b-x}{b-m}, & m < x < b \\ 0, & x \geq b \end{cases} \quad (5)$$

Table 5. PCC value between attributes in AA-ACO and MAP

S. No	Attribute_name	Value of PCC
1	Age	0.405146
2	Anger_level	0.569344
3	Anxiety_level	0.709547
4	Obesity_level	0.328565
5	Cholesterol_level	0.287602

Table 6. Priority Value between attributes in AA-ACO and MAP

S. No	Attribute_name	Priority value	Priority in fuzzy form
1	Age	3	Moderate
2	Anger_level	4	High
3	Anxiety_level	5	Very high
4	Obesity_level	2	Low
5	Cholesterol_level	1	Very low

Initially, as part of the data collection process, the continuous values attributes such as age, obesity, and cholesterol level are discretized as low, medium, and high using a heuristic approach. Then apriori algorithm is used to extract yes class and no class rules separately. The attributes in the antecedent part of the rule are further fuzzified triangular fuzzy membership function based on rules imposed; Fig. 6 shows the fuzzification of attribute anger level using a meta-heuristic-based triangular fuzzy membership function. The top 10 meta-heuristic-based fuzzy rules extracted are summarized in the study. The fuzzy rules are extracted using modified apriori constitute the fuzzy inference system.

The model proposed in this paper is data-driven, hybrid, and dynamic. Initially, the model pre-processes the dataset and determines the PCC value between AA-ACO and MAP. The PCC value is used to determine the attribute's priority while extracting association rules. Figure 7 shows the architecture of the apriori algorithm. If a person's age is 31, it is unclear whether this age should be replaced with young or middle-aged, because it is close to both intervals. This uncertainty is resolved using the fuzzy membership function, in this study the triangular membership function is considered to get the fuzzified values of AA-ACO. If a person has an anger level of either 1.9, or 2.1, his/her anger level can be mild or serious as shown in Fig. 4, to assign the right value triangular fuzzy membership function is used. The yes class records and no class

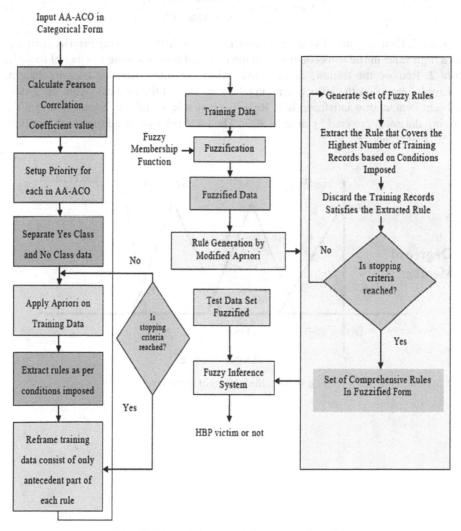

Fig. 5. The architecture of the proposed model

records are separated to form the fuzzy dataset. Then apriori algorithm [39] is applied to this fuzzy dataset to generate the association rules, from these rules, qualitative rules are extracted to build a fuzzy inference system based on the priority and coverage of the rule. The experiments are carried out initially with the support count (SC) and confidence (C) set at 1, but no rules are generated. Then SC, C is decremented by 0.1 in each iteration. At C of 0.9 and SC of 0.3, the yes-class rules begin to appear, and no-class rules, popped up at SC of 0.35 and C of 0.9.

$$SC(A \Rightarrow B) = \frac{\text{Occurrence of (A, B)}}{\text{Occurrence (N)}} \tag{6}$$

$$C(A \Rightarrow B) = \frac{\text{Occurrence of (A, B)}}{\text{Occurrence (A)}} \tag{7}$$

Rule 1. From one item frequent item set, extract a rule that has a top priority attribute, has a high value in the antecedent part of the rule, and covers a more number of records.
Rule 2. Remove the training records covered by the rule1 from the training dataset, and apply apriori on the leftover training data set, extract the next rule from the 2-item frequent item set that satisfies rule 1. **Rule 3.** Apply rule 1, and rule 2 recursively till the training dataset is covered by at least 90%. The same rules are used to extract yes class and no class rules.

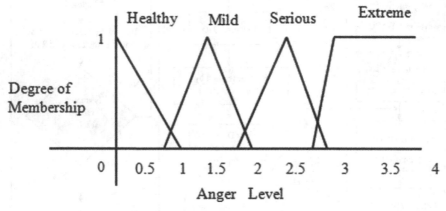

Fig. 6. Fuzzified values of anger level

3.3 Pseudo Code of the Proposed Model

Algorithm 1: Pseudocode for the proposed hybrid model

Input: Yes class and **No class** Data set in Categorical Form, and specified, SC, C

Output: Fuzzy inference System

  Begin:

  Step 1: Calculate the PCC between AA-ACO and MAP

  Step 2: Assign the priority for each attribute in AA-ACO

  Step 3: Separate No class and Yes class data

  Step 4: Run apriori (SC, C) on each class and extract rules based on conditions
          imposed

  Step 5: Fuzzify the antecedent part of each rule and generate new fuzzy training
          data

  Step 6: Apply modified apriori (SC, C) on newly obtained training data to
          generate fuzzy rules and constitute a fuzzy inference system

  Step 7: The extracted rule set is used to classify the victims of HBP

  End

---

4 Results

The dataset is divided into a training dataset and a testing dataset, 715 records are used for training, and 385 records are used for testing. 100 more records are used for the validation of the model being built. The accuracy of the model is compared with the different state-of-the-art existing ML models using the same dataset [40], but the model proposed in this paper is exceptional in terms of precision, recall, and accuracy. The comparative analysis is done with decision tree-based classifiers; such kinds of trees are constructed using entrophy as shown in Eq. 6.

$$Information\ Gain(S, A) = Entropy(S) - \sum_{v \in Values(A)} \left(\frac{|S_v|}{|S|} Entropy(S) \right) \qquad (8)$$

$$Entrophy(S) = \sum_{i=1}^{n} -p_i log_2 p_i \qquad (9)$$

$$P(X|Y) = \frac{P(Y|X) * P(X)}{P(Y)} \qquad (10)$$

$$w_0 + w1_{x1} + w_2 x_2 + \ldots \ldots + w_k x_k = \sum_{i=0}^{k} w_i x_i \qquad (11)$$

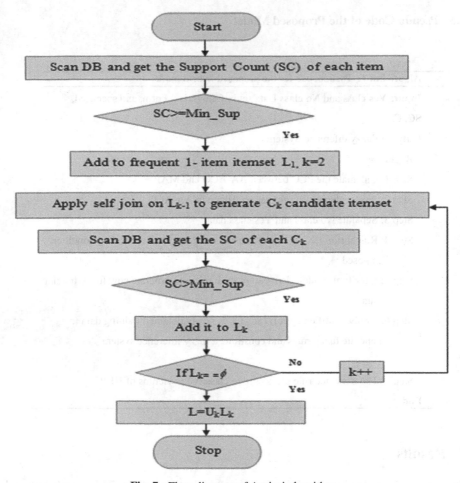

Fig. 7. Flow diagram of Apriori algorithm

The proposed model's performance is also compared with the performance of the Naïve Bayes classifier, and linear regression, these models work based on Eq. 8, and Eq. 9 as shown above. Figure 8 shows the accuracy of different classifiers. The fuzzy inference system was built using the extracted top 10 association rules to classify the test dataset and unseen samples of the dataset are summarized below (Table 7).

1. Obesity = Over Weight $\Rightarrow$ Victim_HBP = yes
2. Anger = Serious $\Rightarrow$ Victim_HBP = yes
3. Cholesterol = Normal && anxiety = Severe $\Rightarrow$ Victim_HBP = yes
4. Anger = Mild && anxiety = Severe $\Rightarrow$ Victim_HBP = yes
5. Obesity = Over Weight && Anger = Mild && anxiety = Severe $\Rightarrow$ Victim_HBP = yes
6. anxiety = Mild $\Rightarrow$ Victim_HBP = no
7. Cholesterol = Normal && anxiety = Mild $\Rightarrow$ Victim_HBP = no

8. Age = Young && Cholesterol = Normal && anxiety = Mild ⇒ Victim_HBP = no

9. Obesity = Over Weight && Cholesterol = Normal && Anger = Mild ⇒ Victim_HBP = no

10. Cholesterol = Normal && Anger = Healthy && anxiety = Mild ⇒ Victim_HBP = no

Table 7. The performance measure of the classifier

Classifier accuracy	$\frac{TP+TN}{(P+N)}$
Classifier error rate	$\frac{FP+FN}{(P+N)}$
Recall	$\frac{TP}{P}$
Precision	$\frac{TP}{(TP+FP)}$
F-measure	$\frac{(2\times precision\times recall)}{(precision+recall)}$

P is the total positive records, N is the total negative records, and TP is the number of positive records correctly labeled by the classifier, TN is the negative records that the classifier correctly labels, FP stands for negative records that have been incorrectly labelled as positive, and FN stands for positive records that have been incorrectly labelled as negative. Figure 9, and Fig. 10 represent the performance of the Yes class and No class predictions of the model (Tables 8 and 9).

Table 8. Accuracy of classifiers considered

Model used	Accuracy	Error rate
Logistic regression	84.6753	15.3247
Naïve Bayes	82.8571	17.1429
J48	87.2727	12.7273
Random forest	90.3896	9.6104
PART	86.4935	13.5065
JRip	89.3506	10.6494
AA-ACO proposed approach	91.1688	8.8312

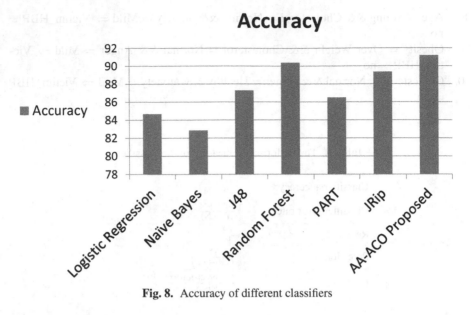

Fig. 8. Accuracy of different classifiers

Table 9. Classwise performance characteristics

Classifier	Class	Precision	Recall	F-measure
Logistic regression	Yes	0.689	0.775	0.728
	No	0.915	0.873	0.893
Naïve Bayes	Yes	0.623	0.892	0.734
	No	0.954	0.806	0.874
J48	Yes	0.715	0.863	0.782
	No	0.947	0.876	0.910
Random forest	Yes	0.849	0.775	0.810
	No	0.921	0.951	0.936
PART	Yes	0.705	0.843	0.768
	No	0.939	0.873	0.905
JRip	Yes	0.835	0.745	0.788
	No	0.912	0.947	0.929
Proposed AA-ACO	Yes	0.821	0.853	0.837
	No	0.946	0.933	0.940

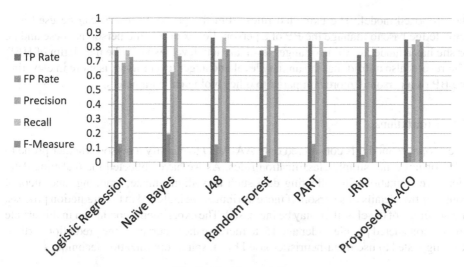

Fig. 9. Yes class details

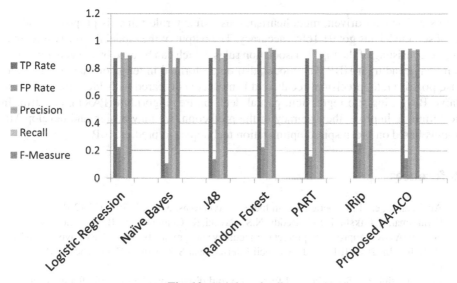

Fig. 10. No class details

5 Discussion

From the experimental analysis, it is obvious that each attribute in AA-ACO has an impact on the elevation of blood pressure. In terms of accuracy, the proposed model outperformed the existing classifiers. The proposed model is exceptional in terms of F-measure, and more accurate in No class predictions. Though J48 is exceptional in precision, it is poor in recall. The accuracy of the random forest is close to the accuracy of the proposed model, but the random forest is not good at F-measure compared with the proposed model. The extracted rules from the proposed model can be used as a knowledge base to manage the BP of a person. For example, if a person is obese and he or she has a moderate value of anger level, anxiety level also may be the victim of HBP. The results also unfold that the anxiety level and anger level impact is more in elevating the BP of a person is more compared to other biological parameters.

5.1 Limitations

The proposed model is considered only AA-ACO to classify a person whether prone to HBP or not using simple classification rules. As we have collected the real-time data, there are limitations in collecting data such as sodium intake, smoking, and alcohol consumption details of a person. If these attributes are included in the prediction process, the accuracy of the classifier may be increased. The experiments conducted in this article are not considered people under age 15, to increase the accuracy of the prediction further, it is suggested to use meta-heuristic-based bio-inspired optimization techniques.

6 Conclusion and Future Work

In this article data-driven, meta-heuristic-based fuzzy rule miner is proposed, and the proposed model has got 91.168% accuracy. The output of the model is a fuzzy inference engine consisting of the top 10 association rules, which can be used by the general public to manage and treat HBP. The model also outperformed in terms of true positive rate, false positive rate, precision, recall, and F-measure compared with J48, random forest, Naïve Bayes, logistic regression, partial decision tree algorithm (PART), and Jrip. In the future, to improve the accuracy of the prediction, we may design and develop ML models based on bio-inspired optimization techniques to predict HBP.

References

1. Anchala, R., et al.: Hypertension in India. J. Hypertens. **32**(6), 1170–1177 (2014)
2. Sivakumar, P., Lakshmi, T.U., Reddy, N.S., Pavani, R., Chaitanya, V.: Breast cancer prediction system: A novel approach to predict the accuracy using majority-voting based hybrid classifier (MBHC). In: 2020 IEEE India Council International Subsections Conference (INDISCON) (2020)
3. Priyadharsini, D., Sasikala, S.: Efficient thyroid disease prediction using features selection and meta-classifiers. In: 2022 6th International Conference on Computing Methodologies and Communication (ICCMC) (2022)
4. Zang, P., Jin, Z.: Prediction analysis of the prevalence of alzheimer's disease in China based on Meta Analysis. OALib **07**(05), 1–13 (2020)
5. Belur Nagaraj, S., Pena, M.J., Ju, W., Heerspink, H.L.: Machine learning based early prediction of end-stage renal disease in patients with diabetic kidney disease using clinical trials data. Diabetes Obes. Metab. **22**(12), 2479–2486 (2020)
6. Jan, M., Ahmad, H.: Image features based intelligent apple disease prediction system. Int. J. Agric. Env. Inform. Syst. **11**(3), 31–47 (2020)
7. Gupta, R.: Chapter-012 hypertension in india: trends in prevalence, awareness, treatment, and control, vol. 2, pp. 61–69. CSI: Cardiol. Update 2015 (2016)

8. Sassi, M.: Solving feature selection problems built on population-based meta-heuristic algorithms. Optim. Mach. Learn. 55–90 (2022)

9. Gupta, P., Kumar Goyal, M.: Machine Learning, Deep Learning-Based Optimization in Multilayered Cloud, pp. 15–32 (2022)

10. Yahyaoui, K.: Hybrid approach based on multi-agent system and Fuzzy Logic for mobile robot autonomous navigation. Optim. Mach. Learn. 169–199 (2022)

11. Agarwal, D., Agrawal, S., Gupta, P.: Fault-aware machine learning and deep learning-based algorithm for Cloud Architecture. Mach. Learn. Optim. Models Optim. Cloud 119–136 (2022)

12. World Health Organization: Blood Pressure, 27 Dec 2018. https://www.who.int/gho/ncd/risk_factors/blood_pressure_prevalence/en/. Accessed: 16 Jan 2019

13. HBP: www.heart.org. en/health-topics/high-blood-pressure. Accessed 18 Apr 2017

14. Reshamwala, A.: Improving efficiency of apriori algorithms for sequential pattern mining. Bonfring Int. J. Data Min. 4(1), 01–06 (2014)

15. Gupta, V., Logerfo, J.P., Raingsey, P.P., Fitzpatrick, A.L.: The prevalence and associated factors for prehypertension and hypertension in Cambodia. Heart Asia 5(1), 253–258 (2013)

16. Alonso, Y.: The biopsychosocial model in medical research: the evolution of the health concept over the last two decades. Patient Educ. Couns. 53(2), 239–244 (2004)

17. Viceconti, M., Kohl, P.: The virtual physiological human: computer simulation for integrative biomedicine I. Philos. Trans. Royal Soc. A: Math., Phys. Eng. Sci. 368(1920), 2591–2594 (2010)

18. Montani, J.-P., Vliet, B.N.V.: Understanding the contribution of Guytonsfrequent circulatory model to long-term control of arterial pressure. Exp. Physiol. 94(4), 382–388 (2009)

19. S. Dalvand, et al.: An examination of factors effecting systolic blood pressure, diastolic blood pressure, and total cholesterol simultaneously using mixed responses model. Iranian Red Crescent Med. J. 19(10) (2016)

20. Narayan, S., Gobal, J.: Optimal decision tree fuzzy rule-based classifier for heart disease prediction using improved cuckoo search algorithm. Int. J. Bus. Intell. Data Min. 15(4), 408 (2019)

21. Halls Dally, J.F.: Fundamental physiological and physical factors in blood pressure. In: High Blood Pressure, pp. 70–80. Elsevier (2013)

22. Salt and blood pressure: the concept of salt sensitivity. In: Burnier, M. (eds.) Sodium in Health and Disease, pp. 285–310, CRC Press (2007)

23. Floras, J.S., Hassan, M.O., Jones, J.V., Osikowska, B.A., Sever, P.S., Sleight, P.: Factors influencing blood pressure and heart rate variability in hypertensive humans. Hypertension 11(3), 273–281 (1988)

24. Yadav, D.: Blood coagulation algorithm: a novel bio-inspired meta-heuristic algorithm for global optimization. Mathematics 9(23), 3011 (2021)

25. Pandurangi, B., Bhat, C., Patil, M.: Comparison of bio-inspired and transform based encryption algorithms for satellite images. In: 2018 International Conference on Electrical, Electronics, Communication, Computer, and Optimization Techniques (ICEECCOT), pp. 1412-1417, Msyuru, India (2018)

26. Uniyal, N., Pant, S., Kumar, A., Pant, P.: Nature-inspired metaheuristic algorithms for optimization. In: Meta-heuristic Optimization Techniques, pp. 1–10 (2022)

27. Krishnanand, K.R., Nayak, S.K., Panigrahi, B.K., Rout, P.K: Comparative study of five bio-inspired evolutionary optimization techniques. In: 2009 World Congress on Nature & Biologically Inspired Computing (NaBIC) (2009)

28. Yang, X.-S., Chien, S.F., Ting, T.O.: Bio-inspired computation and optimization. In: Bio-Inspired Computation in Telecommunications, pp. 1–21 (2015)

29. Fong, S.: Opportunities and challenges of integrating bio-inspired optimization and data mining algorithms. In: Yang, X.-S., Cui, Z., Xiao, R., Hossein Gandomi, A., Karamanoglu, M. (eds.) Swarm Intelligence and Bio-Inspired Computation, pp. 385–402. Elsevier, Oxford (2013)
30. Anger Test – Psychologist World. https://www.psychologistworld.com/stress/anger-test
31. Sukenda, Wahyu, A.P., Sunjana: Medicine product recommendation system using apriori algorithm and Fp-growth algorithm. Int. J. Psychosoc. Rehabil.**24**(02), 3208–3211 (2020)
32. Muhajir, M., Kesumawati, A., Mulyadi, S.: Apriori algorithm for frequent pattern mining for public librariesin united states. In: Proceedings of the International Conference on Mathematics and Islam (2018)
33. Singh, N., Singh, P.: Rule based approach for prediction of chronic kidney disease: a comparative study. Biomed. Pharmacol. J. **10**(02), 867–874 (2017)
34. Berrar: Bayes' Theorem and Naive Bayes Classifier. In: Encyclopedia of Bioinformatics and Computational Biology, pp. 403–412 (2019)
35. Matloff, N.: Regression and classification in big data. In: Statistical Regression and Classification, pp. 431–450 (2017)
36. Jeyasheela, Y., Jinny, S.V.: Reliable disease prediction system based on association rulemining and Pyramid Data Structure (2021)
37. Christopher, J.: The science of rule-based classifiers. In: 2019 9th International Conference on Cloud Computing, Data Science & Engineering (Confluence) (2019)
38. Liu, J., Zhang, Y., Zhao, Q.: Adaptive vibe algorithm based on pearson correlation coefficient. In: 2019 Chinese Automation Congress (CAC) (2019)
39. Wu, X., Zeng, Y.: Using apriori algorithm on students' performance data for Association Rules Mining. In: Proceedings of the 2nd International Seminar on Education Research and Social Science (ISERSS 2019) (2019)
40. Obthong, M., Tantisantiwong, N., Jeamwatthanachai, W., Wills, G.: A survey on machine learning for stock price prediction: algorithms and techniques. In: Proceedings of the 2nd International Conference on Finance, Economics, Management and IT Business (2020)

Implementing Machine Vision Process to Analyze Echocardiography for Heart Health Monitoring

Kishan Kesari Gupta[1], Abhinav Anil[2(✉)], and Parag Ravikant Kaveri[3]

[1] TechVerito Software Solution LLP, Pune, India
[2] Senquire Analytics Pvt. Ltd., Pune, India
abhinav.anil2206@gmail.com
[3] Symbiosis Institute of Computer Studies and Research, Symbiosis International Deemed University, Pune, India

Abstract. Machine vision analysis of echocardiography images (echo) has vital recent advances. Echocardiography images are ultrasound scans that present the cardiac structure and function that becomes helpful in a significant measure of eight standard echo views, namely A2C, A3C, A4C, A5C, PLAX, PSAA, PSAP, PASM of the Cardiac cycle, and also identifies the disorders. In this research, we introduce a vision model for echo analysis with a deep convolutional neural network protected by the U-Net, trained to phase the echoes, and extract information of the right ventricle, left atrium, aorta, septum, and outer internal organ wall. The data includes image bundles; input to the CNN model predicts the cardiac structure by a softmax function into different categories, which becomes an input to a U-Net architecture that encodes and decodes the layers and foretells the functioning of the heart through segmentation. In summary, the research covers designed architecture that presents state-of-the-art for investigating echocardiography information with its benefits and drawbacks continued by future work.

Keywords: Machine vision · Echocardiography · Image annotation · Segmentation · CNN · VGG16 · U-Net · Softmax

1 Introduction

Machine vision deals with object detection and motion recognition that extracts features from digital images and videos and uses an algorithm to learn and analyze similar processes that transpire in biological vision [1]. Machine vision needs to join healthcare for analysis and to give an accurate measurement. There is a possibility to enhance the system to see precise results through the motion of a cardiac structure that provides vast information and becomes straightforward to recognize by natural eyes [6]. Machine vision analysis of echocardiography (echo) images performs a significant role in identifying indications of heart working disorder by analyzing the cardiac structure and functional malformations and evaluating those patients. Error-free echo measurements can be disrupted by a lack of consistency for interpretation and quality of the images

© The Author(s), under exclusive license to Springer Nature Switzerland AG 2023
I. Woungang et al. (Eds.): ANTIC 2022, CCIS 1798, pp. 189–204, 2023.
https://doi.org/10.1007/978-3-031-28183-9_13

[7]. Consequently, there is a health care need for a standard system of echo measures to give error-free results. Nowadays, vision-based applications permit the classification of imaging features with the self-learning ability of deep learning models and productive computing power [16].

An echocardiography measurement is a neat path for the practice of deep learning with a segmentation process that begins with splitting an image into sections describing eight view areas of the moving heart that discern from any viewpoint as regions signify similarities in terms of specific picked features [23]. Those regions are a set of pixels. The segment is regularly taken as standard for uniformity of color, texture, and gray level areas that are extensively utilized in image processing to evaluate cardiac structure and function. Echocardiography uses a screening modality for good health, and patients with no symptoms properly diagnose and manipulate patients with complicated heart disorders. Echocardiography is essential and satisfactory to diagnose many heart disorders, and it's relevant for phenotyping, and there is variation in the human understanding of images that could affect health care [28]. Deep learning with segmentation is definite, and even the development of a novel system for precise echocardiographic measurement is heavily dependent on operator competence for a secure echocardiographic analysis procedure. Diagnostic flaws are a primary unsolved puzzle [40].

Moreover, not only do heart specialists vary from one another in image understanding. But the same viewer may get to several judgments when an analysis recurs, and manual interpretation workload in healthcare may drive to this fault and many heart specialists need correct interpretation in this area. Hence, a system needs to point out the heart working disorder from echocardiography images with high accuracy. A need for the online application provides functionality to upload the patient echocardiography image will use for testing with the echo model running behind the application and return the result by highlighting the heart working disorder using the segmentation approach and with a disorder percentage in a graph.

2 Literature Review

From the excerpt of the investigation, Erik Andreas, Andreas Ostvik, presented a method for image sequence in echocardiography consisting of 4 necessary components. A components pipeline uses U-Net architecture commences with cardiac view classification of muscle tissue, left ventricle length semantic partitioning measurement and ventricular adjustment, estimates regional motion, fusion measurement. A dense tissue movement prophesied a stack U-Net framework with images wrapping for mid-flow, developed to tackle variable shifts [20]. The resulting motion and segmentation calculations were welded in a Kalman filter and utilized as a source to estimate global longitudinal strain [37]. Sarvani Gajjala, Pulkit Agarwal, et al. propose a method to analyze pipelines concerning echocardiogram (echo) study using the vision-based technique. A convolutional neural network data pipeline uses image segmentation, tracing particles to calculate longitudinal strain, interpretation of a cardiac cycle, volumes of each chamber and ventricular mass, and constructing an algorithm for extracting cardiac amyloidosis and hypertrophic cardiomyopathy [27]. Riyanto Sigit, Eva Rochmawati proposed a model to track and detect the edge of the cardiac cavity in each frame in the video. They describe the first process as eliminating noise using a median filter. The second process is to determine the edge of a cardiac cavity in image frames using B-Spline. And the closing process is to detect and track the edges in the image frame into an echocardiography video. After extracting outcomes, the researcher optimized the processes and observed the error between the processes is less than 11 percent, and the cardiac activity area is 0.18 standard deviation [32].

Rama Ramaraj, Maxime Taron propose a shape-based variational model for segmentation for ultrasonic images. A process entails modeling, extraction of features, coarse segmentation, and edge detection. We ponder two distinct model locations, one is diastolic, and another is a systolic state. We improve the ordinary shape and the modes of inequalities for every model by (PCA) Principal Component Analysis applying a set of recorded training examples. Extraction of significant features of the valve plane, ventricular walls are practiced to start the time segmentation step [41].

Ali Madani, Rima Arnaout prepared a convolutional neural network to identify fifteen distinct echocardiographic panoramas, twelve b-mode, three continuous-wave & pulsed-wave Doppler, and m-mode records use in validation and training kit of 200,000, test kit of 20,000 pictures. Clustering breakdowns revealed that the neural channels could classify different input images according to a panorama. To prepare specimens per echocardiogram from several patients, and training, validation, and test kits do not overlap through study. Training and test kit of images cover a series of echocardiographic differences with patient implications. The comprehensive health care repository includes inconsistencies in the sector width, chroma map, diastole/systole, image quality, color doppler, strain, and left ventricle [21]. Ahmed I. Shahin, Sultan Almotairi, introduced a deep learning classification model to classify different echocardiography scenes and ferret out their physiological section. And use the model to classify three cardio regions. Moreover, extract novel ephemeral descriptors based on the neutrosophic collections field. And connect spatial and neutrosophic ephemeral descriptors. Though extract characteristics by applying the pre-trained channels as characteristics extractors. After characteristic extraction, a Long Short Term Memory classifier was employed to classify particular echoes (images) into eight cardio scenes [5]. Florian Espinosa, Sarah Leclerc, proposes the CAMUS dataset, the most comprehensively openly obtainable and annotated echocardiographic estimation. And assess how encoder and decoder convolutional neural networks work with two-dimensional echocardiographic images. It includes two-dimensional echocardiographic image series with 2 & 4-chamber scenes from five hundred patients. The five hundred patient's dataset is split into ten sections to complete the cross-validation process and see results obtained from deep learning U-Net models. Every part contains fifty patients with equal allocation in terms of picture quality. The nine sections (450 patients) apply for training the model. And one section (50 patients) practice for the test set [17].

Kusunose Kenya proposed a step-by-step process from image pre-processing to detect abnormalities in echocardiography. A proposed work starts from screening out the poor-quality picture since quality is bound to accuracy. After screening, the detection of appropriate views is categorized into different cardiac structures. Once the image quality is considered and found the accurate viewpoints then utilizes a deep learning technique for estimating ejection fraction. From the variety of patients with low ejection fraction, balance in the Area under curve (AUCs) from per model with the immense AUC base on moderate five viewpoints [10]. Elisabeth S. Lane et al. proposed a convolutional neural network for automatic identifying fourteen distinct anatomical echo viewpoints in a repository of 8732 videos received from 374 heart disease sufferers. A distinct method is used to create a neural network for immediate premise while preserving accurateness. The effect of picture resolution, quality, training set size, echo view categories on the effectiveness of model is analyzed. In disparity to more in-depth categorization, the suggested models had a remarkably low no. of train arguments, achieved comparative classification, real-time execution with inference time for each image [3]. Wei Guo, Dianmin Sun proposed the classification subnetwork to categorize the apical view of two, three, four chambers images and utilize the regression subnetworks to ferret out the left ventricle concomitantly. It shows not just the location of the left ventricle on the testing image. But also show the image viewpoint class that simplifies the diagnosis. The technique used is MIOU (Mean Intersection Over Union) as a sign to estimate the performance of the left ventricle ferret out and the accurateness as a sign to calculate the impact of classification on the three distinct views. Analysis indicates that both classification and ferret-out effects are considerable [11].

Bjoern Menze, Hongwei Li presented a generalized segmentation structure for image segmentation in that multi-disease, multi-vendor, multi-center data repositories are concerned. A productive adversary network with an attendant loss stood to translate the images from origin domains to a mark domain, thus generating a good-quality artificial cardiac structure and enlarging the training data. An accumulation of information augmentation processes is to emulate real-world changeover to promote the segmentation performance for unrecognized domains. We reached an intermediate Dice score of 90.3% for the LV, 86.5% for the RV, and 85.9% for the myocardium on the hidden validation put across four agents. Hence indicates that the field changes in heterogeneous cardiac imaging repository can be brought down by two factors (good-quality artificial data by knowing the underlying mark domain allocation and piled image processing procedures for data enlargement) [12]. Son Kuswadi, Calvin Alfa Roji presented the method to examine the heart rate motion and automatic measure cavity area. The research proposes an improved technique for cardiac segmentation employing an MHBF (Median High Boost Filter) to decrease noise and enrich the light intensity weight of picture quality, pursued by the use of optical flow and active shape model. The segmentation of the heart motion rate and measuring cavity area for interpreting the patient heart state with precision [19].

Patrick Hunziker, Peter Buser proposed a motion mapping multiscale technique based on mathematical image processing. It utilizes echocardiographic data like the human visual technique. It permits Doppler and independent border perseverance of deformation and action in echocardiograms at random zones. And document the proper measures in artificial echocardiograms and phantom experimentations. Exploratory analyses indicated its use in a sequence of complex moves that formed irregular septal movement and estimation of myocardial twisting. The clinical relevance in a consecutive sequence of echocardiograms in which acceptable feasibility, suitable correlation are saved [42].

After reading the literature review, examine the different methods & techniques implemented by researchers so far in the field of echocardiography. We decided to use the VGG16 architecture and our logic to build an algorithm that split the bundle of images into eight categories. Hence images of different classes form into training and test set input to U-Net architecture.

3 Analysis

Here, we have 842 echocardiography videos with a time duration of one or two minutes of the heart functioning, collected from the Mc Graw Hills repository. These 842 videos are split into 660000 images through OpenCV technique of saving video frames. These six lakhs sixty thousand images again split onto a training kit of 528000 images and a testing kit of 132000 images that became an input to the VGG16 arch model. The VGG16 arch model is to classify significant features based on an appropriate image that is dependent on the confidence value [15, 22]. In preprocessing steps, eight tags are provided based on mask creation, namely A2C, A3C, A4C, A5C, PLAX, PSAA, PSAP, and PASM. In the training and testing process, images turned into a NumPy array shape of (224 × 224 × 3). In the below architecture, the layers of the CNN contain the activation function ReLU for the kernel size of 4. The max-pooling layer is placed after every three CNN + ReLU to preserve significant features that transfer to the next set of layers. After information gathering in the next layer, a fully connected layer is applied and supports the layer connections [29]. At last, the softmax function converts the echoes into different categories of images (Fig. 1).

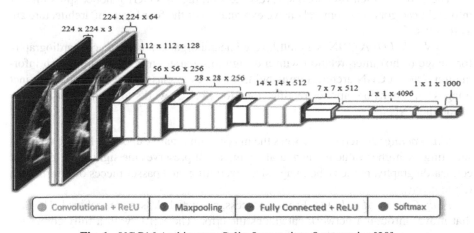

Fig. 1. VGG16 Architecture Splits Images into 8 categories [30]

A pseudocode and comprehensive explanation of the four layers of architecture are as follows:

Training Process. INPUT: labeled training data as $\tilde{X} = \{X^{(1)}, X^{(2)}, \ldots X^{(k)}\}$, N is the class group.

CNN $\leftarrow \tilde{X}$; % the raw training data are sent into CNN to pull out feature vectors
$\tilde{F} = \{F^{(1)}, F^{(2)}, \ldots\ldots F^{(k)}\}$; % the feature vectors are connected into high-dimensional space to be % cover class by class.

for i 1 to N do.

$D^{(i)} \leftarrow F^{(i)}$; % Calculate the pixel values for features in class i

$\{T_{i1}, T_{i2}\} \leftarrow$ arg min($D^{(i)}$); % find the likelihood pixel value from $D^{(i)}$, marked as T_{i1}, and T_{i2}

$F^{(i)} = F^{(i)} - \{T_{i1}, T_{i2}\}$; % of dropout from layer

$(T_{i3}, T_{i4}) \leftarrow$; ; % FindPtoN($F^{(i)}$, $\{T_{i1}, T_{i2}\}$); % Find is a function used to find the minimum distance sum % from $F^{(i)}$ to T_{i1} and T_{i2}

$\theta_1 \leftarrow \{T_{i1}, T_{i2}, T_{i3}, T_{i4}\}$% $T_{i1}, T_{i2}, T_{i3}, T_{i4}$ constitute the first bounding box θ_1.

$F^{(i)} = F^{(i)} - \{T_{i1}, T_{i2}, T_{i3}, T_{i4}\}$;

$j = 1$;

while $F^{(i)} \neq \emptyset$ % repeat the steps above until $F^{(i)}$ is empty

$\theta_{j+1} \leftarrow$ FindPtoN($F^{(i)}$, θ_j);

$j = j + 1$;

end

OUTPUT: $T = \{T_1, T_2, \ldots T_k\}$; % set of all classes.

Classification Process. INPUT: $\hat{x}$ is an image to be classified

$\hat{f} \leftarrow$ CNN $\leftarrow \hat{x}$;

$\rho_i = \min^{Mj}_{j=1} \rho_{ij}$, i = 1, 2, ..., N; % ρ_{ij} is the pixel distance between $\hat{f}$ and the coverage of neuron j in class i

OUTPUT: Class $= \hat{x}$ belongs to the targeted class based on the training equation.

The above written pseudocode revels the working of VGG16 model splits images into eight category and comprehensive explanation of the four layers of architecture are as follows:

CNN + ReLU: A CNN is a multilayered neural organism used in echocardiography for image (echo) interpretation with a design to separate intricate highlights in information. Once a CNN architecture is built, it utilizes to classify the essence of distinct images. In expansion, applies rectifier function (ReLU) works to extend non-linearity inside the CNN.

Max Pooling: A step is to process the max-pooling matrix upon the feature map and selecting the higher value in the neural net matrix. It preserves the significant feature of echocardiography, reduces the image size, overfitting, and passes pieces of information to the layers.

Fully Connected + ReLU: From a process, predicted classes are archived. The data that moves through a network calculates the error. The ReLU with a fully connected layer helps to transfer significant features to the output layer.

Softmax: A final process contains an activation function that classifies in binary form shows the probability of each class.

According to the above architecture and their function, convert the echocardiography image dataset into eight different categories with its predicted accuracy value shown below in the pictures [26] (Fig. 2).

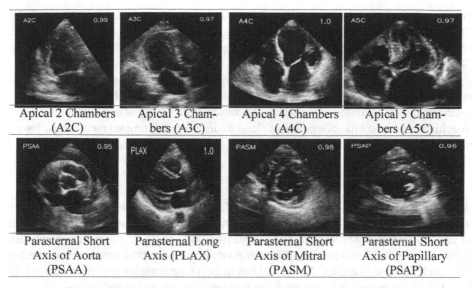

Apical 2 Chambers (A2C)	Apical 3 Chambers (A3C)	Apical 4 Chambers (A4C)	Apical 5 Chambers (A5C)
Parasternal Short Axis of Aorta (PSAA)	Parasternal Long Axis (PLAX)	Parasternal Short Axis of Mitral (PASM)	Parasternal Short Axis of Papillary (PSAP)

Fig. 2. Eight different categories of echocardiography images.

The preceding architecture splits 660000 images (echoes) into eight different categories. From these eight different categories of images considering only those images having confidence value greater than 0.75 for segmentation processing in further steps. There are 375,808 images of eight categories process for segmentation to know the heart working disorder. The training and test sets details are given below in a Table 1.

Table 1. Image count of eight classes.

	A2C	A3C	A4C	A5C	PLAX	PSAA	PSAP	PASM
Training	26439	11257	109371	5502	89790	13900	29079	15308
Testing	6610	2814	27343	1376	22447	3475	7270	3827
Total	33049	14071	136714	6878	112237	17375	36349	19135

4 Proposed Work

The proposed work commences with the annotation of training images become input to U-Net Architecture. After the complete running of the U-Net model, API bundle the U-Net model, VGG-16, and annotation results into JSON format and return to the web application [33]. Here, the annotation process commences with annotating training images listed above in a table. Annotation in machine learning is a means of marking the information on pictures. The pictures may additionally incorporate echocardiography, ECG, any parts to make it recognizable for machines [8]. Annotations are of various kinds applied to teach machines about the presence of distinct entities within the world. Therefore, annotating eight categories of images using point polygon, creating a mask, and saving those mask categories is sent as input to the U-Net architecture for training [9, 38, 39].

In order to create a mask, which is essentially a binary image made up of zero or nonzero values, the U-Net architecture is used. This procedure helps us to reach the necessary outcome for the segmentation operation. With the aid of annotated images and matching mask, the images significant element discovered during segmentation allowed us to use them to locate the points of heart working abnormalities.

4.1 U-Net Model Architecture

An architecture design seems a "U" form explains a U-Net model. The U-Net structure includes three parts: contraction, bottleneck, and expansion. A contraction part is a form of various contraction blocks. Each block exerts input to two 3 × 3 convolution network layers follows 2 × 2 max pooling. The kernels numbers & function maps became double after each block so that the U-Net model can interpret the complex structures adequately [13, 35]. The bottom-most layer mediates between the contraction and extension layer. It makes use of a couple of 3 × 3 CNN layers examined by a 2 × 2 up convolution network layer. The Echocardiography UNet model is essential as it can locate and differentiate borders by classifying each pixel, then the input and output are of identical size [4, 14] (Fig. 3).

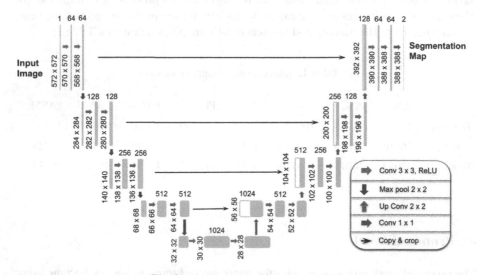

Fig. 3. U-net model architecture [35].

The U-Net architecture explains how the downsampling and upsampling processes perform a significant role in echocardiography as follows.

Downsampling: Every process forms a couple of layers, and the number of channels switched from 1 to 64 as a convolutional process will enhance the depth of an image.

The max-pooling in the first layer decreases the dimension of the image and obtains high pixel information. This process of decoding is continuing longer than three-time. And the channel switches in each layer like $64 \Rightarrow 128$, $128 \Rightarrow 256$, and so forth as per the number of layers is considered [18]. The formula uses to train the model for echocardiography.

$$\text{Convolutional\_layer1} \Rightarrow \text{Convolutional\_layer2} \Rightarrow \text{Max} - \text{pooling} \Rightarrow \text{dropout(optional)}$$

In echocardiography, we have three layers, and it is decoding each pixel in the Conv2D from 1–64 to 512. The max-pooling layers downsize the image in taking into consideration the strides.

Upsampling: Conv2DTranspose is the technique that is required for the expansion of the image. It applies padding on the original image following the convolutional procedure. The image passed from Conv2D becomes upsized and is concatenated with similar pictures from the contracting path. It's necessary to merge the information with the previous layer to get precise prophecy information [36]. The formula is used as follows:

$$\text{Conv2D\_Transpose} \Rightarrow \text{Concatenate} \Rightarrow \text{ConvLayer\_1} \Rightarrow \text{ConvLayer\_2}$$

The last layer is the convolutional layer by a filter size of 1×1, and there is no dense layer.

4.2   Web Application System Architecture

The system architecture of web apps includes frontend service (User Interaction), Backend Service (APIs), a running model instance of VGG16 & the U-Net model. A journey starts when the user uploads the raw echo images by interacting with to UI form, necessary details sent through post request to backend service [25]. The backend service validates the echo image from the running instance of the VGG16 model and returns the image with its category name become input to the running instance of the U-Net model. The model returns a segmentation map results to backend service, combines the VGG16, annotation, segmentation results in JSON format returned to frontend service for visualization [24, 31, 34].

Here represents the system architecture and pseudocode of web applications as discussed in the above lines (Fig. 4).

The below pseudocode shows the processes that start executing when the user uploads the echocardiography image and gets the resulting image.

Frontend Service:
echoImage = Read the uploaded echocardiography image from user.

Call asynchronous function getEchoResults() and passing echoImage object as parameter
 function getEchoResult (echoImage)
  Post request to API and sending echoImage parameter in body.
  if post request status is success then

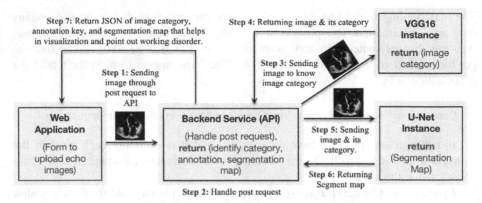

Fig. 4. Web Application System Architecture represents image flow.

Assign image category, segmentation, annotation value to variables.
Compute data to draw line graph to showcase heart disorder percentage.
Assign value to line graph variable
Render html & css code to showcase the transformed image to user.

Backend Service:
Handle post request.

Call function to permit parameters received from frontend service.

After permit is success then call process_echo function and pass image as parameter.

function process_echo (image)

image_category = calling function vgg16_instance and passing image as parameter.

annotation_key_numbers = calling a function have logic of image annotation.

segmentation_result = calling function unet_instance and passing image as parameter.

process_result = Combining the image_category, annotation_key, segmentation_result.

Converting process_result into JSON format.

return process_result

function vgg16_instance (image)

image_type = process and validate the image from running instance of VGG16 model.

return image_type

function unet_instance (image)

segmentation_map = process and passing image to running instance of unet model.

return segmentation_map

The above web application system architecture and pseudocode represents the user journey from uploading raw echocardiography pictures to get the segmented results, pointing out the heart working disorder, and showing the disorder percentage with a line graph.

5   Result and Discussion

According to the segmentation in the proposed work, the sensitivity of the heart by echocardiography (echo) images is envisioned and shows working disorder. The graph represents the heart malfunctioning percentage used for the instance level of each segmented mask score computation. The segmentation outcome represents a malfunctioning percentage higher than 4 percent becomes a severe problem. Here the mask rates are used for detection and sorted in descending outlier score order.

An outlier that appears in classified images classes is inaccurate for some pixels. In echocardiography, eight categories of images have some heart working disorder. An echocardiography-trained model validates normal heart functioning with malfunctioning and segmenting heart diseases on an image, treating them as outliers to exhibit the percentage value of eight parts of heart malfunctioning [2].

In graphs, all eights parts A2C, A3C, A4C, A5C, PLAX, PSAA, PSAP, PASM, reveals Heart Disordering Rate on Y-axis explains the percentage of the segmented region of that relative part of the echocardiography image. And On X-axis explains the mask of segmented region values defines the error rate in that particular heart region.

The visualization helps in interpreting the heart disorder in each segmented region that assists healthcare to know the actual root cause and provide correct treatments (Figs. 5, 6, 7, 8, 9, 10, 11 and 12).

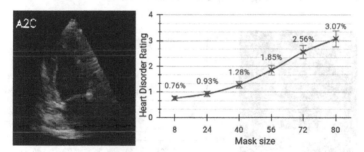

Fig. 5. Apical 2 chambers (A2C)

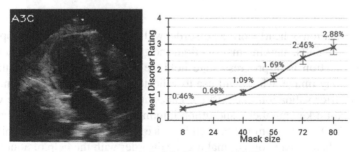

Fig. 6. Apical 3 chambers (A3C)

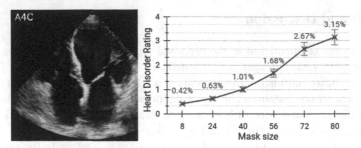

Fig. 7. Apical 4 chambers (A4C)

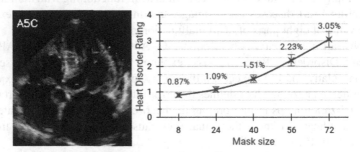

Fig. 8. Apical 5 chambers (A5C)

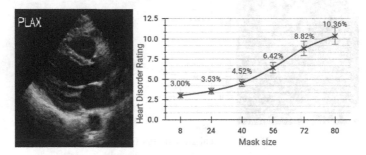

Fig. 9. Parasternal long axis (PLAX)

The visualization of heart working disorder will be visible through web applications. The segmented results, marking malfunction, and graph represents the disorder percentage. The application is in-progress state hold the functionality to upload the patient echocardiography image, which will use to validate with the deep learning model running behind. After validation, the API combines model data and returns the validation results, annotation key numbers, and graph information in JSON format. The application receives JSON data from the backend service containing the deep learning model and creates the heart image on UI, making the disorder with the help of annotation key numbers, and presenting the graph showing disorder percentage. This application will help the user and healthcare to know the working disorder point and avoid the sundry interpretation.

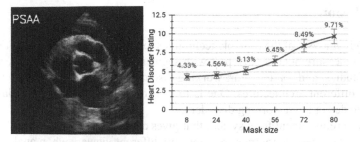

Fig. 10. Parasternal short axis of arota (PSAA)

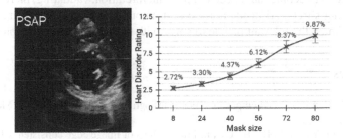

Fig. 11. Parasternal short axis of papillary (PSAP)

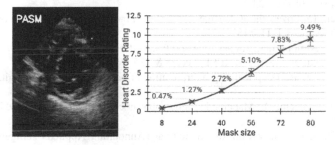

Fig. 12. Parasternal short axis of mitral (PASM)

6 Future Work

Nowadays, AI has evolved to flaws interpretation, will be visible to end-user only when the AI model is connected to a web application through API and showcase its result. The application is in a development state consisting of form to upload the image, backend service (API), and running instance of VGG16 & U-Net model that will perform their task and return the result.

In subsequent work, we will research heart wall motion and thickness abnormalities based on shape and size. Additionally, We'll put forth an approach that improves the accuracy of identifying the root of heart working disorders.

The future development of web applications will make it easier to eliminate discrepancies amongst cardiac specialists, and all specialists will offer the same opinion for image understanding and diagnose patients effectively.

7 Conclusion

A meticulous analysis of the possible techniques for echocardiography category classification and measurement of each part with segmentation, computerized interpretation of echoes studies, and foretell heart working disorders, shown in this paper. The paper shows two different architectures. One is to categorize echoes in distinct classes, and another is to detect heart working disorders.

There is a requirement for a system that gives correct interpretation results to heart specialists and eludes sundry interpretations by different viewers when analysis recurs. An upcoming system provides consistent results for numbers of analysis reappears.

Therefore, AI becomes advanced to flaws interpretation, validating, increasing security, and giving surety. AI needs a close-knit among healthcare clinics and computer scientists to know the relevant puzzle to solve with the most suitable approach.

References

1. Akkus, Z., Kane, G.C.: AI empowered echocardiography interpretation. Clin. Med. J. **10**(7), 1391 (2021)
2. Zhu, M., Hu, Y., Yu, J., He, B., Liu, J.: Find outliers of image edge consistency by weighted local linear regression with equality constraints. Sensors **21**, 2563 (2021)
3. Azarmehr, N., et al.: Neural architecture search of echocardiography view classifiers. J. Med. Imaging **8**(3), 034002 (2021)
4. Shi, J., et al.: Improvement of damage segmentation based on pixel-level data balance using VGG-Unet. Appl. Sci. **11**, 518 (2021)
5. Shahin, A.I., Almotairi, S.: An accurate and fast cardio-views classification system based on fused deep features and LSTM. IEEE Access **8**, 135184–135194 (2020)
6. Ghorbani, A., et al.: Deep learning interpretation of echocardiograms. J. Digit. Med. **3**, 10 (2020)
7. Sabeetha, K., Saleem, M.: Machine learning and echocardiogram. J. Crit. Rev. **7**(15), 5879–5882 (2020)
8. Guo, W., Chen, Y.: A Survey on Automatic Image Annotation. Applied Intelligence, Springer (2020)
9. Bouchakwa, M., Ayadi, Y., Amous, I.: A review on visual content-based and users' tags-based image annotation: methods and techniques. Multimed. Tools Appl. **79**(29–30), 21679–21741 (2020)
10. Kusunose, K.: Steps to use artificial intelligence in echocardiography. J. Echocardiogr. **19**, 21–27 (2021)
11. Huang, C., et al.: Deep RetinaNet for dynamic LV detection in multi-view echocardiography classification. Hindawi J. **2020**, 7025403 (2020)
12. Menze, B., Li, H.: Generaliseable cardiac structure segmentation via attentional & stacked image adaptation. In: IWSACMH, LNCS, vol. 12592. Springer, Cham (2020). https://doi.org/10.1007/978-3-030-68107-4_30
13. Singh, V., Chandra, V., Sarkar, P.G.: A survey on role of DL in two dimensional transthoracic echocardiography. Int. J. Sci. Technol. Res. **9**, 7060–7065 (2020)
14. Kurt, D., Demetris, M., Bashford-Rogers, T.: Spectrally Consistent U-Net for High Fidelity Image Transformations. Cornell University (2020)

15. Rawat, J., Logofătu, D., Chiramel, S.: Factors affecting accuracy of convolutional neural network using VGG-16. In: Iliadis, L., Angelov, P.P., Jayne, C., Pimenidis, E. (eds.) EANN 2020. PINNS, vol. 2, pp. 251–260. Springer, Cham (2020). https://doi.org/10.1007/978-3-030-48791-1_19

16. Takashi, A., Kenya, K., Akihiro, H.: Utilization of AI in echocardiography. Circ. J. **83**, 1623–1629 (2019)

17. Leclerc, S.: DL for segmentation using open large scale dataset in 2Dimension echocardiography. Trans. Med. Imaging IEEE **38**, 2198–2210 (2019)

18. Dumitrescu, D., Boiangiu, C.-A.: A study of image upsampling and downsampling filters. Computers **8**, 30 (2019)

19. Sigit, R., Roji, C., Harsono, T., Kuswadi, S.: Improved echocardiography segmentation using active shape model & optical flow. TELKOMNIKA (Telecommun. Comput. Electron. Control) **17**, 809 (2019)

20. Erik, A., Andreas, O.: Automatic myocardial strain imaging in echocardiography using deep learning. In: International Workshop on Deep Learning in Medical Image Analysis (2018)

21. Madani, A., Arnaout, R., Mofrad, M., Arnaout, R.: Fast and accurate view classification of echocardiograms using deep learning. NPJ. Digit. Med. **1**, 6 (2018)

22. Jiang, H., Daigle, H., Tian, X.: Feature detection for digital images using ML algorithms & image processing. In: Unconventional Resource Technology Conference (2018)

23. Alsharqi, M., et al.: Artificial intelligence and echocardiography. Echo Res Pract. **5**(4), R115–R125 (2018)

24. Breje, A.-R., Gyorodi, R., Győrödi, C., Zmaranda, D., Pecherle, G.: Comparative study of data sending methods for XML and JSON models. Int. J. Adv. Comput. Sci. Appl. **9**, 198–204 (2018)

25. Angelini G.: Current practices in web application programming interface documentation. Eur, Acad. Colloquium (2018)

26. Qassim, H., Verma, A., Feinzimer, D.: Compressed residual-VGG16 CNN model for big data places image recognition. In: 2018 IEEE 8th Annual Computing and Communication Workshop and Conference (CCWC), pp. 169–175. Las Vegas, NV, USA (2018)

27. Zhang, J.: A CV Process for Automated Determination of Cardiac Structure and Function & Disease Detection by 2D Echocardiography. Cornell University (2017)

28. Gao, X., Li, W., Loomes, M., Wang, L.: A fused DL architecture for viewpoint classification of echocardiography. Inform. Fusion **36**, 103–113 (2017)

29. Lu, J., Ma, W.: An Equivalence of Fully Connected Layer and Convolutional Layer. Cornell University (2017)

30. Yang, C.K., Sugata, T.L.I.: Leaf recognition with deep CNN. Mater. Sci. Eng. IOP J. **273**, 012004 (2017)

31. de Jong, W.A., Harris, C.J., Hanwell, M.D.: RESTful web APIs, JSON, NWCHEM & the modern web application. J. Cheminform. **9**, 55 (2017)

32. Sigit, R., Rochmawati, E.: Segmentation echocardiography video using B-Spline and optical flow. In: 2016 International Conference on Knowledge Creation and Intelligent Computing (KCIC), pp. 226–231. Manado, Indonesia (2016)

33. Tramèr, F., Zhang, F., Juels, A., Reiter, M.K., Ristenpart, T.: Stealing ML model via prediction APIs. In: Usenix Security Symposium (2016)

34. Izquierdo, J.L.C., Cabot, J.: Visualizing the schema lurking behind JSON document. Knowl. Based Syst. **103**, 52–55 (2016)

35. Ronneberger, O., Fischer, P., Brox, T.: U-Net: convolutional networks for biomedical image segmentation. In: Navab, N., Hornegger, J., Wells, W.M., Frangi, A.F. (eds.) MICCAI 2015. LNCS, vol. 9351, pp. 234–241. Springer, Cham (2015). https://doi.org/10.1007/978-3-319-24574-4_28

36. Zhao, Y., Wang, R., Wang, W., Gao, W.: High resolution local structure-constrained image upsampling. IEEE Trans. Image Process. **24**(11), 4394–4407 (2015)
37. Snare, S.R., Torp, H., Orderud, F., Haugen, B.O.: Real-time scan assistant for echocardiography. IEEE Trans. Ultrason. Ferroelectr. Freq. Control. **59**(3), 583–589 (2012)
38. Yuen, J., Torralba, A.: Online Image Annotation & Application. MIT Open Access, IEEE Xplore (2010)
39. Russell, B.C., Torralba, A., Murphy, K.P., Freeman, W.T.: A database and web-based tool for image annotation. Int. J. Comput. Vis. **77**, 157–173 (2008)
40. Catherine, M.O.: The Practice of Clinical Echocardiography Book. Echocardiography Laboratory, University of Washington (2007)
41. Paragios, N., Jolly, M.-P., Taron, M., Ramaraj, R.: Active shape models and segmentation of the left ventricle in echocardiography. In: Kimmel, R., Sochen, N.A., Weickert, J. (eds.) Scale-Space 2005. LNCS, vol. 3459, pp. 131–142. Springer, Heidelberg (2005). https://doi.org/10.1007/11408031_12
42. Hunziker, P., Buser. P.: MMM: a novel CV technique for quantitative objective echocardiographic MM independent of Doppler. J. Circ. **29**, 926–934 (2004)

Social Media Bot Detection Using Machine Learning Approach

Prathamesh Bhongale[✉], Om Sali, and Shraddha Mehetre

Computer Engineering, Sanjivani College of Engineering, Kopargaon 423601,
Maharashtra, India
bhongaleprathamesh@gmail.com

Abstract. Nowadays, social media platforms are thronged with social bots spreading misinformation. Twitter has become the hotspot for social bots. These bots are either automated or semi-automated, spreading misinformation purposefully or not purposefully is influencing society's perspective on different aspects of life. This tremendous increase in social bots has aroused huge interest in researchers. In this paper, we have proposed a social bot detection model using Random Forest Classifier, we also used Extreme Gradient Boost Classifier, Artificial Neural Network, and Decision Tree Classifier on the top 8 attributes, which are staunch. The attribute is selected after analyzing the preprocessed data set taken from Kaggle which contains 37446 Twitter accounts having both human and bots. The overall accuracy of the proposed model is above 83%. The result demonstrated that the model is feasible for high-accuracy social bot detection.

Keywords: Social bots · Bot detection · Feature selection · Random forest classifier · XGBoost · ANN · Decision tree classifier

1 Introduction

A bot is a computer program that is designed to do certain simple, automated tasks repeatedly and is done in a proper format and more efficiently than a human [1]. A bot that acts like a human in the social ecosystem is termed a social bot. Social bots are of different types, used for various purposes such as advertising, influencing, etc. [2]. A social bot exists on a social media platform that generates and floods social media platforms with misinformation to alter or manipulate human behavior [3]. Social bots differ in their complexity some are just used to spam content which is easy to point out, while some are used to interact with humans and mimic the same behavior as humans making them difficult to detect [4].

A botnet is referred to a network of bots that are controlled as a group in a coordinated manner. A study analyses the coordination structure of the bots on

---

O. Sali and S. Mehetre—These authors contributed equally to this work.

I. Woungang et al. (Eds.): ANTIC 2022, CCIS 1798, pp. 205–216, 2023.
https://doi.org/10.1007/978-3-031-28183-9_14

certain important events such as the natural disaster in 2017 events like (Mexico Earthquake, Hurricane Harvey, etc.) and the Winter Olympics in 2018 at PyeongChang, South Korea [2]. Tweets that flooded during the US Presidential Election in 2016 were used to change public perception of political entities or even to try to affect the outcome of political elections [5]. All such events demanded services for bot detection and led to a significant increase in bot detection studies. And the development of many machine learning-based, DeepSBD-based, and graph-based techniques for bot detection. On the other hand, programmers began to develop more advanced bots. The most complex bot is hacked account of a genuine user, or concealing a bot under an authentic user account. The cheaper way of advancing the bot is to use account legal privacy settings that will restrict obtaining information that is used in bot detection. Thus bot detection becomes challenging.

Bot detection becomes paramount for the human ecosystem. Detecting and eradicating bots from social platforms is of greater concern nowadays. Maxim et al. [6] have delivered a technique for camouflaged bot detection using a friend list. In this paper, we have proposed a model that uses parameters like followers count, friends list, favourites count, tweets per day, statuses count, account age days, verified, and geo-enabled for bot recognition. These attributes can be obtained even though the account is secured under privacy settings.

The originality of the model is that selecting multiple attributes leads us to higher precision and more elevated accuracy. We have sorted out the top features that are dependable.

This paper is arranged as follows. The second section is the Literature Review in this particular section, we have flashed comprehensive summary of previous developed models used for bot detection. The third section is the Methodology - in which we created the data set and showcased the methods - classification techniques we used in this model. The forth section is Experimental Results, where we will summarize and discuss the result obtained. The fifth section is Conclusion, where we wrap the model and the future scope of the model.

2   Literature Review

Authors in [7] define a "social bot" as a computer program that automatically generates the content and interacts with humans on social media, trying to manipulate their behavior. Nowadays people buy bots for different reasons, some buy just for advertising while some to alter human behavior. Researchers [8] have found that bot comes with different types of properties, that depends on the quality of the bots, some bots are just to flood social media platforms trying to promote something, and these type of bots are simple bots and are easy to detect. Some bots are of high quality, it is a hacked real user accounts or some people do it for money and are hard to detect. Social bots played a critical role in US presidential election in 2016. These bots can alter the ecosystem of different social media platforms such as Twitter and Facebook. They can flood to promote a public figure with a favorable image, to increase their followers by retweeting the post of the user [9].

3   Existing Social Media Bot Detection Technologies

Researchers in [10] recognized reliable features such as invitation frequency, out-going requests accepted, network clustering coefficient, and utilized network-based techniques, crowd sourcing strategies, hybrid systems, and feature-based supervised learning to detect bots and developed a tool called BotOMeter, for-merly known as BotOrNot [11]. Yebo Feng et al. in [12] studied the traffic flow of social bots and proposed a method called BotFlowMon. It takes input as traffic flow information to differentiate social bot traffic real user traffic from social bot traffic. This method's approach is privacy-preserving and can be deployed by Internet/network service providers.

Structure-Based (Social-Network-Based) Bot detection. One of the technique is "Sybilbelif", it is a semi supervised learning approach for structure-based bot detection technique [13].

4   Methodology

4.1   Data Set

In this paper, we have used the raw data set taken from Kaggle, a labeled data set of bots and human users on Twitter. The data set initially contains 37,446 Twitter accounts. We have pre-processed the data set using various pre-processing techniques described below:

4.1.1   Data Cleaning

Firstly, we have checked null values in the data set. After analysing the result, we dropped a few columns such as "description", "lang", "profile_background_ image_url" which had a large number of null values and has less signifi-cance. The attributes with the least null values such as "favourites_count", "fol-lowers_count", "friends_count", "statuses_count", "verified", "average_tweets_ per_day", "account_type" were taken which may come up with the considerable significance and eliminated null values in such columns. The next step was to convert all the values into a numeric type.

The negative values need to be checked. To diagnose the data, we used a Correlation matrix with a Heatmap for some of the staunch attributes (Fig. 1).

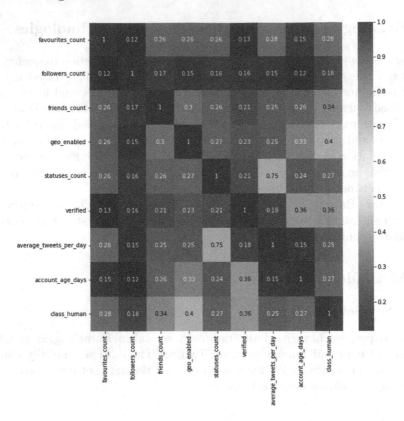

Fig. 1. Correlation matrix with heatmap

4.1.2   Data Balancing

Data balancing is a vital step in data preparation. Having a balanced data set for a model would generate a higher accuracy model, higher balanced accuracy, and a balanced detection rate. Hence, it is crucial to have a balanced data set for a classification model.

One approach to addressing imbalanced datasets is to oversample the minority class. The simplest approach involves duplicating examples in the minority class, although these examples don't add any new information to the model. Instead, new examples can be synthesized from the existing examples. This is a type of data augmentation for the minority class and is referred to as the Synthetic Minority Oversampling Technique, or SMOTE for short. To balance the our imbalance data we have used this technique.

Before balancing, the count was humans (25011) and bots (12423), with a ratio of almost 2:1. Figure 2 shows unbalanced data and a comparison of bot/human. After data balancing, the ratio was reduced to 3:2, humans (21547) and bots (15860). Figure 3 shows the data set after balancing, and a comparison of bot/human.

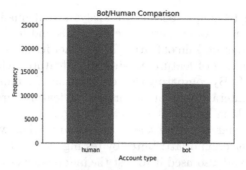

Fig. 2. Data set before balancing

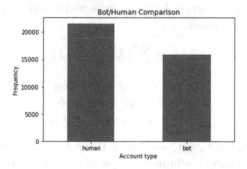

Fig. 3. Data set after balancing

4.1.3   Feature Selection

We filtered the data set to evaluate the attribute through multiple filters.

1. Information Gain Ranking Filter
   Information gain is a method in feature selection used for the transformation
   of the dataset by calculating the reduction of the entropy. Mostly this method
   is used in the formation of the decision tree from a training dataset by calculating the information gain for each attribute of the dataset and selecting
   the attribute which provides the maximum gain, hence the dataset is split
   into groups for effective classification and minimizes the entropy. In Feature
   selection, by evaluating the gain of each attribute with the context of the
   target attribute we can find the rankings of each attribute.

$$E = -\sum_{0}^{1} p_i log_2 p_i \tag{1}$$

   where pi, is the probability of randomly picking an element of class i.
2. Symmetrical Uncertainty Ranking Filter
   Symmetrical uncertainty is mostly used to measure the degree of relevance
   between the feature and the particular class label. It is considered the key

feature selection technique because it analyses and qualifies the relevance, redundancy, and irrelevance between class labels and features.

The average interaction gain of feature X, all other features, and the class label reflect the interaction of feature X with other features when calculated in a given feature set F. By comparing the combination of symmetrical uncertainty and normalized interaction gain, the irrelevant features are removed.

3. Chi-squared Ranking Filter

We use the Chi-squared feature selection technique when we have to solve the problem in the selection of attributes by testing the relationship between the given attributes and also used it to test the independence of the two features. This technique is probably used to find the rankings of the attributes in the given dataset. Given the data of two variables, the Chi-square feature selection technique measures how the expected count C and observed count D deviate from each other.

$$\chi_c^2 = \sum (X_i - Y_i)^2 / Y_i \tag{2}$$

$c =$ degree of freedom
$X =$ observed value(s)
$Y =$ expected value(s)

After filtering the data set, we found the reliable features by Gain Ratio Feature Evaluator. Thereby eliminating less important attribute from the data set. These features were:

- Followers count - Followers are people who subscribed to your account.
- Friends count - To make friend, a user must send a request, and another user must accept it.
- Favourites count - it is the number of times the tweet has been favorited.
- Status count - The number of status the user had posted till date.
- Account age days - Time period from the creation of the user account till the present time.
- Verified - Is the account verified or not by the platform.
- Geo-enabled - If enabled shares the location with the tweet.

The above features are the most reliable features (Fig. 4).

The following diagram shows the architecture of proposed work:

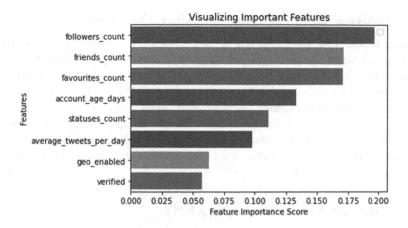

Fig. 4. Top 8 attributes

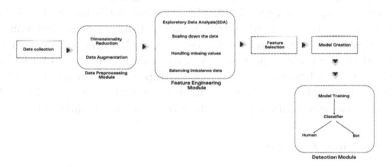

Fig. 5. Architecture diagram

4.2 Methods

In this study, we used several ready-made classifier machine learning methods for classification on the extracted features on Twitter account from the data set, and evaluate the best model on the trade-off, thereby helping us to detect bots and stop polluting the social media space. The classifier we used are, namely:

4.2.1 Random Forest Classifier

Random Forest Classifier is a supervised machine learning algorithm that is used in classification as well as in regression problems. It is one of the most powerful, scalable, and highly accurate models that does not depend on a single decision. It takes many randomized decisions into consideration and makes a final decision based on the majority of decisions. This helps to deliver better results in classification problems. That's why we have used the Random Forest Classifier in our model. Bagging and bootstrapping are used in Random Forest which helps in working parallelly.

4.2.2 Extreme Gradient Boost Classifier (XGBoost)

XGBoost is also a supervised learning model used for classification as well as for regression on large datasets. As our dataset is quite large, XGBoost is a good choice to handle such data. It uses sequentially-built shallow decision trees to prepare accurate results and a highly-scalable training method that overcomes overfitting. XGBoost combines the results of many weak classifiers, called base learners to build a strong result. Along with the Random Forest, we have also used XGBoost Classifier for model creation. While using XGBoost in our model we took care of some of the things that numeric features are scaled and categorical features are encoded.

4.2.3 Artificial Neural Network (ANN)

Along with the Random Forest Classifier and XGBoost with have also used an Artificial Neural Network model i.e. ANN. It is a machine-learning model which learns from a sample data set. Artificial Neural Networks are used in situations where we're trying to detect patterns in data. In our data set, we are trying to find a common pattern or common behavior between the bot accounts on Twitter that separates them from human accounts. Artificial neural networks are used because there is a need to understand complex relationships between inputs and outputs as we want to separate bot accounts from genuine human accounts. Using Artificial Neural Networks is a common practice to retain knowledge and data.

4.2.4 Decision Tree Classifier

We have also used another supervised learning algorithm which is the Decision Tree Classifier, this also operates in both classifications as well as regression. It handles data accurately and works best for a linear pattern. It efficiently handles large data. So, these are some of the reasons why we chose a decision tree algorithm for our dataset. Tree depth is an important aspect. Shallower the depth better the performance. Recursion is used in traversing the tree. But one of the major drawbacks of the Decision Tree is it is very unstable, as a slight change in the data may result in a large deflection in the result.

We performed a couple of experiments with the data set described in Sect. 5. In the first experiment, we used some of the data to train and evaluate the mentioned classifier. We divided the data into two portions in the ratio of 70% to 30%. The first 70% of data was used to train the model. In the second experiment, we used the second chunk of the divided data, which is 30% of the data for testing purpose.

5 Experimental Results

In this study, we implemented four models; The first is the Random Forest Classifier that was fed by the features, which we gathered from feature engineering, and the feature extraction process shows us the accuracy of 99.99% on the training data and the test data accuracy of 87.21%. Figure 5 shows the Receiver Operating Characteristics (ROC) Curve of the Random Forest implementation (Fig. 6).

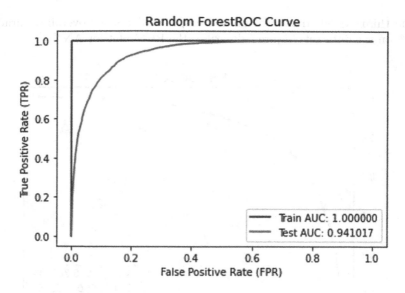

Fig. 6. ROC curve for random forest classifier

The second classifier is the XGBoost, that gives an accuracy of 84.34% on testing data and 84.75% on training data which is less than Random Forest Classifier but still the overall accuracy of the trained model is good. Figure 5 shows the ROC curve for the XGBoost Classifier.

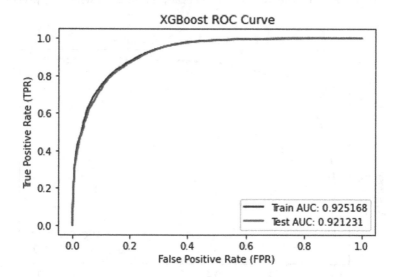

Fig. 7. ROC curve for XGBoost classifier

The third model Artificial Neural Network delivers the overall accuracy of 84.33% on the data set. Figure 7 describes the ROC plot for ANN.

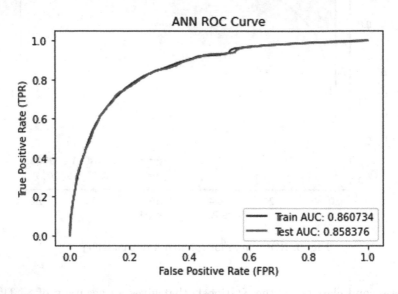

Fig. 8. ROC curve for ANN

The last is the Decision Tree Classifier shows us the accuracy of 85.86% on the training data, and the test data accuracy is 84.28% which is pretty good

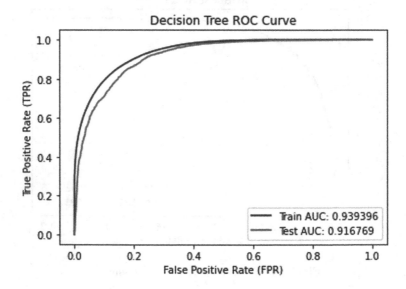

Fig. 9. ROC curve for decision tree classifier

with the default parameters. Figure 8 shows the ROC curve for Decision Tree classifier (Fig. 9).

As we can see the algorithm implemented, we have drawn the table which shows the comparison between accuracy score and training and test set (Table 1).

Table 1. Accuracy scores of classifiers

Sr. No	Accuracy scores	Training data set	Testing data set
1	Random Forest	99.99%	87.32%.
2	XGBoost	83.34%	84.75%.
3	ANN	84.65%	84.33%.
4	Decision Tree	85.86%	84.28%

Random forest shows the best performance because in multi-class object detection random forest is considered the best technique for the classification of the data, and also works well with lots of missing data and more noise. The random forest also consists of multiple single trees, each based on a random sample of the training data, so they are more accurate than the single decision trees. In the random forest, the leaves of the trees are equally weighted, and with the available data accuracy and precision can be obtained easily. Even random forest also handles the outliers automatically.

Conclusion

A study has found that in the Presidental elections of the US in 2016 the 20% of political decisions on social media were generated by over 400,000 social media bots. Similarly, there are many cases where social media bots have there influenced in bad as well as good ways.

In this paper, we have analyzed social media bot detection using machine learning algorithms and designed a machine learning model that can detect social media bots. With the effect of, the given dataset we have identified some attributes and used the feature selection techniques to identify the rankings of the attributes and select the top 80% of attributes from the given dataset. Using a Random Forest algorithm the accuracy of the training data is 99.99% and the testing data is 87.32%, as well as the testing accuracy of XGBoost, ANN and Decision Tree algorithms have accuracy of 84.75%, 84.33% and 84.28%.

The limitation of proposed work is that it only works upon social media account profile attributes like followers count, following count, frequency of posting contents. It fails to work upon the contents posted by social media user like texts, images, videos or voice message to identify the type of contents and type of behaviour of that particular account user through the contents posted.

For future work, we are going to analyze the description attribute, on the basis of the description provided by the account we can detect whether it is a bot or not using natural language processing techniques.

References

1. Gayer, O.: Understanding bots and how they hurt your business. Imperva Blog (2016)
2. Khaund, T., Bandeli, K.K., Hussain, M.N., Obadimu, A., Al-Khateeb, S., Agarwal, N.: Analyzing social and communication network structures of social bots and humans. In: 2018 IEEE/ACM International Conference on Advances in Social Networks Analysis and Mining (ASONAM), pp. 794–797. IEEE (2018)
3. Jiang, M., Cui, P., Faloutsos, C.: Suspicious behavior detection: current trends and future directions. IEEE Intell. Syst. **31**(1), 31–39 (2016)
4. E&T: Social media bots becoming more human and difficult to detect, study shows. E&T article (2019)
5. Bessi, A., Ferrara, E.: Social bots distort the 2016 us presidential election online discussion. First Monday **21**(11-7) (2016)
6. Kolomeets, M., Tushkanova, O., Levshun, D., Chechulin, A.: Camouflaged bot detection using the friend list. In: 2021 29th Euromicro International Conference on Parallel, Distributed and Network-Based Processing (PDP), pp. 253–259. IEEE (2021)
7. Ferrara, E., Varol, O., Davis, C., Menczer, F., Flammini, A.: The rise of social bots. Commun. ACM **59**(7), 96–104 (2016)
8. Subrahmanian, V.S., et al.: The DARPA twitter bot challenge. Computer **49**(6), 38–46 (2016)
9. Al-khateeb, S., Agarwal, N.: Examining botnet behaviors for propaganda dissemination: a case study of ISIL's beheading videos-based propaganda. In: 2015 IEEE International Conference on Data Mining Workshop (ICDMW), pp. 51–57 (2015)
10. Varol, O., Ferrara, E., Davis, C.A., Menczer, F., Flammini, A.: Online human-bot interactions: detection, estimation, and characterization. In: Eleventh International AAAI Conference on Web and Social Media (2017)
11. Davis, C.A., Varol, O., Ferrara, E., Flammini, A., Menczer, F.: BotOrNot: a system to evaluate social bots. In: Proceedings of the 25th International Conference Companion on World Wide Web, pp. 273–274 (2016)
12. Feng, Y., Li, J., Jiao, L., Wu, X.: BotFlowMon: learning-based, content-agnostic identification of social bot traffic flows. In: 2019 IEEE Conference on Communications and Network Security (CNS), pp. 169–177 (2019)
13. Gong, N.Z., Frank, M., Mittal, P.: SybilBelief: a semi-supervised learning approach for structure-based Sybil detection. IEEE Trans. Inf. Forensics Secur. **09**, 976–987 (2014)

Detection of Homophobia & Transphobia in Malayalam and Tamil: Exploring Deep Learning Methods

Deepawali Sharma[1(✉)], Vedika Gupta[2], and Vivek Kumar Singh[1]

[1] Department of Computer Science, Banaras Hindu University, Varanasi, India
deepawali21@bhu.ac.in
[2] Jindal Global Business School, O.P. Jindal Global University, Sonipat, Haryana, India

Abstract. The increase in abusive content on online social media platforms is impacting the social life of online users. Use of offensive and hate speech has been making social media toxic. Homophobia and transphobia constitute offensive comments against LGBT + community. It becomes imperative to detect and handle these comments, to timely flag or issue a warning to users indulging in such behaviour. However, automated detection of such content is a challenging task, more so in Dravidian languages which are identified as low resource languages. Motivated by this, the paper attempts to explore applicability of different deep learning models for classification of the social media comments in Malayalam and Tamil languages as homophobic, transphobic and non-anti-LGBT + content. The popularly used deep learning models-Convolutional Neural Network (CNN), Long Short Term Memory (LSTM) using GloVe embedding and transformer-based learning models (Multilingual BERT and IndicBERT) are applied to the classification problem. Results obtained show that IndicBERT outperforms the other implemented models, with obtained weighted average F1-score of 0.86 and 0.77 for Malayalam and Tamil, respectively. Therefore, the present work confirms higher performance of IndicBERT on the given task on selected Dravidian languages.

Keywords: Deep learning · Homophobia · Malayalam · Tamil · Transphobia

1 Introduction

People share and post their views/opinions/thoughts about various topics on various social media platforms. The freedom to create such content also results in a large amount of displeasing data on racism, homophobia, transphobia, targeting particular communities and organizations, posted on the Web. Unfortunately, LGBT + people are being abused online by other communities resulting into problems of mental disorders (anxiety disorders, behavioural and emotional disorders, depression) in them. Sometimes, campaigns are initiated against these vulnerable communities when they come online for support and these campaigns are often converted into bullying [8]. Automatic detection of such content is a challenging task, more so if the text is in a low resource language.

I. Woungang et al. (Eds.): ANTIC 2022, CCIS 1798, pp. 217–226, 2023.
https://doi.org/10.1007/978-3-031-28183-9_15

Many studies have been done on the detection of hate speech [9–11], offensive and abusive content [12–14], cyberbullying [15–17] and many more on content in some selected languages. However, there is very little effort towards detecting racism, homophobia, transphobia in online texts from low resource Indian languages.

This paper presents an attempt towards this direction. Different deep learning-based models (CNN, LSTM, mBERT and IndicBERT) are implemented on data from two languages, namely Tamil and Malayalam. Both languages belong to the family of Dravidian languages and are low-resourced languages. The dataset provided by Dravidian-LangTech [8] is used for the purpose of the experiment. The comments are classified as Homophobic, Transphobic and Non-anti-LGBT + content. Those comments that contain pejorative labels or denigrative phrases against the gay, lesbian or any other community are classified as Homophobic [8]. People who can be homosexual, or can be transphobic without being homophobic, are identified as transphobic persons. Therefore, the comments that advocate or proposes anything unfavourable for transgender people are classified as transphobic [8]. Those comments that do not include homophobic, transphobic and have positive influence on readers are classified as non-anti-LGBT + content.

Different deep learning-based models are implemented to detect homophobia and transphobia in comments. More specifically, the paper performs the following tasks:

- Implementation of deep learning models (CNN, LSTM) with GloVe embedding for data in both languages (Malayalam and Tamil).
- Implementation of transformer-based models (mBERT, IndicBERT) for data in both languages (Malayalam and Tamil)
- Performance evaluation of the different models implemented on a standard dataset using standard metric.

The rest of the paper is organized as follows: Sect. 2 discusses the related work for the detection of homophobia and transphobia. Section 3 describes the dataset and its dimensions. Section 4 presents the experimental set up. Results are presented in Sect. 5. Section 6 concludes the paper with a brief summary of the results and major conclusions drawn.

2   Related Work

There is very limited previous work on detecting homophobia and transphobia in social media comments, particularly on low resource Indian languages. In one study, the ensemble transformer-based model was implemented to classify homophobia and transphobia on social media comments in Tamil and Tamil-English datasets [1]. Similarly, to classify the comments as homophobia and transphobia in English, different transformer-based models (BERT, RoBERTa and HateBERT) were implemented [2]. For detecting homophobia and transphobia, different monolingual and multilingual transformer-based models experimented on English, Tamil and Tamil-English datasets [3]. Another study experimented with transformer-based model (RoBERT-base) for English, Tamil and English-Tamil code-mixed datasets [6]. A study implemented neural network using sentence embedding and ensemble model in Tamil, English and Tamil-English [4]. Some of the studies implemented different classification algorithms using TF-IDF to classify the YouTube comments as homophobic and transphobic in English, Tamil and Tamil-English [5]. Similarly, the combination of word embeddings and Support Vector Machine (SVM) are implemented along with BERT-based models in English, Tamil and English-Tamil [7]. There is, however, no previous work on detecting homophobia and transphobia on social media comments in Malayalam language. Further, the previous studies have not explored the newer methods like IndicBERT. Therefore, the present study explores the suitability of various deep learning-based models, including the recently proposed IndicBERT model, for the task of detecting homophobia and transphobia on social media comments in Malayalam and Tamil languages.

3 Dataset Description

The dataset used in the study was launched by DravidianLangTech and is available online at https://codalab.lisn.upsaclay.fr/competitions/. The dataset contains the comments in two Dravidian languages namely Malayalam and Tamil. There are two attributes in the dataset: comment and category. The comment attribute consists of the sentiment/opinion of the people in form of text and the category tells that which of the three classes the comment belongs to: Homophobic, Transphobic, and Non-anti-LGBT + content. The Malayalam dataset contains 3,114 comments and the Tamil dataset contains 2,662 comments. Table 1 shows the category-wise distribution of comments in the Malayalam dataset. Table 2 shows the distribution of comments in each category of the Tamil dataset.

Table 1. Category-wise distribution of comments of Malayalam Dataset

Category	No. of comments
Homophobic	2434
Transphobic	491
Non-anti-LGBT + content	189

Table 2. Category-wise distribution of comments in Tamil Dataset

Category	No. of comments
Homophobic	2022
Transphobic	485
Non-anti-LGBT + content	155

3.1 Data Pre-processing

Since data pre-processing is a very important step in NLP applications and model building, we performed the following steps to pre-process the original text:

- Removing punctuations
- Removing Numbers
- URLs given in comments are removed.
- Repeated characters that do not add any information are removed.
- Extra blank spaces, that are created during pre-processing or if some comments already have that, are removed.

4   Experimental Setup

4.1   CNN

CNN was initially developed for image processing but in the past years, CNN showed good results in NLP tasks as well. When CNN is applied to text rather than the image, then 1-dimensional convolutional neural networks are used. To work with $1 - D$ CNN, a word embedding layer is required. GLoVe word embedding is used in this paper. For preparing the word embedding for the model, firstly all punctuations, links, etc. are removed, the text is tokenized and padding the text using the pad_sequences() to make equal length sequences. Figure 1 shows the implementation of CNN. From the word embedding, the words are represented as vectors. The embedding matrices are passed to the embedding layer. After that, the convolutional layer is added using "relu" as an activation function. Now, a pooling layer is added to reduce the complexity of the dimensions, and to be more specific MaxPooling is used. At last, the fully connected layer is added which is also called the dense layer in which the "Softmax" is used as an activation function since the dataset is multi-class classification. So, it classifies the comments into three categories: Homophobic, Transphobic and Non-anti-LGBT + content. The model is trained on 100 epochs for both languages (Malayalam and Tamil) and "Adam" is used as an optimizer. The loss is" Categorical Cross-entropy" to classify the tweets.

4.2   LSTM

LSTM is used for text classification because LSTM memorizes the information effectively and removes unwanted information. The LSTM model is able to find out the meaning of the input string and classify the text to the most precise output class if the appropriate layers of embedding are used. Before adding the embedding layer, firstly the data is pre-processed and the text is tokenized into tokens. After that, the sequence is padded by adding zero at the end of the sequence to make the sequence of the same length. Now, the word embedding (GLoVe) is used to represent the words into vectors. The padded sequence are passed to embedding layer as an input. The LSTM layer has been added after embedding layer using ReLu as an activation function. The dense layer is added at the end with activation function as softmax to classify the comments into more than two classes. Figure 2 shows the block diagram for LSTM to classify the comments. The model is trained on 100 epochs using the categorical cross-entropy as a loss function and "Adam" as an optimizer for both languages.

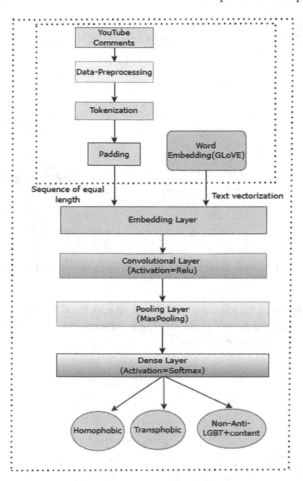

Fig. 1. Implementation of CNN to detect homophobia and transphobia

4.3   mBERT

BERT was developed in 2018 by Jacob Devlin and his colleagues from Google. BERT was trained on large-corpus of English data whereas mBERT was trained on 104 different languages including English [19]. It is not feasible to have separate BERT model for each language and therefore mBERT was introduced as a single BERT for 104 languages. In this paper, BERT base is used that has 12 layers of transformer encoder. Firstly, the comments are converted into tokens with the help of BERT tokenizer. Figure 3 shows the framework of BERT to classify the comments. Two special tokens [CLS] and [SEP] are added at the starting and end of the sequence, respectively. Vocabulary IDs for each of the tokens are token embeddings. Sentence embedding is used to distinguish between the sentences; and positional embedding is used to show the position of each word in the sequence. The model is build using the pre-trained BERT-base multilingual-cased

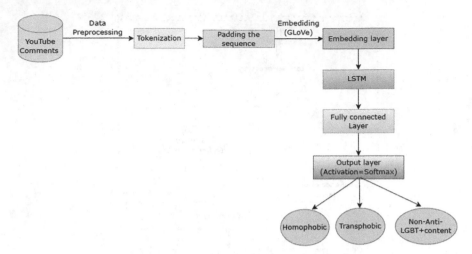

Fig. 2. Block diagram to show the implementation of LSTM model

model. The batch size is 32, learning is 3e-5 and the epochs = 5 is used to train the model on the dataset. At last the classifier classify the comments into homophobic, transphobic and non-anti-LGBT + content classes.

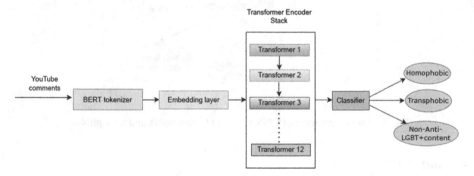

Fig. 3. Framework of transformer-based BERT model

4.4 IndicBERT

IndicBERT is a multilingual model trained on 12 Indian languages: Tamil, Malayalam, Bengali, Marathi, Punjabi, English, Hindi, Gujarati, Assamese, Oriya, Telugu and Kannada. As compared to other models like mBERT and XLM-R, it has a smaller number of parameters but even then gives the state-of-the-art (SOTA) performance for various tasks [18]. IndicBERT is based on the ALBERT model which is the derivative of the BERT. The text is tokenized using the Autotokenizer and the [CLS] token is added at the beginning of the sequence and [SEP] tokens are added at the end of the sequence similar to the BERT model. IndicBERT also has the ability to consider more than one sentence into a single sequence for input. As the dataset is in Indian languages: Malayalam and Tamil. For this dataset, the IndicBERT outperformed the other models and reported the weighted average F1 score for Malayalam and Tamil is 0.86 and 0.77, respectively. The parameters are fine-tuned: learning rate is set to be 3e-5, epochs = 5 and batch size is 32. At the end, the model classifies the comments into the three given categories: Homophobic, Transphobic and non-anti-LGBT + content.

5   Results

The CNN and transformer-based models are implemented to classify the comments from two languages into one of the three classes: 'Homophobic', 'Transphobic', and 'Non-anti-LGBT + content'. This section shows the performance of the implemented models. Table 3 shows the performance analysis of the CNN, LSTM and transfer learning models (mBERT and IndicBERT) for Malayalam. It can be observed that the weighted F1-score for CNN, LSTM, mBERT and IndicBERT are 0.80, 0.81, 0.83 and 0.86, respectively. For the Malayalam language, IndicBERT outperformed the other models. Table 4 shows the performance analysis of the implemented models for Tamil. The weighted average F1-score for deep learning models: CNN and LSTM are 0.71 and 0.72, respectively. The transformer-based model (IndicBERT) performs better than the other three implemented models (CNN, LSTM, mBERT), with a weighted F1 score of 0.77.

Table 3. Performance analysis for implemented models for Malayalam Dataset

Model	Homophobic			Transphobic			Non-anti-LGBT + content			Weighted average F1-score
	P	R	F1-score	P	R	F1-score	P	R	F1-score	
CNN(GloVe)	0.65	0.35	0.45	0.86	0.32	0.46	0.84	0.96	0.89	0.80
LSTM(GloVe)	0.69	0.45	0.54	0.60	0.32	0.41	0.86	0.95	0.90	0.81
mBERT	0.74	0.47	0.58	0.67	0.32	0.43	0.86	0.96	0.91	0.83
IndicBERT	0.79	0.49	0.59	0.70	0.39	0.50	0.88	0.97	0.91	**0.86**

[*] P = Precision, R = Recall

5.1   Comparison with Existing Studies

A comparative analysis of the deployed method is also done in order to understand the performance level of the method. Table 5 presents a comparative study of major previous studies on Tamil dataset with the performance obtained by the IndicBERT model. Studies experimented with transformer-based models. One study experimented with simple transformer model tamillion to classify the comments and reported weighted average F1-score is 0.75 [7]. Similarly, another study used RoBERTa-Base approach for the detection of comments into 3 classes: Homphobic, Transphobic and Non-anti-LGBT + content and obtained macro F1-score is 0.29 [6]. Similarly, the transformer- based

Table 4. Performance analysis for implemented models for Tamil Dataset

Model	Homophobic			Transphobic			Non-anti-LGBT + content			Weighted Average F1-score
	P	R	F1-score	P	R	F1-score	P	R	F1-score	
CNN(GloVe)	0.57	0.08	0.14	1.00	0.27	0.42	0.78	0.99	0.88	0.71
LSTM(GloVe)	0.67	0.12	0.21	0.80	0.27	0.40	0.79	0.98	0.87	0.72
mBERT	0.70	0.15	0.24	0.79	0.30	0.43	0.81	0.96	0.87	0.74
IndicBERT	0.72	0.18	0.28	0.76	0.34	0.46	0.84	0.94	0.88	**0.77**

* P = Precision, R = Recall

model (mBERT) experimented for the detection of homophobia and transphobia and reported F1-score is 0.64 [3]. There is no existing work on detecting homophobia and transphobia on social media comments in Malayalam language. The proposed approach (IndicBERT) is found to be outperforming other models and obtained weighted average F1-score for Malayalam and Tamil are 0.86 and 0.77 respectively. The obtained results of the IndicBERT model are better for both languages (Tamil and Malyalam) to classify the comments in given categories: homophobic, transphobic and non-anti-LGBT + content.

Table 5. Results of some of the previous studies

S. No.	Authors	Approach		F1-score	
		Tamil	Malayalam	Tamil	Malayalam
1	Swaminathan, K., Bharathi, B., Gayathri, G. L., & Sampath, H. (2022, May) [7]	Transformer monsoon-nlp/tamillion	N/A	0.75	N/A
2	Maimaitituoheti, A. (2022, May) [6]	RoBERTa-Base	N/A	0.29	N/A
3	Bhandari, V., & Goyal, P. (2022) [3]	mBERT	N/A	0.64	N/A
4	Proposed Approach (in this paper)	IndicBERT (Proposed Approach)	IndicBERT (Proposed Approach)	**0.77**	**0.86**

6   Conclusion

The paper presents the performance analysis of the different deep learning models (CNN, LSTM, mBERT and IndicBERT) on the task of homophobia and transphobia detection of the Malayalam and Tamil texts. The goal was to classify each comment into given three categories: Homophobic, Transphobic and Non-anti-LGBT + content. Experimental results show that the IndicBERT model outperformed the other models for both languages: Malayalam and Tamil, with reported weighted average F1-score of 0.86 and 0.77, respectively. While the other models also show reasonable performance, but the IndicBERT model is the best among all in terms of measured performance values. Thus, the IndicBERT model emerges as the superior of the various proposed methods for the tasks of Homophobia and Transphobia detection in the selected Dravidian languages. The present work can also be extended to data from other Indian languages. Further, ensemble-based models can also be explored for the given task.

Acknowledgement. This work is supported by an extramural research grant by HPE Aruba Centre for Research in Information Systems at BHU (No. M-22-69 of BHU).

References

1. Upadhyay, I.S., Srivatsa, K.A., Mamidi, R.: Sammaan@ lt-edi-acl2022: ensembled transformers against Homophobia and Transphobia. In: Proceedings of the Second Workshop on Language Technology for Equality, Diversity and Inclusion, pp. 270–275 (2022)
2. Nozza, D.: Nozza@ LT-EDI-ACL2022: ensemble modeling for homophobia and transphobia detection. In: Proceedings of the Second Workshop on Language Technology for Equality, Diversity and Inclusion, pp. 258–264 (2022)
3. Bhandari, V., Goyal, P.: bitsa_nlp@ lt-edi-acl2022: leveraging pretrained language models for detecting homophobia and transphobia in Social Media Comments. arXiv preprint arXiv: 2203.14267. (2022)
4. García-Díaz, J., Caparrós-Laiz, C., Valencia-García, R.: UMUTeam@ LT-EDI-ACL2022: Detecting homophobic and transphobic comments in Tamil. In: Proceedings of the Second Workshop on Language Technology for Equality, Diversity and Inclusion, pp. 140–144 (2022)
5. Ashraf, N., Taha, M., Abd Elfattah, A., Nayel, H.: Nayel@ lt-edi-acl2022: homophobia/transphobia detection for Equality, Diversity, and Inclusion using Svm. In: Proceedings of the Second Workshop on Language Technology for Equality, Diversity and Inclusion, pp. 287–290 (2022)
6. Maimaitituoheti, A.: ABLIMET@ LT-EDI-ACL2022: a RoBERTa based approach for homophobia/transphobia detection in social media. In: Proceedings of the Second Workshop on Language Technology for Equality, Diversity and Inclusion, pp. 155–160 (2022)
7. Swaminathan, K., Bharathi, B., Gayathri, G.L., Sampath, H.:Ssncse_nlp@ lt-edi-acl2022: homophobia/transphobia detection in multiple languages using Svm classifiers and Bert-based Transformers. In: Proceedings of the Second Workshop on Language Technology for Equality, Diversity and Inclusion, pp. 239–244 (2022)
8. Chakravarthi, B.R., et al. Dataset for identification of homophobia and transophobia in multilingual YouTube comments. arXiv preprint arXiv:2109.00227
9. Khan, S., et al.: HCovBi-caps: hate speech detection using convolutional and Bi-directional gated recurrent unit with Capsule network. IEEE Access **10**, 7881–7894 (2022)
10. Khan, S., et al.: BiCHAT: BiLSTM with deep CNN and hierarchical attention for hate speech detection. J. King Saud Univ.-Comput. Inform. Sci. **34**(7), 4335–4344 (2022)
11. Sap, M., Card, D., Gabriel, S., Choi, Y., Smith, N.A.: The risk of racial bias in hate speech detection. In: Proceedings of the 57th annual meeting of the association for computational linguistics, pp. 1668–1678 (2019)

12. Koufakou, A., Pamungkas, E. W., Basile, V., Patti, V.: HurtBERT: incorporating lexical features with BERT for the detection of abusive language. In: Fourth Workshop on Online Abuse and Harms, pp. 34–43. Association for Computational Linguistics (2020)

13. Susanty, M., Rahman, A.F., Normansyah, M.D., Irawan, A.: Offensive language detection using artificial neural network. In: 2019 International Conference of Artificial Intelligence and Information Technology (ICAIIT), pp. 350–353. IEEE (2019)

14. Wiedemann, G., Ruppert, E., Jindal, R., Biemann, C.: Transfer learning from lda to bilstm-cnn for offensive language detection in twitter. arXiv preprint arXiv:1811.02906 (2018)

15. Cheng, L., Li, J., Silva, Y. N., Hall, D. L., Liu, H.: Xbully: Cyberbullying detection within a multi-modal context. In: Proceedings of the Twelfth ACM International Conference on Web Search and Data Mining, pp. 339–347 (2019)

16. Balakrishnan, V., Khan, S., Fernandez, T., Arabnia, H.R.: Cyberbullying detection on twitter using Big Five and Dark Triad features. Personal. Individ. Differ. **141**, 252–257 (2019)

17. Hani, J., Mohamed, N., Ahmed, M., Emad, Z., Amer, E., Ammar, M.: Social media cyberbullying detection using machine learning. Int. J. Adv. Comput. Sci. Appl. **10**(5) (2019). https://doi.org/10.14569/IJACSA.2019.0100587

18. Kakwani, D., Kunchukuttan, A., Golla, S., Gokul, N. C., Bhattacharyya, A., Khapra, M. M., Kumar, P.: IndicNLPSuite: Monolingual corpora, evaluation benchmarks and pre-trained multilingual language models for Indian languages. In: Findings of the Association for Computational Linguistics: EMNLP 2020, pp. 4948–4961 (2020)

19. Devlin, J., Chang, M. W., Lee, K.,Toutanova, K.: Bert: Pre-training of deep bidirectional transformers for language understanding. arXiv preprint arXiv:1810.04805 (2018)

Coffee Leaf Disease Detection Using Transfer Learning

Anshuman Sharma[1]([✉]), Noamaan Abdul Azeem[2], and Sanjeev Sharma[2]

[1] Kalinga Institute of Industrial Technology, Bhubaneswar, India
anshumansharma179@gmail.com
[2] Indian Institute of Information Technology, Pune, India

Abstract. Recognizing disease in coffee leaves is an important aspect of providing a better quality of coffee across the world. Economies of many countries in the world depend upon the export of coffee and if we fail to recognize the disease in the coffee plant it will have a negative impact on them. The objective of this paper is to propose models for recognizing disease in coffee leaf plants. For achieving our objective we used various pre-trained models. We used transfer learning approach to identify coffee leaf detection. There were several models that achieved great results on both training and testing data. However, the best-achieving model was VGG19 due to less memory utilized and less time required for execution.

Keywords: Deep learning · Transfer learning · Coffee leaf disease detection

1 Introduction

After water coffee is the most widely used commodity in the world. Arabica Coffee makes up 60% or more of coffee production in the world. There was an increase in the production of green coffee beans by 17% and the consumption of coffee increased by 2% at an annual rate during the previous decades. Recognizing diseases in coffee [19] in its growing stage is an important task as we can avoid the loss in the production of coffee leaves in the early stage. Even a small reduction in coffee yields due to disease in coffee leaves will have a large impact on coffee production. Failing to recognize the diseases in coffee leaves will also affect the economies of countries [31] that are mostly dependent on the export of the coffee commodity. If we fail to recognize the diseases in coffee leaves the production of coffee will get reduced by around 10% from one season to next season. Recognizing diseases in coffee will increase the productivity and the quality of coffee production. Hence disease recognition plays an important role in defining the quality of the coffee.

Disease detection through our naked eyes is a time-consuming activity and requires a lot of expertise. So we will be developing models using transfer learning methods or CNNs. Transfer learning is a technique where we use the knowledge gained while learning the classes of one dataset to a different dataset. Convolutional Neural Networks are special kinds of neural networks that are used in processing data which are having a grid or matrix-like structure, for example if we think of time-series data that is a 1-D grid that takes samples at regular time intervals and if we think of image data that is a 2-D matrix or grid of pixels.

I. Woungang et al. (Eds.): ANTIC 2022, CCIS 1798, pp. 227–238, 2023.
https://doi.org/10.1007/978-3-031-28183-9_16

Today CNN's play a vital role in image classification [12], object detection [21]. In terms of Convolution Neural Networks or CNNs, the first argument is considered as input, the second argument is considered as Kernel, and the output is sometimes known as feature maps. CNN learn feature vectors with weight sharing and local connectivity which detects patterns at all locations in the image. The initial layers of a CNN learn simple features and the deeper ones learn more complex features. In transfer learning, the top-most layer of the pre-trained models is removed and the model with the remaining layers is used as a feature vector. After removing the top layer the softmax layer is connected to the remaining network for classification. Then this network is trained on training data set. The intention is that the remaining layers or feature vector of the neural network that we developed is trained on one kind of data set that can be further used to extract useful features on another data set. If we want to reduce the time of learning all the weights of neural networks then transfer learning is a useful technique to learn all the weights at a minimum time. As we know that diseases are shapeless quality so we will be using the texture quality of leaves to determine the disease that is present in coffee leaves.

The real motivation behind the research was the recent emergence of deep learning architectures. The preference for deep learning over machine learning was due to the fact that deep learning algorithms give better performance as compared to machine learning algorithms. As if in machine learning an algorithm provides an inaccurate prediction, we need to adjust the algorithms manually. Whereas in deep learning models the algorithm determines the prediction is accurate or not using its in-built neural network. After the win of AlexNet [14] in 2012. The use of Convolution Neural Networks has grown for image classification. Here we are provided with a dataset containing images of coffee leaves. So using these images as our model input and image classification as our technique we will predict the correct labels that will help us to identify the conditions of coffee plant leaves. The pre-trained models used in this paper are Inception-V3, Mobile-Net, VGG16. We are performing the models using different parameters that will help us to identify the model which will provide us the best accuracy on this work.

The motivation behind this study was to implement different deep learning models that will help us to recognize the disease in coffee leaves on basis of pictures corresponding to coffee plant leaves.

This article is structured as follows. The following segment begins with an Introduction of the work, followed by Literature Review in which all the related works of this study are included. The next segment discusses the dataset and data preprocessing, as well as the proposed Models in detail. In the next Section, we conduct all of the experiments and publish the results of the work, This paper comes to a conclusion in Sect. 5 where we discuss the conclusion and future scope of this work.

2   Literature Review

There has been a lot of research work done in coffee leaves disease detection owing to the importance it holds in the field of computer vision. In 2019 a similar research was made in this domain. Due to the small size of the images, this research work [18] proposed a model with a fewer number of layers than traditional CNNs. They used the Dice coefficient (D) [25] to measure how similar the two images are. The training of the model took 10003 global steps and 500 epochs and it achieved a 95% accuracy and 0.10 loss. In 2016 another work was done, In this work [27] the authors used pretrained CaffeNet model [13]. This framework was used, along with the set of weights learned on a very large dataset, ImageNet. After the 100th epoch, their accuracy achieved was 96.3%. In 2021 a research was done on unsupervised neural networks. This research [34] used technique of u2net for image detection [23]. This research changed the background into something meaningful and easy to analyze As a result the model achieved 98% accuracy.

In 2019 a research [1] was made based on texture attributes of coffee leaves. This approach is based on the Grey Level Co-Occurrence Matrix (GLCM), GLCM is a matrix that considers the counting of the number of neighbouring pixels with a given grey level that occurs considering a reference pixel with its own grey level.

In 1973 another paper, [7] was published in of similar dataset. The authors of the paper used ResTS [24] architecture. ResTS structure comprises ResTeacher, Decoder, and ResStudent. The general architecture of ResTS is identical to that of Teacher/Student [2]. The accuracy of this work was found to be 99.91% which is pretty impressive. Further research was made on similar dataset in [17]. In which Generative Adversarial Networks (GANS) approach was initiated. GANs is a kind of generating model proposed by Goodfellow et al. [6] in 2014. The major goal is to generate synthetic samples with the same characteristics as the given training distribution. The GANs models mainly consist of two parts, that is, generator and discriminator. The achieved accuracy of the work was 98%.

In 2017 study [4] was made which integrated multiple CNN classifiers to study high-resolution corn disease images. The experimental results showed that when a single CNN classifier was used, the accuracy rate was 90.8%, when two first-level classifiers were used, the accuracy rate rise to 95.9%, and when three first-level classifiers were used, the accuracy rate was 97.8%. In 2020 another study was done of Disease Detection in coffee plants [15] the authors in this work used Sequential model for classification and achieved accuracy of 97.61%. In 2021, research article was published on Coffee disease detection [32] in this work authors used fast Hue, Saturation, and Value (HSV) color space segmentation and a MobileNetV2 architecture trained by transfer learning this study resulted in accuracy of 96%. In recent 2022, a research was made [8] in this work authors attempted to overcome certain drawbacks of traditional segmentation approaches to generate masks for deep disease classification models objective of this research was to label datasets based on a semi-automated segmentation of leaves and disordered regions. In May 2022 [5] paper was published in which authors present a general framework for recognizing plant diseases by proposing a deep feature descriptor based on transfer learning to obtain a high-level latent feature representation Then, integrating the deep features with traditional handcrafted features by feature fusion to capture the local texture information in plant leaf images. In July 2022 a paper [20] was published in which authors proposed a novel 14-layered deep convolutional neural network (14-DCNN) to detect plant leaf diseases using leaf images.

3   Materials and Methods

The following flowchart Fig. 1 illustrates the step by step process of this research. The first step involves the problem identification. In which we identified the problem of this research related to coffee leaves disease detection. After that we randomly split the data into three sets that were training, validation and testing in the ratio of 60%, 20% and 20% respectively. After collection and distribution, the images were prepossessed the prepossessing step included data augmentation and data rescaling. In data rescaling section the data was rescaled in desirable size and in augmentation part the data was augmented to overcome over-fitting of data in the model. After preprocessing, models were designed. Then after the development of models the model was trained on training data. After achieving good accuracy on training data, models were evaluated on testing dataset.

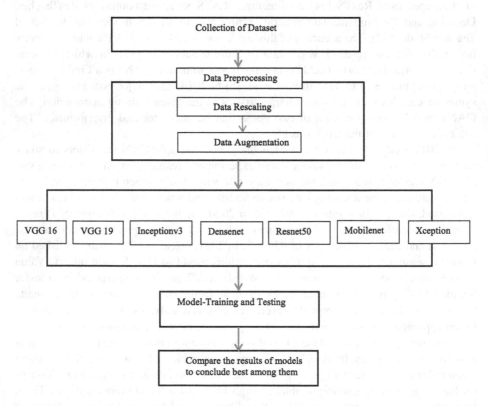

Fig. 1. Overall flow chart of this work

3.1   Dataset

In this research work of coffee disease detection we used JMuBEN2 and JMuBEN datasets, These datasets are publicly available. The combined dataset contains five classes [Healthy, Miner, Cescopora, Phoma, Coffe Rust]. These data were published on 27 March 2021 by Chuka University, University of Embu, and Jomo Kenyatta University of Agriculture and Technology. The following section is the summary of dataset that we used in this work.

JMuBEN2 Dataset. This part of main dataset contain 2 classes (healthy Fig. 2 and Miner Fig. 3) were taken from Arabica coffee plantation using a camera and with the help of a plant pathologist. Then these images were cropped with the purpose of focusing on the target region. Image augmentation was done with the aim of increasing the dataset size and preventing over-fitting problems.

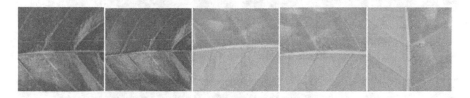

Fig. 2. Sample images of class healthy

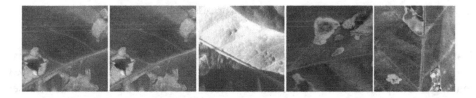

Fig. 3. Sample images of class miner

JMuBEN Dataset. This part of dataset conatins 3 classes (Cescospora Fig. 4, Phoma Fig. 5 and Coffee Rust Fig. 6) The Arabica dataset (JMuBEN) contains images that are useful in training and validation during the utilization of deep learning algorithms used in plant disease recognition and classification. The dataset contains leaf images which were collected from Arabica coffee type and it shows three sets of unhealthy images. In total, 22591 images of Arabica coffee are included in JMuBEN dataset (Fig. 7).

3.2 Data Prepossessing

After collection of required dataset data is preprocessed which contains basically 2 factors that is data rescaling and splitting and data augmentation.

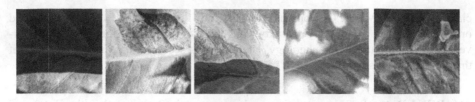

Fig. 4. Sample images of class cercospora

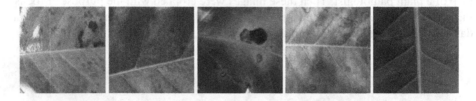

Fig. 5. Sample images of class phoma

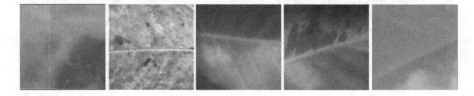

Fig. 6. Sample images of class coffee rust

Data Rescaling and Splitting. This step converts the data into a compatible format with deep learning model in which. The images are then resized to a size of $224 \times 224 \times 3$ making it compatible with the pretrained model. After rescaling of data the dataset is distributed among training and testing dataset. In Which training set have 60% of images validation dataset have rest 20% images and testing dataset contains 20% data.

Data Augmentation. Data augmentation refers to the act where we try to create new data out of the existing data. The purpose is that the image of the coffee leaves is rotated by an angle or flipped along an axis. Basically more images are produced by rotating the original images by different angles.

3.3 Proposed Model

This research paper uses the methodology of transfer learning that is using predefined models. The purpose is to use the knowledge gained by the model on the problem to solve similar other problems. This technique reduces the time while training the model from scratch. In this research paper, we used VGG16, Mobilenet, VGG19, Inception-V3, Xceptionv3, Densenet [121] and Resnet50. For each predefined model, the last

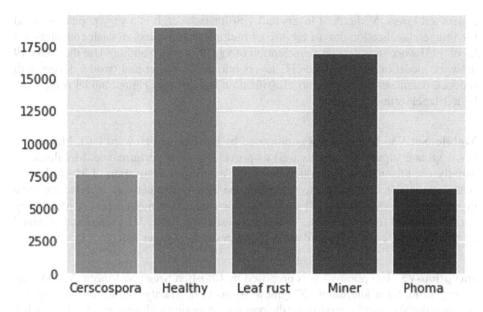

Fig. 7. Number of images of different types

layer which is the classification layer has been replaced by a softmax layer that is suitable for the classification of the given dataset that is number of the classes that are present in our dataset.

Transfer Learning. Transfer learning is a technique where we work with predefined models rather than building models from scratch. In this approach we basically train the model on a large data-set and after training them we use the learnt models to solve different dataset problems. Many a times collecting data can be a complicated and expensive process so in these scenarios we use transfer learning as transfer learning can be a more productive and useful technique as compared to building model from scratch. One of the examples of transfer learning a better approach as compared to model from scratch is face detection, breast cancer and pedestrian.

VGG16. Vgg model was proposed by K. Simonyan and A. Zisserman from the University of Oxford the paper "Very Deep Convolutional Networks for Large-Scale Image Recognition" [26]. The model achieves around 92.7% accuracy in Image-net, containing over 14 million images belonging to 1000 classes. The basic architecture of vgg is vgg have large kernel-sized filters (11 and 5 in first and second CNN layer respectively). Also having 3 × 3 kernal-sized filters. This pre-defined model was trained for weeks using NVIDIA Titan Black GPU's.

VGG19. VGG19 is one of the versions of the VGG model which contains a total of 19 layers. The layer breakdown for vgg19 is that it has 16 convolution layers, 3 fully connected layers, 5 MaxPool layers and 1 Softmax layer. It is a very popular method for image classification due to the use of multiple 3 × 3 filters in each convolutional layer. [33] work shows an implementation of vgg19 in which authors Use the VGG-19 network model to optimise three FC layers into one flat layer and two FC layers with reduced parameters. The softmax classification layer of the original model is replaced by a 2-label softmax classifier.

Mobile-Net V3. MobileNet was proposed by Sandler, and Howard [10]. Mobile-net has a great computation cost as well as provides a great performance. Mobile-net is usually used for mobile-embedded devices. The primary innovation of MobileNetV3 is the application of AutoML to determine the ideal neural network architecture for a given problem. This study [28] shows the implementation mobile net for identifying various types of freshwater fish. The authors used MobileNet V1 trained and obtained an accuracy rate of 90% in the detection of types of freshwater fish.

Inception-V3. Inception-v3 was proposed by Christian Szegedy, Vincent Vanhoucke, Sergey Ioffe, Jonathon Shlens, Zbigniew Wojna [29]. Mainly focuses on burning less computational power by modifying the previous Inception architectures. Model that has been shown to attain greater than 78.1% accuracy on the ImageNet dataset. In an Inception v3 model, several network optimization techniques have been proposed to relax the restrictions and simplify model adaptation. The methods include regularisation, dimension reduction, factorised convolutions, and parallelized computations. In 2019 a study was done [30] using inception-v3 in this work authors used the Inception v3 model in classifying images of human faces into one of five basic face shapes.

Resnet50v2. Resnet was proposed by Kaiming He, Xiangyu Zhang, Shaoqing Ren, Jian Sun [9] ResNet has numerous implementations that use the same idea but varies in the number of layers. The form that can operate with 50 neural network layers is referred known as Resnet50. The ResNet 50 model achieved a top-1 error rate of 20.47% and achieved a top-5 error rate of 5.25%, This is reported for a single model that consists of 50 layers not an ensemble of it. [22] works represents implementation of Resnet50v2.

XceptionV3. XceptionV3 model was proposed by François Chollet [3]. It uses concept Depthwise Separable Convolutions. It is a convolutional neural network that is 71 layers deep. Data first passes via the entering flow, after which it goes to middle flow which repeats eight times and then finally the exit flow.

Densenet. Densenet was proposed by Gao Huang, Zhuang Liu, Laurens van der Maaten, Kilian Q. Weinberger [11]. In DenseNet, each layer obtains additional inputs from all preceding layers and passes on its own feature maps to all subsequent layers. Concatenation is used. Each layer is receiving a "collective knowledge" from all preceding layers. In 2021 a study was made on Facial expression recognition in which authors used Densenet121 as their state of the art form [16].

Table 1. Models comparison table

Model name	Trainable parameters	Non trainable parameters	Memory	Execution time
VGG16	1,52,45,125	0	174.613 MB	7678.6 s
VGG19	2,05,54,821	0	235.398 MB	7907.7 s
DenseNet121	2,00,65,157	2,29,056	93.551 MB	9630.2 s
Xception	2,29,10,253	54,528	263.031 MB	8300.1 s
MobileNetV2	35,40,741	34,112	263.031 MB	9113.8 s
ResNet50V2	2,56,22,661	45,440	41.354 MB	8496.5 s
InceptionV3	2,38,71,653	34,432	274.367 MB	7682.9 s

4   Experiments and Results

4.1   Software Setup

The software used for training the model is GPU version: Tesla T, Ram used for this work is 1.21 GB. The model is coded in the python 3.7.1 version on google Colaboratory. Tensorflow version 2.8.2 and Keras version 2.8.0 was used during this work.

4.2   Evaluation Metrics

In the evaluation part, six quantitative performance measures were computed on the trained models, they are precision, recall, f1-score, accuracy, macro-avg and weighted-avg. These metrics are computed based on True Positive (TP), True Negative (TN), False Positive (FP), and False Negative (FN).

4.3   Results

Each model was trained using the training and validation set of data. The test dataset, which was divided prior to the training of the data train and validation set, was used to consider the model predictions after the model parameters had been trained on the given set of data. It was tested to see how well the given fresh set of images could be predicted. For all the experiments, the dataset is divided into 60%, 20%, and 20% as training, validation and testing set respectively. The comparative performance of testing accuracy for different transfer learning models used in this work is shown in Table 2, from this table it is clear that lowest memory consumed is by ResNet50V2 and highest memory is used by InceptionV3. It can be found that Vgg19, Xception, MobilenetV2, and InceptionV3 produced the highest testing accuracy which is 100% accuracy among all the models used in the work Table 1 shows us the comparison of all the models used in this work on basis of parameter [Trainable and Non-Trainable], Memory used and execution time. From the above table it is clear that VGG-19 is giving as it is achieving 100% accuracy and at the same time consuming least memory and low execution time as compared to all other models that are also giving 100% accuracy (Fig. 8).

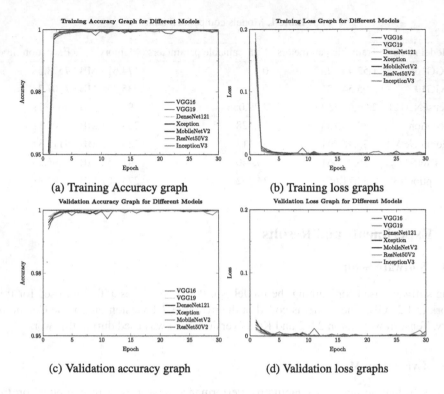

(a) Training Accuracy graph

(b) Training loss graphs

(c) Validation accuracy graph

(d) Validation loss graphs

Fig. 8. Graphs for different parameters

Table 2. Results comparison table

Model	Test accuracy	Precision (WA)	Recall (WA)	F1 Score (WA)	Precision (MA)	Recall (MA)	F1 Score (MA)
VGG16	99.949	0.999	0.999	0.999	1.000	0.999	0.999
VGG19	100	1	1	1	1	1	1
DenseNet121	99.863	0.999	0.999	0.999	0.999	0.998	0.998
Xception	100	1	1	1	1	1	1
ResNet50V2	99.974	1.000	1.000	1.000	1.000	1.000	1.000
MobileNetV2	100	1	1	1	1	1	1
InceptionV3	100	1	1	1	1	1	1

5   Conclusion and Future Scope

As discussed earlier, Recognizing diseases in coffee in its growing stage is an important task as we can avoid the loss in the production of coffee leaves in the early stage. Even a small reduction in coffee yields due to disease in coffee leaves will have a large impact on coffee production. Failing to recognize the diseases in coffee leaves will also affect the economies of countries that are mostly dependent on the export of the coffee commodity. Image classification for coffee leaves disease detection is an important area of research in medical domain. A lot of research have been done in this domain In future we would like to test our models on more similar dataset and even use it for practical applications in real life We would also like to wish to further develop our models to attain more better accuracy for the dataset used in this work.

References

1. Sorte, L.X.B., Ferraz, C.T., Fambrini, F., dos Reis Goulart, R., Saito, J.H.: Coffee leaf disease recognition based on deep learning and texture attributes. Procedia Comput. Sci. **159**, 135–144 (2019). Knowledge-Based and Intelligent Information Engineering Systems: Proceedings of the 23rd International Conference KES2019
2. Brahimi, M., Mahmoudi, S., Boukhalfa, K., Moussaoui, A.: Deep interpretable architecture for plant diseases classification. In: 2019 Signal Processing: Algorithms, Architectures, Arrangements, and Applications (SPA), pp. 111–116. IEEE (2019)
3. Chollet, F.: Xception: deep learning with depthwise separable convolutions. In: 2017 IEEE Conference on Computer Vision and Pattern Recognition (CVPR), pp. 1800–1807 (2017)
4. DeChant, C., et al.: Automated identification of northern leaf blight-infected maize plants from field imagery using deep learning. Phytopathology **107**(11), 1426–1432 (2017)
5. Fan, X., Luo, P., Mu, Y., Zhou, R., Tjahjadi, T., Ren, Y.: Leaf image based plant disease identification using transfer learning and feature fusion. Comput. Electron. Agric. **196**, 106892 (2022)
6. Goodfellow, I., et al.: Generative adversarial nets. In: Advances in Neural Information Processing Systems, vol. 27 (2014)
7. Haralick, R.M., Shanmugam, K., Dinstein, I.H.: Textural features for image classification. IEEE Trans. Syst. Man Cybern. **6**, 610–621 (1973)
8. Hasan, R.I., Yusuf, S.M., Mohd Rahim, M.S., Alzubaidi, L.: Automated masks generation for coffee and apple leaf infected with single or multiple diseases-based color analysis approaches. Inform. Med. Unlocked **28**, 100837 (2022)
9. He, K., Zhang, X., Ren, S., Sun, J.: Identity mappings in deep residual networks. CoRR abs/1603.05027 (2016)
10. Howard, A.G., et al.: MobileNets: efficient convolutional neural networks for mobile vision applications (2017)
11. Huang, G., Liu, Z., van der Maaten, L., Weinberger, K.Q.: Densely connected convolutional networks (2016)
12. Jaswal, D., Vishvanathan, S., Kp, S.: Image classification using convolutional neural networks. Int. J. Sci. Eng. Res. **5**, 1661–1668 (2014)
13. Jia, Y., et al.: Caffe: convolutional architecture for fast feature embedding. In: Proceedings of the 22nd ACM International Conference on Multimedia, pp. 675–678 (2014)
14. Krizhevsky, A., Sutskever, I., Hinton, G.E.: ImageNet classification with deep convolutional neural networks. In: Advances in Neural Information Processing Systems, vol. 25, pp. 1097–1105 (2012)
15. Kumar, M., Gupta, P., Madhav, P.: Disease detection in coffee plants using convolutional neural network. In: 2020 5th International Conference on Communication and Electronics Systems (ICCES), pp. 755–760 (2020)
16. Li, B.: Facial expression recognition by DenseNet-121 (2021)
17. Li, L., Zhang, S., Wang, B.: Plant disease detection and classification by deep learning a review. IEEE Access **9**, 56683–56698 (2021)
18. Marcos, A.P., Rodovalho, N.L.S., Backes, A.R.: Coffee leaf rust detection using convolutional neural network. In: 2019 XV Workshop de Visão Computacional (WVC), pp. 38–42. IEEE (2019)
19. Muller, R., Berry, D., Avelino, J., Bieysse, D.: Coffee diseases, pp. 491–545 (2008)

20. Pandian, J.A., Kumar, V.D., Geman, O., Hnatiuc, M., Arif, M., Kanchanadevi, K.: Plant disease detection using deep convolutional neural network. Appl. Sci. **12**(14) (2022)

21. Pathak, A.R., Pandey, M., Rautaray, S.: Application of deep learning for object detection. Procedia Comput. Sci. **132**, 1706–1717 (2018). International Conference on Computational Intelligence and Data Science

22. Qazi, E., Zia, T., Almorjan, A.: Deep learning-based digital image forgery detection system. Appl. Sci. **12**, 2851 (2022)

23. Qin, X., Zhang, Z., Huang, C., Dehghan, M., Zaiane, O.R., Jagersand, M.: U2-Net: going deeper with nested U-structure for salient object detection. Pattern Recogn. **106**, 107404 (2020)

24. Shah, D., Trivedi, V., Sheth, V., Shah, A., Chauhan, U.: ResTS: residual deep interpretable architecture for plant disease detection. Info. Process. Agric. **9**, 212–223 (2021)

25. Shamir, R.R., Duchin, Y., Kim, J., Sapiro, G., Harel, N.: Continuous dice coefficient: a method for evaluating probabilistic segmentations. arXiv preprint arXiv:1906.11031 (2019)

26. Simonyan, K., Zisserman, A.: Very deep convolutional networks for large-scale image recognition. In: ICLR (2015)

27. Sladojevic, S., Arsenovic, M., Anderla, A., Culibrk, D., Stefanovic, D.: Deep neural networks based recognition of plant diseases by leaf image classification. Comput. Intell. Neurosci. **2016** (2016)

28. Suharto, E., Widodo, A., Sarwoko, E.: The use of MobileNet V1 for identifying various types of freshwater fish. J. Phys. Conf. Ser. **1524**, 012105 (2020)

29. Szegedy, C., Vanhoucke, V., Ioffe, S., Shlens, J., Wojna, Z.: Rethinking the inception architecture for computer vision (2015)

30. Tio, A.E.: Face shape classification using inception V3 (2019)

31. Villarreyna, R., Barrios, M., Vílchez, S., Cerda, R., Vignola, R., Avelino, J.: Economic constraints as drivers of coffee rust epidemics in Nicaragua. Crop Prot. **127**, 104980 (2020)

32. Waldamichael, F.G., Debelee, T.G., Ayano, Y.M.: Coffee disease detection using a robust HSV color-based segmentation and transfer learning for use on smartphones. Int. J. Intell. Syst. **37**(8), 4967–4993 (2022)

33. Xiao, J.Z.X.G.S., Wang, J., Cao, S., Li, B.: Application of a novel and improved VGG-19 network in the detection of workers wearing masks. J. Phys. Conf. Ser. **1518** (2020)

34. Yebasse, M., Shimelis, B., Warku, H., Ko, J., Cheoi, K.J.: Coffee disease visualization and classification. Plants **10**(6), 1257 (2021)

Airline Price Prediction Using XGBoost Hyper-parameter Tuning

Amit Kumar$^{(\boxtimes)}$ [ID]

Government of Andhra Pradesh, Visakhapatnam, India
amitkumar@andhrauniversity.edu.in

Abstract. In order to determine ticket prices, airlines use dynamic pricing methods which are based on demand estimation models. Since airlines only have a limited number of seats to sell on each flight, they usually regulate the price of the seats according to the required demand. During periods of high demand, airlines usually increase the fares of traveling and thus the rate of filling the seats gets slowed down. Whenever the seats gets unsold as the demand goes down, the airlines usually reduce the traveling fares in order to attract the customers. Since unsold seats represent loss of revenue, it will be more advantageous to sell those seats for a price above the cost of service per passenger. A major objective of this study was to determine the factors responsible for airline ticket price fluctuations, and explore the relationships between them (basically, predict how airlines will price their tickets). Thus a model was built which predicts air ticket prices in the future and thus consumers will be able to make better purchasing decisions. Data was downloaded from an online website and data pre-processing and the exploratory data analysis of the data set was done. Later, three different machine learning algorithms i.e., Linear regression, Random Forest and XGBoost regressor were used in this study to predict the price of airline tickets in India. Hyperparameter tuning was also done in order to achieve the best and accurate results for prediction. XGBoost regressor performed best results by achieving highest accuracy with R^2 of about 84% and least RMSE of about 1807.59.

Keywords: Airline price prediction · Machine learning · Linear regression · Random forest · XGboost regressor

1 Introduction

Corporations with standing inventories often use complex and dynamic pricing methods to maximize their revenue. Airline companies use dynamic pricing strategies based on proprietary algorithms and hidden variables in order to fix the price of the ticket. Because of this, it becomes difficult for consumers to predict future price of airline tickets [1]. When buyers have access to information about flight prices then they monitor price changes over a certain period of time and thus can predict future price fluctuations. Observations alone, however, do not allow one to predict the price of the flight with much precision.

I. Woungang et al. (Eds.): ANTIC 2022, CCIS 1798, pp. 239–248, 2023.
https://doi.org/10.1007/978-3-031-28183-9_17

The seats in a flight are divided into several buckets, each with a different fare price. These seats are rearranged across buckets by the airlines to earn more money, which increases the price of the flight tcikets for customers. As a result, different customers pay different prices for the same flight. The price of an airline ticket depends on several different factors such as the price of the fuel in the international market, the distance traveled by the flight, the time at which the customer is purchasing the ticket etc. Prices of airfares are set by each carrier according to its own rules and algorithms.

As airline ticket prices change over time, it can be a very lucrative business to predict when tickets are cheapest. A number of papers have discussed the prediction of ticket prices and worked on the buy-wait strategies [2]. A major way that airlines manage their standing inventory is through yield management, in which they change prices up and down to increase their yield according to historical demand and airplane capacity. Traditional yield management was done by hand, but is now largely automated through YMS (Yield Management Systems). As a result, YMS tries to sell the right seat to the right customer at the right price at the right time so as to maximize revenue. Yield management is not only applicable to airlines, but to hotel bookings, ship cruises and car rentals as well [3]. An YMS attempts to predict demand based on historical data and adjust prices accordingly, and applied a multi-strategy data mining technique called HAMLETT to web-crawled airfare data to predict airline ticket prices. They built a model using several data mining techniques that could predict the price of the airfares and thus was able to save a substantial amount of money for the customers. In their study they used a total of 12,000 observations over a period of 41 d. Also, according to the authors, the price of the tickets are strongly affected by the number of seats left in a flight. [4] used clustering techniques and regression techniques too in order to help the customers to make prudent decisions. Initially in order to group similar airlines groups whose prices were almost similar they used k-means clustering technique and later used Random forest to determine the feature importance for predicting airline fares. [4] has suggested another approach, based on the theory of (marked) point processes and random tree forest algorithm [5,6], which should have less computational difficulty than the HAMLETT approach. Results showed they perform almost as well as HAMLETT, but do have a more useful prediction because of a given circumstance and possible interpretation of the prediction.

This paper uses three different machine learning algorithms to predict the price of flight tickets many days before the departure time fairly well. Thus, the use of this approach could aid future air travelers in deciding to purchase a ticket at a certain price.

Objectives of the study

The main objectives of this paper are as follows.

- To identify the most important features that influence the airline ticket price.
- To predict the airline prices using three different machine learning (ML) algorithms.
- To compare the accuracy of all the ML models used in this study.

The rest of the paper is organized as follows. Section 2 discusses the literature review. Sections 3 and 4 describes the exploratory data analysis of the dataset and the methodologies used in this study respectively. Section 5 contains the results and accuracy comparison of all the models. Finally, Sect. 6 summarizes and concludes the findings.

2 Literature Review

The use of machine learning algorithms and data mining strategies to model airline prices has increased significantly over the last decade. There are several regression models that are frequently used in predicting accurate airfare prices, including Support Vector Machines (SVM), Linear Regression (LR), Decision trees (DT) and Random Forests (RF) [7–11]. [7] applied eight machine learning models, including ANN, RF, SVM and LR to predict the airline ticket prices. In their study, Bagging Regression tree outperformed all other machine learning algorithms with a highest R^2 of about 88% accuracy. [8] used four statistical regression models on data containing more than a lakh observations to predict the price of the airline ticket. Their model recommends the traveler whether to buy a ticket at a particular price or else to wait till the price falls. A limitation to their work was that this model would work only on economy tickets and that too on flights from San Francisco to Kennedy Airport. According to them, mixed linear models with linear quantile were the most effective way to predict ticket prices many days before departure. [9] tried to predict the price of the airline tickets using Linear Regression, Naive Bayes, Softmax Regression and Support vector machine (SVM). About 9,000 observations in which six different attributes like the total number of stops, the duration from the booking and departure date etc. were used to build a model. The linear regression model outperformed other models with the least error rate of about 22.9%, while the SVM performed worst in their study. However, SVM was used to classify the airfares into two categories i.e., whether the price was "lower" or "higher" than the mean price. Based on the type of flight, i.e whether the flight is non-stop, one stop or direct, [10] built a model which predicted the air fares. [12] proposed a mathematical model which would predict the minimum air fares on particular routes. They used a data of two months and by using isotonic regression technique, which basically is a non parametric technique they built a model which would suggest the customers to buy the air fares at a particular time period. The authors of [13,14] examined how airline ticket prices fluctuate over a certain period of time using factors like total stops, total days to the departure etc. [13] used Support Vector Machine to predict the price of the airline tickets in future and achieved an accuracy of about 69.4%. [14] used Partial least squares regression model to optimize flight ticket purchasing and obtained an accuracy of 75.3%.

[15] used Genetic Algorithms (GA) and Artificial Neural Networks (ANN) to predict the revenue from airline tickets. As input features, Taiwan's monthly unemployment rate, the international oil price and the Taiwan stock market weighted index were included. By selecting the optimum input features,

the GA improves the performance of ANN. The model performed well with a mean absolute percentage error of 9.11%. The use of advanced machine learning models are being implemented for improving a model that would more accurately predict the price of airline tickets. To achieve more accurate predictions, Deep Regressor Stacking was proposed by [16]. They used ensemble models including Random forest and SVM to improve the accuracy of the model.

3   Exploratory Data Analysis

The dataset for this study was downloaded from the Kaggle website and it consists of 11 different attributes namely Airline, Date_of_Journey, Source, Destination, Route, Dep_Time, Arrival_Time, Duration, Total_Stops, Additional_Info and Price as shown in Table 1. Initially there were 10,683 observations and 11 columns. The dataset was checked for any null values or duplicate values. Data processing was done for the attributes Date_of_journey, Arrival_Time and Dep_Time as it was object types. So, they were converted into date and time for proper prediction. Pre-processing was done on duration column, hence duration hours and minute were separated from duration. As there were some outliers in Price feature, it was replaced using the median value. In order to handle categorical data, two main encoding techniques were used to convert categorical data into numerical format. The first technique was one hot encoding which was used for nominal data which were not in any order. The second technique was the label Encoder which was used for the ordinal data which were in some order.

Table 1. Dataset description

Sl. No.	Variable name	Description	Data type
1	Airline	Name of the Airline	Object
2	Date_of_Journey	Date on which the journey starts	Object
3	Source	Boarding place	Object
4	Destination	The landing place	Object
5	Route	Route from which the flight travels	Object
6	Dep_Time	The departure time of the flight	Object
7	Arrival_Time	The arrival time of the flight	Object
8	Duration	Total duration of journey	Float
9	Total_Stops	Total number of stops	Object
10	Additional_Info	Any additional information	Object
11	Price (dependent variable)	Price of the airline ticket in Indian rupees (INR)	Int

The relationship between the average price and the airlines is as shown in Fig. 1. From Fig. 1 it can be seen that average price of Jet Airways Business class is highest and the average price for rest of the airlines is almost same while the average price for SpiceJet is lowest. Figure 2 shows the relationship between the price and the source. There is a little bit more outliers in Bangalore and in the rest of the sources the average prices is almost same. Figure 3 shows the relationship between the price and the month. It can be seen that flight fares in the month of April are little bit cheaper than other months of the year.

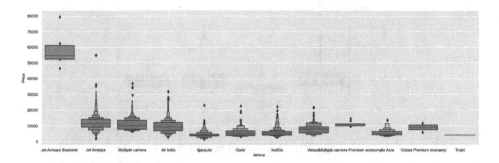

Fig. 1. Average price of all the airlines

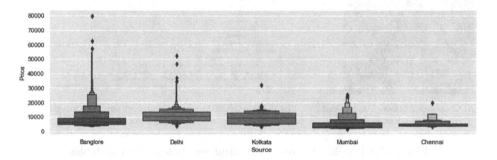

Fig. 2. Average price vs sources

Figure 4 shows the relationship between the dependent and independent variables. Figure 4(a) and 4(b) shows the heatmap of all the variables and the importance of all the independent variables respectively. As shown in Fig. 4(a) total stops is highly correlated with price with a correlation value of about 0.60. The correlation between total stops and duration hours is 0.74 and the correlation between price and duration hours is 0.51. From Fig. 4(b) it can be interpreted that total stops and journey day plays very important role to predict the price of airline tickets.

4   Methodologies

4.1   Linear Regression

It explains the relationship between a dependent variable and one or more independent variables. Linear regression (LR) tries to find a best fit straight line

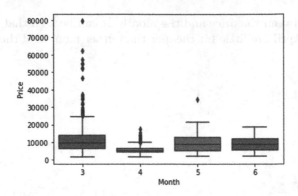

Fig. 3. Price vs month

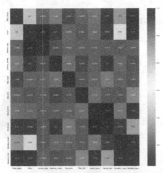

(a) Correlation between dependent
and independent variables

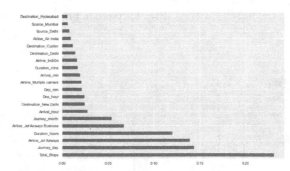

(b) Feature importance of independent variables using Extra
Tree Regressor

Fig. 4. Relationship between dependent and independent variables

between independent and the dependent variable. The mathematical representation of the multiple linear regression is shown in equation-1.

$$y_i = \beta_0 + \beta_1 x_1 + \beta_2 x_2 + \ldots\ldots + \beta_n x_n + \varepsilon_i \tag{1}$$

where,

$y_i \in \mathbb{R}$ is dependent variable,
$x_i \in \mathbb{R}$ is independent variables,
β_0 is the intercept,
$\beta_i \in \mathbb{R}$ is the set of parameters,
$\varepsilon_i \sim N(0, \sigma^2)$ is residual (error).

To estimate the unknown parameters of equation-1, one of the most popular methods which the Ordinary Least Squares (OLS) uses is to minimize the Residual Sum of Squares (RSS) is as shown in equation-2.

$$\widehat{\beta} = min \sum_{n=1}^{n} (y_i - (\beta_0 + \beta_1 x_1 + \beta_2 x_2 + \ldots\ldots + \beta_n x_n))^2 \tag{2}$$

4.2 Random Forest Regressor

Random Forest (RF) are ensembles of decision trees where it has a set of decision trees called Random Forest. Firstly, RF tries to make the subsets of the original dataset. Then the row sampling and feature sampling with replacement is done and later it creates subsets of the training dataset. In the next step, it creates an individual decision tree for each subset and it will give an output. Decision tree algorithm faces an issue of low bias in training dataset and high variance in testing dataset. But, Random forest eliminates this drawback by using bagging technique which tries to deal with bias-variance problem by decreasing the variance in the testing dataset.

In order to train the tree learners, bootstrap aggregation technique is used for the training dataset by Random forests. Given a training set $X = x_1, ..., x_n$ and its outputs as $Y = y_1, ..., y_n$, bagging repeatedly (B times) selects a random sample and fits trees to these samples. For $b = 1, ..., B$, with replacement, it creates n training examples from X, Y, known as X_b and Y_b. Then it trains a classification or regression tree f_b on X_b, Y_b. By averaging the predictions from all the individual regression trees on x', predictions for unseen samples x' can be made. Since this is a regression problem, final output is considered based on average of all the outputs of the decision tree which is given as $\widehat{f} = \frac{1}{B} \sum_{b=1}^{B} f_b(x')$.

4.3 XGBoost Regressor

The Extreme Gradient Boosting (XGBoost) approach implements gradient boosting in an efficient manner which can be applied to regression predictive modeling. This algorithm is used when large data is available to make a prediction with high accuracy. Boosting is actually an ensemble of learning algorithms that combine the prediction of several estimators in order to enhance robustness over a single estimator [17,18]. To build a strong predictor, it combines several weak or average predictors. he main difference between this technique and the other gradient boosting methods is the objective function as shown in equation-3, which basically consists of two components. The first one is the training loss and the second one is the regularization term.

$$\mathcal{L}(\varnothing) = \sum_{i=1}^{n} \ell(\widehat{y_i}, y_i) + \sum_{k} \Omega(f_k) \tag{3}$$

$$where, \Omega(f) = \gamma T + \frac{\|w\|^2}{2}\lambda \tag{4}$$

For hyper parameter [19–21] tuning RandomizedSearchCV was used. The learning rate was from 0.01 to 0.1, maximum depth per tree was between 3 to 10, n_estimators which represents the number of trees for ensemble was 100 to 200, subsample which represents the fraction of observations to be sampled for each tree was between 0.3 to 0.9, colsample_bytree was between 0.5 to 1. Random search of parameters, using 5 fold cross validation was done and the number of iterations used was 10.

5 Results

5.1 Evaluation Metrics

Metrics such as mean absolute error (MAE), mean square error (MSE), root mean square error (RMSE) and R^2 are used to evaluate the models. Mean absolute error (MAE) as shown in equation-5 is the difference between the target value and the predicted value. MAE penalizes errors less severely and is less susceptible to outliers. It gives equal weightage to all individual differences.

$$MAE = \frac{1}{n} \sum_{i=1}^{n} |y_i - \widehat{y_i}| \tag{5}$$

A mean squared error (MSE) or mean squared deviation (MSD) of an estimator (of a procedure to estimate an unobserved quantity) is the average of the squares of the errors, i.e., the average squared difference between the estimated and actual values. Errors are penalized even if they are small and the model's performance is overestimated. A smaller MSE value implies a better fit since a smaller value indicates a smaller magnitude of error. MSE is given as shown in equation-6.

$$MSE = \frac{1}{n} \sum_{i=1}^{n} |y_i - \widehat{y_i}|^2 \tag{6}$$

The root mean squared error (RMSE) as shown in equation-7, is calculated by taking the square root of the difference between the target value and the predicted value. An error is squared before averaging and a penalty is applied for large errors. Therefore, RMSE is helpful whenever large errors are not intended.

$$RMSE = \sqrt{\frac{1}{n} \sum_{i=1}^{n} |y_i - \widehat{y_i}|^2} \tag{7}$$

Coefficients of determination (R^2) as shown in equation-8, is a statistical measure that examines how changes in one variable can be explained by a change in a second variable, when predicting the outcome of an event.

$$R^2 = 1 - \frac{RSS}{TSS} \tag{8}$$

where,

y_i = actual values,
$\widehat{y_i}$ = predicted values,
n = total number of data points,
RSS = Residual sum of squares and
TSS = Total sum of squares

5.2 Accuracy Comparison of Models

The preprocessed data was divided into training and testing datasets. 80% of the data was used for training dataset while the rest of the 20% of the dataset was used for testing dataset. Later, all three machine learning algorithms were passed on both training and testing dataset and the accuracy of these models were calculated based on the evaluation metrics. Table 2 shows the accuracy comparison of all the models used in this study. The R^2 obtained for Linear regression, Random forest and XGBoost regressor were 59%, 80% and 83% respectively. After hyperparameter tuning of XGBoost regressor, we get a model with highest R^2 of about 84% and least RMSE of about 1807.59. Thereby, XGBoost regressor after hyperparameter tuning has outperformed rest of the machine learning algorithms in this study.

Table 2. Accuracy of all the models

Sl. No.	Model	MAE	MSE	RMSE	R^2
1	Linear regression	1961.25	8432989.82	2903.96	59%
2	Random forest regressor	1190.76	4011116.33	2002.77	80%
3	XGBoost regressor	1159.96	3307070.72	1818.53	83%
4	XGBoost regressor after hyperparameter tuning	1190.63	3267398.24	1807.59	84%

6   Conclusion

In this paper, the prices of different airline tickets in India has been analysed. It was seen that the average price of Air India, Jet Airways, Multiple carriers were the most expensive flights while IndiGo and Air Asia were the most cheapest flights. Source wise average price were almost same for all the sources. Also, the airline prices were little bit low in the month of April. The prices of airlines were predicted using three different machine learning (ML) algorithms i.e., Linear regression, Random forest and XGBoost regressor. Feature selection was used to find the most important feature and thus elimination of redundant and irrelevant variables was done. Thus the issue of dimensionality reduction was also done. Based on the evaluation metrics, the XGBoost regressor with hyperparamater tuning predicts the price of the airline ticket with highest accuracy. Thereby, hyperparameter tuning increased the accuracy.

References

1. Etzioni, O., Tuchinda, R., Knoblock, C.A., Yates, A.: To buy or not to buy: Mining airfare data to minimize ticket purchase price. In: Proceedings of the Ninth ACM SIGKDD International Conference on Knowledge Discovery and Data Mining, 24 Aug 2003, pp. 119–128 (2003)

2. Ambite, J.L., Barish, G., Knoblock, C.A., Muslea, M., Oh, J., Minton, S.: Getting from here to there: Interactive planning and agent execution for optimizing travel. In: AAAI/IAAI, 28 Jul 2002, pp. 862–869 (2002)
3. Kimes, S.E.: The basics of yield management. Cornell Hotel Restaur. Admin. Quart. **30**(3), 14–19 (1989)
4. Wohlfarth, T., Clémençon, S., Roueff, F., Casellato, X.: A data-mining approach to travel price forecasting. In: 2011 10th International Conference on Machine Learning and Applications and Workshops, 18 Dec 2011, vol. 1, pp. 84–89. IEEE (2011)
5. Jacobsen, M., Gani, J.: Point process theory and applications: Marked point and piecewise deterministic processes
6. Breiman, L.: Random forests. Mach. Learn. **45**(1), 5–32 (2001)
7. Tziridis, K., Kalampokas, T., Papakostas, G.A., Diamantaras, K.I.: Airfare prices prediction using machine learning techniques. In: 2017 25th European Signal Processing Conference (EUSIPCO) Aug 2017, pp. 1036–1039. IEEE (2017)
8. Janssen, T., Dijkstra, T., Abbas, S., van Riel, A.C.: A linear quantile mixed regression model for prediction of airline ticket prices. Radboud University, 3 Aug 2014
9. Ren, R., Yang, Y., Yuan, S.: Prediction of Airline Ticket Price. University of Stanford (2014)
10. Rama-Murthy, K.: Modeling of United States Airline Fares-Using the Official Airline Guide (OAG) and Airline Origin and Destination Survey (DB1B) (Doctoral dissertation, Virginia Tech)
11. A Regression Model For Predicting Optimal Purchase Timing For Airline Tickets, Groves and Gini (2011)
12. Domínguez-Menchero, J.S., Rivera, J., Torres-Manzanera, E.: Optimal purchase timing in the airline market. J. Air Transp. Manag. **1**(40), 137–43 (2014)
13. Papadakis, M.: Predicting Airfare Prices (2014)
14. Groves, W., Gini, M.: An agent for optimizing airline ticket purchasing. In: Proceedings of the 2013 International Conference on Autonomous Agents and Multiagent Systems, 6 May 2013, pp. 1341–1342 (2013)
15. Huang, H.C.: A hybrid neural network prediction model of air ticket sales. Telkomnika Indonesian J. Electric. Eng. **11**(11), 6413–9 (2013)
16. Santana, E., Mastelini, S.: Deep regressor stacking for air ticket prices prediction. In: Anais do XIII Simpósio Brasileiro de Sistemas de Informação 17 May 2017, pp. 25–31. SBC (2017)
17. Chen, T., Guestrin, C.: XGboost: A scalable tree boosting system. In: Proceedings of the 22nd ACM SIGKDD International Conference on Knowledge Discovery and Data Mining 13 Aug 2016, pp. 785–794 (2016)
18. Friedman, J.H.: Greedy function approximation: A gradient boosting machine. Annal. Statist. **1**, 1189–232 (2001)
19. Putatunda, S., Rama, K.: A comparative analysis of hyperopt as against other approaches for hyper-parameter optimization of XGBoost. In: Proceedings of the 2018 International Conference on Signal Processing and Machine Learning, 28 Nov 2018, pp. 6–10 (2018)
20. Wang, Y., Ni, X.S.: A XGBoost risk model via feature selection and Bayesian hyper-parameter optimization. arXiv preprint arXiv:1901.08433 (2019)
21. Qiu, Y., Zhou, J., Khandelwal, M., Yang, H., Yang, P., Li, C.: Performance evaluation of hybrid WOA-XGBoost, GWO-XGBoost and BO-XGBoost models to predict blast-induced ground vibration. Eng. Comput. **22**, 1–8 (2021)

Exploring Deep Learning Methods for Classification of Synthetic Aperture Radar Images: *Towards NextGen Convolutions via Transformers*

Aakash Singh[✉] and Vivek Kumar Singh

Department of Computer Science, Banaras Hindu University, Varanasi 221005, India
aakash.singh10@bhu.ac.in

Abstract. The Images generated by high-resolution Synthetic Aperture Radar (SAR) have vast areas of application as they can work better in adverse light and weather conditions. One such area of application is in the military systems. This study is an attempt to explore the suitability of current state-of-the-art models introduced in the domain of computer vision for SAR target classification (Moving and Stationary Target Acquisition and Recognition (MSTAR)). Since the application of any solution produced for military systems would be strategic and real-time, accuracy is often not the only criterion to measure its performance. Other important parameters like prediction time and input resiliency are equally important. The paper deals with these issues in the context of SAR images. Experimental results show that deep learning models can be suitably applied in the domain of SAR image classification with the desired performance levels.

Keywords: SAR images · SAR image classification · Deep learning

1 Introduction

Synthetic Aperture Radar (SAR) is a kind of active and coherent data collection system which is mostly airborne or spaceborne. It utilizes the long-range propagation properties of radar signals and works by analyzing the strength of reflected signals after interacting with objects/ surfaces. It is employed in tasks that require imaging of broad areas at high resolutions. In such use cases, most of the time the light and the weather conditions remain unfavorable for optical imagery. However, the SAR technique attracts more noise than its optical counterparts. The noise here is called Speckle which comprises granular noise patterns that distort the quality of the image. The application domain of this technique is very vivid containing areas like earth-resource monitoring, disaster management, and military systems.

With the advancement in technology, high-resolution SARs are now coming into the picture. This has made the manual classification of the images a tedious and unremunerative task, thus highlighting the necessity of Automatic Target Recognition (ATR).

I. Woungang et al. (Eds.): ANTIC 2022, CCIS 1798, pp. 249–260, 2023.
https://doi.org/10.1007/978-3-031-28183-9_18

The approaches used in ATR have been greatly influenced by machine learning techniques since their introduction. An ATR framework for SAR is composed of typically three phases: detection, discrimination, and classification [1]. The first phase evolves the detection of regions of interest (ROI) in an image. It is followed by the discrimination phase whose task is to filter out natural clutters. The last phase is the classification phase where we try to predict a label for the objects obtained from previous phases. This paper primarily deals with the classification phase. Some well-known state-of-the-art models are explored for their suitability in SAR image classification task. Thus, the paper presents an experimental study of application of deep learning models in the SAR image classification domain.

The rest of the paper is organized as follows: Sect. 2 presents related work comprising of the previous studies that explored this problem domain. A brief description of the dataset (MSTAR) is provided in Sect. 3. Section 4 gives a glimpse of deep learning models explored in presented analysis. The experimental approach followed in the study is presented in Sect. 5. The key results of the experimentation are presented in Sect. 6 followed by key conclusions and implications in Sect. 7.

2   Related Work

Several previous studies have tried to look into the classification problem of SAR images. One such classification benchmark dataset i.e., Moving and Stationary Target Acquisition and Recognition (MSTAR) came in the late'90s. This led to researchers starting to work on this problem as early as 1998. One of the initial studies [2] used Bayesian pattern theory to deduce the importance of matching noise models to the noise statistics in classification. Later in 1999, another work [3] tried to explore the 3-class classification problem of MSTAR with polynomial Support Vector Machine (SVM) and managed to achieve an accuracy of 93.4%. A similar machine learning-based study [4] has applied SVM with the gaussian kernel on the same 3-class classification task and has compared the results with other traditional methods. Another research work [5] analyzed various feature extraction techniques namely Principal Component Analysis (PCA), Independent Component Analysis (ICA), and Hu moments, and clubbed it with popular classification techniques, and has touched classification accuracy of 98% on 8-class classification. The deep learning-based methods were seen to be employed in the domain in the year 2016. An AlexNet-based classifier network was created [6] and was modified with dropout layers. They called it "AFRLeNet" and have managed to score an accuracy of 99% on 7-class classification. Another research work [7] has applied deep convolutional neural networks (CNN) as the classifier. This work considered phase information along with amplitude information and claimed to reach an accuracy of 91% on 10-class classification. Few other studies also tried to further improve the accuracy of the classification. However, most of the studies ignored the parameter of responsiveness of the classification model, seen in terms of time required for prediction and the model resiliency. This work attempts to bridge this research gap by exploring the applicability of convolution and transformer-based models in SAR image classification.

3   Dataset

This study utilizes the MSTAR (Motion and Stationary Target Acquisition and Recognition)[1] dataset. The dataset contains SAR radar images of targets (mainly military vehicles). It was collected and released in the public domain by Sandian National Laboratory[2]. The data was the outcome of a project jointly supported by Defense Advanced Research Projects Agency (DARPA) and the Air Force, USA. The collection of data was done in 2 phases i.e., in September 1995 (Collection #1) and in November 1996 (Collection #2). There are different versions of the datasets available. The version used in the study is the mixed variant of both the collection phases. It has SAR images of 8 different tank targets Fig. 1.

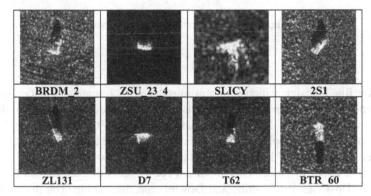

Fig. 1. Sample images from MSTAR dataset

The images generated for the same target at different depression angles may show wide variations. Hence the classification task is a challenging task. The distribution of data inside the classes is also visualized in Fig. 2. It is done as the data distribution is known to largely affect the model training process and also in understanding the performance of the model in the evaluation stage [8].

4   The Explored Models

The recent deep learning-based models used in the comparative analysis have been briefly described in this section. The pre-trained versions of these models were obtained from either the Keras applications library or from the TensorFlowHub. The study used base versions of these models to ensure an unbiased comparative study. The models were used in their vanilla form by fine-tuning their feature vectors only. The top layers of these models were neglected and instead, instead a dense prediction layer was added to suit the target classification needs.

---

[1] Https://www.sdms.afrl.af.mil/index.php?collection=mstar.

[2] Https://www.sandia.gov/.

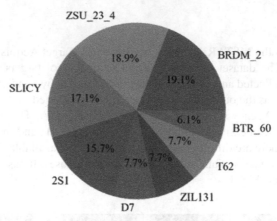

Fig. 2. Class distribution among dataset

4.1 BiT

It stands for Big Transfer, which is a term introduced by researchers of Google brains in their paper [9]. The purpose behind devising this technique was to tackle the problem of scarcity of labeled data. The standard method i.e., transfer learning has been known to struggle when applying patterns learned on a large dataset to smaller datasets. The model architecture of BiT employs standard ResNet with their depth and width increased. The paper discusses two important components that are crucial for transfer learning i.e., Upstream pre-training and Downstream fine-tuning. The first utilizes the fact that "larger datasets require larger architectures to realize benefits and vice-versa". The batch normalization of ResNet is replaced with GroupNorm and Weight Standardization (GNWS). For the second one, they have proposed their cost-effective fine-tuning protocol called "BiT-HyperRule". For the case, the study used BiT-S R50x1 version of the model pre-trained on the ImageNet dataset available on TensorFlow Hub.

4.2 ConvNext

Since the introduction of transformers and their variants applicable to computer vision tasks, a lot of attention has been given by researchers to these models. This has even led to the negligence of mainstreamed convolutional neural network (CNN) based approaches. But, the recent paper [10] by researchers at Facebook AI Research (FAIR) has led to the revival of CNN. The researchers here have tried to improve the residual network-based architecture on the path of the hierarchical transformer. The ConvNext blocks are defined in terms of the transformer's self-attention block. ConvNext has been demonstrated to have rivaled the performance of most vision transformers. In addition, as they work on CNN backbone, they are not restricted by the size of the input image and can be trained feasibly on larger-size images. Out of several versions available the study used the base version of ConvNext downloaded from TensorFlow Hub.

4.3 DenseNet121

DenseNets are among the most popular CNN-based architectures to be used in the computer vision domain. When first introduced in CVPR 2017 [11], it won the best paper award. It tends to harness the power of skip-connections, initially introduced for residual networks. Here, each layer is provided with an extra input made of feature maps of all the layers preceding it. To make feasible concatenation operation of previous inputs, the architecture is divided into Dense Blocks where the dimensions of the feature map do not change. There exist Transition layers between 2 Dense blocks. The DensNet121 version of the architecture was chosen from Keras application library for this study.

4.4 MobileNetV3

This model was proposed keeping two key objectives in mind i.e., efficiency and light weightiness. The mobile applications were the target deployment of this model. It is also quoted as "TensorFlow's first mobile computer vision model" [12]. The proposed architecture uses depth-wise separable convolutions which reduces the number of parameters by many folds when compared with the regular convolution of the same depth. The presented analysis used the V3 [13] version of MobileNet which was introduced much later in 2019 with significant improvements over the original structure. The pre-trained model feature extractors were loaded from TensorFlow Hub.

4.5 ViT

The transformer was initially developed for NLP problems in 2017 in the paper titled "Attention is all you need" [14]. Soon with its introduction, it became the new state-of-the-art in the NLP domain. Later in 2020, the work of Dosovitskiy et al. 2020 [15] showed that the concept may also be applicable in the computer vision domain. This led to the birth of the Vision Transformer (ViT). The concept proved that dependency on CNNs can be removed completely by the introduction of a pure self-attention-based mechanism. ViT works by dividing the image into patches. These patches are embedded with the position vectors. This is then passed to the transformer encoder where each patch is weighted differently according to its significance. The encoder is made up of Multi-Head Self-Attention layers (MSP), Multi-Layer Perceptron layer (MLP), and Layer Norms (LN). ViT-B32 version provided by the ViT_Keras library was utilized for this study.

4.6 Xception

Xception is another CNN-based architecture that relies solely on depth-wise separable convolutions. It was introduced by F. Chollet [16] who also happens to be the creator of Keras library. It is considered an improvement over the InceptionV3 network. It outperforms InceptionV3 by utilizing fewer parameters. The fact that it runs on depth-wise separable convolutions makes it ideologically similar to MobileNets. However, the motivation for developing these two architectures was very distinct Xception was built to keep the model's accuracy in focus, while MobileNets emphasize more on light weightiness property of the model. The pre-trained version of the model available with the Keras application library was employed for the analysis.

5 Experimental Setup

This section discusses the experimental setup and the configurations used while training and evaluating the models. A glimpse of the methodology employed is given in Fig. 3. The experimentation was performed on a competent GPU i.e., Nvidia RTX A5000 24GB. The images retrieved from the dataset were of different dimensions that have to be converted into a dimension of (224,224,3) as all models selected for the comparative study were pre-trained on similar sizes of images. This process was covered under the data pre-processing step. Data augmentation is the next step in line. Here, the study tried to induce randomness into the data set by transposing, flipping, rotating, and saturating the pixels of images. Augmenting data in general cases is known to improve learning performance and reduce problems like overfitting [17]. The pre-processed and augmented data is then fed to the selected models, discussed in section IV, individually for training purpose. The evaluation of all the models were done using 5-fold cross-validation [18]. It was done to get a better statistical idea of the performance of individual model. Model's mean accuracy and mean prediction time were the primary parameters under observation. Where accuracy was calculated using the predefined function available in Keras.metrics, the prediction was calculated by noting TensorFlow's model.predict for the entire test set and averaging it to get the time required for a single prediction.

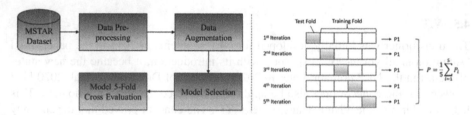

Fig. 3. Block diagram of the experimental design

Now, the configurational aspect of the training process involved are discussed. The same configurations were used with all the models discussed to facilitate a non-partial performance comparison. Popular python frameworks Keras and TensorFlow 2.0 were used to perform the study. The process initiates with loading of the pixel values of the images along with their respective classes using ImageDataGenerator utility of Keras into 32-size batches.

Various standardization and normalization techniques were applied to these batches. These include (1) rescaling the pixel intensity from 0–255 to 0–1, (2) performing sample wise centre, and (3) sample wise standard normalization.

Here, the second step shifts the origin of intensity distribution by subtracting with its sample's mean. The third step scales the intensity by dividing the value by its sample's standard deviation. It helps in reducing the chances of exploding gradient problems along with ensuring a faster convergence of the model [19]. The batch pixel intensity is visualized in the Fig. 4 (before and after normalization).

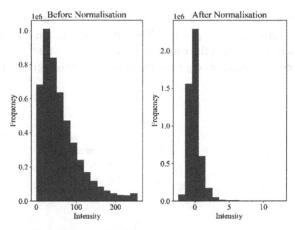

Fig. 4. Histogram plot of batch pixel intensities

5.1 Model Compilation

The loss function used here was cross-entropy loss, since the problem was of a categorical type. Label smoothing option was set to a factor of 0.2 to make learning more generalized. Optimizer is also one of the other important compilation parameters. Here the study used rectified adam (RAdam) for the case. RAdam is proved to be better in handling large variance problems of Adam optimizer for the limited dataset at an early stage of training [20]. The learning rate (lr) required by the optimizer was provided in a discriminative way. A smaller lr $(1 * e-5)$ was chosen to fine-tune the pre-trained models on the target dataset, while a larger lr $(1 * e-3)$ was used for the last prediction dense layer. The rationale behind this was to preserve more information from the feature vector of the trained models by slowly updating it to adapt to the target problem, and also to let the randomly initialized dense layer learn at a faster pace to decrease overall model training time. The lr rate was also dynamically reduced using modified ReduceLROnPlateau callback utility from Keras. It reduces the lr by the factor of 0.33 for feature vector and 0.1 for top dense layer if the validation accuracy does not improve for 2 consecutive epochs. The other callbacks used in the training were EarlyStopping (built-in) to stop model from overtraining, GC callback to handle garbage collection and memory leaks and a Time callback to save intermediate training variables like epoch count and epoch time for every training fold.

6 Results

The results obtained from the study are detailed in this section. This study is an attempt to explore the suitability of current state-of-the-art models introduced in the domain of computer vision for SAR target classification. Here, the results of DenseNet121 are used as the baseline for the comparative study. First, a glance at the training process of these models is discussed. Figure 5 and Fig. 6 represent the validation loss and accuracy curves of all the models. These curves broadly indicate that all models have performed well compared with the baseline. The baseline's validation curves were quite bumpy indicating a less stable learning process. The other models, on the other hand, have performed quite smoothly. On a finer look, It may be observe that ConvNext model has the smoothest curve and has converged in the least number of epochs. It is followed by BiT and ViT.

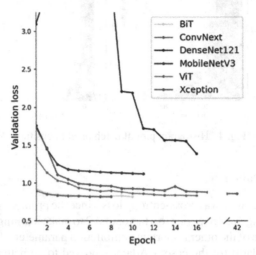

Fig. 5. Loss curves of trained models

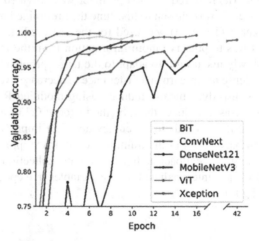

Fig. 6. Accuracy curves of trained models

The Table 1 summarises the performance of individual models after 5-fold cross-validation process. Model accuracies and losses at various steps (training, validation, and test) were captured. These values represent the mean of all the 5 folds that the models have gone through. It may be noted from these values that ConvNext with test accuracy (mean) 99.87 ± 0.09% was the model that outperformed the rest of the models. It was found to have about 4% more test accuracy than the baseline model. Again, it was seen to be closely trailed by BiT and ViT respectively.

Table 1. The loss and accuracy of the trained models.

Target classification models	Training loss mean (Std)	Training accuracy mean (Std)	Validation loss mean (Std)	Validation accuracy mean (Std)	Test loss mean (Std)	Test accuracy mean (Std)
BiT	0.8106 (0.0023)	0.9994 (0.0005)	0.8182 (0.0039)	0.9971 (0.0013)	0.8170 (0.0031)	0.9971 (0.0015)
ConvNext	0.8174 (0.0110)	0.9993 (0.00105)	0.8195 (0.0105)	0.9995 (0.0005)	0.8193 (0.0108)	**0.9987** (0.0009)
DenseNet121	1.5688 (0.2681)	0.9711 (0.0040)	1.6320 (0.2807)	0.9575 (0.0052)	1.6680 (0.4253)	0.9583 (0.0096)
MobileNetV3	1.0979 (0.0086)	0.9957 (0.0018)	1.1100 (0.0070)	0.9906 (0.0016)	1.1116 (0.0045)	0.9899 (0.0016)
ViT	0.8329 (0.0108)	0.9949 (0.0023)	0.8340 (0.0099)	0.9951 (0.0026)	0.8352 (0.0076)	0.9941 (0.0020)
Xception	0.8497 (0.0104)	0.9951 (0.0023)	0.8767 (0.0116)	0.9850 (0.0031)	0.8800 (0.0140)	0.9792 (0.0070)

The study also tried to include the second most important dimension i.e., prediction time of comparison. The Fig. 7 represents a bubble chart where the y-axis denotes the mean test accuracies of the model (in %), and the x-axis denotes the mean prediction time required to classify a single data point (in milliseconds). The size of the bubble represents a separate dimension i.e., the training time required by individual models. It is calculated by the average time required to complete a training epoch (Et) multiplied by the average number of epochs taken by a model to converge (En). Thus the training time would be "Et*En". It is used as a comparative quantity, and we are not interested in its absolute numbers here.

Now, comprehension of the Fig. 7 is discussed. The observation from Table 1 inferred that ConvNext was the best model so far in terms of test accuracy. But, the "Fig. 7" shows the other side of the picture. The accuracy achieved by ConvNext comes with the cost of increased prediction time. It may be seen to have almost double the prediction time when compared to the fastest in the figure i.e., MobileNetV3. Even the baseline model has performed better than ConvNext in terms of prediction time. One probable explanation for the observation could be that the complicated architecture of the ConvNext allows it to learn better features from the target, which on the other hand complicates the prediction process and increases its prediction time as well. If responsiveness is considered the primary objective of a mission, then one may recommend (from the Fig. 7) the MobileNetV3 model for the task. However, if the objective requires a blend of high accuracy and good response time, then BiT would be an obvious choice. The other parameter that can be noted from the same figure is bubble size (training time).

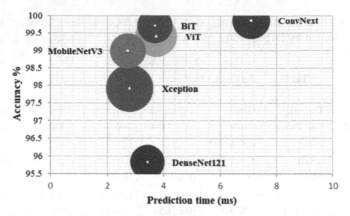

Fig. 7. Accuracy vs. prediction time plot, where bubble size represents the training time of a model.

DenseNet121 (baseline) was seen to have the least training time while Xception had the largest training time among all.

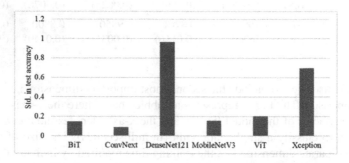

Fig. 8. Standard deviation from mean test accuracy.

The Fig. 8 is plotted to show the variation in test accuracy percentage as models are tested on every data point in successive validation folds. Standard deviation is the statistical measure used to track this variation. ConvNext was observed to have the least deviation from mean test accuracy followed by BiT. This may be interpreted as it has shown the least input sequence dependency in the training phase and was found to be the most input resilient when compared with other models. However, the difference here is not much prominent. Two probable reasons could be that the dataset used contained a limited number of images and that the images were too simplistic/ idealistic (contained only one object per image). The results may turn very useful when considering a bigger and more complex dataset of the task.

7   Conclusion

The paper explores the application of deep learning models in the domain of SAR image classification. It produces an in-depth comparative analysis of the different models applied to SAR image classification. Apart from accuracy, the study tried to include other important dimension of prediction time. To add further, the dependency between a model's training and its input sequence was also analyzed. The results revealed that ConvNext was the most accurate classification model. It was also found to be most input resilient. However, it lacked drastically on the parameter of responsiveness. BiT appeared to be the best choice when considering a blend of accuracy and responsiveness. It has also shown good input resilient characteristics. The results thus present a useful insight on application of deep learning models for SAR image classification. The finding of the study could be utilized by agencies and departments working in strategic sectors to develop a state-of-the-art SAR system. All models compared are in their vanilla state and hence have the scope of further improvement in their performance by considering other domain-specific customizations.

Acknowledgements. This work is partly supported by extramural research grant from Ministry of Electronics and Information Technology, Govt. of India (grant no: 3(9)/2021-EG-II) and by HPE Aruba Centre for Research in Information Systems at BHU (No. M-22-69 of BHU).

References

1. Thiagarajan, J.J., Ramamurthy, K.N., Knee, P., Spanias, A., Berisha, V.: Sparse representations for automatic target classification in SAR images. In: 2010 4th International Symposium on Communications, Control And Signal Processing (ISCCSP), pp. 1–4. IEEE (2010, March)
2. Mehra, R.K., Ravichandran, R.B., Srivastava, A.: MSTAR target classification using Bayesian pattern theory. In: Algorithms for Synthetic Aperture Radar Imagery V, vol. 3370, pp. 675–684. SPIE (1998)
3. Bryant, M. L., Garber, F. D.: SVM classifier applied to the MSTAR public data set. In: Algorithms for Synthetic Aperture Radar Imagery VI, vol. 3721, pp. 355–360. SPIE (1999)
4. Zhao, Q., Principe, J.C.: Support vector machines for SAR automatic target recognition. IEEE Trans. Aerosp. Electron. Syst. **37**(2), 643–654 (2001)
5. Yang, Y., Qiu, Y., Lu, C.: Automatic target classification-experiments on the MSTAR SAR images. In: Sixth International Conference on Software Engineering, Artificial Intelligence, Networking and Parallel/Distributed Computing and First ACIS International Workshop on Self-Assembling Wireless Network, pp. 2–7. IEEE. (2005)
6. Profeta, A., Rodriguez, A., Clouse, H.S.: Convolutional neural networks for synthetic aperture radar classification. In: Algorithms for Synthetic Aperture Radar Imagery XXIII, vol. 9843, pp. 185–194. SPIE (2016)
7. Coman, C.: A deep learning sar target classification experiment on mstar dataset. In: 2018 19th International Radar Symposium (IRS), pp. 1–6. IEEE. (2018)
8. Weiss, G. M., Provost, F.: The Effect of Class Distribution on Classifier Learning: An Empirical Study. Rutgers University (2001)
9. Kolesnikov, A., et al.: Big transfer (bit): general visual representation learning. In: Vedaldi, A., Bischof, H., Brox, T., Frahm, JM. (eds.) European Conference on Computer Vision, LNCS, vol. 12350, pp. 491–507. Springer, Cham (2020). https://doi.org/10.1007/978-3-030-58558-7_29
10. Liu, Z., Mao, H., Wu, C.Y., Feichtenhofer, C., Darrell, T., Xie, S.: A convnet for the 2020s. In: Proceedings of the IEEE/CVF Conference on Computer Vision and Pattern Recognition, pp. 11976–11986 (2022)

11. Huang, G., Liu, Z., van der Maaten, L., Weinberger, K. Q.: Densely connected convolutional networks, vol. 1608. arXiv 2016. arXiv preprint arXiv:1608.06993, (2018)
12. Howard, A.G., et al.: Mobilenets: efficient convolutional neural networks for mobile vision applications. arXiv preprint arXiv:1704.04861 (2017)
13. Howard, A., et al.: Searching for mobilenetv3. In: Proceedings of the IEEE/CVF International Conference on Computer Vision, pp. 1314–1324 (2019)
14. Vaswani, A., et al.: Attention is all you need. Adv. Neural Inform. Process. Syst. **30** (2017)
15. Dosovitskiy, A., et al.: An image is worth 16x16 words: Transformers for image recognition at scale. arXiv preprint arXiv:2010.11929 (2020)
16. Chollet, F.: Xception: deep learning with depthwise separable convolutions. In: Proceedings of the IEEE Conference on Computer Vision and Pattern Recognition, pp. 1251–1258 (2017)
17. Perez, L., Wang, J.: The effectiveness of data augmentation in image classification using deep learning. arXiv preprint arXiv:1712.04621 (2017)
18. Anguita, D., Ghelardoni, L., Ghio, A., Oneto, L., Ridella, S.: The 'K' in K-fold cross validation. In: 20th European Symposium on Artificial Neural Networks, Computational Intelligence and Machine Learning (ESANN), pp. 441–446. i6doc. com publ. (2012)
19. Bishop, C.M.: Neural Networks for Pattern Recognition. Oxford University Press (1995)
20. Liu, L., et al.: On the variance of the adaptive learning rate and beyond. arXiv preprint arXiv: 1908.03265 (2019)

Structure for the Implementation and Control of Robotic Process Automation Projects

Leonel Filipe Santos Patrício[1,4]([✉]), Carlos Roberto de Sousa Costa[1,2,4], Lucas Pimenta Fernandes[3], and Maria Leonilde Rocha Varela[1,4]

[1] Department of Production and Systems Engineering, Universidade do Minho, 4800-058 Guimarães, Portugal
leonelfilipepatricio@gmail.com, carlos.sousa@ifmg.edu.br, leonilde@dps.uminho.pt
[2] Federal Institut of Minas Gerais (IFMG), Varginha Farm, Bambuí/Medeiros Highway, Km 05, PO Box 05, Bambuí, MG, Brazil
[3] UNOPAR - Universidade Norte do Paraná, Av. Paris, 675, Jardim Piza, Londrina, PR 86041-100, Brazil
[4] ALGORITMI Research Centre, Universidade do Minho, 4804-533 Guimarães, Portugal

Abstract. Robotic Process Automation known as RPA aims to automate business processes by reproducing human interactions with the graphical user interface. The implementation of a technology such as Robotic Process Automation (RPA) allows all these routines to be executed by software "robots". The objective of this work is to develop a structural management framework for the implementation and control of RPA projects, based on the PDCA cycle and the RPA life cycle. To achieve this objective, a bibliographical analysis was carried out using key terms related to the theme. Few works related to the theme were identified. An analysis of the works was carried out, verifying that none of the works addresses all phases of the PDCA cycle. However, what is new is a structural framework that covers all phases of the PDCA cycle and the RPA lifecycle. In addition, this framework presents the functions of each of the stages of the RPA life cycle, necessary for the implementation and control of RPA projects, and presents the external/internal structure of the organization chart of an RPA team, passing through the various levels of implementation of RPA, given the complexity of this technology. Finally, a proposed methodology was also presented in the framework to assist in the creation of RPA KPI's. In short, this framework stands out from the others for being quite complete and being able to have good proposals for managing the implementation and control of RPA projects, in teams that are at different levels of RPA implementation.

Keywords: Robotic Process Automation (RPA) · PDCA cycle · Control RPA projects · RPA life cycle

1 Introduction

The implementation of good management and governance practices has become one of the main focuses within organizations. Therefore, it is necessary for each sector/area to

I. Woungang et al. (Eds.): ANTIC 2022, CCIS 1798, pp. 261–274, 2023.
https://doi.org/10.1007/978-3-031-28183-9_19

make adaptations to ensure better adaptation to the management policies adopted by the business organization [1]. This work will focus on the adequacy of these management policies within the Robotic Process Automation (RPA) area, one of the IT (Information Technology) areas.

The management of processes in the IT (Information Technology) area seeks to develop policies, standards, norms, and guidelines that ensure everything is done correctly. In this way, it contributes to the guarantee of increasingly reliable and robust processes [2].

The governance and management of IT end up harmonizing and combining the activities that the IT area develops according to the needs and strategic objectives established by the organization. Always looking to develop reliable and available services to achieve business excellence where management processes are implemented [3].

The implementation of a management structure in the RPA area should contribute to a greater effectiveness of all the processes developed, in addition to directing efforts to then achieve the defined results.

Robotic Process Automation (RPA) aims to automate business processes or parts of them with software robots, through the reproduction of human interactions with the graphical user interface [4, 5]. In addition to productivity and improvement of administrative processes, it helps to relieve employees of tedious and repetitive work. Despite being a tool that significantly contributes to improving the quality of life at work, a critical point related to this technology is the rejection by employees for fear of losing their jobs due to the implementation of robots [6].

RPA is about using digital robots and artificial intelligence to eliminate/minimize human errors in repetitive processes and make them faster and more efficient. It is a technology that mimics the way a human interacts with the machine, performing tasks through configured software or another technological aspect, such as one (or more) robots [7].

The implementation of RPA reduces the manual burden within companies, in their various administrative or operational sectors. In this way, it guarantees greater autonomy to the teams, to focus on strategic issues that lead the company to fulfil its objectives [8].

To manage the quality of products, several tools and techniques are used, among them the PDCA cycle, which is also called the Deming cycle. Initially it was created for the process of quality improvement in the production area, however, this is a tool capable of being used in any management process [10].

The PDCA was developed in the 17th century by Francis Bacon when he proposed inductive studies, which went through stages that were later identified in the PDCA cycle.

The application of the PDCA cycle is possible when:

- Starting a new improvement project;
- Developing a new or improved design of a process, product, or service;
- Defining a repetitive work process;
- Planning data collection and analysis in order to verify and prioritize problems or root causes;
- Implementing any change;
- Working toward continuous improvement.

In its currently used version, the PDCA cycle presents steps for the execution of a process, promoting continuous and incremental improvements, as a managerial decision-making tool, promoting the standardization of processes [11]. As the cycle repeats itself, the process is confirmed or adjusted, generating improvements and learning, involving the stages of: Planning (Plan), in which strategies and objectives are defined. Paths to be followed, the re-sources to be used, the attribution of responsibilities, and the definition of objectives in a measurable way; Execution (Do), in which the implementation of the planning occurs, promoting the implementation of the strategy; Control (Check), to study and examine the results, check if the objectives were met, monitor to identify if there were deviations from what was planned; Act, in which the strategy is confirmed or re-thought, lessons about the results of the process are identified, and the standardization of results is carried out, in the search for continuous improvement [12].

The use of the PDCA in the Governance process applied to RPA, Fig. 1, was carried out from the definition of the actions to be carried out in each of the stages of the PDCA, as shown below:

- **Planning:**

  - Identify the Objectives of the Business Area
  - Define Your Company's RPA Goals

- **Execution:**

  - Definition of Necessary Actions (Internal or External to Your Organization)

- **Control:**

  - Definition of Measuring mechanisms of the performance achieved, comparing it with the objectives defined in the planning.

- **Action:**

  - Analyze cycle results to complete the process or restart and analyze failures.

The management process of IT processes is constantly evolving, so the development of management/governance methods must be adapted to the specificities of technology, thus ensuring an improvement in the quality of the projects developed. With this idea as a reference, this work seeks to answer a key question:

- *How is it possible to guarantee the quality of implementation and control of Robotic Process Automation (RPA) projects?*

The importance of using management methodologies is directly related to the results achieved by the organization. Regardless of the management model used, planning and monitoring the strategies adopted is the key to achieving the expected results.

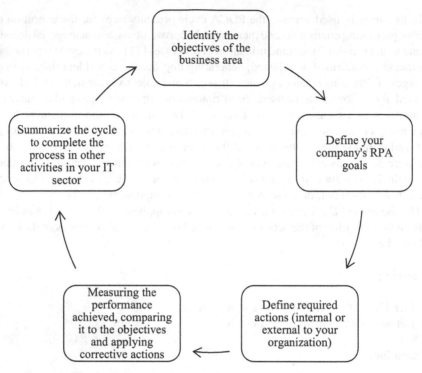

Fig. 1. Steps to Implement a Governance Process in RPA.

The objective of this work is to develop a structure for the implementation and control of Robotic Process Automation projects.

2 Methodology

The methodology for the present work is based on the analysis of a set of data sources considered very important. Through the set of contributions analyzed throughout this work, with investigations of reference authors who investigate this theme or part of it. The set of articles and investigations that were verified and analyzed here were obtained through the database of the online library "B-on". This platform was selected because it allows reaching the full content of a wide range of scientific publications in relevant and indexed journals, together with publications in international scientific conferences, also indexed in the ISI WOS and/or Scopus systems. "B-on" is one of the most extensive databases, which includes thousands of peer-reviewed journals in a wide range of fields from different scientific fields. Through the online scientific library "B-on", of the Portuguese Foundation for Science and Technologies, researchers can access the best-known international scientific databases, so this library was used to carry out the research process underlying this work, based on the following three groups (Group 1, Group 2 and Group 3) shown in Table 1.

Table 1. Groups of searched through "B-on".

Group 1	Group 2	Group 3
"RPA" Or "Robotic Process Automation" Or "Intelligent Process Automation" Or "Tools Process Automation" Or "Artificial Intelligence in Business Process" Or "Machine Learning in Business Process" Or "Cognitive Process Automation"	"Governance" Or "Management" Or "process control" Or "management tools" Or "project management" Or "team management" Or "cycle PDCA"	"Implementation" Or "Model" Or "analysis" Or "development" Or "framework"

Four research tests were carried out through the "B-on" by using the three groups and the OR operator as a connector between the Title or the Keywords (KW) of the intended sets. In Table 2 are expressed the number of articles found in each research test.

Table 2. Research tests performed through the "B-on".

	Title	OR	Keywords (KW)	
Set 1	(Group 1 AND Group 2 AND Group 3)	OR	(Group 1 AND Group 2 AND Group 3)	n = 7
Set 2	(Group 1 AND Group 2)	OR	(Group 1 AND Group 2)	n = 47
Set 3	(Group 1 AND Group 3)	OR	(Group 1 AND Group 3)	n = 1675

After the applied filters (Fig. 2), a reading of the title, the key terms and the resume of each of the articles was carried out to verify which articles were directly related to the research. From the carried-out research, 1729 papers were obtained, applied the filters we verified a total of 948 articles and of which only 18 were framed with the theme.

Next, throughout the research process, a set of filters were applied, based on the sets of publications obtained, and the results obtained, in terms of number of publications, are summarized in Table 3.

The following Sect. 3 the analysis and synthesis of the articles. Here, data about the articles we consider relevant to the subject of this work are presented.

3 Articles Analysis

The following Table 4 presents an analysis of the 18 articles identified related to the subject under study and the phases of the PDCA governance life cycle. We can see the table below.

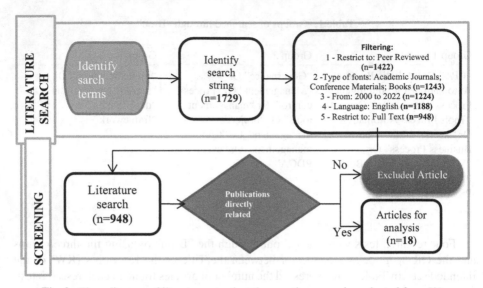

Fig. 2. Flow diagram of literature search and respective screening adapted from [9].

Table 3. Publications obtained through the B-on, after the application of some filters.

	Set 1	Set 2	Set 3
Initial result:	7	47	1675
1 - Restrict to: Peer Reviewed	5	22	1395
2 -Type of fonts: Academic Journals; Conference Materials; Books	5	21	1217
3 - From: 2000 to 2022	5	19	1200
4 - Language: English	5	18	1165
5 - Restrict to: Full Text	5	18	925
Final result:	5	18	925

3.1 Synthesis Results

After analyzing the previous table, you can verify the following observations:

- The phases that are most addressed by the investigations found are, respectively, with 61%, at 3 - Define the necessary actions (internal or external to your organization); and 4 - Measure the performance achieved, comparing it with the objectives and applying corrective actions.
- None of the identified works addresses phase 5 - Summarize the cycle to complete the process in other activities in your IT sectoring their investigation.
- There is no work that addresses all phases of the PDCA governance life cycle, that is, there is a possibility here for the creation of this work, that is, a model proposal that covers all these phases of the PDCA life cycle governance.

Table 4. Studies carried out in RPA and the implementation phases of the governance model based on PDCA.

PDCA Cycle / Papers References	1- Identify the objectives of the business area	2- Define your company's RPA goals	3 - Define the necessary actions (internal or external to your organization)	4 - Measure the performance achieved, comparing it with the objectives and applying corrective actions	5 - Summarize the cycle to complete the process in other activities in your IT sector
[13]				x	
[14]			x		
[15]			x		
[16]		x	x		
[17]			x	x	
[18]			x	x	
[19]		x		x	
[20]				x	
[21]		x	x		
[22]	x	x			
[23]			x	x	
[24]				x	
[25]				x	
[26]		x	x	x	
[27]	x	x	x		
[3]			x	x	
[28]		x	x		
% Articles / phase	11%	39%	**61%**	**61%**	0%

- The works with the reference [26, 27] were the ones that addressed more phases of the PDCA cycle in their investigations.
- The works with the reference [13–15, 20, 24, 25] were the ones that addressed fewer phases of the PDCA cycle in their investigations.

4 Implementation and Control RPA Projects: Framework Proposal

In this section, the proposed framework will be presented.

Through this proposal for a Robotic Process Automation management model, an organization can implement its exact functions and have the human resources indicated, knowing exactly what each of the functions must perform in its day-to-day work. Determine which are the process indicators and monitor the development of each project in an optimized way.

After identifying the conclusions of the analysis table of the identified works, we move on to the presentation of the proposal for the Robotic Process Automation framework.

4.1 Identify the Objectives of the Business Area

In the first stage, the objective of the RPA area was identified, as observed in the literature review [22, 27] and the definition adopted for this work.

- Perform routine activities, normally performed by humans, in an automatic, simple and flexible way, making organizations more effective in business processes.

4.2 Define Your Company's RPA Goals

In the second stage, the main goals that guarantee the achievement of the pro-posed objective were defined, according to the works [16, 19, 21, 22, 27, 28].

- Increase in service productivity;
- Processing improvements;
- Reduce service costs;
- Operational efficiency gains;
- Greater service profitability.

4.3 Define the Necessary Actions (Internal or External to Your Organization)

In the stage, a definition was created for the organization of the tasks carried out from the analysis of the RPA life cycle and from there different levels of implementation and organization of work were defined.

4.4 Organizational Structure of the Teams

After the articles, the need to create different levels of complexity of the governance process in the area of RPA analysis was defined. Because according to the number of processes, the structure needs a greater organization and specialization of the team in each of the operational and management processes. This was based on the literature and on-site organization of RPA processes in companies using this technology.

Firstly, we identified the various phases of the Robotic Process Automation life cycle (Table 5).

Each of these phases presented has specific characteristics, which are described below:

1. Analysis – here the main objective is to identify new project opportunities and carry out an analysis of the same project.
2. Requirements gathering – here the main objective is to carry out all the requirements gathering (access/inputs/outputs/details) associated with the project.
3. Design – Project development – here the main objective is to carry out the final design of the solution and the development of the project.
4. Testing phase – here the main objective is, after the end of development, to start testing the project.

Table 5. RPA lifecycle stages.

RPA lifecycle stages
1 - Analysis
2 - Requirements gathering
3 - Design - Project development
4 - Testing phase
5 - Deployment & Hyper care
6 - Go-live and Support

5. Deployment & Hyper care – here the main objective is the deployment of the project in production and its follow up, and final approval of the project.
6. Go-live and Sustentation – here the main objective is to get the project into support, that is, its monitoring, and the accomplishment of some necessary evolution to the project.

After identifying the various phases of the RPA lifecycle, it was proposed, for the implementation of RPA, three levels of Robotic Process Automation state in an organization (Level 1; Level 2; Level 3). Level 1 is the basic level, that is, the moment when an organization is in an initial state of implementation of Robotic Process Automation technology. Level 2 is the intermediate level, that is, the moment when an organization has left Level 1 and is in an intermediate state, with some workload, where there is a need for more functions for the Robotic Process Automaton. Finally, Level 3 is the advanced state, that is, the moment when an organization has left Level 2 and is in an advanced state, with a lot of work, where it has the need to create sub-stations. Teams within the RPA team to do specific tasks.

To this end, specific jobs were identified for each of the team levels, a demonstrated in Tables 6, 7 and, 8.

Table 6. Level 1 functions.

Workplace - Level 1
Senior RPA Developer (DS)
RPA Team Manager (TM)

After identifying the jobs for each of the different levels, we present a set of specific tasks associated with each of the phases of the Robotic Process Automation life cycle, and we classify them for each of the different levels (Level 1; Level 2; Level 3) who are responsible for each of the functions identified for each phase of the life cycle.

Table 7. Level 2 functions.

Workplace - Level 2
Business Analyst (BA)
Full RPA Developer (DP)
Senior RPA Developer (DS)
RPA Team Manager (TM)
RPA Project Manager (PM)

Table 8. Level 3 functions.

Workplace - Level 3
Business Analyst (BA)
Full RPA Developer (DP)
Senior RPA Developer (DS)
RPA Solution Architect (SA)
RPA Team Manager (TM)
RPA Project Manager (PM)
RPA Support Leader (SL)
RPA Support(s)

The Table 9 summarizes the organizational structure considering the RPA lifecycle and the roles identified in each of the phases of the cycle. In addition, 3 levels of RPA implementation are presented where the roles for the various identified positions were distributed. Regarding the structures worked on, the RPA team was considered as an internal structure and the client's integration/responsibility as an external structure.

4.5 Governance Frameworks

RPA acts at the tactical and operational level within an organization, for the implementation of efficient indicators it is necessary to develop medium and short-term goals. In order to make clear to the whole team the objectives to be achieved. Thus, one must question the objectives to be achieved and the results that should have been generated as governance in the RPA area is being implemented.

By setting clear goals, it becomes simpler to identify the best KPIs (Key Performance Indicator) for your RPA governance. Due to its form, we present here a set of methodologies that will help each one of the organizations to identify the most suitable KPIs for them. Knowing the frameworks (work models) responsible for providing the metrics and guiding the path to be followed is essential to ensure the effectiveness of the implemented practice.

Table 9. Accountability for RPA lifecycle tasks.

1 - Analysis	Level 1	Level 2	Level 3
- Identify opportunities;	DS	BA	BA
- Analyze As-Is process;	DS	BA	BA
- Initial estimation of development effort;	DS	DS	DS, SA
- Initial estimate of return on investment (ROI) & project benefits;	TM	BA, TM	BA, TM, PM
- Assessment document with all the analysis done;	DS	BA	BA
- Customer approval to start the project;	Customer	Customer	Customer
2 - Requirements gathering	Level 1	Level 2	Level 3
- Deep analysis of the As-Is process;	DS	BA	BA
- Risk assessment and contingency plans;	TM	BA	BA, PM
- Construction of the PDD (Process Definition Document);	DS	BA	BA
- Approval of PDD - client;	Customer	Customer	Customer
3 - Design - Project development	Level 1	Level 2	Level 3
- Analysis and construction of the To-be process;	DS	BA	SA
- Construction of the SDD (solution design document);	DS	DS	SA
- Project development;	DS	DS	DS, PM
- Unit tests/Integration tests;	DS	DS	SA, DS; PM
4 - Testing phase	Level 1	Level 2	Level 3
- UAT construction report (user acceptance test);	DS	DS	SA, DS
- End-to-end testing of the project;	DS	DS	SA, DS, PM
- Test approval - UAT report;	Customer	Customer	SA, PM, Customer
5 - Implantation and Hyper care	Level 1	Level 2	Level 3
- Implementation of the project in Production;	DS	DS	SA, DS, PM
- Monitoring the project in Production;	DS	DS	DS, PM
- Construction of the Manual;	DS	DS	SA, DS
- Approval Manual;	Cliente	Cliente	Cliente
- Final approval of the project;	Customer	Customer	Customer
6 - Go-live and Support	Level 1	Level 2	Level 3
- Construction of Business Case;	TM	BA, TM	BA, TM, PM
- Handover for Support time;	DS	DS	DS, SL
- Project monitoring;	DS	DP	s, SL
- Management of evolutions (changes);	TM	BA, DS	BA, DS, SL

The main enabling frameworks you have implementing RPA governance are:

- COBIT (Control Objectives for Information and related Technology) = Work model most used when implementing IT governance.

This framework presents resources that include objective controls, audit maps, executive summary, goal and performance indicators and a guide with management techniques. The management practices of this framework are used to test and guarantee the quality of the IT services provided and it uses its own metrics system.

- ITIL (Information Technology Infrastructure Library) - defines the set of practices for managing IT services through "libraries" that are part of each management module.

This is a customer-oriented framework and unlike Cobit it is a more focused model for the IT services themselves.

- PmBOK (Project Management Body of Knowledge) - Focuses on the management of projects in the area, in order to improve the development and performance of information technology professionals.

Therefore, all definitions, sets of actions and processes of PmBOK are described in its manual, which exposes the skills, tools and techniques needed to manage a project.

5 Conclusion

The framework proposal for the implementation and control of RPA projects, which is presented here, is a very important topic because the value resulting from the management of RPA technology projects can compromise the flow of operation of a business area.

This work analyzed the works available in the literature and identified some gaps that served to propose complementary guidelines to the structural framework proposed in this work. The indicated guidelines covered the phases of the PDCA governance cycle, which served as the basis for the design of the model.

Considering the results of the work, the presented structure was developed from the definition of the RPA life cycle. Then, the various functions associated with each of the stages of the RPA life cycle were identified, and the external and internal structure of the organization chart was presented, by RPA implementation levels, given the complexity of this technology. Finally, a proposal of methodologies that help in the creation of RPA KPI's was also presented.

As a suggestion for future work, the implementation and validation of this structure is verified, as well as the elaboration of a research work associated with the identification of KPI's linked to RPA.

References

1. Brown, C.V.: The IT organization of the future. In: Competing in the Information Age: Align in the Sand: Second Edition (2003)
2. Almeida, A.P.: Boas práticas de gestão de serviços de ti com o uso de ferramentas automatizadas no gerenciamento de ativos de ti. Datacenter: projeto, operação e serviços-UnisulVirtual (2017). https://repositorio.animaeducacao.com.br/handle/ANIMA/4022
3. Herm, L.V.: A framework for implementing robotic process automation projects. Inf. Syst. E-bus. Manag. (2022)
4. Leopold, H., van der Aa, H., Reijers, H.A.: Identifying candidate tasks for robotic process automation in textual process descriptions. In: Gulden, J., Reinhartz-Berger, I., Schmidt, R., Guerreiro, S., Guédria, W., Bera, P. (eds.) BPMDS/EMMSAD -2018. LNBIP, vol. 318, pp. 67–81. Springer, Cham (2018). https://doi.org/10.1007/978-3-319-91704-7_5
5. Hallikainen, P., Bekkhus, R., Pan, S.L.: How OpusCapita used internal RPA capabilities to offer services to clients. MIS Q. Exec. **17**, 41–52 (2018)
6. de Lange, D.E., Busch, T., Delgado-Ceballos, J.: Sustaining sustainability in organizations. J. Bus. Ethics **110**, 151–156 (2012)
7. Zhang, X., Wen, Z.: Thoughts on the development of artificial intelligence combined with RPA. J. Phys. Conf. Ser. **1883**, 12151 (2021)
8. William, W., William, L.: Improving corporate secretary productivity using robotic process automation. In: Proceedings - 2019 International Conference on Technologies and Applications of Artificial Intelligence, TAAI 2019 (2019)
9. Neves, A., Godina, R., Azevedo, S.G., Matias, J.C.O.: A comprehensive review of industrial symbiosis. J. Clean. Prod. **247**, 119113 (2020)
10. Moen, R.: Foundation and history of the PDSA cycle. Assoc. Process Improv. 2–10 (2009)
11. Feltraco, E.J.: Análise da adoção de normas para a qualidade ISO 9001: um estudo de caso com base no ciclo PDCA na visão dos envolvidos no processo. Navus - Rev. Gestão e Tecnol. **2**, 43–56 (2012)
12. Pietrzak, M., Paliszkiewicz, J.: Framework of strategic learning: the PDCA Cycle: find articles, books, and more. Management 149–161 (2015)
13. Kazim, A.: Enhancement of government services through implementation of robotic process automation- a case study in Dubai. theijbmt.com **4**, 119–124 (2020)
14. Borghoff, V., Plattfaut, R.: Steering the robots: an investigation of IT governance models for lightweight IT and robotic process automation. In: Marrella, A., et al. (eds.) Business Process Management: Blockchain, Robotic Process Automation, and Central and Eastern Europe Forum: BPM 2022 Blockchain, RPA, and CEE Forum, Münster, Germany, 11–16 Sept 2022, Proceedings, pp. 170–184. Springer, Cham (2022). https://doi.org/10.1007/978-3-031-16168-1_11
15. Kämäräinen, T.: Managing Robotic Process Automation: Opportunities and Challenges Associated with a Federated Governance Model (2018)
16. Petersen, J., Schröder, H.: HMD Praxis der Wirtschaftsinformatik **57**(6), 1130–1149 (2020). https://doi.org/10.1365/s40702-020-00659-y
17. Kedziora, D., Penttinen, E.: Governance models for robotic process automation: the case of Nordea Bank. J. Inf. Technol. Teach. Cases **11**, 20–29 (2020)
18. Asatiani, A., Kämäräinen, T., Penttinen, E.: Unexpected Problems Associated with the Federated IT Governance Structure in RPA Deployment, vol. 2. Aalto University publication series (2019)
19. Wang, S., Sun, Q., Shen, Y., Li, X.: Applications of robotic process automation in smart governance to empower COVID-19 prevention. Procedia Comput. Sci. **202**, 320–323 (2022)

20. Rogers, S., Zvarikova, K.: Big data-driven algorithmic governance in sustainable smart man-
    ufacturing: robotic process and cognitive automation technologies. Anal. Metaphys. **20**,
    130–144 (2021)
21. Bhuyan, P.K., Dixit, S., Routray, S.: Integration of robotic process automation with. ijisrt.com
    3, 315–319 (2018)
22. Anagnoste, S.: Setting up a robotic process automation center of excellence. Manag. Dyn.
    Knowl. Econ. **6**, 307–322 (2013)
23. Vasarhelyi, M.A.: Formalization of standards, automation, robots, and IT governance. J. Inf.
    Syst. **27**, 1–11 (2013)
24. Feio, I.C.L., Santos, V.D.: A strategic model and framework for intelligent process automation.
    In: Iberian Conference on Information Systems and Technologies, CISTI vols 2022-June
    (2022)
25. Rutschi, C., Dibbern, J.: Towards a framework of implementing software robots: transforming
    human-executed routines into machines. Data Base Adv. Inf. Syst. **51**, 104–128 (2020)
26. Marciniak, P., Stanisławski, R.: Internal determinants in the field of RPA technology imple-
    mentation on the example of selected companies in the context of industry 4.0 assumptions.
    Inf. **12** (2021)
27. Asatiani, A., Copeland, O., Penttinen, E.: Deciding on the robotic process automation
    operating model: a checklist for RPA managers. Bus. Horiz. (2022)
28. Nitin Rajadhyaksha, C., Saini, J.R.: Robotic process automation for software project man-
    agement. In: 2022 IEEE 7th International Conference for Convergence in Technology, I2CT
    2022 (2022)

Shrinkable Cryptographic Technique Using Involutory Function for Image Encryption

Mousumi Karmakar[2] , Annu Priya[1]([✉]) , Keshav Sinha[2] , and Madhav Verma[3]

[1] Chitkara University, Rajpura, Punjab, India
annu.priya12@yahoo.com
[2] University of Petroleum and Energy Studies, Dehradun, India
[3] B.I.T Sindri, Dhanbad, Jharkhand, India

Abstract. Cryptography is the technique of hiding and transmitting confidential information via the internet. There are various traditional cryptographic approaches have been presented by different researchers. Still, these techniques have several limitations, including huge computational times (during key generation, encryption, and decryption) and a high level of complexity (during permutation and substitutions). In the current scenario, Lightweight electronic devices (mobile, IoT, Smart Home devices) are becoming increasingly popular today. These devices create massive amounts of data, making it necessary to seek shrinkable and lightweight cryptographic techniques to ensure security. In this paper, we employ the property of an Involutory Function and a Pseudorandom Number Generator (PRNG) for encryption and decryption. The Involutory functions overcome the permutation and combinations encryption process and shrink the cryptographic operations using Functional Based Encryption. The XORed and Bit-Level Encryption processes are used to acquire the encrypted image. The encryption process is examined in terms of Execution Time. The encrypted image is evaluated using standard NIST statistical testing, Correlation coefficient, and Histogram analysis, demonstrating that the encrypted data has excellent statistical properties and security performance in cryptographic applications.

Keywords: Pseudorandom Number Generator (PRNG) · Functional based encryption · XOR · Involutory function · Light Weight Cryptographic (LWE) · NIST

1 Introduction

The demand for multimedia data has grown in tandem with the advancement of communication technologies. All the e-content on the internet is classified as multimedia data. This data is collected from various industries such as education, medicine, the military, trade, and entertainment. Accessing and sharing huge amounts of sensitive data on the internet requires security. The multimedia data is classified into two types (i) Resolution Dependent, where Bitmap format stores digital material such as movies and photos. It consists of a (0–255) pixel value range. It saves 3 bytes for the RGB picture, 1 byte for the grayscale image, and (ii) Resolution Independent, where mathematical algorithms generate the images for video games and logos.

© The Author(s), under exclusive license to Springer Nature Switzerland AG 2023
I. Woungang et al. (Eds.): ANTIC 2022, CCIS 1798, pp. 275–289, 2023.
https://doi.org/10.1007/978-3-031-28183-9_20

1.1 Multimedia Data and Security

The security of data requires cryptographic algorithms. The modern electronic security system uses cryptography techniques to protect multimedia data on intranets, extranets, and the internet. The encryption methods allow authorized users to decode and encode data. Several conventional cryptographic algorithms exist, such as RC4, RC6, RSA, Advanced Encryption Standard (AES), and Data Encryption Standard (DES). These techniques are mainly focused in-depth by different researchers on textual data encryption. For practical applications, traditional cryptographic algorithms are not effective for Lightweight Devices [30]. The multimedia data generated from these devices are large and take longer to encode than textual data. Multimedia encryption is different from textual encryption methods, and it is true even if the approaches use textural characteristics. A Moving Picture Experts Group (MPEG) formatted one-hour movie, which weighs around 1 G.B., takes two hours to encrypt using the AES algorithm on a 2.6 GHz CPU. The conventional encryption method is inadequate for large file sizes of multimedia data because of its processing complexity.

Based on the above discussion, this paper's work is motivated to reduce the complexity of traditional cryptographic techniques. The pseudorandom number generator and lightweight cryptographic technique provide security for electronic devices. The paper aims to develop efficient mechanisms that overcome the drawbacks of traditional security approaches to facilitate the secure transmission and storage of multimedia data files. The paper is organized as follows: In Sect. 1, introduces various types of multimedia data and data security. In Sect. 3, presents the research methodology based on PRNG and functional-based encryption, followed by Sect. 2, which presents the various methods for multimedia data security. In Sect. 4, presents the result and discussion section. In Sect. 5 presents the statistical analysis. Finally, the entire work conclusion is presented in Sect. 6.

2 Literature Review

The origins of English word "cryptography" came from the Greek words "kryptós," which means "secret writing or solution," and "logos," which means "secret communication." The study of cryptography and cryptanalysis together is known as "Cryptology." Cryptography is the practice of transforming data into an incomprehensible format so that unauthorized users will not be able to decode it. The inverse of cryptography is cryptanalysis, which means transforming unreadable information into readable form without understanding how it was encrypted.

This paper's encryption strategy is based on a Pseudorandom Generator and Involutory Functional-based encryption. In Table 1 compares PRNG based on the length of the generated random stream and running time. In Table 2 compares various encryption techniques using the properties of PRNG.

In [14], the author developed an RNG system using Recurrent Neural Networks and Long Short-Term Memory (LSTM). The purpose of this generator is to produce a random stream that mimics the characteristics of irrational numbers. Huang and Yang [15] employed a Hyperchaotic System with two random-phase masks for image encryption. In [16], the authors propose the use of Deoxyribonucleic Acid (DNA) and Binary

Table 1. Comparison of traditional pseudorandom number generator

PRNG	PRNG mathematical model and performance
Middle-Square Method (MSM) [1]	The middle 'n' digit is square and used for the next round The very short range of sequence generation
Blum Blum Shub (BBS) [2] [8]	$X_{n+1} = (X_n)^2 \bmod M$ X_n = seed value, and M = (p × q) large prime number Short range for sequence generation
Linear Congruential Generator (LCG) [3, 8]	$X_{n+1} = (a \times X_n + c) \bmod M$ Where, m = modules, a = multiplier, and c = increment Long range for sequence generation
Fibonacci based PRNG [4]	$F_k = (A \times k) \bmod B$ $k = [1, 2, \ldots, B-1]$, and 'A' & 'B' are the Fibonacci number It is easy to compute, remember, and analyze Generate a random number in between the interval of [0, 1]
Irrational Number-based PRNG [5]	$X_j = \left(\dfrac{(X_{j-1}+n) \times K_1 \times (M-j)}{K_2} \right) \bmod n$ X_j = Seed value, j ∈ {1, 2, ..., N}, n = positive integer (natural number), $K_1 \& K_2$ = set of irrational numbers, M = N + p (Here, 'N' is the maximum number of elements 'X_j' and 'p' belongs to a natural number). It generates long-range but is not cryptographically secure
Logistic Map based PRNG [6]	$X_n = \Phi(X_{n-1}) + \alpha X_{n-1}(1 - X_{n-1})$ $\alpha \in [3.57, 4]$, a = 3.99999, x_0 = 0.12345678912342, and y_0 = 0.87865765433212. It generates a long range of sequences and takes a longer execution time
Two-dimensional Chaotic System [7]	$\begin{cases} X_{n+1} = sin(\pi(F(a, X_n) + G(b, Y_n))) \\ Y_{n+1} = cos(\pi(F(a, Y_n) + G(b, X_n))) \end{cases}$ Here $F(a, X_n)$ and $G(b, Y_n)$ are 1D chaotic Maps (seed maps), where 'a' and 'b' are parameters, and 'n' is the iteration number. It generates a long range of sequences and takes a longer execution time

Table 2. Comparison of encryption technique based on PRNG

Author's	Technique	Contributions	Advantages	Disadvantages
Benlashram et al., (2020) [9]	3D Chaotic Map XOR for Image Encryption	Encoded using Pixel Shuffling	High Entropy, Fast Key Generation	High Space Complexity
Chen et al. (2020) [10]	Four-wing Memristive Hyperchaotic Systems	Matrix Scrambling and XOR Operation	High Sensitivity, Fast Generation	Take Longer Execution Time
Wang et al. (2020) [11]	Chaotic Sequence Random Integer Cycle Shift	Image scrambling and Bit-level Encryption	Sensitivity of Encrypted Data, Fast Generation	High Space Complexity
Sivakumar and Venkatesan (2020) [12]	Calligraphy and Random Numbers, XOR and Scrambling	Scrambled by Pixel Position Permutation	Highly Sensitive, Fast Key Generation	High Encryption Time
Zhu et al. (2018) [13]	Chaotic System SHA-256	Scrambling of Image Pixel Feedback and Dynamic Index for Diffusion	Highly Sensitive, Fast Key Generation	High Encryption Time

Search Tree (BST) for image encryption. The technique takes up more room, creating an algorithmic limitation. In [17], the author proposed a PRNG based on the properties of a non-integral irrational number. The random stream is used for image padding and encryption. In [18], the authors present the Elliptic Curves (E.C.s) based PRNG technique for image encryption. The NIST standard is used to measure the statistical properties of encrypted images. In [19], the authors present the Memristive Hopfield Neural Network (MHNN) based PRNG generator. The generated stream is examined with 32-bit floating point values with high precision. The proposed model is designed for the Internet of Things (IoT) system. In [20], the authors present a PRNG generator based on the Discrete-Time Model of a simple Memristive Chaotic System. The method uses Euler's and Runge-Kutta's to obtain the chaotic sequence.

2.1 Limitations and Drawbacks of Traditional Cryptographic Techniques

The modern cryptographic algorithms (DES, 3DES, BLOWFISH, IDEA, AES, RC6, and RSA) are selected and evaluated based on their structure, security, and potential for future expansion [31]. The analysis of cryptographic techniques is shown in Table 3.

The traditional algorithms have various limitations and will not suit electronic devices due to their computational time. To cope with the problem, we proposed the shrinkable cryptographic technique. The term shrinkable focuses on the cryptographic structure and

Table 3. Drawbacks and limitations of traditional generators

Encryption technique	Structure	Message block	Key size	Number of rounds
DES [21]	Feistel	64 bits	56 bits	16 rounds
3DES	Feistel	64 bits	168 bits	48 rounds
RC6 [22]	Feistel	128 bits	128, 192, and 256 bits	20 rounds
BLOWFISH [23]	Feistel	64 bits	32–448 bits	16 rounds
CAST-128 [24]	Feistel	64 bits	40–128 bits	12–16 rounds
IDEA [25]	Substitution and Permutation	64 bits	128 bits	8 rounds
AES [26]	Substitution and Permutation	128 bits	128, 192, and 256 bits	10, 12, and 14 rounds
RSA [27]	Factorization	–	p, q, and n (512, 512, and 1024 bits)	–

block size. The functional-based encryption uses the feature of the Involutory function, which consists of a small key size for the encryption, reducing computational time.

3 Research Methodology

After thoroughly examining various research articles, the strategy for encryption is proposed based on PRNG and Functional-Based Encryption, as shown in Fig. 1.

i.   The proposed strategy uses the edge server connected with various lightweight electronic devices. The users can upload the original data ($I_{original}$) to the server for secure storage and transmission.

ii. The next step is Rand Generation Phase which generates the random stream (R_1), which is finite, non-repeatable, and cryptographically secure (Sinha et al., 2022). The K.M. generator's mathematical foundation is presented by using Eq. 1.

$$X_{n+1} = (X_n \times M \times I) \ mod \ m \tag{1}$$

where, X_n = Seedvalue, I = non-integral positive values, M = Multiplier "Maddy Constant", m = Moduli (Any natural number). The binary sequences range lies between $[0, 1]^*$.

iii. The generated random stream's objective is to XOR with the original image. It will create redundancy in the original data. The formulation of the operation is given in Eq. 2.

$$\text{Optimal Encryption Padding(OEP)} = New_{Data} = f(R_1 \oplus I_{original}) \tag{2}$$

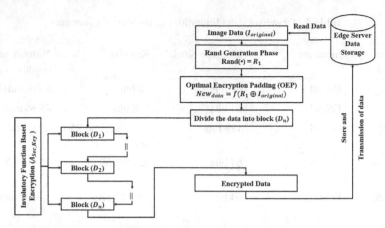

Fig. 1. Strategy for encryption

iv. The data is divided into sub-blocks, and each sub-block consists of a similar size to increase the performance. The sub-block division is based on a user-defined input variable.

$$New_{Data} = New_{Data_1} + New_{Data_2} + \cdots + New_{Data_n} \tag{3}$$

v. Lightweight Functional Encryption (LWFE) encrypts the data file on the edge server. The server uses the Involutory function for bit-level encryption. The Involutory function system is based on the bijection or bijective function. The bijection function is defined as Set 'M' and Set 'N', with the inverse function from Set 'N' to Set 'M,' assuming that both sets have the same elements [29]. The element's inverse property is shown in the mapping:

$$f : G \rightarrow G' \tag{4}$$

$$f(M.N.) = f(N)f(M) \tag{5}$$

For every 'M' and 'N' in group 'G,' the function 'f' is said to have Anti-homomorphism. The involution function is written as follows:

$$f(x) = X \tag{6}$$

and the inverse is written as:

$$f(f(x)) = X \tag{7}$$

Anti-involution is another name for the inverse involution function (or Anti-homomorphism). The encryption process uses a similar approach with a symmetric key for encryption and decryption.

$$Encryted_{Data} = f(X) = \sum_{i=0}^{n} \frac{E_{key}}{New_{Data_i}} \tag{8}$$

$$Original_{Data} = f(f(X)) = \sum\nolimits_{i=0}^{n} \frac{E_{key}}{(Encrypted_{Data})_i} \qquad (9)$$

Here OEP Data = $New_{Data\,i}$, E_{key} = Symmetric Key, 'i' = number of blocks. The involution function uses the stream of data for encryption. The property of the involution function is discussed above, and we know that it has a unique property used to give back the original content when it functions again.

vi. Finally, the encrypted data is stored at the edge server for secure transmission. It will create the optimum strategy for data encryption for lightweight devices.

The algorithm for generating PRNG is presented below as K.M. Generator (Sinha et al. 2022) [6].

Algorithm 1: K.M. Generator (Sinha et al., 2022) [6]

01: Start
02: Select seed value (X_n)
03: Initialized non-integral (I), multiplier (M), moduli (m), and n.
04: for i = 1 to n, do
05: Generate: float $S_{dec} \leftarrow X_{n+1} = (X_n \times M \times I)$ mod m, {Sequence} $\in$ {0 to m}
06: Convert: int $I_n \leftarrow$ as.integer (S_{dec}), integer output $\in$ {0 to m}
07: Convert: int $B_i \leftarrow$ (I_n mod 2), bits $\in$ [0, 1]*
08: end for
09: Stop

---

4 Result and Discussion

This section is concerned with PRNG generator and encryption, which is done on a local system. We ran the pseudorandom sequence generator (PRSG) on the Linux Mint 19.1 platform, with 4 GB RAM, a 64-bit operating system, and an Intel core i5, the single-core processor running at 1.70 GHz. The statistical test ensures that the encrypted data is uniformly distributed and cryptographically secure.

4.1 Pseudo Random Number Generator

Figure 2 represents the pseudorandom number generation for the random bit's generation. Figure 2(a) represents the generation of random bits in (256 × 256) bit of frame, and Fig. 2(b) presents the random bit pixel.

4.2 Image Encryption and Decryption

The foundation of this case study is image (.jpg) encryption. The benchmark images are taken from the website (http://www.imageprocessingplace.com/rootfilesV3/image databases.htm). We'll utilize five grayscale photos of resolution (256 × 256) pixels—Lena, House, Cameraman, Boat, and Jetplane—XOR and function-based encryption is used to create the encrypted image. Figure 3 presents the encryption/decryption process of the boot image.

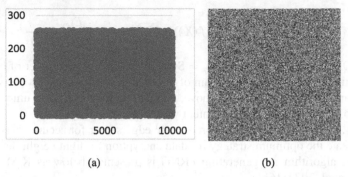

(a)   (b)

Fig. 2. Pixel representation (a) 256 × 256 bit of random pixels, (b) random bit pixel image

(a) Original   (b) Encrypted Image   (c) Decrypted Image

Fig. 3. Encryption and decryption process of boot image

5   Statistical Analysis

5.1   Histogram Analysis

In Table 4 shows a comparison of encrypted and original data. According to the observation, the pixels of the original file are not uniformly distributed. However, the frequencies of the pixels in encrypted files are evenly distributed over the histogram graph plot. It illustrates the exceptional quality of cipher images and reveals no relationship between neighboring pixels after encryption.

5.2   NIST Statistical Analysis

The encrypted data is tested to the NIST statistical suite for randomness. In Table 5 illustrates the testing input parameters based on the NIST SP 800 standard.

A statistical tool called the NIST suite has 16 tests for evaluating the randomness of generated sequences. The focus of these tests is on various forms of non-randomness in the sequence [8]. The tests are listed below:

- A block frequency test determines the proportion of ones in an M-bit block. A frequency test determines the proportion of ones in the entire sequence.
- Block frequency test is used to determine the proportion of ones in the entire sequence.

Table 4. Histogram analysis of original and encrypted image

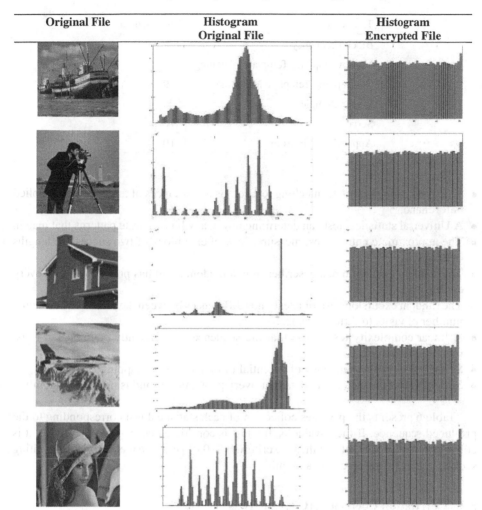

Original File	Histogram Original File	Histogram Encrypted File

- The most significant deviation of 0's in the random walk is the focus of the cumulative sum test.
- If the oscillation of 0's and 1's is too rapid or sluggish, the Runs test is utilized.
- The test for the longest run of ones in a block looked for irregularities in sequence length.
- The rank test examines the linear relationships between fixed-length substrings and the initial sequence.
- FFT test finds repeating patterns close to one another.
- Non-overlapping template matching tests identify non-periodic patterns that recur too frequently.

Table 5. Input parameters

Test name	Block length
Block Frequency	128
Non-overlapping Template Matching	9
Overlapping Template Matching	9
Linear Complexity	500
Serial	16
Approximate Entropy	10

- The overlapping template matching test counts the instances of target strings supplied beforehand.
- A Universal statistical test can determine how many bits separate patterns that match.
- The approximate entropy test measures how often a block of two successive lengths overlaps.
- The random excursion test describes how a random stroll has precisely k trips every cycle.
- The random excursion variation test finds differences between the predicted and actual number of visits to different states.
- A linear complexity test shows that the sequence is sufficiently complicated to be regarded as random.
- Serial 1 detects the frequency of potential m-bit pattern overlapping.
- Serial 2 looks for patterns in data that overlap by 2 m bits and is ordered randomly.

Table 6 presents the p-values collection of each statistical test corresponding to the produced sequence. If the P-value is, the test is considered successful; otherwise, it is considered failed. The set significance criterion (>0.01) must be met before the resulting sequence may be accepted as random.

5.3   Correlation Coefficient (C.F.) Analysis

The correlation coefficient analysis is a statistical approach used to compare neighboring pixels in the original and encrypted images. The correlation is calculated using the mean and variance of neighboring pixels. The findings are evaluated so that the surrounding pixel correlation coefficient for the original image is the highest (closest to 1) and the lowest for the encrypted image (closest to 0). The conclusions are based on the pixels' diagonal, vertical, and horizontal correlations. The correlation coefficient is calculated using Eq. 10.

$$Corr_{(x,y)} = \frac{\left| \frac{1}{N} \sum_{i=1}^{n} (x_i - E(x))(y_i - E(y)) \right|}{\sqrt{\frac{1}{N} \sum_{i=1}^{n} (x_i - E(x))^2 \times \frac{1}{N} \sum_{i=1}^{n} (y_i - E(y))^2}} \tag{10}$$

Table 6. NIST SP 800-22 statistical test on encrypted image

Statistical test	Encrypted images				
	Cameraman	House	Jet plane	Lena	Boat
Frequency	0.8043	0.8842	0.9241	0.8904	0.8014
Block Frequency	0.9103	0.9423	0.9236	0.9273	0.8921
Cumulative sums	0.8123	0.8711	0.8164	0.8155	0.8911
Runs	0.9774	0.9213	0.9183	0.9113	0.9123
Longest runs	0.8331	0.8160	0.8236	0.8452	0.8332
Rank Test	0.7633	0.7162	0.7032	0.7422	0.7321
FFT	0.8315	0.8421	0.8442	0.8764	0.9523
Non-overlapping Templates	0.9187	0.8719	0.8944	0.7919	0.8293
Overlapping Templates	0.8311	0.8887	0.8121	0.8623	0.8123
Universal	0.4256	0.4231	0.4123	0.4632	0.4321
Approximate entropy	0.9521	0.9328	0.9128	0.9268	0.9628
Random excursions ($x = -4$)	0.3714	0.3499	0.3564	0.3465	0.3654
Random excursions variant ($X = -9$)	0.3312	0.3590	0.3991	0.3949	0.3360
Linear Complexity	0.9321	0.9139	0.9335	0.9245	0.9451
Serial 1	0.9753	0.9663	0.9264	0.9532	0.9253
Serial 2	0.9133	0.9440	0.9242	0.9642	0.9520

Here the parameter like E(x) and E(y) is the mean of the x-axis and y-axis of the pixels vector, and it is calculated by Eq. 11.

$$E(x) = \frac{1}{N} \sum_{i=1}^{n} x_i \& E(y) = \frac{1}{N} \sum_{i=1}^{n} y_i \qquad (11)$$

The output is based on the evaluation of 16384 neighboring pixel pairs. Table 7 presents the five different grayscale pictures of size (256×256) benchmarks. The statistical results revealed the difference between encrypted and original images, where original data ($New_{Data\,i}$) is closer to 1, while encrypted data ($Encrypted_{Data}$) is closer to 0. It is determined that the suggested functional-based encryption provides high entropy among nearby pixels.

5.4 Comparison of Encryption Time

The traditional cryptographic technique takes a significant amount of computational time. Table 8 compares various encryption techniques based on the encryption time.

As the file size increases, the encryption times for the AES, Blowfish, and XOR methods increase, as shown in Table 8. The encryption times for the AES and blowfish algorithms are almost equal. When utilizing the XOR approach, the encryption rates for all sample file sizes are essentially the same. RSA takes much longer for all sizes than

Table 7. Comparison of correlation coefficient

Algorithm	Images	Direction	Plane	Encrypted
Proposed LWE Technique	Cameraman (256 × 256)	Horizontal	0.9688	−0.0027
		Vertical	0.9725	−0.0018
		Diagonal	0.9997	−0.0004
	House (256 × 256)	Horizontal	0.9954	−0.0019
		Vertical	0.9932	−0.0039
		Diagonal	1.0000	−0.0045
	Jet Plane (256 × 256)	Horizontal	0.9664	−0.0013
		Vertical	0.9661	−0.0018
		Diagonal	1.0000	−0.0006
	Lena (256 × 256)	Horizontal	0.9419	−0.0031
		Vertical	0.9615	−0.0032
		Diagonal	0.9993	−0.0037
	Boat (256 × 256)	Horizontal	0.9962	−0.0018
		Vertical	0.9721	−0.0021
		Diagonal	0.9215	−0.0007
		Diagonal	0.9592	0.0011
DNA-BST [16]	Cameraman (256 × 256)	Horizontal	0.9688	0.0024
		Vertical	0.9725	0.0042
		Diagonal	0.9997	0.0019
	House (256 × 256)	Horizontal	0.9954	0.0053
		Vertical	0.9932	0.0091
		Diagonal	1.0000	0.0032
	Jet Plane (256 × 256)	Horizontal	0.9664	0.0055
		Vertical	0.9661	0.0086
		Diagonal	1.0000	0.0092
	Lena (256 × 256)	Horizontal	0.9419	0.0015
		Vertical	0.9615	0.0019
		Diagonal	0.9993	0.0012
	Boat (256 × 256)	Horizontal	0.9962	0.0084
		Vertical	0.9721	0.0084
		Diagonal	0.9215	0.0012

Table 8. Comparison of encryption time

File name resolution (256 × 256)	Size in (kb)	Encryption time (Sec)				
		Blowfish [28]	AES [28]	XOR [28]	RSA [28]	Proposed LWE technique
Cameraman	112	2.12	1.76	1.98	5.14	0.95
House	45	1.19	1.05	0.96	3.21	0.63
Lena	116	2.32	1.82	1.54	5.24	0.98
Jet Plain	76	1.73	2.15	1.17	4.12	0.72
Boat	92	1.93	2.32	1.26	4.76	0.92

other techniques, whereas the proposed LWE Technique requires much less time than other cryptographic techniques. The proposed technique is cryptographically secure, fast, and efficient for lightweight devices.

6 Conclusion

This paper proposed the Shrinkable lightweight cryptographic technique using a Pseudo-random number generator and Functional based encryption for multimedia data. The data is collected from various lightweight electronic sources. These devices are more compatible with edge servers for storage and transmission. This paper uses the K.M. generator for random stream generation, XORed with the original image. Further, Functional-based encryption is used for bit-level encryption. NIST statistical test is used for the performance analysis, which shows that the encrypted data is cryptographically secure. The result of the proposed method is also compared with the traditional cryptographic technique. The results show that the proposed method is suitable for lightweight devices. In the future, we will also conduct trials to combine our system with IoT devices to check the cryptographic algorithm performance.

References

1. Meiser, L.C., Koch, J., Antkowiak, P.L., Stark, W.J., Heckel, R., Grass, R.N.: DNA synthesis for true random number generation. Nat. Commun. **11**(1), 1–9 (2020)
2. Laia, O., Zamzami, E.M., Sutarman: Analysis of combination algorithm Data Encryption Standard (DES) and Blum-Blum-Shub (BBS). J. Phys. Conf. Ser. **1898**(1), 012017 (2021)
3. Ivanov, M.A., Konnova, I.G., Salikov, E.A., Stepanova, M.A.: Obfuscation of logic schemes of pseudorandom number generators based on linear and non-linear feedback shift registers. Bezopasnost informacionnyh Tehnol. **28**(1), 74–83 (2021)
4. Anderson P.G.: A Fibonacci-Based Pseudorandom Number Generator. Applications of Fibonacci Numbers, pp. 1–8 (1991)
5. Milinković, L., Antić, M. and Čiča, Z.: Pseudorandom number generator based on irrational numbers. In 10th International Conference on Telecommunication in Modern Satellite Cable and Broadcasting Services (TELSIKS), vol. 2, pp. 719–722. IEEE (2011)

6. Man, Z., et al.: A novel image encryption algorithm based on least squares generative adversarial network random number generator. Multimedia Tools Appl. **80**(18), 27445–27469 (2021). https://doi.org/10.1007/s11042-021-10979-w
7. Huang, H., Yang, S., Ye, R.: Efficient symmetric image encryption by using a novel 2D chaotic system. IET Image Proc. **14**(6), 1157–1163 (2020)
8. Rukhin, A., Soto, J., Nechvatal, J., Smid, M., Barker, E.: A statistical test suite for random and pseudorandom number generators for cryptographic applications. Booz-allen and hamilton inc mclean va. NIST (2000). https://doi.org/10.6028/nist.sp.800-22
9. Benlashram, A., Al-Ghamdi, M., AlTalhi, R., Laabidi, P.K.: A novel approach of image encryption using pixel shuffling and 3D chaotic map. J. Phys. Conf. Ser. **1447**(1), 012009 (2020). (IOP Publishing)
10. Chen, X., et al.: Pseudorandom number generator based on three kinds of four-wing memristive hyperchaotic system and its application in image encryption. In: Muñoz-Pacheco, J.S. (ed.) Complexity, pp. 1–17 (2020). https://doi.org/10.1155/2020/8274685
11. Wang, X.Y., Gu, S.X., Zhang, Y.Q.: Novel image encryption algorithm based on cycle shift and chaotic system. Opt. Lasers Eng. **68**, 126–134 (2015)
12. Sivakumar, T., Venkatesan, R.: A novel image encryption using calligraphy based scan method and random number. KSII Trans. Internet Inform. Syst. **9**(6), 2317–2337 (2015)
13. Zhu, S., Zhu, C., Wang, W.: A new image encryption algorithm based on chaos and secure hash SHA-256. Entropy **20**(9), 716 (2018)
14. Jeong, Y.S., Oh, K., Cho, C.K., Choi, H.J.: Pseudo random number generation using LSTMs and irrational numbers. In: 2018 IEEE International Conference on Big Data and Smart Computing (BigComp), pp. 541–544. IEEE (2018)
15. Huang, H., Yang, S.: Image encryption technique combining compressive sensing with double random-phase encoding. Math. Probl. Eng. **2018**, 1–10 (2018)
16. Nematzadeh, H., Enayatifar, R., Yadollahi, M., Lee, M., Jeong, G.: Binary search tree image encryption with DNA. Optik **202**, 163505 (2020)
17. Sinha, K., Paul, P., Amritanjali: An improved pseudorandom sequence generator and its application to image encryption. KSII Trans. Internet Inform. Syst. **16**(4), 1307–1329 (2022)
18. AbdElHaleem, S.H., Abd-El-Hafiz, S.K., Radwan, A.G.: A generalized framework for elliptic curves based PRNG and its utilization in image encryption. Sci. Rep. **12**(1), 1–16 (2022)
19. Yu, F., Zhang, Z., Shen, H., Huang, Y., Cai, S., Du, S.: FPGA implementation and image encryption application of a new PRNG based on a memristive Hopfield neural network with a special activation gradient. Chin. Phys. B **31**(2), 020505 (2022)
20. Haliuk, S., Krulikovskyi, O., Vovchuk, D., Corinto, F.: Memristive structure-based chaotic system for PRNG. Symmetry **14**(1), 68 (2022)
21. Wu, Y., Dai, X.: Encryption of accounting data using DES algorithm in computing environment. J. Intell. Fuzzy Syst. **39**(4), 5085–5095 (2020)
22. Sohal, M., Sharma, S.: BDNA-A DNA inspired symmetric key cryptographic technique to secure cloud computing. J. King Saud Univ. Comput. Inform. Sci. **34**(1), 1417–1425 (2022)
23. Jasim, Z.M.: Image encryption using modification blowfish algorithm. Int. J. Adv. Sci. Res. Eng. **06**(03), 182–186 (2020)
24. Aggarwal, K., Kaur Saini, J., Verma, H.K.: Performance evaluation of RC6, blowfish, DES, IDEA, CAST-128 block ciphers. Int. J. Comput. Appl. **68**(25), 10–16 (2013)
25. Rahim, R., Mesran, M., Siahaan, A.P.U.: Data Security with International Data Encryption Algorithm (2017). https://doi.org/10.31227/osf.io/r98e5
26. Singh, A.: Comparative analysis of reduced round dynamic AES with standard AES algorithm. Int. J. Comput. Appl. **183**(10), 41–49 (2021). https://doi.org/10.5120/ijca2021921407
27. Cao, N., O'Neill, A., Zaheri, M.: Toward RSA-OAEP without random oracles. In: Kiayias, A., Kohlweiss, M., Wallden, P., Zikas, V. (eds.) PKC 2020. LNCS, vol. 12110, pp. 279–308. Springer, Cham (2020). https://doi.org/10.1007/978-3-030-45374-9_10

28. Chaddha, R., Kumar, A., Sinha, K., Paul, P., Amritanjali: Selection on various traditional image encryption techniques: a study. In: Nath, V., Mandal, J. (eds.) Nanoelectronics, Circuits and Communication Systems. NCCS 2018. LNCS, vol 642, pp. 219–228. Springer, Singapore (2020). https://doi.org/10.1007/978-981-15-2854-5_20
29. Pranav, P., Dutta, S., Chakraborty, S.: An involution function-based symmetric stream cipher. In: Nath, V., Mandal, J.K. (eds.) Proceedings of the Fourth International Conference on Microelectronics, Computing and Communication Systems. LNEE, vol. 673, pp. 61–68. Springer, Singapore (2021). https://doi.org/10.1007/978-981-15-5546-6_5
30. Nayancy, Dutta, S., Chakraborty, S.: A survey on implementation of lightweight block ciphers for resource constraints devices. J. Discrete Math. Sci. Cryptograph. 25(5), 1377–1398 (2022)
31. Suresh, D., Odelu, V., Reddy, A.G., Phaneendra, K., Kim, H.S.: Provably secure pseudo-identity three-factor authentication protocol based on extended chaotic-maps for lightweight mobile devices. IEEE Access 10, 109526–109536 (2022)

Implementation of Deep Learning Models for Real-Time Face Mask Detection System Using Raspberry Pi

V. Vanitha[1]([✉]), N. Rajathi[1], R. Kalaiselvi[2], and V. P. Sumathi[3]

[1] Department of Information Technology, Kumaraguru College of Technology,
Coimbatore 641049, India
{vanitha.v.it,rajathi.n.it}@kct.ac.in
[2] Department of Information Science and Engineering, Kumaraguru College of Technology,
Coimbatore 641049, India
kalaiselvi.r.cse@kct.ac.in
[3] Department of Computer Science and Engineering, Kumaraguru College of Technology,
Coimbatore 641049, India
sumathi.vp@kct.ac.in

Abstract. Amidst this COVID-19 pandemic, it is of utmost importance to wear facemasks and follow precautionary and preventive measures to decrease the further spread of this virus. In recent years Convolutional Neural networks (CNN) has impacted tremendously in various fields for classification and detection systems. In this paper we propose a facemask detection system using deep learning algorithms and a comparative study of various metrics for these deep learning algorithms. Algorithms like VGG, Resnet, Inception, Nasnet and Densenet, and its variations have been used. Using these deep learning models as a base and fine tuning the output layers of these models we construct an architecture for deep learning. Hyperparameter tuning and other methods like data augmentation have also helped in achieving better results. Various metrics like precision, recall, F1score, Average precision, accuracy and hamming loss has been evaluated for the models trained. An accuracy of 93.76% and average precision of 90.99% is achieved for the Denset201. Furthermore, we propose a standalone facemask detection system using the Raspberry Pi and a camera by fitting in the Nasnet mobile model into the detection system. Many applications for this system can be foreseen in places like hospitals, malls, restaurants and other places of public interest as an authentication or entry access criteria system.

Keywords: Deep learning · Convolution neural network · Face mask detection · Computer vision · Artificial Intelligence · Raspberry Pi

1 Introduction

Coronavirus or COVID-19 is a viral disease caused by SARS-Cov-2 (Severe Accurate Respiratory Syndrome Coronavirus 2) which leads to symptoms such as breathing difficulties, fevers, colds, muscle pain etc. This virus spreads through water droplets through

I. Woungang et al. (Eds.): ANTIC 2022, CCIS 1798, pp. 290–304, 2023.
https://doi.org/10.1007/978-3-031-28183-9_21

the air medium and anyone in contact with such surroundings have high chances of getting infected. In 2020, due to the viral spread of COVID-19 across countries and continents, the World Health Organisation (WHO) had declared it as a global pandemic. This pandemic is causing a global health crisis and it is of high importance that the spread of the disease be stopped by preventive measures like social distancing, maintaining personal hygiene, and to wear facemask.

As per the current situation, with the increase in the number of cases all around the world, WHO recommends the public to wear facemasks as a precaution and a preventive way to come in contact with this virus. Furthermore, people facing symptoms of COVID-19 are mandatorily required to wear facemask to stop further spread of the virus.

In this paper, we propose a novel face mask detection system using Deep learning algorithms to detect if the person is wearing a facemask or not. This is a standalone system on Raspberry Pi and it would accurately detect and classify the above. Many deep learning algorithms have been trained and compared in the process and we provide a comparison on the metrics of various model results obtained.

Facemask detection finds its applications in many areas such as hospitals, containment zones, places of public interests, airports, railways and surveillance. One of the most interesting applications is issuing entry access based on whether the person is wearing facemask. This is one of the preventive methods that can be implemented in malls, restaurants and other public places to tackle the current situation of further spread of the virus.

The term deep learning refers to the training of large Neural Networks (NN). It is basically an extension of Machine Learning (ML). Deep learning was developed by taking inspiration from the network of the human brain. Some of the common application areas are object detection, speech recognition, autonomous driving, etc. In recent days, deep earning has experienced a great boom. Some of the main reasons are the availability of the dataset [4]. Dataset is crucial in both machine learning and deep leaning. Also, the emergence of parallel computing and GPU clusters has a bigger impact on the growth of deep learning. Object detection can be performed by various methods but why deep learning is special?

As the size of the dataset increases, there is a huge spike in the performance of deep learning algorithms compared to other algorithms. As stated earlier there is a huge amount of dataset getting uploaded on the internet every day. Thus, in today's scenario, deep learning outperforms other learning algorithms due to the availability of large datasets and computers with high computational powers. The key contributions of this work are:

a) Implementation of face mask detection using various CNN models.
b) Comparative study of all trained model's using different evaluation metrics.
c) Deploying a real-time stand-alone face mask detection system in Raspberry Pi.

This paper is organized as follows. The next section describes the recent advancements in CNN and face mask detection. Section 3 deals with the dataset processing and the architectural designs of many models. Section 4 talks about the environmental setup used for training the models and implementation of a real-time face mask detection system in Raspberry Pi. In Sect. 5, the deep learning model's evaluation metrics are compared. Finally, in Sect. 5, the work is concluded, and the possible future scopes are discussed.

2 Literature Survey

Deep learning models have faced a lot of advancements in the coming years. Deep learning uses the concept of CNN and has performed better than the many machine learning techniques in various domains, such as speech recognition, object detection, face detection, etc. [3, 5]. Deep learning is a model where utilizing various layers known as convolutional layers tries to learn and grasp the data it receives [6]. This follows the concept of mimicking the human brain and the nervous system for sending and receiving data and learning from them. Deep learning finds its application in so many domains for the reason being its better performance metrics and mostly being reliable in detection analysis.

Various state-of-the-art CNN models have been put forth over the years and many models have derived from other models [18]. The VGG model is a state-of-the-art model that led the way in revolutionizing the deep learning era. In [7] the authors showcased the VGG architecture and how it has been implemented to yield results, but due to its disadvantage of non-scaling of the depth of the convolutional layers, it led to the advancement of ResNet and Inception models. As portrayed in this paper [8], the ResNet model uses the shortcut connections to tackle this problem while the inception model as shown in [9] has used a different technique of stacking up of all convolution units. Further derivations are from these models such as DenseNet and NASNet [10, 11]. We have used the models VGG, ResNet, Inception, NASNet and DenseNet along with its variation for the purpose of our paper.

As the world around is changing amidst this pandemic, we have drawn the inspiration from [1] wherein the author has used a deep learning model to detect the virus from chest X-ray images. Furthermore, as a precautionary measure, it is important to wear a face mask for the prevention of this disease. The paper [12] has allowed us to work in the ease with its open-source dataset of facemask images of people. Moreover, many models like the Retinamask [13] and other works like [2, 22] which also deal with the detection of facemask on people have also showcased a great amount of work in combining the deep learning concept with the facemask detection.

3 Raspberry Pi Based Face Mask Detection

The proposed methodology in the detection of the face mask using CNN consists of data collection followed by processing, augmentations, evaluation and implementing it using RPi. The steps in the proposed work is given by Fig. 1 and explained below in detail.

3.1 Data Set Collection

In any deep learning problem, the first and foremost task is dataset collection. The dataset used for face mask detection is taken from X-zhangyang's real world masked

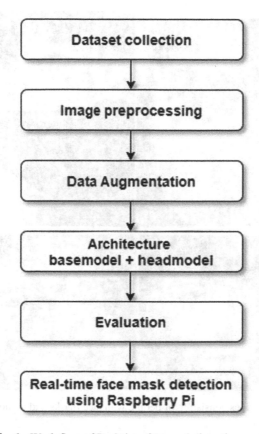

Fig. 1. Work flow of Real-time facemask detection system

dataset GitHub repository. It is one of the most popular datasets available for face mask detection. It has both simulated and real-world images of people wearing face mask. In this work, only the real-world image dataset is used for training the neural networks. It has around 2000 positive images (face with mask) and 90000 negative images (face without mask). In order to maintain balance in data, only 2000 negative images are used. Some of the sample images are shown in Fig. 2. The dataset is divided into two classes: People wearing mask and not wearing mask respectively and each class contains 2000 images.

3.2 Image Preprocessing

The next step is image preprocessing. In order to generate a good performing model, its highly essential to reduce errors from the input data and therefore image preprocessing is one of the crucial steps. Preprocessing converts the input data according to the modal format. Also, it reduces errors such as corrupted images, wrong format, mismatched labels and missing values in input data. TensorFlow's built in preprocess_input() function is used for preprocessing the dataset [14]. This function converts the image from RGB

Fig. 2. Dataset images consisting of people with face masks and without face masks.

to BGR format and each color channel is zero-centered. Also, it raises an error in case of unknown data format.

3.3 Data Augmentation

Deep learning algorithms perform well with large datasets. Large dataset helps to optimize the weights of the neural network and thus enhances the accuracy. But in reality, there is a lack of availability of large dataset for many object detection problems. In this work as mentioned above there are only 2000 images with face mask. Therefore, data augmentation is used to increase the dataset size.

Data Augmentation can improve accuracy of the model under two circumstances, 1) when the dataset size is not large enough. 2) when there is an imbalance of data between classes [15]. Using data augmentation, synthetic data can be added to the dataset. Some of the traditional transformations used for data augmentation are rotation, zooming, translation, blurring and flipping of images. Furthermore, some other methods include color transformations and adding random white noise to images. Of course, these methods have proven in improving the accuracy of the model, but in many recent advancements there has been a growing interest in image style transfer. In style transfer two images are taken, one for content and another is for style. The content of the first image and the style of the second image are fused together to generate the synthetic image. The content and style weights can be altered based on the dataset requirement.

3.4 Model Fitting

After performing the necessary image fine tunings, we then fit them into the architectural model as shown in Fig. 3. In the base model, we train various deep learning architectures and finally the output of the base model architecture is fine-tuned by fitting it into the head model to achieve better results. Further, the base model architectures and head model details are explained below.

VGG Architecture

The motive of this architecture revolves around the concept of investigating the accuracy in a large-scale image recognition system when increasing the network depth of convolutional units. For this purpose, an image of fixed size 224 × 224 RGB image has been taken and is passed through a stack of Convolutional layers, where the filter size is 3 × 3. The padding is 1 so that the spatial resolution is retained after the convolutional process. This is called as the "same" convolutions, where the spatial resolution of the convolutional layer is preserved. Also, five max-pooling layers are carried out with a 2 × 2-pixel window, with stride of 2.

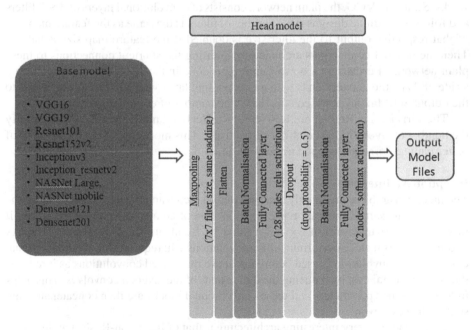

Fig. 3. Architecture model design

Finally, this stack of convolutional layers is then connected to three fully connected (FC) layers, where the first two have 4096 channels each and third is a SoftMax layer with the number of nodes matching the number of classes to be classified.

The hidden layers use the Rectified Linear Unit (ReLU) as the activation function. This state-of-the-art technique has been a tremendous insight for many deep learning and machine learning approaches. The variations of VGG are the VGG-16 and VGG-19 where the number of parameters learnt in each are 138 M and 144 M respectively. With these many numbers of parameters learnt, it led to the ideology of increasing the number of convolutional layers to achieve a good accuracy.

Resnet Architecture

Training a neural network is a very difficult task. Especially deeper networks are even harder to train as they face the problem of exploding gradients also commonly known as vanishing gradients. When the number of layers is increased, due to these vanishing gradients, a degradation problem arises wherein the accuracy tends to saturate and lead to higher training errors. Hence the concept of Residual Networks (ResNet) emerged.

The ResNet model has a building block where instead of assuming that the layers will learn better parameters by stacking layers, an underlying learnt parameter is directly fit to the present layer. This way even if the present layer does not learn much or tends to saturate, the previous layer's parameters will be added on to it, preventing it from degrading and causing the gradients to vanish. Due to this model, deep residual networks can easily have better accuracy from increased depth giving better results.

The implementation of this architecture consists of plain networks and residual networks. Similar to VGG, the plain network consists of convolutional layers of 3×3 filters and follow two simple designs i) the number of filters is the same as the feature map size of that respective output ii) the filter size is doubled if the feature map size is halved. Then the residual connections are made by inserting the shortcut connections to these plain networks. Furthermore, down sampling is done in the convolutional layer with a stride of 2 and the network ends with a max pooling layer which in turn is connected to the output SoftMax layer which consists of the number of classes required.

The variations in ResNet are ResNet50, ResNet101, and ResNet152 which specify the number of layers 50, 101 and 152 respectively. This model has led to the learning of better parameters yielding good training accuracy.

Inception Architecture

The inception architecture mainly concentrates on increasing the depth and width of the network, at the same time improving the utilisation of computational resources [16]. It involves stacking up results of 1×1, 3×3 and 5×5 convolutional layers and also a max pooling layer. But since performing this convolutions will require a lot of computational cost, a 1×1 convolution is used before the above mentioned convolutions as it reduces the computational cost by reducing the dimensions of the layers it convolves. This helps in learning better parameters and these convolutional blocks are then concatenated and sent to the next layer.

Furthermore, a very interesting architecture is that of Inception-ResNet architecture where there is a combination of Inception and the ResNet models together. The motive of this architecture is that the residual connections improve the training accuracy of the Inception networks. This architecture thus combines the low-cost computation and addresses the vanishing gradients problem. Hence the architecture will proceed with inception layers and then added with the residual connections from the previous layers. This model performs better than the inception models without the residual connections.

NASNet Architecture

One of the highlighting aspects of Neural Architecture Search Network (NASNet) is that the architecture is not fixed. Over time the architectures are finetuned to generate a better performance based on the dataset. NASNet has two major networks namely Recurrent Neural Network (known as the controller) and child networks. The RNN controls the child network by sampling different architectures and further the child network is trained to attain some accuracy (say R) on validation set. The controller is updated with the generated accuracy and thus helping it to learn the dataset better. In turn, the accuracy obtained from the learned architecture mentioned above surpasses the human framed models.

In NASNet, the global architecture remains predetermined but the individual cells are optimized by the search process. It has two types of blocks namely Normal cell and Reduction cell which are stacked upon each other to form the network. Normal cell outputs a feature map of the same dimension. On the other hand, Reduction cell outputs a feature map where its height and width are reduced to half.

NASNet comes with a wide range of models ranging from mobile to large. Models can be selected based on the computational performance of the system. Moreover, NASNet's mobile model (with low computational cost) outperforms many other state-of-the-art classifiers and makes a perfect fit for embedded platforms.

DenseNet Architecture

Starting from VGG16, the number of layers in current networks has been steadily increasing making it deeper. This leads to an issue of information from initial layers not reaching the end. ResNet and many other networks has connections only between the subsequent layers. On the contrary, In DenseNet each layer has a direct connection to every other layer in the network having the same feature-map size. An L layer DenseNet has a total of $L(L + 1)/2$ connections.This unique feature mitigates the vanishing gradients and overfitting issues and thus enhances feature propagation. In addition, to improve computational efficiency in dense block, a 1 * 1 convolutional layer is added before each 3 * 3 convolution.

DenseNet has 4 dense blocks interlinked by a transition layer (contains batch normalization layer followed by a 1 * 1 convolutional layer and a 2 * 2 average pooling layer). It comes with different architectures namely, DenseNet121, DenseNet169 and DenseNet201 where the numbers represent the total layers.

3.5 Head-Model

The output of the base model from all the different architectures is fed into the head model. The head model consists of max-pooling layers and fully connected layers with regularisation and batch normalisation.

The output of the base model is then fed into the Max pooling layer [3] with a pool size of 7×7. The purpose of pooling is to down sample the input representation and by using the Max pooling technique we get the maximum value over the 7×7 pool window from the output of the base model. It is given with the same padding format so that the layer is evenly padded in all the sides maintaining the dimensions of the input fed through it. This is further flattened and is connected to couple a fully-connected layer (FC) with 128 nodes using the ReLu activation function.

Then a dropout function with a probability of 0.5 is introduced to add the regularisation term to deal with the overfitting of data and high variance problem. Finally, it is connected to another FC layer with two output nodes with a softmax activation function. The two output nodes namely are used to classify whether the person is wearing a facemask or not.

Furthermore, batch normalisation has been implemented in the head model before every FC layer. The authors in [17] highlighted the purpose of batch normalisation (BN) is that it accelerates the training procedure by normalising the layer outputs of each mini-batch. BN helps for deep neural networks to fasten its training procedure and now exists as a standard block in almost all deep convolutional network. In-fact, many state of the art architectures like Resnet, Inception, DenseNet etc. imbibe BN into them.

As depicted in Fig. 3, the dataset is trained for various base model architectures and their respective model files are generated. Next step is facemask detection and determining how well it performs on different base model architectures. Various metrics such as precision, recall, accuracy, average precision score, hamming loss etc. have been evaluated and compared for each of the different base model architectures.

4 Face Detection and Classification

The main objective is to classify whether a person is wearing face mask or not. For this it is required to perform a localisation search on a given image to extract the face image. This can be done using the pretrained weights from the caffe model. With the help of the caffe model, the system detects the face and draws bounding boxes around it. From this crop, we use our model files to predict whether the cropped-out face image is classified under the "No mask" or "Mask" category. Furthermore, this work implements the system in Raspberry Pi. With the help of camera and the Raspberry Pi a standalone facemask detection system is implemented. The applications of this system can be used in many health centres and places of public interest.

4.1 Experimental Setup

As deep learning networks require more computational power, the required system specification is pretty high. Also, for a faster training GPU parallelization can be used. Therefore, Google Colab is used for training purposes. Google Colab is a cloud-based GPU provider with a Jupyter environment. It provides 12.72 GB RAM and 100 GB disk space.It offers a great support to many deep learning libraries. Training the network with large architecture like DenseNet201 consumes a lot of space but architectures like NASNet-Mobile consume very less space. The models are trained for 50 epochs with a batch size of 32.

TensorFlow is used for training the deep learning models. In recent days, TensorFlow is used in many Artificial Intelligence and Deep learning applications. Moreover, Keras-one of the most famous deep learning library is now officially integrated with TensorFlow in its 2.3.0 version update. This turns the training process easier and more efficient.Also, OpenCV package is used to perform many image processing and real-time computer vision functions required for the face mask detection.

Embedded devices are known for their compact size and affordable price. In today's world, it plays a major role in many automation processes. One of the most famous single-board computers is Raspberry Pi [19, 21]. In this project, Raspberry Pi 3 model B with a dedicated camera is used for implementing the trained models and achieve a stand-alone face mask detection system. Figure 4 shows the Real-time face mask detection system using Raspberry Pi 3 and camera. Indeed, this setup drastically cut down the cost of the whole product and thus making it more affordable. It has a 1.2 GHz quad-core ARM Cortex A53 CPU equipped with 1GB of RAM and the operating system is Raspbian. Additionally, it has both wireless LAN and Bluetooth modules.

The Virtual Network association (VNC) tool is used for remote access of the Raspberry Pi. In VNC tool, Raspberry Pi is configured as server and the laptop as client. Initially, Raspberry Pi installed with dependencies such as TensorFlow, OpenCV, matplotlib, etc. Then, the pre-trained models are deployed in Raspberry Pi. As the focus is to achieve a real-time detection system, detection time is a crucial parameter. Considering the limitation in computational power of Raspberry Pi, tiny model such as NASNet mobile is used.

Fig. 4. Real-time face mask detection system using raspberry Pi 3 and camera

4.2 Results

Evaluation is one of the crucial tasks in any deep learning project. It helps to filter out the best model based on the requirements. Table 1 summarizes the evaluation metrics of all the trained models. In order to understand the metrics used in Table 1, a clear knowledge of confusion matrix is required. Confusion matrix consists of four parameters namely, True Positive (TP), False Positive (FP), False Negative (FN), True Negative (TN). Each predicted output falls under any of the four categories. When both the ground truth and prediction detect face mask then it's a TP. On the other hand, when both are negative its classified as TN. When the model prediction says no mask but the ground truth says there is a face mask then it comes under FN. Conversely, when the predicted output is positive while the ground truth says there is no mask then it's a FP.

Table 1. Performance metrics achieved for various models

Models	Evaluation metrics					
	Average precsion	Accuracy	F1 score	Precision	Recall	Hamming loss
VGG16	81.45	86.88	86.87	87.00	86.87	0.13
ResNet101	83.28	88.31	88.30	88.40	88.30	0.12
NASNet mobile	84.52	88.96	88.96	88.97	88.96	0.11
VGG19	84.66	89.22	89.22	89.26	89.21	0.11
ResNet152 v2	86.85	90.65	90.65	90.65	90.65	0.09
DenseNet121	88.77	92.21	92.21	92.21	92.21	0.08
NASNet large	89.18	92.34	92.34	92.34	92.34	0.08
Inception _Resnet v2	89.40	92.34	92.34	92.34	92.34	0.08
Inception v3	90.46	92.60	92.59	92.69	92.61	0.07
DenseNet201	91.00	93.77	93.77	93.77	93.76	0.06

Precision is nothing but the ability of our model to identify only the relevant objects [20]. The recall says about the percentage of finding out all the positives. F1 score is defined as the harmonic mean of precision and recall. Hamming loss is defined as the fraction of negative labels to the total number of labels. The mathematical formulas for precision, recall, f1 score and accuracy are given in Eqs. 1, 2, 3, 4 respectively.

$$\text{Precision} = \frac{\text{True Positive}}{\text{True Positive} + \text{False Positive}} \tag{1}$$

$$\text{Recall} = \frac{\text{True Positive}}{\text{True Positive} + \text{False Negetive}} \tag{2}$$

$$\text{F1score} = 2 * \frac{\text{precision} * \text{recall}}{\text{precision} + \text{recall}} \tag{3}$$

$$\text{Accuracy} = \frac{\text{True Positive} + \text{True Negetive}}{\text{Total population}} \tag{4}$$

With so many parameters defined it's tough to analyse the models. Therefore, a single crucial parameter named Average Precision (AP) is used for comparing the model performance. Average Precision is the area under the precision-recall curve and thus, it summarises both precision and recall. Greater AP implies better the model performance. Thus, from Fig. 5 it's clear that the best AP is generated by Densenet201 (91%) followed by Inceptionv3 (90.46%), Inception_resnetv2 (89.4%) and NASNet Large (89.18%). Furthermore, Densenet201 outputs the highest accuracy of 93.77%. Due to the issues such as, vanishing gradient and overfitting problems in VGG, Average Precision is comparatively low.

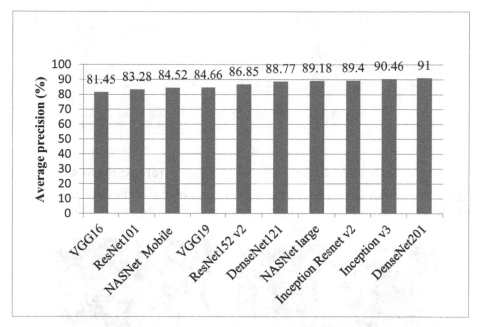

Fig. 5. Comparison of average precision for different models

The Fig. 6 shows the training loss and accuracy of few top performing models such as Densenet201, InceptionResnetv2, NASNet-large and NASNet-mobile. The plot consists of train accuracy, validation accuracy, train loss and validation loss. As the number of epochs increase there is a smooth decrease in loss function which says that the model's hyperparameters are tuned perfectly and doesn't have any overfitting issues. Training is ended when the loss saturates and no longer decreases. Densenet201 has the most optimized hamming loss with a saturation value of 0.06. Also, its highest overall accuracy of 93.77% authenticates the effectiveness of data augmentation. Therefore, it clearly says that the model has an exceptional classification capacity.

Figure 7 shows some sample output detection from the Real-time face mask detection system. Bounding boxes in red indicate that the person has not wearing a mask and those in green indicate the person wearing a mask. Further, it also displays the confidence score of its respective class.

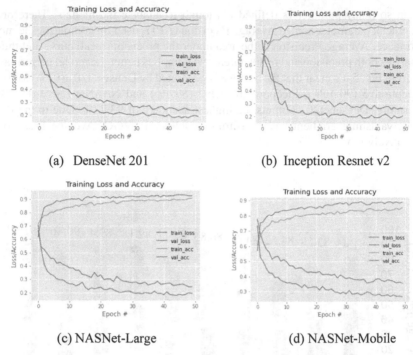

(a) DenseNet 201   (b) Inception Resnet v2

(c) NASNet-Large   (d) NASNet-Mobile

Fig. 6. Training loss and accuracy graph for (a) DenseNet-201 (b) Inception-Resnet-v2 (c) NASNet-Large (d) NASNet-Mobile. Loss/Accuracy evaluated for the number of Epochs trained

Fig. 7. Sample face mask detection output

5 Conclusion

In this paper, a realtime deep convolutional neural network based face mask detection is implemented using Raspberry Pi. Automating the face mask detection system will have a vast use cases in the time of pandemic situation. It can be deployed in public places, offices, hospitals, etc. to monitor people in order to minimize the spread of virus. Furthermore, implementing face mask detection in a stand alone system using Raspberry Pi has a two fold benefit, 1) Its compact and easy to install, 2) highly affordable. The models show excellent detection results. Comparing the models, Densenet201 produces the best average precision of 90.99%. Inceptionv3 has the second best average precision of 90.45% followed by inceptionresnetv2 and NASNetlarge. Nasnetmobile is used for realtime face mask detection in Raspberry pi due to its reduced number of layers which in turn requires very less computational power. Data Augmentation has been a key in improving the accuracy of the models.

As a futurework, deeper transfer learning can be used to improve feature extraction. Furthermore, the research can be extended to find out the incorrectly worn mask and face recognition of people wearing face mask can be detected.

References

1. Martínez, F., Martínez, F., Jacinto, E.: Performance evaluation of the NASNet convolutional network in the automatic identification of COVID-19. Int. J. Adv. Sci. Eng. Inform. Technol. **10**(2) (2020)
2. Loey, M., Manogaran, G., Taha, M.H.N., Khalifa, N.E.M.: A hybrid deep transfer learning model with machine learning methods for face mask detection in the era of the COVID-19 pandemic. Measure. J. Int. Measure. Confed. **167**(2021). https://doi.org/10.1016/j.measurement.2020.108288
3. Pathak, A.R., Pandey, M., Rautaray, S.: Application of deep learning for object detection. Procedia Comput. Sci. **132**, 1706–1717 (2018). https://doi.org/10.1016/j.procs.2018.05.144
4. Zhao, Z.-Q., Zheng, P., Xu, S., Wu, X.: Object Detection with Deep Learning: A Review (2018). http://arxiv.org/abs/1807.05511
5. Voulodimos, A., Doulamis, N., Doulamis, A., Protopapadakis, E.: Deep learning for computer vision: a brief review. Comput. Intell. Neurosci. **2018** (2018). https://doi.org/10.1155/2018/7068349. (Hindawi Limited)
6. Lecun, Y., Bengio, Y., Hinton, G.: Deep learning. Nature **521**(7553), 436–444 (2015). https://doi.org/10.1038/nature14539. (Nature Publishing Group)
7. Simonyan, K., Zisserman, A.: Very Deep Convolutional Networks for Large-Scale Image Recognition (2014). http://arxiv.org/abs/1409.1556
8. He, K., Zhang, X., Ren, S., Sun, J. Deep residual learning for image recognition. In: Proceedings of the IEEE Conference on Computer Vision and Pattern Recognition, pp. 770–778 (2016)
9. Szegedy, C., et al.: Going deeper with convolutions. In: Proceedings of the IEEE Conference on Computer Vision and Pattern Recognition, pp. 1–9 (2015)
10. Iandola, F., Moskewicz, M., Karayev, S., Girshick, R., Darrell, T., Keutzer, K.: Densenet: implementing efficient convnet descriptor pyramids (2014). arXiv preprint arXiv:1404.1869
11. Zoph, B., Vasudevan, V., Shlens, J., Le, Q.V.: Learning transferable architectures for scalable image recognition. In: Proceedings of the IEEE Conference on Computer Vision and Pattern Recognition, pp. 8697–8710 (2018)

12. Wang, Z., et al.: Masked Face Recognition Dataset and Application (2020). http://arxiv.org/abs/2003.09093

13. Jiang, M., Fan, X., Yan, H.: RetinaMask: A Face Mask detector (2020). http://arxiv.org/abs/2005.03950

14. Abadi, M., et al.: Tensorflow: a system for large-scale machine learning. In: 12th {USENIX} Symposium on Operating Systems Design and Implementation ({OSDI} 16), pp. 265–283 (2016)

15. Mikołajczyk, A., Grochowski, M.: Data augmentation for improving deep learning in image classification problem. In: 2018 International Interdisciplinary PhD Workshop (IIPhDW), pp. 117–122 (2018)

16. Szegedy, C., Ioffe, S., Vanhoucke, V., Alemi, A.: Inception-v4, inception-resnet and the impact of residual connections on learning. arXiv preprint arXiv:1602.07261 (2016)

17. Kalayeh, M.M., Shah, M.: Training faster by separating modes of variation in batchnormalized models. IEEE Trans. Pattern Anal. Mach. Intell. **42**(6), 1483–1500 (2019)

18. Jia, Y., et al.: Caffe: convolutional architecture for fast feature embedding. In: Proceedings of the 22nd ACM International Conference on Multimedia, pp. 675–678 (2014)

19. Shiddieqy, H.A., Hariadi, F.I., Adiono, T.: Implementation of deep-learning based image classification on single board computer. In: 2017 International Symposium on Electronics and Smart Devices (ISESD), pp. 133–137 (2017)

20. Dharneeshkar, J., Aniruthan, S.A., Karthika, R., Parameswaran, L.: Deep Learning based Detection of potholes in Indian roads using YOLO. In: 2020 International Conference on Inventive Computation Technologies (ICICT), pp. 381–385 (2020)

21. Ikram, B.A.O., et al.: Real-time facemask detector using deep learning and raspberry Pi. In: 2021 International Conference on Digital Age & Technological Advances for Sustainable Development (ICDATA). IEEE (2021)

22. Peter, S., et al.: Intelligent real-time face-mask detection system with hardware acceleration for COVID-19 Mitigation. Healthcare **10**(5), 873 (2022). (MDPI)

Depression Detection on Twitter Using RNN and LSTM Models

Abhyudaya Apoorva[(✉)], Vinat Goyal, Aveekal Kumar, Rishu Singh,
and Sanjeev Sharma

Indian Institute of Information Technology, Pune, Pune, India
abhyudayaapoorva19@ece.iiitp.ac.in

Abstract. Social media mainly provides an unparalleled chance to
detect depression early in young adults. Depression is an illness that
so often requires the self-reporting of symptoms. Social networking sites
can provide an ample amount of data and information to train an efficient deep learning model. We aim to perform depression analysis on
Twitter by analyzing its linguistic markers, making it plausible to create
a deep learning model capable of providing an individual discernment
into their mental health much earlier than the traditional approaches.
We use two models to detect depressive users using their tweets on this
conquest, a simple Recurrent Neural Network (RNN) and Long-Short
Term Memory (LSTM). The LSTM model outperforms simple RNN by
having a validation accuracy of 96.21 and a validation loss of 0.1077.
Both models were trained on a single customized dataset, half of which
was from sentiment140, and the other half was extracted from Twitter
using the Twitter API.

Keywords: Sentiment analysis · Depression · Deep learning · CNN ·
LSTM · Social media

1 Introduction

The growth of the internet and communication technologies, especially online
social networks, has rejuvenated how people interact and communicate electronically. The applications such as Facebook, Twitter, Instagram and alike not only
host the written and multimedia contents but also offer their users to express
their feelings, emotions, and sentiments about a topic, subject or an issue online
Md. Rafiqul Islam and Ulhaq (2018). A study concludes that there is a causal
link between the use of social media and adverse effects on well-being, primarily
depression and loneliness. "What we found overall is that if you use fewer social
media, you are less depressed and less lonely, meaning that the decreased social
media use is what causes that qualitative shift in your well-being", as stated by
Melissa G. Melissa G. Hunt and Young (2018). Out of 300 million people suf-
fering from depression, only a fraction of them can receive adequate treatment.
Nearly 800,000 people die every year due to suicide, proving depression to be
the leading cause of disability worldwide. Among 15–30-year-olds, suicide is the

I. Woungang et al. (Eds.): ANTIC 2022, CCIS 1798, pp. 305–319, 2023.
https://doi.org/10.1007/978-3-031-28183-9_22

second leading cause of death. Subsequent treatment for mental health diseases is often imprecise, delayed or utterly missed (https://www.who.int/news-room/fact-sheets/detail/depression).

Social media provides an unparalleled chance to detect depression early in young adults. Every second, approximately 9,000 Tweets are tweeted on Twitter, which corresponds to over 540,000 tweets sent per minute, 800 million tweets per day and around 300 billion tweets per year (https://www.internetlivestats.com/one-second/#tweets-band). Depression is an illness that so often requires the self-reporting of symptoms. Social networking sites can provide an ample amount of data and information that can be used to train an efficient deep learning model. There have been various depression-related studies on social media, and they have primarily relied on Facebook posts. However, very few have focused on Twitter posts. These two platforms have several key differences that lead to different types of content. Users often use their alias name to remain anonymous, which allows them to relate to users they have never met and provide an unbiased insight into their mental state or thoughts and experiences. The last few years have seen a growing interest in the use of social networking sites as a tool for public health, such as detecting the spread of flu symptoms or gaining insights about new diseases using Twitter content. However, this method of analyzing mental health disorders is still in its infancy. This project works on expanding the scope of mental health measures with the help of social media and a deep learning model to predict the text-based signs of depression which uses the proven correlation between specific linguistic features and mental health disorders, specifically depression.

The rest of the paper is organized as follow: Related works are described in Sect. 2, proposed models are presented in Sect. 3, Results and discussions are depicted in Sect. 4, and lastly, Sect. 5 concludes the paper.

2   Literature Survey

Social media offers a considerable amount of accessible common language, attracting the attention of those who study the language of individuals with mental health conditions. Twitter is a natural source, a popular platform enabling users to share short messages publicly. Early work used crowd-sourcing to identify Twitter users who report a depression diagnosis in a survey and proposed features to locate depressed users before the onset of depression. Over the last few years, there has been growing interest in using social media as a tool for public health, ranging from identifying the spread of flu symptoms Adam Sadilek and Vincent (2012) to building insights about diseases based on postings on Twitter Paul and Dredze (2011). However, research on harnessing social media for understanding behavioural health disorders is still in its infancy. Kotikalapudi et al. Raghavendra Katikalapudi and Lutzen (2012) analyzed patterns of web activity of college students that could signal depression. Similarly, Moreno et al. Megan A Moreno and Cox (2011) demonstrated that status updates on Facebook could reveal symptoms of major depressive episodes.

Choudhury et al. Michael Gamon and Horvitz (2013) considered online networking as a good instrument for public health, concentrating on the utilization of Twitter presents on fabricating predictive models about the forthcoming impact of childbirth on the conduct and disposition of new mothers. Utilizing Twitter posts, they measured postpartum changes in 376 mothers along with measurements of social engagement, feeling, informal community, and phonetic style.

O'Dea et al. Bridianne O'Dea and Calear (2015) examined that Twitter is progressively researched as a method for recognizing psychological well-being status, including depression and suicidality in the population. Their investigation revealed that it is conceivable to identify the level of worry among suicide-related tweets, utilizing both human coders and a programmed machine classifier.

Bachrach et al. Yoram Bachrach and Stillwell (2012) studied how users' activity on Facebook identifies with their identity, as measured by the standard Five-Factor Model. They analyzed relationships between users' identities and the properties of their Facebook profiles. For instance, the size and thickness of their friend's network, number of transferred photographs, number of occasions went to, number of gathering enrolment's, and number of times the user has been tagged in pictures. Ortigosa et al. Ortigosa A and RM (2014) have exhibited a new strategy for sentiment examination in Facebook that suggests that starting from messages composed by users, as to extract data about the users' assessment extremity (positive, unbiased or negative), as transmitted in the messages they write; and to show the users' standard conclusion extremity and to distinguish massive, passionate changes.

Zhang et al. Lei Zhang and Zhu (2014) have shown that if individuals with a severe danger of suicide can be recognized through online networking like a microblog, it is conceivable to actualize a dynamic intervention system to save their lives.

Orabi et al. AH et al. (2018) used a combination of CNN and RNN to detect depression in Twitter data using Adam as an optimizer. The word embedding training was performed using CBOW, Skip-gram, and Random word embedding with a uniform distribution range from −0.5 to +0.5.

Zogan et al. H et al. (2020) proposed a new method for identifying depressed users based on their online timeline tweets and behaviors. The hybrid model, which combines CNN and Bi-GRU, was tested on a benchmark dataset. The model extracted semantic features representing user behaviors and showed improved classification performance compared to state-of-the-art techniques.

Suman et al. SK et al. (2020) used deep learning models and a cloud-based smartphone application to detect depression in tweets. The sentence classifier used in the study was RoBERTa, which was associated with the provided tweet or query and a standard corpus of tweets. The use of a standard corpus improved the model's reliability. The model was able to estimate the patient's depression status and predict their mental health. Additionally, the authors used random noise factors and a larger set of tweet samples to improve depression prediction.

3   Methodology

Depression detection takes on a little different approach than sentiment analysis. While the latter determines the polarity of a text, the former is much more specific as the tweets indicating depression generally contains certain linguistic cues related to depression. Moreover, there is a growing body of literature addressing the role of social networks on the structure of social relationships such as break up in a relationship, mental illness ('depression', 'anxiety', 'bipolar' etc.), smoking and drinking relapse, sexual harassment and for suicide ideation, Liu (2011); Olivier (2017). The overall methodology of the work is given in flow graph Fig. 1.

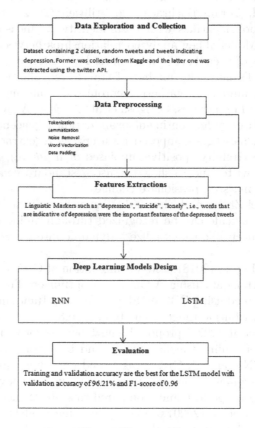

Fig. 1. Flow graph

3.1   Data Exploration and Collection

We relied on Twitter in this phase. Twitter users often use pseudonyms and are more likely to be connected with users they have never met. This allows for a more anonymous means of communication, which may provide a less biased account of an individual's thoughts and experiences.

Two types of tweets were utilised to build the model: random tweets that do not necessarily indicate depression (Sentiment140 data-set on Kaggle) and depressed tweets extracted using the Twitter API. Since there are no publicly available Twitter data-set that shows depression, the tweets were removed according to the linguistic markers indicative of depression such as "Hopeless", "Lonely", "Suicide", "Antidepressants", "Depressed", etc.

The Tweets were searched and scraped in a random 24-h period and saved as separate csv files. Information that could identify the Twitter user was removed, including username, name, conversation_id, created_at, place, and geolocation. Additionally, timezone, likes count, links, retweets, quote URLs, videos, photos, user retweet id, replies count, and retweet counts were dropped as they were unnecessary for the classifier. Null values were removed as well.

3.2 Data Cleaning

This step aims to clean noise those are less relevant to find the sentiment of tweets such as punctuation, special characters, numbers, and terms that won't carry significant weightage in context to the Tweet. Initial data cleaning requirements that we can think of are:

1. The Twitter handles are already masked as @user due to privacy concerns. So, these Twitter handles are hardly giving any information about the nature of the tweet.
2. We can also think of getting rid of the punctuations, numbers and even special characters since they wouldn't help differentiate different kinds of tweets.
3. Most of the smaller words do not add much value. For example, 'her', 'his', 'all'. So, we will try to remove them as well from our data.
4. Once we have executed the above three steps, we can split every tweet into individual words or tokens, an essential step in any NLP task.
5. In the rest of the data, we might have terms like loves, loving, lovable, etc. These terms are often used in the same context as "love". If we can reduce them to their root word 'love', we can reduce the total number of unique words in our data without losing significant information.

3.3 Data Preprocessing

To feed our text data to our LSTM model, we'll have to go through several extra preprocessing steps. Most neural networks expect numbers as inputs. Thus, we'll have to convert our text data to numerical data.

1. *Tokenization* - To feed our text data to a classification model, we first need to tokenize it. Tokenization is splitting up a single string of text into a list of individual words or tokens.
2. *Lemmatization* - The process of reducing the different forms of a word to one single form, for example, reducing "builds", "building", or "built" to the lemma "build". This will significantly help our classifier by treating all variants of a given word as references to the original lemma word.

3. *Noise Removal* - Stopwords are frequently-used words (such as "the", "a", "an", "in") that do not hold any helpful meaning to extract sentiment. Such words are removed from the tweet. Also, a custom function is defined to fine-tune the cleaning of the input text. This function is highly dependent on each use case.

4. *GloVe Word Embeddings* - Word embeddings are a way for us to convert words to representational vectors. Instead of mapping each word to an index, we want to map each word to a vector of real numbers representing this word.

5. *Data Padding* - Further in our training, we would like to speed the process up by splitting data into mini-batches. Batch learning is the process of training on several examples simultaneously, which significantly decreases the training time. Figure 2 shows the embedding layer.

For the model, both random Tweets and Tweets indicating depression were necessary. Tweets indicating depression were retrieved using the Twitter scraping tool Tweepy, requiring the Twitter API. These tweets were extracted according to linguistic cues indicative of depression. Those terms were:

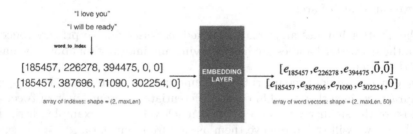

Fig. 2. Embedding layer

- Depressed
- Depression
- Hopeless
- Lonely
- Antidepressant
- Antidepressants
- Suicide

They were scrapped in a random 24 h period, saved as separate CSV files, and then concatenated, resulting in a dataset of 300,000 tweets. They proved to be highly indicative of depression. However, some tweets did not necessarily indicate depression, such as tweets linking to sites related to depression or maybe lyrics of a song. VADER sentiment analysis was performed to separate such tweets, which gave each text a VADER score (score less than 0.05 means negative polarity, more than 0.05 means a positive polarity). VADER (Valence Aware Dictionary and sEntiment Reasoner) is a lexicon and rule-based sentiment analysis tool that is specifically tuned to sentiments expressed in social media E.E. (2014). The positive tweets were removed from the dataset. Thus the total number of tweets were reduced to 160,000.

The remaining negative tweets were thus saved in a CSV file. Next, in the random tweets, the text labelled positive, i.e., 4, were separated and sliced to get a total of 160,000 tweets, equal to the number of depressive tweets. Both types of data were then concatenated to obtain a final data set, each type being assigned its respective label (0 for depressive and 1 for random).

3.4 Deep Learning Models

Simple Recurrent neural networks (RNN) are a class of neural networks that is powerful for modelling sequence data such as time series or natural language Abdullahi et al. (2021).

Schematically, an RNN layer uses a for loop to iterate over the timesteps of a sequence while maintaining an internal state that encodes information about the timesteps it has seen so far. Figure 3 shows the model of simple RNN. Table 1 shows the model summary for the simple RNN model.

Long Short-Term Memory usually just called "LSTMs" - are a special kind of RNN, capable of learning long-term dependencies. They were introduced by Hochreiter & Schmidhuber (1997) and were refined and popularized by many

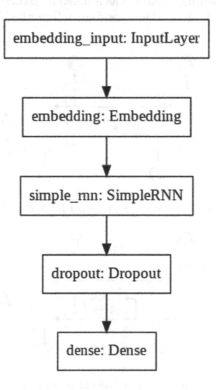

Fig. 3. Simple RNN model

Table 1. Simple RNN model summary

Layer Type	Outer shape	No. of parameters
Embedding	(None, 49, 300)	120000300
Simple RNN	(None, 64)	23360
Dropout	(None, 64)	0
Dense	(None, 1)	65
Total params: 120,023,725		
Trainable params: 23,425		
Non-trainable params: 120,000,300		

people in the following work. They work tremendously well on a large variety of problems and are now widely used Sepp Hochreiter (1997); Sherstinsky (2018).

LSTMs are explicitly designed to avoid the long-term dependency problem. Remembering information for long periods is practically their default behaviour, not something they struggle to learn. All recurrent neural networks have the form of a chain of repeating modules of a neural network. In standard RNNs, this repeating module will have a straightforward structure, such as a single *tanh* layer. Figure 4 depicts a repeating module in a standard RNN containing a single layer taken fromGhosh et al. (2019) LSTMs also have this chain like structure, but the repeating module has a different structure. Instead of having a single neural network layer, there are four, interacting in a very special way.

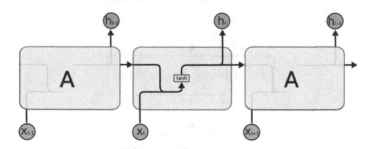

Fig. 4. The repeating module in a standard RNN contains a single layer

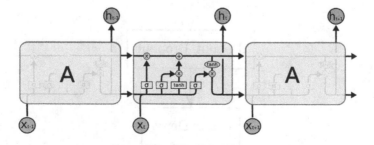

Fig. 5. The repeating module in an LSTM contains four interacting layers

Olah. Figure 5 depicts a repeating module in a standard LSTM containing a single layer taken fromGhosh et al. (2019)

Unfortunately, this simple RNN suffers from the exploding, and vanishing gradient problem during the backpropagation training stage Hochreiter (1998). LSTMs solve this problem by having a more complex internal structure that allows LSTMs to remember information for either long or short terms Sepp Hochreiter (1997). The hidden state of an LSTM unit is computed by

$$f_t = \sigma(W_f \cdot x_t + U_f \cdot h_{t-1} + b_f)$$

$$i_t = \sigma(W_i \cdot x_t + U_i \cdot h_{t-1} + b_i)$$

$$o_t = \sigma(W_o \cdot x_t + U_o \cdot h_{t-1} + b_o)$$

$$c_t = f_t * c_{t-1} + i_t * tanh(W_c \cdot x_t + U_c \cdot h_{t-1} + b_c)$$

$$h_t = o_t * tanh(c_t)$$

where i_t is called the input gate, o_t is the output gate, f_t is the forget gate, c_t is the cell state, h_t is the regular hidden state, σ is the sigmoid function, and $*$ is the Hadamard product. Figure 6 shows the model for LSTM. Table 2 shows the LSTM model summary.

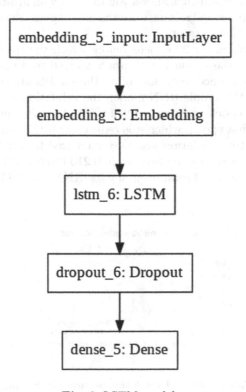

Fig. 6. LSTM model

Table 2. LSTM model summary

Layer Type	Outer shape	No. of parameters
Embedding	(None, 49, 300)	120000300
LSTM	(None, 16)	20288
Dropout	(None, 16)	0
Dense	(None, 1)	17

Total params: 120,020,605

Trainable params: 20,305

Non-trainable params: 120,000,300

4   Model Evaluation and Validation

Once the models were compiled, there are now ready to be trained using the fit() function of the Sequential class of Keras API. Since too many epochs can lead to overfitting of the training dataset, whereas too few may result in an underfit model, we give the argument of early stopping to the "callbacks", which provides a way to execute code and interact with the training model process automatically, Early stopping is a method that allows you to specify an arbitrarily large number of training epochs and stop training once the model performance stops improving on a holdout validation dataset.

Models were trained for 20 epochs before which the training was automatically called off since the validation accuracy started to drop from thereon. The training and validation accuracy/loss of all the models are compared in the following figures. For the simple RNN model, the validation accuracy started from 94.01% on the first epoch and reached 95.90% on the 17th epoch. Validation loss was 0.1765 on the first epoch, which was reduced to 0.1176 on the last epoch. For the LSTM model, the validation accuracy increased from 94.25% to 96.22% in 20 epochs and validation loss reduced from 0.2106 to 0.1077. Figure 7 and Fig. 8 show the training and validation accuracy for RNN and LSTM respectively.

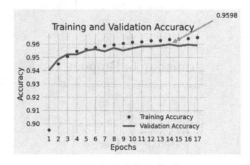

Fig. 7. Training and validation accuracy of Simple RNN

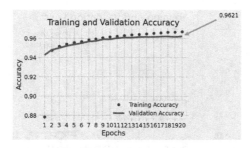

Fig. 8. Training and validation accuracy of LSTM

Figure 9 and Fig. 10 show the training and validation loss for RNN and LSTM respectively.

Since accuracy is not always the metric to determine how good the model is. Therefore, 3 other metrics, precision, recall and F1-score are also calculated.

– Precision talks about how precise/accurate the model is out of those predicted positive, how many of them are positive. Precision is an excellent measure to determine when the costs of False Positive is high.

$$Precision = \frac{TruePositive}{TruePositive + FalsePositive}$$

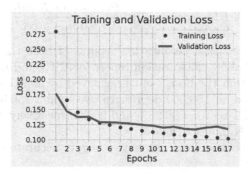

Fig. 9. Training and validation loss of Simple RNN

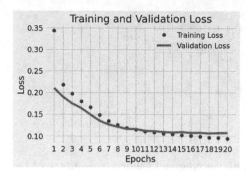

Fig. 10. Training and validation loss of LSTM

– Recall calculates how many of the Actual Positives our model capture through labelling it as Positive (True Positive). Applying the same understanding, we know that Recall shall be the model metric we use to select our best model when there is a high cost associated with False Negative.

$$Recall = \frac{TruePositive}{TruePositive + FalseNegative}$$

– F1 Score might be a better measure to use if we need to seek a balance between Precision and Recall AND there is an uneven class distribution (a large number of Actual Negatives)

$$F1 - score = 2 \times \frac{Precision * Recall}{Precision + Recall}$$

Considering these metrics, Classification reports of both the models are tabulated. Table 3 and 4 show classification report for RNN and LSTM respectively.

It clearly shows that the best result is achieved by model 2 (LSTM) which is trained and validated on 150,000 depressive tweets and 150,000 random tweets with accuracy and F1-score of 96.28% and 96% respectively. It performs better than the simple RNN model (Table 5).

Finally testing the model on custom tweets gave accurate polarities (Fig. 11).

Table 3. Classification Report of Simple RNN

	Precision	Recall	F1-Score	Support
Class 0	0.97	0.95	0.96	29314
Class 1	0.95	0.97	0.96	29877
Accuracy			0.96	59191
Macro Avg	0.96	0.96	0.96	59191
Weighted Avg	0.96	0.96	0.96	59191

Table 4. Classification Report of LSTM

	Precision	Recall	F1-Score	Support
Class 0	0.98	0.95	0.96	29314
Class 1	0.95	0.98	0.97	29877
Accuracy			0.96	59191
Macro Avg	0.96	0.96	0.96	59191
Weighted Avg	0.96	0.96	0.96	59191

Table 5. Comparison of both the models

Models	Val. Accuracy	Precision	Recall	F1-Score	Loss
Simple RNN	95.98%	0.96	0.96	0.96	0.1176
LSTM	96.21%	0.96	0.96	0.96	0.1077

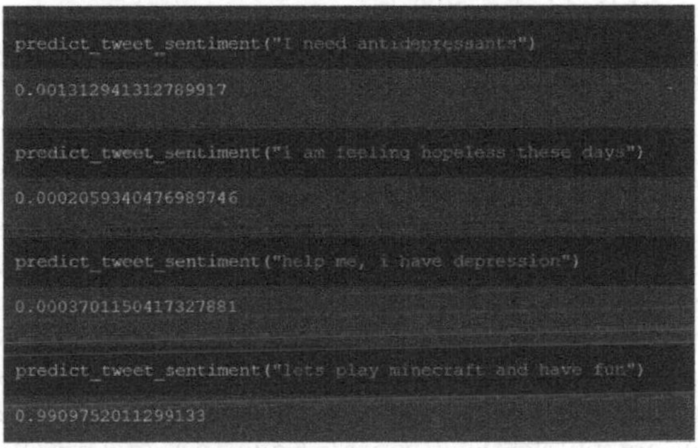

Fig. 11. Prediction on custom tweets

5 Conclusion and Future Scope

The use of linguistic markers as a tool in analysing and diagnosing depression has enormous potential. Depression can so quickly be seen in the text, even without complex models. Visual analysis alone can illuminate the difference between random Tweets and Tweets that have depressive characteristics by simply collecting, cleaning, and processing available data. The potential of linguistic analysis in the arena of mental health cannot be overstated. By analysing a person's words, you have a clear and valuable window into their mental state. Even the most straightforward analysis of social media can provide us with unprecedented access into individuals thoughts and feelings and lead to substantially greater understanding and treatment of mental health.

We intend to improve our detector by including some more psychological factors in the future. Since the model's accuracy has been excellent, it can be concluded that with sufficient data and hardware, a reliable program can be developed to check for signs of depression in a message. These programs can be deployed to analyse real-life messages and blogs to check if the person writing is depressed or not. Many psychologists, along with AI developers, are still working on algorithms that could give more intuition about the depression of the person concerned. Finally, we would like to develop efficient data processing algorithms that could reduce the errors caused by the use of slang more efficiently.

References

Abdullahi, S.S., Sun, Y., Muhammad, S.H.: Deep sequence models for text classification tasks. In: International Conference on Electrical, Communication, and Computer Engineering (ICECCE) (2021)

Kautz, A.S.H., Bernard, M., Vincent, S.: Modeling spread of disease from social interactions. In: Association for the Advancement of Artificial Intelligence (AAAI) (2012)

Orabi, A.H., Buddhitha, P., Orabi, M.H., Inkpen, D.: Deep learning for depression detection of twitter. In: Proceedings of the Fifth Workshop on Computational Linguistics and Clinical Psychology (2018)

Ng, A., Katanforoosh, K., Mourri., Y.B." Sequence models | coursera. https://www.coursera.org/learn/nlp-sequence-models

O'Dea, B., Wan, S., Batterham, P.J., Calear, A.L.: Detecting suicidality on twitter. Internet Intervent. **2**, 183–188 (2015)

Hutto, C., Gilbert, E.: Vader: a parsimonious rule-based model for sentiment analysis of social media text. In: Eighth International Conference on Weblogs and Social Media (ICWSM-2014) (2014)

Ghosh, A., Bose, S., Maji, G., Debnath, N., Sen, S.: Stock price prediction using lstm on Indian share market. In: Yuan, Q., Shi, Y., Miller, L., Lee, G., Hu, G., Goto, T. (eds.) Proceedings of 32nd International Conference on Computer Applications in Industry and Engineering, vol. 63 of Epic Series in Computing, pp. 101–110 (2019). EasyChair. https://easychair.org/publications/paper/LKgnhttps://doi.org/10.29007/qgcz

Goodfellow, I., Bengio, Y., Courville, A.: Deep Learning. MIT Press, Cambridge (2016). http://www.deeplearningbook.org

Zogan, H., Wang, X., Jameel, S., Xu, G.: Depression detection with multi-modalities using a hybrid deep (2020). arXiv preprint arXiv:2007.02847

Heaton, J., Ian, G., Bengio, I., Courville, A.: Deep learning. Genet. Program. Evol. Mach. **19**(1), 305-307. https://doi.org/10.1007/s10710-017-9314-z

Hochreiter, S.: The vanishing gradient problem during learning recurrent neural nets and problem solutions. Int. J. Uncertain. Fuzz. Knowl.-Based Syst. **6**(02), 107–116 (1998)

Pennington, J., Socher, R., Manning, C.D.: Glove: global vectors for word representation. Stanford (2014)

Zhang, J., Li, Y., Tian, J., Li, T.: Lstm-cnn hybrid model for text classification. In: IEEE 3rd Advanced Information Technology, Electronic and Automation Control Conference (IAEAC) (2018)

Kingma, D.P., Ba, J.: Adam: a method for stochastic optimization. In: 3rd International Conference for Learning Representations, San Diego (2014)

Zhang, L., Huang, X., Liu, T., Zhu, T.: Using linguistic features to estimate suicide probability of Chinese microblog users. In: International Conference on Human Centered Computing (2014)

Liu, B.: Social network analysis. Web Data Mining (2011)

Maheshwari, A.: Report on text classification using cnn, rnn and han. https://medium.com/jatana/report-on-text-classification-using-cnn-rnn-han-f0e887214d5f

Islam, M.R., Kabir, M.A., Ahmed, A., Ulhaq, A.: Depression detection from social network data using machine learning techniques. Health Inf. Sci. Syst. **6**, 1–12 (2018)

Moreno, M.A., Jelenchick, L.A., Egan, E.G., Cox, E.: Feeling bad on facebook: depression disclosures by college students on a social networking site. Depress. Anxiety **28**, 447–455 (2011)

Hunt, M.G., Marx, R., Lipson, C., Young, J.: No more FOMO: limiting social media decreases loneliness and depression. J. Social Clin. Psychol. **37**(10), 751–768 (2018)

Gamon, M., de Choudhury, M., Counts, S., Horvitz, E.: Predicting depression via social media. In: Association for the Advancement of Artificial Intelligence (AAAI) (2013)

Olah, C.: Understanding lstm networks. https://colah.github.io/posts/2015-08-Understanding-LSTMs/

Olivier, S.: Social network analysis. In: Knowledge Solutions (2017)

Ortigosa, A., Martín, J.M., Carro, R.M.: Sentiment analysis in facebook and its application to e-learning. Comput. Human Behav. **31**, 527–541 (2014)

Paul, M.J., Dredze, M.: You are what you tweet: analyzing twitter for public health. In: Proceedings of the Fifth International Conference on Weblogs and Social Media (2011)

Phung, V.H., Rhee, E.J.: A high-accuracy model average ensemble of convolutional neural networks for classification of cloud image patches on small datasets. Appl. Sci. **9**(21) (2019). https://www.mdpi.com/2076-3417/9/21/4500. https://doi.org/10.3390/app9214500

Raghavendra, K., Chellappan, S., Montgomery, F., Lutzen, K.: Associating internet usage with depressive behavior among college students. IEEE Technol. Soc. Maga. **31**, 73–80 (2012)

Sardogan, M., Tuncer, A., Ozen, Y.: Plant leaf disease detection and classification based on cnn with lvq algorithm. In: 2018 3rd international conference on computer science and engineering (ubmk), pp. 382–385 (2018). https://doi.org/10.1109/UBMK.2018.8566635

Sawant, M.: Text sentiments classification with cnn and lstm. https://medium.com/@mrunal68/text-sentiments-classification-with-cnn-and-lstm-f92652bc29fd/

Hochreiter, S., Schmidhuber, J.A.: Long short-term memory. Neural Comput. (1997)

She, X., Zhang, D.: Text classification based on hybrid cnn-lstm hybrid model. In: 11th International Symposium on Computational Intelligence and Design (ISCID) (2018)

Sherstinsky, A.: Fundamentals of recurrent neural network (rnn) and long short-term memory (lstm) network. Elsevier Physica D: Nonlinear Phenomena J.: Special Issue Mach. Learn. Dyn. Syst. **404** (2018)

Suman, S.K., Shalu, H., Agrawal, L.A., Agrawal, A., Kadiwala, J.: A novel sentiment analysis engine for preliminary depression status estimation on social media (2020)

Yin, W., Kann, K., Yu, M., Schutze, H.: Comparative study of cnn and rnn for natural language processing. In: Computation and Language (cs.CL) (2017)

Bachrach, Y., Kosinski, M., Kohli, P., Stillwell, D.: Personality and patterns of facebook usage. In: ACM Conference on Web Sciences (2012)

Depression. https://www.who.int/news-room/fact-sheets/detail/depression

Internet live stats. https://www.internetlivestats.com/one-second/#tweets-band

Understanding nlp word embeddings – text vectorization. https://towardsdatascience.com/understanding-nlp-word-embeddings-text-vectorization-1a23744f7223

Performance Assessment of Machine Learning Techniques for Corn Yield Prediction

Purnima Awasthi[1]([✉])[iD], Sumita Mishra[2][iD], and Nishu Gupta[3][iD]

[1] Amity School of Engineering and Technology, Amity University, Lucknow, India
purnima.awasthi@s.amity.edu
[2] Amity School of Engineering and Technology, Amity University, Lucknow, India
smishra3@lko.amity.edu
[3] Department of Computer Science, Faculty of Information Technology and Electrical Engineering, Norwegian University of Science and Technology, 2815 Gjøvik, Norway
nishugupta@ieee.org

Abstract. Agriculture Industry has evolved tremendously over the past few years. Numerous obstacles have been raised in the agricultural fields including change in climate, pollution, lack of land and resource, etc. To overcome these hurdles and increase the crop productivity, agricultural practices need to adopt smarter technologies. Crop Yield prediction at an early stage is an significant task in precision farming. The yield of any crop depends on many factors including crop genotype, climatic conditions, soil properties, fertilizers used, etc. In this work, we propose a framework based on machine learning technique to predict the yield of corn in 46 districts of Uttar Pradesh, the largest Indian state in terms of population over a period of 37 years. We combine weather data, climatic data, soil data and corn yield data to help farmers to predict the annual production of corn in their district. We implement Linear Regression (LR), Decision Tree (DT) Regression, Random Forest (RF) Regression, and ensemble Bagging Extreme Gradient Boosting (XGBoost) model. Upon evaluation of all models and comparing them we observe that Bagging XGBoost Regression model outperforms all other models with the accuracy of 93.8% and RMSE= 9.1.

Keywords: Corn yield prediction · Machine learning · Linear regression · Decision Tree Regression · Random Forest Regression · Bagging XGBoost

1 Introduction

Agricultural industry plays a significant role in the global economy. As the population is increasing day by day, the pressure on food supply is also increasing. In future, the food demand will be higher among the people, which would require an efficient food production system [1]. Nowadays people are unaware in growing the right crop at the right place and time, which ultimately leads to reduced crop productivity or crop loss. As a solution, crop yield prediction carries important

I. Woungang et al. (Eds.): ANTIC 2022, CCIS 1798, pp. 320–335, 2023.
https://doi.org/10.1007/978-3-031-28183-9_23

agricultural concern. The yield of any crop majorly depends upon the climatic conditions, soil health, pesticides, etc. Accurate crop yield prediction helps in the management of risk associated with the crop loss [2].

Corn is called the queen of all cereals as it is one of the most versatile crop among all crops grown globally. It is cultivated in more than 168 countries having wide variety of climate, soil, and biodiversity. In India corn (maize) is the third most important crop after rice and wheat. Uttar Pradesh is the third highest producer of corn in India. It is mainly a rainy crop. Prediction of corn yield will help the farmers to analyse and take necessary measures to improve its production.

Over the past years Machine Learning (ML) has been proved to be a promising technique to forecast the crop yield and has helped in improving the quality and productivity of the crops [3]. ML has the ability to analyse patterns and correlation between different parameters and discover knowledge from the data sets [4,5]. ML predictive models help to make predictions for the future [6,7]. For a high performance predictive model, it is important to choose the right algorithm as well as efficient data handling [8,9].

In this work, we propose four ML models: Linear Regression, Random forest, Decision Tree Regression, and an ensemble model named Bagging XGBooost Regression for predicting the yield of corn in the 46 districts of Uttar Pradesh. Features analysed include annual average temperature, annual rainfall, soil moisture, specific humidity, area under cultivation and annual production. The metrics used for evaluation of the models are accuracy and root-mean-square error (RMSE). Further this paper is organised as: Sect. 2 which represents the past related work in this field; Sect. 3 explains data collection and data set; Sect. 4 represents Methodology; Sect. 5 presents Results and Discussion; and finally Sect. 6 concludes the article with discussing the Future Scope.

2   Related Work

In the past few years ML has gained a lot of importance by the researchers in the fields of agriculture. Some of the works explaining the implementation of ML in the prediction of crop yield are discussed as under:

Farnaz et al. [10] exploited different ML algorithms: Decision Tree, Gradient Boosting Machine, Adaptive Boosting, Random Forest, XGBoost, and ANN to predict the corn hybrid yield. They used the data provided in Syngenta Crop Challenge, 2020. XGBoost model gave best result than all other algorithms with RMSE = 0.0524.

Lontsi et al. [11] proposed a ML based prediction system to predict the crop yield of maize, rice, seed cotton, cassava, bananas, and yams in the countries of West Africa throughout the years. They used weather data, climatic data, agricultural data, and chemical data for prediction of crop production. They have implemented multiple ML algorithms including decision tree, multi variant logistic regression, and K-Nearest Neighbor (KNN). They applied hyper parameter tuning with cross validation to obtain better results. Among all, the decision tree algorithm gave best result with 95.3% accuracy.

Javed et al. [12] proposed an interaction regression model for predicting the crop yields. They studied corn and soyabean crops in the three states of Midwest (Indiana, Illinois, and Lowa) of US. The factors under consideration for crop yield prediction were: environment, management and their interaction, and genotype. Their model achieved RMSE of 8% or less.

S. Vinson et al. [13] performed a study on paddy fields of 28 districts of wide spectrum of Tamil Nadu over a time period of 18 years. They developed ML models named: Back Propagation Neural Network(BPNN), SVM, and General Regression Neural Network(GRNN). As a result they found that GRNN achieved highest accuracy of 97% ($R^2 = 95.3$).

R. Usha et al. [14] proposed a crop recommendation system based on soil factors using various ML models like Logistic Regression, Naive Bayes, and Random Forest. They analysed the features like N, P, K, temperature, humidity, and rainfall and suggested the best crop that could be grown in that soil condition. Accuracy achieved were 95.2% by Logistic Regression, 90.2% by Naive Bayes, and 99.09% by Random Forest.

P.S. Nishant et al. [15] implemented various regression models including Efficient Neural Network (ENet), Lasso, and Kernel Ridge to predict the crop yield of almost all the crops grown in India. The parameters used were state, district, season, and area. They used the stacking regression concept which improved the performance of models with RMSE less than 1%.

S. Khaki et al. [16] designed a model based on Deep Neural Network for the prediction of maize crop. They used 2018 Syngenta Crop Challenge data set built across 2,247 locations of US and Canada between 2008 and 2016. The factors included crop genotype, yield performance and environment(Soil and weather) data. The model showed high performance with RMSE=12% of average yield and 50% of STD (with predicted weather data) and RMSE=11% of average yield and 46% of STD (with perfect weather data).

Ali Farjam et al. [17] implemented Artificial Neural Networks (ANNs) to predict the yield of seed and grain of corn. They collected data from 144 farms in 2011. They used Multi layer perceptron (MLP) ANNs. Their ANNs contain six neurons in the input layer. They used fertilisers, biocides, human labour, machinery, and diesel fuel as energy inputs. As a result, the model obtained R^2 score of roughly 0.9998 and 0.99978 for seed and grain respectively.

Khadijeh et al. [18] estimated two deep learning algorithms namely: Long Short-Term Memory and Gated Recurrent Units for the prediction to tomato and potato crops. For the analysis, they used crop simulation outputs, remote sensing data, weather, and soil data from MCYFC database. As a result they found that Bidirectional Long Short Term Memory (LSTM) model outperformed all other models with MSE= 0.017 to 0.039 and $R^2 = 0.97$ to 0.99.

Han et al. [19] implemented six ML models to predict the crop yield of wheat in winter season which include Support Vector Machine (SVM) Regression, K-Nearest Neighbor (KNN) Regression, Artificial Neural Network (ANN) Regression, Decision Tree and Gaussian Rrocess Regression (GPR), and Random Forest Regression. They integrated remote sensing data, climatic data, and soil data for analysis. Their result showed that SVM, GPR, and RF gave best performance with $R^2 > 0.75$.

3   Data Set

3.1   Data Collection

Data is very important for any ML based predictive system. This system uses a historical corn yield data, weather data, climatic data, and soil data of 46 districts of Uttar Pradesh, India as an input.

The data set used here is not publicly available as a whole. We created this data set by combining data from two different sources. The data for temperature (average-annual), humidity (average-anuual) and soil moisture factors is obtained from Data Access Viewer-NASA POWER [20] portal. Here, we can find the solar and meteorological data of any geographical location by specifying the latitudes, longitudes and timelime. The data for rainfall(annual), area under the corn production, total annual corn production is obtained from International Crops Research Institute for Semi-Arid Tropics (ICRISAT) [21] portal, which provides the district level database for Indian agriculture and allied sectors. The data provided here is till year 2017 only.

We merged the data from these two sources with respect to the district and year parameter. We further removed all missing and null values and standardised it into a standard format which made the merged data set feasible for analysis.

The variable of the data set and their sources are described below:

- **Corn Production:** Total annual corn production obtained from International Crops Research Institute for Semi-Arid Tropics (ICRISAT) [21].
- **Corn Area:** Total area under corn production obtained from ICRISAT.
- **Rainfall:** Total annual rainfall obtained from ICRISAT.
- **Temperature:** Average annual temperature of the district obtained from Data Access Viewer-NASA POWER [20].
- **Humidity:** Average annual specific humidity of the district obtained from Data Access Viewer-NASA POWER.
- **Soil Moisture:** Soil Moisture of the district obtained from Data Access Viewer-NASA POWER.

The preview of the data set prepared is shown in Fig. 1.

	A	B	C	D	E	F	G	H
1	Dist Code	Year	RAINFALL (Average)	Temperature (C)(Average)	Humidity(g/kg)	Soil moisture (1)	CORN AREA (1000 ha)	CORN PRODUCTION (1000 tons)
2	189	1981	861.3	24.3	9.46	0.48	29	29.1
3	189	1982	635	23.54	9.95	0.47	27.1	26.6
4	189	1983	1389.7	24.09	8.97	0.41	30.5	36.9
5	189	1984	602.3	24.8	8.54	0.42	29.4	45.3
6	189	1985	803.9	24.61	8.97	0.47	28.7	32.5
7	189	1986	794.9	24.56	8.24	0.41	26	37.7
8	189	1987	517.8	26.23	7.02	0.35	21.2	19.1
9	189	1988	1569.2	25.01	9.28	0.47	21.2	27.3

Fig. 1. Data set preview

3.2   Data Pre-processing

Pre-processing of data is very important for any data set before its actual use. In the collected data set, there are few 'NA' values which are removed using python. Further, the values of data set are standardised into a standard format.

3.3   Data Visualization

After the data set is cleaned, further it is recommended to do an Exploratory Data Analysis. Here, we have used pair-plot (Scatter Matrix) tool to see the relationships between the variables.

Fig. 2 represents the pair plot of the variables of the Data Set.

Another tool to analyse data set is Correlation Matrix. The correlation matrix of our data set is shown in Fig. 3.

The above figure represents the degree to which one variable coordinates with other. Here, in our data set, area under production has the highest correlation with the total annual corn production.

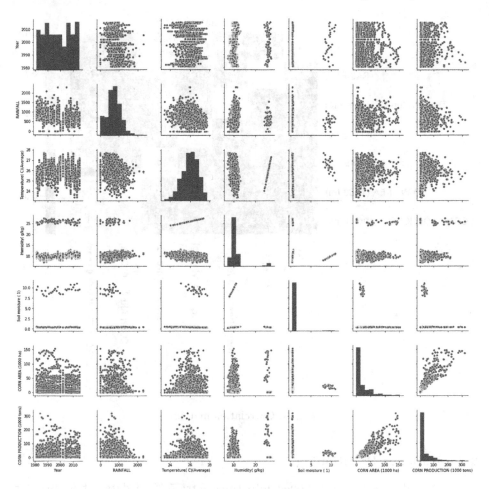

Fig. 2. Pair plot of the data set

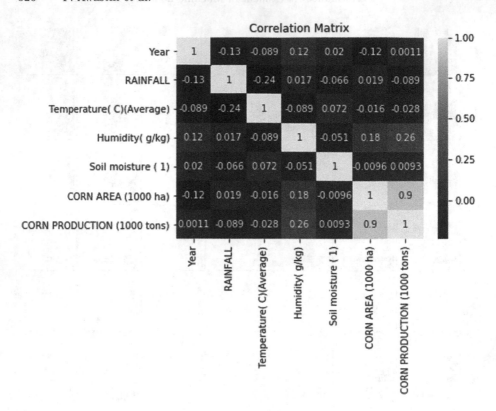

Fig. 3. Correlation matrix

3.4   Data Set Partitioning

The entire data set is partitioned into three sets: 70% of data set is used for training the model, 20% of data set is used as validation set and 10% of data set is used for testing the model which is shown in Fig. 4.

Data Set

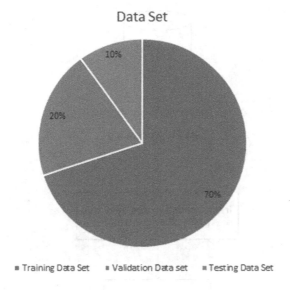

■ Training Data Set   ■ Validation Data set   ■ Testing Data Set

Fig. 4. Data set split

4 Methodology

We have proposed a corn yield prediction model which is based on ML. Figure 5 represents the flowchart of the complete work. It consists of six steps: Data Collection, Data Pre-processing, Data set splitting, Training of models, Performance Assessment of all models, and Comparative analysis of performance of all models.

We first collected data of rainfall, temperature, specific humidity, area under production, annual corn production of 46 districts of Uttar Pradesh over a time of 37 years. After collection, we prepossessed the data set by removing 'NA' values and performing the standard normalization. Further the prepossessed data was splitted into three subsets for training, validation, and testing purpose. The ratio of training, validation, and testing set is 70%, 20%, and 10% respectively. After splitting data set we implemented and trained four ML models namely: Linear Regression (LR), Decision Tree (DT) Regression, Random Forest (RF) Regression, and Bagging Extreme Gradient Boosting (XGBoost).

Linear Regression: Linear Regression (LR) is a simple Regression based on statistics for predictive analysis. It depicts the linear relationship between the independent variable (represented on X-axis) and the dependent variable (represented on Y-axis). In the event that there are more than one info variable, then it is called Multiple Linear Regression. Linear Regression uses slope-intercept form for the calculation of best fit line

$$y = mx + c \qquad (1)$$

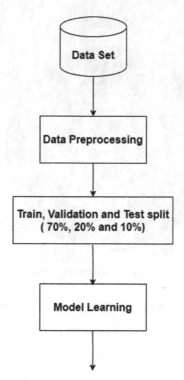

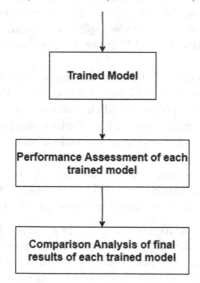

Linear Regression, Descision Tree, Random Forest, Bagging XGBoost

Fig. 5. Flowchart of methodology of the work

$$y = a_0 + a_1.x \tag{2}$$

where, y= Dependent variable, x= Independent variable, a_0 = Intercept of the line, a_1 = Linear regression coefficient.

Decision Tree Regression: It is commonly used algorithm for both regression and classification problems. Decision Tree Regression provides a tree based decision structure to predict the target values. The target values are contiguous values. The basic structure of decision tree is shown in Fig. 6.

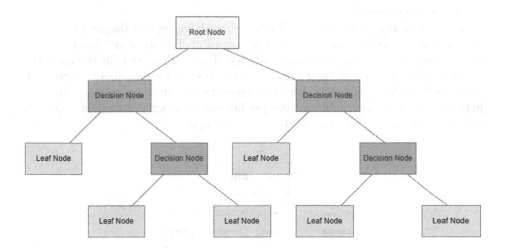

Fig. 6. Structure of a decision tree

Here, root note represents the whole data points, decision node represents the intermediate results and the leaf node represents the final results(values).

Random Forest Regression: In Random Forest, multiple decision trees are merged together to predict some results. It uses Ensemble model for learning. In Random Forest, we solve problems using mean squared error.

$$MSE = \frac{1}{N}.\sum_{n=1}^{\infty}.(f_i - y_i)^2 \tag{3}$$

By using the above MSE approach we can calculate the distance of each node from the actual predicted value, which further help us to decide which decision branch is better in our forest.

Bagging XGBoost Regression: Extreme Gradient Boosting is a powerful technique for building supervised ML models. It is an Ensemble learning which is tree based. It gives best tree model by using more accurate approximations. Mathematically, XGBoost model can be represented in the form of Eq. 4.

$$y_i = \sum_{k=1}^{K} \cdot (f_k)(x_i), f_k \in F \tag{4}$$

where, K represents number of trees, f denotes functional space of F, and F is the set of all possible CARTs.

To increase the performance of XGBoost, we have applied Bagging technique on it. Bagging refers to Bootstrap and Aggregation. This approach has the capability to improve the accuracy and stability of any ML model. In Bagging, the data set is divided into n equal subsets. On each subset a base model is created. Then each model is trained with their respective training set and finally predictions are made by combining the predictions from all the models. Figure 7. represents the basic structure of Bagging technique.

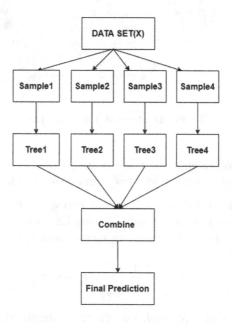

Fig. 7. Structure of bagging XGBoost regression

After implementing the ML models, performance of each model was assessed and finally a comparison was done among all.

5   Results and Discussion

We used the computer hardware with windows 10 operating system with a core i3 processor and 8GB RAM. We implemented our work in Anaconda 2.1.1 environment using Python 3.10 (Jupyter Notebook). The Libraries used for implementation, data preprocessing and data visualization are Scikit-Learn, Pandas and Numpy.

We have used two metrics to evaluate the performance of our system: Model Accuracy and Root Mean Squared Error(RMSE). Accuracy is defined as the percentage of predictions which are made correct for the test data set. It is calculated as:

$$Accuracy = \frac{No. of\, correct\, predictions}{Total\, no. of\, predictions} \tag{5}$$

RMSE is the standard deviation of the errors occur while making prediction on a data set. It shows how the data is spread out around the best-fit line. The formula to calculate RMSE is represented in Eq. 6.

$$RMSE = \sqrt{\frac{1}{n} \cdot \sum_{i=1}^{n} \cdot (f_i - o_i)^2} \tag{6}$$

where, f is the predicted value, o is observed value, and N is sample size.

Finally, after evaluation of each implemented model we conclude that Linear Regression achieved the accuracy of 87.9% with RMSE = 12.9. Performance of Decision Tree was comparatively less with accuracy of 78.8% and RMSE = 16.9. Random Forest Regression achieved accuracy of 87.9% with RMSE = 12.7. Lastly, Bagging XGBoost outperformed all other models with accuracy of 93.8% and RMSE = 9.1. Table 1 shows the final results.

Table 1. Performance metrics of ML models

ML Model	Accuracy	RMSE
Linear regression	87.9%	12.9
Decision tree	78.8%	16.9
Random forest	87.9%	12.7
Bagging XGBoost	93.8%	9.1

Figure 8 represents the distribution plot of predicted values vs. actual values for Linear Regression model. We can see clearly there is a deviation between the predicted values and the true values.

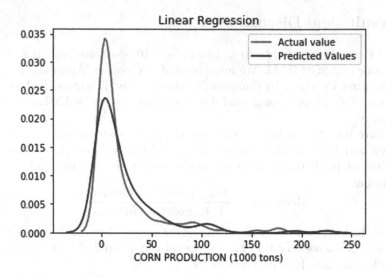

Fig. 8. Distribution plot for linear regression

Fig. 9 represents the distribution plot of predicted values vs. actual values for Decision Tree model. Here we can see that there is less deviation between the predicted values and the true values.

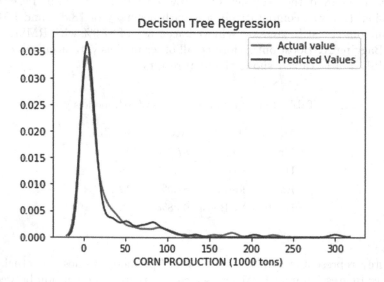

Fig. 9. Distribution plot for decision tree

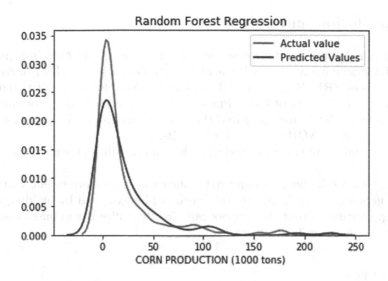

Fig. 10. Distribution plot for random forest

Fig. 10 represents the distribution plot of predicted values vs. actual values for Random Forest Regression model. Here again we can see that there is more deviation between the predicted values and the true values.

Fig. 11 represents the distribution plot of predicted values vs actual values for Bagging XGBoost Regression model. This model gave the highest accuracy of 93.8% with RMSE of 9.1. Here we can see that there is very less deviation between the predicted values and the true values.

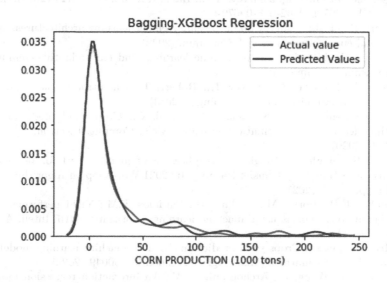

Fig. 11. Distribution plot for Bagging XGBoost regression

6   Conclution and Future Scope

ML is a popular tool for future prediction. In this work, we have implemented four ML model namely: Linear Regression (LR), Decision Tree (DT) Regression, Random Forest (RF) Regression and Bagging XGBoost for the prediction of corn yield in the 46 districts of Uttar Pradesh. We have evaluated the performance of all the four models and compared them. As a conclusion, the performance of Ensemble Bagging XGBoost gave best results.

The limitation of this work includes the unavailability of some data beyond year 2017.

This framework can give improved results assuming more recent year information gets accessible. In future, this work can be extended by building a GUI based application so that the farmers can directly utilize it and make wise decision for growing corn in their area.

References

1. Jayanarayana Reddy, D., Rudra Kumar, M.: Crop yield prediction using machine learning algorithm. In 2021 5th International Conference on Intelligent Computing and Control Systems (ICICCS), pp. 1466–1470 (2021)
2. Gupta, N., Gupta, V., Chauhan, B.S., Singh, A.P., Singh, R.P.: Comparison of organochlorine pesticides levels in soil and groundwater of Agra, up, India. I Control Pollut. **29**(1), (2012)
3. Chen, Y., et al.: Strawberry yield prediction based on a deep neural network using high-resolution aerial orthoimages. Remote Sens. **11**(13), 1584 (2019)
4. Nguyen, G., et al.: Machine learning and deep learning frameworks and libraries for large-scale data mining: a survey. Artif. Intell. Rev. **52**(1), 77–124 (2019). https://doi.org/10.1007/s10462-018-09679-z
5. Balhara, S., et al.: A survey on deep reinforcement learning architectures, applications and emerging trends. IET Commun. (2022)
6. Alpaydin, E.: Introduction to machine learning, 2nd edn. adaptive computation and machine learning (2010)
7. Gareth, J., Daniela, W., Trevor, H., Robert, T.: An introduction to statistical learning: with applications in R. Spinger (2013)
8. Van Klompenburg, T., Kassahun, A., Catal, C.: Crop yield prediction using machine learning: a systematic literature review. Comput. Electron. Agric. **177**, 105709 (2020)
9. Mishra, S., Singh, A., Singh, V.: Application of mobilenet-v1 for potato plant disease detection using transfer learning. In: 2021 Workshop on Algorithm and Big Data, pp. 14–19 (2021)
10. Sarijaloo, F.B., Porta, M., Taslimi, B., Pardalos, P.M.: Yield performance estimation of corn hybrids using machine learning algorithms. Artif. Intell. Agric. **5**, 82–89 (2021)
11. Cedric, L.S., et al.: Crops yield prediction based on machine learning models: case of west African countries. Smart Agric. Technol. **2**, 100049 (2022)
12. Ansarifar, J., Wang, L., Archontoulis, S.V.: An interaction regression model for crop yield prediction. Sci. Rep. **11**(1), 1–14 (2021)

13. Joshua, S.V.: Crop yield prediction using machine learning approaches on a wide spectrum (2022)
14. Devi, U., Selvakumari, S.: Crop prediction and mapping using soil features with different machine learning techniques. Available at SSRN 4097213 (2022)
15. Nishant, P.S., Venkat, P.S., Avinash, B.L., Jabber, B.: Crop yield prediction based on Indian agriculture using machine learning. In: 2020 International Conference for Emerging Technology (INCET), pp. 1–4 (2020)
16. Khaki, S., Wang, L.: Crop yield prediction using deep neural networks. Front. Plant Sci. **10**, 621 (2019)
17. Farjam, A., Omid, M., Akram, A., Fazel Niari, Z.: A neural network based modeling and sensitivity analysis of energy inputs for predicting seed and grain corn yields. J. Agric. Sci. Technol. **16**(4), 767–778 (2014)
18. Alibabaei, K., Gaspar, P.D., Lima, T.M.: Crop yield estimation using deep learning based on climate big data and irrigation scheduling. Energies **14**(11), 3004 (2021)
19. Han, J., et al.: Prediction of winter wheat yield based on multi-source data and machine learning in china. Remote Sens. **12**(2), 236 (2020)
20. Data access viewer-nasa power. https://power.larc.nasa.gov/data-access-viewer/index.html
21. International crops research institute for semi-arid tropics. http://data.icrisat.org/dld/index.html

Detection of Bird and Frog Species from Audio Dataset Using Deep Learning

R. S. Latha⬤, G. R. Sreekanth⬤, and K. Suvalakshmi$^{(\boxtimes)}$ ⬤

Kongu Engineering College, Erode, India
grsreekanth@kongu.ac.in, suva1798@gmail.com

Abstract. There are over 9000 bird and frog species in the globe. Some of the species are rare to find, and even when they are, predicting their behaviour is challenging. There is an efficient and simple technique to recognise these frog and bird species contingent on their traits to solve this challenge. Also, humans are better at recognising birds and frogs through sounds than they are at recognising them through photographs. As a result, employed various CNN models including CNN-Sequential, CNN-ResNet, CNN-EfficientNet, CNN-VGG19 and a hybrid model Convolution Neural Networks with Long Short-term Memory (CNN-LSTM). It is a powerful deep learning model that has shown to be effective in image processing.

Compared to standard alone models, hybrid model produces better accuracy. A hybrid system for classifying bird and frog species is provided in this study, which employs the Rainforest Connection Species Audio Detection dataset from Kaggle repository for both training and testing. The classification of bird or frog species by using audio dataset after processing it and convert it into spectrogram images. Among all the deployed models CNN-LSTM system has been shown to achieve satisfactory results in practise by building this dataset and achieves accuracy of 92.47.

Keywords: Bird species · Machine learning · Convolutional Neural Networks

1 Introduction

Animals make the world better in more ways than just chirping. The abundance of rainforest species is a reliable indicator of how climate change and habitat loss are affecting the environment. Bird and frog species behavior and population dynamics have recently become a major concern. These species assist us in recognizing various living forms on the planet by reacting quickly to environmental changes.Because, it is easier to hear than to sight these species, it is critical to employ universal acoustic technologies. The identification of species can be done via a photograph, sound, or videography. It is possible to detect distinct species using an audio processing technology that captures their sound signature [1]. However, because of the diversed noises in the habitat, such as creepy crawlies, physical world items, and so on, the interpretation of such data becomes increasingly complicated.

© The Author(s), under exclusive license to Springer Nature Switzerland AG 2023
I. Woungang et al. (Eds.): ANTIC 2022, CCIS 1798, pp. 336–350, 2023.
https://doi.org/10.1007/978-3-031-28183-9_24

Conventional ways of assessing species biodiversity are boundaries constrained. Nonetheless, organizing and accumulating data on large species necessitates a great deal of human effort and is a very expensive method. In this scenario, a strong framework is needed that will allow for large-scale data processing regarding birds and frogs while also functioning as an important tool for legislators, scientists, and other stakeholders. Deep learning has been successful in automatic auditory identification; models require a significant amount of data per species for training. This restricts its use to endangered species, which are critical to preservation efforts. The solution is to develop methods for automating greater accuracy wild species detection in clamorous soundscapes with limited amount of training samples. Bird and frog species identification entails classification of bird or frog species by using audio dataset after processing it and convert it into spectrogram images.Real-time data, such as that supplied by machine learning algorithms, could allow for early recognition of human environmental consequences. This finding could lead to better preservation management strategies.

2 Literature Survey

Ecologists keep an eye on them in particular to figure out what causes population fluctuations and to aid in the conservation and management of rare and endangered wildlife species. The numerous surveys, as well as data collection procedures, were briefly discussed. A rapidly expanding group of experts have been discovered to have investigated the need for computer vision for vegetation surveillance. This study aims at assessing descriptions of studies discovered in the literature that deal with species surveillance and classification. It focuses on evaluating birds and frogs techniques for these species, which are often comparable, as well as motion aspects, which this study aims to analyze for species classification [2]. Offer a wide-scale prognosis and estimation of acoustics out of 100 distinct bird species using deep learning. On the Cornell Bird Challenge (CBC) 2020, studies shows that a hybrid modelling approach involving a CNN for recognizing the depiction of spectrograms and a RNN for the extraction of temporal attribute and to merge throughout time-points in order to produce the error-free methodology. The best acting method obtains an accuracy percentage of 67% over distinct bird species.

Reference [3] starting with raw, unprocessed audio, build a convolutional network for multispecies multi-label categorization of landscape records for training. The group of species involved in a recording is then predicted using a CNN contingent on mel-spectrograms of accent. Across the 24 unique species, the model has achieved precision of 0.893. Reference [4] provides a new feature learning method for identifying concurrent vocalising frog calls that uses a deep learning model. Finally, to categorize frog species, a binary significance based multiple-label classification technique is applied. Reference [5] illustrated that the addition of ambient recordings to the customary xeno-canto recordings which focuses on a prominent category was the key novelty of this article which also details the evaluation process, a summary of the tested systems that were put into practise by the six research groups, together with the results.

Reference [6] briefly showcase two current real-world application case studies of long-term, large-scale ecological tracking and biological resources exploitation. These findings show that AudioMoth has the ability to facilitate a major drift beyond passive uninterrupted recording by single or multiple devices towards proactive recognition by neural networks of components flooding enormous and isolated environs. Reference [7] compares different setups, such as the count of target labels (bird species) and the spectrogram palette. The findings imply that selecting a colour map that matches the images used to train the neural network delivers a measurable benefit. Reference [8] discovered wherein each augmentation set influences the deployed model's performance differently for every audio class, implying that the architectures performance can be enhanced further by using the class conditional data augmentation techniques.

The advantages of employing NMF-dependent feature value as input to DNN models rather than time-frequency estimates or extraction of manual feature have been explored. The use of NMF is more efficient and better was demonstrated in an experimental evaluation done by [9]. Table 1 depicts the systematic literature review and meta-analysis for sound classification.

Reference [10] findings revealed that the tested systems may achieve extremely high identification rates, even when dealing with a huge number of other species (as far as 10,000 species in range). Reference [11] gave information about the attempt to classify bird sounds on a broad scale using several CNN architectures. The introduction of these new CNN architectures made the most notable breakthrough, proving the techniques' rapid advancement. The task is approached using three distinct network topologies and a ensemble model, in which the ensemble approach attains a precision of 41.2% (official score) and 52.9% for salient species which was proposed by [12, 13] put forwards a method that employs unlabeled data learning, which is a technique for learning patterns in spectro-temporal information without using the training labels, allowing a classifier to extrapolate to similar content. References [14–16] develops a convolutional neural networks which were created for image classification, but they've proved to be successful in the audio domains as well.

3   Dataset Desrciption

The data was obtained from the Kaggle source and the URL is https://www.kaggle.com/c/rfcx-species-audio-detection. The dataset consists of features which are described below in Table 2. Given sound recordings containing audios from a number of wildlife. To forecast the likelihood that every one of the supplied species is detectable in the audio clip for every test's audio file.

Exploratory Data Analysis. The number of distinct species is 24 and the number of distinct records is 1132. Figure 1 shows that the majority of the train sound clips are unique species. Figure 2 depicts that excluding the species 23 and the species 17, the dataset is nearly equal.

The data consists of the length of time (tmin and tmax) that the animal species audio was recorded. It is analysed that the entire time duration of species recordings and discovered that the majority of species sounds are between 1 and 3 s long in the sound version. This is portrayed in Fig. 3.

Table 1. Systematic literature review and meta-analysis for sound classification

S.no	Researcher name	Title	Dataset	Models implemented	Year of publication	Accuracy	Limitations
1	Gupta G. et al. [17]	Recurrent Convolutional Neural Networks for large scale Bird species classification	Cornell Bird Challenge (CBC) dataset	CNN and RNN	2021	90%	Multiple species of bird calls can't be detected
2	JIE XIE et al. [18]	Investigation of Different CNN-Based Models for Improved Bird Sound Classification	Public dataset CLO-43DS	VGG	2019	86.31%	Only 43 bird species are classified using this framework
3	Dan Stowell et al.[19]	Automatic acoustic detection of birds through deep learning: The first Bird Audio Detection challenge	1.Chernobyl dataset 2.freefield1010 dataset 3.Warblr dataset 4.PolandNFC dataset	GMM	2019	93.8%	Lack of broad-scale recognition
4	LorisNanni et al. [20]	Data augmentation approaches for improving animal audio classification	1. BIRDZ 2.Xeno-canto Archive	CNN	2020	91.08%	Detect only the limited trained sounds
5	Hasan Abdullah Jasim et al. [21]	Classify bird species audio by Augment convolutional neural Network	1. BIRDZ 2.Xeno-canto Archive	CNN	2022	98%	Definite categorization labels don't really represent the shape of bird species precisely
6	Stefan Kahl et al [22]	BirdNET: A deep learning solution for avian diversity monitoring	Xeno-canto	ResNet	2021	79%	Because there is no standardised benchmark dataset and standard evaluation metrics
7	Museum fuer Naturkunde et al. [23]	Acoustic bird detection with deep convolutional neural networks	IEEE AASP Challenge	DCNNs	2018	95%	Spectrograms are not considered

(continued)

Table 1. (*continued*)

S.no	Researcher name	Title	Dataset	Models implemented	Year of publication	Accuracy	Limitations
8	Jack LeBien et al. [3]	A pipeline for identification of bird and frog species in tropical soundscape recordings using a convolutional neural network	Recordings from El Yunque National Forest	CNN	2020	97%	Considered large parameters and thus increasing memory and decreasing prediction speed

Table 2. Dataset description

Features used	Description
recording_id	Distinctive recording id
species_id	Distinctive species id
songtype_id	Distinctive song id
t_min	Beginning second of signal

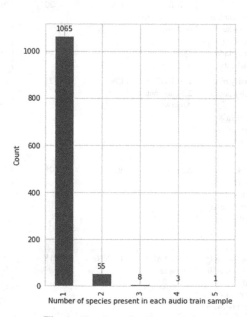

Fig. 1. Number of unique species

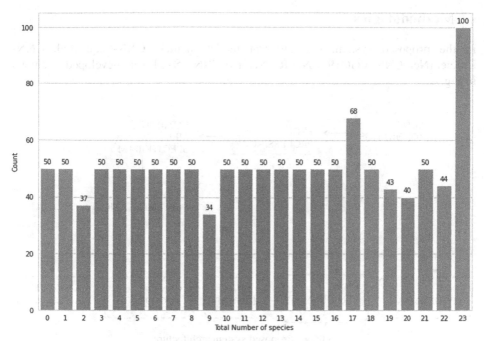

Fig. 2 Species count

Distribution of length of audio clips containing any species

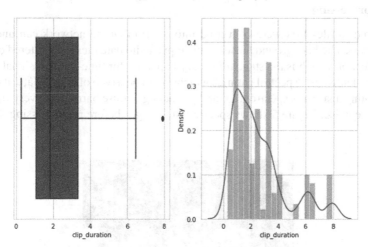

Fig. 3. Time duration of audio records

4   Methodologies

In the proposed system, five different models namely CNN-Sequential, CNN-EfficientNet, CNN-VGG19, CNN-ResNet and CNN-LSTM were developed as shown in Fig. 4.

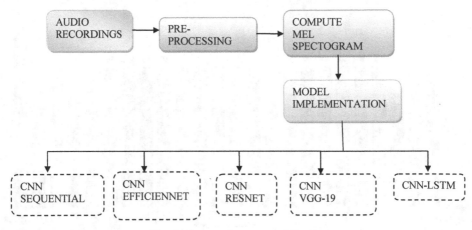

Fig. 4. Proposed system architecture

4.1   Preprocessing

The audio data files first were converted into a form that the network can understand and then train. The background noises in the input audio data files were filtered out using Noise reduction which is the standard library in python for time-domain signals. It uses a technique known as "spectral gating," which would be a type of Noise Gate. It operates by calculating a signal's spectrogram and predicting a noise barrier for every frequency range of the noise. Figure 5 shows spectrogram images before preprocessing the audio data files.

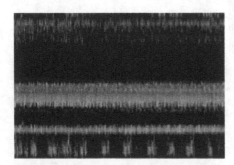

Fig. 5. Spectrogram image before preprocessing audio files

4.2 Generating Spectrograms

In previous studies, mel-spectrograms were found to be superior to the short time Fourier transform (STFT) and mel-frequency cepstral coefficients (MFCCs) for frequency translation of a time-domain signals. Figure 6 shows the spectrogram images after preprocessing and removing the background noises. By using librosa library the 2 s clipped audio samples, were converted into mel-spectrogram images. An average of 128 mel filter banks were employed to resample the audio. The hop-length is fixed to 694 for generating the spectrograms, and then the length of Fast Fourier Transform (FFT) is given to 2560.

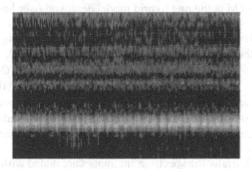

Fig. 6. Spectrogram image after preprocessing and removing noises

4.3 Evaluation

Estimating the species present in each sample test audio track is the task. A few test sound files only contain one species, whereas others contain several. The estimations are to be performed at the audio file level, which means that no beginning and end timestamps are provided. The label-weighted average precision is the performance measure, that serves as a generalisation of the average reciprocal rank indicator for the specific instance where there may be numerous true labels per given test.

4.4 Experimental Setup

DCNNs pretrained on Lstm are fine-tuned with mel spectrogram images representing brief recording chunks to establish an bird and frog detection system. Python is used for both training and testing, with built in package named librosa that used for audio file recognition and computation. For large data, the same basic pipeline is used, which can be summarised as follows:

- Pull out recording chunk from folder with a duration of about 4 s
- Use short-time Fourier transform for convertion to mel spectrogram remove frequencies.

• Reconfigure the spectrogram to best suit the network's input perspective

The challenge organisers highly suggest using detailed development sets for training and one for effectiveness validation.

4.5 Models Implemented

Adam optimizer and softmax activation function has been used to train every single model in this proposed architecture. For testing, the model with the highest training and validation accuracy is considered. The variation of CNN architecture including EfficientNet, ResNet, Sequential and VGG19 are implemented which are standalone models and CNN-LSTM is the one hybrid model deployed over here.

CNN-Sequential. The Pre-trained Sequential model is build using ten layers. First the input layer accepts the input image of width 100 and height 200. Then the inputs are resized into the size of 32×32 and it is followed by two CONVO 2D layers. Pooling operation is performed by fifth layer using MaxPooling function. All the pooled features of two-dimensional arrays are converted into linear vector by using Flattening layer. The last three layers of the models are constructed using dense and dropout layers. The model's total parameters are 1,628,248, and the trainable parameters are 1,628,248.

CNN-Efficientnet. Initially the spectrogram images are added with some random gaussian noises and then given as an input to EfficientNetB2 layer. The obtained convenient wav output obtained is saved and Global Average Pooling layer is added for doing pooling operations. Dense layer, is the final layer in the model and serves as the output layer.

CNN-Vgg19. It is made up of eight layers. The first layer is made up of a 224×224 input image. It is convolved using six size 32 filters, resulting in a size of 111×111. Again, Convolution is added as the subordinate layer, with a stride of 2 and size of convolutional filter is 64. As a result, the final image size will be 55×55. Similarly, the third layer also performs convolution, followed by a flattening and dropout layers.Dense and dropout 1 layers are used to build the last three layers of the models. The total parameters is 95,670,360 and the trainable parameters is 95,670,360 of the model.

CNN-Resnet. It is one of the most basic ResNet architecture which comprises of seven layers. The first block is an input layer and following two blocks are used to perform convolutional operation and the resultant image is of size 96×196. The fourth layer is MaxPooling layer follwed by CONVO 2D layer. Global Average Pooling function is used for pooling Atlast a dropout layer with a 0.5 moderate frequency range is connected to prevent overfitting of the data. There are 822,808 total parameters in the model, with 820,248 trainable parameters.

CNN-LSTM. A composite approach was incorporated in this work to impulsively classify different species by utilizing spectrogram images. This architecture's framework has been developed by fusion of CNN and LSTM networks (Hybrid) which is shown in Fig. 7,

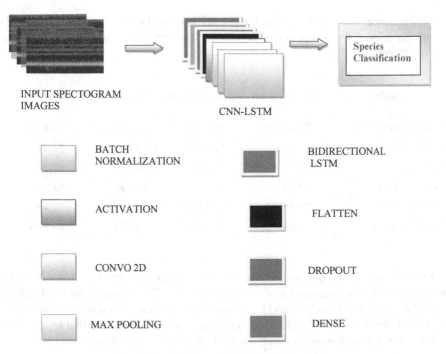

INPUT SPECTOGRAM
IMAGES

CNN-LSTM

Species
Classification

BATCH
NORMALIZATION

BIDIRECTIONAL
LSTM

ACTIVATION

FLATTEN

CONVO 2D

DROPOUT

MAX POOLING

DENSE

Fig. 7. Architecture of CNN-LSTM model

with the LSTM serving as a classifier and the CNN retrieving intricate information from images.

There are Thirty layers in the network: 7 batch normalisation layers,1 bidirectional LSTM layer,1 resizing layer,1 lambda layer,4 convolution layers, 5 activation layers, 4 max pooling layers,3 drop out layers, 1 flatten layer, and two dense layers. Every convolution block is made up of two dimensional CNNs and batch normalization layers ordered into a stack of depth. Accompanied by a dropout layer with 20% and 30% dropout rate. The convolutional layer of 3×3 filter size is activated, that are used for extraction of features by the activation function. To minimise the dimensions of an input image size, the max-pooling layer are added with a 2×2 filter. In the last stage of the design process, the activation map is directed to the LSTM layer to extract data.The output shape is $12 \times 12 \times 256$ at the end of all convolution process.

5 Result

5.1 Result Analysis

The findings of an additional investigation of the preceding experiment are shown in Table 2. In this study, the test set is formed by accounting for percentage variations of 20% and 30%; the remaining instances are utilized for training. It is also observed that the retention of accuracy outcomes in fluctuations of test ratios. The Table 3 shows the performance analysis of various CNN models trained on 6719 flac recordings. The models are trained for 50 epochs with both the learning rate set to 0.001 and the batch size is 128 respectively.

Table 3. Result analysis by varying the percentage of train and test data set

Model implemented	Train 80%	Test 20%	Train 70%	Test 30%
CNN-Efficient Net	60.56%	56.96%	58.60%	54.99%
CNN-Res Net	73.54%	70.45%	71.26%	67.76%
CNN-Sequential	78.05%	74.12%	76.09%	73.02%
CNN-VGG19	80.75%	76.84%	77.65%	72.43%
CNN-LSTM (Hybrid)	94.09%	92.47%	90.77%	86.39%

From the results it is cleared that the proposed model gives good accuracy of 92.47% for batch size 16 with sensitivity of 82% and recall of 92%. Figure 8 shows the change in validation accuracy analysis and Fig. 9 shows the variation in validation loss analysis graph for CNN-LSTM with reference to training epoch. It is evident that hybrid model is best suited for rainforest species classification without over fitting and bias.

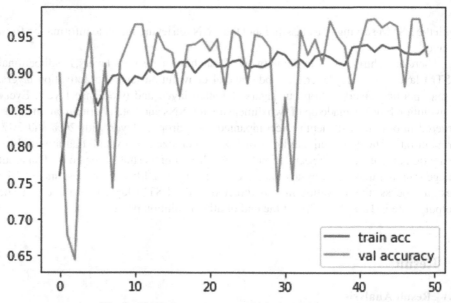

Fig. 8. Validation accuracy analysis for CNN-LSTM

The various sound components observed at various points in the audio clip are derived primarily and easily distinguished. When compared to fully connected CNN networks

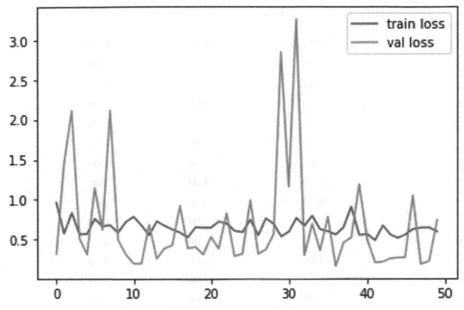

Fig. 9. Validation loss analysis for CNN-LSTM

the results shows that hybrid network can achieve good results on audio classification. From the accuracy analysis of both standard alone CNN models and hybrid models, it is clear that CNN with LSTM (Hybrid) model performs better classification of task when compared to conventional approaches. Based on bird and frog sounds, the network learns to categorize species accordingly. The classification report for species detection illustrated in Table 4.

Table 4. Classification report

	Precision	Recall	F1-score
0	1.00	1.00	1.00
1	1.00	1.00	1.00
2	1.00	1.00	1.00
3	0.00	0.00	0.00
4	1.00	1.00	1.00
5	1.00	1.00	1.00
6	0.97	1.00	0.99

(continued)

Table 4. (*continued*)

	Precision	Recall	F1-score
7	1.00	1.00	1.00
8	0.52	1.00	0.69
9	1.00	1.00	1.00
10	1.00	1.00	1.00
11	1.00	1.00	1.00
12	1.00	1.00	1.00
13	1.00	1.00	1.00
14	0.00	0.00	0.00
15	1.00	1.00	1.00
16	0.97	1.00	0.99
17	1.00	1.00	1.00
18	0.52	1.00	0.69
19	0.50	1.00	0.66
20	1.00	1.00	1.00
21	1.00	1.00	1.00
22	1.00	1.00	1.00
23	1.00	1.00	1.00
Accuracy			0.92
Macro Avg	0.87	0.92	0.89
Weighted-Avg	0.88	0.92	0.89

6   Conclusion

The introduction of automated tracking systems that produce actual information could allow for early identification of human environmental implications, allowing for more rapid and effective environmental conservation. Presented a complete analysis of hybrid deep learning techniques on a huge tropical soundscape dataset, the Rainforest Species Audio Detection challenge (2020). The purpose of this study was to enhance on the current species classification system and robotize the identification of bird and frog species.

A number of standard alone CNN models and hybrid modelsare investigated, with deep nets demonstrating improved performance over some conventional machine learning models for autonomous classification of endangered mammalian species using spectrogram images. From the studies, it is analyzed that the hybrid models have outperformed baseline CNN-only models on a variety of sound recognition tasks [20]. If more computing resources are provided, the described solution's effectiveness could be enhanced even more.

The hybrid model is trained and tested using audio data files. In terms of tropical species identification, the model is producing an accuracy of 92.47%. If additional information on animal species is acquired [21], the models' performance can be enhanced and a larger number of other species can be also be easily classified. In the tropical rainforest, IoT devices might be employed to achieve this strategy.

7 Future Work

As for future work, trying to introduce a unique hybrid model incorporating variations of RNNs such as Gated recurrent units (GRU) and Legendre memory units (LMU).Implementing hybrid models with variations of RNNs using the Rainforest connection species detection dataset, by adding attention layers in order to enhance the accuracy for classification of tropical species. Extending the present models to detect distinct bird and frog species and implementation of the same technique to different audio datasets.

References

1. Kahl, S., et al.: Overview of birdclef 2020: bird sound recognition in complex acoustic environments. In: CLEF 2020-Conference and Labs of the Evaluation Forum (2020)
2. Gupta, G., et al.: Recurrent Convolutional Neural Networks for large scale Bird species classification (2021)
3. LeBien, J., et al.: A pipeline for identification of bird and frog species in tropical soundscape recordings using a convolutional neural network. Eco. Inform. **59**, 101113 (2020)
4. Xie, J., et al.: Multi-label classification of frog species via deep learning. In: 2017 IEEE 13th International Conference on e-Science (e-Science). IEEE (_2017)
5. Goëau, H., et al.: Lifeclef bird identification task 2016: the arrival of deep learning. In: CLEF: Conference and Labs of the Evaluation Forum (2016)
6. Hill, A.P., et al.: AudioMoth: evaluation of a smart open acoustic device for monitoring biodiversity and the environment. Methods Ecol. Evol. **9**(5), 1199–1211 (2018)
7. Incze, A., et al.: Bird sound recognition using a convolutional neural network. In: 2018 IEEE 16th International Symposium on Intelligent Systems and Informatics (SISY). IEEE (2018)
8. Salamon, J., Bello, J.P.: Deep convolutional neural networks and data augmentation for environmental sound classification. IEEE Signal Process. Lett. **24**(3), 279–283 (2017)
9. Bisot, V., et al.: Leveraging deep neural networks with nonnegative representations for improved environmental sound classification. In: 2017 IEEE 27th International Workshop on Machine Learning for Signal Processing (MLSP). IEEE (2017)
10. Joly, A., et al.: Lifeclef 2017 lab overview: multimedia species identification challenges. In: International Conference of the Cross-Language Evaluation Forum for European Languages, LNCS, vol. 10456. Springer, Cham (2017). https://doi.org/10.1007/978-3-319-65813-1_24
11. Kahl, S., et al.: Large-scale bird sound classification using convolutional neural networks. In: CLEF (working notes) (2017)
12. Piczak, K.J.: Recognizing bird species in audio recordings using deep convolutional neural networks. In: CLEF (working notes) (2016)
13. Stowell, D., Plumbley, M.D.: Audio-only Bird Classification Using Unsupervised Feature Learning. CLEF (Working Notes), vol. 1180 (2014)

14. Sprengel, E., et al.: Audio based bird species identification using deep learning techniques (2016)
15. Martinsson, J.: Bird species identification using convolutional neural networks (2017)
16. Han, Y., Lee, K.: Acoustic scene classification using convolutional neural network and multiple-width frequency-delta data augmentation. arXiv preprint arXiv:1607.02383 (2016)
17. Gupta, G., et al.: Comparing recurrent convolutional neural networks for large scale bird species classification. Sci. Rep. **11**(1), 1–12 (2021)
18. Xie, J., et al.: Investigation of different CNN-based models for improved bird sound classification. IEEE Access **7**, 175353–175361 (2019)
19. Stowell, D., et al.: Automatic acoustic detection of birds through deep learning: the first Bird Audio Detection challenge. Methods Ecol. Evol. **10**(3), 368–380 (2019)
20. Nanni, L., Maguolo, G., Paci, M.: Data augmentation approaches for improving animal audio classification. Eco. Inform. **57**, 101084 (2020)
21. Jasim, H.A., et al.: Classify bird species audio by augment convolutional neural network. In: 2022 International Congress on Human-Computer Interaction, Optimization and Robotic Applications (HORA). IEEE (2022)
22. Kahl, S., et al.: BirdNET: a deep learning solution for avian diversity monitoring. Eco. Inform. **61**, 101236 (2021)
23. Lasseck, M.: Acoustic bird detection with deep convolutional neural networks. In: DCASE (2018)

Lifestyle Disease Influencing Attribute Prediction Using Novel Majority Voting Feature Selection

M. Dhilsath Fathima[1]($\boxtimes$) (iD), Prashant Kumar Singh[1] (iD),
M. Seeni Syed Raviyathu Ammal[2] (iD), and R. Hariharan[1] (iD)

[1] Department of Information Technology, Vel Tech Rangarajan Dr.Sagunthala R&D Institute of Science and Technology, Chennai, India
dhilsathfathima@veltech.edu.in
[2] Department of Information Technology, Mohamed Sathak Engineering College, Kilakarai, , Chennai, TamilNadu, India

Abstract. In humans, Lifestyle Disease (LSD) is caused by an improper way of life such as less physical activity, sleeplessness, unhealthy eating habits, liquor drinking, and smoking. LSD leads to gastric problems, indigestion of food, and prognosis to heart problems, Type II diabetes, and lung diseases. LSD treatment and medication lead to high expenditure for patients and country through LSD management and policies. Patients who suffer from LSD need lifelong treatment. The solution to reducing mortality due to Lifestyle Diseases is early detection and effective treatment. LSDs are low progressive in nature and need an effective and accurate early prediction method for effective treatment. The most prevalent LSD, based on World Health Organization (WHO) statistics, are heart disease and diabetes problems. This proposed model identifies the influencing attributes for contributing disease risk such as diabetes and heart attack and their associations using novel feature selection techniques such as Novel Majority Voting Ensembled Feature Selection (NMVEFS) for heart disease (HD) and diabetes. The influencing attributes are used to build a Clinical Decision Support System (CDSS) for LSD using a deep neural network, which helps physicians in identifying heart disease and diabetes at an early stage with 97.5% prediction accuracy and decreases treatment cost.

Keywords: Lifestyle disease · Majority vote · Deep neural network · Heart disease · Diabetes

1 Introduction

Chronic diseases, which are strongly associated with way of life living, termed as Lifestyle Disease (LSD). Lack of physical exercise, improper eating habits, drinking alcohol, and smoking are the causes of LSD. LSDs have a significant percentage of health-care expenditures. Globally, LSDs kill over 40 million people every year, and responsible for 70% of deaths. Early identification of LSD and effective treatment are

I. Woungang et al. (Eds.): ANTIC 2022, CCIS 1798, pp. 351–364, 2023.
https://doi.org/10.1007/978-3-031-28183-9_25

primary methods for reduction of mortality rates. The slow progression nature of LSD is undiagnosed at an early stage [1]. LSD is caused by three types of risk factors: modifiable behavioural risk factors, non-modifiable risk factors, and metabolic risk factors. Modifiable behavioural risk factors, such as excessive alcohol consumption, unhealthy diets, smoking, being physically inactive, and disrupted human biological clocks, enhance the high probability of developing LSD. Risk factors that are never managed or changed through activity are non-modifiable risk factors such as Genetics, Gender, Race, and Age. Metabolic risk factors are caused due to modifications in the metabolic systems, such as blood pressure, overweight, high diabetes, and increases blood lipid levels, which develop LSD [2].

The most common types of LSD include diabetes, heart disease, cancer, and respiratory conditions. Two of the most prevalent causes of LSD are diabetes and heart disease. Heart Disease (HD) is the major reason of LSDs mortality, accounting for 17.9 million fatalities per year in the world, outnumbers both respiratory diseases and cancer. Heart disease and diabetes affects the majority of people in the world.

1.1 Biological Link Between Heart Disease and Diabetes

Diabetes Mellitus is the major lifestyle disease, which leads to chronic illnesses in humans. Diabetes and Cardiovascular Disease (CVD) cause death in people. Hypertension, obesity, and lipids are risk factors for diabetic individuals, which shows elevated risk for cardiac attack. Diabetic person is prone to high risk of CVD, and death rate from cardiovascular disease is more in number than non-diabetics. WHO database and statistics show high correlation between diabetes and cardiovascular disease. Diabetes patients with CVD mortality rates are high. High blood glucose due to diabetes damages heart arteries, resulting in heart disease. Diabetes patients develop heart disease at a younger age than non-diabetics.

HD affects the blood vessels in heart of the patient. Myocardial infarction, coronary artery disease, angina (chest pain), stroke, and block in heart are major types of cardiovascular disease. According to the WHO, 23 million will be affected by heart disease by 2030 in the whole world. Heart disease has risen as the top disease, which causes death in developing countries like India. In India, particularly in poor states and rural regions people are affected by diabetes and heart disease. In Western countries, 23% of CVD fatalities occur before the age of 70, whereas in India, the ratio is close to 52% [3]. Patients with uncontrolled diabetes are likely to suffer from heart disease. HD diagnosed at an early stage, reduces the risk of mortality, and treatment costs [4].

1.2 Limitations of Prior Work

CDSS uses patient data from clinical datasets for disease analysis and prediction, which improves decision-making in the treatment of LSD. The clinical dataset is large, and it contains a significant number of disease markers (input features). Many disease markers are irrelevant to the disease and may have a negative influence when used in the prediction of LSD. It is possible to eliminate irrelevant disease markers by selecting the influencing attributes of LSD. This elimination improves the efficacy of CDSS significantly by reducing the system learning time. Thus, the novel feature selection technique is required for selection of influencing attributes of heart disease and diabetes which enhances CDSS prediction accuracy.

1.3 Motivation of the Proposed Model

This proposed model aims to develop an enhanced CDSS for early diagnosis of heart disease and diabetes using a novel feature selection technique. Doctors often need to undertake blood test to diagnose heart disease and diabetes, which takes time, money, and effort. This automated CDSS accurately predict diabetes and heart disease and save time and effort by utilizing the Novel Majority Voting Ensembled Feature Selection (NMVEFS) technique with the Modified Deep Neural Network (MDNN). The NMVEFS technique outperforms the single feature selection process as it combines multiple feature selection methods.

1.4 Research Contributions

The research contribution of the proposed work:

(1) The Novel Majority Voting Ensembled Feature Selection (NMVEFS) is proposed for identifying the influencing attributes of LSD from HD and diabetes dataset.
(2) The majority voting process used in the NMVEFS to choose influencing attributes of LSD by combining the predictive capability of six feature selection methods.
(3) Developing a customized DNN for the LSD prediction.
(4) Implementing an efficient CDSS for Lifestyle diseases (LSD) primarily for HD and diabetes using NMVEFS and MDNN.
(5) Analyzation of complex medical data related to heart disease and diabetes in less time with highest prediction accuracy of 97.5%.

1.5 Organization of This Proposed Work

The following sections compose the remaining contents of the paper: Sect. 2 describes the state-of-the-art analysis to LSD prediction; Sect. 3 details the proposed NMVEFS - MDNN model; and Sect. 4 displays and evaluates the experimental results of the proposed model. Section 5 defines the conclusion of this proposed work.

2   State-of -Art Analysis of LSD Prediction

This section explains the Machine learning approaches used in CDSS for diabetes and heart disease prediction. Ali et al. [5] develops a two-stage HD diagnosis model and reduces over-fitting and improve generalization. It has two stages: statistical mutual information and the neural networks. The results shows that this prediction system improved generalization and minimized Mean Percent Error (MPE) to 8.8%, lower than prior research. VirenViraj Shankaret et al. [6] developed a HD prediction model with Convolutional Neural Network (CNN) [7] for training and modelling. Model works on real world clinical data gathered from the hospital for model training. CNN compared to the K-Nearest Neighbour classifier and Naive Bayes model [8, 9]. CNN has high prediction accuracy.

CDSS improve health care quality. However, unified clinical approach and inadequate clinical resource management, and erroneous preventive medicine are the problems in CDSS [10]. Frontoni et al. [11] developed an integrated solution based on building and sharing an Electronic Health Record (EHR) in Netmedica Italian cloud architecture. This system uses ML to analyze shared EHR, allowed to deal with EHR variability. The CDSS measured chronic care performance efficiently over time and increased diabetic patient's quality of life by up to 12%. Diabetes is caused by the malfunctioning of insulin release. The diagnosis and comprehensive study of this fatal condition need the use of ML algorithms with low rates of error in order to be successful diabetes prediction model [12]. Aftab et al. [13] suggested a cloud-based ML fusion method that combines machine algorithms with fuzzy systems to provide highly accurate result on the early diagnosis of diabetes.

Recent research in ML techniques detect and diagnose heart disease and diabetes. However, lack of a smart framework is required for heart disease prediction. These systems are not able to deal large-scale, high-dimensional data effectively. Farman et al. [14] developed feature fusion method with Ensemble Deep Learning (DL) for heart disease classification to provide healthcare services to the general public. This feature fusion integrates features of electronic medical data and sensor, generates significant healthcare data and used to improve patient care. Conditional probability technique calculates feature weight of class and improves performance of system. Finally, Ensemble DL model predict the heart disease and the accuracy is about 98.5 percent, greater than the accuracy of existing systems. This section describes how researchers developed an automated LSD diagnosis model using machine classifiers. The goal of this proposed model is to identifying the influencing attributes of the LSD and increase the accuracy of the LSD prediction model using NMVEFS and MDNN classifier.

3 Proposed Methodology

The proposed model predicts LSD such as HD and diabetes. This model uses NMVEFS - MDNN for LSD prediction. This model utilizes NMVEFS to select influencing attributes of HD and diabetes, and MDNN classifier is used for predicting HD and diabetes in people.

3.1 Novel Majority Voting Ensemble Feature Selection (NMVEFS)

Deep Neural Network (DNN), includes all attributes of input dataset, which is unnecessary, leads to overfitting. Unnecessary features are removed to improve DNN performance. Three types of feature selection methods are used: filter-based method, which use a criterion such as correlation, information value and determine the significance of a feature, Wrapper-based method identifies the significant features by using greedy search methods such as stepwise selection, recursive feature elimination, and backward elimination, and Embedded approaches use classification models such as random forest (RF), lasso regression, & extra tree classifiers to evaluate features. NMVEFS combines filter, wrapper, and embedded methods for finding the influencing attributes of LSD.

NMVEFS uses six feature selection (FS) techniques, such as Information Value (IV), RF, Lasso Regression (LAR), Recursive Feature Elimination (RFE), Extra Tree Classifier (ETC), and chi-square (χ^2) and handle with local optima and individual biases of single feature selection method. When multiple FS techniques are combined, the ensemble feature selection process outperforms single FS model. NMVEFS use a majority vote and combines outcome of the various feature selection & identify the top 'N' ranked attributes (features). Figure 1 shows the proposed NMVEFS approach.

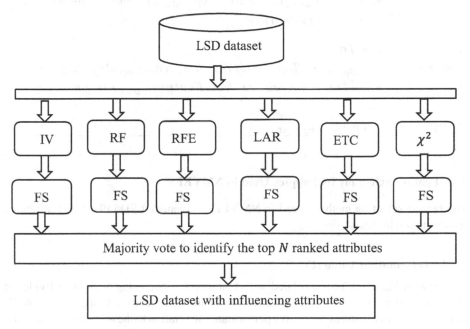

Fig. 1. Novel majority voting ensemble feature selection (NMVEFS)

The working procedure of the NMVEFS is shown in Algorithm 1.

Algorithm 1: Novel majority voting ensemble feature selection (NMVEFS)

Input	:	D_s: Input dataset of N training samples
		$FS \rightarrow \{IV, RF, RFE, LAR, ETC, \chi^2\}$; #Set of feature selection
Output	:	$D1_{relevant} \rightarrow p_1, p_2, ..., p_N$; # Top N ranked features

Step 1	:	Initialize an empty set: $Feature_{subset} = \emptyset$; best =0
Step 2	:	**for** t in FS do
		1. Apply FS techniques to D_s and rank the features;
		2. Sort the ranked features in descending order;
		3. Select the $Top_{feature}$; # Top N features;
		4. $Feature_{subset}$. INSERT $(Top_{feature})$; #insert the Top N features to $Feature_{best}$
		end **for**
Step 3	:	$D1_{relevant} \leftarrow$ Top N features $(Feature_{subset}, Majority\ vote)$; # Find the top N features from $Feature_{subset}$ using majority vote
Step 4	:	Return $D1_{relevant}$

3.2 Feature Selection Techniques Used in NMVEFS

The feature selection methods used in NMVEFS to identify LSD influencing attributes are discussed in this section.

3.2.1 Information Value (IV)

Information Value (IV) is calculated with feature relevance using Weight of Evidence (WOE) to identify the significant attributes of the HD dataset. Using Eq. 1, WOE evaluates an input features predictive performance in relation to the output class variable.

$$IV = \sum_{j=1}^{n} \left(WOE_j * (\% \text{ of positive event} - \% \text{ of negative event}) \right) \qquad (1)$$

Awhere n represent output class label, and WOE_j represent weight of evidence determined by Eq. 2.

$$WOE_j = ln\left(\frac{percentage\ of\ positive\ event}{percentage\ of\ negative\ event} \right) \qquad (2)$$

3.2.2   Random Forest (RF)

The RF-based FS technique ranks relevant attributes (features) based on their node impurity. The Gini Impurity (GI) calculates the probability value of each input feature. The feature with the lowest GI is chosen relevant, whereas those with a high Gini index are removed. Equation 3 shows the mathematical derivation of the GI of the input feature P.

$$GI(p) = Gini(D) - Gini_p(D) \qquad (3)$$

Awhere $GI(p)$ represent total GI, $Gini(D)$ represents is the GI of dataset D through Eq. 4, and $Gini_p(D)$ represents GI of input feature p.

$$Gini(D) = 1 - \sum_{j=1}^{n} prob_j^{2} \qquad (4)$$

Awhere $prob_j$ represents probability of class label n in p is calculated as $p_n = \frac{|c_n, N|}{|N|}$ where $|N|$ is a sample of a feature p and $|c_n, N|$ is a class label. If n is divided into 2 sets like n_1 and n_2, $Gini_p(D)$ is specified in Eq. 5.

$$Gini_p(D) = \frac{|n_1|}{|n|} Gini(n_1) + \frac{|n_2|}{|n|} Gini(n_2) \qquad (5)$$

3.2.3   Recursive Feature Elimination (RFE)

RFE uses Logistic Regression (LR) and select relevant input features. LR used a logit function and determine the importance of the input feature (p_i), as shown in Eq. 6.

$$logit(p_i) = log\left(\frac{prob}{1 - prob}\right) = \beta_0 + \beta_i p_i \qquad (6)$$

where $prob$ is the probability of input feature, β_0 and β_i are the logistic regression parameters.

3.2.4   Lasso Regression

The cost function of Lasso regression selects the best features by minimizing the absolute value of weight coefficient, as in Equation 7. It chooses the optimal features by giving irrelevant features zero weight and relevant features a non-zero weight.

$$Costfunction(Lasso) = \sum_{i=0}^{N} (q_i - \sum_{j=0}^{M} p_{ij} w_j)^2 + \lambda \sum_{j=0}^{M} |W_j| \qquad (7)$$

where q_i is the class attribute, p_{ij} is the input feature, w_j represents weight coefficient, λ represents regularization term, and $|W_j|$ represents sum of absolute weight coefficients.

3.2.5 Extra Tree Classifier (ETC)

This technique builds a random number of tree models from the input dataset D and selects the most popular features to be relevant features. The extra tree classifier selects features based on information gain, with the best feature having the highest information gain.

3.2.6 Chi-Square (chi^2)

Chi-square score determines the relevant input feature by evaluating the association among each input feature & the output variables, as shown in Eq. 8. The attribute (feature) with the highest χ^2 depends on output variable, suitable for training the model.

$$\chi^2 = \sum_{i=1}^{n} \frac{(o_i - E_i)^2}{E_i} \tag{8}$$

where o_i represents observed sample, E_i represents expected sample.

3.3 Modified Deep Neural Network (MDNN)

The proposed LSD prediction model customizes the default Deep Neural Network (DNN) layers; hence it is called Modified DNN (MDNN). In MDNN, the DNN architecture [15] is modified with the dropout layer, batch normalization, and bootstrap aggregation. MDNN analyzes the training data pattern and build a hypothesis $hyp_z(D1)$ with a goal of minimizing total errors across all training samples, which improves prediction accuracy of LSD. The MDNN classifier is depicted diagrammatically in Fig. 2.

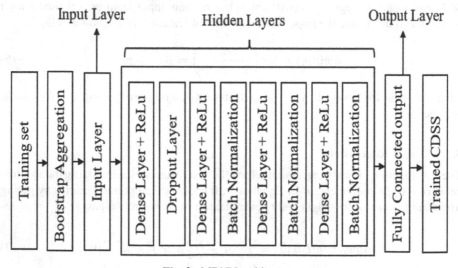

Fig. 2. MDNN architecture

Dropout is a regularization technique used in the proposed MDNN and prevent overfitting by random dropping off hidden layer neurons, reducing model complexity and the overfitting problem. Batch normalization speeds up model training by reducing epochs and training the MDNN model. The MDNN is batch normalized before using activation function. Batch normalized neuron is computed as in Eq. 9:

$$z1^{normalized} = \left(\frac{z1 - m_{z1}}{s_{z1}}\right) * \gamma + \beta \qquad (9)$$

where $z1^{normalized}$ is the batch normalization function, $z1$ is the input parameter, m_{z1} represents mean of the neuron output, s_{z1} represents standard deviation, and β and γ are batch normalization parameters. Bootstrap aggregation increases model stability and prediction with high accuracy of MDNN model. Bootstrap aggregation has resampling function which generate multiple training subsets by randomly sampling the training dataset with replacement.

4   Experimental Result of LSD Prediction Model

4.1   Dataset Description

The Cleveland HD dataset from the UCI repository [16] and the PIMA Indian diabetes dataset [17] are two open datasets which are utilized to evaluate the proposed LSD prediction model. Cleveland HD Dataset has 303 samples, and 13 heart disease-related variables. Table 1 displays the name (attribute code) and description of the HD dataset input attributes. Diabetes dataset has 768 samples and eight input attributes, which describe diabetes diagnoses factors with a class variable that specifies each individual parameter, such as diabetes presence or absence. Table 2 describes the input features of diabetes dataset.

Table 1. Input attributes of HD dataset

S. No	Attribute code	Feature description
1	AGE	Age
2	GENDER	Gender
3	CPT	Chest pain type
4	REBP	Resting blood pressure
5	SECHOL	Serum cholesterol
6	FABS	Fasting blood sugar
7	ECGREST	ECG at resting
8	MAXHRT	Maximum heart rate
9	EXIA	Exercise included angina
10	OLPK	Old Peak Value
11	PESTS	Peak exercise ST segment
12	NMV	Number of major vessels
13	THALAS	Thalassemia

Table 2. Input attributes of diabetes dataset

S. No	Attribute code	Feature description
1	PREGN	Pregnancy
2	GLUC	Glucose level
3	BLPR	Blood Pressure level
4	THSK	Thickness of skin fold
5	INSUL	Insulin
6	BDMSIN	Body mass Index
7	PDFN	Pedigree function
8	AGE	Age

4.2 Performance Metrics of the LSD Prediction Model

The performance of the proposed LSD prediction model is evaluated using classification performance measures which are depicted in Table 3.

Table 3. Performance metrics of the proposed LSD model

Performance metrics	Formula
Model Accuracy (*Model.Acc*)	$Model.Acc = \frac{No of samples predicted correctly}{No of training samples}$
Sensitivity (*Sen*)	$Sen = \frac{TruePositive}{TruePositive + FalseNegative}$
Specificity (*Spe*)	$Spe = \frac{TrueNegative}{TrueNegative + FalsePositive}$
Precision (*Pre*)	$Pre = \frac{TruePositive}{TruePositive + FalsePositive}$
Model Execution time (*ExeTime*)	$ExeTime = Model development time$

4.3 Experimental Results of NMVEFS – MDNN Classifier

NMVEFS selects influencing attributes from the HD and diabetes dataset for LSD prediction which is shown in Table 4.

MDNN model is executed for several epochs with these influencing attributes. The performance of the MDNN classifier is compared to the simple DNN classifier. Tables 5 and 6 show the DNN and MDNN classifier results, respectively.

Tables 5 shows that DNN achieves 75.3% accuracy on the LSD dataset. Table 6 illustrates, MDNN model is more efficient than the DNN model achieving 97.5 percent accuracy on the LSD dataset. The MDNN excellent performance shows that combining dropout regularization, batch normalization, and bootstrap aggregation improves LSD

Table 4. LSD Influencing Attributes

Influencing attributes of heart disease	Influencing attributes of diabetes
Gender	Pregnancy
Chest pain type	Glucose level
Maximum heart rate	Blood Pressure level
Exercise included angina	Body mass Index
Old Peak Value	Pedigree function
Number of major vessels	Age
Thalassemia	

Table 5. DNN performance without modifying the default layers

Classifier	Epochs	Exe Time (M: S)	Model Acc	Sen	Spe	Pre
DNN	50	0:27	69.4	46.2	82	58.1
	100	1:00	72.7	59.2	8	61.5
	300	3:30	75.3	64.8	81	64.8

Table 6. MDNN performance with LSD influencing attributes

Classifier	Epochs	Exe Time (M: S)	Model Acc	Sen	Spe	Pre
MDNN	50	0:14	87.6	83.3	9	81.8
	100	0:18	92.8	87.0	96	92.1
	300	0:36	97.5	98.1	97	94.6

model predictive performance. MDNN takes less time than DNN to develop an LSD prediction model.

As seen in Fig. 3, the MDNN generates the LSD prediction model faster than the DNN. The suggested model, MDNN, gives good accuracy at a lower execution time due to an ensemble of bootstrap aggregation, batch normalization, and dropout regularization. This proposed NMVEFS-MDNN model could be used in a CDSS to diagnose heart disease and diabetes at earlier stage.

4.4 Comparative Analysis of NMVEFS-MDNN Model

Table 7 compares the proposed NMVEFS-MDNN classifier to other recent HD and diabetes prediction models. This analysis evidenced that the NMVEFS-MDNN classifier is better for predicting lifestyle disease than the existing techniques.

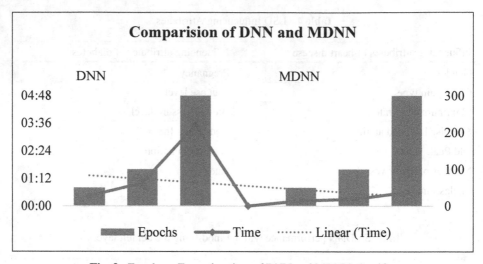

Fig. 3. Epoch vs. Execution time of DNN and MDNN classifier

Table 7. Performance comparison of NMVEFS-MDNN with LSD dataset

Dataset	Year of publication	Reference work	Classifier	Accuracy in (%)
HD dataset	2022	Al Bataineh et al. [18]	Multilayer perceptron & particle swarm optimization	84.61
	2020	Gazeloglu et al. [19]	Naive Bayes and Fuzzy RoughSet	84.81
	2022	Subahi et al. [20]	Modified Self - Adaptive Bayesian algorithm	90
	2022	Nagarajan et al. [21]	Crow search algorithm	94
	2022	Rajendran et al. [22]	Ensemble algorithm	92.7
Diabetes dataset	2022	Mohideen et al. [23]	Optimized Gaussian Naïve Bayes	81.85
	2022	Kumar et al. [24]	CatBoost algorithm	86
	2022	Mahesh et al. [25]	Blended ensemble algorithm	97.11

(continued)

Table 7. (*continued*)

Dataset	Year of publication	Reference work	Classifier	Accuracy in (%)
	2022	Azad et al. [26]	Decision tree and Genetic Algorithm	82.12
	2022	Gupta et al. [27]	Deep learning	95
HD and diabetes dataset	–	Proposed work	NMVEFS-MDNN	97.5

5 Conclusion

Diabetes person are twice as likely to get heart disease. Heart disease caused by lifestyle disorder, significant problem across the world, particularly in developing countries like India, Bangladesh, Sri Lanka. Diagnosing diseases earlier reduces risk of losing lives and treatment costs. This proposed NMVEFS-MDNN develops an LSD prediction model for heart disease and diabetes which is significantly precise than the existing LSD prediction models. LSD influencing attributes are identified such as Gender, old peak value, maximum heart rate, chest pain type, major vessels, exercise included angina, Thalassemia, blood pressure, old peak value, pregnancy, pedigree value, glucose, body mass index, and age. The primary objectives of this study are achieved by predicting LSD with high accuracy of 97.5%. The small input dataset (300 and 800 samples) limits the generalization performance of this proposed model. The model performs better as data amount and quality increase. Furthermore, the LSD prediction can be extended based on demography, occupation, and microclimate.

References

1. Barrett-Connor, E., Wingard, D., Wong, N., Goldberg, R.: Heart Disease and Diabetes (2021)
2. Şahin, B., İlgün, G.: Risk factors of deaths related to cardiovascular diseases in World Health Organization (WHO) member countries. Health Soc. Care Community **30**(1), 73–80 (2022)
3. Allarakha, S., Yadav, J., Yadav, A.K.: Financial Burden and financing strategies for treating the cardiovascular diseases in India. Social Sciences & Humanities Open **6**(1), 100275 (2022)
4. Nibali, L., Gkranias, N., Mainas, G., Di Pino, A.: Periodontitis and implant complications in diabetes. Periodontology 2000 **90**(1), 88–105 (2022)
5. Ali, L., Bukhari, S.A.C.: An approach based on mutually informed neural networks to optimize the generalization capabilities of decision support systems developed for heart failure prediction. Irbm **42**(5), 345–352 (2021)
6. Shankar, V., Kumar, V., Devagade, U., Karanth, V., Rohitaksha, K.: Heart disease prediction using CNN algorithm. SN Computer Science **1**, 1–8 (2020)
7. O'Shea, K., Nash, R.: An Introduction to Convolutional Neural Networks. arXiv preprint arXiv:1511. 08458 (2015)
8. Sharma, A., Mishra, P.K.: State-of-the-art in performance metrics and future directions for data science algorithms. Journal of Scientific Res. **64**(2), 221–238 (2020)
9. Sharma, A., Mishra, P.K.: Performance analysis of machine learning based optimized feature selection approaches for breast cancer diagnosis. Int. J. Inf. Technol. **14**(4), 19491960 (2022)

10. Sutton, R.T., Pincock, D., Baumgart, D.C., Sadowski, D.C., Fedorak, R.N., Kroeker, K.I.: An overview of clinical decision support systems: benefits, risks, and strategies for success. NPJ Digital Med. **3**(1), 1–10 (2020)

11. Frontoni, E., et al.: A Decision Support System for Diabetes Chronic Care Models Based on General Practitioner Engagement and EHR Data Sharing. IEEE J. Translational Eng. Health Med. **8**, 1–12 (2020)

12. Larabi-Marie-Sainte, S., Aburahmah, L., Almohaini, R., Saba, T.: Current techniques for diabetes prediction: review and case study. Appl. Sci. **9**(21), 4604 (2019)

13. Aftab, S., Alanazi, S., Ahmad, M., Khan, M.A., Fatima, A., Elmitwally, N.S.: Cloud-Based Diabetes Decision Support System Using Machine Learning Fusion (2021)

14. Ali, F., et al.: A smart healthcare monitoring system for heart disease prediction based on ensemble deep learning and feature fusion. Information Fusion **63**, 208–222 (2020)

15. Papernot, N., McDaniel, P., Goodfellow, I., Jha, S., Celik, Z.B., Swami, A.: Practical black-box attacks against machine learning. In: Proceedings of the 2017 ACM on Asia Conference on Computer and Communications Security, pp. 506–519 (2017)

16. UCI Machine Learning: Pima Indians Diabetes Database [Internet] - [Accessed on 23 Sep 2022]. https://www.kaggle.com/uciml/pima-indians-diabetes-database

17. Janosi, A., Steinbrunn, W., Pfisterer, M., Detrano, R.: Heart Disease Data Set. https://archive.ics.uci.edu/ml/datasets/Heart+Disease. Accessed 23 Sep 2022

18. Al Bataineh, A., Manacek, S.: MLP-PSO hybrid algorithm for heart disease prediction. Journal of Personalized Med. **12**(8), 1208 (2022)

19. Gazeloglu, C.: Prediction of heart disease by classifying with feature selection and machine learning methods. Prog. Nutr. **22**(2), 660–670 (2020)

20. Subahi, A.F., Khalaf, O.I., Alotaibi, Y., Natarajan, R., Mahadev, N., Ramesh, T.: Modified Self-Adaptive Bayesian Algorithm for Smart Heart Disease Prediction in IoT System. Sustainability **14**(21), 14208 (2022)

21. Nagarajan, S.M., Muthukumaran, V., Murugesan, R., Joseph, R.B., Meram, M., Prathik, A.: Innovative feature selection and classification model for heart disease prediction. J. Reliable Intelligent Environments **8**(4), 333–343 (2022)

22. Rajendran, R., Karthi, A.: Heart disease prediction using entropy based feature engineering and ensembling of machine learning classifiers. Expert Syst. Appl. **207**, 117882 (2022)

23. Mohideen, D.F.M., Raj, J.S.S., Raj, R.S.P.: Regression imputation and optimized Gaussian Naïve Bayes algorithm for an enhanced diabetes mellitus prediction model. Brazilian Archives of Biology and Technol. **64** (2022)

24. Kumar, M., et al.: Machine learning–derived prenatal predictive risk model to guide intervention and prevent the progression of gestational diabetes mellitus to type 2 diabetes: prediction model development study. JMIR Diabetes **7**(3), e32366 (2022)

25. Mahesh, T.R., et al.: Blended ensemble learning prediction model for strengthening diagnosis and treatment of chronic diabetes disease. Computational Intelligence and Neuroscience 2022 (2022)

26. Azad, C., Bhushan, B., Sharma, R., Shankar, A., Singh, K.K., Khamparia, A.: Prediction model using SMOTE, genetic algorithm and decision tree (PMSGD) for classification of diabetes mellitus. Multimedia Syst. **28**(4), 12891307 (2022)

27. Gupta, H., Varshney, H., Sharma, T.K., Pachauri, N., Verma, O.P.: Comparative performance analysis of quantum machine learning with deep learning for diabetes prediction. Complex Intelligent Syst. **8**(4), 30733087 (2022)

Sample Size Estimation for Effective Modelling of Classification Problems in Machine Learning

Neha Vinayak$^{(\boxtimes)}$ (iD) and Shandar Ahmad (iD)

Jawaharlal Nehru University, New Delhi, India
nehavinayak25@gmail.com, shandar@jnu.ac.in

Abstract. High quality and sufficiently numerous data are fundamental to developing any machine learning model. In the absence of a prior estimate on the optimal amount of data needed for modeling a specific system, data collection ends up either producing too little for effective training or too much of it causing waste of critical resources. Here we examine the issue on some publicly available low-dimensional data sets by developing models with progressively larger data subsets and monitoring their predictive performances, employing random forest as the classification model in each case. We try to provide an initial guess for optimum data size requirement for a considered feature set size using Random Forest Classifier. This sample size is also suggested for other machine learning (ML) models, subject to their trainability on the dataset. We also investigate how the data quality impacts its size requirement by introducing incremental noise to original class labels. We observe that optimal data size remained robust for up to 2% class label errors, suggesting that ML models are capable of picking up the most informative data instances as long as there are sufficient number of objects to learn.

Keywords: Sample size estimation · Training data size · Machine learning models · Learning curve · Random forest · Noisy data

1 Introduction

Having large and diverse volumes of data are the basic driving force behind effective machine learning models. However, collecting large amounts of data is expensive in terms of time and cost. The need for having sufficient training data at a minimal cost is therefore a critical question for developing an end-to-end ML-based modeling strategy. Researchers have tried to estimate a good sample size in individual systems such as autism [10,26], ADHD [21], medical imaging [3], eye-tracking [24], examples of the systems where compiling large data sets is difficult. Intuitively the data size requirements depend on the diversity of data objects. In another example, pixel-wise description of images in medical diagnosis and single nucleotide level variations in genomics data are high dimensional problems where correspondingly large volumes of samples are impossible to acquire. Based on these observations, having a prior estimate of data size needed to develop a suitable machine learning model with high generalization is critical in

© The Author(s), under exclusive license to Springer Nature Switzerland AG 2023
I. Woungang et al. (Eds.): ANTIC 2022, CCIS 1798, pp. 365–378, 2023.
https://doi.org/10.1007/978-3-031-28183-9_26

data-driven knowledge generation. In recent work [6], we have explored this question for MRI images by having a data pool and developing ML methods from a sample drawn randomly from this dataset. By varying the size of this randomly drawn sample, insights on real data size requirements may be developed.

Literature review shows that there is no general guideline for how much sample size is sufficient to get a generalized model with good results, irrespective of the model or type of data involved. Only model-specific and data-specific studies and reviews have been conducted to answer this question in individual focused contexts. Among the studies available on this issue are the works of Indranil Balki et. al. [3], who conducted a review of the Sample Size Determination Methods (SSDMs) in medical imaging research and classified the SSDMs as pre-Hoc (model based) or post-Hoc (curve-fitting) approaches. A study conducted by [11] on model-based approaches proposed by [4,13] suggested upper bounds on the training set size as 1580 and 240 using LDA and Classification tree models respectively, for classification error less than $\frac{1}{8}$ and a neural network with 12 units and 30 hidden nodes. Curve fitting approaches evaluated the model performance at available sample sizes and extrapolated the performance based on learning-curve or linear-curve fitting approaches, at larger sample sizes. The learning-curve based studies suggested a need of 10,000 images per class to attain a classification accuracy of 82% [18] and 4092 images per class for achieving accuracy of 99.5% in a separate study [7]. The authors in [3] have attributed this difference to the selected models and hyperparameters used in the studies.They also pointed out that there are no international standards on sample size considerations for machine learning studies. Rosa L Figueroa et al. [9] used the learning-curve fitting approach on annotated medical data and found that 80 to 560 samples were required to achieve an average root mean square error less than 0.01 and Claudia Beleites et al. [5] reported that in annotated biospectroscopy data, 5 to 25 samples per class were sufficient to achieve acceptable model performance but 75 to 100 test samples were needed to validate a good, but not perfect classifier. In a biomarker study [19], the authors noted that sample size depends on the type of study being conducted. Studies involving biomarker analysis for psychiatric disorders showed heterogenous patient data when the sample size was large. Smaller sample size of 100 subjects resulted in accuracy of 90% or higher, which dropped to less than 70% for the number of subjects more than 300. They concluded from the study that models with smaller sample size had less generalizing capability over other samples but gave higher accuracy within the sample.

The above studies have been performed on specific problems using a single model. Moghaddam et al. in [14] studied the effect of sample size on the accuracy in mapping of ground-water potential on multiple models like Random Forest and Decision Tree among a few others. They found that Random Forests were least sensitive to change in sample size and gave the best performance in terms of area under the ROC curve (AUC). Noi et al. [22] analyzed the effect of sample size on land cover classification using sentinel-2 image data. Among the classifiers Support Vector Machine (SVM), Random Forest (RF) and k-Nearest Neighbors (k-NN), all three resulted in high accuracy scores ranging from 90% to 95% and

SVM was found to be least sensitive to training sample size, followed by RF and k-NN.

As per our knowledge, the above sample size estimation works do not take into account the effect of noise in the data collected for a study. Presence of noise in the datasets is known to impact the performance of ML models and affect their trainability. For example, Zhou et al. [28] studied the impact of noisy data on achieving the local and global optimum and have numerically proved that noise helps the models to overcome local optima problems. Guozhong [1] studied the effect of noise in the backpropagation algorithm and concluded that for classification problems, noisy inputs and weights increased the generalization of the model, whereas other forms of noise had no effect on model generalization. Studies in [12,15,23,25] have successfully trained models in the presence of noisy data and [2,27] suggest that noisy data leads to decreased performance of their models in addition to overfitting on the noisy labels. Owing to the importance of noise in the data, we have taken into account the effect of noisy labels while estimating the data size. Finally, the existing studies on sample size estimation are problem specific and do not remark on the general sample size requirement. We have tried to estimate the sample size requirement on the basis of multiple datasets from an open repository, which have similar characteristics in terms of the data and feature size while being from diverse backgrounds.

In summary, this work attempts to determine sample size requirements, in general and in the pretense of various proportions of noisy labels and through a variety of data sets, thereby integrating currently three independently studied issues of data science. The objectives of the study are:

1. To establish a benchmark regarding how many samples are sufficient to conduct a supervised classification study in a selected number of dataset.
2. To investigate the effect of bias due to the data and study the effect of noise the sample size requirements reported above.

2 Methodology

2.1 Bird-eye View of the Process

Fig. 1 shows the overall flow diagram of the study. Data is collected from OpenML repository (Sect. 2.2) and sanity checks are performed on different sample sizes to evaluate whether the models (Sect. 2.3) are able to train or not. We see that few models are able to perform at lower sample sizes while others are not. Test AUC score has been used as the performance metric. Other experimental details are described in Sect. 2.4.

2.2 Datasets

All the experiments in this paper are performed using datasets from OpenML [17], an open repository of datasets. It contains around 4000 data sets for supervised learning problems (as on the date this research was started). For conducting

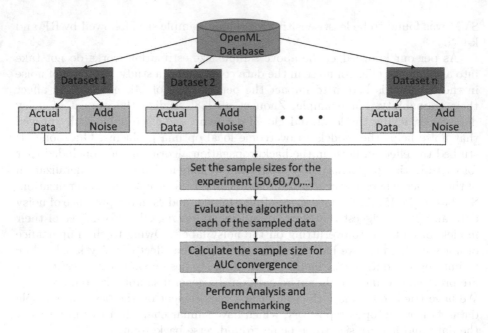

Fig. 1. Overall flow of the study

this experiment, datasets with the following properties have been selected from the OpenML repository:

1. Number of features ranging from 15 to 30
2. Number of instances ranging from 5000 to 50000. Large datasets have been chosen for the study to calculate the performance metrics at a varied range of sample sizes.
3. No missing values
4. Binary Classification problems

Twelve datasets meet the above criteria, which include both balanced and imbalance datasets. The attributes of the selected datasets are described in Table 1.

2.3   Machine Learning Algorithms

Based on the reviews by [16,20], supervised machine learning algorithms for binary classification problems can be broadly grouped into following categories:

1. **Logically learning algorithms**: This class of algorithms deal with solving the problem in a step by step manner, where each step forward is taken based on the evaluation of a logical condition. **Decision Tree** is a classical example of this class of algorithms and **Random Forest** uses an ensemble of decision trees on different samples and takes majority voting to come to a decision.

Table 1. Details of the 12 datasets selected for the study.

ID	Dataset name	Description	Features	Majority class	Minority class
761	Cpu_act	Computer activity data	22	5715	2477
821	House_16H	US census house details data	17	16040	6744
846	Elevators	Details of controlling an F16 aircraft	19	11469	5130
847	Wind	Daily wind speeds in Republic of Ireland	15	3501	3073
976	JapaneseVowels	Discrete time series of uttering Japanese vowels	15	8347	1614
1019	Pendigits	Handwritten digits collected from many writers	17	9848	1144
1471	Eeg-eye-state	EEG measurements from the head	15	8257	6723
1496	Ringnorm	Data with different mean and covariance	21	3736	3664
1507	Twonorm	Data with different means and unit variance	21	3703	3697
40701	Churn	Telephone account features and usage details	21	4293	707
41146	Sylvine	Dataset from the Automated ML challenge	21	2562	2562
42477	Default-of-credit-card-clients	Defaults of credit card clients in Taiwan	24	23364	6636

2. **Support Vector Machines**: This is an advanced supervised classification technique which maps n features from a data set into an n-dimensional hyper space and segregates the points in classes by a decision boundary.

3. **Statistics based algorithms**: These algorithms use statistics based distribution functions to predict the output labels for the task. **Gaussian Naive Bayes** classifier assumes all features to be continuous and following a gaussian distribution. It calculates the probability for each case and the outcome with maximum probability is labeled as the output. **Logistic Regression** is another statistics based algorithm which predicts the probability of occurrence of each class at the output layer and assigns the output labels based on the sigmoid function.

4. **Lazy Learning algorithms**: This type of algorithm uses distance based computations for labelling the outputs. It is called lazy because it does not proactively perform the classification task. Only when a new instance has to be labelled, it computes the distance from the existing points and assigns the maximum likelihood label to the instance. **k Nearest Neighbor** belongs to this class.

5. **Multi Layer Perceptron (MLP)**: MLPs are simple models capable of modeling complex relationships between data and predicting the outcomes of new instances. They are represented by layers through which the features flow and the training takes place. The input layer represents the input data and the output layer represents the final class labels assigned to them. In between there can be multiple hidden layers with any number of nodes.

Earlier studies regarding sample size estimation show that the non-parametric machine learning algorithms Random Forest (RF), Support Vector Machine (SVM) and k-Nearest Neighbors (kNN) perform well on the datasets. In addition to these, three parametric algorithms have been also included in our experiments based on the above classification: Gaussian Naive Bayes (GNB), Multi Layer Perceptron (MLP) and Logistic Regression (LR). The trainability of each model on the datasets and the sample size required for training these models will help to determine whether the sample size is independent of the chosen model or model specific. In case, the sample size is model dependent, the best performing model is chosen for determining the sample size requirements. For this study, we have used multiple models from these groups at the outset and then proceeded the detailed benchmarking with the model that performed best across data sets. This model was found to be Random Forest, as discussed in the Results section.

2.4   Experimental Setup

Training and Test Data: The data samples have been created using the Nx Repeated Cross Validation [3] technique. The dataset is shuffled and randomly sampled into training and test sets. The selected samples compose the training set and remaining samples form the test set. The sample sizes used for this study are: 50 to 200 with an interval of 10 samples; 200 to 1000 with an interval of 100 samples and 1000 to 4000 with an interval of 500 samples. So the studied sample sizes are [50, 60, ... 190, 200, 300, ... 900, 1000, 1500 ... 3500, 4000]. The model is trained using 10-fold cross-validation.

Evaluating Performance Scores: Learning curves show the performance of a model with increasing sample sizes. They can help us to estimate the required sample size to achieve a desired performance. In this study, the performance scores for each given sample size for the models are calculated using the learning_curve method of scikit learn library. For each algorithm in the study, the scikit learn implementation has been used as input to the learning_curve function. *It should be noted that the learning curve in the study is used to calculate the performance metrics at different sample sizes for the analysis and no curve fitting is being performed.*

Once the data is partitioned into training and test sets, the model is trained on the training set and its performance is evaluated over the remaining test data [8] using a 10-fold cross validation technique. This forms one experiment. Each such experiment is performed five times and average scores are calculated. Based on these scores of the learning curve, the sample size requirement is analyzed.

Instead of training the model till an absolute AUC is reached, we look for model convergence. The test AUC score is noted for the previous sample sizes or last 10 consequent sample sizes, whichever is less. These consequent scores tell us whether the model is still learning or has converged. The difference in score from the previous sample is noted and convergence is checked by calculating the average difference in the scores achieved in the converging samples. If this average is less than the error threshold, we conclude that the model has converged. Experiments have been conducted for error thresholds ranging from 0.001 to 0.01 and most datasets converge at the selected threshold of 0.01. So, 0.01 has been selected as the error threshold to report results.

Models which do not achieve convergence till the last sample size in the study (4000) are treated as not converged. Models which converge at a score < 0.6 are also treated as not successfully trained. All models do not perform well on all datasets, so the best performing model in each case is chosen to analyze the sample size requirement.

Rank-based Evaluation of the Best Model: Choice of the best performing model is done on the basis of a ranking system. The best model is the one with highest test AUC score after attaining convergence. So, once we have determined that convergence for the model has been achieved, we note this score as the model score. Some models are seen to achieve high test AUC scores but convergence is not detected. Ranks are assigned to each model for each dataset and the best performing model is selected.

Introduction of Synthetic Noise: It is possible that the convergence achieved in the above experiments is due to clean datasets of OpenML. The effect of input noise has been explored in their study by different authors as discussed in Sect. 1. There are reports of successful training of models in the presence of input noise [12,15,23,25] as well as degraded performance [2,27]. This input noise may be in the form of noise in the input data features or input data labels.

We have conducted further experiments to see the generalization of the results in case of noise in the data. The noise has been manually and incrementally introduced in randomly selected class labels of the training data (only), in the proportions of 1%, 2%, 3%, 4%, 5%, 10%, 20% and its effect on the sample size requirements has been analyzed.

3   Results

Random Forest algorithm reported the best performance for 7 out of 12 models, other well performing algorithms being MLP, Gaussian Naive Bayes and k-Nearest Neighbor.

To evaluate the overall performance, rank of each algorithm has been evaluated in Table 2, for every dataset and it is noticed that the Random Forest algorithm is the best performer.

Table 2. Rank of each algorithm for all datasets based on their test AUC performance scores.

Algorithm	Average rank
RandomForest	**1.83**
MLP	3.33
GaussianNB	3.58
LogisticRegr	3.67
SVC	3.67
K-Neighbors	4.92

As shown in Fig. 2, on comparing the test AUC of Random Forest with the best performing model for each dataset, the difference is in the range 0.0 to 0.01 with a mean of 0.0018. Based on this, Random Forest has been used to analyze the sample size requirement.

The convergence of the OpenML datasets in their original form, without introduction of noise, has been computed at an average test AUC error threshold of 0.01. Then the sample size at which the model converges is noted. It is seen that most datasets converge at sample sizes < 200 and very few at larger sample sizes. For better visualization, the latter are grouped and cumulative distribution plot of fraction of datasets converging at each sample size is shown in Fig. 3.

In cases where convergence is achieved in the original data, it may be possible that they converge at small sample sizes due to good and clean data of OpenML. To check the robustness and generalization capability of the models, noise has been introduced in the data by randomly selecting 1%, 2%, 3%, 4%, 5%, 10% and 20% of the training data and swapping their output labels.

Similar analysis is again performed for all the cases of noise in the data. Figure 4 shows the effect of noise on the fractions of datasets converging in case of Random Forest algorithm. It is noticed that the number of datasets which converge at noise levels 1% and 2% are the same as the original data. So, noise introduction upto 2% does not affect the prediction of the models. On increasing the noise from 3% to 5%, the fraction of datasets converging at lower sample sizes is seen to increase. On increasing the noise further to 10% the fraction of converging datasets increases marginally as compared to the original data, while at 20% noise, the fraction of converging datasets decreases drastically. Figure 5 shows the sample sizes for which 85% of the datasets are seen to converge.

4   Discussion

For studies where collection of data is expensive or difficult, it will be beneficial to have a guideline on the minimum number of data to be collected for conducting the experiments. Table 3 shows the sample size guidelines provided by the existing studies in this area along with our proposal.

The study to gauge this requirement has been conducted with the help of selected datasets from OpenML and popular machine learning algorithms. All the algorithms in the study do not perform well for all datasets. Random Forest algorithm is found to be the best performing model across all datasets with an average rank of 1.83. For datasets where it is not the best performer, it is close behind the best one. The model which performed worst in terms of test AUC score of test data is k-Nearest Neighbors with an average rank of 4.92.

For the Random Forest algorithm, more than 60% of datasets converge at sample size 60, while the other datasets converge at higher sample sizes 180–200. One dataset - 40701: churn, converges at a larger sample size (3500) whereas one dataset - 1471: EEG eye state dataset, does not converge at all. Further investigation shows that the EEG eye state dataset does not converge for any of the datasets in the study. Overall, it can be said a sample size of 200 is good

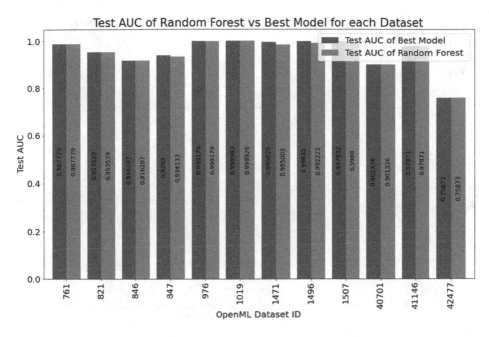

Fig. 2. Comparison of test AUC scores of random forest with that of the best scoring model for each dataset.

Table 3. Sample size guidelines by existing studies and proposed model.

Paper	Sample size	Dataset	Model details
Beleites, Claudia, et al. (2013)	5–25 per class	Raman spectra of single cells	Linear Discrimant Analysis (LDA) & Partial-least sq LDA
Schnack, Hugo G. et al. (2016)	100	Neuroimages of Schizophrenia	Machine Learning on images
Figueroa, Rosa L., et al. (2012)	80–560	Clinical text (smokers) and waveform-5000	Weighted learning curve fitting
Proposed Model	**200**	Multiple binary classification datasets	Random Forest Classifier
Hitzl et al. (2003)	240	Glaucoma	Classification Tree
Hitzl et al. (2003)	1580	Glaucoma	Linear Discrimant Analysis
Rokem et al. (2017)	4092 per class	Healthy vs AMD retina images	Learning curve fitting on CNN
Hitzl et al. (2003)	10000 per class	Glaucoma	Learning curve fitting on Neural Network

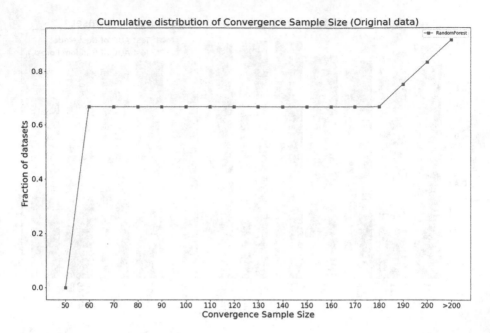

Fig. 3. Cumulative distribution of datasets converging at different sample sizes for Random Forest algorithm. X-axis: Sample sizes in the study; Y-axis: Fraction of datasets that converge. Observation: One dataset (ID: 1471) is not able to converge. More than 60% datasets converge at sample size 60 while most of the other datasets converge at higher sample sizes 180–200. One dataset converges at very high sample size of 3500. All the sample sizes more than 200 are clubbed into one label.

for any dataset to be modeled using Random Forest algorithm. Table 4 shows the training data sizes of various problems solved using RandomForestClassifier in the Kaggle data repository. It may be noted that in some cases data volume is very high, although less amount of data may also result in well generalized models.

Investigation of other models also led to a similar conclusion. All models converge at sample size ≤ 200 for most datasets, although convergence doesn't guarantee a well trained model in terms of performance.

When noise is introduced in the data, the number of datasets converging for upto 2% noise, follows the same pattern as the original data. So, it can be said that the sample size requirement is not dependent on the dataset and whether it is clean or noisy to some extent. Data with upto 2% noise also results in a well trained model. Adding further noise of 3–5%, reduces the sample size requirement to 100 data samples. This decreased sample size requirement on addition of further noise, needs to be investigated.

On adding further noise upto 10%, the sample size requirement increases marginally, whereas the model couldn't train well at 20% noise.

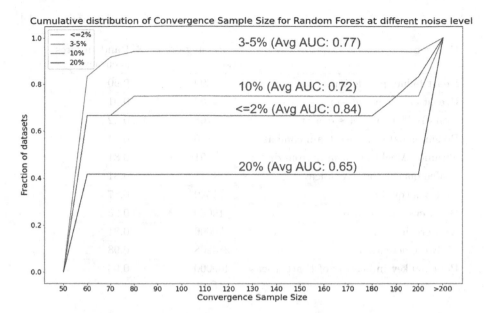

Fig. 4. Cumulative distribution of convergence sample sizes for Random forest algorithm for all 12 openML algorithms at noise levels <=2%, 3–5%, 10% and 20%

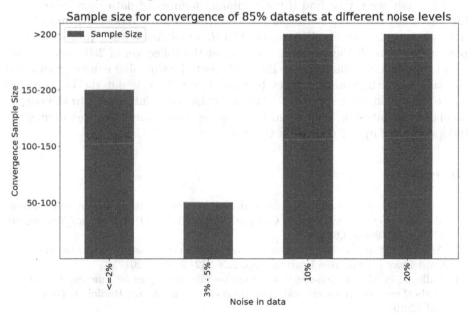

Fig. 5. Sample Size for convergence of 85% of the datasets at different noise levels introduced in the data labels (<=2%, 3–5%, 10%, 20%)

Table 4. Training data size and accuracy reported in kaggle for random forest model.

Dataset	Training data size	Random forest accuracy
Heart failure prediction	299	0.90
Breast cancer wisconsin	569	0.91
Pima Indians diabetes dtaset	768	0.92
Pokemon dataset with team combat	800	0.94
Titanic - Machine learning from disaster	891	0.81
Coffee quality data Arabica	1311	0.81
Red wine quality	1599	0.87
Bank customer churn	10000	0.86
UCI credir card	30000	0.81
Malware detection	284268	0.98
Personal key indicators of heart disease	400000	0.93

5 Conclusion

In this study we try to find if the minimum number of data samples required for any study can be generalized for a well performing model. All models are not able to train well on all datasets. The Random Forest algorithm is found to perform well on all the datasets. We suggest the collection of 200 data samples for any study using the Random Forest dataset. This number can be generalized to other algorithms also, subject to trainability. To rule out the bias created due to the clean datasets of OpenML, noise has been introduced in the output labels of the datasets. It is found that the reported sample size requirement is independent of upto 2% noise in the data.

References

1. An, G.: The effects of adding noise during backpropagation training on a generalization performance. Neural Comput. **8**(3), 643–674 (1996). https://doi.org/10.1162/neco.1996.8.3.643
2. Arpit, D., et al.: A closer look at memorization in deep networks. In: International Conference on Machine Learning, pp. 233–242. PMLR (2017)
3. Balki, I., et al.: Sample-size determination methodologies for machine learning in medical imaging research: a systematic review. Can. Assoc. Radiol. J. **70**(4), 344–353 (2019)
4. Baum, E., Haussler, D.: What size net gives valid generalization? In: Advances in Neural Information Processing Systems, vol. 1 (1988)
5. Beleites, C., Neugebauer, U., Bocklitz, T., Krafft, C., Popp, J.: Sample size planning for classification models. Anal. Chim. Acta **760**, 25–33 (2013)
6. Chauhan, S., et al.: A comparison of shallow and deep learning methods for predicting cognitive performance of stroke patients from MRI lesion images.

Front. Neuroinf. **13** (2019). https://doi.org/10.3389/fninf.2019.00053, https://www.frontiersin.org/articles/10.3389/fninf.2019.00053

7. Cho, J., Lee, K., Shin, E., Choy, G., Do, S.: How much data is needed to train a medical image deep learning system to achieve necessary high accuracy? arXiv preprint arXiv:1511.06348 (2015)

8. Dinga, R., Penninx, B.W., Veltman, D.J., Schmaal, L., Marquand, A.F.: Beyond accuracy: measures for assessing machine learning models, pitfalls and guidelines. BioRxiv p. 743138 (2019)

9. Figueroa, R.L., Zeng-Treitler, Q., Kandula, S., Ngo, L.H.: Predicting sample size required for classification performance. BMC Med. Inf. Decis. Making **12**(1), 1–10 (2012)

10. Gutiérrez, J., Che, Z., Zhai, G., Le Callet, P.: Saliency4asd: challenge, dataset and tools for visual attention modeling for autism spectrum disorder. Sig. Process. Image Commun. **92**, 116092 (2021)

11. Hitzl, W., Reitsamer, H., Hornykewycz, K., Mistlberger, A., Grabner, G.: Application of discriminant, classification tree and neural network analysis to differentiate between potential glaucoma suspects with and without visual field defects. J. Theor. Med. **5**(3–4), 161–170 (2003)

12. Huang, N., Chen, Q., Cai, G., Xu, D., Zhang, L., Zhao, W.: Fault diagnosis of bearing in wind turbine gearbox under actual operating conditions driven by limited data with noise labels. IEEE Trans. Instrument. Measur. **70**, 1–10 (2021). https://doi.org/10.1109/TIM.2020.3025396

13. Kubat, M.: Neural networks: a comprehensive foundation by Simon Haykin, Macmillan, 1994, isbn 0-02-352781-7. Knowl. Eng. Rev. **13**(4), 409-412 (1999)

14. Moghaddam, D.D., Rahmati, O., Panahi, M., Tiefenbacher, J., Darabi, H., Haghizadeh, A., Haghighi, A.T., Nalivan, O.A., Bui, D.T.: The effect of sample size on different machine learning models for groundwater potential mapping in mountain bedrock aquifers. Catena **187**, 104421 (2020)

15. Namysl, M., Behnke, S., Köhler, J.: Nat: Noise-aware training for robust neural sequence labeling (2020). https://doi.org/10.48550/ARXIV.2005.07162, https://arxiv.org/abs/2005.07162

16. Osisanwo, F., Akinsola, J., Awodele, O., Hinmikaiye, J., Olakanmi, O., Akinjobi, J.: Supervised machine learning algorithms: classification and comparison. Int. J. Comput. Trends Technol. (IJCTT) **48**(3), 128–138 (2017)

17. van Rijn, J.N., et al.: OpenML: a collaborative science platform. In: Blockeel, H., Kersting, K., Nijssen, S., Železný, F. (eds.) ECML PKDD 2013. LNCS (LNAI), vol. 8190, pp. 645–649. Springer, Heidelberg (2013). https://doi.org/10.1007/978-3-642-40994-3_46

18. Rokem, A., Wu, Y., Lee, A.: Assessment of the need for separate test set and number of medical images necessary for deep learning: a sub-sampling study. bioRxiv p. 196659 (2017)

19. Schnack, H.G., Kahn, R.S.: Detecting neuroimaging biomarkers for psychiatric disorders: sample size matters. Front. Psychiatry **7**, 50 (2016)

20. Sen, P.C., Hajra, M., Ghosh, M.: Supervised classification algorithms in machine learning: a survey and review. In: Mandal, J.K., Bhattacharya, D. (eds.) Emerging Technology in Modelling and Graphics. AISC, vol. 937, pp. 99–111. Springer, Singapore (2020). https://doi.org/10.1007/978-981-13-7403-6_11

21. Tenev, A., Markovska-Simoska, S., Kocarev, L., Pop-Jordanov, J., Müller, A., Candrian, G.: Machine learning approach for classification of ADHD adults. Int. J. Psychophysiol. **93**(1), 162–166 (2014)

22. Thanh Noi, P., Kappas, M.: Comparison of random forest, k-nearest neighbor, and support vector machine classifiers for land cover classification using sentinel-2 imagery. Sensors **18**(1), 18 (2017)

23. Vahdat, A.: Toward robustness against label noise in training deep discriminative neural networks. In: Guyon, I., et al. (eds.) Advances in Neural Information Processing Systems, vol. 30. Curran Associates, Inc. (2017). https://proceedings.neurips.cc/paper/2017/file/e6af401c28c1790eaef7d55c92ab6ab6-Paper.pdf

24. Vila, J., Gomez, Y.: Extracting business information from graphs: an eye tracking experiment. J. Bus. Res. **69**(5), 1741–1746 (2016)

25. Xu, Y., Du, J., Dai, L.R., Lee, C.H.: Dynamic noise aware training for speech enhancement based on deep neural networks. In: Fifteenth Annual Conference of the International Speech Communication Association (2014)

26. Yang, X., Schrader, P.T., Zhang, N.: A deep neural network study of the abide repository on autism spectrum classification. Int. J. Adv. Comput. Sci. Appl. **11**(4) (2020)

27. Zhang, C., Bengio, S., Hardt, M., Recht, B., Vinyals, O.: Understanding deep learning (still) requires rethinking generalization. Commun. ACM **64**(3), 107–115 (2021)

28. Zhou, M., Liu, T., Li, Y., Lin, D., Zhou, E., Zhao, T.: Toward understanding the importance of noise in training neural networks. In: Chaudhuri, K., Salakhutdinov, R. (eds.) Proceedings of the 36th International Conference on Machine Learning. Proceedings of Machine Learning Research, vol. 97, pp. 7594–7602. PMLR 09–15 June 2019. https://proceedings.mlr.press/v97/zhou19d.html

A Generative Model Based Chatbot Using Recurrent Neural Networks

Vinay Raj[1]($\boxtimes$)(iD) and M. S. B. Phridviraj[2](iD)

[1] Department of Computer Applications, National Institute of Technology
Tiruchirappalli, Tiruchirappalli, India
vinayraj@nitt.edu
[2] Department of Computer Science and Engineering, Kakatiya Institute
of Technology and Science, Warangal, India
msbp.cse@kitsw.ac.in

Abstract. Conversational modeling is an important task in natural language understanding and machine intelligence. It makes sense for natural language to become the primary way in which we interact with devices because that is how humans communicate with each other. Thus, the possibility of having conversations with machines would make our interaction much more smooth and human-like. The natural language techniques need to be evolved to match the level of power and sophistication that users expect from virtual assistants. Although previous approaches exist, they are often restricted to specific domains and require handcrafted rules. The obvious problem lies in their inability to answer questions for which the rules were not written. To overcome this problem, we build a generative model neural conversation system using a deep LSTM Sequence to Sequence model with an attention mechanism. Our main emphasis is to build a generative model chatbot in open domain which can have a meaningful conversation with humans. We consider Reddit conversation datasets to train the model and applied turing test on the proposed model. The proposed chatbot model is compared with Cleverbot and the results are presented.

Keywords: Chatbot · Recurrent Neural Networks · LSTM

1 Introduction

Advances in end-to-end neural network training have resulted in significant advances in a variety of fields, including speech recognition, computer vision, and language processing. Recent research implies that neural networks may be used to map intricate structures to other complicated structures, rather than merely categorization [18]. Because it necessitates mapping between inquiries and replies, conversational modelling may directly benefit from this approach. Conversational modelling had traditionally been developed to be highly confined in domain because to the intricacy of this mapping, with a substantial

I. Woungang et al. (Eds.): ANTIC 2022, CCIS 1798, pp. 379–392, 2023.
https://doi.org/10.1007/978-3-031-28183-9_27

endeavour on feature engineering [19]. In this paper, we use recurrent networks to experiment with the conversation modelling job by transforming it into a goal of predicting the future sequence given the prior sequence or sequences.

In recent years, chatbots, which are programmes that simulate human beings in discussions, have received a lot of attention in the tech industry. Researchers have attempted to construct and execute such systems since Michael Maudlin created the first Verbot, Julia, in 1994. Conventional dialogue systems, such as rule-based chatbots, continue to confront considerable hurdles in terms of robustness, scalability, and domain adaption [5], despite the rising relevance of conversational agents in promoting seamless interaction between humans and their electronic gadgets. As a result, researchers have begun to concentrate their efforts on creating data-driven conversational bots that largely rely on machine learning. Typically, there are three types of chatbots [6], (i). Rule based Chatbots. (ii). Retrieval based models. (iii). Generative models.

1. Rule-Based Chatbots: In this kind of approach, the conversational agent generates replies based on the rules written by programmers [10]. These rules can vary from being very simple to extremely complex. Though the implementation of chatbots following this approach is straightforward, they are very inefficient in answering questions which have a pattern different from the rules on which we train the bot. AIML, a language based on XML, is one such language which allows users to write rule based chatbots. Also, writing rules for all the infinite possibilities is impossible. The main advantage of these kinds of chatbots lies in their simplicity to implement and understand. Nevertheless, for developing complex chatbots they are not very useful.

2. Retrieval based models: In retrieval based models, the model is provided with a repository of questions and answers on which it is trained [11]. For each question asked, a set of responses are selected from the repository which are then scored by the model. The response with the highest score is then returned as the answer. The disadvantage of these kinds of models is similar to that of rule based models i.e., they cannot generate responses to completely new kind of questions. But, if the model is trained on a lot of data and if the data-set is pre processed smartly, it will be able to generate fairly good answers. The heuristic on which the responses are selected range from a simple rule-based expression match to complex machine learning classifiers. Also, there is no need to worry about the grammar of the answers generated as no new answers will be generated by the bot but the ones in the dataset are only used.

3. Generative models: Generative models differ from the previous two model in such a way that they can generate responses to completely new questions [12]. They don't need any rules or pre defined repository of responses. Machine translation techniques are typically used for training generative models. These advantages come an obvious disadvantage i.e. the replies generated by these models might not be grammatically or syntactically correct all the time. Also, they need lots of data to generate decent responses. These models have the capability to pass Turing Test. Hence most of the current research on conversational bots is focused on generative models. The main disadvantage with

generative models is they require huge amounts of data sets but can outperform every other model once trained. Hence, our emphasis in this project is to develop a generative model chatbot which must be able to give a near human responses. A generative model trained on open domain is Artificial General Intelligence (AGI) because of its ability to handle all possible scenarios. Even though we are far away from that, a lot of active research is being carried out to make it possible.

Motivation of the Work: For a company with a large consumer base, with lots of customer queries generating every second, answering all of them involves a large force of employees which is not always feasible. In most of the cases, these queries are quite trivial which might not require the intervention of humans. Development of conversational agents is a perfect solution to solve these problems. Also, with the advent of personal agents like Alexa, Google Now etc. machines which are able to converse with humans in an open domain are becoming increasingly prevalent. All these agents work on the basis of conversational models. Despite these uses, conversational agent development is still in its early phases and has a long way to go. Since a result, now is an excellent moment to begin building these models, as they may soon be integrated into many aspects of our lives.

Problem Statement: In this paper, we develop a neural network model called LSTM Encoder- Decoder that consists of two Long Short-Term Memory (LSTM) networks. The first LSTM network encodes a sequence of symbols into a fixed-length vector representation, while the second LSTM network decodes the representation into another sequence of symbols. The proposed model's encoder and decoder are both trained together to optimise the conditional probability of a target sequence given a source sequence. The primary aim is to develop a generative model chatbot in an open domain (not confined to a particular domain like sports, news etc.) which can have a meaningful conversation with humans thus by improving upon the existing metrics. The idea is to use Sequence to Sequence model which in turn uses LSTM layers. This provides the advantage of retaining useful information over long periods compared to Recurrent Neural Networks (RNN).

Structure of the Paper: The preliminaries about the different neural networks are discussed in Sect. 2. The related work of this paper is presented in Sect. 3 and Sect. 4 presents the proposed approach. The evaluation of the proposed approach is presented in Sect. 5 and Sect. 6 concludes the paper.

2 Preliminaries

2.1 Recurrent Neural Networks

Traditional neural networks (vanilla neural networks) does not have persistence [10]. That is, every output it generates is completely independent of the previous generated outputs. This might not appear to be a major issue but for solving some problems like predicting the next scene in a movie or the next word in a sentence, this lack of persistence seems to be a major shortcoming. Recurrent neural networks address this issue of neural networks. Recurrent networks are the networks with loops in them, allowing information to persist. These loops may appear daunting at first but with a moment of thought, it will be clear that recurrent neural networks can be thought of multiple copies of the same network, each passing the output as the input to its successor. Thus recurrent neural networks comes as a natural choice for solving sequence to sequence problems.

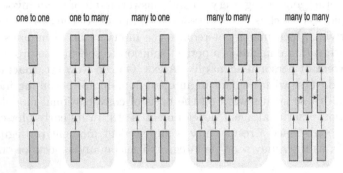

Fig. 1. Different types of RNNs

Different Types of Recurrent Neural Networks Architectures: There are different types of RNN architectures as shown in the Fig. 1. 1. One to One Recurrent Neural Networks 2. One to Many Recurrent Neural Networks 3. Many to Many Recurrent Neural Networks with same number of input and outputs. 4. Many to Many Recurrent Neural Networks with different number of input and output timesteps. The first type of RNN is the most trivial one. One to Many RNNs are used for sequence generation whereas many to one are used for different applications like sentiment classification etc. where a sequence of words is given as input and a single output is generated which describes the sentiment of the sentence. When it comes to many to many RNN architectures, there are two types of them, one where the input length and output length are identical and the other where the lengths of input and outputs differ. Since the length of the output generated is different from the input length, we will use many to many Recurrent Neural Network architecture with different input and output lengths.

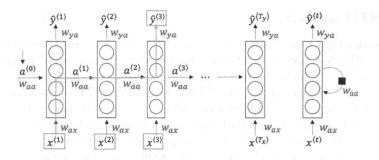

Fig. 2. Forward propagation in RNN

Forward Propagation in Recurrent Neural Networks: The forward propagation mechanism is presented in Fig. 2 and the activations and outputs at each time step are calculated as given in the equations below. Initial state is usually initialized to an all zero vector. At every time step, the previous activation and the current input are used to calculate the current activation which in turn is used to calculate the output of the current timestep. The new activation calculated in this time step is further propagated. This ensures that the outputs calculated at each time step are affected not only by their respective inputs but also by the previous inputs of the sequence as well. Also, another important feature of RNNs is that they use the same set of weights and biases and every time step.

$$a^{(t)} = \tanh(W_{ax}x^{(t)} + W_{aa}a^{(t-1)} + b_a)$$
$$\hat{y}^{(t)} = soft\max(W_{ya}a^{(t)} + b_y)$$

Backpropagation Through Time: In backpropagation through time, we will get error at each time step. The sum of errors at all the time steps gives us the total error. We are using weighted cross entropy loss in our model to calculate the loss. The error gets backpropagated, upon which gradients of all the parameters are calculated and their values are updated. The most significant recursive calculation occurs when the error is backpropagated through the activations from left to right. When the sequence is really large, multiplying with similar values over and over again might result in vanishing or exploding the gradient. This problem is called Vanishing/Exploding gradient problem. Exploding gradient problem is easy to identify as it will result in NaN(Not a number errors) and can be fixed using gradient clipping. But solving vanishing gradients problem is a little more tricky and the structure of Recurrent Neural Networks is to be modified to tackle that problem. Two of these structures are very popular are LSTM and Gated Recurrent Units(GRU) [7]. Since, LSTMs are observed to provide better results than GRUs, we used LSTMs for our model.

2.2 LSTM Networks

Long Short-term Memory are an extension of Recurrent Neural Networks. They are explicitly designed to overcome the long-dependency problem of RNNs. Essentially, both form a chain of repeating modules but the repeating module of RNN is a lot simpler than that of LSTM [8]. In RNN, the repeating module typically has a single layer whereas in LSTM there are four layers. LSTM has a candidate cell, a memory cell and three gates namely update gate, forget gate and output gate as shown in Fig. 3. These gates are used to update the values of different LSTM cells. Candidate cell captures the new information that needs to be included to the memory of LSTM. Memory cell depends both on the memory of the previous time step and the current candidate cell. Update and forget gate together with the memory of the previous time step and the current candidate cell calculates the memory value of the current timestep. Finally, output gate specifies what all parts of the memory cell needs to be included in the memory cell. It is able to capture the information over a long sequence much better than the Vanilla Recurrent Neural Networks because of these gates [20]. For example, setting update gate to 0 and forget gate to 1 retains the memory cell and this can be continued for as long as possible. Similarly to update the memory cell by completely discarding the previous memory value, update gate can be set while the forget gate can be reset to 0.

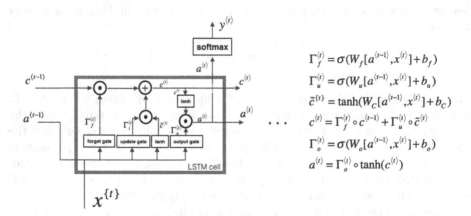

$$\Gamma_f^{\langle t\rangle} = \sigma(W_f[a^{\langle t-1\rangle}, x^{\langle t\rangle}] + b_f)$$

$$\Gamma_u^{\langle t\rangle} = \sigma(W_u[a^{\langle t-1\rangle}, x^{\langle t\rangle}] + b_u)$$

$$\tilde{c}^{\langle t\rangle} = \tanh(W_c[a^{\langle t-1\rangle}, x^{\langle t\rangle}] + b_c)$$

$$c^{\langle t\rangle} = \Gamma_f^{\langle t\rangle} \circ c^{\langle t-1\rangle} + \Gamma_u^{\langle t\rangle} \circ \tilde{c}^{\langle t\rangle}$$

$$\Gamma_o^{\langle t\rangle} = \sigma(W_o[a^{\langle t-1\rangle}, x^{\langle t\rangle}] + b_o)$$

$$a^{\langle t\rangle} = \Gamma_o^{\langle t\rangle} \circ \tanh(c^{\langle t\rangle})$$

Fig. 3. LSTM Network architecture

2.3 Sequence to Sequence Models

Since its debut in Learning Phrase Representations using RNN Encoder-Decoder for Statistical Machine Translation, the Sequence To Sequence paradigm has been the de facto standard for Dialogue Systems and Machine Translation [22]. It consists of two Recurrent Neural Networks (these can be Vanilla Recurrent Neural Networks, Long Short-term memory networks or Gated Recurrent Units). The first network is called an encoder and the second is called a decoder. Encoder takes a sequence of inputs, one at each time step and produces a final state vector called thought vector. The initial state of encoder network is randomly initialized or can be initialized to a zero vector. The decoder network then takes this thought vector as its initial state vector. It then uses this thought vector and its inputs(which are targets pushed forward by one time step and appended a 'START' token at the beginning) to generate outputs until an 'EOS' (End of Sentence token is generated). There are several modifications [21] to vanilla sequence to sequence networks such as beam search, attention models, etc. which provide a much better output than the vanilla seq2seq networks.

2.4 Attention Models

The main idea of attention model is to have direct connections between the target and the source by paying attention to relevant intermediate states produced in the encoder networks as shown in Fig. 4. In vanilla seq2seq only the final thought vector is passed as initial state of the decoder networks and all the other intermediate state vectors of the encoder are discarded. This way of passing a single fixed hidden state vector might for medium and small sentences [23]. However, it becomes an information bottleneck for long sentences. To overcome this, the attention mechanism allows decoder states to peek into the hidden states of encoder rather than discarding them. This improves the model's ability to output long sentences as well.

The current hidden state is compared with all the hidden states of the encoder network and the corresponding attention weights are obtained. Then, a weighted average source is computed using the attention weights which acts as a thought vector. The target hidden and the weighted thought vector and combined which acts as the final attention vector. This vector, is then fed as input to the next time step. These steps are described by the following equations.

In the above equation, score is calculated by comparing the target hidden state with the source hidden state and the values are combined to fetch attention vectors. There are various choices for the calculation of score including additive and multiplicative function given by Bahdanau and Luong respectively [13,14].

3 Related Work

Though chatbots have existed for a long time, even until recently most of them were rule based (hardcoded with rules). Developing neural dialogue systems using neural networks seemed quite challenging because of the lack of enough data and computational resources. But with the advancements in GPUs and exponential increase in computational power, and generation of large amounts of data, a lot of research is going into the development of neural dialogue systems. In [3], Kelvin Kyung Kun et al. showed that reasonably good outputs can be developed using Encoder Decoder models. Sordoni et al. [17] used LSTM introduced by Sepp Hochreiter et al. [15] in place of RNNs in the encoder-decoder

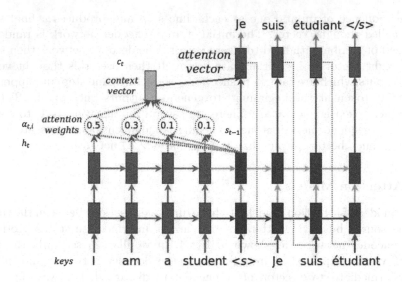

Fig. 4. Attention model architecture

$$\alpha_{ts} = \frac{\exp\left(\text{score}(\boldsymbol{h}_t, \bar{\boldsymbol{h}}_s)\right)}{\sum_{s'=1}^{S} \exp\left(\text{score}(\boldsymbol{h}_t, \bar{\boldsymbol{h}}_{s'})\right)} \qquad \text{[Attention weights]}$$

$$\boldsymbol{c}_t = \sum_s \alpha_{ts} \bar{\boldsymbol{h}}_s \qquad \text{[Context vector]}$$

$$\boldsymbol{a}_t = f(\boldsymbol{c}_t, \boldsymbol{h}_t) = \tanh(\boldsymbol{W}_c[\boldsymbol{c}_t; \boldsymbol{h}_t]) \qquad \text{[Attention vector]}$$

architecture which produced better results. Nowadays, GRUs introduced by Jun-young Chung et al. [16] are used interchangeably with LSTM though LSTM are observed to be giving better outputs. This comes at the cost of additional complexity of LSTM. For mappings from full sequences of words or characters to other sequences, Sequence to Sequence models have garnered a lot of attention [4]. In [1], Vinyals et al. exhibit their neural conversation system on multiple datasets. They show, for example, that when educated on an IT help desk training set, their model correctly includes contextual knowledge in dialogue, such as discussing operating systems. Li et al. demonstrate how common Seq2Seq networks estimate the likelihood of a target phrase given a source sentence [9]. They improve on this by integrating the output of the Seq2Seq model with an anti-language model and penalising over-generic replies given by their conversation model. In [2], Jiwei Li et al. worked on how to include a personality to a chatbot to generate consistent replies over long conversations. Also with the introduction of Attention models by Bahdanau et.al. [13] and its refinement by Luong et al. [14] encoder decoder models became the go to models for machine translation related tasks.

4   Proposed Approach

In this section, the procedure followed for generating the model, the design and implementation of the proposed approach are discussed.

4.1   Procedure

1. **Dataset collection** Reddit conversation datasets are used for the training of our model. The conversation datasets for the months of September to December 2016, including all the comments on the Reddit, their replies, replies of those replies and comments and so on are scraped from Reddit using Reddit's API.
2. **Reddit Dev API** In order to obtain JSON formatted data of a specific Reddit request, we need add .json at the end of the request. For example, if we want to obtain the JSON data of the request "https://www.reddit.com/r/relationships/top/", we add .json at the end of it i.e. "https://www.reddit.com/r/relationships/top/.json". In order to prevent Cross-Site Request Forgery (CSRF) attacks, first we need to create a User Agent and then we can start requesting for data. Another limitation is that the number of requests is limited to 30 per minute.
3. **Data preprocessing** The next step is the preprocessing of the data. Only the questions which have answers were taken for training. All the other replies and comments were removed. The questions asked were saved in input file and the answers/replies were saved to an output file. Also, those questions and answers which satisfy the limitation of the maximum sequence length were retained. Further, before training all of the questions and their respective answers were batched according to the model's batch size. Also certain subreddits like announcements, blog etc. are blacklisted and substrings "http:// etc" are blacklisted as they do not provide any additional information to the model.
4. **Word level feature extraction** There are different word embeddings available out of which GloVe is being extensively used now-a-days and because of the availability of GloVe vectors pre trained on a large number of tokens, we used it for our model.

4.2   Design and Implementation

1. **Construction of sequence to sequence model:** We implemented a seq2seq model by considering the hyperparameters according to certain standards and recommendations.
   The four layers of deep LSTM network with each layer consisting of 1500 units are used. Batch size is fixed at 40 and the number of epochs for which the data is trained on is 50 epochs. Since the dataset size is huge (millions of question-answer pairs), around 100GB, we couldn't train it for any more number of epochs. Also, for every 10000 batches, the learning rate decreases by a factor of decay rate. The reason for such a small learning rate is the availability of massive amount of data.

Table 1. Hyper parameters of the implemented model.

Type of rnn_cell used	Long short-term memory
Number of LSTM layers in encoder	4
Number of LSTM layers in decoder	4
Number of rnn)units per layer	1500
Number of epochs	50
Batch size	40
Learning rate	6e^5
Decay rate	0.95

2. **Generation of thought vector:** The input is given as a sequence of words, one at each time step. At the end of the input, the encoder layer generates a state at for each of the timesteps. In vanilla RNN, only the last hidden state, called thought vector would have been provided to the decoder network, but since the attention model is used, all these states are used to calculate the attention vectors at each of the timesteps in the decoder layer.

3. **Projection layer:** The above mentioned model is trained on the Reddit data for the enough number of epochs. There is a small difference on how the outputs are calculated between training and testing. During training, decoder inputs are the target words pushed right side by a timestamp of 1, regardless of the output generated in the decoder. But during testing, the output generated at the current timestep is fed as input to the next timestep. Also, the decoder units won't generate the outputs directly. There exists a projection layer which does that. The projection is a dense matrix vector which turns the top hidden layers into logits of vocabulary size dimension.

4. **Softmax output:** Finally, once the logits are obtained from the projection layer, softmax is applied on it and the word index with the highest probability is the predicted word. The formula to calculate softmax is as given in Eq. 1.

$$\sigma(\vec{z})_i = \frac{e^{z_i}}{\sum_{j=1}^{K} e^{z_j}} \tag{1}$$

where σ = softmax,
$\vec{z}$ = input vector,
e^{z_i} = standard exponential function for input vector,
K = number of classes in the multi-class classifier,
e^{z_j} = standard exponential function for output vector.

The vector representation of this word is obtained from the embedding matrix which in turn is given as input to the next text step and this goes on until an End Of Sentence token is generated or we reach the maximum length of the response (Table 1).

5 Evaluation of the Proposed Approach

In this section, we present the evaluation and testing results of the proposed chatbot model and compared it with an existing chatbot mechanism.

5.1 Turing Test

The turing is a binary test which classifies the response generated as either human or non-human. The Turing test has the potential to penalise errors excessively. The biggest issue with the test is that it might conceal progress because it is a binary test ("human" or "not human"). A conversational model, for example, might have poor syntax and semantics. However, if we update the model to produce better grammar but the semantics remain poor, the turing test may still label all generated replies as "not human," obscuring the progress achieved in the grammar part of the model. Since the model is still in the nascent stages, most of the answers it is giving are classified as not human.

5.2 Sample Conversations with the Model

The below table lists a sample conversation with the bot. These responses are not cherry picked (Table 2).

Table 2. Conversation with chatbot

Questions	Chatbot response
Hi, How are you?	I'm good. I have a feeling that you are in minority
That's great	Haha thank you!
Where are you from?	Northern Carolina
You don't know what you are talking	I'm sorry. I gotta be really stupid
It's okay	It's okay. I just feel it's a good thing
Where are you from?	Chicago
I hate you	Well, you've got your point across

5.3 Comparison with Cleverbot

We compared the results of our chatbot with Cleverbot which was used for similar purposes by Oriol Vinyals [1]. The sample conversation with Cleverbot is as shown in Table 3.

Table 3. Responses given by CleverBot

Human: *Is sky blue or black?*
CleverBot: *I am 200 years old.*
Human: *What is the color of a yellow car?*
CleverBot: *Brown*
Human: *What is the usual color of a leaf?*
CleverBot: *What is the color of the apple in the fridge?*
Human: *What is the purpose of life?*
CleverBot: *My purpose is to forward my species, in other words to make it easier for future generations of mankind to live.*
Human: *What do you think about tesla?*
CleverBot: *I am tesla*
Human: *What do you think about cleopatra?*
CleverBot: *Cool is cool*

The first major hurdle of any generative model chatbot is to be able to understand the language and generate semantically and syntactically correct results. As can be observed from the results, our chatbot is able to give responses with no grammatical error. Also it is able to generate contextually correct responses to a wide range of questions as opposed to the Cleverbot.

6   Conclusion

In this paper, we developed a generative model chatbot using encoder decoder architecture. Further, we used Deep LSTM networks for each of the encoder and decoder. The main goal was to develop a conversationalist which will be able to have a decent conversation with humans on any generic topic i.e. a chatbot for open domain. Our model was able to give decent answers for some questions but failing to maintain any context over a series of conversations. Even the best in the industry such as Google now, Amazon Echo are still using statistical based methods to converse with humans. Artificial Intelligence which will be able to think and converse like humans and it will be embedded into all the applications. But this is still in its most primal stages and its requires further investigation. Future work can be done to improve this model will be to embed a personality into the chatbot to attain consistent replies over a span of conversation.

References

1. Vinyals, O., Le, Q.: A neural conversational model. arXiv preprint arXiv:1506.05869 (2015)
2. Li, J., Galley, M., Brockett, C., Spithourakis, G.P., Gao, J., Dolan, B.: A persona-based neural conversation model. arXiv preprint arXiv:1603.06155 (2016)

3. Wu, Y., Wu, W., Xing, C., Xu, C., Li, Z., Zhou, M.: A sequential matching framework for multi-turn response selection in retrieval-based chatbots. Comput. Linguist. **45**(1), 163–97 (2019)
4. Sutskever, I., Vinyals, O., Le, Q.V.: Sequence to sequence learning with neural networks. Adv. Neural Inf. Process. Syst. **27** (2014)
5. Raj, V., Sadam, R.: Patterns for migration of SOA based applications to microservices architecture. J. Web Eng. **10**, 1229–46 (2021)
6. Chander, G.P., Das, S.: Decision making using interval-valued pythagorean fuzzy set-based similarity measure. In: Singh, B., Coello Coello, C.A., Jindal, P., Verma, P. (eds.) Intelligent Computing and Communication Systems. AIS, pp. 269–277. Springer, Singapore (2021). https://doi.org/10.1007/978-981-16-1295-4_28
7. Raj, V., Sadam, R.: Performance and complexity comparison of service oriented architecture and microservices architecture. Int. J. Commun. Netw. Distrib. Syst. **27**(1), 100–117 (2021)
8. Raj, V., Chander, G.P.: Monitoring of microservices architecture based applications using process mining. In: 2022 9th International Conference on Computing for Sustainable Global Development (INDIACom), 23 March 2022, pp. 486–494. IEEE (2022)
9. Li, J., Galley, M., Brockett, C., Gao, J., Dolan, B.: A diversity-promoting objective function for neural conversation models. arXiv preprint arXiv:1510.03055 (2015)
10. Dhyani, M., Kumar, R.: An intelligent Chatbot using deep learning with Bidirectional RNN and attention model. Mater. Today: Proc. **1**(34), 817–24 (2021)
11. Pennington, J., Socher, R., Manning, C.D.: Glove: global vectors for word representation. In: Proceedings of the 2014 Conference on Empirical Methods in Natural Language Processing (EMNLP), pp. 1532–1543 (2014)
12. Shivakumar, P.G., Georgiou, P.: Confusion2vec: towards enriching vector space word representations with representational ambiguities. PeerJ Comput. Sci. **10**(5), e195 (2019)
13. Song, J., Kim, S., Yoon, S.: Alignart: non-autoregressive neural machine translation by jointly learning to estimate alignment and translate. arXiv preprint arXiv:2109.06481 (2021)
14. Luong, M.T., Pham, H., Manning, C.D.: Effective approaches to attention-based neural machine translation. arXiv preprint arXiv:1508.04025 (2015)
15. Hochreiter, S., Schmidhuber, J.: Long short-term memory. Neural Comput. **9**(8), 1735–80 (1997)
16. Weerakody, P.B., Wong, K.W., Wang, G., Ela, W.: A review of irregular time series data handling with gated recurrent neural networks. Neurocomputing **21**(441), 161–78 (2021)
17. Sordoni, A., et al. A neural network approach to context-sensitive generation of conversational responses. arXiv preprint arXiv:1506.06714 (2015)
18. Guo, Y., et al.: Topic-aware chatbot using Recurrent Neural Networks and Nonnegative Matrix Factorization. arXiv preprint arXiv:1912.00315 (2019)
19. Akkineni, H., Lakshmi, P.V.S., Sarada, L.: Design and development of retrieval-based chatbot using sentence similarity. In: Nayak, P., Pal, S., Peng, S.-L. (eds.) IoT and Analytics for Sensor Networks. LNNS, vol. 244, pp. 477–487. Springer, Singapore (2022). https://doi.org/10.1007/978-981-16-2919-8_43
20. Saab, S., Fu, Y., Ray, A., Hauser, M.: A dynamically stabilized recurrent neural network. Neural Process. Lett. **54**(2), 1195–209 (2022)
21. Pandey, S., Sharma, S., Wazir, S.: Mental healthcare chatbot based on natural language processing and deep learning approaches: ted the therapist. Int. J. Inf. Technol. **2**, 1 (2022)

22. Shi, T., Keneshloo, Y., Ramakrishnan, N., Reddy, C.K.: Neural abstractive text summarization with sequence-to-sequence models. ACM Trans. Data Sci. **2**(1), 1–37 (2021)
23. Chaudhari, S., Mithal, V., Polatkan, G., Ramanath, R.: An attentive survey of attention models. ACM Trans. Intell. Syst. Technol. (TIST). **12**(5), 1–32 (2021)

Pixel Attention Based Deep Neural Network for Chest CT Image Super Resolution

P. Rajeshwari[✉] and K. Shyamala

CSE Department, Osmania University, Hyderabad, Telangana, India
raji.nooka@gmail.com
http://www.uceou.edu

Abstract. The High-Resolution chest CT scan images help to diagnose lung related diseases accurately. In general, the more advanced hardware used in CT Scan machines, the more high resolution images will be generated. But it is a costlier approach. This limitation can be overcome with the post processing of the images generated from the CT machine. Even when the image is upscaled, the quality of the image should be retained. So, the process of reconstructing the High-Resolution images from the Low-Resolution images is known as Image Super-Resolution. The recent advancements in hardware and Super Resolution deep neural networks enabled reconstructing High-Resolution images in an efficient way. The objective quality metric Peak-Signal-to-Noise-Ratio evaluates the performance of a SR deep model. In this paper, proposed a pixel attention based deep neural network, MediSR for chest CT scan medical image Super-Resolution. The model is trained with two chest CT datasets and the experimental results showed an improvement of 1.78% and 18.23% for the 2× and 4× scale factors over the existing literature.

Keywords: Attention networks · Chest CT scans · Deep neural networks · Medical imaging · Residual networks · Super resolution

1 Introduction

Single Image Super-Resolution (SISR) is a process of reconstructing a High-Resolution image (HR) from a single Low-Resolution (LR) input image [1]. There are wide ranges of Super Resolution(SR) applications including medical Imaging, Satellite Imaging, HD Video Surveillance, Astronomy, and many more to consider. In Medical field, there are certain limitations in CT scan hardware devices to obtain HR images. The more sensors used in CT Scan machines, the more high resolution CT images, the machine can produce. But the cost of the sensors used in CT scan machines is highly expensive. To avoid this limitation, post processing of CT images is desirable. To obtain high resolution images, many SISR Deep Learning models were evolved, which significantly improved the quality of the reconstructed HR image from a single LR image with different

© The Author(s), under exclusive license to Springer Nature Switzerland AG 2023
I. Woungang et al. (Eds.): ANTIC 2022, CCIS 1798, pp. 393–407, 2023.
https://doi.org/10.1007/978-3-031-28183-9_28

scale factors like 2× and 4× which are greatly useful in diagnosing chest related diseases accurately.

In this paper, MediSR, a Deep Learning Model based on the Pixel Attention mechanism [2] was proposed. This model was trained and tested with two different CT Scan Image datasets, The Cancer Imaging Archive (TCIA) Non-Small Cell Lung Cancer (NSCLC) Chest CT Scan Images [3] and Covid-19 Chest CT Scan Image Datasets [4]. The implementation outcome shows the notable improvement in Peak-Signal-to-Noise-Ratio (PSNR) [5], an objective quality measurement compared to the existing deep learning models. The significant contribution in this paper is the use of a modified Enhanced Deep Super Resolution residual structure with pixel attention mechanism, which improved quality of SR image.

This paper organized as follows. Section 2 describes the literature related to Single Image Super Resolution Deep Models, Sect. 3 discuss the proposed network design details, Sect. 4 describe the experiment results and Sect. 5 discusses the conclusion.

2   Existing SISR Techniques

In Literature, many SISR techniques were proposed. These are basically categorized as Interpolation based techniques [6,7], Reconstruction based techniques [8,9], Learning based methods [10–13] and Deep Learning Based Methods [14]. The simple traditional interpolation techniques like bi-linear, bi-cubic and nearest neighbour methods upscale the image by increasing number of pixels and applies simple mathematical formulas to replace the missing pixel values. But these techniques suffer with blur artefacts in reconstructed image and repeated pixels which lead to poor quality HR image. To overcome the problems with interpolation methods, reconstruction-based methods were proposed. These methods use prior values like soft cuts [8], gradient profile prior [9] to produce sharp details in the reconstructed image. These methods use high computational cost and degrade the reconstructed image quality when the upscale factor is high.

Then the learning-based methods were proposed which are based on machine learning and derive the statistical relation between the LR and HR Images. These methods include Nearest Neighbour Embedding [11], Markov Random Field [10], Random Forest [13] and sparse representation methods [12]. As these methods require manual pre-processing of the input LR images during training, which requires more computational time.

The significant advancement in hardware like GPUs and various technologies made it possible to overcome the computational time limitations by applying deep neural network models and proved that these methods outperformed than traditional SR Methods. In this regard, many neural networks were designed and evaluated.

The various Deep Neural Network Models evolved for SISR, at the first the Linear deep models evolved like SRCNN [14], FSRCNN [15], ESPCNN [16] and more, Residual Networks like VDSR [17], EDSR [18], SRResNet [19] and more , Adversarial Networks like SRGANs [20], Attention based Networks like Channel Attention [21,22], Spatial Attention [23] and Pixel Attention Networks(PAN) [2] and many more evolved in recent years and solve the SR problem with improved performance [23]. The detailed explanation of Pixel Attention presented in Sect. 3.1.

3   Proposed Model: MediSR Network

3.1   Pixel Attention Mechanism

The use of a pixel attention mechanism for super resolution is a technique that can be used to improve the quality of LR image. A pixel attention mechanism can help a super resolution model focus on important parts of the image, such as edges or high-frequency details, and use this information to generate a higher-resolution version of the image. This can help improve the visual quality of the generated image and make it appear more realistic.

The recent network models based on pixel attention mechanism [2], which significantly improved 17.92% performance gain comparatively SRResNet [19] and it is a light-weight Network model with 272K parameters generated during training the model. Attention techniques are popular because a "second order" feature multiplication can effectively boost feature representation capacity [24].

The network achieved improved performance with the same computational load with the use of a powerful feature propagation approach. For network compression, this is a potential direction in pixel attention. By using spatial global pooling, channel attention pools the preceding features into a vector, whereas spatial attention combines the features into a single feature map via channel-wise pooling.

These systems perform poorly in the SR process, which needs pixel level examination. Moreover omitting the pooling operation could boost performance dramatically. The modified attention approach is called pixel attention since the features are amplified in a pixel-by-pixel manner.

The Pixel Attention Networks (PAN) has shown significant improvement over the channel and spatial attention models [2]. The pixel attention generates 3D attention maps compare to 1D attention maps or 2D attention maps generated from channel and spatial attention networks respectively. Figure 1 [2] shows the three attention mechanisms. Pixel attention produces pixel coefficients for every pixel in the generated feature maps. The various methods [25–34] applied on CT medical image for performance improvement. The proposed model MediSR was trained with chest CT medical images and it is observed that a notable improvement in reconstructed HR image quality. To measure the objective quality of the up-scaled HR image, the quantitative performance measure PSNR is used, and it has significantly improved with proposed MediSR PAN.

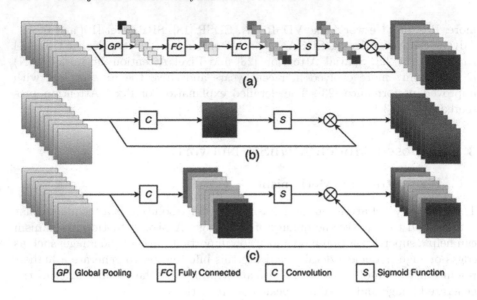

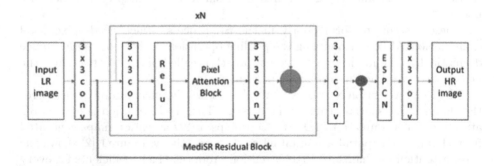

Fig. 1. Channel, Spatial and Pixel Attention

3.2 Network Design

In Fig. 2, the proposed MediSR network module has shown. The proposed MediSR deep model has designed based on the modified residual network Enhanced Deep Residual Networks for Single Image Super-Resolution(EDSR) [18] architecture with Pixel Attention mechanism.

Fig. 2. The proposed MediSR Deep Learning Model

The model has been divided into three blocks namely feature extraction block, consisting input LR image with 3×3 convolution to generate feature maps as input, set of N-MediSR Residual blocks with Pixel Attention block to learn the features at pixel level and post up sampling block to upscale and generates HR output image from MediSR residual block using Efficient Sub

Pixel Convolutional Network (ESPCN) [16] with 3×3 convolution to generate the output SR image.

The pixel attention block in MediSR residual block is a 1×1 convolution with sigmoid function to map the entire pixels into a small range as shown in Fig. 3.

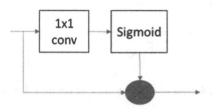

Fig. 3. Pixel Attention Block

3.3   Working of Proposed Network

The proposed deep network model has been shown in Fig. 2. This network uses a local Residual Network Structure like EDSR [18]. First, the network goes through a first convolution layer consisting of the number of input channels 1, with 64 filters of 3×3 filter size for an input image with stride $= 1$ and padding as 1. The output of this layer will be the input for a stack of N $= 4$ number of MediSR residual blocks, composed of the Pixel Attention mechanism.

In each MediSR residual block, a 3×3 convolutional layer is followed by the ReLu activation layer, and the output is fed as input to the pixel attention block, shown in Fig. 2. This output is given as input to the 3×3 convolution layer. The output generated from this layer is concatenated with the first 3×3 convoluted input image. This process will be repeated four times to learn the important features at pixel level and generates the feature maps accordingly. The output from the MediSR Residual block is now fed as an input to the 3×3 convolution layer.

The output from this layer is again concatenated with the input convolved image. The outcome of this layer is input to ESPCN [16] network model for up-scaling image. The proposed network is a post-up-sampling Model. The up-sampled image is applied with 3×3 convolution, and finally, it generates an up-scaled HR output image.

As shown in Fig. 4, the training process of proposed model starts from the LR input image X_{lr} and Y_{hr} is the output of the model. The first output in network is F_0, and the mapping function is shown in Eq. (1) where $H_{fe}(.)$ represents the convolution process in the first convolutional layer. The F_0 feature map used as input to the MediSR Residual Block (MediSRRB). Let rd is the number of residual blocks. In proposed model, four residual blocks (MediSRRB) were

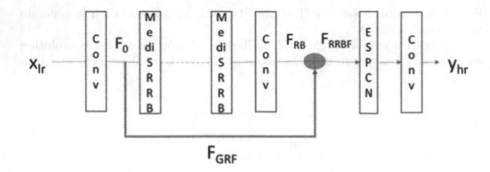

Fig. 4. Network Structure of proposed model

considered. The output from four MediSRRB residual blocks is fed as input to second convolution layer. Now, the resultant feature map F_{RB} is shown in Eq. (2).

$$F_0 = H_f e(x) \tag{1}$$

$$F_{RB} = H_{RB,rd}(F_{MediSRRB-1}) \tag{2}$$

where $H_{MediSRRB,rd}$ represents the operations of the rd^{th} MediSRRB. The inner layers of the MediSRRB consists of three Residual Blocks(RB), the features of the MediSRRB are calculated using Eq. (3).

$$F_{MediSRRB} = H_{RB,rd}((H_{RB,rd-1}(F_{rd}-1))(..)(H_{RB,rd2}(F_{rd2}))) + F_{rrl} \tag{3}$$

where $H_{RB,rd}$ represents the operations of the rd^{th} RB. As $H_{RB,rd}$ is a joint operation of the convolution and ReLU. As $F_{MediSRRB}$ is calculated using all MediSRRBs and residual in residual learning (F_{rrl}). The output of the dth RB can be obtained using the input of F_{d-1} as shown in Eq. (4).

$$F_d = H_{RB,d}(F_{d-1}) \tag{4}$$

where, F_d is the local features of the RB. As F_d is calculated using all convolutional layers and the ReLU, and the inner layers of the dense block are formulated using Eq. (5).

$$F_{RRBF} = F_0 + F_{GRF} \tag{5}$$

where F_{GRF} is the global residual learning and F_0 is the feature extraction of the first convolution layer. Final output Y_{hr} of the network can be obtained by the Eq. (6).

$$Y_{hr} = H_{MediSR}(X_{lr}) \tag{6}$$

Section 4 discusses the results, which shows the proposed model significantly improved the reconstruction of SR image.

4   Experimental Results

4.1   Datasets Details

The proposed model was trained with two different Chest CT Scan Image Datasets and tested. One dataset is from TCIA Non-Small Cell Lung Cancer (NSCLC) Chest CT Scan Images [3]. This Dataset has clinical findings of 56 patients' CT images, and each image size is 512×512 pixels. Each CT Scan has multiple slices. The TCIA NLCSC dataset includes a collection of chest CT scan images from the National Lung Cancer Screening Trial (NLST). These images are annotated and indexed to facilitate research in the field of lung cancer screening and diagnosis. The dataset includes a wide range of imaging modalities, such as CT scans, chest x-rays, and PET scans, among others. The dataset is divided in 80:20 ratio, where 100 images used for training and validation, 10 images used for testing.

The second dataset is COVID-CT Dataset [4]. This Dataset has 349 clinical findings of COVID-19 CT images collected from 216 patients. The Dataset also divided by 80:20 ratio for training and validation.

4.2   Performance Metric

PSNR is a useful metric for evaluating the quality of an image after super resolution.

The formula for calculating the PSNR of a reconstructed image is:

$$PSNR = 10log_{10}(M^2/MSE) \tag{7}$$

Here M is the maximum possible pixel value in an image, and MSE is the mean squared error between the ground truth image and output images. The MSE is calculated as the sum of the squared differences between each pair of corresponding pixels in the original and output images, divided by the total number of pixels. The formula for calculating the MSE of an image is:

$$MSE = (1/N) * sum((I1(x,y) - I2(x,y))^2) \tag{8}$$

where N is the total number of pixels in the image, I1 is the original image, I2 is the reconstructed image, and (x,y) are the coordinates of each pixel in the image. Higher PSNR values indicate better image quality after super resolution, and are generally considered to be desirable.

4.3   Training Details

For training, Selected 100 images and 10 images for testing from TCIA Dataset. A total of 280 training images and 69 validation images from COVID-CT Dataset. A 32×32 image patch size was extracted from each image in both datasets.

The network hyper parameters for the proposed model was selected based upon the experiments done with different filter sizes, number of residual blocks, Learning rates, batch size and calculated PSNR value, an objective quality metric for HR image, training and validation losses. Table 4 shows the experimental results. The hyper parameters are selected with stable PSNR value and reduced training and validation losses.

The different number of filter sizes considered were 16, 32 and 64 with different residual block sizes 4 and 8, tested with TCIA Dataset on the proposed model during training and noted the training and validation losses with PSNR value. It is observed that at filter size 64 and residual blocks 4, the PSNR value is higher and decreased in training/validation loss. For other filter and residual blocks, the values are decreasing. So, the hyper parameters for number of filters and residual blocks are chosen as 64 and 4 respectively. The results were shown in Table 1.

Table 1. Hyper parameter selection - no. of filters and residual blocks (TCIA dataset)

No. of filters	Residual blocks	PSNR (dB)	Training loss/Validation loss
16	4	31.79	0.0008/0.0006
32	4	35.52	0.0003/0.0002
64	4	**37.04**	0.0002/0.0001
64	8	36.90	0.0001/0.0002

In the similar way, the learning rates 0.001, 0.0001, 0.00001 and 0.000001 are tested. The learning rate 0.00001 has selected which has stable PSNR value and the results were presented in Table 2. Similarly, with the batch sizes 4, 8, 16 and 32 were tested. The batch size 4 has given stable PSNR value, so it's selected as one of hyper parameter. It's shown in Table 3.

Finally, the Network hyperparameters chosen are the Loss function is Mean Square Error (MSE), the Optimizer applied is Adam, the Learning rate = 0.00001 with Batch Size as 4, the number of filters is 64 and Number of Residual Blocks considered is 4. The Proposed network model is implemented using the PyTorch machine learning framework. The Number of EPOCHs run is 100, 200, 400, 500 and 1000 for scaling factors 2× and 4×.

With the selected hyper parameters, the proposed model was trained with two datasets TCIA and COVID-19. After 500 Epochs, it is observed that a stable PSNR and training/validation loss. So the PSNR value for upscale factors 2× and 4× are **38.01 dB** and **36.06 dB** for TCIA dataset, **33.94 dB** and **27.56 dB** for Covid-CT dataset are achieved. The inferences were plotted for different

Table 2. Hyper parameter selection - learning rate (TCIA dataset)

No. of filters	Residual blocks	Learning rate	PSNR (dB)	Training loss/Validation loss
64	4	0.001	35.72	0.0001/0.00062
64	4	0.0001	37.02	0.0001/0.0001
64	4	0.0001	**37.04**	0.0002/0.0001
64	8	0.000001	30.15	0.0011/0.0010

Table 3. Hyper parameter selection - batch size (TCIA dataset)

Batch size	PSNR (dB)
4	**37.04**
8	35.08
16	32.30
32	30.42

Epochs vs training/validation losses for the scale factors 2× and 4× and it is inferred that as the epoch number increases, the training and validation losses are gradually decreases and stabilizes after 500 epochs as shown in Figs. 5 and 6. The Fig. 5a, 5b and 5c are plotted for the 100, 200 and 400 no. of epochs vs training/validation losses and it is observed that as the epoch number increases, the corresponding losses are reduced and stabilized which leading to good fit and the same can be observed in Fig. 6a, 6b, and 6c.

Figure 7 shows that for different Epochs of the scale factor 2×, it is deduced that as the epoch number increases, PSNR value increases and stabilizes after 500 epochs.

Figures 8 and 9 shows the input LR image and output SR image with 2× scale factor respectively. The resultant SR image shows the details of input image clearly with objective PSNR value though it may not be clear perceptually.

The proposed model was implemented on the Windows 10 operating system. In the hardware configuration, the processor is an Intel Core i7 with 16 GB of RAM embedded with NVIDIA GPU GeForce GTX 1060 of 6 GB RAM. The model was implemented using the python PyTorch machine learning framework.

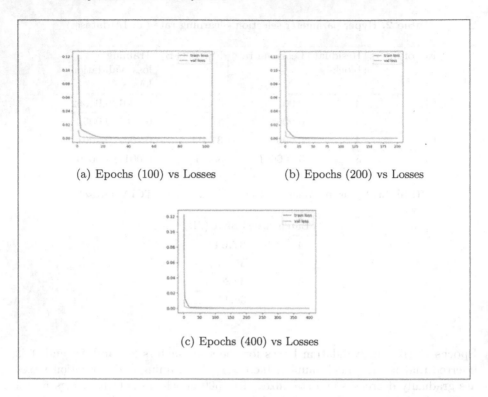

(a) Epochs (100) vs Losses   (b) Epochs (200) vs Losses

(c) Epochs (400) vs Losses

Fig. 5. Epochs vs Losses (MSE) for 2× scale factor

4.4   Comparative Results

The Table 4 shows the results of training the TCIA and COVID-19 Data sets with 2× scale and Table 5 shows results of 4× scale. The results obtained by the authors of [30] and the proposed model are compared and the results were listed in Table 6. The PSNR achieved for the scale factors of 2× and 4× for TCIA dataset are **38.01(2×)** and **36.06(4×)** and for COVID-19 dataset are **33.94(2×)** and **27.56(4×)**.

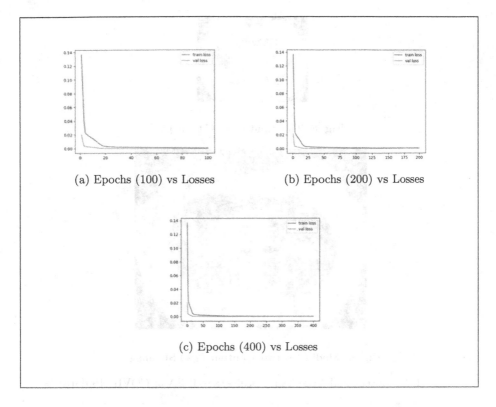

Fig. 6. Epochs vs Losses (MSE) for 4× scale factor

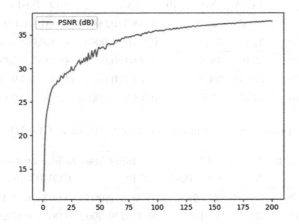

Fig. 7. Epochs vs PSNR for 2× Scale factor

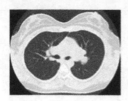

Fig. 8. The input chest CT image

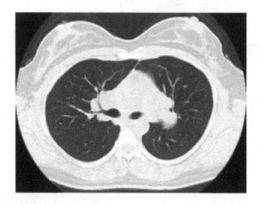

Fig. 9. MediSR network output (2×) SR image

Table 4. Proposed model results for Scale-2× - TCIA & COVID-19 datasets

Epochs	PSNR (dB)		Training loss/Validation loss	
	TCIA	COVID-19	TCIA	COVID-19
100	35.57	32.23	0.0003/0.0003	0.0010/0.0009
200	37.04	33.37	0.0002/0.0001	0.0008/0.0007
400	37.91	33.85	0.0001/0.0001	0.0006/0.0006
500	**38.01**	**33.94**	0.0001/0.0001	0.0006/0.0005
1000	37.75	33.76	0.00009/0.0001	0.0005/0.0006

Table 5. Proposed model results for Scale-4× - TCIA & COVID-19 datasets

Epochs	PSNR (dB)		Training loss/Validation loss	
	TCIA	COVID-19	TCIA	COVID-19
100	34.50	26.39	0.0006/0.0003	0.0035/0.0033
200	35.66	27.10	0.0003/0.0002	0.0030/0.0029
400	35.98	27.55	0.0002/0.0002	0.0023/0.0025
500	**36.06**	**27.56**	0.0002/0.0002	0.0021/0.0025
1000	35.95	27.37	0.0001/0.0002	0.0015/0.0026

Table 6. Results comparison

Author name	Dataset and model	PSNR (dB) scale-2×	Performance gain-2×	PSNR (dB) scale-4×	Performance gain-4×
Umehara et al. [30]	TCIA with 89 CT images, SRCNN	37.42 dB	1.78%	30.50 dB	18.23%
Proposed Model - MediSR	TCIA with 100 CT images	38.01 dB		36.06 dB	

5   Conclusion

CT medical image super resolution helps in diagnosing the lung diseases accurately by up-scaling the image without loss of its quality with different deep learning models for super resolution [25–34]. The recent advances in pixel attention based networks proved a significant improvement in HR image quality [2]. This paper discusses proposed model MediSR, a pixel attention based residual network. This model trained and validated with TCIA NSCLC [3] and COVID-CT [4] datasets and tested. The experimental results shows that PSNR value for 2× scale factor improved 1.78% and for 4× scale factor improved 18.23% compared to Umehara et al. [30].

References

1. Irani, et al.: Improving resolution by image registration. CVGIP: Graph. Model. Image Process. **53**(5), 231–239 (1991)
2. Zhao, H., Kong, X., He, J., Qiao, Y., Dong, C.: Efficient image super-resolution using pixel attention. In: Bartoli, A., Fusiello, A. (eds.) ECCV 2020. LNCS, vol. 12537, pp. 56–72. Springer, Cham (2020). https://doi.org/10.1007/978-3-030-67070-2_3
3. Bakr, et al.: A radiogenomic dataset of non-small cell lung cancer. Scientific Data **5**(1), (1–9) (2018)
4. Zhao, et al.: COVID-CT-dataset: A CT scan dataset about COVID-19 (2020)
5. Wang, Z., et al.: Image quality assessment: From error visibility to structural similarity. TIP (2004)
6. Keys, R., et al.: Cubic convolution interpolation for digital image processing. IEEE Trans. ASSP **29**(6), 1153–1160 (1981)
7. Lukin, et al.: Image interpolation by super-resolution. Procd of GraphiCon, vol. 2006, No. Citeseer (2006)
8. Dai, S., et al.: SoftCuts: A soft edge smoothness prior for color image super-resolution. IEEE Trans. IP **18**(5), 969–981 (2009)
9. Sun, J., et al.: Image super-resolution using gradient profile prior. In: IEEE Conference on CVPR, pp. 1–8 (2008)

10. Wei, W., et al.: Single-image super-resolution based on Markov random field and contourlet transform. JEI **20**(2), 023005 (2011)
11. Hong, et al.: Super-resolution through neighbor embedding. In: Proceedings of IEEE Computer Society Conference on CVPR, p. I (2004)
12. Yang, J., et al.: Image super-resolution via sparse representation. IEEE Trans. IP **19**(11), 2861–2873 (2010)
13. Schulter, S., et al.: Fast and accurate image upscaling with super-resolution forests. IEEE Conference on CVPR, pp. 3791–3799 (2015)
14. Dong, C., et al.: Image Super-Resolution Using Deep Convolutional Networks, CVPR, NE. ACM (2016)
15. Dong, C., Loy, C.C., Tang, X.: Accelerating the super-resolution convolutional neural network. In: Leibe, B., Matas, J., Sebe, N., Welling, M. (eds.) ECCV 2016. LNCS, vol. 9906, pp. 391–407. Springer, Cham (2016). https://doi.org/10.1007/978-3-319-46475-6_25
16. Shi, et al.: Real-time single image and video super-resolution using an efficient sub-pixel convolutional neural network. In: Proceedings of the IEEE Conference on CVPR (2016)
17. Kim, J., et al.: Accurate image super-resolution using very deep convolutional networks. In: Proceedings of the IEEE Conference on CVPR, pp. 1646–1654 (2016)
18. Lim, B., et al.: Enhanced deep residual networks for single image super-resolution. In: Proceedings of the IEEE Conference on CVPR (2017)
19. Balduzzi, et al.: The shattered gradients problem: If resnets are the answer, then what is the question. In: International Conference on ML, PMLR (2017)
20. Ledig, et al.: Photo-realistic single image super-resolution using a generative adversarial network. In: Proceedings of the IEEE Conference on CVPR (2017)
21. Liu, et al.: An attention-based approach for single image super resolution. In: IEEE, ICPR (2018)
22. Zhang, et al.: Image super-resolution using very deep residual channel attention networks. In: Proceedings of the European Conference on CV (ECCV), pp. 286–301 (2018)
23. Dai, et al.: Second-order attention network for single image super-resolution. In: Proceedings of the IEEE/CVF Conference on CVPR (2019)
24. Zheng, et al.: Upsampling Attention Network for Single Image Super-resolution. VISIGRAPP (2021)
25. Zhang, et al.: Hierarchical patch-based sparse representation-A new approach for resolution enhancement of 4D-CT lung data. IEEE Trans MI **31**(11), 1993–2005 (2012)
26. Yan, et al.: Super resolution in CT. IJIST **25**(1), 92–101 (2015)
27. Wang, T., et al.: Adaptive patch-based POCS approach for super resolution reconstruction of 4D-CT lung data. PMB **60**(15), 5939 (2015)
28. Tran, et al.: Example-based super-resolution for enhancing spatial resolution of medical images. In: International Conference of the IEEE EMBC (2016)
29. Yu, et al.: Computed tomography super-resolution using convolutional neural networks. In: IEEE International Conference on IP (2017)
30. Umehara, et al.: Application of super-resolution convolutional neural network for enhancing image resolution in chest CT. JDI **31**, 441–450 (2018)
31. Li, M., Shen, S., Gao, W., Hsu, W., Cong, J.: Computed tomography image enhancement using 3D convolutional neural network. In: Stoyanov, D., et al. (eds.) DLMIA/ML-CDS -2018. LNCS, vol. 11045, pp. 291–299. Springer, Cham (2018). https://doi.org/10.1007/978-3-030-00889-5_33

32. Van der Ouderaa, et al.: Chest CT Super-Resolution and Domain-Adaptation Using Memory-Efficient 3D Reversible GANs (2019)
33. Zhang, et al.: CT Super Resolution via Zero Shot Learning (2020)
34. Park, et al.: Computed tomography super-resolution using deep convolutional neural network. PMB **63**, 145011 (2018)

Evaluation of Various Machine Learning Based Existing Stress Prediction Support Systems (SPSSs) for COVID-19 Pandemic

Poonam[✉] and Neera Batra

Department of Computer Science and Engineering, M. M. Engineering College, MMDU,
Mullana, Haryana, India
saini24poonam@gmail.com

Abstract. COVID-19 profoundly impacts human beings in various ways, i.e., psychological, socioeconomic, fear, social isolation, etc., augmenting the prevailing inequalities in mental health. The role of machine learning (ML) can be understood through its various potential applications in Stress Prediction in mental health. This literature survey uncovered various related articles, which were utilized to determine the essential structure for analysis. The gathered information helped in providing the new ideas and the concepts, which were incorporated with the support of literature and classified under broad themes based on mental health during the pandemic COVID-19. This study emphasized assessing various existing "Stress Prediction Support Systems" based on machine learning. This article also addresses the mental health issues that were emerged due to COVID-19 pandemic, further; also analysed the previously available stress prediction Machine Learning based models.

Keywords: COVID-19 · Decision Support Systems · Machine Learning · Mental Health

Research subjects that Were Used to Channel the Assessment:

- How does the recent Pandemic offer a situational advantage to design, develop and deploy ML and AI-based technological solutions?
- How has technology in mental health evolved in India during COVID-19?
- What are the different ways to use ML (Machine Learning) and AI (Artificial Intelligence) to support mental health issues?
- How can ML be incorporated with various COVID-19 caused stress prediction solutions?

1 Introduction

On December 31st, 2019, cases of pneumonia of unknown etiology were detected in Wuhan City, China. After that, it was named a coronavirus (2019-nCoV) [1]. The WHO called the virus COVID-19, and was declared a pandemiconMarch11th, 2020 [2, 3]. In

I. Woungang et al. (Eds.): ANTIC 2022, CCIS 1798, pp. 408–422, 2023.
https://doi.org/10.1007/978-3-031-28183-9_29

the third week of March, UNESCO suggests that almost all colleges and universities stay closed [4]. India locked down itself in the third week of March 2020. COVID-19 and its immediate aftermath present a critical threat to human beings' mental health, including our school students, who may suffer from stress, depression, anxiety, and many other psychological disorders.

Various scientific studies and surveys concluded that the coronavirus (SARS-CoV-2) and its consequent Pandemic (COVID-19 disease) have drastically impacted people's mental health and behavior [5, 6]. Due to COVID-19, the government-imposed many restrictions that lead the human being towards economic threats, career uncertainties, living situations, etc. Mental health issues were dramatically increased during this stage of the COVID-19 Pandemic when people were under lockdown. COVID-19 caused many psychosomatic and mental health gestures in human nature such as fear, anxiety, depressive moods, and lack of confidence, substance violence, and suicidality [6]. Many deaths were reported from suicide, apparently due to pitiable mental health, then from Pandemic.

The sudden outbreak of COVID-19, Lockdown, and social distancing led to the closures of schools and educational institutes in India. It dragged the traditional teaching-learning system into an emergency which can be addressed as "Education in Emergency" [7, 8]. The paradigm of face-to-face learning (offline classroom teaching) environment shifted to an entirely different experience of e-learning (online learning), where students and educators struggled to cope with several work related stress issues. Educators were unaware of the technological gap, lack of mastering inappropriate online teaching methods, examination conduction, inadequate measures to check plagiarism of answer sheets, huge teacher-student ratio, etc. Like teachers, the students also faced challenges, i.e., online assessments/examinations, trial and error methods during online activities, uncertainty, and confusion among the teachers, students, and parents [9].

In the current era, ML and AI are two impressive models that have been evolved to provide automated, diverse, and application-based algorithms for multimodal and multidimensional analysis and prediction on any specific COVID-19 dataset [10]. Machine learning algorithms are intelligent enough to deal with a dataset (data collected to train the machine); these algorithms can predict the cost functions or a relative objective over the training datasets [10–14]. ML has already revealed potential in diagnosing stress, anxiety, and therapeutic monitoring of many diseases [15, 16] in different age groups. Machine Learning approaches could be hope in dealing with these mental health issues. ML techniques can be classified in four ways (Fig. 1) [12, 15]:

i.   **Supervised Machine Learning:** In this learning, the machine is trained with examples (known dataset). Input and output are passed to the model along with feedback. Regression and Classification are supervised learning methods.
ii. **Unsupervised Machine Learning:** The machine must learn from an unlabeled dataset (identifying meaningful patterns in the dataset) and no training provided to the machine. Clustering and Dimension reduction falls under the supervised learning category.
iii. **Semi-supervised Machine Learning:** Semi-supervised learning is similar to supervised learning, using both labeled and unlabeled data. Labeled data is essential information that has meaningful tags so that the algorithm can understand the data,

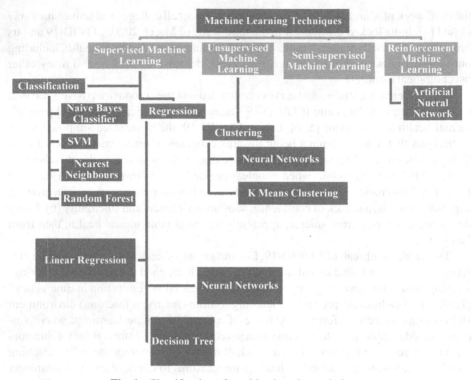

Fig. 1. Classification of machine learning techniques

while unlabeled data lacks that information. By using this combination, machine learning algorithms can learn to label unlabeled data.

iv. **Reinforcement Machine Learning:** This is another category of ML algorithm that deals with software agents to study how these agents perform actions in an environment to improve their performance, i.e., correct input and output are not provided to the system, and the system has to improve itself on behalf of actions.

The machine learning route goes through various essential steps, from data collection to producing fact-full prediction results. These steps are as follows (Figs. 2 and 3):-

A. **Creating the dataset:** ML process starts with collecting a dataset from various resources, i.e., online questionnaires, surveys, professional datasets like Kaggle, etc. [17]. This collected data should be framed into a data structure for features selection and data labelling [15].

B. **Training and Model Finalization:** This step is to choose an appropriate algorithm to train the machine learning model, separate the dataset into the training dataset, test the dataset and finalize the prediction model [18].

C. **Testing the Dataset and Predictions:** This is the final step of the ML prediction process where finalized model has loaded for the operation of the dataset, and final prediction results are collected [15, 17, 18] These results are open for implementation in any diagnostic solutions.

ML Techniques are being used in various areas such as stress prediction, treatment, engineering, education, teaching methods, manufacturing and production, forecast, traffic management, etc. Figures 2 and 3 collaboratively indicate the generalized learning process for developing any ML-based stress prediction models.

This study emphasized assessing various existing "Stress Prediction Support Systems (SPSSs)" for predicting post-covid-19 stress in students. This study also describes that machine learning and AI are comprehensive and critical techniques to fight against the COVID-19 crisis, behavioral change prediction, diagnosis, and disease progression. Various researchers have been using supervised ML techniques to develop the predictive stress models for COVID-19, using labeled dataset and ML algorithms, i.e., decision tree, logistic regression, naive Bayes, support vector machine, and artificial neural network.

This article is organized as follows:- Section II covers related prior work (literature review) about stress/anxiety/depression predictive machine learning models. Section III enlists some identified research gaps after reviewing the related literature. Research methodology is described in section-IV. Section V describes statistical discussions and performance assessments. Section-VI concludes the overall efforts put for formulating the research and future directions.

2 Literature Review

Researchers have already been proposed numerous ML and AI-based prediction models to diagnose and predicate stress/anxiety caused by COVID-19. Here comprehensive research about the current era technology of AI and ML is presented about how these technologies have managed to predict the stress/anxiety in students and front line workers during COVID and how this automation technology can transform the mental health area.

This type of analysis can identify the gap and may empower the mental health care system. The analysis also revealed varying impacts on a segment of the population who already suffer from different types of mental illness, and their symptoms burst out when COVID-19 encountered.

Table 1 enlisted the related literature analysis introduced so far by many researchers indicating that ML algorithms and AI techniques have played significant roles in stress prediction and diagnosis solutions during the COVID - 19 pandemic. Further, ML and AI can diminish the massive liability of inadequate health care systems. Until now, no such research study has been investigated in India which can help predict the stress and anxiety in school students during COVID-19. This assessment examines the gaps in these models and to find out the scope of implementing COVID-19 based stress predictive models.

Table 1. Summary of contributing articles in assessment of stress/anxiety predictive machine learning models.

Article	Summary & Contribution	Analyzed Sentiments/Features
[19]	A cross-sectional-based anxiety and depression finding model (SMOTE) has been introduced for college students. The samples have been divided into five equal parts to perform a 5-fold cross-validation	• Anxiety and depression finding model (SMOTE) • Tested for College Students
[20]	The model is divided into five phases; HCWs' stressor experience during the COVID-19, subjective estimation of stress practiced by HCWs, unique stimulation paradigms, computed neuron-physiological features, and statistical and Machine Learning data study	• Stress and anxiety Prediction Model • Tested for Health Care Workers
[21]	This article analyzes the psychological impact of COVID-19, psychosomatic influence, socio-demographic imbalance, impact on lifestyle, and awareness about risk factors of COVID-19	• COVID-19 risk factor model • Tested for seven U.S. university students
[22]	KAGGLE dataset has been used for assessment, and the dataset has been divided into four classes: 1) Mobility & Social Distancing, 2) COVID & Health, 3) Financial Impact, and 4) Vulnerable Population	• Clustering of COVID-19 KAGGLE dataset
[23]	PRISMA-ScR (Preferred Reporting Items for Systematic reviews and Meta-Analyses extension for Scoping Reviews) guidelines was used for framing questions for the cross-sectional study	• PRISMA-ScR method for cross-sectional study on mental health model
[24]	Two models of machine learning algorithms are used to predict two essential variables, i.e., fear and health, linear model LASSO, and non-linear ERT. The models were evaluated with a nested cross-validation procedure	• ML algorithms LASSO (linear model) and ERT (non-linear) are used • Predicted variables are fear and health

(continued)

Table 1. (*continued*)

Article	Summary & Contribution	Analyzed Sentiments/Features
[25]	2787 participants were assessed for predicting psychological distress during the COVID-19 Pandemic. The demographics, history of adverse childhood activities, and current psychological distress were analyzed with the ML-based model. The authors found that anxiety, depression, and stress levels were much higher than clinical observations among healthcare workers	• Psychological distress model during the COVID-19 • Random forest algorithm to find strongest predictors of distress • Regression trees for identifying the individuals at greater risk for anxiety, depression, stress
[26]	DSM-IV-TR is a repository of stress solutions used to map the description of a patient's mental health status. The complete methodology uses several ML concepts, i.e., genetic algorithm and classification data mining	• Semi-automated psychological disorder model • Genetic algorithm, classification data mining and machine learning approaches
[27]	KAGGLE dataset of size 334 participants with 31 separate fields about unemployment and mental illness was assessed via implementing ML-based Logistic Regression, SVM, Decision Tree, K-Nearest Neighbor, and Naïve-Bayes algorithms for creating ensemble models	• Algorithms and classifiers of machine learning • Ensemble models for testing mental health on KAGGLE dataset
[28]	Decision Trees, SVM, Naive Bayes Classifier, Logistic Regression, and KNN Classifier are analyzed to identify the state of mental health	• Mental health testing Model • Students of high school, college students and working professionals
[29]	In this article, the authors have analyzed the general population (sample size of 2119 online participants) of the Philippines and tried to find out the potential contributing factors to stress, anxiety, and depression using ML-based approaches	• Analysis of adverse psychological impact using ML techniques
[30]	A dataset of 647 participating students' for online classes during COVID-19 was investigated and analyzed for students' mental health well-being	• Sensitivity, specificity, and accuracy were analyzed with ML-based clustering and classification methods

(*continued*)

Table 1. (*continued*)

Article	Summary & Contribution	Analyzed Sentiments/Features
[31]	The authors tried to enlist the significant parameters directly related to the stress level of online workers. A real-time AI desktop application has been introduced to identify the users' stress levels. The proposed application provides more than 70% accuracy	• An IoT-based device was developed, which is bettered with a computer mouse for monitoring the heart rate variability in real-time

3   Research Gaps

ML and AI technologies perform much better compared to the traditionally subjective prediction model where a person has to travel to a psychiatrist during mental illness. Researchers have targeted ML-based prediction models; some of these models have been summarized in Table 1. There are some critical issues (gaps) that can be picked up to investigate in various ways, i.e., presenting the existing model with a new algorithm, analyzing any existing prediction model with available dataset with different parameters, etc. While studying the various research articles under the literature survey, several gaps were identified, i.e.

- Availability of original related dataset, dataset consideration.
- Demographic features of students, socioeconomic background, anxiety, career uncertainty, difficulties with concentration and attention, changes in appetite, energy, desires, and interests, feelings of fear, anger, sadness, worry, numbness, or frustration etc.
- Selection of appropriate parameters and ML-based algorithm that closely suits the dataset.
- Implementation of ML based prediction analysis into AI based applications for spreading the benefits.
- Technological Challenges: Unavailability of skilled technical personnel and lack of support in installation, operation, maintenance, network administration and security, slow internet etc.

Among all these challenges availability of original datasets, identifying the feature selection machine learning algorithm on the COVID-19 dataset,and implementing ML-based prediction analysis into AI-based applications are some critical gaps that can be picked up for further investigation.

4   Proposed Methodology

After analyzing vast literature, we proposed a generalized machine learning (ML) based prediction model (Fig. 2) to analyze and predict the stress level in human beings. By applying these types of models, various researchers have approved many findings like level of stress, approved diagnostic solutions, etc. The proposed model includes dataset collection, data labeling, preprocessing, feature extraction, applying suitable machine learning algorithms, and comparing them to performance parameters (Fig. 3).

The general methodology for developing the machine learning models for prediction stress caused by COVID-19 is depicted in Fig. 2; further, Fig. 3 shows the generalized event flow diagram (detailed diagram based on Fig. 2). During COVID-19, data collection was done online, i.e., through online questioners, surveys, pre-ready datasets, etc. The dataset has essential information like demographic details, cause of stress, and students' socioeconomic background, and this information needs to be prepared for the ML algorithm through data labeling.

Some critical terminologies used in Fig. 2 and Fig. 3 is as follows:

Dataset
ML process starts with collecting a dataset from various resources, i.e., online questionnaires, surveys, professional datasets like Kaggle, etc. This collected data should be framed into a data structure for features selection and data labelling.

Data Labelling
In machine learning, data labeling is the method of identifying raw data (images, text files, videos, etc.) and appending one or more expressive and informative labels to provide context so that a machine learning model can learn from it.

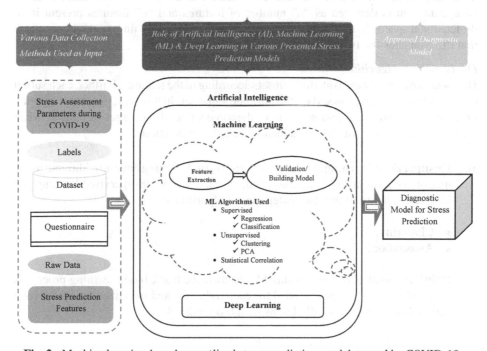

Fig. 2. Machine learning-based generalized stress prediction model caused by COVID-19.

Architecture/Algorithms to Train the Model

i. **Supervised learning:** In supervised learning, we provide sample labeled data to the machine to train it, and on that basis, it predicts the output. Various algorithms fall under these subcategories (Fig. 1).

Naïve Bayes Algorithm
This supervised classification algorithm is used for classification tasks in which dataset instances are categorized based on the specified feature. It is mainly used in *text* classification that includes a high-dimensional training dataset. The formula for Bayes' theorem is given as:

$$P(X|Y) = \frac{P(Y|X)P(X)}{P(Y)}; Where, \tag{1}$$

P(X|Y) = Probability of hypothesis X on the observed event Y.

P(Y|X) = Probability of the evidence given that the Probability of a hypothesis is true.

P(X) = Probability of hypothesis before observing the evidence.

P(Y) = Probability of Evidence.

Support Vector Machine
SVM algorithm can be used for both classification and regression ML models. Here, each data item is depicted as "n" number of features and "n" features present in n-dimensional space. In this way, Classification is performed by finding the hyper-plane that differentiates the two classes very well.

Decision Tree Algorithm
Datasets can be bifurcated into tree subsets according to the features. Further, each subset can be split into a subset based on the attribute value set. In this way, the subset creation procedure continued until all nodes have the same value of the target variable or when the bifurcation process no longer added value to the predictions.

ii. **Unsupervised learning:** Datasets of unsupervised learning have no additional information, i.e., not labeled, not classified, or categorized. Unsupervised learning can be further classified into two categories of algorithms:

- Clustering,
- Association.

iii. **Reinforcement learning:** In this ML method feedback-based learning process is used, where an agent is rewarded for each right task and penalized for each wrong action. ML agent repeatedly learns with this feedback.

In the current era, the modern machine learning prediction models may be used to make various fact-full predictions, including stress prediction during and after COVID-19 among multiple stakeholders, weather prediction, disease prediction, stock market analysis, etc.

Training and Model Finalization
This step is to choose/develop an appropriate architecture/algorithm to train the machine learning model, separate the dataset into a training dataset, test the dataset, and finalize the prediction model.

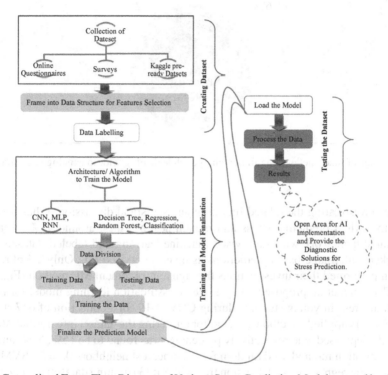

Fig. 3. Generalized Event Flow Diagram of Various Stress Prediction Models caused by COVID-19.

Testing the Dataset and Predictions
This is the final step of the ML prediction process, where the finalized model is loaded to process the dataset, and final prediction results are collected. These results are open for implementation in any AI application-based diagnostic solution.

5   Statistical Discussions and Performance Assessments

Various factual findings have been presented by researchers that can help in better understanding of ML's importance in mental health, stress predictions, and COVID-19 management. Researchers have attempted all three types of ML techniques, i.e., supervised, unsupervised, and reinforcement prediction learning models. The majority of research communities have focused on supervised learning-based datasets and prediction models. Statistical discussion and performance assessment is presented in this section.

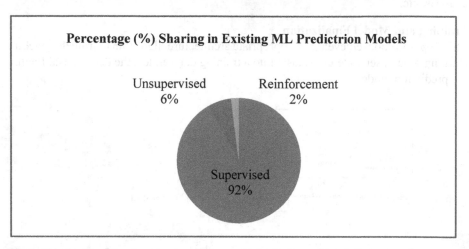

Fig. 4. Usage of machine learning in percentage while dealing with in existing stress prediction models.

After investigating the related literature and statistical discussion, it has been concluded that while predicting stress and mental health issues, around 92% researchers investigated their work with supervised machine learning and labeled datasets, while 6% worked with image-based predictions using unsupervised ML. Only 2% of research has been performed their investigations through reinforcement ML method (Fig. 4).

K. Parthiban et al. proposed a supervised classification learning model for predicting mental stress in young students during COVID-19. In a collection of 647 students, dataset authors applied the elbow method for clustering the dataset into normal, stressed, and highly depressed, and respectively percentage was found to be 15%, 63%, and 22%. The classification method used random forest, k-nearest neighbors (k = 5), SVM, naïve Bayes, logistic regression, and decision tree with 84:33 (training dataset: testing dataset) data separation technique. These algorithms are analyzed with three performance parameters sensitivity, specificity, and accuracy. Among all the algorithms SVM performed better with almost 88% accuracy, 94% specificity, 80% sensitivity; further, Logistic regression with 82%, 89%, 78% sensitivity; Naïve Bayes with 78%, 84%, 78%; Random forest (500 tress construction) with 85% accuracy, 70% specificity, 76% sensitivity; Decision tree with 58%, 65%, 62%; k-nearest (k = 5) with 58%, 45%, 63% sensitivity.

T. A. Prout et al. presented a dataset of 2787 participants and tried to determine psychological distress during COVID-19. A random forest supervised ML algorithm was implemented to identify the highest predictors of distress among younger participants less than 45 years. A regression tree identifies individuals at greater risk for anxiety, depression, and post-traumatic stress. Age, gender, race/ethnicity, country, education, socioeconomic class, marital status, etc., are essential dataset factors in the demographic sample.

C. V. P. Palattao et al. presented a study determining the factors contributing to the psychological and mental health impact of COVID-19 using a machine learning approach. A dataset of 2119 participants was collected during an online survey—the best first and ranker algorithm used for feature selection. The four stress, anxiety, depression, and event impact factors are analyzed using supervised learning-based random forest, Naïve Bayes, SVM, and Logistic Regression. Analysis of results shows that logistic regression achieved the best accuracy with an average of 83.25%, 81.25% average precision, and recall of 73.53%. Naïve Bayes was the worst predictor, with 81.44% accuracy, 80.88% average precision, and 68.65% recall.

Using a labeled dataset, L. J. Muhammad et al. proposed a supervised ML model by implementing logistic regression, decision tree, SVM, Naïve Bayes, and ANN. Before developing the actual model, dependent and independent features were analyzed with the help of the correlation coefficient method. The training and testing dataset were in 80:20 ratios for testing the model. Result analysis shows that the decision tree algorithm has the highest accuracy of 95% following logistic regression with 91.35%, Naïve Bayes with 90.5%, SVM with 90%, and ANN with 87% accuracy. SVM has the highest sensitivity of 93%, following ANN with 92.2%, decision tree with 88%, logistic regression with 83.35%, and Naïve Bayes with 82.75% sensitivity. Naïve Bayes has the highest specificity of 94.3%, decision tree algorithm with 91% following logistic regression with 83.5%, ANN with 81.75%, and the lowest was SVM with 78% of specificity.

S. J. Eder et al. presented a cross-national study where fear is mentioned as a mental health issue during COVID-19. 533 participants (345 females, 188 male, mean age 30.48, SD = 12.18) participated in a weekly self-report survey dataset. Psychological factors, socioeconomic factors, and vulnerability to COVID-19are some essential features that have been analyzed. Overall analysis shows that 23% variance is predicted due to fear of the virus; 5% was anticipated due to perceived health.

M. H. E. M. Browning et al. proposed a study on the psychological impacts of COVID-19 among university students. A dataset of 2534 (1546 women, 988 men, 507 were graduates) respondents was prepared. After analyzing the dataset through ML technology, the authors found that 45% of students were highly psychologically impacted; further, 40% were moderately affected and 14% were affected at a low level.

D. Sharma and S. Chaudhary presented a dataset of 220 undergraduates, and postgraduate examinations investigated for natural, social, mental, and scholarly postgraduate and doctoral understudies. ML-based algorithms, i.e., SVM, KNN, Random Forest, Naive Bayes, Logistic Regression, and Decision Tree, have been analyzed for stress prediction. The naive Bayes classifier gives the highest accuracy of 88%.

While investigating the supervised prediction models, we found that 87% of researchers examined its dataset with a decision tree algorithm, SVM was used by 79% of researchers, random forest by 82%, Naïve Bayes by 95%, 24% by ANN and k-nearest neighbors while using logistic regression this percentage lend to 78% (Fig. 5).

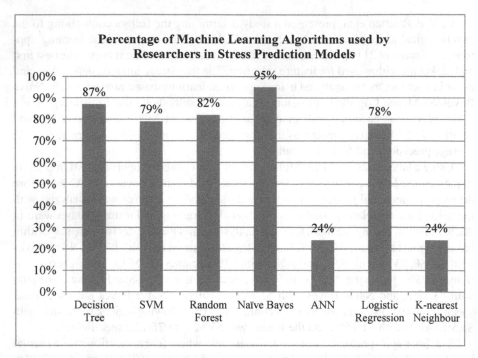

Fig. 5. Percentage of machine learning algorithms used by researchers in stress prediction models.

6   Conclusions and Future Directions

This assessment deals with stress prediction among students during COVID-19. While investigating, we found that 87% of researchers examined its dataset with a decision tree algorithm, 79% with SVM, random forest by 82%, Naïve Bayes by 95%, ANN and k-nearest neighbors by 24% while using logistic regression this percentage lend to 78%. The proposed model will accommodate various ML algorithms that will lead us to design a specific mental stress prediction model for students. Furthermore, we have discussed the challenges that should be overcome for ML-based stress prediction models' success. Focus of this study is to find out how the manual (visiting to a doctor) assessment of a stress-detected patient can be shifted to a self-assessment ML prediction model.

References

1. Novel coronavirus (2019-ncov) situation report – 1. Accessed 9 Dec 2020
2. Novel coronavirus (2019-ncov) situation report – 22. Accessed 9 Dec 2020
3. Coronavirus disease 2019 (covid-19) situation report – 51. Accessed 10 Dec 2020
4. Covid-19 weekly epidemiological update. Accessed 5 Feb 2021
5. Javed, B., Sarwer, A., Soto, E.B., Mashwani, Z.U.: The coronavirus (COVID-19) pandemic's impact on mental health. Int. J. Health Plann. Manage. **35**(5), 993–996 (2020). https://doi.org/10.1002/hpm.3008

6. Ganesan, B., Al-Jumaily, A., Fong, K., Prasad, P., Meena, S., Tong, R.-Y.: Impact of coronavirus disease 2019 (COVID-19) outbreak quarantine, isolation, and lockdown policies on mental health and suicide. Front. Psych. **12**, 1–12 (2021). https://doi.org/10.3389/fpsyt.2021.565190

7. Alqabbani, S., Almuwais, A., Benajiba, N., Almoayad, F.: Readiness towards emergency shifting to remote learning during COVID-19 Pandemic among university instructors. E-Learning and Digital Media. **18**(5), 460–479 (2021). https://doi.org/10.1177/2042753020981651

8. Khanna, D., Prasad, A.: Problems faced by students and teachers during online education due to COVID-19 and how to resolve them. In: 2020 6th International Conference on Education and Technology (ICET), pp. 32–35 (2020). https://doi.org/10.1109/ICET51153.2020.9276625

9. Elberkawi, E.K., Maatuk, A.M., Elharish, S.F., Eltajoury, W.M.: Online Learning during the COVID-19 pandemic: issues and challenges. In: 2021 IEEE 1st International Maghreb Meeting of the Conference on Sciences and Techniques of Automatic Control and Computer Engineering MI-STA, pp. 902–907 (2021). https://doi.org/10.1109/MI-STA52233.2021.9464505

10. Triantafyllidis, A., Tsanas, A.: Applications of machine learning in real-life digital health interventions: review of the literature. J. Med. Internet Res. **21**(4), e12286 (2019). https://www.jmir.org/2019/4/e12286. https://doi.org/10.2196/12286

11. Cousins, A., Nakano, L., Schofield, E., et al.: A neural network approach to optimising treatments for depression using data from specialist and community psychiatric services in Australia, New Zealand and Japan. Neural. Comput. Appl., pp. 120 (2022). https://doi.org/10.1007/s00521-021-06710-3

12. Madhuri, V.J., Mohan, M.R., Kaavya, R.: Stress management using artificial intelligence. In: 2013 Third International Conference on Advances in Computing and Communications, pp. 54-57 (2013). https://doi.org/10.1109/ICACC.2013.97

13. Akhtar, F., Bin Heyat, M.B., Li, J.P., Patel, P.K., Guragai, B.: Role of machine learning in human stress: a review. In: 2020 17th International Computer Conference on Wavelet Active Media Technology and Information Processing (ICCWAMTIP), pp. 170–174 (2020). https://doi.org/10.1109/ICCWAMTIP51612.2020.9317396

14. Reddy, U.S., Thota, A.V., Dharun, A.: Machine learning techniques for stress prediction in working employees. In: 2018 IEEE International Conference on Computational Intelligence and Computing Research (ICCIC), pp. 1-4 (2018). https://doi.org/10.1109/ICCIC.2018.8782395.

15. Mange, J.: Effect of training data order for machine learning. In: 2019 International Conference on Computational Science and Computational Intelligence (CSCI), pp. 406-407 (2019). https://doi.org/10.1109/CSCI49370.2019.00078

16. Waheed, A., Shafi, J.: Successful role of smart technology to combat COVID-19. In: 2020 Fourth International Conference on I-SMAC (IoT in Social, Mobile, Analytics and Cloud) (I-SMAC), pp. 772–777 (2020). https://doi.org/10.1109/I-SMAC49090.2020.9243444

17. Pandey, D., Khurana, P., Misra, A.: Towards understanding the psychological effects of the COVID-19 pandemic on the indian population. In: 2021 20th IEEE International Conference on Machine Learning and Applications (ICMLA), pp. 1449–1454 (2021). https://doi.org/10.1109/ICMLA52953.2021.00233

18. Bansal, V., Buckchash, H., Raman, B.: Computational intelligence enabled student performance estimation in the age of COVID-19. SN Computer Sci. **3**(1), 1–11 (2021). https://doi.org/10.1007/s42979-021-00944-7

19. Ren, Z., et al.: Psychological impact of COVID-19 on college students after school reopening: a cross-sectional study based on machine learning. Frontiers in Psychol. **12**, 641806 (2021).https://doi.org/10.3389/fpsyg.2021.641806

20. Cosic, K., Popovic, S., Šarlija, M., Kesedžić, I., Jovanovic, T.: Artificial intelligence in prediction of mental health disorders induced by the COVID-19 Pandemic among health care workers. Croat. Med. J. **61**, 279–288 (2020). https://doi.org/10.3325/cmj.2020.61.279
21. Browning, M.H.E.M., et al.: Psychological impacts from COVID-19 among university students: Risk factors across seven states in the United States. PLoS ONE **16**(1), e0245327 (2021)
22. Wolfe, G., Elnashar, A., Schreiber, W., Alsmadi, I.: COVID-19 candidate treatments, a data analytics approach. In: 2020 Fourth International Conference on Multimedia Computing, Networking and Applications (MCNA), pp. 139–146 (2020). https://doi.org/10.1109/MCNA50957.2020.9264290
23. Thenral, M., Annamalai, A.: Telepsychiatry and the role of artificial intelligence in mental health in Post-COVID-19 India: a scoping review on opportunities. Indian J. Psychol. Med. **42**, 428434 (2020). https://doi.org/10.1177/0253717620952160
24. Eder, S.J., et al.: Predicting fear and perceived health during the COVID-19 Pandemic using machine learning: a cross-national longitudinal study. PLoS ONE **16**(3), e0247997 (2021)
25. Prout, T.A., et al.: Identifying predictors of psychological distress during COVID-19: a machine learning approach. Front Psychol. **5**(11), 586202 (2020)
26. Azar, G., Gloster, C., El-Bathy, N., Yu, S., Neela, R.H., Alothman, I.: Intelligent data mining and machine learning for mental health diagnosis using genetic algorithm. In: 2015 IEEE International Conference on Electro/Information Technology (EIT), pp. 201-206 (2015). https://doi.org/10.1109/EIT.2015.7293425
27. Kumar, P., Chauhan, R., Stephan, T., Shankar, A., Thakur, S.: A machine learning implementation for mental health care. application: smart watch for depression detection. In: 2021 11th International Conference on Cloud Computing, Data Science & Engineering (Confluence), pp. 568–574 (2021). https://doi.org/10.1109/Confluence51648.2021.9377199
28. Narayanrao, P.V., Kumari, P.L.S.: Analysis of machine learning algorithms for predicting depression. In: 2020 International Conference on Computer Science, Engineering and Applications (ICCSEA), pp. 1–4 (2020). https://doi.org/10.1109/ICCSEA49143.2020.9132963
29. Palattao, C.A.V., Solano, G.A., Tee, C.A., Tee, M.L.:Determining factors contributing to the psychological impact of the COVID-19 Pandemic using machine learning. In: 2021 International Conference on Artificial Intelligence in Information and Communication (ICAIIC), pp. 219-224 (2021). https://doi.org/10.1109/ICAIIC51459.2021.9415276.
30. Parthiban, K., Pandey, D., Pandey, B.K.: Impact of SARS-CoV-2 in online education, predicting and contrasting mental stress of young students: a machine learning approach. Augmented Human Res. **6**(1), 1–7 (2021). https://doi.org/10.1007/s41133-021-00048-0
31. Amarasinghe, A.A.S.M., Malassri, I.M.S., Weerasinghe, K.C.N., Jayasingha, I.B., Abeygunawardhana, P.K.W., Silva, S.: Stress analysis and care prediction system for online workers. In: 2021 3rd International Conference on Advancements in Computing (ICAC), pp. 329–334 (2021). https://doi.org/10.1109/ICAC54203.2021.9671106

Machine Learning Approaches for the Detection of Schizophrenia Using Structural MRI

Ashima Tyagi$^{(\boxtimes)}$, Vibhav Prakash Singh, and Manoj Madhava Gore

Department of Computer Science and Engineering, Motilal Nehru National Institute
of Technology Allahabad, Prayagraj, India
{ashima.2020rcs01,vibhav,gore}@mnnit.ac.in

Abstract. The reproducibility of *Computer Aided Diagnosis (CAD)* in detecting schizophrenia using neuroimaging modalities can provide early diagnosis of the disease. Schizophrenia is a psychiatric disorder that can lead to structural abnormalities in the brain, causing delusions and hallucinations. Neuroimaging modality such as a *structural Magnetic Resonance Imaging (sMRI)* technique can capture these structural abnormalities in the brain. Utilizing *Machine Learning (ML)* as a potential diagnostic tool in detecting classification biomarkers can aid clinical measures and cater to recognizing the factors underlying schizophrenia. This paper proposes an ML based model for the detection of schizophrenia on the structural MRI dataset of 146 subjects. We sought to classify schizophrenia and healthy control using five ML classifiers: Support Vector Machine, Logistic Regression, Decision Tree, k-Nearest Neighbor, and Random Forest. The raw structural MRI scans have been pre-processed using techniques such as image selection, image conversion, gray scaling of MRI images, and image flattening. Further, we have tested the performance of the model using hold-out cross-validation and stratified 10-fold cross-validation techniques. The results showed that the SVM achieved high accuracy when the dataset was validated using a stratified 10-fold cross-validation technique. On the other hand, k-Nearest Neighbor performed better when the hold-out validation method was used to evaluate the classifier.

Keywords: Schizophrenia · Machine Learning · Detection · Magnetic Resonance Imaging · Classification · Cross validation

1 Introduction

Schizophrenia is a neurodegenerative disorder that hampers the functioning of the human brain. The primary symptoms of *Schizophrenia (SZ)* are delusions, social isolation, and hallucinations, including seeing unreal things and hearing imaginary voices. A person with schizophrenia bears a significant burden due to the inability to distinguish what is real and what is not. Schizophrenics might

I. Woungang et al. (Eds.): ANTIC 2022, CCIS 1798, pp. 423–439, 2023.
https://doi.org/10.1007/978-3-031-28183-9_30

show signs of agitation, violence, unusual postures, social withdrawal, irrelevant speech, bizarre behavior, and hearing or smelling things that are not there. According to World Health Organisation (WHO), the disease is prevalent among 1% of the population in the world, i.e., 24 million [1]. It is diagnosed during late adolescence, and men are diagnosed with the disease more often than women. The condition can occur due to stress, depression, genetics, and other life factors. Schizophrenia patients are vulnerable to dying 2–3 times more likely than normal people because of not seeking aid [2]. However, psycho-social support and medicines have proved to be successful in the treatment of schizophrenia [1]. It takes lifelong medication compliance if schizophrenia is identified in the advanced stages [3].

The diagnosis of schizophrenia can be done by a psychiatrist using various methods, including the patient's medical history and conducting interviews based on symptoms [4]. Neuroimaging techniques such as *Magnetic Resonance Imaging (MRI)* also aid in detecting schizophrenia. MRI, a powerful clinical tool, is an imaging technology used to produce 3-D structural images of the body [5]. It uses radio waves and magnets to produce intense magnetic fields to construct complete body images. An MRI is of two types, *structural MRI (sMRI)* and a *functional MRI (fMRI)*. Structural and functional neuroimaging techniques aid in diagnosing severe psychotic disorders because the development of these disorders occurs due to the deformity and abnormality present in the structure and function of the brain [6,7]. An sMRI is the most widely used neuroimaging technique in clinical practice and research to determine the brain's anatomical structure.

The rapid growth of science and technology in medical science has improved the diagnosis and treatment of serious diseases. The application of *Artificial Intelligence (AI)* in *Computer-Aided Diagnosis (CAD)* has been widely employed in MRI research such as ADHD diagnosis [8], Alzheimer's detection [9], and brain tumor segmentation [10]. *Machine Learning (ML)*, a branch of AI, gives computers the capability to learn from experience with minimum human intervention. ML has shown promising results in the detection of schizophrenia. Researchers have been utilizing ML approaches to detect schizophrenia using sMRI to find the classification pattern of psychiatric patients [11–13]. A study done in [14], used random forest, kernel ridge regression, *Support Vector Machine (SVM)* and randomized neural network algorithms for the detection of schizophrenia where SVM performed better than other classification models. One of the studies [15] used two-sample t-tests for feature selection and applied an SVM classifier to the data reaching an accuracy of 85%. Sequential backward elimination (SBE) based SVM (SBE-SVM) [16] showed the presence of amygdaloid and hippocampal structural changes in the patients. The SBE-SVM model achieved an accuracy of 81.75% with an AUC of 0.8241. Another study [17] applied *Logistic Regression (LR), Linear Discriminant Analysis [LDA]*, and SVM to test the performance of the model using 10-fold cross-validation along with a hold-out cross-validation set. 73.5% of accuracy was achieved by cortical thickness (CT) SZ data using SVM. The subject-level classification was performed in [18] using hierarchical clustering by dividing the data into three clusters based on symptom burden. Stratified nested 5-fold cross-validation was performed on RF, LR, and SVM, where RF performed better with an accuracy of 75%. Another study [19] utilized sMRI and applied an ensemble of trees with 3-fold cross-validation for detecting schizophrenia and achieved 64.2% accuracy.

In this paper, we have proposed an ML based model on sMRI dataset for the detection of schizophrenia. Schizophrenia classification is done into two separate classes, mainly schizophrenia and healthy control. We have used image pre-processing methods to first preprocess the MRI scans using techniques such as selection of relevant images, image conversion, gray scaling and image flattening. Five ML classifiers, including SVM, LR, decision tree, k nearest neighbor, and random forest are used to classify schizophrenia and healthy control. Furthermore, we used Hold-out cross-validation and Stratified k-fold cross-validation techniques to estimate the performance of the ML classifiers. The paper is structured as follows; the second section describes the methods and models, such as image pre-processing techniques, validation techniques, and classifiers used in the paper for the detection of schizophrenia. The third section describes the SZ dataset used in the study. This section also explains the results obtained by applying validation techniques on the dataset using five classifiers. The last section of this paper concludes the work.

2   Methods and Models

Figure 1 depicts the framework of the paper. At first, we performed pre-processing of the dataset, followed by the analysis of the data. After analyzing the image dataset, we applied the cross-validation method to perform splitting of the dataset into training and testing. Five ML models were created based on the cross-validated data set. The proposed framework is explained in Subsects. 2.1 to 2.3.

2.1   Pre-processing

An ML algorithm requires high-quality data to provide accurate results. Hence, the images must be converted to a form that an ML model can understand. Computer Vision is a domain of AI that allows computers to extract insights from visual inputs, videos, and digital images. Computers are able to think due to AI and they are able to see due to computer vision [20]. Computer vision tasks are acquiring image data, processing it, and analyzing it to understand the data for extracting meaningful insights [21].

During image acquisition, various external conditions and interference might affect the images. The raw images might contain some redundant or unwanted data. Therefore, analyzing the neuroimaging modalities is complex, time-taking, and exacting. These images need to be first processed using pre-processing techniques for better analysis. Therefore, image pre-processing is a crucial step in

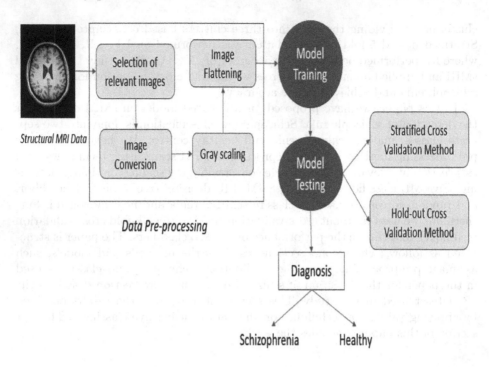

Fig. 1. Proposed framework

analyzing the data and developing models based on it. The pre-processing tasks performed on the dataset are explained below.

- *Selection of Relevant Images:* This is a process of selecting relevant images from a large dataset before feeding it to the ML model. Some images might not be appropriate and can confuse the ML model. Hence, we select only those images which will be appropriate for the model.
- *Image Conversion:* Any data science task requires an image to be converted to an array to understand the distinct features present in the image. The ML algorithms work on numerical array data. In ML, image data is represented in height, width, and channel format.
- *Gray scaling:* With a focus on increasing the operation speed of the computer and reducing the computer resources, the images are first converted into grayscale. Before digitally processing the images, the RGB (Red Green Blue) image must be converted to grayscale. Generally, the brightness of a grayscale image is divided into 0 to 255 levels, where 0 is for black and 255 is for white [22]. RGB color technology is commonly used to represent images. There are three components in RGB mode, including red, green, and blue and each of these pixels value represent the brightness values of the colors. The color depicted by the pixel is the color superfetation of the three brightness.

The total variations of color possible are $256 * 256 * 256$ per pixel because each color has 256 types of values. However, only 256 variations are possible per pixel in a grayscale image. The grayscale image retains the characteristics such as brightness and chromaticity of the original RGB image [23].

- *Image Flattening:* Flattening of the images is a process of converting a multi dimensional array to a one dimensional array in order to feed the 1-D array to the classification model. A multi-dimensional array consumes more memory as compared to a 1-D array. Generally, the dataset is huge and contains thousands of images. Hence, image flattening will help in reducing the memory as well as space to train the model [24].

2.2   Classifiers

The base classifiers used in this paper to classify schizophrenia and healthy control are described below.

- Support Vector Machines (SVM): SVM works on data that is linearly separable by dividing the data into a two-dimensional space [25]. Both regression and classification problems can be solved by SVM. The classes are divided by a hypothesis or a hyperplane which is a separating surface for the different classes in an n-dimensional space [26]. The hyperplane is used for the error-free dissociation of the target classes [25]. The SVM algorithm's main aim is to find a hyperplane that can divide the n-dimensional space into different classes [27].
- Logistic Regression (LR): LR is an algorithm that uses some features of linear regression algorithm [28,29]. LR estimates the relationship between independent variables with a dependent variable (outcome) that is binary. A binary variable consists of two categories. The major task of LR is to determine the probability of the outcome variable based on the independent variables [30].
- Decision Tree: Decision tree algorithms are used in data mining because they are unambiguous, robust, and easy to use [31]. The independent or dependent variables can either be continuous or discrete. The elements of a decision tree consist of nodes and branches. The root node represents a decision to divide into two or more subsets. Internal nodes denote the choices of the decision. The end nodes, also called leaf nodes, shows the result by combining all the decisions at each node [32].
- k-Nearest Neighbors (kNN): kNN is a widely used algorithm for classifying data into classes. It classifies the data on the basis of similarity meaning similar things (points) are close to each other. In this algorithm, k number of neighbors are determined that are nearest to a data point let's say x. These k neighbors form a neighborhood of the point x [33]. The nearest distance of x to the neighbors is calculated using a distance formula such as euclidean distance [34]. The label and the class of the neighbors that have a small distance from x are taken. The point x will then belong to the class of the maximum number of nearest neighbors to x.

- Random Forest: It is an ensemble or a collection of *Classification and Regression Trees (CART)* [35]. Both classification and regression problems can be solved by a random forest algorithm. Random Forest creates a tree by dividing the data into subsets which are called as bootstraps. Random sampling is used on the training set to create the bootstraps [36]. The subsets are given to different decision trees for training the models. Random Forest uses majority voting to predict the final output. Instead of taking the result of one decision tree, it uses the result of each decision tree and outputs the result based on the majority votes of predictions. Accuracy of a random forest algorithm increases on increasing the number of decision trees.

2.3   Cross Validation Method

Cross validation (CV) is employed in ML and data mining to estimate the performance and selection of model. CV method is a way of testing an algorithm statistically. This method divides the data into separate sets: one set is utilized for model training and other for model validation [37]. CV has two objectives- one is to evaluate the model's performance and the second is to compare the performances of different models to determine the most appropriate algorithm for the given dataset [37]. In this paper, we have used two cross-validation techniques, hold-out and stratified k-fold cross-validation. These techniques are explained below.

Hold-Out CV: We have applied hold-out cross-validation to validate the performance of the classifiers to diagnose schizophrenia. This type of cross-validation is the simple validation technique used on large datasets because the training process occurs only once. In this technique, the dataset is randomly split into two subsets that are mutually exclusive. The subsets are called as a training set and a test set. The test set is also referred as a hold out set. The training set is fed to an ML classifier which is then tested on a hold-out or a test set [38]. Generally, the splitting of the data is done in the ratio of 90:10 or 80:20 [39]. Let us consider 'd' be the dataset. The training set is denoted by 'd_t' and the test or hold out set is denoted by 'd_h'. Figure 2 below illustrates the division of the dataset in the hold out validation method.

The disadvantage of the hold out validation method is that test error depends on the train and test data [39]. If all the data belonging to one class is put into the training set entirely during partitioning, then the test set would contain the data entirely of another class. This means that the classifier would be trained on one class only and not on the other class. Due to this limitation of random sampling, the model built would be erroneous. To overcome this limitation, the hold-out validation method can be repeated multiple times and then average of the results can be calculated. This can be done using another technique of data partitioning called as k-fold CV.

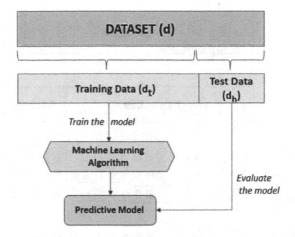

Fig. 2. Splitting dataset in hold-out validation method

Stratified K-fold CV: We have applied stratified k-fold cross-validation for evaluating the performance of the classifier. The limitation of k-fold cross-validation is that it uses random sampling, which means the data is split randomly. Hence, there can be a situation where the test set gets the data belonging to only one class. This problem can be resolved with the help of stratification. The stratified k-fold cross-validation technique works the same way as k-fold cross-validation. However, in this method, stratified sampling is performed rather than choosing samples randomly. In this method, the dataset is split into k folds so that each fold contains the same percentage of the target class as given in the dataset [40]. The algorithm of this technique is explained below.

- Split the dataset into k folds.
- The same percentage of the target class as given in the dataset is present in each fold.
- Choose one fold as a test set. The left k-1 folds will be given to the train set.
- Train the classifier/model on train set. Train a new model on each iteration of cross-validation.
- Evaluate the classifier on test set.
- Save the score of the validation.
- Now, choose another k-2 fold as the test dataset for another iteration and again perform training, evaluating, and saving validation score. This should be performed k times.
- Model has been validated on every fold of the data.
- Calculate the average of all the scores.

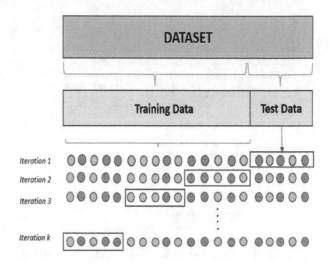

Fig. 3. Splitting dataset in stratified K-fold CV method

Figure 3 shows the splitting of dataset in stratified k-fold cross-validation. In this paper, we have analyzed both hold-out cross-validation and stratified k-fold cross-validation methods for evaluating the model's performance.

3   Analysis and Discussion of Results

3.1   Dataset and Pre-processing

The benchmark dataset included in this study for detecting schizophrenia is- *Center for Biomedical Research Excellence (COBRE)* dataset which has been acquired from The Mind Research Network for Neurodiagnostic Discovery [41]. COBRE dataset was collected and shared by the Mind Research Network and the University of New Mexico funded by a National Institute of Health COBRE grant. The dataset contains anatomical (structural) and functional magnetic resonance image data of 148 subjects. The subjects underwent screening and the subjects having neurological disorder, history of mental retardation, substance abuse and head trauma were excluded. Structured Clinical Interviews used for DSIM Disorders (SCID) were used for collecting diagnostic information from the subjects.

The dataset was created using a multi-echo MPRAGE (MEMPR) sequence with the parameters: flip angle $= 7°$, TR/TE/TI $= 2530/[1.64, 3.5, 5.36, 7.22, 9.08]/900$ ms, Slab thickness $= 176$ mm, FOV $= 256 \times 256$ mm, Matrix $= 256 \times 256 \times 176$, Number of echos $= 5$, Voxel size $= 1 \times 1 \times 1$ mm, Pixel bandwidth $= 650$ Hz, and Total scan time $= 6$ min. Single-shot full k-space echo-planar imaging (EPI) with ramp sampling correction was utilized to acquire the fMRI data or the Rest data using the intercomissural line (AC-PC) as a reference (voxel size: $3 \times 3 \times 4$ mm^3, matrix size: 64×64, TR: 2 s, TE: 29 ms, 32 slices) [41]. The rest scans were obtained in the axial plane where the upper part of the body is separated from lower part. While MPRAGE sequence was obtained in the sagittal plane where the body is divided into left and right sides.

COBRE dataset consists of anatomical MRI scans, resting fMRI scans, and the phenotype information of each subject. The anatomical scans include the sMRI data of 148 subjects specifying the structure of the brain. The resting fMRI depicts the functional aspects of the brain at rest. Phenotype data consists of the information of 148 subjects such as subject id, age, gender, handedness, and diagnosis i.e. whether the subject is a patient or a control. Two subjects were dis-enrolled in the data, hence the total subjects included for the prediction were 146. Out of these 146 subjects 72 patients were having schizophrenia (SZ) while 74 subjects were healthy controls (HC) as shown in Fig. 4. Figure 5 shows that number of male patients was higher than number of female patients. The age range of the patients was 18–65 years old.

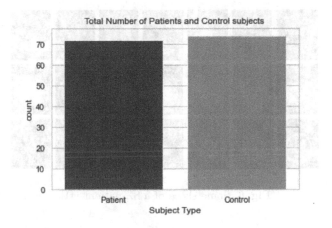

Fig. 4. Total number of SZ patients and control subjects

Each of the 146 subjects consists of 256 sMRI scans, which are referred to as slices of a brain volume. An MRI machine scans the brain of a person in slices. When a brain MRI is captured, the patient's brain is divided into a set of slices. These slices are then further divided into a matrix of voxels. The total number of scans for 146 subjects was 37,376. Figure 6 shows the first few, last few and some middle slices of one subject. Figure 6 only represents some of the slices from a total of 256 slices of a subject. Here, we can observe that the first and last slices of the brain do not contain the full image of the brain. The full structure of the brain is only captured in the middle slices by the MRI scan.

The first and last slices of a brain volume are ambiguous and can confuse the model. Hence, during the first pre-processing step, we selected 30 slices of brain volume for each subject. Figure 7 shows the selected 30 slices of one SZ patient. Now, the total number of slices or images for 146 subjects are 4,380. This is also

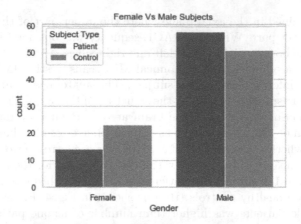

Fig. 5. Distribution of female and male subjects

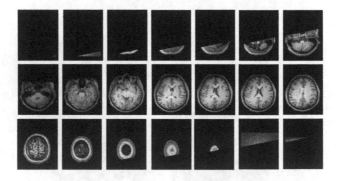

Fig. 6. Some slices of a SZ patient [41]

shown in Table 1, depicting that there were 37,376 images before pre-processing while there are only 4,380 images after pre-processing.

Table 1. Selection of relevant slices in the dataset

	Total subjects	SZ	HC	Volumes	Images
Before pre-processing	146	72	74	256	37,376
After pre-processing	146	72	74	30	4,380

The next step in image pre-processing is image conversion. In this process, the image is converted in an array form because the algorithms of ML work on numerical data. Figure 8 shows the sMRI scan of a subject (left) along with the corresponding array of the same scan (right). This array form of the image will be able to create the whole image. After converting the images into an array

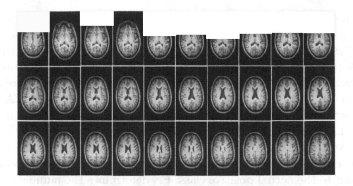

Fig. 7. Selected 30 slices of an SZ patient [41]

form, the RGB array was converted into grayscale. The images are originally in RGB mode containing some pixel values. These pixels determine the brightness values of colors. These images are then converted into a grayscale image with less color variations possible. At last the image array is flattened meaning that the multi-dimensional array is converted to feed the model with a 1-D array. This is done to give the 1-D array to the model for classification of subjects into schizophrenia and healthy control.

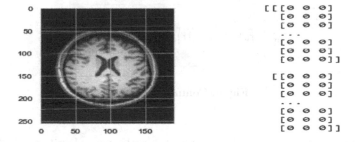

Fig. 8. Image conversion. Left: sMRI scan of a patient. Right: corresponding image array.

3.2   Performance Metrics

The performance metrics are used to test the trained classifier. These metrics measure the classifier's quality when tested with the unseen data [42]. One of the widely used evaluation metrics among researchers is accuracy. However, other metrics such as precision and recall are also used for that matter. The types of performance metrics that can be employed for evaluating the performance of a classifier are briefly explained below.

Confusion Matrix: One of the popular metric for classification problems is confusion matrix which can be used for binary classification as well as and multi-class classification problems. The training of a ML model is done on the training data, while testing is done on an unseen data. The model predicts some values of a target class for the unseen data with some actual values. The task of confusion matrix is to determine the count of predicted and actual values [43]. A confusion matrix is represented in the form of positives and negatives, including True Negative (TN), False Negative (FN), True Positive (TP), and False Positive (FP). TN determines the number of examples of negative class which belong to the actual negative class. TP determines the number of examples of positive class which belong to the actual positive class. FN determines the number of examples of negative class which belong to the actual positive class. FP determines number of examples of negative class which belong to the actual positive class. Figure 9 shows a confusion matrix containing predictive and actual values.

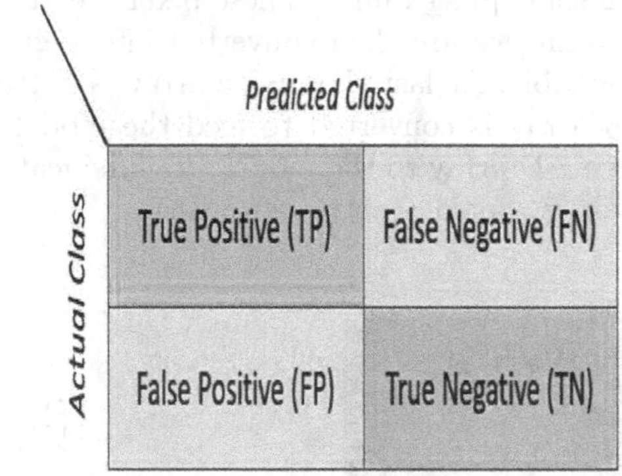

Fig. 9. Confusion matrix

Accuracy: Accuracy is another metric for evaluating classifier's performance and it is calculated from the confusion matrix. It defines the percentage of accurate predictions by dividing accurate predictions to the total number of predictions [44]. Equation 1 defines accuracy where (TP+TN) are the accurate predictions and (TP+TN+FP+FN) are the total number of predictions.

$$Accuracy = \frac{TP + TN}{TP + TN + FP + FN} \tag{1}$$

Precision: Precision is used to check whether the positively identified values made by the model are actually correct. Equation 2 defines precision where TP are the positive values identified by the model correctly and (TP+FP) are the total values that were positively identified by the model.

$$Precision = \frac{TP}{TP + FP} \qquad (2)$$

Recall: Recall is used to check the proportion of actual positives that are identified correctly by the ML model. Equation 3 defines recall where TP are the positive values identified by the model correctly and (TP+FN) are the total number of actual positive samples.

$$Recall = \frac{TP}{TP + FN} \qquad (3)$$

3.3   Discussion

Performance Measures Using Hold-Out Cross-Validation Method. The hold-out cross-validation method is used to test the performance of an ML model by randomly dividing the dataset into training and testing sets. The test size taken in this study is 0:2 i.e. 80:20. This means that the training set is 80% of the data and testing set is 20% of the data. The training set is given to the five different ML classifiers viz SVM, LR, Decision Tree, k-NN, and Random Forest. These five ML classifiers performed the classification of schizophrenia and healthy control. It was observed that k-NN classifier with the number of neighbours as 4 achieved higher accuracy of 99.3% as compared to other classifiers. The precision and recall achieved by k-NN was 99.5% and 99%, respectively. Table 2 shows the accuracy, precision, and recall achieved by different classifiers when validated with hold-out method.

Table 2. Performance measures (%) using Hold-out and Stratified 10-fold CV methods

Model	Validation techniques					
	Hold-out CV			Stratified 10-fold CV		
	Accuracy	Precision	Recall	Accuracy	Precision	Recall
SVM	98.8	98.39	99.3	98.6	98.6	98.6
LR	98.8	98.39	99.3	98.4	98.1	98.6
Decision Tree	87.2	86.6	87.4	83.5	84.9	81
k-NN	99.3	99.5	99	98.4	99	97.6
Random Forest	98.4	98.1	98.6	98.1	98.1	98.1

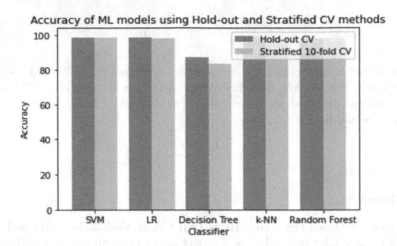

Fig. 10. Accuracy of ML models using hold-out and stratified CV methods

Performance Measures Using Stratified K-fold CV Method. Hold-out CV splits the dataset randomly. Due to this, it might be possible that the training set gets all the data of one class and testing set gets the data entirely from another class. Stratified k-fold cross-validation guarantees that each fold of the dataset contains the same percentage of classes. In our study, we have used 10-fold cross-validation, which means that the division of the data is done into 10 folds. Five ML classifiers viz SVM, LR, Decision Tree, k-NN, and Random Forest were used to classify schizophrenia and healthy control. According to the results, SVM performed better with an accuracy of 98.6%. The precision and recall achieved by SVM were 98.6% and 98.6%, respectively. Table 2 shows the accuracy, precision, and recall achieved by different classifiers when validated with stratified 10-fold CV method. The accuracies achieved by ML classifiers using hold-out and stratified 10-fold cross-validation techniques is illustrated in Fig. 10.

Although high accuracy was achieved by the ML classifiers when evaluated using hold-out validation method, stratified 10-fold CV method gives accurate results. This is because in stratified k-fold validation method, stratified sampling is used which divides the dataset with equal percentage of target classes into training and testing set. This removes the possibility of the subsets getting data of same class. Hence, stratified k-fold cross-validation method is preferred over hold-out validation method.

4   Conclusion

ML, an important field of AI, has been widely utilized in medical imaging research. Because of the ability of ML algorithms to perform classification, the detection of various diseases is now possible. Computer Aided Diagnosis systems aid doctors and radiologists in diagnosing different kinds of mental disorders. CAD can be utilized in diagnosing psychiatric disorders such as schizophrenia using neuroimaging techniques such as an MRI. Schizophrenia is a severe mental disease that leads to defacement in brain functions. It is generally diagnosed from sMRI.

In this paper, we performed the detection of schizophrenia on sMRI dataset using ML techniques. We performed various pre-processing methods on the sMRI brain scans of 146 subjects. Firstly, we selected relevant slices from a large set of brain scans of a single subject. This was repeated for all the subjects. As a result, only 30 slices of each subject were selected from 256 slices. Secondly, we converted the images into an image array to feed them to the ML model. Thirdly, the image array was converted from an RGB mode to a grayscale mode. At last, the image flattening method was performed in which the multi-dimensional image array was converted to a one-dimensional image array. After completing the pre-processing of the images, the data was given to five ML models - SVM, LR, decision tree, k-nearest neighbor, and random forest. The validation was performed using two validation techniques. Firstly, we applied hold-out cross-validation technique, and then we applied the stratified 10-fold cross-validation techniques. Results revealed that the SVM classifier performed better than other classifiers with an accuracy of 98.6% when evaluated with stratified 10-fold cross-validation method. Although the learning classifiers performed better with hold-out CV method, stratified k-fold CV is preferred to evaluate the performance of the classifiers. This is because stratified k-fold CV uses stratified sampling instead of random sampling.

The limitation of the paper is that we have not applied any feature extraction algorithm to extract the relevant features. In this study, raw pixels from the MRI scans are used as features and given to the ML model. Hence, a feature extraction algorithm can be used to extract features from the MRI scans. In addition to this, the future scope of this work can include using a feature selection algorithm to select appropriate set of features from the features extracted using a feature extraction algorithm. Based on the selected features, an ML model can provide more accurate results.

References

1. World health organization on schizophrenia. Schizophrenia. https://www.who.int/news-room/fact-sheets/detail/schizophrenia. Accessed 04 Oct 2022
2. Laursen, T.M., Nordentoft, M., Mortensen, P.B.: Excess early mortality in schizophrenia. Annu. Rev. Clin. Psychol. **10**(1), 425–448 (2014)
3. Abinaya Sundari, R., Sujatha, C.M.: Identification of schizophrenia using LSTM recurrent neural network. In: 2021 Seventh International conference on Bio Signals, Images, and Instrumentation (ICBSII), pp. 1–6 (2021)
4. Spitzer, R.L., Kroenke, K., Williams, J.B.W.: Diagnostic and statistical manual of mental disorders, 3rd edn. American Psychiatric Association (1980)
5. National Institute of Biomedical Imaging and Bioengineering (NIH). Magnetic resonance imaging (MRI). https://www.nibib.nih.gov/science-education/science-topics/magnetic-resonance-imaging-mri. Accessed 04 Oct 2022

6. Borgwardt, S., Andreou, C.: Structural and functional imaging markers for susceptibility to psychosis. Mol. Psychiatry **25**, 2773–2785 (2020)
7. Tyagi, A., Singh, V.P., Gore, M.M.: Towards artificial intelligence in mental health: a comprehensive survey on the detection of schizophrenia. Multimedia Tools Appl. (2022)
8. Chang, C.-W., Ho, C.-C., Chen, J.-H.: ADHD classification by a texture analysis of anatomical brain MRI data. Front. Syst. Neurosci. **6**, 66 (2012)
9. Sarraf, S., Tofighi, G.: Classification of Alzheimer's disease using FMRI data and deep learning convolutional neural networks, March 2016
10. Xiao, Z., et al.: A deep learning-based segmentation method for brain tumor in MR images, pp. 1–6 (2016)
11. Zhu, Y., et al.: Application of a machine learning algorithm for structural brain images in chronic schizophrenia to earlier clinical stages of psychosis and autism spectrum disorder: a multiprotocol imaging dataset study. Schizophrenia Bull. **48**(3), 563–574 (2022)
12. Schwarz, E., et al.: Reproducible grey matter patterns index a multivariate, global alteration of brain structure in schizophrenia and bipolar disorder. Transl. Psychiatry **9**, 01 (2019)
13. Koshiyama, D., et al.: Neuroimaging studies within cognitive genetics collaborative research organization aiming to replicate and extend works of enigma. Hum. Brain Mapp. **43**(1), 182–193 (2022)
14. Tanveer, M., Jangir, J., Ganaie, M.A., Beheshti, I., Tabish, M., Chhabra, N.: Diagnosis of schizophrenia: a comprehensive evaluation. IEEE J. Biomed. Health Inform. 1 (2022)
15. Chen, Z.H., et al.: Detecting abnormal brain regions in schizophrenia using structural MRI via machine learning. Comput. Intell. Neurosci. 13 (2020)
16. Guo, Y., Qiu, J., Lu, W.: Support vector machine-based schizophrenia classification using morphological information from amygdaloid and hippocampal subregions. Brain Sci. 10(8) (2020)
17. Winterburn, J.L., et al.: Can we accurately classify schizophrenia patients from healthy controls using magnetic resonance imaging and machine learning? A multi-method and multi-dataset study. Schizophrenia Res. **214**, 3–10 (2019)
18. Talpalaru, A., Bhagwat, N., Devenyi, G.A., Lepage, M., Chakravarty, M.M.: Identifying schizophrenia subgroups using clustering and supervised learning. Schizophrenia Res. **214**, 51–59 (2019)
19. Skjerbæk, M.W., Foldager, J., Ambrosen, K.S., et al.: A machine-learning framework for robust and reliable prediction of short- and long-term treatment response in initially antipsychotic-Naïve schizophrenia patients based on multimodal neuropsychiatric data. Transl. Psychiatry **10**(276) (2020)
20. IBM: Computer vision. https://www.ibm.com/in-en/topics/computer-vision. Accessed 27 Sept 2022
21. Stockman, G., Shapiro, L.G.: Computer Vision, 1st edn. Prentice Hall PTR, Hoboken (2001)
22. Liu, L., Wang, Y., Chi, W.: Image recognition technology based on machine learning. IEEE Access, 1 (2020)
23. Abbas Malik, M.G., Bashir, Z., Iqbal, N., Imtiaz, Md.A.: Color image encryption algorithm based on hyper-chaos and DNA computing. IEEE Access **8**, 88093–88107 (2020)
24. Impact of image flattening. https://www.geeksforgeeks.org/impact-of-image-flattening/. Accessed 28 Sept 2022

25. Zhang, Y.: Support vector machine classification algorithm and its application. In: Liu, C., Wang, L., Yang, A. (eds.) Information Computing and Applications, pp. 179–186 (2012)

26. Gandhi, R.: Support vector machine - introduction to machine learning algorithms. In: Towards Data Science, 7 June 2018. Accessed 30 Sept 2022

27. Tyagi, A., Singh, V.P., Gore, M.M.: Improved detection of coronary artery disease using DT-RFE based feature selection and ensemble learning. In: Woungang, I., Dhurandher, S.K., Pattanaik, K.K., Verma, A., Verma, P. (eds.) ANTIC 2021. CCIS, vol. 1534, pp. 425–440. Springer, Cham (2022). https://doi.org/10.1007/978-3-030-96040-7_34

28. Vetter, S.P., Regression, T.R.: The apple does not fall far from the tree. Anesthesia Analgesia **127**(1), 277–283 (2018)

29. Vetter, T.R., Schober, P.: Linear regression in medical research. Anesthesia Analgesia **132**, 108–109 (2021)

30. Vetter, T.R., Schober, P.: Logistic regression in medical research. Anesthesia Analgesia **132**, 365–366 (2021)

31. Hastie, T., Tibshirani, R., Friedman, J.H., Friedman, J.H.: The Elements of Statistical Learning. SSS, Springer, New York (2009). https://doi.org/10.1007/978-0-387-84858-7

32. Song, Y.-Y., Lu, Y.: Decision tree methods: applications for classification and prediction. Shanghai Arch. Psychiatry **27**, 130–135 (2015)

33. Guo, G., Wang, H., Bell, D., Bi, Y., Greer, K.: KNN model-based approach in classification. In: Meersman, R., Tari, Z., Schmidt, D.C. (eds.) On the Move to Meaningful Internet Systems 2003: CoopIS, DOA, and ODBASE, pp. 986–996 (2003)

34. Larose, D.T.: Discovering Knowledge in Data an Introduction to Data Mining, 2nd edn. Wiley, Hoboken (2005)

35. Breiman, L.: Classification and Regression Trees, 1st edn. Taylor and Francis Group, Boca Raton (1984)

36. Sarica, A., Cerasa, A., Quattrone, A.: Random forest algorithm for the classification of neuroimaging data in Alzheimer's disease: a systematic review. Front. Aging Neurosci. **9** (2017)

37. Refaeilzadeh, P., Tang, L., Liu, H.: Cross-Validation, pp. 532–538 (2009)

38. Kohavi, R.: A study of cross-validation and bootstrap for accuracy estimation and model selection. In: Proceedings of the 14th International Joint Conference on Artificial Intelligence - Volume 2, IJCAI 1995, pp. 1137–1143 (1995)

39. DataVedas: HOLDOUT CROSS-VALIDATION, 14 June 2018. Accessed 01 Oct 2022

40. Lyashenko, A.J.V.: Cross-Validation in Machine Learning: How to Do It Right. Neptune, 21 July 2022. Accessed 01 Oct 2022

41. The Mind Research Network for Neurodiagnostic Discovery. COBRE. https://www.mrn.org/common/cobre-phase-3. Accessed 25 Sept 2022

42. Hossin, M., Sulaiman, M.N.: A review on evaluation metrics for data classification evaluations. Int. J. Data Min. Knowl. Manag. Process **5**, 01–11 (2015)

43. Kulkarni, A., Chong, D., Batarseh, F.A.: 5 - foundations of data imbalance and solutions for a data democracy. In: Batarseh, F.A., Yang, R. (eds.) Data Democracy, pp. 83–106 (2020)

44. Wenxin, X.: Heart disease prediction model based on model ensemble. In: International Conference on Artificial Intelligence and Big Data (ICAIBD), pp. 195–199 (2020)

A Hybrid Model for Fake News Detection Using Clickbait: An Incremental Approach

Sangita Patil$^{(\boxtimes)}$, Binjal Soni, Ronak Makwana, Deep Gandhi, Devam Zanzmera, and Shakti Mishra

Pandit Deendayal Energy University, Gandhinagar, India
Sangita.pmtds22@sot.pdpu.ac.in

Abstract. In this paper, we have developed a hybrid model to predict fake news that includes clickbait detection as a parameter. The correlation between two different labels has been computed using a chi-square test. After establishing the correlation, the clickbait implementation was done on the heading of the dataset, and a fake news detection model has been executed on the content of the dataset. Then, the results of both the models were combined to generate a hybrid model through a regex equation. Our model is successful in enhancing the accuracy of the existing models by 1–2%.

CCS Concepts • Artificial Intelligence • Natural Language Processing • Information Extraction.

Keywords: Clickbait · Fake news detection

1 Introduction

Over the past few years, the consumption of the internet has increased drastically. This change has affected us and the things we do in our day-to-day life. One of the biggest changes is how we gather information. Currently, we rely more on articles and blogs on the internet rather than the newspaper. This habit has caused concern among people, as the news on the internet might not be authentic and could lead to misinformation or misunderstanding and might lead to some unfortunate consequences. Also, with the rapid spread of the internet, everyone is connected through social media platforms. As a result, sharing information has been much easier. We can send information with just one click to an ample number of people around us, and they can share it with the people they know, and this can go further on [1]. If misinformation is spread in such a way, then it can be drastic. Nowadays, people generally do not have time to verify the fake news and believe it to be correct due to their busy schedules. This is how misinformation is spread these days like wildfire. This misinformation is generally known as fake news which is a major problem.

Fake news articles are intentionally crafted to mislead the readers. It can also be defined as a type of yellow journalism or propaganda. Fake news has been used by traditional news agencies since 1439 [2, 3]. The main reason behind this is the unethical

I. Woungang et al. (Eds.): ANTIC 2022, CCIS 1798, pp. 440–454, 2023.
https://doi.org/10.1007/978-3-031-28183-9_31

reporters who are paid to publish these articles. Fake news often fabricates headlines to increase its readership and mislead people. These headlines are called clickbaits. Every news agency has to compete with a lot of agencies for reader's attention, also they generate money from the clicks of the users. So, to grab users' attention, they employ various techniques to make the headline catchy [4]. Clickbaits exploit the cognitive phenomenon known as the Curiosity Gap [5]. They generally provide forward references in the heading to generate enough information gaps to increase user's curiosity. This will affect the user's attention abilities in the short term. As clickbaits are highly associated with fake news, detection of clickbait will also give us an idea about whether the news is fake or real. Due to these reasons, we have also tried to predict clickbaits and use them for the detection of fake news.

1.1 Study of the Existing Solutions

For the detection of clickbait, given methods are used ranging from detection based on similarities between content and heading as well as on the basis of heading only. For the first method, NLP models are used. TF-IDF, Count Vectorizer, Word2Vec, Doc2Vec, and N-grams are used for the classification of the dataset and cosine similarity, etc. are used to predict the similarity between the heading and the content. For the second approach, various NLP models like n-grams + TF-IDF, CFG + TF-IDF, LIWC, word2vec, Doc2Vec, N-gram, Count Vectorizer for classification of the heading and machine learning models and deep learning models like Naive Bayes, SVM, Linear regression, CNN, RNN, LSTM, etc. are used for comparison of the classification and prediction [8].

For fake news detection NLP, Machine learning models and deep learning models are used in previous research [13]; they have also used TF-IDF, Count Vectorizer, Word2Vec, Doc2Vec, and N-grams, porter stemmer for classification and used hybrid models for comparison of the classification and prediction. Some research papers have used different hybrid models where they predict fake news on the basis of one parameter from one model and in the second model, they use another parameter for fake news prediction, and then they will concatenate the result using a Deep learning model or using regex equations. These are the approaches that we have seen in different research papers [2].

1.2 Research Gap/Problems Found with Existing Solutions

There are a lot of parameters from which can be helpful in predicting the fake news. Some of these are, sentence structures, stop words, hyperbolic, Common phrases, subjects, determiners, possessive cases, N-grams, POS tagging, systemic N-grams, word patterns, clickbait, etc. The accuracy of the model can be significantly enhanced if these can be considered while modelling. We could not find any work where these parameters can be combined and hence, this paper presents a novel work of combining the clickbait and fake news detection model to enhance the accuracy.

2 Literature Review

Various models and methodologies have been used to find fake news, which varies from NLP models, Machine learning models to multiple deep learning models. One of the important aspects that has been found while going through research papers is that the presence of numerous clickbait titles is a detriment to the perceived credibility of a source [6]. With a significant amount of clickbait present in a news article, authors in [3] also tested how much clickbait headlines can affect the model, and the accuracy of the model was increased by 2–3%. Further, clickbait detection was applied on each source of the news and then combined the detected results of each source. Linear SVM for clickbait detection and a feed-forward deep averaging network (FFDAN) for fake news detection has been used in the paper. However, the authors failed to include the credibility score of the source, as nowadays, there are many propaganda-driven news websites.

Another approach for clickbait detection was to classify the content into related or unrelated content using n-gram lemmatization and then classify it to agree or disagree based on linear regression [7].

2.1 Clickbait Detection

As clickbait detection is one of the important aspects of fake news detection to increase its accuracy, a deep literature survey has been carried out using number of research papers and articles for clickbait detection. There are models and methodologies which are used for clickbait detection. Broadly, those methodologies can be classified into two parts [4, 8, 13]:

2.1.1 Clickbait on the Similarity Between the Title and the Content Within

The first approach is detecting clickbait on the similarity between the title and the content within. If the clickbait headings are used, there is most likely to grab the attention to it, but the content within it will be different. Various NLP models are used for this approach like TF-IDF, Bag of Words, N-Gram etc. for classification, and then, machine learning models like SVM, Naive Bayes, etc. are used for comparison of the classifiers [8, 13].

The following is the formula for naive Bayes classification uses the probability of the previous event and compares it with the existing event. Each and every probability of the event is calculated and at last the overall probability of the news as compared to the dataset is calculated. Therefore on calculating the overall probability, we can get the approximate value and can detect whether the news is real or fake.

$$P(A|B) = P(B|A) \cdot P(A)/P(B),$$

Finding the probability of event, A when event B is TRUE.

P (A) = PRIOR PROBABILITY
P (A|B) = POSTERIOR PROBABILITY
FINDING PROBABILITY:
P (A|B1) = P (A1||B1). P (A2||B1). P (A3||B1)
P (A|B2) = P (A1||B2). P (A||B2). P (A3||B2)

If the probability is 0 P (Word) = Word count + 1/ (total number of words + No. of unique words).

Therefore, by using this formula one can find the accuracy of the news [14].

2.1.2 Clickbait Based on the Headlines

The second approach is to predict the clickbait based on the headlines only. This approach is fast and effective with various NLP and machine learning models. There are many parameters that can be extracted from a headline for its classification like "Starting with Number", "punctuation patterns", "hyperbolic words", "N-grams", "POS tagging for both", etc. [4]. To classify clickbait, NLP models like" N-Grams", "TF-IDF", "n-grams + TF-IDF", "word2vec", "Doc2Vec", "Bag of words", "count vectorizer", etc. are used for the classification, and machine learning models and deep learning models like naive Bayes, SVM, Linear Regression, CNN, RNN, LSTM, etc. have been used for comparison of the classifiers and prediction.

Long Short-Term Memory networks (LSTM) are a special type of RNN competent in learning long-term dependencies [15]. LSTM is a very effective solution for addressing the vanishing gradient problem (Fig. 1).

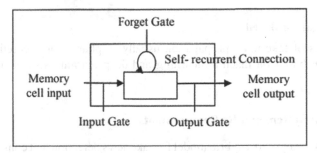

Fig. 1. Structure of LSTM cell [15]

Our proposed approach for classification of headlines is based on the TF-IDF vectorizer and the N-gram approach. For prediction and comparison of the classification, we have used the Naive Bayes model.

2.2 Fake News Prediction

Once the clickbait is calculated successfully, the next objective is to predict fake news. Fake news detection studies can generally be grouped into content-based and propagation-based methods depending on whether the approaches detect fake news by exploring its content or by exploring how it propagates on social networks [9].

2.2.1 Content-Based

In content-based, various machine learning models, deep learning models and NLP models are used. Different NLP methods are used for vectorization like word2vec, fast text, pos tagging, etc. We have used porter stemmer for dividing sentences into words and have used One Hot Encoding for vectorization of the words list. With more computational capabilities and to handle massive datasets, deep learning models present a finer performance over traditional text mining techniques and machine learning techniques. Convolutional Neural Network (CNN) and Recurrent Neural networks (RNN) are widely explored Deep Neural Network (DNN) architectures to handle various NLP tasks [10]. The authors in [10] used word2vec for vectorization of the sentence and then used CNN, RNN, Unidirectional LSTM and Bidirectional LSTM in their model, and the most accurate was the Bi-LSTM model.

A number of research studies have compared machine learning models and deep learning models and concluded that the data with a huge number of articles is beneficial for LSTM, and it will perform very well in it while overcoming the model overfitting. In [3], a naive Bayes model with N-Gram has been implemented and performed equally as deep learning models.

Hybrid models with one deep learning model predicting based on one parameter and another model predicting based on another parameter are also widely used now. In [2], authors have used a CNN for the author profile validation and Bi-LSTM prediction based on content. Then, the predictions have been concatenated to a single vector to generate one output.

2.2.2 Propagation Based

Current studies of fake news propagation usually emphasize on theoretical modeling of propagation based on machine learning and deep learning such as Graph Neural Network.

2.3 Proposed System and Its Requirements

In this paper, we proposed a hybrid model for fake news detection that considers clickbait as one of the parameters. The main goal is to predict whether the given news is fake news or not. To achieve this, we first predicted if the heading is clickbait or not, and then we predicted if the content was fake news or not. Then, we concatenated two results through a regex equation to predict the output of the model.

The major challenge appeared in identifying a complete dataset that will contain article headings, content, clickbait label and fake news label, so two separate datasets for the models of fake news and clickbait detection have been used.

To generate the required dataset, we saved the model of clickbait detection and applied it to the dataset containing fake news labels and generated a predictive column clickbait. Now, we have applied the Chi_square test as both label columns contains binary. After applying the test, we got p-value equal to 0.0000000018603149, which is far lower than the determining score of 0.5. In the chi-square test, if the value is less than 0.5, the variables are dependent on each other. Hence, we have established that they both are dependent on each other.

After having the required dataset, we implemented our proposed model by combining the two models for fake news and clickbait detection respectively, which have detected the output on the basis of the same dataset. To concatenate the results of two predictions, a Regex equation has been found out after careful analysis of the outputs. The final array of predictions of fake news is compared with the fake news column in the dataset.

The proposed hybrid model boosts the accuracy of existing models 1–2% in the prediction depending on the size of the input data.

2.4 Assumption and Dependencies

We do not have such many dependencies although there are a few things that we have to take care of:

1. To increase the efficiency of clickbait detection, we have used the max feature in the Tf-Idf Vectorizer, while classifying the data into vectors. The max features are considered as equal to the number of words that are coming in the dataset at least two times. So, we have to calibrate the max feature according to that dataset.
2. There is no proper data set available to generate the required dataset. Therefore, we need to build and save the model of clickbait first and then run it on the fake news label containing the dataset.
3. In order to generate the hybrid model and do regex equation, following operations have been performed iteratively:

   a. Remove any row that contains errors or unwanted data prior to applying two models for fake news and clickbait detection respectively
   b. Divide it to train and test the dataset before applying both models.

The main reason behind this is that we need an equal number of features in the output array from both the models and in the same order to apply the regex equation properly.

2.5 Advantages Offered by Proposed System

- As fake news and clickbait are related to each other, clickbait can also be used as a parameter in predicting fake news.
- The model is able to verify that including more parameters that are relevant to fake news can affect the accuracy of the model, so including them will definitely increase the accuracy of the model.
- To detect fake news with 84% accuracy only on the basis of the content and the title.

3 Design

3.1 System Architecture

The first step of Fake News Detection model is pre-processing of Fake News Dataset. After completing pre-processing, the vectorization is done. Then, dataset is divided into two parts. First one is used for training the model, and another one is for testing. Training of model is done using Bi-LSTM process method. When the model is trained for prediction, the outcome of test data will be predicted. The trained model of Bi-LSTM is saved for further process, and accuracy will be calculated.

After implementing the proposed architecture, the accuracy of 82% has been observed. The next step was to propose a methodology to predict clickbait based on article headings from a different dataset and saved the trained model for further usage. The architecture for the same is shown in Fig. 2.

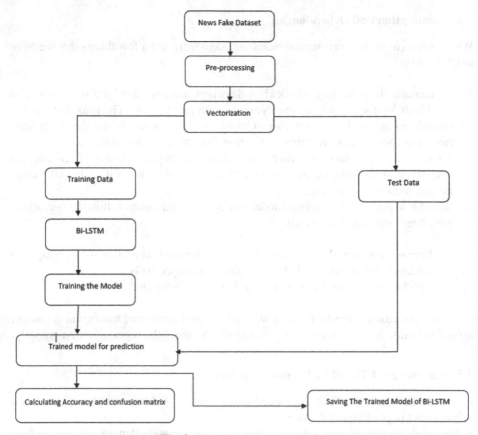

Fig. 2. Fake News detector model

In the first stage, the clickbait dataset is taken and divided into two parts as train and test. After that, train and test data is followed by tokenization, preprocessed and lemmatization sequentially. Then, the train data is going for extracting ferquency_dictionary and TfidVectorizor with maximum_features is followed for it. At that moment, naïve bayes classifier is used for the classification of training dataset; however, TfidVectorizor with maximum_features is directly taken from testing dataset and it has been test on trained model along with checking the accuracy using confusion matrix.

After completing the clickbait detection, the fake news dataset has been used to predict clickbait values for each article, and this is embedded as a new column in the dataset labelled as clickbait label. The architecture for the same is presented in Fig. 3. In the first stage, dataset with fake news and clickbait label is taken and divided into two parts as train and test. Then, on training dataset, we have applied two methods for predicting fake news label array namely Bi-LSTM and Naïve Bayes Classifier and merge them. Later, the fake news label array has been predicted and accuracy has been checked with confusion matrix.

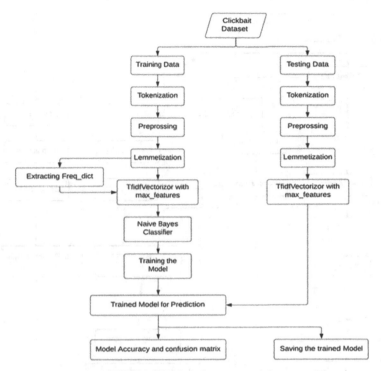

Fig. 3. Clickbait detector model

After getting the required dataset, we have trained both the models of fake news detection and clickbait detection on the same dataset and find the correlation between them based on the predicted values and have generated Regex equation accordingly. The merged output of both models was used to generate final predicted array of fake news labels. The flow diagram for this combined approach is shown in Fig. 4 (Fig. 5).

3.2 Data Dictionaries

3.2.1 Clickbait Dataset

The Clickbait dataset consists of four different columns, i.e. ID, Title, Text, and Clickbait are shown in Table 1. The first column ID provides each entry with a different number so that we can identify it. The next column title has the title of all the articles which are present in the database. The text column has the content of the title, and the last column has values 0s indicating it is not a clickbait and 1 indicating it is a clickbait.

3.2.2 Fake News Dataset

The fake news detection dataset has five columns ID, Title, Author and Text and Label are shown in Table 2. The column ID provides each row with a number to identify them individually. The column title has the title of the article, and the text column consists of the content of the article. The name of the author is provided in the author column, and

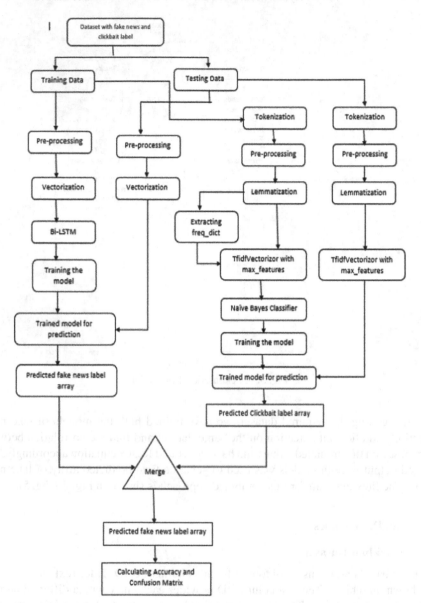

Fig. 4. Combined dataset model (fake news and clickbait datasets)

the last column Label has values 0s and 1s indicating whether the article is fake or not, where 0 suggests that the article is real and 1 the opposite.

3.2.3 Clickbait and Fake News Combined Dataset

The combined dataset has a total of six columns which are shown in Table 3. Different identification numbers are written in the ID column. The title and the inside text of the

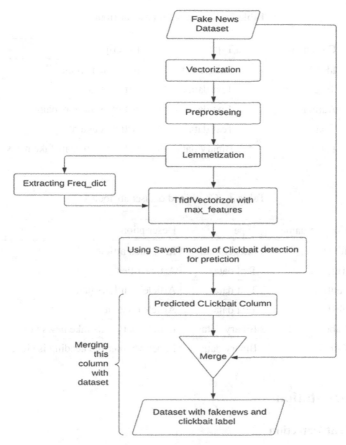

Fig. 5. Proposed hybrid model using clickbait

Table 1. Clickbait dataset attributes

Sr. no.	Column name	Type	Description
1	Id	Integer data	Id number of each article
2	Title	Text data	Article heading
3	Text	Text data	Article content
4	Clickbait	Binary data	Label whether the heading is clickbait or not

article are provided in the title and text columns respectively. The name of the author is in the author column. The details of whether the text is fake or not and the title is clickbait or not are given in the Label and Clickbait column respectively, where 0 indicates it is not clickbait and real news, and 1 dictate that the title is clickbait, and the news is fake.

Table 2. Fake news dataset attributes

Sr. no.	Column name	Type	Description
1	Id	Integer data	Id of each article
2	Title	Text data	Article titles
3	Author	Text data	Article's authors name
4	Text	Text data	Article content
5	Label	Binary data	Label whether its fake news or not

Table 3. Combined dataset attributes

Sr. no.	Column name	Type	Description
1	Id	Integer data	Id of each article
2	Title	Text data	Article titles
3	Author	Text data	Article's authors name
4	Text	Text data	Article content
5	Label	Binary data	Label whether its fake news or not
6	Clickbait	Binary data	Label whether the heading is clickbait or not

4 Implementation

4.1 Clickbait Detection

To create a clickbait detector to detect clickbait, we have used the Naive Bayes Classifier and N-gram model for better outcomes. Then, the dataset was loaded into the data frame and removed the rows which have null values and removed the columns like 'Author', 'Text' and 'label', as we do not require that data to make the clickbait detector. Then, we split the data for training and testing. Here, we have used 75% of the data for testing, and the remaining 25% will be used for testing. In the next step, we have pre-processed the training and the testing dataset. Following methods are used for data pre-processing,

- tokenizing the text,
- converting it into lowercase,
- removing punctuation marks,
- stop words, numbers and spaces and
- Lemmatizing the text using the WordNet lemmatizer present in the NLTK library.

The pre-processed text data is vectorized using tf-idf and then trained using Naive Bayes model. After the training, unigram model is used to further enhance the accuracy of the trained model.

4.2 Implementing Fake News Detector

As per the proposed methodology, next step is to create a Fake news detector to detect fake news. A bi-directional LSTM based approach is used for a better outcome. We have used open-source platform Tensor flow and deep learning library KERAS to implement the same. The fake news dataset is transformed into data frame. For better visualization, we have removed all the rows which had null values. Other column information like 'Author', and 'clickbait' was also removed as this data is not required to make the fake news detector. 'Stop words', stemming words and split words were also removed.

Next, the categorical data is converted into numeric data with help of One Hot Encoding. To do the same, first, a vocabulary of size = 5000 was created. Further, onto representation was used followed by conversion of all the sequences in the same length which is 20. After preprocessing the data and converting it into vector form, we built a Bidirectional LSTM model. For that, three layers have been added: 'Embedding Layer', 'Bidirectional layer' and 'Dense layer'.We will split the data for training and testing, here we have used 80% of the data for testing, and the remaining 20% will be used for testing.

The dataset was divided into the batches of size 64 and the training was done on dataset in 20 epochs.

4.3 A Hybrid Model of Fake News Detection with Clickbait Detection

To find the correlation between both the labels in merged dataset, we have first applied the chi_square as the variables are binary in nature. In the chi_square method if the value p-value is less than 0.5, then the variables are correlated. The p-value has been recorded as 0.0000000018603149. Therefore, it can be concluded that both clickbait labels and fake news are correlated. Figure 7 represents a graph to visualize the relation between clickbait and fake news (Fig. 6).

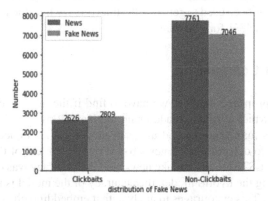

Fig. 6. Chart showing relation between fake news and clickbait

So, if the clickbait is present in the database, then there is a 52 percent chance that the news is fake and if it is not present 47% chance that it's fake news. These results are constrained due to the non-availability of a proper dataset as the amount of clickbait in this dataset is lesser than the non-clickbait headings. From this graph, it can be analyzed that chances of being fake news increase by 5% if clickbait is present.

Data cleaning has been performed by removing the rows containing null data and separating them into two data frames one containing the title, content and author's name and another containing label of fake news and clickbait. The dataset is splitted with 80% of the data for testing, and the remaining 20% for testing. We have generated the corpus from the content of the article, after removal of stop words, stemming and split the sentences into lists. This was carried out for test and train dataset. The categorical data was converted into the numeric data with help of One Hot Encoding. First, a vocabulary of size 5000 was created followed by onto representation. Then, all sequences have been converted to the fixed length of 20. To build a Bi-LSTM model, we add three layers: 'Embedding Layer', 'Bidirectional layer' and 'Dense layer'. The model was trained into batches with batch size $= 64$ in 20 epochs.

For Clickbait detection, first training and the testing dataset were pre-processed with the help of different methods such as tokenizing the text, converting it into the lowercase, removing punctuation marks, stop words, numbers and spaces and lemmatizing the text using WordNet lemmatizer present in the NLTK library.

After doing lemmatization, a frequency dictionary was generated for each word. After generating this dictionary count the number of words are counted that are occurring minimum two times in the corpus. This is used while tokenization in the "max_features" parameter. Next, TfidfVectorizer was used for converting the data into vectors. We take a parameter called "max_features" which will only take into consideration that number of features and generate vectors based on that number of features only. This will help us in increasing the accuracy of the model. The max_feature are taken as 6105.

To implement the hybrid model, first both the models were successfully executed. The resultant for both the models was two arrays of equal length containing the prediction of clickbait and fake news. This helped in knowing clickbait is not present and there is 47% chance of the news being fake. Henceforth, in the regex equation, a weighted average approach has been used to generate the final array, where the fake news prediction accuracy is 55% and 45% for clickbait.

5   Results and Comparison

According to our proposed method, we have to find if the title is clickbait or not. The clickbait detector which we have made using the Naive Bayes and Tf-Idf while using parameters such as max_features and unigram model got us an accuracy of 83%. As our second step is to detect the fake news based on the context of the article, we have used Bidirectional-LSTM to detect fake news, and the accuracy was observed as 82.8%. While implementing the hybrid model, the accuracy of the model is increased by 1.2%, observed as 84.1%. This encourages to analyze that embedding clickbait as a parameter is beneficial for the fake news detection model's accuracy.

From the hybrid model, we observed an accuracy of 84.1% which is approx. 1.3% higher than the previous model. Table 4 presents a comparative analysis between Bi-LSTM Model and the proposed model for performance metrics such as Accuracy, Precision, Recall and F1-Score. To elaborate, Accuracy is 82.82% and 84.08 for Bi-LSTM model and Hybrid model respectively.

Table 4. Model comparison table

Sr. no.	Models	Precision		Recall		F1 score		Accuracy
		1	0	1	0	1	0	
1	Bi-LSTM Model	0.85	0.80	0.84	0.81	0.85	0.80	0.8282
2	Hybrid Model	0.86	0.80	0.84	0.82	0.85	0.81	0.8408

6 Conclusion

This work can be considered as an incremental approach to enhance the accuracy of fake news detection using Clickbait and the fake news content. Though the research is constrained by the non-availability of the combined dataset, we have successfully created a dataset and applied the proposed hybrid model on the same. Our results are encouraging as using clickbait increases the accuracy of fake news by 1–2%. In future, we would like to extend this work with inclusion of fake news detection using propagation-based methods.

References

1. Balwant, M.K.: A closer look at fake news detection: a deep learning perspective (2019). https://doi.org/10.1145/3369114.3369149
2. Abedalla, A., Al-Sadi, A., Abdullah, M.: Bidirectional LSTM based on POS tags and CNN architecture for fake news detection (2019). https://doi.org/10.1109/ICCCNT45670.2019.8944460
3. Khan, J.Y., Khondaker, M. Islam, T., Iqbal, A., Afroz, S.: A benchmark study on machine learning methods for fake news detection (2019). https://www.researchgate.net/project/A-Benchmark-Study-on-Machine-Learning-Methods-for-Fake-News-Detection
4. Chakraborty, A., Paranjape, B., Kakarla, S., Gangulyh, N.: Stop clickbait: detecting and preventing clickbaits in online news media (2016). https://doi.org/10.1109/ASONAM.2016.7752207
5. Loewenstein, G.: The psychology of curiosity: a review and reinterpretation. Psychol. Bull. **116**, 1994 (1994). https://doi.org/10.1037/0033-2909.116.1.75
6. Bourgonje, P., Schneider, J.M., Rehm, G.: DFKI GmbH from clickbait to fake news detection: an approach based on detecting the stance of headlines to articles (2017). https://doi.org/10.18653/v1/W17-4215

7. Li, Q.: Clickbait and emotional language in fake news (2019). www.ischool.utexas.edu/~ml/papers/li2019-thesis.pdf
8. Pujahari, A., Sisodia, D.S.: Clickbait detection using multiple categorization techniques. J. Inf. Sci. **47**(1), 118–1128 (2019). https://doi.org/10.1177/0165551519871822
9. Zhou, X., Jain, A., Phoha, V.V., Zafarani, R.: Fake news early detection: a theory-driven model (2019). https://www.researchgate.net/publication/332726212_Fake_News_Early_Detection_A_Theory-driven_Model
10. Bahada, P., Saxenaa,P., Kamalb, R.: Fake news detection using bi-directional LSTM-recurrent neural network (2020).https://doi.org/10.1016/j.procs.2020.01.072
11. Kaggle Community Prediction Competition. Fake News (2018). https://www.kaggle.com/competitions/fake-news/data. (As accessed on May 11, 2022)
12. Kaggle Community Prediction Competition. Clickbait news detection (2020). https://www.kaggle.com/competitions/clickbait-news-detection/data. (As accessed on May 11, 2022)
13. Oshikawa, R., Qian, J., Wang, W.Y.: A survey on natural language processing for fake news detection (2018). arXiv preprint arXiv:1811.00770
14. Poovaraghan, R.J., Priya, M.K., Vamsi, P.S.S., Mewara, M., Loganathan, S.: Fake news accuracy using naive Bayes classifier. Int. J. Recent Technol. Eng. (IJRTE) **8**(1C2), 2277–3878 (2019)
15. Bahad, P., Saxena, P., Kamal, R.: Fake news detection using bi-directional LSTM-recurrent neural network. Procedia Comput. Sci. **165**, 74–82 (2019)

Building a Multi-class Prediction App
for Malicious URLs

Vijayaraj Sundaram[(✉)] [iD], Shinu Abhi[iD], and Rashmi Agarwal[iD]

REVA Academy for Corporate Excellence, REVA University, Bangalore, India
vijayraj.cs04@race.reva.edu.inh, {shinuabhi,
rashmi.agarwal}@reva.edu.in

Abstract. The page that houses a malicious snippet that could misuse a user's computing resources, steal confidential data, or carry out other forms of assaults is known as a malicious host URL. They are generally distributed across the world wide web under various usage categories like spam, malware, phishing, etc. Although numerous methods or fixes (to identify URLs) have been developed in recent years, still cyberattacks continue to occur.

This study contributes towards implementing three tiers of the system for detection and protection from harmful URLs. The first tier focuses on evaluating the performance of discriminative features in model creation. Discriminative features are derived from URL details and *"Whois"* webpage information that helps in improving detection performance with less latency and low computational complexity. The influence of feature variation on Parametric (neural network) and non-parametric classifier detection results are assessed to narrow down to the most prominent features to be adapted in the best model for the task of identifying URLs with multi-categorization. The study reveals that non-parametric ensemble models like Light GBM, XGBoost, and Random Forest performed well with a detection accuracy of over 95%, which facilitated building a real-time detection system and differentiating multiple attack types (such as Malware, Phishing, and spam).

The second tier focuses on validation with a global database to know, if entered URL is reported as suspicious by various detection engines already. If not, it enables the user in updating the global database with URL details that are new and not reported yet. Finally, the two modules are integrated to create a web application using *Streamlit* that provides full system protection against malicious URLs.

Keywords: Multiclass classification · Malicious URLs · Ensemble learning · Nonparametric models · Prediction

1 Introduction

During the Covid phase, the predominant of our daily work transformed towards online and online platforms. This behavior continued even after covid period due to the convenience it brings to end users fulfilling their individual needs with a click away. As

I. Woungang et al. (Eds.): ANTIC 2022, CCIS 1798, pp. 455–475, 2023.
https://doi.org/10.1007/978-3-031-28183-9_32

more people, organizations, and services turn to the Internet to meet their needs, it has turned into a breeding ground for various forms of fraudulent activities [1]. Malicious attacks including phishing, spamming, and malware infection have all been carried out by adversaries using the Internet as a delivery system [2].

It can be challenging for Internet users to stay on top of the most recent dangers, frauds, viruses, malware, and other forms of malevolent activity. Cybercriminals take benefit of this situation by employing phishing webpages. Spyware, Malware, and a virus are implanted in those websites [1]. Online scams have become more prevalent, mostly as a result of malicious Uniform Resource Locators (URLs) that lead to dangerous websites. As per CISCO's report on cybersecurity threat trends for 2021, approx. 85 percent of firms have one employee who clicks on a phishing link which led to 90% of data breaches [2]. Users clicking on bad URLs are reported as the second most expensive cause of data breaches. Compromised credentials ranked 5th costliest cause of data breach in an organization [3].

Different methods are suggested to identify malevolent weblinks and detrimental content by extracting discriminative rules or features from their URLs [4, 5]. Most of the methods depend on the manual derivation of the URL features [6, 7] while other solutions used deep learning techniques to mechanize feature creation [8, 9]. Attackers bypass security countermeasures easily by using deceptive tactics. The URL-based features may not be sufficient for effective representation because they can be dynamically altered and are open to manipulation by attackers. Therefore, elements that are outside the control of attackers can increase detection accuracy and brings down false alarms.

Domain attributes are one such element that can enrich statical URL features to improve the precision of detection and a lower false alert rate. As deep learning and ensemble algorithms get powerful in reading complex patterns and getting profound insights, it brings a need to explore the adaptability of those algorithms to apply in multi-classification and detection of malevolent URLs with suitable features generated for it.

This work explores the impact of URL and domain features influence on multi-class detection accuracy of Deep Learning (DL) and ensemble models. Having the right classifier in conjunction with global knowledge bases from the web brings the double benefit of detection and protection to end users.

The four primary objectives of this study are to evaluate the performance of discriminative features derived from URL details while building a multiclassification model for detecting URLs. Explore the influence of domain feature variation on the detection result of parametric (Artificial Neural Network) and nonparametric (Ensemble) models. Build integration with a third-party tool (Virus Total) for parallel validation with various detection engines and finally build a single go-to concept web portal focusing on simplified user input for detecting malicious URLs with a basic web User Interface (UI).

The rest of the manuscript is structured as follows. Related literature works are reviewed in Sect. 2. Section 3 explains the detection system design methodology, data preprocessing, feature generation methods, and algorithm selection process for building multi-category URL classification. Section 4 explains feature visualization, performance on model detection, and development of a web predictor app. Section 5 describes the experimental outcome and discusses in detail the results. Section 6 concludes the paper and shares future work.

2 Literature Review

The identification of malicious URLs has drawn a lot of attention from researchers in recent years. The most alluring research techniques among these many techniques rely on machine learning. As a result, it is gradually becoming a common practice to use machine learning algorithms in the detection activities of fraudulent domain names [10–13].

The machine learning features are gleaned from a variety of sources, including Domain Name System (DNS) traffic, *whois* data, search engine results, and online content. The authors of [14] used a mix of google features along with static URL and host features to build ensemble models utilizing Random Forest and Multilayer Perceptron (MLP) algorithms for binary classification. The deep learning and ensemble algorithms getting powerful in reading complex patterns and getting profound insights which are explored by authors of [9, 15–17].

Web content analysis involves visiting the page and performing content analysis for detecting if the website is malicious or not. It brings a huge performance bottleneck, and it is too late to prevent an attack since URL is already opened for study. Hence methods focusing on filtering in advance explored by authors of [18] to identify highly suspect malevolent URLs in massive networks to ease the computational load on back-end systems for detecting bad URLs based on content analysis. Their solution achieved a high recall rate by utilizing simple features.

I. Qabajeh et al. focused on comparing conventional and automated anti-phishing techniques in their work. In addition to highlighting the differences, similarities, and good and bad elements of these approaches from the users' and performance perspectives, they presented methods to counteract phishing by both conventional and intelligent means [19]. Author R. S. Rao et al. built a desktop program named PhishShield that focuses on phishing page URL and Website Content in [20]. PhishShield accepts a URL as an input and returns information about whether it is a real or phishing website.

The heuristics for phishing detection include copyright content, title content, zero links in the HyperText Markup Language (HTML) body, etc. Malicious URLs in the email are detected through the reduced feature set method since hackers pose as a legitimate sender purporting to be from a legitimate institution and ask the recipient for his personal information. A training dataset of harmful phishing URLs and trustworthy URLs is taken for the classifier validation [21].

The authors proposed a machine learning-based approach using a logistic regression algorithm to identify adversaries from the URL input data in the study [22]. Their framework is evaluated further against conventional malicious URL models to measure performance in terms of time taken for training and testing the algorithms. Global Vector for Word Representation (GloVe) is used as a feature to enhance the accuracy of the ML model in detecting malevolent URLs has been proposed by [23]. Features used in their work include work vector representation which is obtained from GloVe alongside statistical cues and running n-gram on blacklists words. Thus, they achieved a prediction accuracy of 89 percent using the ANN algorithm along with GloVe features.

Hevapathige, Asela, et al. work centered on developing an ML classifier model using the Super Learner ensemble to categorize dangerous URLs in [24]. Using the dataset, they built both a binary classification model and multiclassification model which delivered an accuracy rate of 95% and a prediction rate of 96% as against multi classifiers which gave accuracy and prediction rate of 94% and 96% respectively. A Multilayer ML model is proposed for detecting malicious URL by authors in [25]. Four filters or layers are constructed in the work composing black and whitelist, Naïve Bayesian, Classification and Regression Trees (CART) Decision Tree (DT), and Support Vector Machine (SVM) classifier. This improved URL detection in terms of accuracy in their work.

The authors built a phishing webpage using FLASK for detecting harmful URLs by exploring various ML classifiers using three approaches for text feature extraction, count vectorizer, hashing Inverse Document Frequency (IDF) vectorizer, and built models with Decision Tree, K-Nearest Neighbors (KNN), Random Forest, and Logistic Regression in [26]. An accuracy of 97.5% was achieved from the model which used a hash vectorizer together with a random forest algorithm. The outcome of this work also covered building a web application using Flask to check if the entered URL is malevolent or not.

Authors T. Alsmadi, N. Alqudah et al. studied various methods used for malware detection and explored heuristic detection techniques for malware identification in their study [27]. The work reviewed extensively various features used in methods like Application Programming Interface (API) Calls, N-Grams, OpCodes, etc. and lists down in detail the disadvantages and advantages of features applied in the heuristic methods. Verma, Manisha et al. [28] present a comprehensive study and fundamental understanding of non-benevolent URL detection techniques under machine learning tasks. Authors sort and evaluate the contributions of literary works that take into account the various aspects of the issue such as feature representation, algorithm design, etc.

In conclusion, a variety of approaches have been suggested for identifying fraudulent URLs using binary classification i.e., good, or bad. For categorization, the majority of these systems use supervised-based machine learning methods. Investigations have also been done into the deep learning strategy. Very few works are done to the best of knowledge on multi-class classification of URLs.

A threat actor can cause harmful cyber-attacks by sending Malicious URLs for different purposes under various categories. To evaluate and find these URLs, one must be able to recognize them. Recognition of attack kinds is important since it enables us to respond appropriately and take relevant countermeasures against threats by understanding their nature. For instance, malware infection needs immediate response whereas spamming may be overlooked conveniently. Hence, this study focuses on the top 3 frequent and prominent attacks namely malware, spam, and phishing. The next section offers a thorough explanation of the suggested methodology.

3 Proposed Methodology

As described in much of the literature, experimental studies on certain lexical and host features including link structures that are highly discriminative in nature are not only detecting malicious URLs but also identifying various attack kinds or types (Malware, Phishing, and Spam). Hence this study adapts a large set of discriminative URL features related to link structures, textual patterns, domain information, and URL content composition. Many of these features' effectiveness needs to be explored for a good understanding of classifying URLs under various types in the context of algorithm performance.

The Artificial Neural Network (ANN) classifier which is also a parametric and non-parametric ensemble classifiers are taken into consideration in this work to examine and choose a suitable detection model to be incorporated into a web application. This is done to have better classification and to understand classifier's ability to extract effectiveness patterns from textual-based features. Figure 1 illustrates the proposed methodology for building a detection system of a web application with the integration of multiple modules.

To the best of knowledge, the novelty in this methodology is application of DL and ensemble classifiers and the use of both lexical and host features for the multi-classification of URLs. Using the Python *Streamlit* framework for building web applications and integration of Virus Total in the prediction results adds uniqueness to the solution.

3.1 Data Preprocessing and Feature Engineering

Various steps are involved in the design phase starting with data collection and pre-processing. Real-world data contains noise, errors, partial information, missing values, and other forms of corruption. Properties of the data are key for an ML model to produce accurate and exact predictions. For this study, a dataset of total of 1,06,230 URLs with various attack types of Malware, Phishing, spam, and Benign is collected from Kaggle [30]. Dataset consists of 27424 Malware URLs, 26773 Phishing URLs, 25889 Spam URLs, and 26144 benign URLs. After exploring the data through data visuals and summaries, the next step involves is to add more information to variables for increasing their significance and make them more meaningful.

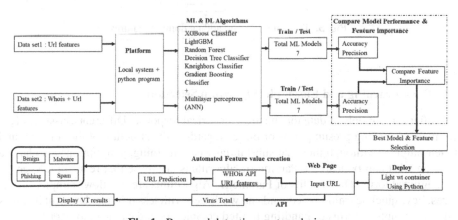

Fig. 1. Proposed detection system design

Two datasets with the difference in features are created for the study. Static lexical features are created from each URL by applying text preprocessing techniques to the raw data. Tokenization, word embedding, and term frequency methods are used in the process of feature engineering steps to generate Dataset1 with 27 features as shown in Fig. 2.

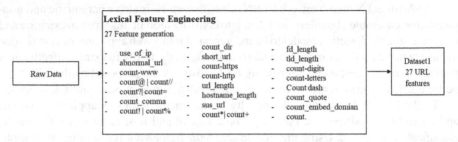

Fig. 2. Dataset1 creation with URL features

An in-house developed python program is used to collect domain registration details of each URL from the *whois* portal [31]. Information like domain registration date, expiration date, and registered nation are used to create two features relating to domain age and host country. These 2 *whois* features are added to dataset 1 to create dataset 2 illustrated in Fig. 3.

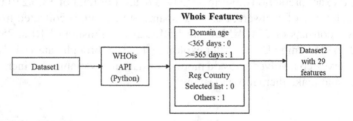

Fig. 3. Dataset2 creation adding domain features

3.2 Deep Learning and Ensemble Algorithm Selection

Classifiers are models of data that have a categorical response. Different classifier algorithms hold varying presumptions or biases regarding the structure of the function and its learnability. Although they can substantially ease learning, assumptions also have a limit on what can be learned. Parametric algorithms are those that reduce the event to a recognized form. The benefits of Parametric Algorithms are it follows simpler procedures, have quick learning speed, and can work well with less training data. But it comes with constraints in terms of handling limited complexity and can lead to poor fit.

Whereas Nonparametric algorithms are the one that does not make up any firm theories about the structure of the mapping function. They are allowed to discover any functional pattern from the training dataset because they are not making any assumptions. These classifier algorithms are able to fit a wide variety of functional forms and can lead to prediction models with greater performance. But it also comes with limitations like the demand of more data volume for training purposes and comes with the risk of overfitting the training data.

In this study, a combination of parametric and non-parametric algorithms is considered to derive a suitable model for multi-class URL detection. Multilayer perceptron (MLP) is taken for study under the parametric algorithm category which is also eventually the Artificial Neural Network (ANN) algorithm. Decision Tree (DT) classifier, K-Nearest Neighbor (KNN) Classifier, Gradient Boosting (GB) Classifier, Random Forest (RF) Classifier, Light Gradient Boosting Machine (LGBM) Classifier, and Extreme Gradient Boosting (XGBoost) Classifiers are taken for an experiment under nonparametric category. XGBoost, LGBM, GB and RF are also eventually ensemble algorithms.

3.3 Experimental Procedures and Model Performance Validation

Two datasets with differentiating features are taken for study to understand the discriminative nature of lexical and host features applicability in detecting malicious URLs and also to identify various attack types efficiently. This enabled, the analysis of the influence of feature variation on the detection result of parametric and non-parametric models that suit to be considered for building URL predictor web application. Experiments run with 7 algorithms on each dataset, to understand the discriminative nature of features. The high-level workflow of the experiment is shown in Fig. 4.

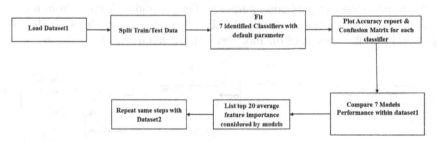

Fig. 4. High-level workflow of model experiments

The model's prediction accuracy of classes in runtime and in training are considered as model performance. It makes it noticeable for the model to show its effective exploitation of the dataset's scoring. A total of four performance, assessment metrics are considered for model validations as Accuracy rate (1), Precision (2), F1 Value (3), and Recall rate (4). False Positive, True Positive, False Negative, and True Negative are used to indicate detection findings which are abbreviated as FP, TP, FN, and TN respectively.

$$Accuracy = \frac{(TP + TN)}{TP + TN + FN + FP} \tag{1}$$

$$Precision = \frac{TP}{TP + FP} \tag{2}$$

$$F1score = \frac{TP}{TP + \frac{1}{2}(FP + FN)} \tag{3}$$

$$Recall = \frac{TP}{TP + FN} \tag{4}$$

Dataset is split into ratio 80:20 for train and test purposes. Two experiments are done using two datasets employing 7 algorithms each time. A total of 14 models are created in the study to compare the performance metrics of models. Also, the top 20 average feature importance considered by models are measured to check the list of features having the maximum impact on model performance. In experiment one with dataset1 carrying only URL lexical features, XGBoost classifiers and Random Classifier gave maximum prediction accuracy and precision rate of 95% each.

The impact of adding the *whois* feature in dataset2 is reflected in enabling additional model LGBM to provide maximum performance together with XGBoost and RF classifiers. In addition, the performance of the ANN MLP classifier increased by 1% but not equal to or exceeding the top 3 models mentioned above. It provides the inference that 29 features extracted from domain and URL links maximizes model performance accuracies.

3.4 Build Web Predictor for URL Categorization

Web application enable users to have the live user interface for the purpose it is built. In this study, a web predictor is designed to host deployed model along with 3 other modules which are integrated for prediction purposes. For generating features from user input URL, the *Whois* connector module and URL feature builder modules are developed. High-level workflow design of the modules is illustrated in Fig. 5 and Fig. 6.

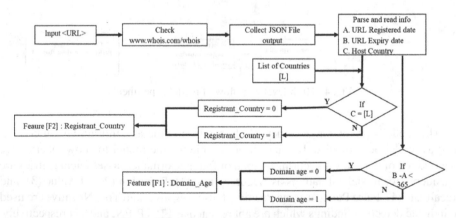

Fig. 5. *Whois* feature builder module workflow

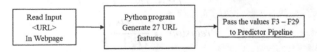

Fig. 6. URL feature builder module workflow

Virus Total (VT) web page provides free service that scans files and URLs for malware such as viruses, worms, and trojan horses. They collaborate with various antivirus organizations and researchers for utilizing scanners to provide safe internet for all users. In this work, a third module is built using a python program to ingest the URL entered in the input field of the web app and the value is passed to Virus Total for a check, consuming free tier API. The received output value is displayed in the web app. This provides a second layer of protection to end users in our solution. The workflow of this module is depicted in Fig. 7.

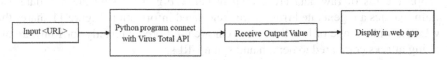

Fig. 7. Virus total module workflow

An open-source Python framework called *Streamlit* is used to create predictor web application by integrating all modules along with a machine learning model as shown in Fig. 8. Using *Streamlit*, one can quickly design and launch web applications. *Streamlit* can create apps in the same manner that one creates with Python code. Working on the interactive cycle of coding and watching outcomes on the web app is made simple by *Streamlit*.

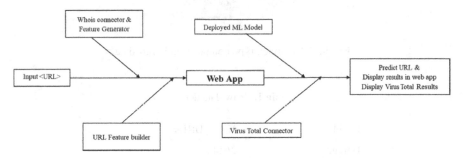

Fig. 8. URL predictor web app workflow and module integrations

3.5 Experimental Settings

The experimental setup is created using computer configuration: Windows 11, 32 GB DDR4 3200 MHz of memory, CPU AMD Ryzen™ 5 4600 H (3.00 GHz base frequency, up to Max. Boost Clock 4.0 GHz, 8 MB cache, 6 cores, 12 Threads), 256 GB PCIe® NVMe™ M.2 SSD + 1 TB HDD of hard disk; Python version:3.9.12; Anaconda Navigator, Jupyter IDLE, Scikit Learn, *Streamlit*.

4 Visualization, Performance Evaluation and Results

4.1 Datasets

Comprehensive details on the dataset are provided in this area. A publicly accessible URL dataset in Kaggle is used for this investigation. Using data visualization tools and exploratory data analysis approaches, it is understood that datasets have an equal distribution of benign, malware, phishing, and spam URLs as shared in Figure 9 and Table 1.

Top5 records of raw data are shown in below Fig. 10. Using the raw data, two domain features are generated from *whois* registered information. Figure 11 shares that new URLs with an age of less than one year are used predominantly for Malware and phishing attacks compared to benign and spam URLs.

Post-generating URL lexical features, it is inferred that a particular URL length is used for creating malware and phishing websites which is illustrated in graph Fig. 12.

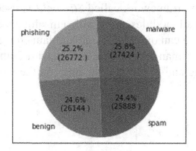

Fig. 9. URL attack type composition in raw data.

Table 1. Raw data details

Label	No. of URLs
Benign	26144
Malware	27424
Phishing	26773
Spam	25889
Total URLs: 1,06,230	

Out[7]:		url	type
	0	http://www.keve-kiserdo.hu/portal/index.php?op...	spam
	1	www.agdealer.com/keystone	phishing
	2	sbcspa.tripod.com/sbcs/	phishing
	3	hockeydraft.ca/players/profile.aspx?id=4132&na...	benign
	4	210.37.11.238/jm32/includes/site/config.bin	malware

Fig. 10. Top 5 records of raw data.

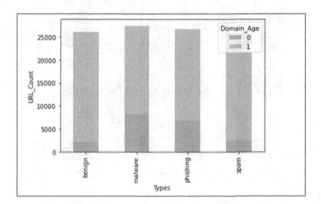

Fig. 11. URLs with age less than 365 days.

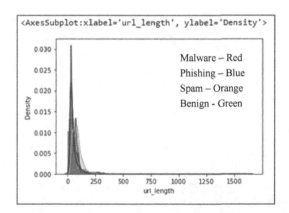

Fig. 12. URLs length as per Labels

4.2 Experiment with Lexical Features (Dataset1)

Total of 7 models are constructed using 27 URL features from Dataset 1. RF, DT, KNN, LGBM, Gradient Boost, XGBoost, and MLP classifiers are used with the default parameters as it is. Figure 13 illustrates the accuracy of all Models and Table 2 shares the performance metrics of different classifiers. Nonparametric classifiers such as XGBoost and Random Forest gave maximum accuracy and precision of 95% each.

Figure 14 depicts top 20 features which influenced model performance when using Dataset1. First directory length, hostname length, URL length, and directory counts are the top 4 features that influenced model performances. Figures 15, 16, 17, 18, 19, 20 and 21 shows the confusion matrix of various models.

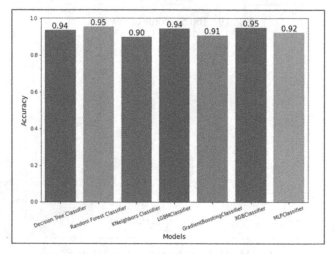

Fig. 13. Accuracy of models when using Dataset1.

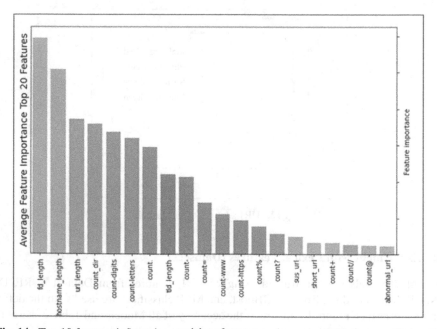

Fig. 14. Top 10 features influencing model performance when using URL features (Dataset1)

Table 2. Performance metrics of classifiers when using URL features (Dataset1).

Classifier Type	Classifier Name	Accuracy	Precision	Recall	F1
Non-parametric	DT	94%	90%	87%	89%
	RF	95%	93%	90%	91%
	KNN	90%	88%	80%	83%
	LGBM	94%	92%	88%	90%
	GB	91%	89%	81%	85%
	XGBoost	95%	93%	95%	94%
Parametric	MLP	92%	90%	82%	87%

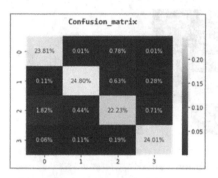

Fig. 15. XGBoost Confusion matrix

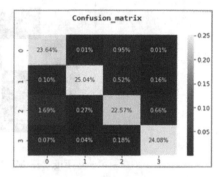

Fig. 16. RF Confusion matrix

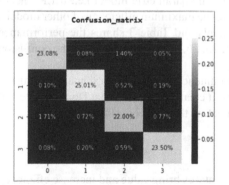

Fig. 17. DT Confusion matrix

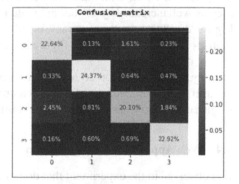

Fig. 18. KNN Confusion matrix

4.3 Experiment with Domain and Lexical Features (Dataset2)

The impact of adding two domain features along with 27 URL features are studied by employing the same list of 7 classifiers with default parameters by building seven experiment models. It resulted in increasing more model's prediction accuracy compared to

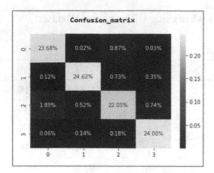

Fig. 19. LGBM Confusion matrix

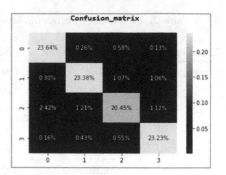

Fig. 20. GB Confusion matrix

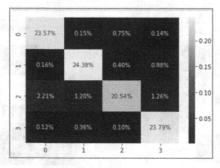

Fig. 21. MLP Confusion matrix

the experiment with Dataset 1. Again, nonparametric models like LGBM, XGBoost, and RF performed well with maximum accuracy. The parametric model i.e., MLP's accuracy as well increased by 1% but not matching the maximum efficiency of other models. Figure 22 illustrates the accuracy of all Models and Table 3 shares the performance metrics of different classifiers. Figure 23, 24, 25, 26, 27, 28 and 29 shows the confusion matrix of all models.

Figure 30 depicts top 20 features which influenced model performance when using Dataset2 i.e., with addition of *whois* features. It clearly illustrates that Domain Age and Registrant country has a relatively good impact on the model performance.

4.4 Web Application for Prediction

It is observed in the experiment that domain features bring value and increase efficiency in model prediction. Since nonparametric classifiers are performing well for multi-class classification of detecting URLs, the XGBoost model is selected for deployment along with *whois* and lexical URL features.

Streamlit is an open-source Python framework that makes it simple to develop and distribute personalized web applications for data science and machine learning. Since they reduce our technical debt by over 80%, using *Streamlit* for Machine Learning applications has shown to be more cost-effective in terms of maintenance. Hence the

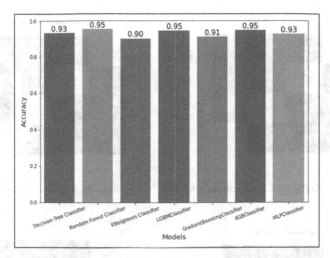

Fig. 22. Accuracy of models when using Dataset 2.

Table 3. Performance metrics of classifiers when adding whois features (Dataset2).

Classifier Type	Classifier Name	Accuracy	Precision	Recall	F1
Non-parametric	DT	93%	93%	87%	88%
	RF	95%	93%	88%	92%
	KNN	90%	88%	80%	84%
	LGBM	95%	96%	88%	91%
	GB	91%	90%	82%	86%
	XGBoost	95%	95%	96%	97%
Parametric	MLP	93%	93%	90%	89%

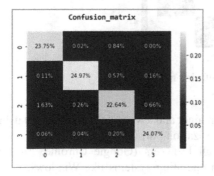

Fig. 23. RF Confusion matrix

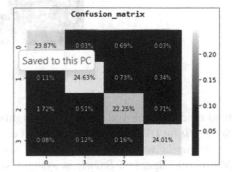

Fig. 24. LGBM Confusion matrix

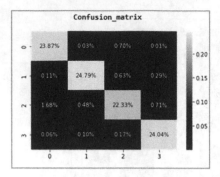

Fig. 25. XGBoost Confusion matrix

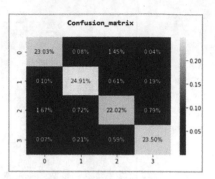

Fig. 26. DT Confusion matrix

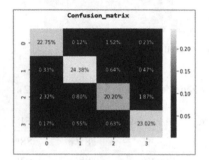

Fig. 27. KNN Confusion matrix

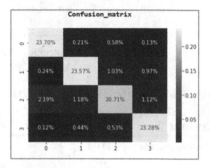

Fig. 28. GB Confusion matrix

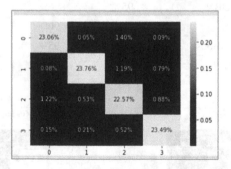

Fig. 29. MLP Confusion matrix

final model is deployed using a lightweight container and a web application is built using *Streamlit* for URL prediction and multi categorization purposes.

Streamlit web app is compatible with all browsers (Google Chrome, Firefox, Microsoft Edge, and Safari) in systems with operating systems like Windows, Unix, and macOS. Prerequisites for a web server hosting environment are Python 3.7 – 3.10 and PIP.

Virus Total connector is developed and integrated as a background service along with two feature builder modules that use domain and URL lexical information for dynamic feature creation from input URL. Figure 31 shows the web app GUI.

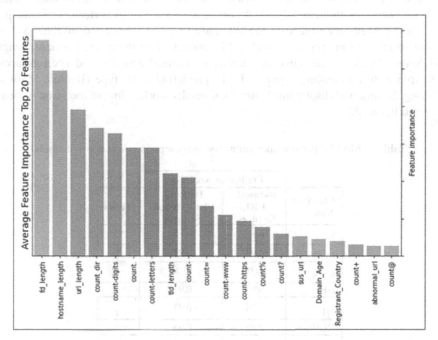

Fig. 30. Top 20 features influencing model performance when adding whois feature (Dataset2)

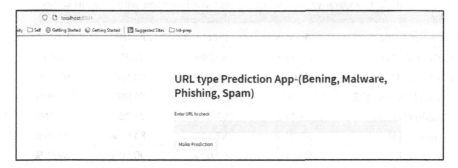

Fig. 31. URL Web Predictor Web app GUI

5   Analysis and Results

It is important to note that both the Nonparametric (ensemble) classifier LGBM and Parametric ANN classifier MLP performance increased as the data is enriched with more features. Nonparametric ensemble classifiers like XGBoost and Random Forest models demonstrate performance consistency staying high with maximum prediction accuracy for multi-classification of URLs compared to other models. A summary of the model's performance and comparison across two feature sets are illustrated with a prediction accuracy trend in Table 3. A comparative analysis of performance indicators with similar works referred to in the literature review is illustrated in Table 5. With respect to feature importance considered by models, first directory, hostname length, URL length, directory, and digit counts having maximum impact on model performances. A Simple webpage seeking input as URL, predicting URL type (Benign, Malware, Phishing, Spam), and displaying Virus Total results worked fine in the same webpage as shown in Fig. 32.

Table 4. Models' performance summary and comparison across two datasets.

| Classifier Name | Prediction Accuracy | | Trend |
	Dataset1 URL features	Dataset2 URL + Whois Features	
RF	0.95	0.95	→
LGBM	0.94	0.95	↑
KNN	0.9	0.9	→
GB	0.91	0.91	→
DT	0.94	0.93	↓
XGBoost	0.95	0.95	→
MLP	0.92	0.93	↑

Table 5. Comparative analysis of performance indicators with previous works.

Classifier Name	Accuracy	Precision	Recall	F1
Asela et al. [24]	82.37%	89.78%	58.22%	70.64%
Rohit et al. [23]	89.00%	88.00%	88.00%	92.00%
Chiramdasu et al. [22]	91.00%	62.00%	85.00%	90.00%
Eduardo et al. [9]	93.47%	93.63%	93.28%	93.46%
Chen et al. [8]	85.99%	87.19%	84.66%	85.01%
Zhao et al. [5]	90.31%	90.03%	90.00%	89.00%
Proposed work	**95.02%**	**95.04%**	**96.10%**	**96.99%**

6 Conclusion

This study proposed a unique multi-class detection App for identifying malicious URLs and classifying the same into different attack categories. The model inbuilt into the

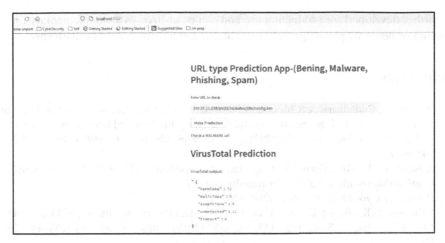

Fig. 32. URL Web Predictor Output results

app was designed and developed based on domain data obtained from the web and using acumen extracted from URL structure. Feature engineering is an important step in malicious URL detection. Each model focuses on an integrated aspect of high dimensional features, leveraging the merits of nonlinear, linear, supervised, parametric and nonparametric models.

The conducted experiments using 106230 instances of web URLs demonstrated that the proposed feature engineering methods are effective and can considerably improve the performances of few types of classifiers in identifying malicious URLs and detecting attack types. We applied six nonparametric classifiers and one parametric artificial neural network algorithm using two datasets. Total of 14 experiments was conducted and investigated. Out of all scenarios, non-parametric classifiers XGBoost, LGBM, and Random Forest models achieved the highest accuracy rate of 95% for URL prediction and XGBoost is used to build multiclass prediction module due to its consistency with high performance in varying features scenario.

This work also focused on developing another module, which validates input URL with a global database (Virus Total) if entered weblink is reported as suspicious or clean by various virus detection engines. This would provide an option to end users and it facilitates them in updating the global database with URL details that are new and not reported as malicious yet. Finally, the two modules are integrated by creating a web app using *Streamlit* and the final application provides full system protection against malicious URLs. This multiclass problem can be considered from the perspective of multilabel learning with little finetune in the methodology keeping class as malicious with labels as Malware, Phishing, and Spam.

Detecting malicious URLs needs continuous data collection, feature selection, and extraction with routine model training. Observation from the study is that DNS feature inclusion and construction of additional features from *whois* information can also be explored as a prominent future study. The predictor app which is built in the study can be further developed for production use and can be utilized as a complementary tool in existing or new anti-phishing, anti-spam, and anti-malware discovery platforms.

References

1. Acharya, J., Chuadhary, A., Chhabria, A., Jangale, S: Detecting malware, malicious URLs and virus using machine learning and signature matching. In: 2021 2nd International Conference on Emerging Technology INCET 2021, pp. 1–5. https://doi.org/10.1109/INCET51464.2021.9456440
2. Rosenthal, M.: Must-Know Phishing Statistics: Updated (2022). https://www.tessian.com/blog/phishing-statistics-2020/#phishing-by-country
3. Public, C.: Cyber security threat trends (2021)
4. Sahingoz, O.K., Buber, E., Demir, O., Diri, B.: Machine learning based phishing detection from URLs. Expert Syst. Appl. **117**, 345–357 (2019). https://doi.org/10.1016/j.eswa.2018.09.029
5. Zhao, H., Chen, Z., Yan, R.: Malicious domain names detection algorithm based on statistical features of URLs. In: 2022 IEEE 25th International Conference on Computer Supported Cooperative Work Design CSCWD 2022, pp. 11–16 (2022). https://doi.org/10.1109/CSCWD54268.2022.9776264
6. George, R., Jalal, R., Raju, R.M., Sunny, S.S., Hari, M.: High responsive plug-in for malicious URL detection. In: Proceedings of International Conference on Trends in Electronics Informatics, ICOEI 2019, pp. 357–359 (2019). https://doi.org/10.1109/ICOEI.2019.8862664
7. Li, T., Kou, G., Peng, Y.: Improving malicious URLs detection via feature engineering: linear and nonlinear space transformation methods. Inf. Syst. **91**, 101494 (2020). https://doi.org/10.1016/j.is.2020.101494
8. Chen, Y., Zhou, Y., Dong, Q., Li, Q.: A malicious URL detection method based on CNN. In: 2020 IEEE Conference on Telecommunications, Optics and Computer Science TOCS 2020, pp. 23–28 (2020). https://doi.org/10.1109/TOCS50858.2020.9339761
9. Anti-Phishing Working Group and Institute of Electrical and Electronics Engineers. Classifying Phishing URLs Using Recurrent Neural Networks
10. Choi, H., Zhu, B.B., Lee, H.: Detecting malicious web links and identifying their attack types. WebApps, no. July 2014, p. 11 (2011). http://dl.acm.org/citation.cfm?id=2002168.2002179
11. Ramesh, K., Bennet, M.A., Veerappan, J., Renjith, P.N.: Performance metric system for malicious URL data using revised random forest algorithm. In: Proceedings of the 5th International Conference on Computing Methodologies and Communication ICCMC 2021, no. ICCMC, pp. 1188–1191 (2021). https://doi.org/10.1109/ICCMC51019.2021.9418480
12. Shantanu, B.J., Arul Kumar, R.J.: Malicious URL detection: a comparative study. In: Proceedings of International Conference on Artificial Intelligent Smart System ICAIS 2021, pp. 1147–1151 (2021). https://doi.org/10.1109/ICAIS50930.2021.9396014
13. Zhang, W., Ren, H., Jiang, Q.: Application of feature engineering for phishing detection. IEICE Trans. Inf. Syst. **E99D**(4), 1062–1070 (2016). https://doi.org/10.1587/transinf.2015CYP0005
14. Alsaedi, M., Ghaleb, F., Saeed, F., Ahmad, J., Alasli, M.: Cyber threat intelligence-based malicious URL detection model using ensemble learning. Sensors **22**(9), 3373 (2022). https://doi.org/10.3390/s22093373
15. Alazab, M., Fellow, S.: Malicious URL detection using deep learning.
16. Yuan, J., Chen, G., Tian, S., Pei, X.: Malicious URL detection based on a parallel neural joint model. IEEE Access **9**, 9464–9472 (2021). https://doi.org/10.1109/ACCESS.2021.3049625

17. Simran, K., Balakrishna, P., Vinayakumar, R., Soman, K.P.: Deep learning based frameworks for handling imbalance in DGA, Email, and URL data analysis. In: Balusamy, S., Dudin, A.N., Graña, M., Mohideen, A.K., Sreelaja, N.K., Malar, B. (eds.) ICC3 2019. CCIS, vol. 1213, pp. 93–104. Springer, Singapore (2020). https://doi.org/10.1007/978-981-15-9700-8_8

18. Tan, G., Zhang, P., Liu, Q., Liu, X., Zhu, C., Guo, L.: MalFilter: a lightweight real-time malicious URL filtering system in large-scale networks. In: Proceedings of the 16th IEEE International Symposium on Parallel and Distributed Processing with Applications, 17th IEEE International Conference on Ubiquitous Computing and Communications, 8th IEEE International Conference on Big Data Cloud Computing, pp. 565–571 (2019). https://doi.org/10.1109/BDCloud.2018.00089

19. Qabajeh, I., Thabtah, F., Chiclana, F.: A recent review of conventional vs. automated cybersecurity anti-phishing techniques. Comput. Sci. Rev. **29**, 44–55 (2018). https://doi.org/10.1016/j.cosrev.2018.05.003

20. Rao, R.S., Ali, S.T.: PhishShield: a desktop application to detect phishing webpages through heuristic approach. Procedia Comput. Sci. **54**, 147–156 (2015). https://doi.org/10.1016/j.procs.2015.06.017

21. Ranganayakulu, D.: Detecting malicious URLs in E-mail – an implementation. AASRI Procedia **4**, 125–131 (2013). https://doi.org/10.1016/j.aasri.2013.10.020

22. Chiramdasu, R., Srivastava, G., Bhattacharya, S., Reddy, P.K., Gadekallu, T.R.: Malicious url detection using logistic regression (2021). https://doi.org/10.1109/COINS51742.2021.9524269

23. Bharadwaj, R., Bhatia, A., Chhibber, L.D., Tiwari, K., Agrawal, A.: Is this URL safe: detection of malicious URLs using global vector for word representation. In: Interenational Conference on Information Networking, vol. 2022, pp. 486–491 (2022). https://doi.org/10.1109/ICOIN53446.2022.9687204

24. Hevapathige, A., Rathnayake, K.: Super learner for malicious URL detection. In: ICARC 2022 - 2nd International Conference on Advanced Research in Computing Towar. a Digit. Empower. Soc., pp. 114–119 (2022). https://doi.org/10.1109/ICARC54489.2022.9753802

25. Dian zi ke ji da xue (Chengdu, Guo jia zi ran ke xue ji jin wei yuan hui (China). Institute of Electrical and Electronics Engineers. Chengdu Section, and Institute of Electrical and Electronics Engineers, MALICIOUS URL DETECTION USING MULTI-LAYER FILTERING MODEL

26. Lakshmanarao, A., Babu, M.R., Bala Krishna, M.M.: Malicious URL detection using NLP, machine learning and FLASK (2021). https://doi.org/10.1109/ICSES52305.2021.9633889

27. Alsmadi, T., Alqudah, N.: A survey on malware detection techniques. In: Proceedings of the 2021 International Conference on Information Technology ICIT 2021, pp. 371–376 (2021). https://doi.org/10.1109/ICIT52682.2021.9491765

28. Verma, M., Ganguly, D.: Malicious URL Detection using Machine Learning: A Survey arXiv: 1701.07179v3. Corr, vol. 1, no. 1, pp. 1281–1284 (2019). 10.1145/

Comparative Performance of Maximum Likelihood and Minimum Distance Classifiers on Land Use and Land Cover Analysis of Varanasi District (India)

Annu Kumari(✉) and S. Karthikeyan

Department of Computer Science, Banaras Hindu University, Varanasi 221005, India
anumanish98@gmail.com

Abstract. Monitoring the Land Use/Land Cover (LULC) changes in this present era has become the most demanding task and it is very crucial for planning, proper resource management, regulating the expansion in the fringe areas in the existing cities, etc. Now the collection of reliable data has become easier as the hyperspectral images captured by various remote sensing satellites are readily available in different spatial and spectral resolutions. Processing this data according to the Region of Interest (ROI) in order to extract meaningful information is challenging. The most crucial part of this process is to identify various land covers very accurately. Only an automatic classification provides a feasible solution, as the manual process is tedious, expensive, and time-consuming. This paper compares two different image classification algorithms in classifying the covers, which can be utilized for land use and land cover changing pattern analysis in the Varanasi district of India. The experiments were carried out with the two most popular classification algorithms, namely: The Maximum Likelihood classifier and the Minimum Distance classifier. The overall accuracy and kappa co-Efficient values computed are 41.67 and 0.12 for the Minimum Distance Classifier and 82.43 and 0.78 for the Maximum Likelihood Classifier. It has been observed that the Maximum Likelihood Classifier outperforms the Minimum Distance Classifier.

Keywords: Land use/land cover · Remote sensing image classifier · Geographic information analysis

1 Introduction

Remote sensing is the science of detecting and gaining information about the earth's surface without actually being in direct contact with it. This is done by recording the reflected and emitted radiation from the remote objects. Geographic information System (GIS) software like QGIS, ArcMap, ArcGIS, etc. are the framework that creates, processes, analyzes, oversees, and visualizes the information about a Region of Interest (ROI). In today's era, remote sensing images play a vital role in analyzing Land Use/Land Cover changes. Various techniques are implemented in remote sensing software to detect land use and land cover change patterns, which can be used for better

I. Woungang et al. (Eds.): ANTIC 2022, CCIS 1798, pp. 476–484, 2023.
https://doi.org/10.1007/978-3-031-28183-9_33

city planning in developed and developing countries. Remote sensing data collected from various satellites like MSS, LANDSAT, MODIS, LISS, etc. can be used to monitor changes in LULC patterns using GIS for proper management of natural resources [1, 2]. The remotely sensed images collected by satellites are normally in the form of multispectral images and each pixel is depicted by a spectral pattern. There are various sequential phases involved in remotely sensed image analysis: importing the image, georeferencing, subsetting the image, geometric correction, and classification of images [5]. Classification of these remotely sensed images is an important part of image analysis [3]. First, image classification techniques are used to obtain automatic pixel categorization, resulting in images with land cover classes and themes. Then, thematic mapping is done on the Region of Interest (ROI). In this remote-sensing image classification, each pixel is represented by a spectral pattern, which is further categorized on a numerical basis [4]. This paper focuses on the classification of the remotely sensed image phase of the image analysis process. Using GIS data and remote sensing, statistical techniques are used to estimate and measure Land Use Land Cover changing patterns. We consider two types of image classification processes: soft image classification and hard image classification. The object-oriented image classification techniques are based on the former one. This technique mainly deals with mixed pixels of the spatially heterogeneous character of Land Cover spreaded on the continuous surface. The images are categorized in terms of location, tone, relational and contextual information, shape, texture, etc. [16]. In this method, the investigator is provided with a measure of degree, also known as a membership grade, in which each pixel is assigned to a few or all of the candidate classes. The user is given the authority to decide to which class the pixel can be attributed. In the hard classification technique, the pixel is represented by the homogeneous area on the earth's surface and shows only the Land Cover type [17]. Each pixel is assigned exclusively to one specific class by using statistical methods. Then the thematic mapping is done on similar objects, giving a dominant scene component for each pixel.

2   Literature Review

Through supervised image classification, the pixels are categorized by specifying various numerical descriptors and then identify the land cover types. The Large Scale Biosphere-Atmosphere (LBA) Experiment was used to evaluate the regional function and determine how land use and climate modify chemical, physical, and biological processes in Amazonia [11]. New techniques were introduced, viz., Automated Monte Carlo Unmixing (AutoMCU) which had new approaches to examine land use and land cover mapping. [12] discussed how multi-scale dynamics, demand-supply relations, and human agencies can better represent land use models, which can be achieved by learning through these model evaluations. Addressing these issues, a new pathway can be outlined that generates land use models that not only allow the assessment of future models for changing patterns of land cover but also provide a sustainable solution that can stimulate the envisioning of future land use by society. [13] assessed deep learning techniques for LULC classification in Southern New Caledonia. The author democratized the satellite data and used high- performance in deep learning techniques to create data automatically. Then, deep learning configuration (viz. Pixel-wise vs. semantic labeling, data augmentation, image processing) was performed for LULC mapping in a complex and sub-tropical environment. [14] examined an accurate assignment of the tree species, that are at risk, which helps in a long-term strategy of forest conversion to a diverse, natural, and climate-resilient forest using Sentinel-2-time series data. [15] has discussed various other alternatives other than the Kappa Index. The author introduces a novel index, QADI (Quantity and Allocation Disagreement Index), that is not sensitive to asymmetric distributions.

3 Materials and Methods

3.1 Image Data Sets

The present study area is Varanasi District in India. Varanasi city is one of the oldest living cities in the world, situated on the banks of the river Ganga and is located at latitude 25 19′18.0624 N and longitude 82 59′14.2404 E. This district has an area of 1535 sq. km. The Land Use Land Cover of the Varanasi district boundary has been collected from India Topographic Sheet No.63k/12 on a scale of 1:50,000 and Google satellite is considered as the base map for the classification. The data has been obtained from the USGS (United States Geological Survey) Earth Explorer data portal and earth imagery satellite data can be downloaded at free of cost (Fig. 1 and Table 1).

Table 1. Satellite data used in this study

Satellite	Sensor	Path	Row	Date of pass	Cloud cover
LANDSAT_8	OLI_TIRS	142	42	17-03-2020	5.18

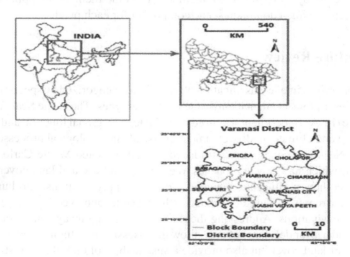

Fig. 1. Study area: Varanasi (Uttar Pradesh, India)

Landsat-8 Images from March 2020 are collected and the images pixels are classified in to 5 major classes as described below:

Class-1 as water bodies.
Class-2 as vegetation and agricultural land.
Class-3 as trees.
Class-4 as built-up.
Class-5 as roadways.

3.2   Image Data Processing

The processing of satellite data starts with collecting spatial as well as non-spatial data, putting it on a common reference system to scanned maps; seamless mosaic; digitization of error elimination, assigning ids, standardization of non-spatial data, integrating; accuracy and quality checking; and finally generating the reports.

Digital Image Processing

It is the process of analyzing the image by assigning and manipulating digital numbers to images by the computer. Digital Image Processing comprises of two process i.e. Pre-Processing of Images and Image Rectification [19].

Pre-processing of Images

Pre-processing is one of the most important phase in satellite image processing. This involves some radiometric correction, which removes the sensor errors and the environmental errors.

Image Rectification

This process is tedious and time-consuming. When new images are created, the distortion has to be removed by recalculating each and every pixel point. Geometric correction and rectification are common and important prior process to image analysis. In this present study we have used the Reference System as: Projection- UTM (Universal Transverse Mercator), Spheroid- WGS 84, Datum-WGS 84, UTM- Zone44, North.

3.3   Image Classification

Unsupervised image classification techniques are less commonly used as they do not match the maps and images produced through these methods. This results in less accuracy, hence it needs to be verified with the field truth. To overcome this drawback, the Maximum Likelihood Classification Technique and Minimum Distance Algorithm of supervised Classification are used in this paper. The Maximum Likelihood classification results are compared with the second supervised classification technique, i.e., the Minimum Distance Algorithm.

The intent of this classification is to categorize all the pixels in a form of digital images comprising one of the several land cover classes, also known as "Themes". This classified data is then used in the thematic mapping of the Region of Interest's land cover class. Here, multi-spectral data need to be classified. So the spectral data for each pixel is used as the basis for the numerical categorization [20, 21]. After the image classification, assign a unique gray level (or color) to each object or the type of land cover that actually represents the ground.

Images Classification Methods

Maximum Likelihood Classifier

The Maximum Likelihood Classification is one of the supervised Learning Algorithms that is most commonly used in Literature works [6, 7]. Considering two different classes, 'i' and 'j'. If the probability of a pixel 'X' position belonging to class 'i' is higher than that of class'j' then the pixels positioned at 'X' is assigned to class 'i' and vice –versa [8]. The Normal Distribution pattern is assigned to the input data and the discriminator for the maximum Likelihood Classification can be defined as:

$$g_i(x) = lnp(w_i) - \frac{1}{2}(x - m_i)^t c_i^{-1}(x - m_i) \tag{1}$$

where,

$g_i(x) = i^{th}$ class discriminant function
$p(w_i) = $ Probability that w_i has occurred
$x = $ A pixel's n-dimensional matrix of digital number value (here n is the total number of bands)
$m_i = $ Mean Vector
$C_i = $ Determinant of Class i's Covariance Matrix
$t = $ transpose of the base matrix

Minimum Distance Classifier

This method also uses supervised classification training techniques that use the center point to represent a specific class in the training set. The class is determined by calculating the Euclidean distance between the center of gravity and the pixel values. The class is assigned to the pixel which is the shortest distance from that class [9].

The Minimum Distance can be calculated as:

$$Min.Dist. = \sqrt{(Dv - M)^2} \tag{2}$$

where,

$Dv \rightarrow$ Digital value of each pixel
$M \rightarrow$ Mean Value of each class

4   Experimental Results and Discussions

Accuracy assessment is the final stage of the image classification process. It is the process of mapping the quantification of remote sensing data to a group classification on the basis of terms and conditions. Accuracy assessment is one of the best techniques to determine the level of error that might have occurred within the classification of images. Accuracy can be computed in the form of an Error Matrix [10].

An error matrix comprises a square array of numbers in which, the rows express the class to which the informational categories have been classified and the columns, represent the informational categories. The sum of the main diagonal elements is expressed in terms of the overall agreement of the classification. When a test area cannot be classified into an informational category, then an omission error might occur. The Commission error occurs when the test area is classified into a different informational category rather than its true category. Thus, information about these types of errors is represented by user accuracy and producer accuracy, respectively. The test area of the same size as training areas are assigned to determine the class of the test area. The overall accuracy and the Kappa statistics are measured by the image classification techniques with the ground truth. Traditionally, the accuracy assessment is done by generating a random polygon set of locations and visiting the ground to verify the actual true land cover type. Then a simple value file is recorded for the true Land over Class (w.r.t. index integer type no.) for each of these locations. Then this value file is used with the vector file of the polygon set of locations, to create the raster image of true classes found for the location to examine. Then this raster image is compared to that of the classified map with the help of the Error Matrix. The Error Matrix is tabulated and comprises the relationship between the true actual land class cover type and the classes mapped. This information is used in assessing the accuracy of the classification, which enhances the supervised classification.

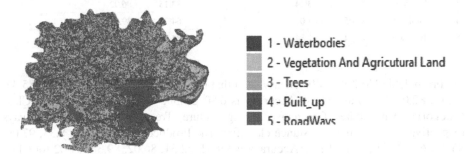

Fig. 2. Maximum likelihood image classification

The description about the legends shown in the above figures Fig. 2 and Fig. 3 are:

- The Blue Color indicates the water bodies (Class-1) which includes rivers, ponds & lakes.
- The Yellow Color signifies the vegetation and agricultural land (Class-2).
- The Green Color signifies trees (Class-3).
- The Red Color signifies built-up areas (Class-4).
- The Purple Color signifies the roadways (Class-5) (Table 2).

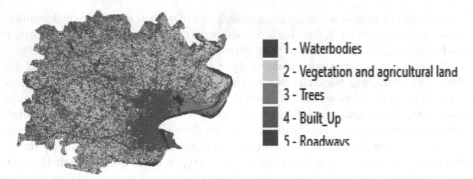

1 - Waterbodies

2 - Vegetation and agricultural land

3 - Trees

4 - Built_Up

5 - Roadways

Fig. 3. Minimum distance image classification

Table 2. Comparative Performance of Minimum Distance and Maximum Likelihood Methods

Sl.No	Classes	Image Classification Methods							
		Minimum Distance Method				Maximum Likelihood Method			
		Producers Accuracy (%)	Users Accuracy (%)	Overall Accuracy (%)	Overall Kappa	Producers Accuracy (%)	Users Accuracy (%)	Overall Accuracy (%)	Overall Kappa
1	Waterbodies	01.17	06.80	41.67	0.12	08.33	99.82	82.43	0.78
2	Green cover & agriculture	85.47	53.39			97.06	92.31		
3	Trees	77.42	43.14			83.15	86.02		
4	Built-up	82.05	67.01			64.73	89.38		
5	Roadways	72.14	41.84			82.39	84.02		

From Table No 2 it can be clearly seen that the Producers Accuracy is 1.17, 85.47, 77.42, 82.05, 72.14 and Users Accuracy is 6.80, 53.39, 43.14, 67.01, 41.84 for Class Categories Waterbodies, Greencover & Agriculture, Trees, Built-ups and Roadways respectively for Minimum distance classifier. The Producers Accuracy is 8.33, 97.06, 83.15, 64.73, 82.39 and Users Accuracy is 99.82, 92.31, 86.02, 89.38, 84.02 for Class Categories Waterbodies, Greencover & Agriculture, Trees, Built-ups and Roadways respectively for Maximum Likelihood Classifier. The Overall accuracy is 41.67 and the Kappa Co-efficient Value is 0.12 for Minimum Distance classifier. The Overall Accuracy is 82.43 and the Kappa Co-efficient value is 0.78 for Maximum Likelihood Classifier. Thus, the above values demonstrate that Overall accuracy and Overall kappa co-efficient values are performed well in the Maximum Likelihood method when compared to that of the Minimum Distance method.

5   Conclusion

This paper analyses the dynamics of Land Use Land Cover Changes for the Varanasi District of Uttar Pradesh in India using Geographical Information Systems (GIS) and Remote

Sensing Tools. The experimental results show that Maximum Likelihood Method yields more precise and accurate performance as compared to the Minimum Distance Method. Further studies can be carried out [18] using the Mahalanobis Distance-and Kernel based Method for spectral dimensionality reduction in hyperspectral images of remote sensing.

References

1. Gregorio, D.: Antonio, and Louisa JM Jansen : A new concept for a land cover classification system. The Land **2**(1), 55–65 (1998)
2. Rutherford, H.: Platt : Land Use and Society: Geography, law, and public policy, 1st edn. Island Press, Washington, DC (2014)
3. Anderson, James Richard : A land use and land cover classification system for use with remote sensor data. 964,. US Government Printing Office (1976)
4. Li, Feng, Xiuping Jia, and Donald Fraser :"Super resolution reconstruction of multispectral data for improved image classification, In: IEEE Geoscience and Remote Sensing Letters 6(4), 689–693(2009)
5. Boucher, A., Kyriakidis, P.C.: Super-resolution land cover mapping with indicator geostatistics. Remote Sens. Environ. **104**(3), 264–282 (2006)
6. Yiğit, Abdurahman Yasin, and Murat Uysal. "NesneTabanlıSınıflandırmaYaklaşımı KullanılarakYollarınTespiti. Türkiye FotogrametriDergisi1(1) 17–24 (2019)
7. Özkan, Coşkun, and Filiz Sunar Erbek. : The comparison of activation functions for multispectral Landsat TM image classification. Photogrammetric Engineering & Remote Sensing 69(11), 1225–1234 (2003)
8. Sisodia, Pushpendra Singh, Vivekanand Tiwari, and Anil Kumar.: Analysis of supervised maximum likelihood classification for remote sensing image. In : International conference on recent advances and innovations in engineering (ICRAIE-2014). IEEE, (2014)
9. Sathya, P., and V. Baby Deepa.: Analysis of supervised image classification method for satellite images. International Journal of Computer Science Research (IJCSR) 5(2), 16–19 (2017)
10. Caprioli, Mauro, and Eufemia Tarantino.: Accuracy assessment of per-field classification integrating very fine spatial resolution satellite imagery with topographic data. Journal of Geospatial Engineering 3(2), 127–134 (2001)
11. Roberts, Dar A., Michael Keller, and Joao Vianei Soares.: Studies of land-cover, land-use, and biophysical properties of vegetation in the Large Scale Biosphere Atmosphere experiment in Amazônia. Remote Sensing of Environment 87(4), 377–388 (2003)
12. Verburg, Peter H., et al.: Beyond land cover change: towards a new generation of land use models. Current Opinion in Environmental Sustainability 38, 77–85 (2019)
13. Rousset, G., et al.: Assessment of deep learning techniques for land use land cover classification in southern new Caledonia. Remote Sensing 13(12), 2257. (2021)
14. Welle, T., et al.: Mapping dominant tree species of German forests. Remote Sensing **14**(14), 3330 (2022)
15. Feizizadeh, B., et al.: QADI as a new method and alternative to kappa for accuracy assessment of remote sensing-based image classification. Sensors **22**(12), 4506 (2022)
16. Foody, G.M.: The role of soft classification techniques in the refinement of estimates of ground control point location. Photogramm. Eng. Remote. Sens. **68**(9), 897–904 (2002)
17. Foody, G.M., Mathur, A.: The use of small training sets containing mixed pixels for accurate hard image classification: training on mixed spectral responses for classification by a SVM. Remote Sens. Environ. **103**(2), 179–189 (2006)

18. Çakmakçı, S.D., et al.: Online DDoS attack detection using Mahalanobis distance and Kernel-based learning algorithm. J. Netw. Comput. Appl. **168**, 102756 (2020)
19. Hall, E.L., et al.: A survey of preprocessing and feature extraction techniques for radiographic images. IEEE Trans. Comput. **100**(9), 1032–1044 (1971)
20. Singh, S.K., Kumar, V., Kanga, S.: Land use/land cover change dynamics and river water quality assessment using geospatial technique: a case study of Harmu river, Ranchi (India). Int. J. Sci. Res. Comput. Sci. Eng. **5**(3), 17–24 (2017)
21. Singh, S.K.: Geospatial technique for land use/land cover mapping using multi-temporal satellite images: a case study of Samastipur District (India). Environ. We an Int. J. Sci. Technol. **11**(4), 75–85 (2016)

Recent Trends and Open Challenges in Blind Quantum Computation

Mohit Joshi[✉], S. Karthikeyan, and Manoj Kumar Mishra

Department of Computer Science, Institute of Science, Banaras Hindu University,
Varanasi 221005, India
joshi.mohit1221@gmail.com

Abstract. Quantum mechanics with radically novel properties: such as superposition, entanglement, and the no-cloning theorem, has begun to open up Quantum Computation beyond the scope of Classical Computation. In recent years, quantum technology has seen tremendous leaps both in academic research and commercial exploration. Quantum computation has started to find applications in many more new domains every day, from disrupting modern cryptography to enabling unconventional security techniques, from quantum chemistry to physical simulations, and from quantum machine learning to financial optimization. This paper first provides the conceptual groundings of quantum computation and explores blind quantum computation, a one-of-its-kind sub-categorization of quantum computing active research. The use of Blind Quantum Computation in Quantum Cryptography is elaborated in detail. Finally concludes with highlights of the applicability of the subject. The paper is an easy-to-follow guide introducing the research trends and open challenges for the new researcher in follow-up on the field.

Keywords: Blind quantum computing · Delegated quantum computing · Quantum cryptography

1 Introduction

Computational science has always been revolutionized by improvements in the understanding of fundamental physics, right from the early days of vacuum tubes to transistor technology and now in the era of advanced fabrication of integrated nano-electronics. The unprecedented success of quantum theories in understanding the physical behaviour of fundamental particles has yet again provided the opportunity for such a kind of evolution in computational techniques. With the announcement of the Nobel Prize in physics in 2022 for the experimental advancements in the field of quantum information science, it is now evident that quantum mechanics has profoundly impacted the founding grounds of computation science. This time the evolution is not just in hardware fabrication but the non-intuitive properties of quantum mechanics have also paved the way for a dynamic rotation of our algorithmic approaches toward practical problem-solving by introducing the statistical nature of inherent physics.

I. Woungang et al. (Eds.): ANTIC 2022, CCIS 1798, pp. 485–496, 2023.
https://doi.org/10.1007/978-3-031-28183-9_34

The idea of using quantum systems for computation emerged, from the impossibility of efficient simulation of certain quantum phenomena on classical simulators [9], and from the possibility of formalizing a quantum mechanical model of Turing computable functions [2]. The theoretical strides were made with the findings of polynomial time integer factorization algorithm [36] in 1994, and quadratic speed up on unordered searching [13] in 1996.

DiVincenzo criteria [8] was proposed in 2000, which laid the principles for the proposal of candidates for a quantum system. This has produced varied contenders in the race to realise fault-tolerant quantum systems like nuclear magnetic resonance, nitrogen-vacancy center in a diamond atom, semiconductor quantum transistors, superconducting qubits, photon polarization, and trapped ions with ytterbium atoms [15]. Although a fault-tolerant quantum computer is still in far sight, commercial zeal has throttled us in the era of Noisy-Intermediate-Scale-Quantum computation (NISQ) [30]. With the open-source quantum simulators and public availability of commercial quantum devices in the cloud, the NISQ era is now taking advantage of the rapid development of hardware and software stack [10]. Quantum availability has proven to be the testbed for fascinating discoveries of applications in the field. The hardware development of quantum computation has sprung upon varied approaches to computation, viz-a-viz the gate model of computation, adiabatic computation, quantum annealers, and measurement-based quantum computation.

The paper gives an introduction to quantum computing principles in Sect. 2 to be self-contained. Blind quantum computation and its techniques are discussed in brief in Sect. 3 and also introduce the trends of BQC, its application, and open problems in the field.

2 Preliminaries

The demarcation of fundamental features of elementary particles from the macroscopic world gives rise to the mathematical description of reality, which is fundamentally probabilistic in nature. The components of classical electronics are either particle-like or wave-like in nature but not both, whereas elementary particles can exhibit both particle and wave-nature simultaneously depending on the type of interaction. The former bifurcates the boundary of digital and analog computers in the classical paradigm, and the latter promises the exponential processing space with the fault tolerance of digital techniques, hence combining the best of both worlds. This theoretical opportunity accounts for the possible advantage of quantum algorithms over classical counterparts. Quantum systems are described by their wave function, given by Schrodinger's wave equation. These wave functions represent the state of the system and computation can be performed by evolving such systems using controlled transformation where measuring the system collapses the wave function. The statistical nature of wave function is manifested in quantum consequences like interference, superposition, entanglement, and tunneling, which do not have any classical analogue.

Quantum computation is hence the branch of computation that harness quantum mechanical principles to establish some algorithmic advantage over its classical counterpart, because of its inherent statistical nature [36] [13]. Quantum bits are the probabilistic representation of information in a special type of complex vector space, called Hilbert space where the state of a qubit represents the probability of finding it in the experiment. For instance, the space for a one-dimensional quantum system can be represented by column vector of $(a_0 \ a_1)^T$ and quantum analogous to classical bit $|0\rangle$ and $|1\rangle$ states can be given as $(1 \ 0)^T$ and $(0 \ 1)^T$, respectively. It is worthwhile to note that row and column vectors are conveniently represented by Dirac notation in the discussions of quantum computation where $\langle.|$ and $|.\rangle$ are respective bracket notation of row and column vectors. Hence, the matrix representation of a two-dimensional quantum system with state $(1 \ 0 \ 0 \ 0)^T$ is ket notation of form $|00\rangle$.

A grave demarcation of properties from classical computation is shown by these qubits in the principle of superposition which permits any linear combination of two or more state vectors as another valid state vector in the given Hilbert space. The mathematical expression for the principle is

$$|\psi\rangle = \begin{pmatrix} \alpha \\ \beta \end{pmatrix} = \alpha|0\rangle + \beta|1\rangle$$

where $\alpha, \beta \in \mathbb{C}$ represent the amplitude of the respective basis component and should follow Born's rule as $|\alpha|^2 + |\beta|^2 = 1$. This validates the intermediate states between $|0\rangle$ and $|1\rangle$ and hence opens exponential space of computation. For instance, $|+\rangle$ is a representation of famous superposition vector $\left(\frac{1}{\sqrt{2}} \ \frac{1}{\sqrt{2}} \right)^T$. Some famous superposition states are given below,

$$|-\rangle = \begin{pmatrix} \frac{1}{\sqrt{2}} \\ \frac{-1}{\sqrt{2}} \end{pmatrix} = \frac{|0\rangle - |1\rangle}{\sqrt{2}}$$

$$i|+\rangle = \begin{pmatrix} \frac{1}{\sqrt{2}} \\ \frac{i}{\sqrt{2}} \end{pmatrix} = \frac{|0\rangle + i|1\rangle}{\sqrt{2}}$$

$$i|-\rangle = \begin{pmatrix} \frac{1}{\sqrt{2}} \\ \frac{-i}{\sqrt{2}} \end{pmatrix} = \frac{|0\rangle - i|1\rangle}{\sqrt{2}}$$

For visual understanding, the superposition states are represented as vectors in the Bloch sphere, which is a three-dimensional method of qubit representation, parameterized by γ, δ, θ. The wavefunction is then represented as $|\psi\rangle = cos(\frac{\theta}{2})|0\rangle + e^{i\varphi} sin(\frac{\theta}{2})|1\rangle$ where $\alpha = e^{i\gamma} cos(\frac{\theta}{2})$, $\beta = e^{i\delta} sin(\frac{\theta}{2})$, $\varphi = \delta - \gamma$.(Note: We neglect complex global phase in the above formula because it do not effect the projection of result to real values). Figure 1 shows the visual representation of Bloch sphere.

The exponential space of computation is not translated into exponential outcomes as the act of measurement in quantum computing is essentially a projection operator which collapses the wave function along the orthogonal subspace of state. It is only an irreversible operator present in the quantum domain.

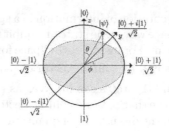

Fig. 1. The Bloch sphere representation of qubit. The conventional choice of basis for computation is z-basis in the Bloch sphere where $|0\rangle$ and $|1\rangle$ are at the opposite end. [16]

The effect of measurement is an inherently probabilistic phenomena where the outcome is dependent on the square of the amplitude of the given component. The mathematical evaluation for finding the probability of $|0\rangle$ in a given wavefunction $|\psi\rangle = \alpha|0\rangle + \beta|1\rangle$ are given as below,

$$prob(|0\rangle) = |\langle 0|\psi\rangle|^2$$
$$= (\alpha\langle 0|\rangle) + \beta\langle 0|1\rangle)^2$$
$$= |\alpha|^2$$

With two or more qubits in a quantum system, a very peculiar property starts to emerge in the computation, which is deemed as "spooky action at a distance" by Einstein himself. This is the entanglement of qubits, which is a special type of superposition where the collective state cannot be represented as individual constituents i.e. $|\psi\rangle \neq |\psi_1\rangle|\psi_2\rangle$. In a two qubit system, there can be four entanglement states, also called bell pairs, that are symbolically represented as $|\phi_+\rangle = \frac{1}{\sqrt{2}}(|00\rangle + |11\rangle)$, $|\phi_-\rangle = \frac{1}{\sqrt{2}}(|00\rangle - |11\rangle)$, $|\psi_+\rangle = \frac{1}{\sqrt{2}}(|01\rangle + |10\rangle)$, $|\psi_-\rangle = \frac{1}{\sqrt{2}}(|01\rangle - |10\rangle)$.

The power and limitations of quantum computation are better understood in terms of impossibility results emerging from the underlying principle of quantum mechanics. The first impossibility result states that a system with n qubits can have 2^n bits equivalent computational space, but only n bits of information can be extracted after computation as the operation of measurement collapses the probability wave function. The second impossibility result comes from the no-cloning theorem, which states that no arbitrary quantum state can be cloned, i.e. there exists no unitary transformation such that $U|\psi, 0\rangle = |\psi, \psi\rangle$. The third impossibility result is the reversibility of quantum operation except measurement which implies that there exists no unitary V such that $V|x, 0, 0\rangle = |x, f(x), g(x)\rangle$i. e. that there is a one-to-one correspondence between the input and output. This introduces the need of including extra qubits in input, which are called ancilla and the result has some extra garbage qubits.

Any quantum algorithm is evolved as a sequence of unitary operations on them in a predefined sequence. The Hadamard gate is among the most important single qubit unitary, which transforms the qubit $|0\rangle$ and $|1\rangle$ into the respective superposition state of $|+\rangle$ and $|-\rangle$. The rotation gates are another set of crucial gates in quantum computing. These include the Pauli rotation gate that rotates the qubit around the three standard axis X, Y, Z with 180°, and special S and T gate which are 90° and 45° around z-axis, respectively. The matrix notation for these gates is given below,

$$X = \begin{pmatrix} 0 & 1 \\ 1 & 0 \end{pmatrix}, \quad Y = \begin{pmatrix} 0 & -i \\ i & 0 \end{pmatrix}$$
$$Z = \begin{pmatrix} 1 & 0 \\ 0 & -1 \end{pmatrix}, \quad H = \frac{1}{\sqrt{2}} \begin{pmatrix} 1 & 1 \\ 1 & -1 \end{pmatrix}$$

Apart from single qubit rotation, some famous multi-qubit rotation gates include the controlled-not gate, abbreviated as CX, whose operation is to apply a NOT operation on a target qubit if the control qubit is active, and the controlled-controlled-not gate, abbreviated as CCX, which has similar functionality in a three-qubit setting.

3 Quantum Cryptography

The advantage of using quantum techniques was first and most profoundly visible in the field of cryptography. With the likes of Shor's [36] and Grover's [13] algorithm, the foundation of classical cryptography was shaken. But quantum computing can not be viewed only as a threat to classical cryptography and should be looked upon as an opportunity that has sprung upon varied unconventional feats impossible in classical cryptography. . Quantum Cryptography has become a broad term for describing the umbrella which branches into quantum key distribution, quantum secure direct communication, semi-quantum cryptography, secure function computation, device-independent cryptography, blind quantum computation, quantum signature, quantum coin flipping, position-based quantum computing, and others [18]. The unique advantage of quantum computing in cryptography is due to their reliance on the underlying statistical nature of physics, which helps them to promise information-theoretic security when modern classical systems are computationally secure at best [4]. Research is also exploring non-quantum alternative for security under the broad category of Post-Quantum cryptography [3].

3.1 Blind Quantum Computation

The security of data has been the topic of research since the dawn of information passing. In the cloud infrastructure, in addition to data, the propriety algorithm has also become a valuable asset that needs to be protected. Due to the properties of quantum computing, early research has now shown promise in securing the computation along with the input and output, a feat that was unheard of in classical cryptography.

In a client-server scheme, blind quantum computation (BQC) is used with a limited resource client to delegate his quantum operations to a remote, sufficiently large quantum server. BQC ensures the safety of the client's input, output, and operation. The most idealistic version of BQC requires a completely classical client and only a single fault-tolerant quantum computer, which has been shown to be impossible without a trusted third party in Ref. [29]. In a realistic situation, a client at least requires quantum memory or access to a quantum channel for a computation protocol to be sufficiently blind.

In a client-server scheme, blind quantum computation (BQC) is used with a limited resource client to delegate his quantum operations to a remote, sufficiently large quantum server. BQC ensures the safety of the client's input, output, and operation. The most idealistic version of BQC requires a completely classical client and only a single fault-tolerant quantum computer, which has been shown to be impossible without a trusted third party in Ref. [29]. In a realistic situation, a client at least requires quantum memory or access to a quantum channel for a computation protocol to be sufficiently blind.

3.2   Single-Server Protocols

First, blind quantum computation protocol was proposed by A. Childs in 2005 [7], which was a circuit-based scheme that required the client to have quantum memory and the ability to perform Pauli operations on qubits. The term blind quantum computation was first used in the work of Arrighi and Pablo [1] who proposed a scheme where clients only need to prepare and measure entangled states.

The first universally blind quantum computing (UBQC) protocol was given in 2009 by Broadbent, Fitzsimons, and Joseph [5], and is popularly known as the BFK protocol. It is based on the measurement-based quantum computing model given by Raussendorf and Briegel [33] which is a model of computing where computation is performed on highly entangled qubit states, called cluster state, and measurement is used to derive the output. UBQC is based on a special type of cluster state, called a brickwork state, and here the client only needs to be able to prepare rotated single-qubit states.

Many variation of these protocols were proposed for different models of quantum computation like Blind Topological computation [25], BQC with teleportation-based computation [6], Continuous-Variable Blind Quantum Computation [23] and ancilla-driven blind quantum computation [37].

In 2013, Morimae et al. presented a blind quantum computation, where the client is only needed to make single-qubit measurements [26]. This protocol achieved several feats by making the UBQC device independent and more secure using the no-signaling principle which is more fundamental than quantum physics. He then showed composable security through the formalism of constructive cryptography in 2018 [28].

3.3 Multi-server Protocols

In an attempt to make the client completely classical, a double server blind quantum computation was proposed using secure entanglement distillation [27]. In this protocol, servers can't communicate with each other to make the client completely classical. Li et al. solved the communication problem using entanglement swapping in 2014 and proposed a triple server protocol where servers can communicate but the client is almost classical with just the ability to access quantum channel [20]. Kong generalized the protocol to multiple servers with the ability to be resilient in the loss of one or more servers during computation [17].

3.4 Verification in Blind Quantum Computation

The problem to verify the computation of Bob had been an open question until Morimae resolved it in 2014 [24] for his protocol of measurement-only client BQC. A simpler protocol of verifiable measurement-only Blind Quantum Computation was presented by Hayashi et al. in 2015 [14] using stabilizer states. Gheorghiu addressed key problems in the experimental implementation of verifiable blind quantum computation [12] Hajdusek proposes a reduced overhead device-independent approach of blind quantum computation using Bell state self-testing with complexity of $O(m^4 \ln m)$ where m is the number of gates. Fitzsimons and Kashefi provided an unconditionally verifiable extension to their universal blind scheme (BFK), allowing clients to detect malicious servers with polynomial overhead [11]. It is still an open problem to establish a conceptual link between blindness and an interactive proof system for verifying high-complexity quantum-theoretic models with a low-complexity classical verifier.

3.5 Authentication in Blind Quantum Computation

Without authenticating the identity of the client, the server may fall prey to threats like man-in-the-middle attacks or denial-of-service attacks. This was solved by Li et al. in 2017 with the introduction of two new quantum-identifiable protocols for single and double servers [19]. Shan et al. in 2021 gave a multi-party blind quantum computation based on measurement device-independent quantum key distribution (MDI-QKD) and certificate authority (CA) [34].

3.6 Circuit-Based Blind Quantum Computation

Child's blind quantum computation protocol was a circuit-based protocol [7] to delegate his operation on a powerful server. Arrighi and Salvail's protocol was also on a circuit-based model [1]. Tan et al. in 2017 proposed a half-blind quantum computing protocol, HDQC which was based on set {H, P, CX, T}. It secured the clients' input and output but not the computation [39]. Liu et al. proposed a full-blind delegated quantum computing scheme using a fixed set of operations (H, P, CZ, CX, CCX) [22].

3.7   Hybrid Models of Computation

The two major models of computation for Blind Quantum Computation are Measurement-based-blind-quantum-computation and Circuit based blind quantum computation. Both models comes with unique advantage and disadvantages. Measurement based BQC usually need large-scale cluster states to delegate the secure computation and circuit based BQC has precise but probabilistic gates. In 2019, Zhang et al. proposed the first hybrid model of computation that tries to resolve probabilistic entanglement in measurement-based and circuit-based blind quantum computing, by combining the operation of both models. [41]. It operates be differentiating rotation and controlled-NOT operation to circuit-based and measurement-based BQC, respectively. Zheng et al. in 2020, [40] divided the computation in two phase where quantum computation, where first phase does the unitary operations and second phase client send auxiliary qubits to carry out gate teleportation.

3.8   Application of Blind Quantum Computing in Newer Domains

In 2012, Barz et al. gave the first demonstrative proof of unconditionally secure quantum computation using measurement-based quantum computation. Using BQC, Barz in 2013, provided an experimental verification protocol for verifier with the minimal quantum resource. In 2014, Fisher et al. did an experimental demonstration of bqc using single photons and linear optics. In 2017, Huang et al. first gave a security demonstration for a completely classical client with access to a quantum channel. It was based on Clauser-Home-Shimony-Holt (CHSH) test and stabilizer states for verification. In recent years, blind quantum computing has started to see various applications in other domains of computation. Major among them are quantum two-party communication [38,43] , quantum multiparty communication [31], blind quantum signature [35], blind quantum machine learning [42], quantum federated learning [21], quantum blind fog computing [32].

4   Conclusion

The rapid advancement in the algorithmic context of quantum computing has started to touch on computationally heavy problems. With the increase of cloud quantum computing infrastructure, security has become of paramount importance. The field of quantum cryptography is rapidly evolving into sub-branches of varied potential. The theoretical discoveries have allowed the field to show promising preliminary results. Among the various domains in quantum cryptography, secure quantum computing has shown a promise of more secure, verifiable, and authenticated networks, analogue of which is not present in the classical domain. Blind Quantum computation is one among many sub-branches of quantum cryptography which enables the limited resource client to delegate his computation on remote powerful quantum server. This protocol is now seeing application from varied branches of practical problems like interactive proof, secure two-party and multi-party computation, quantum signature and many more. The applicability of blind quantum computation is still ongoing research and new leaps are being made every year.

Acknowledgements. This research is supported by seed grant under IoE, BHU[grant no. R/Dev/D/IoE/SEED GRANT/2020-21/Scheme No. 6031].

References

1. Arrighi, P., Salvail, L.: Blind quantum computation. Int. J. Quant. Inf. **04**(05), 883–898 (2006). ISSN 0219–7499, 1793–6918. https://doi.org/ 10.1142/S0219749906002171, https://www.worldscientific.com/doi/abs/10.1142/ S0219749906002171

2. Benioff, P.: Quantum mechanical hamiltonian models of turing machines. J. Stat. Phys. **29**(3), 515–546 (1982). ISSN 0022–4715, 1572–9613. https://doi.org/10. 1007/BF01342185

3. Bernstein, D.J., Lange, T.: Post-quantum cryptography. Nature **549**(7671), 188–194 (2017). ISSN 0028–0836, 1476–4687. https://doi.org/10.1038/nature23461. http://www.nature.com/articles/nature23461

4. Broadbent, A., Schaffner, C.: Quantum cryptography beyond quantum key distribution. Des. Codes Cryptogr. **78**(1), 351–382 (2016). ISSN 0925–1022, 1573–7586. https://doi.org/10.1007/s10623-015-0157-4

5. Broadbent, A., Fitzsimons, J., Kashefi, E.: Universal blind quantum computation. In: 2009 50th Annual IEEE Symposium on Foundations of Computer Science, Atlanta, GA, USA, pp. 517–526. IEEE (2009). ISBN 978-1-4244-5116-6. https:// doi.org/10.1109/FOCS.2009.36. http://ieeexplore.ieee.org/document/5438603/

6. Chia, N.H., Chien, C.H., Chung, W.H., Kuo, S.Y.: Quantum blind computation with teleportation-based computation. In: 2012 Ninth International Conference on Information Technology - New Generations, Las Vegas, NV, USA, pp. 769–774 (2012). IEEE. ISBN 978-0-7695-4654-4. https://doi.org/10.1109/ITNG.2012.149. http://ieeexplore.ieee.org/document/6209084/

7. Childs, A.M.: Secure assisted quantum computation. Quant. Inf. Comput. 5(6) (2001). ISSN 15337146, 15337146. https://doi.org/10.26421/QIC5.6. http://arxiv. org/abs/quant-ph/0111046.arXiv:quant-ph/0111046

8. DiVincenzo, D.P.: The physical implementation of quantum computation. Fortschritte der Physik **48** (9–11), 771–783 (2000). ISSN 00158208, 15213978. https://doi.org/10.1002/1521-3978(200009)48:9/11⟨771::AID-PROP771⟩3.0.CO; 2-E

9. Feynman, R.P.: Simulating physics with computers. In: Feynman and computation, pp. 133–153. CRC Press (2018)

10. Fingerhuth, M., Babej, T., Wittek, P.: Open source software in quantum computing. PLOS ONE **13**(12), e0208561 (2018). ISSN 1932–6203. https://doi.org/10. 1371/journal.pone.0208561

11. Fitzsimons, J.F., Kashefi, E.: Unconditionally verifiable blind quantum computation. Phys. Rev. A **96**(1), 012303 (2017). ISSN 2469–9926, 2469–9934. https://doi. org/10.1103/PhysRevA.96.012303

12. Gheorghiu, A., Kashefi, E., Wallden, P.: Robustness and device independence of verifiable blind quantum computing. New J. Phys. **17**(8), 083040 (2015). ISSN 1367–2630. https://doi.org/10.1088/1367-2630/17/8/083040

13. Grover, L.K.: A fast quantum mechanical algorithm for database search. In: Proceedings of the Twenty-Eighth annual ACM symposium on Theory of computing - STOC 1996, Philadelphia, Pennsylvania, United States, pp. 212–219. ACM Press (1996). ISBN 978-0-89791-785-8. https://doi.org/10.1145/237814.237866. http://portal.acm.org/citation.cfm?doid=237814.237866

14. Hayashi, M., Morimae, T.: Verifiable measurement-only blind quantum computing with stabilizer testing. Phys. Rev. Lett. **115**(22), 220502 (2015). ISSN 0031–9007, 1079–7114. https://doi.org/10.1103/PhysRevLett.115.220502. https://link.aps.org/doi/10.1103/PhysRevLett.115.220502

15. Hidary, J.D .:Quantum Computing: An Applied Approach. Springer, Cham, 2019. ISBN 978-3-030-23921-3. https://doi.org/10.1007/978-3-030-23922-0

16. Kockum, A.F.: Quantum optics with artificial atoms. Chalmers Tekniska Hogskola (Sweden) (2014)

17. Kong, X., Li, Q., Wu, C., Yu, F., He, J., Sun, Z.: Multiple-server flexible blind quantum computation in networks. Int. J. Theor. Phys. **55**(6), 3001–3007 (2016). ISSN 0020–7748, 1572–9575. https://doi.org/10.1007/s10773-016-2932-z

18. Kumar, A., Garhwal, S.: State-of-the-art survey of quantum cryptography. Arch. Comput. Methods Eng. **28**(5), 3831–3868 (2021). ISSN 1134–3060, 1886–1784. https://doi.org/10.1007/s11831-021-09561-2. https://link.springer.com/10.1007/s11831-021-09561-2

19. Li, Q., Li, Z., Chan, W.H., Zhang, S., Liu, C.: Blind quantum computation with identity authentication. Phys. Lett. A **382**(14), 938–941 (2018)

20. Li, Q., Chan, W.H., Wu, C., Wen, Z.: Triple-server blind quantum computation using entanglement swapping. Phys. Rev. A **89**(4), 040302 (2014). ISSN 1050–2947, 1094–1622. https://doi.org/10.1103/PhysRevA.89.040302. https://link.aps.org/doi/10.1103/PhysRevA.89.040302

21. Li, W., Lu, S., Deng, D.L.: Quantum federated learning through blind quantum computing. Sci. China Phys. Mech. Astron. **64**(10), 100312 (2021). ISSN 1674–7348, 1869–1927. https://doi.org/10.1007/s11433-021-1753-3. https://link.springer.com/10.1007/s11433-021-1753-3

22. Liu, W.J., Chen, Z.Y., Liu, J.S., Su, Z.F., Chi, L.H.: Full-blind delegating private quantum computation, p. 13 (2020)

23. Morimae, T.: Continuous-variable blind quantum computation. Phys. Rev. Lett. **109**(23), 230502 (2012). ISSN 0031–9007, 1079–7114. https://doi.org/10.1103/PhysRevLett.109.230502. https://link.aps.org/doi/10.1103/PhysRevLett.109.230502

24. Morimae, T.: Verification for measurement-only blind quantum computing. Phys. Rev. A **89**(6), 060302 (2014). ISSN 1050–2947, 1094–1622. https://doi.org/10.1103/PhysRevA.89.060302. https://link.aps.org/doi/10.1103/PhysRevA.89.060302

25. Morimae, T., Fujii, K.: Blind topological measurement-based quantum computation. Nature Commun. **3**(1), 1036 (2012). ISSN 2041–1723. https://doi.org/10.1038/ncomms2043. http://www.nature.com/articles/ncomms2043

26. Morimae,T., Fujii, K.: Blind quantum computation protocol in which Alice only makes measurements. Phys. Rev. A **87**(5), 050301 (2013). ISSN 1050–2947, 1094–1622. https://doi.org/10.1103/PhysRevA.87.050301. http://arxiv.org/abs/1201.3966.arXiv:1201.3966 [quant-ph]

27. Morimae, T., Fujii, K.: Secure entanglement distillation for double-server blind quantum computation. Phys. Rev. Lett. **111**(2), 020502 (2013). ISSN 0031–9007, 1079–7114. https://doi.org/10.1103/PhysRevLett.111.020502
28. Morimae, T., Koshiba, T.: Composable security of measuring-Alice blind quantum computation (2013). http://arxiv.org/abs/1306.2113. arXiv:1306.2113 [quant-ph]
29. Morimae, T., Koshiba, T.: Impossibility of perfectly-secure one-round delegated quantum computing for classical client (2019). http://arxiv.org/abs/1407.1636.arXiv:1407.1636 [quant-ph]
30. Preskill, J.: Quantum computing in the NISQ era and beyond. Quantum **2**, 79 (2018). ISSN 2521–327X. https://doi.org/10.22331/q-2018-08-06-79. http://arxiv.org/abs/1801.00862. arXiv:1801.00862 [cond-mat, physics:quant-ph]
31. Qu, G.J., Wang, M.W.: Secure multi-party quantum computation based on blind quantum computation. Int. J. Theor. Phys. **60**(8), 3003–3012 (2021). ISSN 0020–7748, 1572–9575. https://doi.org/10.1007/s10773-021-04902-0
32. Qu, Z., Wang, K., Zheng, M.: Secure quantum fog computing model based on blind quantum computation. J. Ambient Intell. Human. Comput. **13**(8), 3807–3817 (2022). ISSN 1868–5137, 1868–5145. https://doi.org/10.1007/s12652-021-03402-7. https://link.springer.com/10.1007/s12652-021-03402-7
33. Raussendorf, R., Browne, D.E., Briegel, H.J.: Measurement-based quantum computation on cluster states. Phys. Rev. A **68**(2), 022312 (2003). ISSN 1050–2947, 1094–1622. https://doi.org/10.1103/PhysRevA.68.022312. https://link.aps.org/doi/10.1103/PhysRevA.68.022312
34. Shan, R.T., Chen, X., Yuan, K.G.: Multi-party blind quantum computation protocol with mutual authentication in network. Sci. China Inf. Sci. **64**(6), 162302 (2021). ISSN 1674–733X, 1869–1919. https://doi.org/10.1007/s11432-020-2977-x
35. Shi, R., Ding, W., Shi, J.: Arbitrated quantum signature with hamiltonian algorithm based on blind quantum computation. Int. J. Theor. Phys. **57**(7), 1961–1973 (2018). ISSN 0020–7748, 1572–9575. https://doi.org/10.1007/s10773-018-3721-7. http://link.springer.com/10.1007/s10773-018-3721-7
36. Shor, P.W.: Algorithms for quantum computation: discrete logarithms and factoring. In: Proceedings 35th Annual Symposium on Foundations of Computer Science, Santa Fe, NM, USA, pp. 124–134. IEEE Computer Society Press (1994). ISBN 978-0-8186-6580-6. https://doi.org/10.1109/SFCS.1994.365700. http://ieeexplore.ieee.org/document/365700/
37. Sueki, T., Koshiba, T., Morimae, T.: Ancilla-driven universal blind quantum computation. Phys. Rev. A **87**(6), 060301 (2013). ISSN 1050–2947, 1094–1622. https://doi.org/10.1103/PhysRevA.87.060301. https://link.aps.org/doi/10.1103/PhysRevA.87.060301
38. Sun, Z., Li, Q., Yu, F., Chan, W.H.: Application of blind quantum computation to two-party quantum computation. Int. J. Theor. Phys. **57**(6), 1864–1871 (2018). ISSN 0020–7748, 1572–9575. https://doi.org/10.1007/s10773-018-3711-9
39. Tan, X., Zhou, X.: Universal half-blind quantum computation. Ann. Telecommun. **72**(9–10), 589–595 (2017). ISSN 0003–4347, 1958–9395. https://doi.org/10.1007/s12243-017-0561-z
40. Zeng, X., Tan, X., Xu, Q., Huang, R.: Blind quantum computation with hybrid model. Int. J. Mod. Phys. B **34**(29), 2050277 (2020). ISSN 0217–9792, 1793–6578. https://doi.org/10.1142/S021797922050277X. https://www.worldscientific.com/doi/abs/10.1142/S021797922050277X
41. Zhang, X., et al.: A hybrid universal blind quantum computation. Inf. Sci. **498**, 135–143 (2019). ISSN 00200255. https://doi.org/10.1016/j.ins.2019.05.057. https://linkinghub.elsevier.com/retrieve/pii/S0020025519304585X

42. Zhou, X., Qiu, D.: Blind quantum machine learning based on quantum circuit model. Quant. Inf. Process. **20**(11), 363 (2021). ISSN 1570–0755, 1573–1332. https://doi.org/10.1007/s11128-021-03301-y

43. Zhu, Y., Li, Q., Liu, C., Sun, Z., Peng, Y., Shen, D.: Secure two-party computation based on blind quantum computation. Int. J. Theor. Phys. **59**(7), 2074–2082 (2020). ISSN 0020–7748, 1572–9575. https://doi.org/10.1007/s10773-020-04479-0

Driving Style Prediction Using Clustering Algorithms

Sakshi Rajput, Anshul Verma$^{(\boxtimes)}$ (iD), and Gaurav Baranwal

Department of Computer Science, Banaras Hindu University, Varanasi, India
anshulverma87@gmail.com

Abstract. Behavior prediction of surrounding vehicles is a critical task. The main goal of this work is the implementation of Gaussian Mixture Model (GMM) and K-means to predict behavior of other vehicles moving on the road and theoretical analysis of their performance. All the vehicles are clustered in three different clusters (aggressive, moderate and conservative) depicting their driving styles. In order to achieve this goal, we implemented GMM and K-means with the help of keras in Python 3.6. The models are tested with NGSIM (Next Generation Simulation) data on the US-101 and I-80 dataset. The results of both the algorithms are visualized using scatter plots. Statistical properties of driving styles are derived using the statistical properties of records belonging to that cluster. The performance of both the algorithms is compared.

Keywords: Vehicular Ad-hoc network · Driving styles prediction · GMM · K-means

1 Introduction

Vehicular Ad-hoc network (VANET) is a subcategory of Mobile Ad-hoc network (MANET) focusing on safety of people travelling on the road and reducing the number of accidents. Vehicles act as nodes of a network that is highly dynamic and self-organized. Motivation for VANET comes from Intelligent Transport Systems which aims at taking driving to its ease and make the journey more relaxing. In VANET, vehicles are equipped with navigation systems, Global Positioning System (GPS), sensors, multimedia systems, and wireless connectivity. Vehicles sense the surroundings using sensors to avoid collisions in the case of emergency. They can use immediate information on road conditions from the network infrastructure. Onboard wireless connectivity with the network provides users with non-safety applications for entertainment on the road.

Communication in VANETs is of various types [1]. Vehicle-to-Vehicle (V2V) communication takes place between a vehicle and rest of the vehicles on the road. It is mainly Onboard Unit (OBU) fixed on vehicle communicating with one or more OBUs. It is used for congestion avoidance and collision control to enhance vehicular safety. Infrastructure-to-Vehicle (I2V) communication or Vehicle-to-Infrastructure (V2I) communication occur during data exchange between infrastructures (like Road Side Units or routers) and vehicles (i.e., their Onboard Units). Traffic information like identification,

© The Author(s), under exclusive license to Springer Nature Switzerland AG 2023
I. Woungang et al. (Eds.): ANTIC 2022, CCIS 1798, pp. 497–509, 2023.
https://doi.org/10.1007/978-3-031-28183-9_35

speed restrictions, locations etc. are shared. Infrastructure-to-infrastructure (I2I) communication is the exchange of data between network infrastructures, important information exchange, and real-time traffic updates. Vehicle-to-Pedestrian or Vehicle-to-Person (V2P) communication is the data exchange between pedestrians and vehicles to remain safe on roads [2].

Vehicles may be interested in predicting the driving behavior of the other vehicles in order to understand the future motion of the moving vehicles better. Behavior prediction of surrounding vehicles is a critical task. Main aim is to provide an efficient algorithm for predicting the driving behavior of the vehicles using time series data describing various attributes of driving routes. Regression and classification are the two types of supervised learning. Unsupervised learning can be further divided into two types: dimension reduction and clustering. In this paper, unsupervised learning, Gaussian Mixture Model, and K-means clustering algorithm are used to achieve the goal. The performance of both the clustering algorithms is analyzed.

2   Literature Review

In VANET, vehicle nodes are highly mobile which leads to frequent changes in network topology. The data-rich environment leads to various issues in the implementation using traditional methods. Various machine learning techniques such as Naive Bayes (NB), k-nearest neighbors (k-NN), k-means clustering, Artificial Neural Network (ANN), and many more can be integrated with VANET to utilize this data efficiently. Different techniques are used for different purposes:

Decision Trees: It is a classification method that can be useful in traffic signal management, detecting misbehaviors of malicious vehicles, and improving routing decisions.

Naive Bayes: It is a supervised machine learning classification method appropriate for handling driver behavior prediction which avoids broad cast storm in VANET and excessive collisions [3].

K-NN: It is a supervised learning algorithm that can be used for both regression and classification. K-NN is suitable for vehicle and incident location detection [26], preserving privacy and intrusion detection (identify when and how many successful internal attempts occur).

Association rules: They belong to both machine learning and data mining because they include performing data processing operations and uncovering patterns to predict future behavior [4].

K-Means: It is unsupervised clustering algorithm useful in early detection of road congestion [5] and improving cluster stability for cluster based VANET techniques.

In [6], Z. Deng et al. analyzed driving styles by conducting experiment on 30 vehicles. Three driving characteristics has been derived by Principal Component Analysis algorithm out of eight driving style evaluation parameters. Then, K-means clustering algorithm is used to classify vehicle into three different driving styles namely caution, moderate and aggressive.

In [7], B. Gao et al. selected 66 random drivers. Values of average, maximum, minimum of relative speed, time-headway, and jerk are used as an input for driving style recognition. Experimental data is clustered through unsupervised machine learning method namely self-organizing feature map neural network followed by K- means to classify vehicles into 3 categories that are conservative, moderate, aggressive.

In [8], Guo et al. used fuzzy logic recognizer to identify driving styles.

3 Design Details and Proposed Algorithm

We implement GMM and K-means to predict driving behavior of other vehicles moving on the road with the help of keras in Python 3.6. The models are tested with NGSIM (Next Generation Simulation) data on the US-101 and I-80 dataset [9]. The dataset is well labeled with the vehicle identity making it suitable for learning. The data consists of various features describing the driving behavior which can be used to predict the behavior. Initially, the data consists of some error values, after applying preprocessing, the data have been trained to predict the behavior to be moderate, conservative or aggressive.

Clustering algorithms such as, Gaussian Mixture Model (GMM) and K-means are used to generate different driving styles. Next Generation Simulation (NGSIM) data on the US101, and I-80 highway dataset is classified in three different driving styles namely Conservative, Moderate, and Aggressive [10].

Vehicle velocity, acceleration, time-headway and space-headway are extracted from the dataset. Using these features, jerk is adopted using the formula:

$$\text{Jerk}(t) = \frac{\text{acc}(t + \Delta t) - \text{acc}(t)}{\Delta t}$$

Algorithms are trained on 16 dimensional vector as shown in Table 1 [11]. Statistical measurements are used to increase the robustness and diversity of the algorithm.

Table 1. Statistical features used for Driving Style Prediction

Features	Statistical measurements	
Velocity	Velocity STD	Mean velocity
Acceleration	Acceleration STD	Mean acceleration
Time headway	Maximum Time-headway	Minimum time-headway
	Time-headway STD	Mean time-headway
Space headway	Maximum Space-headway	Minimum space-headway
	Space-headway STD	Mean space-headway
Jerk	Maximum Jerk	Minimum jerk
	Jerk STD	Mean jerk

[*] STD = Standard Deviation

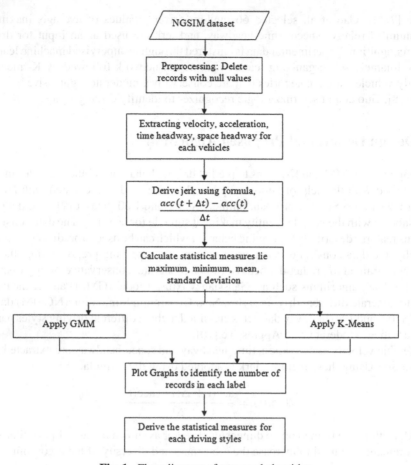

Fig. 1. Flow diagram of proposed algorithm

4 Model Construction and Implementation

The models are trained on the NGSIM dataset. The training objective of models is to estimate the driving styles based on the previous paths and to easily access of vehicle states of the surrounding vehicles based on real-time communication. The dataset consists of 25 columns signifying 25 attributes of the data describing the behavior of vehicle at different time stamps which can be used to predict the driving styles. Implementation is done using Python 3.6.

Size of complete dataset is (11850526, 25). Due to system restrictions, a smaller dataset was required. In order to extract data which is free from missing values and is smaller in size, all the records containing missing values are dropped, making the dataset of (2481206, 25) dimensionality.

A shorter dataframe has been created, consisting of only 6 features. Out of 25 attributes of the dataset, we have considered only 4 attributes namely vehicle velocity, vehicle acceleration, time headway, space headway to predict the driving style. In order to uniquely identify the vehicle and to use these features efficiently, we have used two additional features that are vehicle Id and Global time. Hence, data frame has been to (2481206, 6).

Vehicles have been grouped on Vehicle Id to get all the time stamps of the vehicle together. It is found that there are 1680 vehicles in the dataset and there are multiple number of records for each vehicle.

Additional feature, jerk, is derived using the acceleration values and timestamps. The difference of acceleration value at next time stamp and acceleration value at this timestamp is divided by the difference in both timestamps in order to calculate the jerk values for each record. The jerk value at the last timestamp of each vehicle is explicitly taken to be zero since out of all the calculated values, maximum are zero values. Adding jerk values, the dimensionality of dataset changed to (2481206, 7).

Using these features, 16 dimensional feature vector to train algorithms is produced. All the values of the attribute for a particular vehicle are used to derive statistical values which can be used to train the models. Using velocity, standard deviation and mean of velocity is derived. Using acceleration, standard deviation and mean of acceleration is derived. Using jerk values, maximum and minimum of jerk values are also derived along with standard deviation and mean of jerk. Using space headway, maximum space headway, minimum space headway, mean and standard deviation of space headway are considered [12]. Using time headway, maximum time headway, minimum time headway, mean of time headway and standard deviation of time headway are extracted [13]. These 16 features have been derived for 1680 vehicles.

The final dataset that is used to train the model becomes of dimensionality (1680, 17). The columns consist of vehicle id and 16 statistical features. The GMM model is trained on number of components = 3. Initializations are done using k-means algorithm. The K-means algorithm is trained separately using the same dataset. For visualization, two graphs are plotted. One graph is the representation of driving styles using maximum of time headway, standard deviation of time headway and space headway [14]. Another is the representation of results using standard deviation of speed, mean of time headway, minimum of jerk.

The algorithms divide the complete dataset into three clusters. Based on labels of the records, we classify each vehicle in one of the categories out of moderate, conservative, aggressive. Considering all the records of the cluster, we calculated the statistical measures for the driving styles (see Fig. 1). Statistical measures calculated for the driving styles are the same as the statistical measures we used to train the model. Statistical values are discussed in the Results section.

5 Results and Discussion

The NGSIM dataset is successfully divided into three driving styles. The clusters are visualized using scatter plots. Three different colors are used to depict the driving styles.

The graph illustrated in Fig. 2, shows the distribution of clusters concerning maximum time headway, standard deviation of time headway, standard deviation of space headway using GMM. The points in red color are used to indicate moderate driving, blue are used to indicate conservative driving, green are used to indicate aggressive driving.

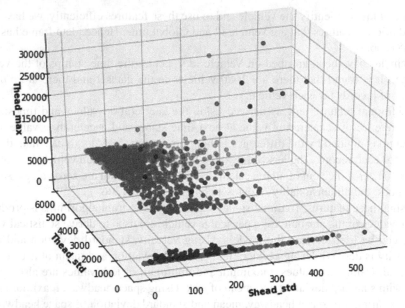

Fig. 2. Plot of Thead_max, Thead_std, Shead_std using GMM. (Color figure online)

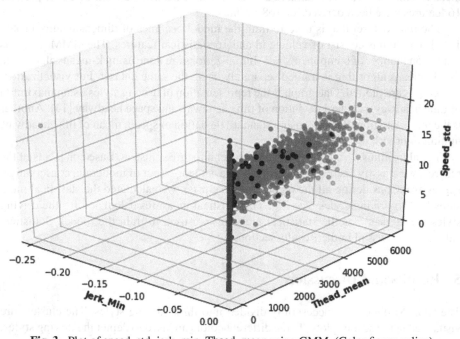

Fig. 3. Plot of speed_std, jerk_min, Thead_mean using GMM. (Color figure online)

The graph illustrated in Fig. 3, shows the distribution of clusters concerning standard deviation of speed, mean of time headway, minimum of jerk using GMM. The points in red color are used to indicate moderate driving, blue points are used to indicate conservative driving, and green points are used to indicate aggressive driving.

Table 2. Statistical values of Speed and Acceleration for each driving style using GMM are shown below:

Label	Spd_std	Spd_mean	Acc_std	Acc_mean
Moderate	10.772	22.510	4.824	0.027
Conservative	16.248	18.588	5.418	0.049
Aggressive	17.041	17.056	5.250	0.032

Table 2 depicts the values of speed and acceleration features using GMM. Statistical measurements considered are mean and standard deviation. For Moderate driving style, the value of standard deviation of speed is 10.772. For conservative driving, the value of standard deviation of speed is 16.248. For aggressive driving style, the value of standard deviation of speed is 17.041. Considering mean of Speed, the value of mean of speed for moderate driving style is 22.510. The value of mean of speed for conservative driving style is 18.588. The value of mean of speed value for aggressive driving style is 17.056.

For Moderate driving style, the value of standard deviation of acceleration is 4.824. For conservative driving, the value of standard deviation of acceleration is 5.418. For aggressive driving style, the value of standard deviation of acceleration is 5.250. Considering mean of acceleration, the value of mean of acceleration for moderate driving style is 0.027. The value of mean of acceleration for conservative driving style is 0.049. The value of mean of acceleration for aggressive driving style is 0.032.

Table 3. Statistical values of Jerk for each driving style using GMM are shown below:

Label	Jerk_max	Jerk_min	Jerk_std	Jerk_mean
Moderate	0.000481	-0.000469	0.000071	0.00
Conservative	0.00	0.00	0.00	0.00
Aggressive	0.00	0.00	0.00	0.00

Table 3 depicts the values of Jerk feature using GMM. Statistical measurements considered are maximum, minimum, mean and standard deviation. For Moderate driving style, the maximum value of jerk is 0.000481. For conservative and aggressive driving styles, the maximum value of jerk is 0.00. For Moderate driving style, the minimum value of jerk is -0.000469. For conservative and aggressive driving styles, the minimum value of jerk is 0.00. For Moderate driving style, the value of standard deviation of jerk is 0.000071. For conservative and aggressive driving styles, the value of standard deviation of jerk is 0.00. For all three driving styles, the mean value of jerk is 0.00.

Table 4. Statistical values of Space headway for each driving style using GMM are shown below:

Label	Shead_max	shead_min	Shead_std	Shead_mean
Moderate	402.003	0.00	92.451	57.747
Conservative	777.132	0.00	171.316	115.832
Aggressive	594.781	0.00	98.197	63.463

Table 4 depicts the values of Space headway feature using GMM. Statistical measurements considered are maximum, minimum, mean and standard deviation. For Moderate driving style, the maximum value of space headway is 402.003. For conservative driving style, the maximum value of space headway is 777.132. For aggressive driving style, the maximum value of space headway is 594.781. For all three driving styles, the minimum value of space headway is 0.00. For Moderate driving style, the value of standard deviation of space headway is 92.451. For conservative driving, the value of standard deviation of space headway is 171.316. For aggressive driving style, the value of standard deviation of space headway is 98.197. Considering mean of acceleration, the value of mean of space headway for moderate driving style is 57.747. The value of mean of space headway for conservative driving style is 115.832. The value of mean of space headway for aggressive driving style is 63.463.

Table 5. Statistical values of Time headway for each driving style using GMM are shown below:

Label	Thead_max	Thead_Min	Thead_std	Thead_mean
Moderate	22.865	0.00	3.558	1.861
Conservative	4937.900	0.00	1020.331	488.150
Aggressive	9999.990	0.00	3524.434	1976.287

Table 5 depicts the values of Time headway feature using GMM. Statistical measurements considered are maximum, minimum, mean and standard deviation. For Moderate driving style, the maximum value of time headway is 22.865. For conservative driving style, the maximum value of time headway is 4937.900. For aggressive driving style, the maximum value of time headway is 9999.990. For all three driving styles the minimum value of time headway is 0.00. For Moderate driving style, the value of standard deviation of time headway is 3.558. For conservative driving, the value of standard deviation of time headway is 1020.331. For aggressive driving style, the value of standard deviation of time headway is 3524.434. Considering mean of time headway, the value of mean of time headway for moderate driving style is 1.861. The value of mean of time headway for conservative driving style is 488.150. The value of mean of time headway for aggressive driving style is 1976.287.

The graph illustrated in Fig. 5 shows the distribution of clusters concerning maximum time headway, standard deviation of time headway, standard deviation of space headway using K-means. The points in red color are used to indicate aggressive driving, blue are used to indicate moderate driving, green are used to indicate conservative driving.

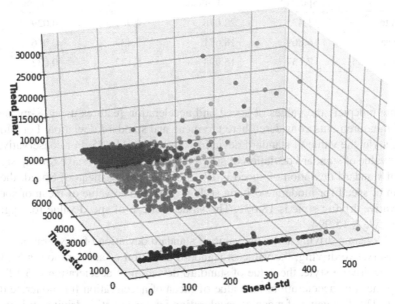

Fig. 5. Plot of Thead_max, Thead_std, Shead_std using K-means. (Color figure online)

The graph illustrated in Fig. 6, shows the distribution of clusters concerning standard deviation of speed, mean of time headway, minimum of jerk using K-means. The points in red are used to indicate aggressive driving, blue points are used to indicate moderate driving, green points are used to indicate conservative driving.

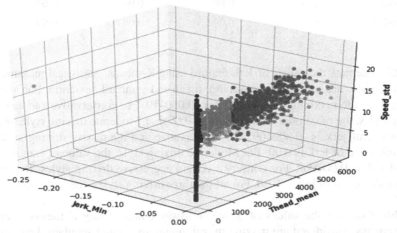

Fig. 6. Plot of Speed_std, Jerk_min, Thead_mean using K-means. (Color figure online)

Table 6. Statistical values of Speed and Acceleration for each driving style using K-means are shown below:

Label	Spd_std	Spd_mean	Acc_std	Acc_mean
Moderate	11.435	22.078	4.909	0.029
Conservative	16.869	18.671	5.437	0.026
Aggressive	17.157	15.994	5.127	0.037

Table 6 depicts the values of speed and acceleration features using K-means. Statistical measurements considered here are mean and standard deviation. For Moderate driving style, the value of standard deviation of speed is 11.435. For conservative driving, the value of standard deviation of speed is 16.869. For aggressive driving style, the value of standard deviation of speed is 17.157. Considering mean of Speed, the value of mean of speed for moderate driving style is 22.078. The value of mean of speed for conservative driving style is 18.671. The value of mean of speed value for aggressive driving style is 15.994.

For Moderate driving style, the value of standard deviation of acceleration is 4.909. For conservative driving, the value of standard deviation of acceleration is 5.437. For aggressive driving style, the value of standard deviation of acceleration is 5.127. Considering mean of acceleration, the value of mean of acceleration for moderate driving style is 0.029. The value of mean of acceleration for conservative driving style is 0.026. The value of mean of acceleration for aggressive driving style is 0.037.

Table 7. Statistical values of Jerk for each driving style using K-means are shown below:

Label	Jerk_max	Jerk_min	Jerk_std	Jerk_mean
Moderate	0.000419	-0.000409	0.000062	0.00
Conservative	0.00	0.00	0.00	0.00
Aggressive	0.00	0.00	0.00	0.00

Table 7 depicts the values of Jerk feature using K-means. Statistical measurements considered here are maximum, minimum, mean and standard deviation. For Moderate driving style, the maximum value of jerk is 0.000419. For conservative and aggressive driving styles, the maximum value of jerk is 0.00. For Moderate driving style, the minimum value of jerk is -0.000409. For conservative and aggressive driving styles, the minimum value of jerk is 0.00. For Moderate driving style, the value of standard deviation of jerk is 0.000062. For conservative and aggressive driving styles, the value of standard deviation of jerk is 0.00. For all the three driving styles, the mean value of jerk is 0.00.

Table 8 depicts the values of Space headway feature using K-means. Statistical measurements considered are maximum, minimum, mean and standard deviation. For

Table 8. Statistical values of Space headway for each driving style using K-means are shown below:

Label	Shead_max	shead_min	Shead_std	Shead_mean
Moderate	436.712	0.00	98.531	62.678
Conservative	679.832	0.00	119.680	74.634
Aggressive	559.546	0.00	91.131	60.843

Moderate driving style, the maximum value of space headway is 436.712. For conservative driving style, the maximum value of space headway is 679.832. For aggressive driving style, the maximum value of space headway is 559.546. For all three driving styles, the minimum value of space headway is 0.00. For Moderate driving style, the value of standard deviation of space headway is 98.531. For conservative driving, the value of standard deviation of space headway is 119.680. For aggressive driving style, the value of standard deviation of space headway is 91.131. Considering mean of space headway, the value of mean of space headway for moderate driving style is 62.678. The value of mean of space headway for conservative driving style is 74.634. The value of mean of space headway for aggressive driving style is 60.843.

Table 9. Statistical values of Time headway for each driving style using K-means are shown below:

Label	Thead_max	Thead_Min	Thead_std	Thead_mean
Moderate	75.875	0.00	12.022	6.192
Conservative	10339.725	0.00	2269.887	711.629
Aggressive	10074.849	0.00	4348.916	2795.324

Table 9 depicts the values of Time headway feature using K-means. Statistical measurements considered are maximum, minimum, mean and standard deviation. For Moderate driving style, the maximum value of time headway is 75.875. For conservative driving style, the maximum value of time headway is 10339.725. For aggressive driving style, the maximum value of time headway is 10074.849. For all three driving styles, the minimum value of time headway is 0.00. For Moderate driving style, the value of standard deviation of time headway is 12.022. For conservative driving, the value of standard deviation of time headway is 2269.887. For aggressive driving style, the value of standard deviation of time headway is 4348.916. Considering mean of time headway, the value of mean of time headway for moderate driving style is 6.192. The value of mean of space headway for conservative driving style is 711.629. The value of mean of space headway for aggressive driving style is 2795.324.

Using GMM, out of 1680 vehicles, 521 are classified as moderate, 107 falls in the conservative cluster and 1052 are in the aggressive cluster. Results indicate that 31.01%

are moderate drivers, 6.36% are conservative drivers, and 62.61% are aggressive drivers. It shows that aggressive drivers form the largest component of traffic.

Total 1680 vehicles have been used in the K-means clustering algorithm, out of which 598 are classified as moderate, 430 are in conservative cluster and 652 fall in the aggressive cluster. According to algorithm, 35.59% are moderate drivers, 25.59% are conservative drivers, 38.80% are aggressive drivers. All the clusters are almost equal indicating there is approximately same distribution of all the three types of drivers.

6   Conclusion and Future Work

In this study, a comparison between K-means and Gaussian Mixture Model is depicted while predicting the driving behavior of vehicles on the road. The model successively classifies the driving behavior of each vehicle as Moderate, Conservative and aggressive. The statistics of derived driving styles have been calculated using averages of values of all the vehicles belonging to the driving style cluster. According to GMM algorithm, aggressive drivers form the largest group on the roads, however, K-means is classifying the records uniformly in approximately equal number.

In Future, focus will be on predicting location using predicted driving styles. This can be done by combining driving styles with LSTM and RNN. An efficient algorithm can be built which can predict the location of vehicles accurately. Predicted location can be used for various purposes like traffic management or collision prevention.

Acknowledgment. This research work is part of the research work funded by "Seed Grant to Faculty Members under IoE Scheme (under Dev. Scheme No. 6031)" at Banaras Hindu University, Varanasi, India.

References

1. Daniel, A., Paul, A., Ahmad, A., Rho, S.: Cooperative intelligence of vehicles for intelligent transportation systems (ITS). Wirel. Pers. Commun. **87**(2), 461–484 (2016)
2. Hossain, M.A., et al.: Comprehensive survey of machine learning approaches in cognitive radio-based vehicular ad hoc networks. IEEE Access **8**, 78054–78108 (2020). https://doi.org/10.1109/ACCESS.2020.2989870
3. Guo, X., Chen, Y., Cao, L., Zhang, D., Jiang, Y.: A receiver-forwarding decision scheme based on Bayesian for NDN-VANET. China Commun. **17**(8), 106–120 (2020)
4. Feng, J., Liu, N., Cao, J., Zhang, Y., Lu, G.: Securing traffic-related messages exchange against inside-and-outside collusive attack in vehicular networks. IEEE Int. Things J. **6**(6), 9979–9992 (2019)
5. Hamida, E.B., Javed, M.A.: Channel-aware ECDSA signature verification of basic safety messages with k-means clustering in VANETs. In: 2016 IEEE 30th International Conference on Advanced Information Networking and Applications (AINA), pp. 603–610. IEEE, March 2016
6. Deng, Z., et al.: A probabilistic model for driving-style-recognition-enabled driver steering behaviors. IEEE Trans. Syst. Man Cybern. Syst. **52**(3), 1838–1851 (2022). https://doi.org/10.1109/TSMC.2020.3037229

7. Gao, B., Cai, K., Qu, T., Hu, Y., Chen, H.: Personalized adaptive cruise control based on online driving style recognition technology and model predictive control. IEEE Trans. Veh. Technol. **69**(11), 12482–12496 (2020). https://doi.org/10.1109/TVT.2020.3020335
8. Guo, Q., Zhao, Z., Shen, P., Zhan, X., Li, J.: Adaptive optimal control based on driving style recognition for plug-in hybrid electric vehicle. Energy **186**, 115824 (2019). https://doi.org/10.1016/j.energy.2019.07.154
9. Xing, Y., et al.: Driver lane change intention inference for intelligent vehicles: framework, survey, and challenges. IEEE Trans. Veh. Technol. **68**(5), 4377–4390 (2019). https://doi.org/10.1109/TVT.2019.2903299
10. Xing, Y., Lv, C., Cao, D.: Personalized vehicle trajectory prediction based on joint time-series modeling for connected vehicles. IEEE Trans. Veh. Technol. **69**(2), 1341–1352 (2020). https://doi.org/10.1109/TVT.2019.2960110
11. Xing, Y., et al.: A Personalized Deep Learning Approach for Trajectory Prediction of Connected Vehicles (2020).https://doi.org/10.4271/2020-01-0759
12. Ngernsukphaiboon, T., Chantranuwathana, S., Noomwongs, N., Sripakagorn, A., Solaphat, M.D.: A Study on Car Following and Cognitive Ability of Elderly Drivers by Using Driving Simulator (2016). https://doi.org/10.4271/2016-01-1737
13. Zhou, H., Saigal, R., Dion, F., Yang, L.: Vehicle platoon control in high-latency wireless communications environment: model predictive control method. Transp. Res. Rec. **2324**(1), 81–90 (2012). https://doi.org/10.3141/2324-10
14. Hosking, S., Young, K., Regan, M.: The effects of text messaging on young drivers. Hum. Factors **51**, 582–592 (2009). https://doi.org/10.1177/0018720809341575

Analyzing Fine-Tune Pre-trained Models for Detecting Cucumber Plant Growth

Pragya Hari[✉] and Maheshwari Prasad Singh

Department of Computer Science and Engineering, National Institute of Technology Patna,
Patna, India
pragyah.phd20.cs@nitp.ac.in

Abstract. Deep learning (DL) models have been used extensively for various applications such as image recognition, virtual chatbots, healthcare, and object detection tasks. DL models are trained with huge data for better prediction ability. It is difficult to collect a lot of data. Thus, use of transfer learning with even lesser samples may yield better recognition rate. However, there exist various pre-trained models which are used for transferring knowledge of one domain to other domain. As, they are trained over specific domain, they need to be fine-tuned as per target domain to improve detection rate. Therefore, this paper proposes six different models by using VGG16, VGG19, Xception, InceptionV3, DenseNet201, and MobileNetV2 respectively. Considering, agriculture domain, monitoring growth of plant is crucial. It may helP_In identifying issues early in plant such as nutrient deficiencies, diseases, weed infections, and affected by pests or insects. Thus, the proposed models are evaluated over cucumber plant stage dataset. Findings show that proposed model using VGG16 (P_VGG16) attains maximum testing accuracy of 97.98%. It is also obtained that P_VGG16 improves accuracy rate by 2% as compared to VGG16. This work also shows the comparison of proposed models with their respective original state-of-the-art pre-trained models.

Keywords: Deep learning · Transfer learning · Convolutional neural network (CNN) · Pre-trained models

1 Introduction

Cucumber (Cucumis sativus L.) is a creeping plant came from Cucurbitaceae gourd family. It is one of the major vegetables grown in greenhouses worldwide, since it is not only high in nutrients with important vitamins and minerals also having antioxidants properties which prevent chronic diseases. This crop promotes hydration because of 96% water composition. The cucumber is most likely originated in India [1]. From India this plant spread quickly to China [2]. China is the highest producer of this croP_In the world. China produces cucumber 77.45% in 2017, 74.84% in 2018, and 37.81 million tonnes in 2019[1].

---

[1] http://www.fao.org/faostat/en/data/QC.

© The Author(s), under exclusive license to Springer Nature Switzerland AG 2023
I. Woungang et al. (Eds.): ANTIC 2022, CCIS 1798, pp. 510–521, 2023.
https://doi.org/10.1007/978-3-031-28183-9_36

Agriculture employs over one-third of the global workforce [3]. One of the most important challenges is the lack of proper monitoring of crops and control mechanisms for efficient farming. To face this issue, modern technologies are empowering farming communities in not only producing better crops, but also monitoring their growth in order to enhance productivity and avoid financial loss. However, there are significant threats to agricultural growth, poverty alleviation, and food security. Crop yields may be severely reduced as a result of frequent climate fluctuations and other meteorological conditions. Climate change not only slows agricultural growth but also eliminates many farmers' work opportunities. Human error, such as the excessive use of herbicides and insecticides, which destroy crops and impair biodiversity, is another factor that contributes to agriculture's downfall.

Thus, plant phenotyping is of great significance in the development of higher yielding plants. This paper aims to improve the state-of-the-art in cucumber plant phenotyping by using publicly available datasets that can be used by researchers to improve their cucumber plant phenotyping ability via machine learning (ML), and DL techniques. Recently, artificial intelligence (AI) has found widespread application in various fields, including industry, agriculture, biology etc. Specifically, DL is increasingly being applied to visual object recognition, text classification, object detection, speech recognition etc.

This paper proposes six different fine-tuned deep learning based pre-trained models using (i) VGG16, (ii) VGG19, (iii) Xception, (iv) InceptionV3, (v) DenseNet201, and (vi) MobileNetV2. For this grading cucumber plant dataset has been used. The remaining of the paper comprises: Section 2 presents related work, Sect. 3 discusses the proposed models, Sect. 4 presents results and discussions, and Sect. 5 presents conclusion and future work.

2 Related Work

Machine Learning and Deep Learning [4] in agriculture have solved many problems. P´erez-P´erez et al. [5] analyze five hyper parameters that is (i) number of layers, (ii) the number of epochs, (iii) the batch size, (iv) optimizer, and (v) learning rate with eight different CNN architectures to determine maturity of ripe Medjool dates, authors found that VGG-19 [6] architecture with a 128 batch size and Adam optimiser with 0.01 learning rate have highest accuracy of 99.32%. Behera et al. [7] use two different approaches for classification of maturity stages of papaya fruit. First approach is based on machine learning where three different features namely (i) Gray Level Co-occurrence Matrix (GLCM) [8], (ii) Histogram Oriented Gradients (HOG) and (iii) Local Binary Pattern (LBP) [9] and three different classifiers viz., (i) Na¨ıve Bayes, (ii) Support Vector Machine (SVM) [10] and (iii) K-Nearest Neighbors (KNN) are used. Combination of KNN and HOG obtains the highest accuracy of 100%. In the second approach, Transfer Learning is used to fine-tune seven different pre-trained models namely, (i) ResNet101 [11], (ii) ResNet50, (iii) ResNet18, (iv) VGG19, (v) VGG16, (vi) Analyzing Deep Architectures for Detecting Cucumber Plant Growth 3 GoogleNet [12] and (vii) AlexNet [12]. VGG19 outperforms all the other pre-trained models and obtains 100% accuracy.

Nasiri et al. [13] study automated sorting of date fruit using deep learning, authors propose CNN [14] model based on VGG-16 which obtains accuracy of 96.98% for classifying healthy date fruits from defective ones. The dataset consists 4 different maturity stages namely (i) Khalal, (ii) Rutab, (iii) Tamar, and (iv) defective ones. Based on maturity feature like color and shape tomato has been classified into eight classes in [15] using AlexNet CNN with 100% accuracy. Pacheco et al. [16] employ supervised algorithms such as K-NN and Multilayer Perceptron (MLP), as well as the unsupervised technique K-Means, to analyse the extracted color space properties of tomatoes images. Mao et al. [17] propose cucumber automatic region detection method using multi-path CNN combined with color component selection and SVM. In past few years, CNN has been used enormously in variety of fields like video classification tasks [18], object detection [19], image classification. In addition to plant growth diagnosis, CNN is applied in leaf disease detection [20, 21], weed detection [22], and yield prediction [23]. Table 1 presents summary of related work.

Table 1. Summary of related works for plant growth detection

Authors	Plants	Classes	Dataset	No. of images	Method	Accuracy
[5]	Mejdool dates	2	Own	1002	VGG-19	99.32%
[7]	Papaya	3	Own	300	VGG-19	100%, and 100%
[13]	Date	4	Supermarket Produce	1357	CNN	96.98%
[15]	Tomato	8	Kaggle	4419	modified AlexNet	100%
[16]	Tomato	6	Own	600	KNN and MLP, and KMeans	95.71% and 94%
[17]	Cucumber	2	Own	450	Multipath-CNN	90%
[24]	Squash	7	Own	–	[LPDBL (Broad Learning Method)	98%
[25]	Paparika	4	Own	–	HSI-DNN	90.9%
[26]	Wheat	3	Own	600	CNN-1D with InceptionV2	90.9%

3 Proposed Models

This section first discusses about six pre-trained models namely, VGG16, VGG19, InceptionV3, Xception, DenseNet201, and MobileNetV2. Further, this section presents the proposed models using these six pre-trained models.

3.1 Transfer Learning

This technique helps in transferring the 'knowledge' of pre-trained models instead of training from scratch. This may reduce training time and computational complexity. The existing pre-trained models are proved to attain outstanding performance on ImageNet datasets. These models are used as feature extractor to train own classifier. Six different pre-trained models used in this paper are as follows:

VGGNet: VGGNet is pre-trained network model based on Visual Geometry Group introduced by oxford. VggNet has more than one version namely VGG16, and VGG19. Both models are trained on Imagenet database. VGG16 includes 16 weighted layers among which 13 layers are convolutional layers and 3 layers are fully connected layers. Whereas, VGG19 consists three additional convolutional layers than VGG16. In both the models, convolutional layers are followed by max pooling layer. Each convolutional layer introduces a small 3×3 kernel. Moreover, both models are trained over 1000 classes of ImageNet dataset. Thus, consisting 1000 units of neurons at softmax layer. They use more than 138 million parameters.

InceptionV3: Szegedy et al [27] introduce the architecture of Inception in 2014. GoogleNet implements the different versions of Inception. The allure of inception module is that, it is a concatenation of convolutional layers with different kernel sizes. That is, instead of having one filter, there are four filters of size 1×1, 3×3, 5×5 at four convolutional layers and one max pooling of size 3×3 in series or parallel are considered. This model uses comparatively lesser parameters than VGG16/VGG19.

Xception: Xception is based on deep convolutional neural networks. This model is inspired from Inception and stands for "Extreme Inception". This variation of Inception model substitutes depthwise separable convolution by pointwise convolution. As a result, the number of connections between neurons was reduced, resulting in a lighter model. This model uses 22,910,480 parameters and is 88 MB in size. On ImageNet dataset, this model attains top1 accuracy of 79% and top5 accuracy of 94.5%.

DenseNet201: This model uses 201 layers and trained over Imagenet database. Huang et al. [28] propose DenseNet, which feeds feature maps of the current layer and all prior layers to the subsequent layers. This model have various advantages such as mitigates vanishing/exploding gradient problem, attains more diversified features, strong gradient flow, and maintains low complexity features.

MobileNetV2: This model consists 53 convolutional layers. Sandler et al. [29] introduce an inverted residual module. This module includes depthwise convolution, pointwise convolution as projection layer and an expansion layer.

3.2 Fine Tuned/Proposed Models

This work presents six different fine-tuned pre-trained models namely P_VGG16, P_VGG19, P_Xception, P_InceptionV3, P_DenseNet201, and P_MobileNetV2. In fine tuning, pre-trained models are used as feature extractor, and helps in classifying new tasks. The fine tune of pre-trained models are done by freezing lower layers of pre-trained models and stacking multiple dense layers at top of the pre-trained models. Figure 1 depicts the proposed architecture for detecting cucumber plant growth stage.

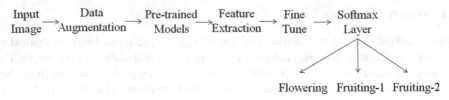

Fig. 1. Proposed architecture for detecting cucumber plant stage

In the proposed models, VGG16 and VGG19 were stacked up using two more dense layers with 512 and 256 neurons respectively. This is done to improve the performance of VGG16 and VGG19 models. These models are having weights of Imagenet database. Thus, to train these models with cucumber datasets for better predictive accuracy two fully connected layers are stacked up. As, the last convolutional layer of both the pre-trained models consists 512 neurons. Thus, in proposed VGG16 and proposed VGG19 are stacked with dense layers of 512 and 256 neurons. This results in utilising the strength of previous convolutional layers completely. Similar, fine-tuned methods for Xception (P_Xception) and InceptionV3 (P_InceptionV3) were stacked up with three dense layers having 256, 128 and 128 neurons. And fine-tuned methods for DenseNet201 (P_DenseNet201) and MobileNetV2 (P_MobileNetV2) were stacked up with three dense layers having 512, 512 and 256 neurons. These layers are added to the top of pre-trained models with one softmax layers having three neurons as the number of classes and keeping rest of the above layers freeze. This paper also utilises early stopping with a patience of 10, which indicates that the model will stop training if the loss does not decreases after 10 epochs.

The existing pre-trained models are trained over one millions of images of ImageNet database for 1000 categories so it consists various features. In the proposed method instead of train these models from beginning which may take huge amount of training time, top head layer are removed and fully connected layer are added with one softmax layer. These fully connected layers are then trained with Adam optimiser and a learning rate of 0.01 on our cucumber plant datasets. In this way the knowledge learned on some different datasets could be transferred to others via transfer learning.

4   Results and Discussions

This section presents Cucumber Plant Stage dataset which is used to evaluate the proposed models. Further, this section discusses the obtained results by six different fine-tuned models (Proposed Models) and six different pre-trained models (without fine-tuning) respectively.

4.1 Dataset

The Cucumber Plant Stage dataset[2] has been collected from Kaggle to evaluate the proposed models. This dataset consists a total of 1232 images comprising three different

---

[2] https://www.kaggle.com/farahseifeld/greenhouse-cucumber-growth-stages.

stages namely, (i) Flowering, (ii) Fruiting-1, and (iii) Fruiting-2. Their respective samples are shown in Figure 2. This figure depicts that most of the images have a white background to eradicate noises.

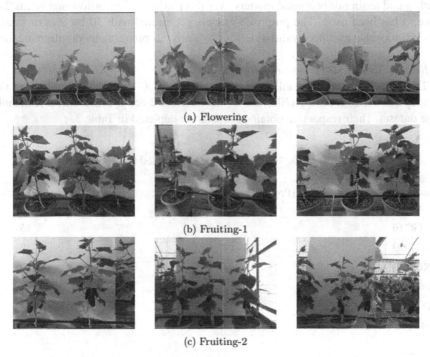

(a) Flowering

(b) Fruiting-1

(c) Fruiting-2

Fig. 2. Few Sample images from cucumber plant dataset

All the images are resized into 224 × 224 for faster computation. In addition to this, techniques like data augmentation have been applied in this work. This includes horizontal flip, shear, and zoom to increase the size of dataset. Further, this dataset has been splitted into training dataset and testing dataset with 80:20 ratio. The detailed statistics are presented in Table 2.

Table 2. Statistics of datasets

Stages	Training Datasets	Testing Datasets
Flowering	289	74
Fruiting-1	342	86
Fruiting-2	352	89

4.2 Results

This work has been implemented using Python language on windows 10 computer with GPU runtime allocated by Google Colaboratory provides 12 GB storage space. For training and testing of proposed models over this platform, Tensorflow and Keras 2.6.0 backend has been used. The proposed models get trained with 30 batches of images. This training also monitors validation loss by Early Stopping method with patience of 10.

Results obtained by Proposed Models

The six different proposed models namely, P_VGG16, P_VGG19, P_Xception, P_InceptionV3, P_DenseNet201, and P_MobileNetV2 are evaluated over Cucumber stage dataset. Their respective obtained results are depicted in Table 3.

Table 3. Results obtained by proposed models

Fine-tune Pre-Trained Models (Proposed Models)	Training accuracy	Testing accuracy	Epochs
P_VGG16	99.80%	97.98%	15
P_VGG19	97.36%	95.97%	10
P_Xception	95.63%	94.35%	10
P_InceptionV3	97.56%	95.97%	10
P_DenseNet201	96.65%	95.16%	5
P_MobileNetV2	98.07%	93.55%	7

This table shows that P_VGG16 attains maximum testing accuracy of 97.98% at epoch 15 followed by P_VGG19 and P_InceptionV3 with 95.97% testing accuracy. P_DenseNet201 attains 95.16% with lesser epochs of 5 which is one-third times of P_VGG16. This infers that P_DenseNet201 attains comparable accuracy with less amount of time followed by P_Xception attaining testing accuracy of 94.35% with 10 epochs. While P_MobileNetV2 attains lower testing accuracy of 93.55%. Moreover, the performance curves are shown using two different metrics: (i) Accuracy vs Epochs and (ii) Loss vs Epochs. These metrics are shown in Figure 3 for all six proposed models. The learning curves in this figure don't show any overfitting or underfitting case.

Results obtained by Pre-trained Models

The six different pre-trained models namely, VGG16, VGG19, Xception, InceptionV3, DenseNet201, and MobileNetV2 are also evaluated over cucumber plant stage dataset. Their respective results are shown in Table 4. These results are obtained without fine tuning the pre-trained models.

Table 4 shows that VGG16 is attaining maximum testing accuracy of 95.97% at 11th epoch. VGG16 followed by VGG19 attaining second highest testing accuracy of 95.57% at 21st epoch. From this, it can be inferred that VGG19 takes maximum time to converge. While Xception and MobileNetV2 is attaining same testing accuracy of 95.16% at epoch 12 and epoch 5 respectively. MobileNetV2 converges faster, due to its

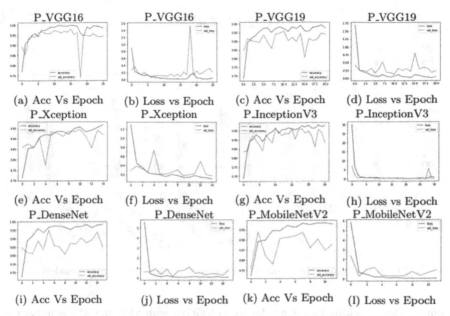

(a) Acc Vs Epoch   (b) Loss vs Epoch   (c) Acc Vs Epoch   (d) Loss vs Epoch
P_Xception   P_Xception   P_InceptionV3   P_InceptionV3

(e) Acc Vs Epoch   (f) Loss vs Epoch   (g) Acc Vs Epoch   (h) Loss vs Epoch
P_DenseNet   P_DenseNet   P_MobileNetV2   P_MobileNetV2

(i) Acc Vs Epoch   (j) Loss vs Epoch   (k) Acc Vs Epoch   (l) Loss vs Epoch

Fig. 3. Learning curves of six different Proposed Models (P_VGG16, P_VGG19, P_Xception, P_InceptionV3, P_DenseNet201, and P_MobileNetV2) are shown using Acc Vs Epoch and Loss Vs Epoch

Table 4. Results obtained by pre-trained models without fine tuning

Pre-trained models	Training accuracy	Testing accuracy	Epochs
VGG16	99.80%	95.97%	11
VGG19	99.70%	95.57%	21
Xception	94.11%	95.16%	12
InceptionV3	96.24%	93.55%	8
DenseNet201	95.63%	92.34%	8
MobileNetV2	96.44%	95.16%	5

drastically lesser number of parameters. Followed by InceptionV3 with 93.55% testing accuracy and DenseNet201 with 92.34% testing accuracy.

The results obtained by proposed models are also compared with the results obtained by original state-of-the-art pre-trained models. Their respective performance comparisons are shown in Figure 4. This figure depicts that proposed models using VGG16, VGG19, Inception V3, and DenseNet201 are attaining better results comparatively to their respective pre-trained models. While original pre-trained models namely, Xception and MobileNetV2 are performing better than their respective proposed models.

P_VGG16 improves the testing performance by 2.01% than VGG16. Considering units of neurons below 256 may underutilize the strength of previous convolutional

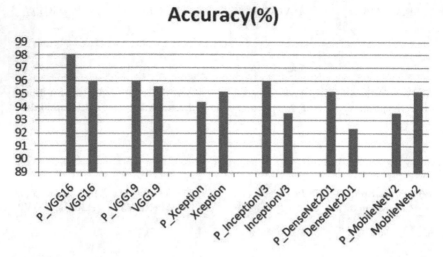

Fig. 4. Performance comparisons of proposed models to pre-trained models

features. Thus, stacking two dense layers to VGG16 with 512, and 256 neurons yield better results. The Table 3 shows that P_VGG16 attains maximum testing accuracy of 97.98%.

Comparative analysis with recent State-Of-The-Art models

This paper presents evaluation of six different proposed models which is based on six different pre-trained models. Among these models, proposed VGG16 with 97.98%, outperforms proposed VGG19, proposed Xception, proposed InceptionV3, proposed DenseNet201, and proposed MobileNetV2 models. Further, proposed VGG16 are compared with S-FPN (shortcut feature pyramid network) [30], Improved U-Net [31], Enhanced YOLOv5 [32], and EFDet (Efficient Detection) [33]. Their respective performances are shown in Table 5.

Table 5. Comparison with recent state-of-the-art over Cucumber Dataset

Authors	Model	Number of samples	Accuracy
Peng et al. [30]	S-FPN	3512	91.5%
Bai et al. [31]	Improved U-Net	349	97.46%
Wang et al. [32]	Enhanced YOLOv5	538	85.19%
Liu et al. [33]	EFDet	7488	85.52%
Proposed	P_VGG16	1232	97.98%

5 Conclusion and Future Work

This work presents six fine-tuned pre-trained models, P_VGG16, P_VGG19, P_Xception, P_InceptionV3, P_DenseNet201, and P_MobileNetV2. The proposed models are evaluated over cucumber plant stage dataset to monitor the growth of cucumber plant. It is obtained from the findings that proposed model using VGG16 attains maximum testing accuracy of 97.98%. Among six proposed models, four proposed models outperform their respective original state-of-theart pre-trained models. These four proposed models are P_VGG16, P_VGG19, P_InceptionV3, and P_DenseNet201 attaining testing accuracies of 97.98%, 95.97%, 95.97%, and 95.16%. This infers that fine tuning of pre-trained models may improve the performance results with lesser amount of time. There are certain limitations of this work, such as tuning hyperparameters of proposed models, and evaluating over different train-test split ratios. In future this work can be extended to detect plant diseases along with plant growth stages. This may results in developing efficient single model to perform multiple tasks. Considering pre-trained models for this work may speed up the process of achieving high accuracy rate.

References

1. Sebastian, P., Schaefer, H., Telford, I.R., Renner, S.S.: Cucumber (Cucumis sativus) and melon (C. melo) have numerous wild relatives in Asia and Australia, and the sister species of melon is from Australia. Proceedings Natl. Acad. Sci. **107**(32), 14269–14273 (2010)
2. Lv, J., et al.: Genetic diversity and population structure of cucumber (Cucumis sativus L.). Public Library of Science San Francisco, USA (2012)
3. James, J.: Plant growth monitoring system, with dynamic user-interface. In: 2016 IEEE Region 10 Humanitarian Technology Conference (R10-HTC), pp. 1–5. IEEE (2016)
4. Bouni, M., Hssina, B., Douzi, K., Douzi, S.: Deep learning identifies tomato leaf disease by comparing four architectures using two types of optimizers. In: International Conference on Advanced Network Technologies and Intelligent Computing, pp. 263–273. Springer, Cham (2021)
5. P´erez-P´erez, B.D., Garcia Vazquez, J.P., Salom´on-Torres, R.: Evaluation of convolutional neural networks' hyperparameters with transfer learning to determine sorting of ripe medjool dates. Agriculture **11**(2), 115 (2021)
6. Simonyan, K., Zisserman, A.: Very deep convolutional networks for large-scale image recognition. arXiv preprint arXiv:1409.1556 (2014)
7. Behera, S.K., Rath, A.K., Sethy, P.K.: Maturity status classification of papaya fruits based on machine learning and transfer learning approach. Inf. Process. Agric. **8**(2), 244–250 (2021)
8. Sebastian, V.B., Unnikrishnan, A., Balakrishnan, K.: Gray level co-occurrence matrices: generalisation and some new features. arXiv preprint arXiv:1205.4831 (2012)
9. Naik, S., Patel, B.: Machine vision based fruit classification and grading-a review. Int. J. Comput. Appl. **170**(9), 22–34 (2017)
10. Semary, N.A., Tharwat, A., Elhariri, E., Hassanien, A.E.: Fruit-based tomato grading system using features fusion and support vector machine. In: Intelligent Systems' 2014, pp. 401–410. Springer, Cham (2015)
11. He, K., Zhang, X., Ren, S., Sun, J.: Deep residual learning for image recognition. In: Proceedings of the IEEE Conference on Computer Vision and Pattern Recognition, pp. 770–778 (2016)

12. Szegedy, C., Vanhoucke, V., Ioffe, S., Shlens, J., Wojna, Z.: Rethinking the inception architecture for computer vision. In: Proceedings of the IEEE Conference on Computer Vision and Pattern Recognition, pp. 2818–2826 (2016)

13. Krizhevsky, A., Sutskever, I., Hinton, G.E.: Imagenet classification with deep convolutional neural networks. Commun. ACM **60**(6), 84–90 (2017)

14. Nasiri, A., Taheri-Garavand, A., Zhang, Y.D.: Image-based deep learning automated sorting of date fruit. Postharvest Biol. Technol. **153**, 133–141 (2019)

15. Kamilaris, A., Prenafeta-Bold´u, F.X.: A review of the use of convolutional neural networks in agriculture. J. Agric. Sci. **156**(3), 312– 322 (2018)

16. Das, P., Yadav, J.P.S.: Transfer learning based tomato ripeness classification. In: 2020 Fourth International Conference on I-SMAC (IoT in Social, Mobile, Analytics and Cloud) (I-SMAC), pp. 423–428. IEEE (2020)

17. Pacheco, W.D.N., L´opez, F.R.J.: Tomato classification according to organoleptic maturity (coloration) using machine learning algorithms K-NN, MLP, and KMeans Clustering. In: 2019 XXII Symposium on Image, Signal Processing and Artificial Vision (STSIVA), pp. 1–5. IEEE (2019)

18. Mao, S., Li, Y., Ma, Y., Zhang, B., Zhou, J., Wang, K.: Automatic cucumber recognition algorithm for harvesting robots in the natural environment using deep learning and multi-feature fusion. Comput. Electron. Agric. **170**, 105254 (2020)

19. Karpathy, A., Toderici, G., Shetty, S., Leung, T., Sukthankar, R., Fei-Fei, L.: Large-scale video classification with convolutional neural networks. In: Proceedings of the IEEE Conference on Computer Vision and Pattern Recognition, pp. 1725– 1732 (2014)

20. Zheng, Y.Y., Kong, J.L., Jin, X.B., Wang, X.Y., Su, T.L., Zuo, M.: CropDeep: the croP_Vision dataset for deep-learning-based classification and detection in precision agriculture. Sensors **19**(5), 1058 (2019)

21. Liu, B., Zhang, Y., He, D., Li, Y.: Identification of apple leaf diseases based on deep convolutional neural networks. Symmetry **10**(1), 11 (2017)

22. Zhang, S., Zhang, S., Zhang, C., Wang, X., Shi, Y.: Cucumber leaf disease identification with global pooling dilated convolutional neural network. Comput. Electron. Agric. **162**, 422–430 (2019)

23. dos Santos Ferreira, A., Freitas, D.M., da Silva, G.G., Pistori, H., Folhes, M.T.: Weed detection in soybean crops using ConvNets. Comput. Electron. Agric. **143**, 314–324 (2017)

24. Nevavuori, P., Narra, N., Lipping, T.: Crop yield prediction with deep convolutional neural networks. Comput. Electron. Agric. **163**, 104859 (2019)

25. Ganesh Babu, R., Chellaswamy, C.: Different stages of disease detection in squash plant based on machine learning. J. Biosci. **47**(1), 1–14 (2022). https://doi.org/10.1007/s12038-021-002 41-8

26. Choi, K., Park, K., Jeong, S.: Classification of growth conditions in paprika leaf using deep neural network and hyperspectral images. In: 2021 Twelfth International Conference on Ubiquitous and Future Networks (ICUFN), pp. 93–95. IEEE (2021)

27. Du, Y., Jiang, J., Liu, Z., Pan, Y.: Combining a crop growth model with cnn for underground natural gas leakage detection using hyperspectral imagery. IEEE J. Selected Topics Appl. Earth Obs. Remote Sens. **15**, 1846–1856 (2022)

28. Szegedy, C., et al.: Going deeper with convolutions. In: Proceedings of the IEEE Conference on Computer Vision and Pattern Recognition, pp. 4510–4520 (2018)

29. Huang, G., Liu, Z., Pleiss, G., Van Der Maaten, L., Weinberger, K.Q.: Convolutional networks with dense connectivity. IEEE Trans. Pattern Anal. Mach. Intell. **44**(12), 8704–8716 (2019)

30. Sandler, M., Howard, A., Zhu, M., Zhmoginov, A., Chen, L.C.: Mobilenetv2: inverted residuals and linear bottlenecks. In: Proceedings of the IEEE Conference on Computer Vision and Pattern Recognition, pp. 4510–4520 (2018)

31. Peng, F., Miao, Z., Li, F., Li, Z.: S-FPN: a shortcut feature pyramid network for sea cucumber detection in underwater images. Expert Syst. Appl. **182**, 115306 (2021)
32. Bai, Y., Guo, Y., Zhang, Q., Cao, B., Zhang, B.: Multi-network fusion algorithm with transfer learning for green cucumber segmentation and recognition under complex natural environment. Comput. Electron. Agric. **194**, 106789 (2022)
33. Wang, N., et al.: An enhanced YOLOv5 model for greenhouse cucumber fruit recognition based on color space features. Agriculture **12**(10), 1556 (2022)
34. Liu, C., Zhu, H., Guo, W., Han, X., Chen, C., Wu, H.: EFDet: an efficient detection method for cucumber disease under natural complex environments. Comput. Electron. Agric. **189**, 106378 (2021)

Home Occupancy Estimation Using Machine Learning

Pragati Kumari, Priyanka Kushwaha, Muskan Sharma$^{(\boxtimes)}$, Pushpanjali kumari, and Richa Yadav

Indira Gandhi Delhi Technical University for Women, New Delhi 110006, India
muskanmodgil0701@gmail.com

Abstract. Today, Smart home technology is commonly used for remote observation and control of devices and systems, for example, heating and lighting for convenience, support, and energy saving. Smart home devices incorporate the Internet of Things (IoT) to help automate activities based on the homeowners' preferences by working together to share the home members' usage data. Many papers are published on home occupancy detection. Occupancy and presence can be used in the contextual smart home to accurately determine the presence of someone in buildings or houses and also able to predict various events and pre-emptive action combines inexpensive, non-intrusive sensors including CO_2, temperature, sound, light, and movement with the aid of supervised learning methods like quadratic random forest and support vector machine (SVM). This method primarily focuses on reliably predicting the total occupants in an area with the help of a combination of heterogeneous sensor nodes and ML algorithms with the greatest 98.4% and the highest 0.953 F1 score. This paper primarily focuses on reliably determining the people in a room utilizing numerous sensor nodes that are heterogeneous in nature and machine learning algorithms, using various parameters such as CO_2, temperature, light, sound, and motion with the help of supervised learning methods like Logistic regression, Naive Bayes, SVM Linear Kernel, KNN, Decision tree, Random Forest, SVM RBF Kernel, with the Maximum Accuracy of 99.62% and F1 score 0.996 The effectiveness of a scaled dimensional data set was further assessed using linear discriminant analysis i.e. LDA and principal component analysis i.e. PCA.

Keywords: Home occupancy · Machine learning · Accuracy

1 Introduction

A "smart home" refers to a home that connects to the internet via mobiles and other connected devices and can automatically control appliances and devices remotely from anywhere. Internet-connected networks connect appliances in smart homes, allowing remote control features such as temperature, sound, home theater, security access, and many more [19–25]. Smart home gadgets are connected are accessible from electronic

Supported by organization IGDTUW.

devices like smartphones, laptops, or game consoles. The system which is installed on users' mobile devices or other network devices can be used to schedule some changes. Smart home devices can learn the homeowners' schedules to adjust to them. Smart home control for lights allows residents to save on utility bills while using less electricity. In case of emergency smart home automation systems can ring alarms or even notify the police or fire brigade in an emergency. One of the most useful pieces of information in the contextual smart home is smart home occupancy and presence, which enables it to precisely detect whether someone is home, who is there, and which rooms they are in. The Home Control System uses this data to influence judgments, eventually enabling it to foresee situations and take preventative action. One of the primary characteristics that define a smart home is an occupancy and presence. It is essentially difficult to transition from basic home automation to a genuinely smart house without them. The actual strength, however, comes from a single, logical model that includes numerous layers of location, proximity, occupancy, and present data. The ability to automatically update the status, which modifies things like target temperatures for rooms, etc., is a major goal for our home. Finding the ideal mix between manual control planned control, and detected occupancy or presence of people in our home, is the largest issue. Thus, the paper focuses on the detection of occupancy. Numerous publications [1–8] have been written about ML-based occupancy estimates. In [1], supervised learning methods like random forest and support vector machine (SVM), are used with the highest 98.4% accuracy and the highest 0.953 F1 score. In [2], a distributed network of sensors was considered to test three machine learning (ML) techniques: the artificial neural network (ANN), the Hidden Markov model (HMM), and the support vector machine (SVM). It has been demonstrated that HMM performs best, with 75% accuracy. However, they acknowledged that the occupancy levels were highly variable and suggested that not all labels might have the same amount of data points. As a result, the confusion matrix and F1 score are better performance indicators for these experiments than the accuracy metric used in [2], which only considered one study. In [3], data from environmental sensor systems located in two laboratories were classified using a radial basis function neural network. However, they did not perform cross-validation. As a result, their model may not perform well at large ranges where single knots are ineffective. Another set of sensors, including CO2, air mass, auxiliary, and temperature sensors, were used in [6]. But, rather than providing a point estimate, the paper binned occupancy levels. Similar binning techniques were employed in [5], which used a bidirectional deep convolutional long-term and short-term memory strategy to obtain excellent accuracy [1].

Following are our contributions and addition to accuracy detection calculation:-

1) Used 7 supervised learning methods such as K-Nearest Neighbors [7, 9], the support vector machine [7], Logistic regression [10, 11], Random Forest [14, 15], Decision tree [14], Kernel SVM [17], Naïve Bayes [13], unlike previously used maximum 4–5 methods to find accuracy.
2) Data processing, feature scaling [18] and dimensionality reduction technique are used such as LDA [16], and PCA [16] in addition to supervised learning approaches.
3) CO2, temperature, slope, sound, and motion used as sensors including light unlikely previous paper devoid the light for accuracy calculation.

2 Methodology

2.1 Data Preprocessing and Scaling

In this research paper, the data set from [1] is taken, and variables that have missing values were excluded. There were 10,000 points and 16 features in the final data set including the slope of CO2 as derived due to the good deviation of CO2 data to the number of people in the room but as few minutes were taken by the reading so it can fall and rise in case of CO2, therefore CO2 slope was taken as variable. Data processing refers to any type of processing algorithm that makes data easier and more effective for applying classification algorithms, and hence it helps to increase accuracy. Data processing includes feature scaling, normalization, and dimension reduction techniques. In this paper feature scaling and normalization are used to scale all the features so that no feature can dominate another and accurate results can be obtained. PCA and LDA techniques were used for dimensionality reduction, PCA generally deals with mathematical analysis, finding patterns, eigenvalues, standard deviation, covariance, variance, and more feature classification while LDA maximizes the difference between the classes and minimizes the separation within the classes and find a vector to discriminate among classes and to do data classification.

2.2 Machine Learning Algorithms

There can be supervised or unsupervised Machine Learning algorithms. The supervised algorithm first trains the model using a labeled training data set and then according to the trained model machine predicts the output, supervised approaches may be used for regression and classification, whereas in the unsupervised machine learning technique there is no labeled training data set to train the model instead the model itself finds patterns for the given data set, unsupervised ML techniques cannot be used for regression or classification directly as unlike the supervised learning input data is present but output data is not present. As the goal of this paper is room occupancy detection, supervised ML classification algorithms will be used for this paper.

The classification algorithms used are Logistic Regression, Support Vector Machine-SVM RBF Kernel, SVM Linear Kernel, KNN, Naive Bayes, Decision Tree, and Random Forest. In logistic regression, the code for the occurrence of an event is 1 and the absence of an event is 0. The linear model classic regression notation is $y = a + bx + e$ Where y is the dependent variable, x is the independent variable, a is the intercept, b is the coefficient of regression and e is an error in the system.

SVM is a classification algorithm by which the solution of the learning problem is found as an "optimal" hyperplane. If the hyperplane is in the space of the input data x it is called linear SVM which is the simplest SVM algorithm. In this, the subsets of all hyperplanes of the form $y = wx + b$ are the hypothesis space. If the hyperplane, different from the input data x is found by the SVM in space, i.e. if the hyperplane is induced by the kernel K in the feature space where the inner product of that space is defined by a kernel, called the SVM kernel. A set of "hyperplanes" in feature space induced by K through the kernel K is called the hypothesis space. In the K-Nearest Neighbor algorithm, no presumptions are made on the dataset, so it is called non-parametric classification.

It is simple and effective with a low computational time. The nearest neighbors are calculated by euclidean distance in case the data is continuous. The value of K plays a major role in the classification of unlabeled data which can be determined by repeated runs of classifiers with different values, to find the most effective value. Therefore the computational cost is high and it is known as a lazy algorithm. The maximum all-likelihood elegance is assigned by Naive Bayes to a given instance, and its characteristic vector is used to define it. If we assume that functions are impartial given elegance we can simplify this algorithm which means it is a characteristic vector and is a class.

$$P(X|C) = PInP(X|C), where X = (x1...............xn) \tag{1}$$

Just like the ordinary tree, the decision tree consists of nodes in the form of circles, and they are connected by branches in the form of segments. The root of the tree from which the decision tree starts is called the root node. From the root node, the decision tree moves downwards and starts from the left towards the right. And the node at the end of the chain is called the leaf node. In the random forest a group of classification or regression trees, where the prediction is made by aggregating the predictions and random selection of samples are used to form the trees.

3 Experiments and Results

The ML algorithms are implemented using the python Scikit-learn library [18], Accuracy, Accuracy, F1 score, Recall, Precision, Sensitivity, Specificity, RMSE, and Kappa are the metrics found. Accuracy refers to the measure of right predictions by the model, but this is not the only parameter to find the best model in case of imbalanced data, so other parameters are also calculated here.

If the positive class is correctly predicted it's true positive else it's a false positive while if the negative class is correctly predicted it is true negative else it is a false negative.

The true positive/(true positive + false positive) is termed as precision, it tells how precise a model is for predicted positive whereas Recall is true posi tive/(true positive+false negative), so it deals with the number of actual positives the model found by giving it label as true positive. Correctly predicted true positives are measured by sensitivity while correctly predicted true negatives are measured by specificity. RMSE is the root mean square error by which the quality of the model can be evaluated, If the RMSE for training is lower than the test set, then the model created is overfitted, so, the RMSE of the training and test set should be similar for good quality of the model, and kappa is more realistic than accuracy and can be used for imbalanced data, it is used to measure the closeness of ground truth data with the data classified by machine learning.

The observations and results for each parameter are calculated algorithm- wise as discussed below, first, the parameters are calculated for individual variables than for groups of variables, and finally by taking all the variables.

3.1 Logistic Regression

In the logistic regression table (Table 1) maximum accuracy is obtained by taking all the parameters i.e. 0.99 and kappa as 0.97 and the most accurate prediction is obtained for light i.e. 0.96 and following after is CO2 and CO2 Slope combined i.e. 0.893 following temperature i.e. 0.867 which means light, temperature and CO2 are the major factors for occupancy detection in this case.

Table 1. Different parameters calculated for Logistic Regression.

Feature	Accuracy	Sensitivity	Specificity	Precision	Recall	f1 Score	RMSE	kappa
Temp1, 2, 3, 4	0.867	1.0	0.171	0.867	0.867	0.867	0.646	0.551
Light1, 2, 3, 4	0.967	0.999	1.0	0.967	0.967	0.967	0.455	0.897
Sound1, 2, 3, 4	0.872	0.999	0.292	0.872	0.872	0.872	0.596	0.556
PIR6, 7	0.871	1.0	0.0	0.871	0.871	0.871	0.599	0.537
CO2	0.825	1.0	0.0	0.825	0.825	0.825	0.891	0.276
Slope	0.871	1.0	0.0	0.871	0.871	0.871	0.596	0.517
CO2, Slope	0.893	1.0	0.0	0.893	0.893	0.893	0.503	0.631
Temp1, 2, 3, 4, CO2,Slope	0.918	0.999	0.428	0.918	0.918	0.918	0.458	0.732
Temp1, 2, 3, 4, CO2, Slope Sound1, 2, 3, 4	0.948	0.999	0.746	0.948	0.948	0.948	0.320	0.837
Temp1, 2, 3, 4, CO2, Slope Sound1, 2, 3, 4, PIR6, 7	0.949	0.998	0.753	0.949	0.949	0.949	0.319	0.841
Temp1, 2, 3, 4, CO2,Slope Sound1, 2, 3, 4, PIR6, 7, Light1, 2, 3, 4	0.990	0.999	1.0	0.990	0.990	0.990	0.139	0.970

3.2 K-Nearest Neighbor

In the KNN (Table 2) accuracy obtained by taking all the parameters is 0.987 and kappa is 0.96 and the most accurate prediction is obtained for light i.e. 0.987 and following after is temperature i.e. 0.983 then CO_2 and CO_2 Slope combined i.e. 0.947 which means light, temperature and CO_2 are the major factors for occupancy detection in this case.

Table 2. Different parameters calculated for KNN.

Feature	Accuracy	Sensitivity	Specificity	Precision	Recall	f1 Score	RMSE	kappa
Temp1, 2, 3, 4	0.983	0.998	0.972	0.983	0.983	0.983	0.204	0.949
Light1, 2, 3, 4	0.987	0.999	1.0	0.987	0.987	0.987	0.286	0.961
Sound1, 2, 3, 4	0.893	0.998	0.636	0.893	0.893	0.893	0.520	0.660
PIR6, 7	0.871	0.998	0.334	0.871	0.871	0.871	0.613	0.537
CO2	0.824	0.958	0.193	0.824	0.824	0.824	0.863	0.402
Slope	0.878	0.996	0.552	0.878	0.878	0.878	0.536	0.606
CO2, Slope	0.947	0.997	0.806	0.947	0.947	0.947	0.331	0.838
Temp1, 2, 3, 4, CO2,Slope	0.989	0.999	0.977	0.989	0.989	0.989	0.133	0.968
Temp1, 2, 3, 4, CO2, Slope Sound1, 2, 3, 4	0.974	0.999	0.944	0.974	0.974	0.974	0.197	0.922
Temp1, 2, 3, 4, CO2, Slope Sound1, 2, 3, 4, PIR6, 7	0.966	0.997	0.937	0.966	0.966	0.966	0.245	0.898
Temp1, 2, 3, 4, CO2, Slope Sound1, 2, 3, 4, PIR6, 7 Light1, 2, 3, 4	0.987	0.998	0.995	0.987	0.987	0.987	0.155	0.961

3.3 Support Vector Machine (RBF Kernel)

In the SVM RBF Kernel (Table 3) accuracy obtained by taking all the parameters is 0.992 and kappa is 0.976 and the most accurate prediction is obtained for light i.e. 0.972 and following after is temperature i.e.0.948 then CO2 and CO2 Slope combined i.e. 0.920 which means light, temperature and CO2 are the major factors for occupancy detection in this case.

Table 3. Different parameters calculated for SVM(RBF Kernel).

Feature	Accuracy	Sensitivity	Specificity	Precision	Recall	f1 Score	RMSE	kappa
Temp1, 2, 3, 4	0.948	1.0	0.788	0.948	0.948	0.948	0.372	0.839
Light1, 2, 3, 4	0.972	0.999	1.0	0.972	0.972	0.972	0.449	0.913
Sound1, 2, 3, 4	0.891	0.999	0.542	0.891	0.288	0.537	0.537	0.644
PIR6,7	0.864	1.0	0.0	0.864	0.864	0.864	0.602	0.509
CO2	0.825	1.0	0.0	0.825	0.825	0.825	0.798	0.272
Slope	0.879	0.996	0.301	0.879	0.879	0.879	0.532	0.583
CO2, Slope	0.920	0.997	0.492	0.920	0.920	0.920	0.399	0.748
Temp1, 2, 3, 4, CO2, Slope	0.969	1.0	0.844	0.969	0.969	0.969	0.248	0.906
Temp1, 2, 3, 4, CO2, Slope Sound1, 2, 3, 4	0.968	0.999	0.902	0.968	0.968	0.968	0.212	0.904
Temp1, 2, 3, 4, CO2, Slope Sound1, 2, 3, 4, PIR6,7	0.965	0.998	0.992	0.965	0.965	0.965	0.233	0.894
Temp1, 2, 3, 4, CO2, Slope Sound1, 2, 3, 4, PIR 6, 7, Light1, 2, 3, 4	0.992	0.999	1.0	0.992	0.992	0.992	0.127	0.976

3.4 Support Vector Machine (Linear Kernel)

In the SVM Linear Kernel (Fig. 3) accuracy obtained by taking all the parameters is 0.994 and kappa is 0.983 and the most accurate prediction is obtained for light
i.e. 0.968 and then CO_2 and CO_2 Slope combined i.e. 0.903 following temperature
i.e. 0.894 which means light, temperature and CO_2 are the major factors for occupancy detection in this case.

Table 4. Different parameters calculated for SVM (Linear Kernel).

Feature	Accuracy	Sensitivity	Specificity	Precision	Recall	f1 Score	RMSE	kappa
Temp1, 2, 3, 4	0.894	0.999	0.201	0.894	0.894	0.894	0.523	0.666
Light1, 2, 3, 4	0.968	0.999	1.0	0.968	0.968	0.968	0.455	0.898
Sound1, 2, 3, 4	0.877	0.999	0.408	0.877	0.877	0.877	0.589	0.580
PIR6,7	0.871	1.0	0.0	0.871	0.871	0.871	0.599	0.537
CO2	0.822	1.0	0.0	0.822	0.822	0.822	0.910	0.221
Slope	0.873	1.0	0.0	0.873	0.873	0.873	0.566	0.545
CO2, Slope	0.903	1.0	0.150	0.903	0.903	0.903	0.464	0.679
Temp1, 2, 3, 4, CO2,Slope	0.932	1.0	0.538	0.932	0.932	0.932	0.404	0.785
Temp1, 2, 3, 4, CO2, Slope Sound1, 2, 3, 4	0.954	0.998	0.814	0.954	0.954	0.954	0.298	0.858
Temp1, 2, 3, 4, CO2, Slope Sound1, 2, 3, 4, PIR6, 7	0.952	0.998	0.791	0.952	0.952	0.952	0.304	0.850

3.5 Naive Bayes

In the Naive Bayes (Table 5) accuracy obtained by taking all the parameters is 0.968 and kappa is 0.905 and the most accurate prediction is obtained for light i.e. 0.914 a then CO_2 and CO_2 Slope combined i.e. 0.904 and following temperature i.e. 0.882 which means light, temperature and CO_2 are the major factors for occupancy detection in this case.

Table 5. Different parameters calculated for Naive Bayes.

Feature	Accuracy	Sensitivity	Specificity	Precision	Recall	f1 Score	RMSE	kappa
Temp1, 2, 3, 4	0.882	1.0	0.053	0.882	0.882	0.882	0.525	0.638
Light1, 2, 3, 4	0.914	0.999	1.0	0.914	0.914	0.914	0.831	0.757
Sound1, 2, 3, 4	0.869	0.997	0.527	0.869	0.869	0.869	0.594	0.568
PIR6,7	0.864	1.0	0.0	0.864	0.864	0.864	0.602	0.509
CO2	0.820	1.0	0.0	0.820	0.820	0.820	0.835	0.363
Slope	0.853	1.0	0.0	0.853	0.853	0.853	0.727	0.395
CO2, Slope	0.904	0.999	0.229	0.904	0.904	0.904	0.462	0.690
Temp1, 2, 3, 4, CO2, Slope	0.898	0.994	0.532	0.898	0.898	0.898	0.476	0.698
Temp1, 2, 3, 4, CO2, Slope Sound1, 2, 3, 4	0.905	0.982	0.760	0.905	0.905	0.905	0.450	0.727
Temp1, 2, 3, 4, CO2, Slope Sound1, 2, 3, 4, PIR6, 7	0.903	0.968	0.795	0.903	0.903	0.903	0.402	0.725
Temp1, 2, 3, 4, CO2, Slope Sound1, 2, 3, 4, PIR6, 7, Light1, 2, 3, 4	0.968	1.0	1.0	0.968	0.968	0.968	0.397	0.905

3.6 Decision Tree

In the Decision Tree (Table 6) accuracy obtained by taking all the parameters is 0.993 and kappa is 0.98 and the most accurate prediction is obtained for light i.e. 0.988 and following after is temperature i.e. 0.955 then CO2 and CO2 Slope combined i.e. 0.934 which means light, temperature and CO2 are the major factors for occupancy detection in this case.

Table 6. Different parameters calculated for Decision tree.

Feature	Accuracy	Sensitivity	Specificity	Precision	Recall	f1 Score	RMSE	kappa
Temp1, 2, 3, 4	0.955	0.992	0.864	0.955	0.955	0.955	0.320	0.866
Light1, 2, 3, 4	0.988	0.999	1.0	0.988	0.988	0.988	0.249	0.961
Sound1, 2, 3, 4	0.871	0.996	0.525	0.871	0.871	0.871	0.562	0.596
PIR6,7	0.864	1.0	0.0	0.864	0.864	0.864	0.602	0.509
CO2	0.837	0.989	0.189	0.837	0.837	0.837	0.839	0.415
Slope	0.874	0.995	0.480	0.874	0.874	0.874	0.557	0.594
CO2, Slope	0.934	0.993	0.801	0.934	0.934	0.934	0.385	0.798
Temp1, 2, 3, 4, CO2, Slope	0.938	0.988	0.725	0.938	0.938	0.938	0.394	0.810
Temp1, 2, 3, 4, CO2, Slope Sound1, 2, 3, 4	0.924	0.992	0.777	0.924	0.924	0.924	0.391	0.766
Temp1, 2, 3, 4, CO2, Slope Sound1, 2, 3, 4, PIR6, 7	0.923	0.992	0.762	0.923	0.923	0.923	0.374	0.766
Temp1, 2, 3, 4, CO2, Slope Sound1, 2, 3, 4, PIR6, 7, Light1, 2, 3, 4	0.993	0.999	1.0	0.993	0.993	0.993	0.173	0.980

3.7 Random Forest

In the Random Forest (Table 7) accuracy obtained by taking all the parameters is 0.996 and kappa is 0.988 and the most accurate prediction is obtained for light i.e. 0.99 and following after is temperature i.e. 0.98 then CO_2 and CO_2 Slope combined i.e. 0.942 which means light, temperature and CO_2 are the major factors for occupancy detection in this case.

Table 7. Different parameters calculated for Random Forest.

Feature	Accuracy	Sensitivity	Specificity	Precision	Recall	f1 Score	RMSE	kappa
Temp1, 2, 3, 4	0.980	0.998	0.920	0.980	0.980	0.980	0.224	0.939
Light1, 2, 3, 4	0.990	0.999	1.0	0.990	0.990	0.990	0.209	0.972
Sound1, 2, 3, 4	0.890	0.997	0.633	0.890	0.890	0.890	0.512	0.656
PIR6,7	0.864	1.0	0.0	0.864	0.864	0.864	0.602	0.509
CO2	0.829	0.985	0.230	0.829	0.829	0.829	0.846	0.420
Slope	0.871	0.994	0.446	0.871	0.871	0.871	0.559	0.587
CO2, Slope	0.942	0.996	0.785	0.942	0.942	0.942	0.344	0.823
Temp1, 2, 3, 4, CO2, Slope	0.984	1.0	0.940	0.984	0.984	0.984	0.196	0.954
Temp1, 2, 3, 4, CO2, Slope Sound1, 2, 3, 4	0.9767	0.998	0.943	0.976	0.976	0.976	0.196	0.929
Temp1, 2, 3, 4, CO2, Slope Sound1, 2, 3, 4, PIR6,7	0.967	0.997	0.942	0.967	0.967	0.967	0.237	0.9000
Temp1, 2, 3, 4, CO2, Slope Sound1, 2, 3, 4, PIR6,7, Light1, 2, 3, 4	0.996	0.999	1.0	0.996	0.996	0.996	0.100	0.988

Table 8. Comparison of accuracy from base paper and using dimensionality reduction PCA and LDA.

Algorithm	Accuracy in base paper	Accuracy	Accuracy with PCA	Accuracy with LDA
SVM Linear Kernel	0.982	0.994	0.994	0.987
Random forest	0.978	0.996	0.986	0.991
Naive bayes	Not given	0.968	0.951	0.984
Logistic regression	Not given	0.990	0.990	0.986
KNN	Not given	0.987	0.987	0.991
SVM RBF Kernel	0.984	0.992	0.992	0.987
Decision tree	Not given	0.993	0.985	0.985

The Bar graph (Table 8) shows the comparison in accuracy by different algorithms, the maximum accuracy is obtained by random forest followed by SVM linear kernel, decision tree, SVM RBF kernel, logistic regression, and KNN, and the least accuracy is obtained by Naive Bayes. Also, a comparison between accuracy with PCA and without PCA is done in Fig. 1, and a comparison between accuracy with LDA and without LDA is done in Fig. 2, both of the graphs show higher results for accuracy without dimensionality reduction techniques for this data set, so it can be concluded that the data set may have lost some spatial information due to the use of dimensionality reduction techniques which is important for classification and hence the accuracy decreased. In Fig. 3, the bar graph shows the increase in accuracy as compared to the base paper for some algorithms which are used in both papers.

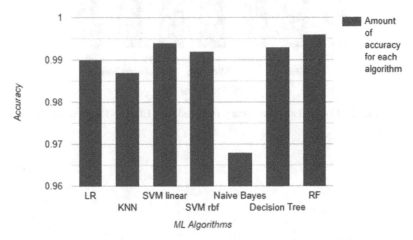

Fig. 1. Comparison of accuracy obtained from various algorithms.

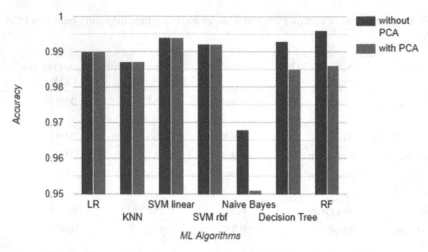

Fig. 2. Comparison of accuracy obtained with PCA and without PCA.

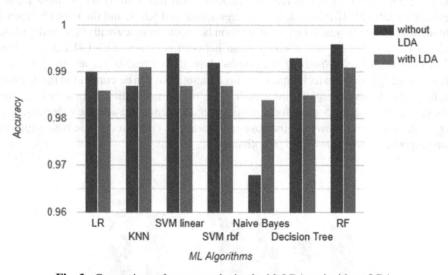

Fig. 3. Comparison of accuracy obtained with LDA and without LDA.

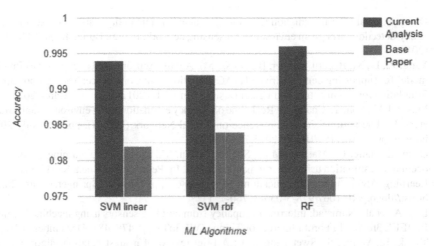

Fig. 4. Comparison of accuracy with the accuracy obtained in the base paper.

4 Conclusion and Future Scope

In this paper, we have calculated the accuracy and other parameters of occupancy by using the various sensors as parameters such as CO_2, temperature, slope, light, sound, and motion with the help of seven supervised learning classification methods like KNN, Logistic regression, the support vector machine (SVM), Naive Bayes, random forest, SVM, Decision tree, Kernel SVM with the Maximum Accuracy of 99.62% and F1 score 0.996 in case of random forest. The effectiveness of a scaled dimensional data set has been further assessed using principal component analysis (PCA) and linear discriminant analysis (LDA). CO_2, temperature, slope, sound, and motion are used as sensors including light unlikely previous papers devoid the light for accurate calculation. An increase in accuracy has been observed as compared to the base paper. The maximum accuracy obtained by Random Forest is much better than the accuracy obtained in the base paper (Fig. 4).

Results for numerous other feature combinations have also been recorded. The future scope will be to create a hardware setup installation and to find the occupancy estimation for larger buildings/workspace [1]. If our dataset will be large, other features that are derived like time and day of the week can be considered too.

Acknowledgements. We are grateful to our renowned college Indira Gandhi Delhi Technical University for Women for motivating us as well as also for providing us with all the much needed guidance and mentorship, we would also like to thank our mentor Dr. Richa Yadav for her support and a special thanks to our guide Pushpanjali Kumari for helping us at every step.

References

1. Singh, A.J., Chaudhari,V., Kraemer, S., Werner, F., Stefan Garg, Vishal.: Machine learning-based occupancy estimation using multivariate sensor nodes, pp. 1–6 (2018). https://doi.org/10.1109/GLOCOMW.2018.8644432

2. Dong, B., et al.: An information technology enabled sustainability test-bed (itest) for occupancy detection through an environmental sensing network. Energy Build. **42**(7), 1038–1046 (2010)

3. Yang, Z., Li, N., Becerik-Gerber, B., Orosz, M.: A multi-sensor based occupancy estimation model for supporting demand driven HVAC operations. In: Conference: The Symposium on Simulation for Architecture and Urban Design (SimAUD) 2012, Orlando, March 2012

4. Masood, M., Soh, Y., Chang, V.: Real-time occupancy estimation using environmental parameters. In: International Joint Conference on Neural Network (IJCNN). pp. 1–8, July 2015. https://doi.org/10.1109/IJCNN.2015.7280781

5. Chen, Z., Jiang, C., Masood, M.K., Soh, Y.C., Wu, M., Li, X.: Deep learning for building occupancy estimation using environmental sensors. In: Pedrycz, W., Chen, S.-M. (eds.) Deep Learning: Algorithms and Applications. SCI, vol. 865, pp. 335–357. Springer, Cham (2020). https://doi.org/10.1007/978-3-030-31760-7_11

6. Dey, A., et al.: Namatad: inferring occupancy from building sensors using machine learning. In: IEEE 3rd World Forum Internet of Things (WF-IoT), pp. 478–483, Dec ember 2016

7. Taunk, K., Verma, S., Swetapadma, A.: A brief review of nearest neighbor algorithms for learning and classification. In: International Conference on Intelligent Computing and Control Systems (ICCS), May 2019. https://doi.org/10.1109/ICCS45141.2019.9065747

8. Yang, B., Haghighat, F., Fung, B.C.M., Panchabikesan, K.: Season-based occupancy prediction in residential buildings using machine learning models. e-Prime **1**, 100003 (2021). https://doi.org/10.1016/j.prime.2021.100003

9. Madson, M., et al.: KNN algorithm and multivariate analysis to select and classify starch films. Food Packaging Shelf Life **34**, 100976 (2022). https://doi.org/10.1016/j.fpsl.2022.100976

10. Alves, A., et al.: Read this paper if you want to learn logistic regression. Revista de Sociologia e Politica. **28**, 1 (2020). https://doi.org/10.1590/1678987320287406en

11. Thorat, A.: Simply Logistic Regression, December 2021

12. Evgeniou, T., Pontil, M.: Support vector machines: theory and applications. In: Paliouras, G., Karkaletsis, V., Spyropoulos, C.D. (eds.) Machine Learning and Its Applications. ACAI 1999. LNCS, vol. 2049, pp. 249–257. Springer, Berlin, Heidelberg (2001). https://doi.org/10.1007/3-540-44673-7_12

13. Sai, F., Kamasani, M., Mitra, S.: A study on naive bayes classifier. Naive Bayers. Chittoor, November 2021

14. Ali, J., Khan, R., Ahmad, N., Maqsood, I.: Random forests and decision trees. Int. J. Comput. Sci. Issues (IJCSI). **9**, 272 (2012)

15. Farhadi, Z., Bevrani, H., Feizi Derakhshi, M.R.: Improving random forest algorithm by selecting appropriate penalized method. In: Communications in Statistics - Simulation and Computation, pp. 1–16, November 2022

16. Shereena, V.B., David, J.: Comparative study of dimensionality reduction techniques using PCA and LDA for content based image retrieval. In: International Conference on Computer Science and Information Technology, April 2015. https://doi.org/10.5121/csit.2015.50905

17. Iliou, T., Anagnostopoulos, C.N., Nerantzaki, M., Anastassopoulos, G.: A novel machine learning data preprocessing method for enhancing classification algorithms performance. In: Conference: Proceedings of the 16th International Conference on Engineering Applications of Neural Networks (INNS), Rhodes, Greece, September 2015. https://doi.org/10.1145/279 7143.2797155

18. Pedregosa, F., et al.: Scikit-learn: Machine learning in python. J. Mach. Learn. Res. **12**, 2825–2830 (2011)

19. Garg, V., Bansal, N.: Smart occupancy sensors to reduce energy consumption. Energy Build. **32**(1), 81–87 (2000)

20. Erickson, V., Achleitner, S., Cerpa, T.: POEM: power effificient occupancy based energy management system. In: Proceedings of 12th International Conference on Information Processing in Sensor Network (IPSN), pp. 203–216, New York, NY, USA (2013)
21. Balaji,B., Xu, J., S., Nwokafor, A., Gupta, R., Agarwal, Y.: Sentinel: occupancy based HVAC actuation using existing WiFi infrastructure within commercial buildings. In: Proceedings of the 11th ACM Conference on Embedded Networked Sensor Systems, pp. 17:1–17:14, November 2013. https://doi.org/10.1145/2517351.2517370
22. Scott, J., et al.: Preheat: controlling home heating using occupancy prediction. In: Proceedings of 13th International Conference on Ubiquitous Computing Series. UbiComp. New York, NY, USA, pp. 281–290. ACM (2011). https://doi.org/10.1145/2030112.2030151
23. Li, N., Calis, G., BecerikGerber, B.: Measuring and monitoring occupancy with an RFID based system for demand-driven HVAC operations. Autom. Constr. **24**, 89–99 (2012)
24. Ang,I.B., Salim, F.D., Hamilton, M.: Human occupancy recognition with multivariate ambient sensors. In: IEEE International Conference on Pervasive Computing and Communication Workshops (PerCom Workshops), pp. 1–6, March 2016. https://doi.org/10.1109/PERCOMW.2016.7457116
25. Yang, T., Zhao, L., Li, W., Wu, J., Zomaya, A.: Towards healthy and cost-effective indoor environment management in smart homes: a deep reinforcement learning approach. Appl. Energy. **300**, 117335 (2021). https://doi.org/10.1016/j.apenergy.2021.117335

A Prediction Model with Multi-Pattern Missing Data Imputation for Medical Dataset

K. Jegadeeswari⬥, R. Ragunath, and R. Rathipriya$^{(\boxtimes)}$⬥

Department of Computer Science, Periyar University, Salem, Tamil Nadu, India
rathipriyar@gmail.com

Abstract. Medical data is over and over again analyzed for disease diagnosis and proper treatment. Medical dataset usually contain missing data it is also treated as error. These missing values possibly will clue to incorrect disease diagnosis result. Meanwhile the medical data collection is costly, time incontrollable and an essential on the way to collected beginning various issues. Therefore get better missing data is an alternative of re-collecting the medical data. In this paper a Prediction Model has been proposed for missing data imputation in medical data. An experiment includes various datasets to validate the model as well as to establish the importance of imputation. A new Method name called enhanced random forest regression predictor is proposed for missing data imputation on medical dataset. Method is validated using 3 datasets named wisconsin, dermatology and breast cancer. All the datasets are downloaded from UCI repository. Missing data are generated manually in the original data from 1% to 15%. The proposed Prediction model is predict the missing values based on enhanced random forest regression predictor and evaluates the model using various classifiers. Classification is assessment of normal and abnormal disease diagnostics and produce the result of this experiment is accuracy. Proposed predictor has been compared with two imputation method as KNN and mice forest. Missing prediction model is perform better compared with other methods. Evaluation is demonstrating the classification and gives accuracy which is compared with original dataset and the imputed dataset. Missing data problem is a serious problem in medical data and can guidance downstream disease analysis. A proposed enhanced missing prediction model for missing data imputation is an application of imputing the missing data and disease analysis using classification in better way.

Keywords: Prediction model · Enhanced random forest regression predictor · Accuracy · Multi pattern and medical dataset

1 Introduction

An analysis of medical data has been commonly used in many researches over the bioinformatics disciplines are including disease prediction [1], diagnosis [2], drug design [3] and therapy identification etc. now a days machine learning techniques are play a vital role for analysis and challenging accountability for numerous medical applications. At the same time practical medical dataset collection is the essential and most first stage

I. Woungang et al. (Eds.): ANTIC 2022, CCIS 1798, pp. 538–553, 2023.
https://doi.org/10.1007/978-3-031-28183-9_38

of analysis process and also number of issues is rise during the collection. The issues are categorized in to two types such as human mistake and machine mistake. Human mistakes are comes from entry error, data unavailability, improper request, incomplete sequence, carelessness etc. machine mistakes are rise from various sources such as software corrupt, hardware failure and power shutdown. According to that the data collection typically contains feature redundancy, irregular patterns, missing values, incorrect values [4]. Missing values are fixed as NaN (Not a Number), null, undefined, incorrect, blanks and any other place holders. Dealing the missing value is important and focused area of analysis process because missing values can lead to inaccurate result. If the large amount of missing values arise, when the dataset massive then the entire dataset will loss the quality and valuable information. Therefore missing data handling is one of the big and concentrated problems whatever the missing value is small or large [5].

One of the ways to handling the missing value issue is collect the data again but that is not assurance to get complete dataset. Moreover if the dataset is massive entire process is expensive and takes large amount of time. Another way to dealing the missing value issue is to removing the missing values from the dataset in analysis process. Removing is a process of delete the entire row or column where the missing value occurred [6]. This removing process said to be loss of information moreover the entire dataset has losing valuable information that is why called as lagging dataset. This is lead to incorrect findings on analysis process in the area of bioinformatics disciplines. Recollect and removing process is not suitable to handling the missing values. Therefor imputation process is one of the computational method and also worthwhile which is filling the missing values in medical dataset for any analysis.

Missing values are generally two types of data one is numerical data and another one is categorical data. Numerical data is defined as numbers like integer values, continuous values [7]. Information is divided in to groups is known as categorical data. Generally imputation is divided in to two parts as single variant imputation and multivariate imputation. Single variate imputation is aimed to fill only one missing value over the row or column in the dataset. Multivariate imputation is to fill the more than one value over the row or column in the dataset. The missingness are three category of missing values called patterns [8] namely Missing Completely at Random (MCAR), Missing at Random (MAR), and Not Missing at Random (NMAR).

Completely at Random (MCAR) [9] pattern is arisen completely random all over the dataset. Missing value of this type pattern is no relationship with other observed values of features. This type of pattern filling is single variate imputation techniques. Some of the single variant imputations are discuss in the background part. Missing at random (MAR) [10] pattern is arisen randomly all over the dataset. Probability of this type pattern, missing value of the tuple belonging to the feature can be depends on observed data of other features. Missing not at random (MNAR) [11] pattern is arisen nonrandomly and entirely intentional motive reasons all over the dataset. Probability of the pattern is missing value and observed of the feature not equal. These two patterns are using multi variate imputation techniques. Some of the multi variate imputation techniques are discuss in the background part.

1.1 Motivation

Generation of missing data is one of the unavoidable problems in the field of bioinformatics. Many machine learning methods and statistical techniques are applied to analysis the medical dataset for specified applications such as disease prediction, diagnosis, drug design etc. Analysis supports to develop an effective drug for a particular disease because treatment process is differ from one and another disease and patient. Hence as an essential preprocess, missing Data imputation is far implemented before analyzing the medical data. It is helping to increases the value of information and quality of the dataset for effective analysis [12]. Missing Data imputation will become ever more important and also a worthwhile effort for effective data analysis in future.

2 Contribution

The summarization of the main contribution in this paper as follows.

- Introducing a Prediction Model to develop Enhanced Random Forest Regression predictor imputation methods using multi pattern missing values which is have four stage.
- Collecting the various medical dataset named Wisconsin, Dermatology and Breast Cancer.
- Decomposing the dataset into three sub dataset based on missing patterns named MCAR, MAR, and MNAR.
- Predict and Imputing the Missing value using Enhanced Random Forest Regression Predictor
- Merge all the imputed dataset after the missing data imputation.

2.1 Background

So far, many efforts have been completed to advance effective imputation methods for missing values in medical dataset. The existing methods were survey to replace the missing values as follows, One simplest early method is to replace the missing value by zero namely zeroimpute. Another one of simplest early method is rowimpute and columnimpute, missing values were filled with average of observed values from the corresponding column or row. In other words, the mean value of the row or column were to fill the missing value and also find the median or mode values over the row or column were to replace the missing value. All these methods are suitable for single variate imputation and does not considered correlation between the features [13]. So many existing literature worked based on single variant imputation, which is not perform feasibly when large missingness occurred. In generally a medical dataset have correlated features but a few existing literatures are worked based on correlation between the features and multi variant imputation [14]. Support vector Mechanism imputation (SVMI) have a two state one is trained state and another one tis test state. Trained state is trained the observed data (do not have missing data) of dataset to predict the missing value over the attribute. Testing state is to predict the missing data as fitting as the class label using other attributes. K Nearest Neighbor Imputation (KNNI) is initially fit the k as missing value then find most common nearest neighbor between all observed attribute. Add the distance of all observed attribute to distance collection. After that takes a mean value of the distance collection to fill the missing value. Local Least Square Imputation (LLSI) is fix the k as missing value, then identifies similar observed attributes from k and fit a least square between observed attributes and knowing record of the missing attribute to replace the missing values. Similarly many methods were used to impute the missing values. According to the existing literatures, different multi variant imputation methods are categorized in to three approaches called L-local, G-Global and H-Hybrid are reviewing of all the existing shown in Table 1.

Table 1. Review of multi variant imputation approaches.

Reference	Methods	Approach	Dataset	Description	Metrics
[15]	KNNimpute	L	DNA Microarrays	Find K neighboring genes with the help of Euclidian distance. Calculate the weighted average of each gene to impute missing values	RMSE
[16]	Sequential KNN	L	DNA Microarrays	Nearest neighbor design based imputed the missing values sequentially. Select further related of K neighbor	Accuracy
[17]	iterative KNNimpute	L	DNA Microarrays, Time Series	Find K neighboring genes with the help of Euclidian distance. In first iteration take missing position is replace by average of coherent gene row	NRMSE
[18]	GMCimpute	L	cell cycle	Each and every target is demonstrated by distribution of multi variant regular. Same as clustering work flow with Gaussian mixture	RMSE, Accuracy

(*continued*)

Table 1. (*continued*)

Reference	Methods	Approach	Dataset	Description	Metrics
[19]	LSimpute	L	Lymphoma	Correlation genes are selected with respect to target. Add weight to the target. Calculate weighted average to fill the missing values	RMSD
[20]	LLSimpute	L	Cyc-a, Alpha, Elu, cDNA	Correlation genes are selected in iteration manner. Difference between the first iteration and the last iteration is to impute at missing position using Euclidian distance	NRMSE
[21]	SLLSimpute	L	(SP.Alpha), Crzlp, RO.Cell-lin	Automatic parameter selection was introduced which is work both correlation basis feature selection and nearby neighbor to impute the missing values	NRMSE
[22]	RLSP	L	ALPHA, ELU	Select K closer gene and apply principle component. Which is work based on correlation between features	NRMSE

(*continued*)

Table 1. (*continued*)

Reference	Methods	Approach	Dataset	Description	Metrics
[23]	CMVE	L	BRCA1, BRCA2	Select complete covariant of target and rank the covariant. Choose effective covariant based on rank to impute at missing position	RMSE
[24]	ARLS	L	DNA Microarrays	Autoregressive constant was collected and sum the collected constant to imputing the missing values. Follow these steps reputedly	NRMSE
[15]	BPCA	G	cDNA microarray	This is works together of principal component, Bayesian and estimation maximization respectively	NRMSE
[25]	SVDimpute	G	DNA Microarrays, Time series	Perform singular values decomposition based on finding identical features of gene expression. Every gene contains Mutual orthogonal pattern which combined together based decomposition	RMSE

(*continued*)

Table 1. (*continued*)

Reference	Methods	Approach	Dataset	Description	Metrics
[26]	LinCmb	H	GeneChip, mRNA, cDNA	Add maximum weight to Limputation method	FRP, FNP, RMSE
[27]	HPM-MI	H	Breast Cancer	In training stage: K-Means, MLP and back propagation. Testing stage: extracts the instance based on patterns and apply MLP classification	Accuracy, sensitivity and ROC
[28]	Tri-imputation	H	Alpha, Elu, Ronen, Tacrc	Proposed RMIH is hybrid three methods are BPCA and LLS and ILLS	NRMSE

Rest of this paper organized as follows. Materials and methods divided in two parts as dataset description which gives the detail explanation about the datasets. Proposed method is demonstrate the detailed derivation of missing patterns and how the proposed Prediction Model works based on both of three patterns and enhanced RFR predictor. After that result and discussion is exploring the analysis report between proposed and exists. Finally conclude the paper.

3　Materials and Methods

3.1　Dataset Description

Author Collect the various medical dataset named Wisconsin, Dermatology and Breast Cancer. All the dataset are available from UCI repository. Missing data are generated manually with the help of random() function from 1% to 15% in the original data. From the literature review it can be seen that missing values or NaN in the dataset can be up to 20% to build better and more accurate machine learning models [29]. Where the 1% to 5% of missing values is treated as single variant missing and 6% to 15% missing values are treated as multi variant missing. The following table shows datasets which has taken for experiment.

3.2　Proposed Method

The proposed Prediction Model have four stages are bring together to improving the missing values imputation an efficiently. After generating missingness, that missing value contained dataset will move to first stage of proposed model for imputing. First stage of the proposed model is used for analyzing and identifying the types of missing

Table 2. Datasets details

Name of the Datasets	Records	Features	Pure Records		
			5%	10%	15%
Wisconsin	699	9	386×9	349×9	219×9
Dermatology	366	35	206×35	186×35	156×35
Breast Cancer	569	30	319×30	279×30	249×30

patterns namely MCAR, MAR, and MNAR. Second stage is decomposing the dataset based on the three patterns. After that the following third stage is imputation which is performing the imputation task to all the decomposed datasets using Enhanced Random forest regression predictor. Final fourth stage is merging all the imputing decomposed datasets. Evaluate the proposed model with relevant existing techniques using classification. Figure 1 shows the architecture of proposed Prediction model. Figure 1 shows the architecture of proposed Prediction model.

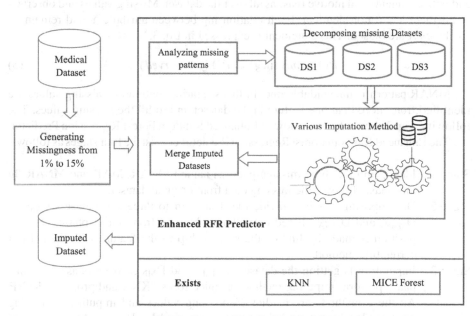

Fig. 1. Proposed Prediction Model

In this experiment consist three patterns namely Missing Completely at Random (MCAR), missing at Random (MAR), and Not Missing at Random (NMAR). Completely at Random (MCAR) pattern is arisen completely random all over the dataset. Missing values of the attribute (take it as Y) is independent of all remaining observed attributes (take it as X). In other words observed and missing values of attribute Y are matching. This statement is expressed in Eq. 1.

$$P(Y|y\ mis\sin g) = P(Y|y\ observed) \tag{1}$$

Missing at random (MAR) pattern is arisen randomly all over the dataset. Probability of this pattern, Missing values of the attribute (take it as Y) is dependent of all remaining observed attributes (take it as X) but not depend on observed value of Y itself. In other words missing values observed values of attribute Y are identical with other observed attribute X. This statement is expressed in Eq. 2.

$$P(Y|y\ mis\sin g,\ y\ observed,\ X) = P(Y|y\ observed,\ X) \tag{2}$$

Another missing pattern is Missing not at random (MNAR) is arisen nonrandomly and entirely intentional motive reasons all over the dataset. Missing values and observed of attribute Y are not identical. Even relationship between attribute Y and remaining attributes X are biased. This statement is expressed in Eq. 3.

$$P(Y|y\ mis\sin g) \neq P(Y|y\ observed) \tag{3}$$

MNAR pattern is unavoidable one. In this scenario, continuous missing values are identified from more than one feature in the dataset and to fill the missing values. The following Fig. 2 shows the work flow of Enhanced Random Forest Regression Predictor.

The Enhanced Random Forest Regression Predictor consist the four stages as follows.

Stage 1. Identifying the three missing patterns named MCAR, MAR and MNAR. In this phase discover the missing data from original dataset.

Stage 2. Decomposing phase is divide the dataset in to three sub datasets D_{MCAR}, D_{MAR}, and D_{MNAR} based on patterns obtained from above phase. Decomposition is made by finding the relationship of the feature with the help of correlation method.

Stage 3. Imputation is getting the datasets D_{MAR}, and D_{MNAR} from phase 2. In this phase perform imputing methods as mice forest, KNN and proposed RFRP. All these methods are predict the missing values and imputing at missing position. Produce the filled sub datasets named MI D_{MCAR}, MI D_{MAR}, and MI D_{MNAR}.

Stage 4. Merge phase collet all the filled sub datasets MI D_{MCAR}, MI D_{MAR}, and MI D_{MNAR} from the phase 3 merge together to form a final imputed dataset.

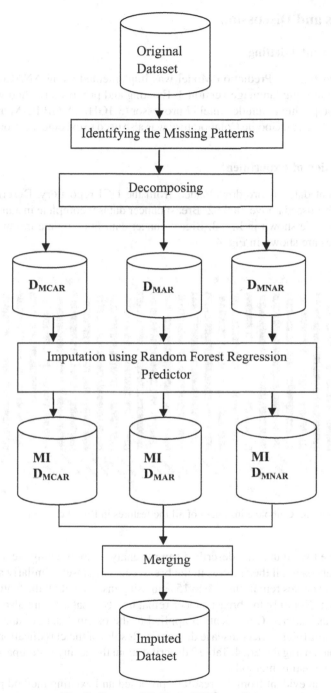

Fig. 2. Proposed Enhanced RFR predictor

4 Results and Discussion

4.1 Experimental Setting

The proposed Missing Prediction Model was implemented using ANACONDA 3 and Python programming language version 3. Existing and proposed method was executed using HP laptop which includes Intel i7 processor (3.1GHz), 8 GB RAM and Windows 10 Operating System. Google Colaboratory was also used to execute the proposed model.

4.2 Evaluation of Experiment

Three different datasets are downloaded from the UCI repository. Description of the dataset has discussed above Table 2. Breast cancer dataset complete instance belonging to the features are shown in Fig. 3. Breast cancer dataset complete instance belonging to the features are shown in Fig. 4.

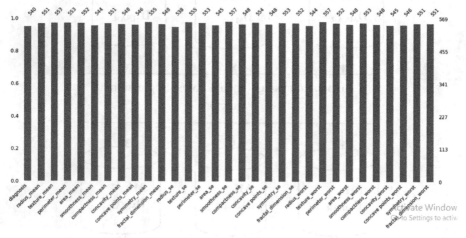

Fig. 3. Complete instances of all the features in Breast cancer dataset

The above two figures are described sample analysis about complete and 1% to 5% missing instances of all the features in the breast cancer dataset. Similarly author would analysis and executes remaining 6% to 15% missing instance of all the features in breast cancer dataset. Not only the breast cancer remaining two datasets are also analysis and execute in this manner. Classification applied to the original dataset and the imputed dataset for identifying cancer disease diagnosis. Results of the classification as accuracy were calculated using the Eq. 4. Table 3 describe about the accuracy comparison between proposed and existing methods.

Table 3 is an evident from the result of proposed and existing method performance. Various classification method were used to identify the disease diagnosis both before (original dataset) generating missing values and after imputing the missing values. SVM is benchmark method which perform the classification task of before generating missing

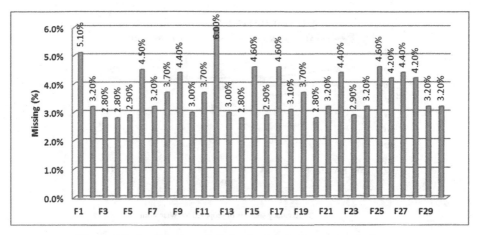

Fig. 4. Missing Instance of all the features in Breast cancer dataset

Table 3. Classification accuracy comparison

Datasets	Classifiers	Enhanced RFR Predictor				KNN				Mice forest			
		Original Dataset	After Imputation			Original Dataset	After Imputation			Original Dataset	After Imputation		
			5%	10%	15%		5%	10%	15%		5%	10%	15%
Wisconsin	SVM	97.1	96.5	96.5	97	90.4	89.9	89.3	90.5	93.4	94.2	94.1	94.3
	KNN	96	96	96.5	96.5	92.5	92.4	91.3	92	94.1	94.1	94	94.8
	NB	95.4	95.4	96	94.8	90.8	91.3	90.8	89.8	92.4	93.4	93.5	92.6
	DT	93.7	93.1	94.8	97.1	89.1	89	89.6	92.1	90.3	91.1	92.3	94.9
	RF	97.1	96.5	96.5	96	91.5	91.4	91.3	91	94.1	94.5	94	93.8
Dermatology	SVM	98.7	98.9	94.2	96.7	92.1	93.7	90.4	92.8	93.5	95.7	93.1	95.6
	KNN	96.7	97.8	95.6	97.8	94.1	94.8	89	91.7	95.7	96.9	91.7	94.5
	NB	84.7	78.2	80	77	80.1	74.1	73.4	75	81.2	76.2	76.1	77.8
	DT	93.4	93.4	90.2	96.7	88.8	89.3	85	91.7	90.4	91.4	87.2	94.5
	RF	92.3	93.4	89	90.2	87.7	89.3	83.8	85.2	89.3	91.4	86.5	88
Breast Cancer	SVM	96.5	96.5	94.4	95.1	91.9	92.4	89.2	90.1	93.5	94.5	91.9	92.9
	KNN	95.8	95.8	93.7	95.1	90.2	91.7	88.5	90.1	92.4	93.8	91.2	91.9
	NB	92.3	93	91.6	92.3	87.7	88.9	86.4	87.3	89.3	91	89.1	90.1
	DT	95.1	94.4	94.6	94.8	90.5	90.3	89.4	89.8	92.1	92.4	92.1	92.6
	RF	96.5	96.5	94.4	95.1	91.9	92.4	89.2	90.1	93.3	94.2	91.3	92.2

value, the accuracy result is 97.1 for Wisconsin, 98.7 for dermatology and 96.5 for breast cancer dataset using SVM classifier. Classification accuracy result for after imputing the missing values using proposed enhanced RFR predictor is 96.5 for 5% missing, 96.5 for 10% missing and 97 for 15% missing of Wisconsin dataset. Similarly take all the dataset accuracy result in this way for proposed method and the existing methods. Whether the missing values are smaller or larger the proposed method maintaining the same accuracy level there is no major difference between 5% and 15% missingness. Similarly all the datasets classification accuracy analyzed based on existing methods both missing

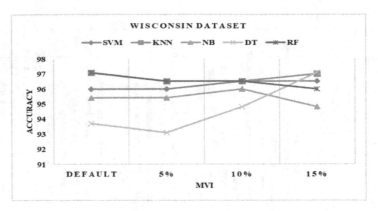

(a) Accuracy analysis of proposed for Wisconsin

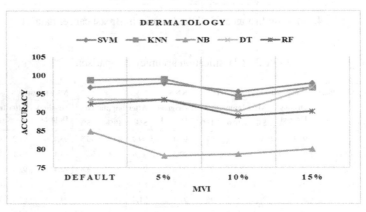

(b) Accuracy analysis of proposed for Dermatology

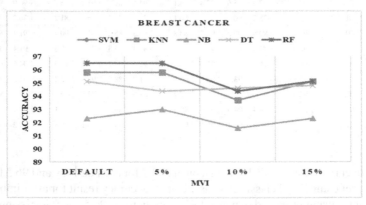

(c) Accuracy analysis of proposed for Breast cancer

Fig. 5. Accuracy analysis of proposed method using various dataset

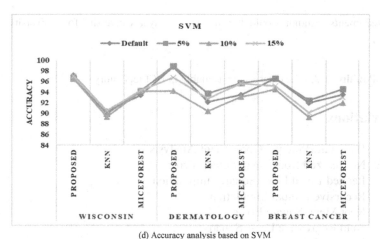

(d) Accuracy analysis based on SVM

Fig. 5. (*continued*)

smaller and larger. According to that analysis the proposed method performance is better to compared with existing KNN and mice forest. Following Fig. 5 a,b,c describe various classifier accuracy of various datasets based on missing percentage and d describe the benchmark method SVM based Proposed method analysis using various dataset.

5 Conclusion

Different types of missing patterns are occurred in real word medical dataset. Dealing the missing value is important and focused area of analysis process because missing values can lead to inaccurate result. Many researchers fail to identify the missing patterns and applying an effective imputation method during analyzes the disease diagnosis. Missing data patterns can decrease the performance of the classifiers. Several missing value imputation methods were developed to fill the missing data however most of the researchers are not satisfy all missing patterns. In this paper proposed Enhanced Random Forest Regression predictor developed to imputing the missing value based on three types of missing patterns. Three different datasets were used to evaluate the proposed method performance. Missing values are generated manually from 1% to 15%.The proposed method is analyzing the missing patterns from the original dataset after that decomposing in to three sub dataset as D_{MCAR}, D_{MAR}, and D_{MNAR}. Perform the imputation task to each sub dataset after that merge all the sub dataset to form an imputed dataset. The proposed method evaluated using different classifiers which produce the accuracy result. The accuracy value has no major difference between original data and the imputed. Therefore the proposed method gave the sufficient result.

In future, Ensemble hybrid imputation model is includes different machine learning techniques. This model can applied to complex dataset like gene expression and micro array dataset. Meanwhile it can also handle different types of missing patterns and this single model can impute the both univariant, multi variant imputation.

Acknowledgments. Author would like to thank Periyar University for University Research Fellowship.

Data Availability:.   All the datasets are available in UCI repository.

Abbreviations

BPCA   Bayesian Principal Component Analysis
NRMSE   Normalized Root Mean Square Error
ILLS   Iterated Local Least Squares imputation
RMI   Recursive Mutual Imputation
RMSE   Root Mean Square Error
ARLS   Auto Regressive Least Square
ILLS   Iterative Local Least Square
RLSP   Robust Least Squares Principal components
GMC   Gaussian Mixture Computing
SLLS   Sequential Local Least Square
SKNN   sequential K Nearest Neighbor

References

1. Muro, S., et al.: Identification of expressed genes linked to malignancy of human colorectal carcinoma by parameteric clustering of quantitative expression data. Genome. Biol. **4**(R21), 1–10 (2003)
2. Mirus, J.E., et al.: Cross-species antibody microarray interrogation identifies a 3-protein panel of plasma biomarkers for early diagnosis of pancreas cancer. Clin. Cancer Res. **21**(7), 1764–1771 (2015)
3. Wang, W., et al.: Microarray profiling shows distinct differences between primary tumors and commonly used preclinical models in hepatocellular carcinoma. BMC Cancer **15**, 828 (2015)
4. Shipp, M.A., et al.: Diffuse large b-cell lymphoma outcome prediction by gene-expression profiling and supervised machine learning. Nat Med. **8**(1), 68–74 (2002)
5. Li, J., Wong, L., Yang, Q.: Guest editors' introduction: data mining in bioinformatics. IEEE Intell. Syst. **20**(6), 16–18 (2005)
6. Ayilara, O.F., Zhang, L., Sajobi, T.T., Sawatzky, R., Bohm, E., Lix, L.M.: Impact of missing data on bias and precision when estimating change in patient-reported outcomes from a clinical registry. Health Quality Life Outcomes, **17**(1) (2019)
7. Dantan, E., Proust-Lima, C., Letenneur, L., Jacqmin-Gadda, H.: Pattern mixture models and latent class models for the analysis of multivariate longitudinal data with informative dropouts. Int. J. Biostat. **4**(1) (2008)
8. Jegadeeswari, K., Ragunath, R., Rathipriya, R.: Missing data imputation using ensemble learning technique: a review. Soft Comput. Secur. Appl. 223-236 (2023)
9. Ramli, M.N., Yahaya, A., Ramli, N., Yusof, N., Abdullah, M.: Roles of imputation methods for filling the missing values: a review. Adv. Environ. Biol. **7**, 3861–3870 (2013)
10. Rezvan, P.H., Lee, K.J., Simpson, J.A.: The rise of multiple imputation: a review of the reporting and implementation of the method in medical research. BMC Med. Res. Methodol. **15**, 30 (2015)

11. Eisemann, N., Waldmann, A., Katalinic, A.: Imputation of missing values of tumour stage in population-based cancer registration. BMC Med. Res. Methodol. **11**, 129 (2011)
12. Rahman, S.A., Huang, Y., Claassen, J., Heintzman, N., Kleinberg, S.: Combining Fourier and lagged k-nearest neighbor imputation for biomedical time series data. J. Biomed. Inform. **58**, 198–207 (2015)
13. Gómez-Carracedo, M.P., Andrade, J.M., López-Mahía, P., Muniategui, S., Prada, D.: A practical comparison of single and multiple imputation methods to handle complex missing data in air quality datasets. Chemom. Intell. Lab. Syst. **134**, 23–33 (2014)
14. Langkamp, D.L., Lehman, A., Lemeshow, S.: Techniques for handling missing data in secondary analyses of large surveys. Acad. Pediatr. **10**(3), 205–210 (2010)
15. Troyanskaya, O., Cantor, M., Sherlock, G., Brown, P., Hastie, T., Tibshirani, R., et al.: Missing value estimation methods for DNA microarrays. Bioinformatics **17**, 520–525 (2001). https://doi.org/10.1093/bioinformatics/17.6.520
16. Kim, K.Y., Kim, B.J., Yi, G.S.: Reuse of imputed data in microarray analysis increases imputation efficiency. BMC Bioinform. **5**, 160 (2004). https://doi.org/10.1186/1471-2105-5-160
17. Brás, L.P., Menezes, J.C.: Improving cluster-based missing value estimation of DNA microarray data. Biomol. Eng. **24**, 273–282 (2007). https://doi.org/10.1016/j.bioeng.2007.04.003
18. Ouyang, M., Welsh, W.J., Georgopoulos, P.: Gaussian mixture clustering and imputation of microarray data. Bioinformatics **20**, 917–923 (2004). https://doi.org/10.1093/bioinformatics/bth007
19. Bø, T.H., Dysvik, B., Jonassen, I.: LSimpute: accurate estimation of missing values in microarray data with least squares methods. Nucleic Acids Res. **32**, e34 (2004). https://doi.org/10.1093/nar/gnh026
20. Cai, Z., Heydari, M., Lin, G.: Iterated local least squares microarray missing value imputation. J. Bioinform. Comput. Biol. **4**, 935–957 (2006). https://doi.org/10.1142/s0219720006002302
21. Zhang, X., Song, X., Wang, H., Zhang, H.: Sequential local least squares imputation estimating missing value of microarray data. Comput. Biol. Med. **38**, 1112–1120 (2008). https://doi.org/10.1016/j.compbiomed.2008.08.006
22. Yoon, D., Lee, E.K., Park, T.: Robust imputation method for missing values in microarray data. BMC Bioinform. **8**, S6 (2007). https://doi.org/10.1186/1471-2105-8-S2-S6
23. Sehgal, M.S.B., Gondal, I., Dooley, L.S.: Collateral missing value imputation: a new robust missing value estimation algorithm for microarray data. Bioinformatics **21**, 2417–2423 (2005). https://doi.org/10.1093/bioinformatics/bti345
24. Choong, M.K., Charbit, M., Yan, H.: Autoregressive-model-based missing value estimation for DNA microarray time series data. IEEE Trans. Inform. Technol. Biomed. **13**, 131–137 (2009). https://doi.org/10.1109/TITB.2008.2007421
25. Oba, S., Sato, M., Takemasa, I., Monden, M., Matsubara, K., Ishii, S.: A Bayesian missing value estimation method for gene expression profile data. Bioinformatics. **19**, 2088–2096 (2003). https://doi.org/10.1093/bioinformatics/btg287
26. Jörnsten, R., Wang, H.Y., Welsh, W.J., Ouyang, M.: DNA microarray data imputation and significance analysis of differential expression. Bioinformatics **21**, 4155–4161 (2005). https://doi.org/10.1093/bioinformatics/bti638
27. Purwar, A., Singh, S.K.: Hybrid prediction model with missing value imputation for medical data. Expert Syst. Appl. **42**, 5621–5631 (2015). https://doi.org/10.1016/j.eswa.2015.02.050
28. He, C., Zhao, C., Li, G.Z., Zhu, W., Yang, W., Yang, M.Q.: A hybrid iterative approach for microarray missing value estimation. In: 2016 IEEE International Conference on Bioinformatics and Biomedicine (BIBM). Shenzhen, pp. 2–1350. IEEE (2016)
29. Emmanuel, T., Maupong, T., Mpoeleng, D., Semong, T., Banyatsang, M., Tabona, O.: A survey on missing data in machine learning (2021)

Impact Analysis of Hello Flood Attack on RPL

Prashant Maurya(✉) ⓘ and Vandana Kushwaha ⓘ

Banaras Hindu University, Varanasi, India
{prashant.maurya17,vandanakus}@bhu.ac.in

Abstract. The Internet of Things (IoT) has a wide range of applications that improve our quality of life with smart things that can connect without human intervention. However, IoT networks face new threats similar to Wireless Sensor Networks. Concerning high risks seriously impact the network topology, security, privacy, and energy levels. A routing protocol for devices with limited resources in the Internet of Things networks is the IPv6 Routing Protocol for Low-Power and Lossy Networks (RPL). The nodes can be subject to several attacks when it transmits packets between nodes. One of the most potent attacks against RPL protocol is the DODAG Information Solicitation (DIS) Flooding attack, which has a detrimental effect on the node's limited processing power and energy level. The impact of the Hello-Flood attack has been examined for several scenarios in this study. The Contiki-Cooja simulation environment is used to carry out the experiments.

Keywords: Hello flood · DIS flood · RPL · IoT · Attack · Security

1 Introduction

The Internet of Things (IoT), a revolutionary networking architecture, promises to improve the quality of life by turning every physical object in our surroundings into a smart object that can sense its surroundings and interact with other smart things in the network. Softwares, wireless network technologies, and sensors-actuators are some of the Internet of Things components. IoT has gained momentum as a result of the fast-expanding number of sensors, actuators, and smart devices connected to the Internet. In particular, it enables data collection and remote control of physical things via the internet, integrating physical and computer-based systems and bringing about improvements in dependability, accuracy, and financial gains. However, the expansion of devices and their incorporation into the network environment has drawn a lot of security risks. Although there are various security risks due to the growing number of devices and their connection with the network environment [1]. For sensitive data, security threats might be very hazardous. Large businesses have been targeted by cyberattacks in particular so that company reports, credit card data, and customer privacy documents can be taken. The long-term viability of the network system depends on IoT security. Due to the inconvenience of the constrained resource structure, it may be vulnerable to the damaging consequences of attacks. Attacks against IoT devices are anticipated to increase in

I. Woungang et al. (Eds.): ANTIC 2022, CCIS 1798, pp. 554–568, 2023.
https://doi.org/10.1007/978-3-031-28183-9_39

the near future as IoT devices become more widely utilized with diversity. The most crucial routing protocol for Internet Protocol version 6 (IPv6)-based Low-power Wireless Personal Area Networks is the Routing Protocol for Low Power and Lossy Networks (LLNs) (RPL). Numerous cyberattacks have been launched against the vast array of IoT applications and their integration services online. The resource utilization of nodes in the IoT ecosystem is the direct target of the most frequent RPL attacks. IoT must therefore overcome the negative impacts of cyberattacks, including the significant loss of data packets, the high computational load, and the consistency of node energy for LLNs [2].

1.1 RPL Overview

RPL uses Destination Oriented Directed Acyclic Graphs (DODAGs) rooted at a single destination named sink to operate on the IP networking layer via the 6LoWPAN protocol stack [3]. The protocol constructs a network of logical channels that lead to the sink using actual network connections. Since a variety of metrics (like link reliability, latency throughput, and throughput) and constraints (like nodes' energy, link colour, and throughput) can be used to evaluate the nodes' rank, parents' selection on paths towards the DODAG root can be thought of as a multi-objective optimization problem [4]. The designated Objective Function (OF) specifies how the RPL nodes pick and optimize routing paths in a DODAG as well as transform metrics and/or limitations into ranks.

RPL Control Messages. RPL primarily uses three types of ICMPv6 control messages to construct and manage the network topology and routing data [5]:

a) DODAG Information Object (DIO) Message. This message promotes the creation of a DODAG, its maintenance, and upward routes from other nodes to the root [6]. It contains crucially updated configuration parameters such as the rank of the sender node, the RPLs instance ID, the DODAGs ID, the version number, the RPLs mode of operation, and other crucial maintenance parameters [3, 6]. Additionally, DIO messages are issued in response to a DODAG information solicitation (DIS) message that has been received [7].

b) DODAG Information Solicitation (DIS) Message. A new node looking to join an existing network uses it as an upward ICMP control message to ask nearby nodes for a DIO message. When a node doesn't get a DIO message after a certain amount of time, it sends one.

c) Destination Advertisement Object (DAO) Message.
When building downward routes, each node advertises to its parent the set of nodes in its sub-DODAG that choose it as their preferred parent. Upward routes are created and maintained via DIO and DIS messages [9]. If necessary, the DAO receiving node may elect to send a DAO acknowledgement message, although RPL Contiki does not. When every node has a way to the root, convergence is achieved. Following convergence, nodes occasionally communicate with one another to maintain the network [8].

DODAG Building. Based on the exchange of routing control messages, such as the DODAG Information Object (DIO), Destination Advertisement Object (DAO), DAO-ACK, and DODAG Information Solicitation, the sink-node begins the (re)construction of the DODAG (DIS). Numerous DIO messages are multicast by nodes joining the graph after the sink has multicast the first DIO message. All nodes, except the sink, utilize DAO messages to spread reverse route information; in contrast, detached or unconnected nodes (due to mobility) send DIS messages to other potentially connected neighbours to join the network. The routing metrics and/or constraints, as well as the OF used to form the routing paths, are all contained in DIO messages, which are crucial for the graph's development [2].

DODAG Maintenance. The most basic functionality of RPL is the maintenance of the DODAG. Therefore, the propagation of DIO messages, which is the basis for the network's convergence time, is synchronized by a special algorithm called the Trickle timer [9]. Any modification to the DODAG, such as the selection of a new parent or an unreachable parent, causes the Trickle timer to reset. The algorithm predicts that DIO messages will be transmitted more frequently when the network is unstable and less frequently when it is stable to save energy [2].

A brief overview of the exchange mechanism for RPL control messages has been represented in Fig. 1. A new node first sends out the DIS to ask adjacent DODAG for data when it wants to join the network. Following that, the network replies to the DIS with a DIO message containing network data. The original network will then be rejoined using DODAG, which is directed by DAO that the new node will then send. The DAO-ACK is the original network's response upon receiving the DAO. Since the original RPL lacks a way to validate control messages, all RPL attacks take advantage of tampering with control messages. To reduce network control traffic and the impact of attacks that modify control messages, RPL employs an adaptive timing mechanism called a Trickle timer [10].

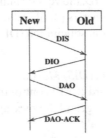

Fig. 1. RPL control messages

2 Literature Review

The WSN experts have examined flooding threats in great detail and have offered numerous defence strategies. However, due to the RPL protocol's unique operating methods and control message formats, similar solutions cannot be directly applied to RPL security [1]. Authors in [11] did an investigation the effects of various routing attacks on

6LoWPAN networks using RPL. In their analysis, the authors took into account rank, local repair, replay, and DIS flooding attacks. The DIS flooding attack, out of the four attacks, is demonstrated as a critical attack against RPL-based 6LoWPAN networks. Critical parameters that are most adversely affected by DIS flooding attacks include control packet overhead, end-to-end delay, and power consumption. Authors in [5] analyzed network performance in terms of power consumption, overhead, packet delivery ratio, and latency under various scenarios and operational settings, and a new flooding version number attack against RPL-based networks have been developed. Authors in [12] studied and examined the RPL IoT Protocol assaults in [8], where they categorised the potential routing attacks against this protocol. Attacks against resources, topology, and data traffic were divided into three broad types, and risk management for these attacks was addressed. Authors in [13] documented difficulties, security issues and several attacks on the RPL protocol. They have also provided an overview of the architecture of IoT routing protocols like 6LoWPAN and RPL. Nevertheless, they did not simulate the attacks, which inspired us to continue and simulate several attacks. The RPL is being examined by [14], for numerous cyberattacks against it, including the Hello Flood, Version Number Modification Attack, and Blackhole attack. Authors of [15] simulated DIS attack, blackhole attack, DIO flood, DAO assault, and version number attack. Authors in [16] studied the impact of DIS flooding attack on RPL with malicious nodes near the root node and far from the root node which is outside the range of communication range of the root node. The study analyzed Packet Delivery Ratio, end-to-end delay, power consumption and overhead. Authors in [17], and [18] reviewed various attacks and techniques to mitigate flooding attacks. Considering all of these RPL attack research and surveys, some writers chose not to replicate any routing attacks, while others simply simulated one or two attacks. Many researchers use a single malicious node while other uses multiple malicious nodes. In this paper single malicious node has been taken for analysis of the hello flood attack against RPL.

3 Attacks on RPL Protocol

Due to the brittle and hackable nature of IoT nodes, RPL protocol is susceptible to a variety of insider and outsider attacks that are challenging to identify and counteract. Control message, encryption, and security modes are among the numerous RPL security techniques [19]. Due to implementation costs and inadequate mechanism specifications, security measures are not taken into account in the majority of RPL implementations [20]. The majority of security measures are successful in thwarting outsider attacks, but they fall short in thwarting insider attacks because an insider can go beyond RPL's security measures. Authors in [21] and [22] have categorized attacks according to their principal target as discussed below.

3.1 Type of Attack on RPL

Various types of attacks can be implemented against the RPL protocol. Attacks can be classified based on their effect on resources, network topology or traffic.

Resources Category Attack. The goal of these kind of attacks is to disrupt network availability by causing legitimate nodes to spend their energy, processing, or memory resources. Attacks on resources can be divided into two basic groups. The first type of attack, known as a direct attack, involves the attacker using nodes to create traffic overhead to directly disrupt the network. The second type of attack is indirect in which the attacker makes use of other nodes to overburden the network. Most significant attacks under this category are as follows [21]:

a) Hello Flood. In this attack excessive amount of discovery packets in a network is produced to destabilize and render the nodes unreachable. It could be carried out either internally or externally. It might also be seen as a topology-based attack [14, 23]. In the DIS Flooding attack, a malicious node transmits DIS messages to nearby neighbours who are within its transmission range regularly. A victim node responds with DIO messages and resets its timer in exchange. Sending multicast or unicast DIS messages might be used to complete this operation. When a node gets a unicast DIS message from the attacker during a unicast DIS flooding attack, it must respond with a DIO message. Like the multicast DIS flooding attack, the attacker broadcasts multicast DIS messages, and each node that receives them sends DIO messages to its neighbours. Increased control packet overhead, node energy depletion, and routing disruption are the results of the hello flood attack [1, 5].

b) Rooting Table Overload. The routing table can be overloaded by sending a bogus route in the DIO message to the target node. The attacker takes advantage of a node that is in storage mode. The routing table will be filled, causing a halt to any attempts to add new routes, and it will interfere with regular network activities [7].

c) Increased Rank Attack. Routing loops are created when a node is purposely modified to have a Rank value that is the same as its sibling node [24].

d) Version Number Modification. To deliver the DIO message to its neighbours, the attackers try to boost the version number value inside of it. As a result, the DODAG had to be rebuilt from the ground up, which had the unfortunate side effects of clogged networks, significant data packet loss, and resource waste [25].

Against Topology. The purpose of these kind of attacks is to topologically degrade the network that is being attacked. According to the outcomes, this attack might also be divided into two sorts. Consequently, a sub-optimization attack precludes optimal network convergence, while an isolation attack aims to isolate a node or a group of nodes from DODAG [10]. These are a few significant attacks against topology:

a) Routing Table Falsification. The rogue node will change the DAO control message to confuse the network with a bogus route. In turn, this would cause the impacted nodes to get incorrect routing information from the routing table, resulting in growing delays and a clogged network [7].

b) Sinkhole. This attack draws in as much traffic as possible through deceptive informational adverts. As a result, network performance will suffer. Additionally, if this attack is paired with other attacks like blackhole or Selective Forwarding attacks, it will become more damaging [26].

c) Blackhole. As much traffic as possible is attracted in this assault, but the attacker isolates nodes from the topology and drops packets through its node. One may classify a blackhole assault as a DoS attack [1].

d) Routing Information Reply. This attack involves transmitting packets while purposefully delaying and repeating them [7].

E) Wormhole. With this assault, a connection between two nodes that would typically have great distances between them is created purposefully. It interferes with the process of creating the best routes and paths [27].

Against Traffic. The goal of these kind of attacks is to take over all information used for communication. Based on its final goal, this attack could potentially be divided into two types. First, to gather all of the network's traffic, and second, to gather important information about the topology and the targeted network [7].

a) Sniffing. This attack involves listening to packets that nodes send over the network, which compromises the transmission's confidentiality [14].

b) Traffic Analysis. A sniffer attack might be combined with a traffic analysis attack. Even though the routing information is already encrypted, it is still possible to extract valuable information from it, such as the relationships between nodes. The goal of this attack is to acquire enough data to execute a different kind of attack [14].

c) Decreased Rank Attack. Nodes that are closer together tend to look more appealing than ones that are farther apart. To attract more traffic for attacks like Blackhole, sinkhole, and eavesdropping, malicious nodes could fraudulently be given a lower Rank value using fake DIO packets [24].

d) Identity Attack. The rogue node would impersonate a legitimate network node. The attacker would be able to locate nodes of interest to impersonate legitimate nodes by forging their addresses if it was used in conjunction with a sniffing attack. An identity assault on a DODAG root would result in the attacker seizing control of the whole network [14].

RPL control messages can be illegitimately manipulated to disrupt routing operations. Similarly, fault tolerance mechanisms can be exploited to target network resources by performing a Denial of Services attack (DoS) [21].

4 Experimental Tool and Simulation Environment

The Contiki OS Java Simulator, widely known as Cooja, enables the simulation of various nodes on which the Contiki operating system and its applications are loaded. With the aid of this tool, programs may be inexpensively evaluated before being loaded into the flash memory of absolute sensors. A versatile, lightweight OS for networked tiny sensors is Contiki. Wireless sensor networks have drawn a lot of attention from the scientific community nowadays. It is conceivable to imagine a wide range of applications in the scientific, military, industrial, and home automation domains thanks to the downsizing of sensors and their relatively inexpensive cost. To make it easier to design these applications Cooja is a memory-efficient, multitasking operating system for wireless sensor networks and embedded networked systems [15, 28].

This experiment was performed on Ubuntu 14.04 in a VirtualBox with two cores processor and 8192MB memory. We use the Contiki-3.0 and the Cooja simulator. Simulation Parameters are summarized in Table 1.

Table 1. Simulation parameters

Parameters	Values
Network layer Protocol	RPL
Operating System	Contiki 3.0
Simulator	Cooja
Emulated Nodes	Zolertia Z1
Number of Sink Nodes	1
Number of Normal Nodes	5, 10, 15, 20, 25
Number of Malicious Nodes	1
Radio model	UDGM
Simulation area	200 m × 200 m
Simulation time	120 s
Attack Implemented	Hello Flood Attack

4.1 Simulation Scenario

In this experiment, five scenarios have been considered. Each scenario has three types of nodes sink node, normal node and malicious node. In each scenario attacker node has been introduced as an extra node in the network. Table 2 summarizes all scenarios used in this experiment. Snapshots of all scenarios with malicious nodes have been illustrated in Fig. 2.

5   Result Analysis and Discussion

This section discusses the effect of the hello flood attack on RPL. Results have been analyzed for nodes, overall energy consumption, and ICMPv6 control messages.

In each scenario power consumption of nodes has been significantly increased after implementing the hello flood attack because these nodes are in the transmission range of rogue nodes. Energy is consumed in the initialization of node (INT), keeping it powered-ON (ON), in Transmission (TX) and in Receiving (RX). In each scenario, all nodes available in the transmission range of rogue node energy consumption for ON,

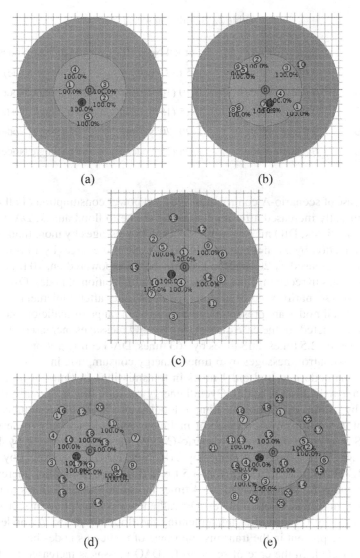

Fig. 2. (a) Scenario-A (b) Scenario-B (c) Scenario-C (d) Scenario-D (e) Scenario-E

TX & RX has been significantly increased. Other nodes which are not in the transmission range of rogue node has not had much impact on their energy consumption. Malicious node consumes energy while transmitting DIS Messages and while it is powered on. On the other hand, nodes affected by hello flood attacks consume energy while it is powered on, receiving DIS and transmitting DIO messages as a response to DIS messages. The number of DAO messages, DIO messages and DIS messages has increased after the attack. But the number of DIS messages increased significantly because the malicious node transmits DIS messages.

Table 2. Simulation scenarios

Scenario	Sink Nodes ID	Normal Nodes ID	Malicious Nodes ID
Scenario-A	0 (Single Node)	1–5 (5 Nodes)	6 (Single Node)
Scenario-B	0 (Single Node)	1–10 (10 Nodes)	11 (Single Node)
Scenario-C	0 (Single Node)	1–15 (15 Nodes)	16 (Single Node)
Scenario-D	0 (Single Node)	1–20 (20 Nodes)	21 (Single Node)
Scenario-E	0 (Single Node)	1–25 (25 Nodes)	26 (Single Node)

In the case of scenario-A control messages and power consumption of all nodes has been significantly increased after implementing the hello flood attack. DAO messages increased by 4 times, DIO messages by 5 times, DIS messages by more than 500 times, DAG configuration by 5 times and total ICMPv6 control messages by 14 times. Energy consumption increased by 20 times in keeping the node powered on, 10 times in transmission, 30 times in receiving, and 10 times in the initialization of nodes. Overall energy consumption in scenario-A has been increased by 24 times after implementing the flooding attack. As all nodes are present in the transmission range of malicious nodes hence all nodes are affected. In the case of scenario-B DAO messages increased by 2.3 times, DIO messages by 2.5 times, DIS times by 263 times, DAG configuration by 3 times and total ICMPv6 control messages by 6 times. Energy consumption increased by 6 times in keeping the node powered on, 4 times in transmission, 14 times in receiving, and 10 times in initialization of nodes. Overall energy consumption in scenario B has been increased by 7 times after implementing a flooding attack. As nodes number 0,1,4,6,7 are present in the transmission range of malicious nodes hence only these nodes are affected. Similarly, In the case of scenario-C DAO messages increased by 1.6 times, DIO messages by 1.7 times, DIS times by 218 times, DAG configuration by 1.6 times and total ICMPv6 control messages by 3.5 times. Energy consumption increased by 5 times in keeping the node powered on, 4 times in transmission, 15 times in receiving, and 14 times in initialization of nodes. Overall energy consumption in scenario C has been increased by 6 times after implementing the flooding attack. As nodes number 0,1,4,5,7,10 are present in the transmission range of malicious nodes hence only these nodes are affected. In the case of scenario D, DAO messages increased by 1.3 times, DIO messages by 1.6 times, DIS times by 140 times, DAG configuration by 1.5 times and total ICMPv6 control messages by 3.2 times. Energy consumption increased by 4 times in keeping the node powered on, 3 times in transmission, 4 times in receiving, and 15 times in initialization of nodes. Overall energy consumption in scenario-D has been increased by 5 times after implementing a flooding attack. As nodes number 0, 3, 4, 5, 6, 10, 13, 15, 17, 18 are present in the transmission range of malicious nodes hence only these nodes are affected. In the case of scenario-E DAO messages increased by 1.2 times, DIO messages by 1.2 times, DIS times by 79 times, DAG configuration by 1.1 times and total ICMPv6 control messages by 2.2 times. Energy consumption increased by 3 times in keeping the node powered on, 2 times in transmission, 2 times in receiving, and 5 times in the initialization of nodes. Overall energy consumption in scenario E has been increased by 2.5 times after implementing a flooding attack. As nodes number 0, 3, 4, 7, 8, 9, 10, 11, 12, 13, 16, 20 are present in the transmission range of malicious nodes hence only these nodes are affected. Overall, Energy consumption increased by 4.4 times in keeping the node powered-ON, 3 times in transmission, 40 times in receiving and 10 times in initialization of the node while total energy consumption has been increased up to 5 times after the hello flood attack.

Overall, DAO messages increased by 1.7 times, DIO messages by 1.84 times, DIS times by 178 times, DAG configuration by 1.8 times and total ICMPv6 control messages by 4 times. Increment of control messages leads to Energy consumption increased by 4.4 times in keeping the node powered-ON, 3 times in transmission, 40 times in receiving and 10 times in initialization of the node while overall energy consumption has been increased up to 5 times (Figs. 3, 4, 5, 6, 7, 8 and 9).

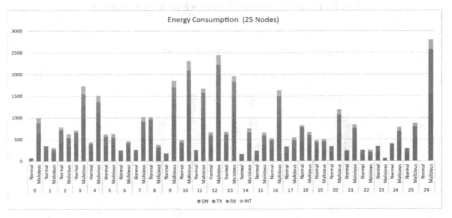

Fig. 3. Energy Consumption of each node in Scenario-E

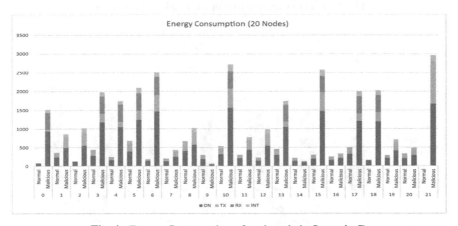

Fig. 4. Energy Consumption of each node in Scenario-D

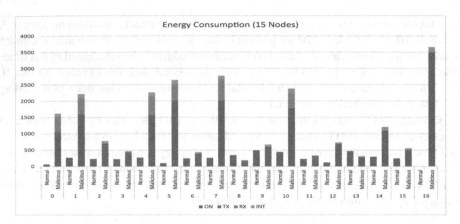

Fig. 5. Energy Consumption of each node in Scenario-C

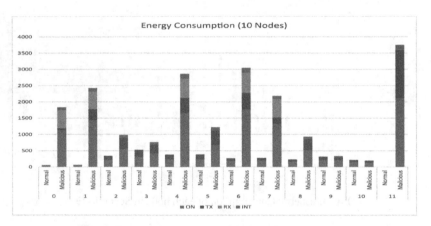

Fig. 6. Energy Consumption of each node in Scenario-B

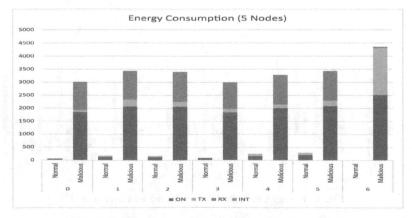

Fig. 7. Energy Consumption of each node in Scenario-A

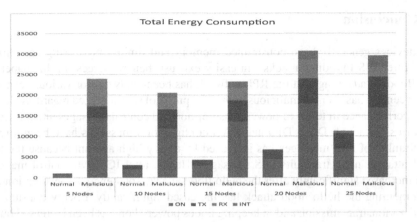

Fig. 8. Total Energy Consumption

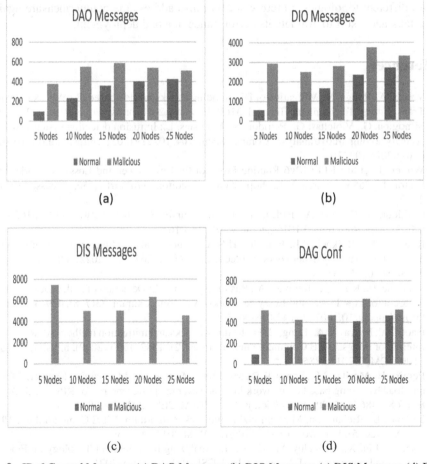

Fig. 9. IPv6 Control Messages (a) DAO Messages (b) DIO Messages (c) DIS Messages (d) DAG Conf

6 Conclusion

IoT devices generally have constrained memory and limited processing capabilities. Therefore, DIS Flooding attacks can easily exhaust their resources. In this paper, the DIS flooding attack against the RPL network has been analyzed for various scenarios. Each scenario has a single malicious node. The protocol was analyzed regarding the network performance in terms of power consumption and control messages under different scenarios. Although DAO, DIO and DAG configuration messages have been affected but Number of DIS messages has increased by a very high amount because the hello flood attacker node transmits DIS messages. Hence, total ICMPv6 control messages have increased significantly after the hello flood attack. Total energy consumption after implementing the hello flood attack has increased significantly. Energy consumed in initialization, transmission and in keeping nodes powered on has been increased but the largest amount of Energy is consumed in receiving DIS messages which are forwarded by the malicious node.

In the future, we plan to study the effect of hello flood under various time intervals, across different topologies. Future work will also address the countermeasure against this attack and test it to evaluate its performance in a real deployment.

References

1. Verma, A., Ranga, V.: Mitigation of DIS flooding attacks in RPL-based 6LoWPAN networks. Trans. Emerg. Telecommun. Technol. **31**(2), February 2020. https://doi.org/10.1002/ett.3802
2. Simoglou, G., Violettas, G., Petridou, S., Mamatas, L.: Intrusion detection systems for RPL security: a comparative analysis. Comput. Secur. **104**, 102219 (2021). https://doi.org/10.1016/j.cose.2021.102219
3. Winter, T., et al.: RPL: IPv6 Routing Protocol for Low-Power and Lossy Networks. RFC Editor, RFC6550, March 2012. https://www.rfc-editor.org/info/rfc6550. Accessed 09 July 2020
4. Gaddour, O., Koubâa, A.: RPL in a nutshell: a survey. Comput. Netw. **56**(14), 3163–3178 (2012). https://doi.org/10.1016/j.comnet.2012.06.016
5. Rouissat, M., Belkheir, M., Belkhira, H.S.A.: A potential flooding version number attack against RPL based IOT networks. J. Electr. Eng. **73**(4), 267–275 (2022). https://doi.org/10.2478/jee-2022-0035
6. Shafique, U., Khan, A., Rehman, A., Bashir, F., Alam, M.: Detection of rank attack in routing protocol for Low Power and Lossy Networks. Ann. Telecommun. **73**(7–8), 429–438 (2018). https://doi.org/10.1007/s12243-018-0645-4
7. Raoof, A., Matrawy, A., Lung, C.-H.: Routing attacks and mitigation methods for RPL-based internet of things. IEEE Commun. Surv. Tutor. **21**(2), 1582–1606 (2019). https://doi.org/10.1109/COMST.2018.2885894
8. Pereira, H., Moritz, G.L., Souza, R.D., Munaretto, A., Fonseca, M.: Increased network lifetime and load balancing based on network interface average power metric for RPL. IEEE Access **8**, 48686–48696 (2020). https://doi.org/10.1109/ACCESS.2020.2979834
9. Djamaa, B., Richardson, M.: Optimizing the trickle algorithm. IEEE Commun. Lett. **19**(5), 819–822 (2015). https://doi.org/10.1109/LCOMM.2015.2408339
10. Zhao, J., Liu, X., Baddeley, M., Haque, I.: Analyzing the Impact of Topology on Flooding Attacks in Low-power IoT Networks. In: DCSI 2021, p. 4, July 2021

11. Le, A., Loo, J., Lasebae, A., Vinel, A., Chen, Y., Chai, M.: The impact of rank attack on network topology of routing protocol for low-power and lossy networks. IEEE Sens. J. **13**(10), 3685–3692 (2013). https://doi.org/10.1109/JSEN.2013.2266399

12. Mayzaud, A., Badonnel, R., Chrisment, I.: A Taxonomy of Attacks in RPL-based Internet of Things. Int. J. Netw. Secur. **18**(3), May 2016. https://doi.org/10.6633/IJNS.201605.18(3).07

13. Stephen, A., Arockiam, D.L.: Attacks against Rplin Iot: A Survey, vol. 25, no. 4, p. 20 (2021)

14. Tonapa, Y.T., Wahidah, I., Karna, N.B.A.: Performance testing of routing protocol for low power and lossy networks (RPL) against attack using cooja simulator, vol. 7, no. 2, p. 9, October 2020

15. Krari, A., Hajami, A., Jarmouni, E.: Study and analysis of RPL performance routing protocol under various attacks, vol. 13, no. 4, p. 10 (2021)

16. Rajasekar, V.R., Rajkumar, S.: A study on impact of DIS flooding attack on RPL-based 6LowPAN network. Microprocess. Microsyst. **94**, 104675 (2022). https://doi.org/10.1016/j.micpro.2022.104675

17. Nisha, A.D., Sindhu, V.: A review of DIS-flooding attacks in RPL based IoT network. In: 2022 International Conference on Communication, Computing and Internet of Things (IC3IoT), Chennai, India, March 2022, pp. 1–6 (2022). https://doi.org/10.1109/IC3IOT53935.2022.976 7875

18. Dhingra, A., Sindhu, V.: A study of RPL attacks and defense mechanisms in the internet of things network. In: 2022 International Conference on Computing, Communication, Security and Intelligent Systems (IC3SIS), Kochi, India, June 2022, pp. 1–6 (2022). https://doi.org/ 10.1109/IC3SIS54991.2022.9885473

19. Perazzo, P., Vallati, C., Arena, A., Anastasi, G., Dini, G.: An implementation and evaluation of the security features of RPL. In: Puliafito, A., Bruneo, D., Distefano, S., Longo, F. (eds.) ADHOC-NOW 2017. LNCS, vol. 10517, pp. 63–76. Springer, Cham (2017). https://doi.org/ 10.1007/978-3-319-67910-5_6

20. Kamgueu, P.O., Nataf, E., Ndie, T.D.: Survey on RPL enhancements: a focus on topology, security and mobility. Comput. Commun. **120**, 10–21 (2018). https://doi.org/10.1016/j.com com.2018.02.011

21. Mayzaud, A., Badonnel, R., Chrisment, I.: A taxonomy of attacks in RPL-based Internet of Things. Int. J. Netw. Secur. **18**(3), 459–473 (2016)

22. Verma, A., Ranga, V.: Security of RPL based 6LoWPAN networks in the internet of things: a review. IEEE Sens. J. **20**(11), 5666–5690 (2020). https://doi.org/10.1109/JSEN.2020.297 3677

23. Pongle, P., Chavan, Gg.: A survey: attacks on RPL and 6LoWPAN in IoT. In: 2015 International Conference on Pervasive Computing (ICPC), Pune, India, pp. 1–6 (2015). https://doi. org/10.1109/PERVASIVE.2015.7087034

24. Boudouaia, M.A., Ali-Pacha, A., Abouaissa, A., Lorenz, P.: Security against rank attack in RPL protocol. IEEE Netw. **34**(4), 133–139 (2020). https://doi.org/10.1109/MNET.011.190 0651

25. Dvir, A., Holczer, T., Buttyan, L.: VeRA - version number and rank authentication in RPL. In: 2011 IEEE Eighth International Conference on Mobile Ad-Hoc and Sensor Systems, Valencia, Spain, pp. 709–714, October 2011. https://doi.org/10.1109/MASS.2011.76

26. Weekly, K., Pister, K.: Evaluating sinkhole defense techniques in RPL networks. In: 2012 20th IEEE International Conference on Network Protocols (ICNP), Austin, TX, USA, pp. 1–6, October 2012. https://doi.org/10.1109/ICNP.2012.6459948

27. Bhawsar, A., Pandey, Y., Singh, U.: Detection and prevention of wormhole attack using the trust-based routing system. In: 2020 International Conference on Electronics and Sustainable Communication Systems (ICESC), Coimbatore, India, pp. 809–814, July 2020. https://doi. org/10.1109/ICESC48915.2020.9156009

28. Dunkels, A., Gronvall, B., Voigt, T.: Contiki - a lightweight and flexible operating system for tiny networked sensors. In: 29th Annual IEEE International Conference on Local Computer Networks, Tampa, FL, USA, pp. 455–462 (2004). https://doi.org/10.1109/LCN.2004.38

Classification of Quora Insincere Questionnaire Using Soft Computing Paradigm

Prachi Vijayeeta[1](✉) [iD], Parthasarathi Pattnayak[1] [iD], and Kashis Jawed[2] [iD]

[1] School of Computer Applications, KIIT Deemed to Be University, Bhubaneswar, Odisha, India
prachi.vijayeeta@gmail.com
[2] School of Computer Applications, KIIT Deemed to Be University, Bhubaneswar, India

Abstract. The global system of interconnection covers an enormous scope of multiple data resources and feasible access mechanisms. It provides a direction for developing robust frameworks to interact and exchange knowledge in a diversified domain. But a major problem arises when a fast response to queries are raised by end users from different corners of the worldwide forum. Quora is one of the web based platform for receiving questions and suggesting answers accordingly. Many a times it is observed that the queries seems to be very irrelevant and creates chaos situation. Researchers are still struggling to equip new policies and mechanisms to deal with virulent and non-virulent queries. The cognition behind this study, aims at designing of a model to classify sincere and insincere questions using soft computing mechanisms. In this paper, seven algorithms out of which three ensemble techniques are employed on the Kaggle dataset.

Keywords: Text classification · Multinomial naive bayes · SVM · Xgboost · Quora · Tokenization · Text classification · Multinomial naive bayes · SVM

1 Introduction

Text classification plays a vital role in devising patterns for distinguishing very categories of textual data. It has now become one of the most important thing to scan a set of documents that are primarily represented in natural languages. The process of classification may be a content based approach or request based approach. However, internet has been successful in supporting the users with many valuable solutions as per the questionnaire put on the website. The response to the questions are made so flexible that people from any part of the world can feel free to answer the questions. The websites that are exclusively dedicated for this purpose are termed as question forums. The easy accessibility and the simplicity of approaches makes it very much admirable. Quora, Red it, Stack Overflow, and Yahoo Answers, Let's Diskuss, Answer, Ask FM, Blur tit, The Answer Book, Superuser, Just Query, Debug.school are few examples of question forum websites.

Let's Diskuss is a recently formed online discussion website hosting question-answers and blogs, that allows texts in both Hindi and English.

© The Author(s), under exclusive license to Springer Nature Switzerland AG 2023
I. Woungang et al. (Eds.): ANTIC 2022, CCIS 1798, pp. 569–576, 2023.
https://doi.org/10.1007/978-3-031-28183-9_40

These websites also acts as careers advisory and suggest some personal opinions. But it suffers with a limitation of people dissipating it. These questions unnecessarily leads to an unhealthy situation, thereby deteriorating the actual significance hosting this kind of website. Keeping an eye to overcome these issues, a learning model is being developed to filter out the relevant questions from a pool of question bank to preserve its optimal weightage. A classification model is simulated, to classify insincere questions and sincere questions to protect the integrity of the website. A question done on a purpose to make a statement instead of looking for helpful answers is termed as an insincere question. It should empower people to exchange knowledge among themselves so that they learn from each other.

Previously, Quora had adopted manual review mechanisms to classify the two types of questions which in the long run became very much cumbersome. The key challenge was to develop an automated system using soft computing tools to generate accurate and effective output.

2 Literature Review

An extensive study on the previous related works is thoroughly carried out and the research gap is explored. In the works done so far, there are challenges associated with data imbalance, and linguistic form of questionnaire posted by the users. Luo et al. [1] carried out experiment on 1033 documents with 4000 features on English text using Rocchio classifier and SVM. Endalie et al. [2] made use of Convolutional Neural Network to extract features. Zhou [4] published an article on text analysis by embedding words with a combination of learning models such as BiLSTM, CNN etc. Along with global vector, document frequency etc. Kaddoura [5] took the help of social media to detect spam by analyzing the texts. Muneer et al. [6] had employed seven ML methods on Twitter dataset and concluded that Logistic Regression achieved an accuracy of 90.57% and F1-score 0.9280. Liu et al. [7] tried their level best to collect information from criminality trend using Ontology based Text classification and could reach an accuracy of 86.67%. Taiwanese et al. [9] identified the intent of the user by employing multinomial NAive Bayes Classifier along with NLP.

3 Problem Formulation

One of the biggest challenge in the field of text classification [3] is the appropriate selection of techniques for generating accurate result. This work is based on implementation of CRISP-DM (Cross-industry Process For Data Mining) methodology which is an extended version of KDD (Knowledge Discovery Database). This model serves as a base for analyzing and extracting valuable data from a large set of know ledge- based-database.

The CRISP-DM is an open standard framework that describes common approaches mostly adopted by data analysts. A large number of task is executed in various sequences thereby allowing to make manipulations in the preceding steps. This framework consists of 7 steps:

Step-1: Business Understanding In this stage the primary objective and the availability of the resources are identified. It is quite helpful for the Quora users to drop queries and collect significant results. But the model needs to be very robust to identify the type of questions that are put forth on the website. There are certain instances where the under-rated questions reduces the quality of the website. To overcome this issue, the learning model has the potential to identify the insincere questions and eliminate it from website for maintaining its quality (Fig. 1).

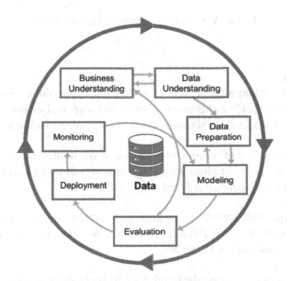

Fig. 1. CRISP-DM Diagram

Step-2: Data Understanding: The dataset used in this work is obtained from https://www.kaggle.com/c/quora-insincere-questions-classification/data. There are three attributes which are as follows:

1. **Q ID**: An identity is allocated to each question to make it distinguishable.
2. **Question Text**: It is the original question.
3. **Target**: It is the class label that is expressed in terms of 0 or 1. If it is 1 denotes that the question belongs to insincere class while 0 denotes that it corresponds to sincere class.

The parameters that plays a very vital role to distinguish the type of questions are:

A. A non-neutral tone, such as an elaboration of remarks Indicating to a specific community of people.
B. Is disparaging or inflammatory referring to a discriminatory Remark.
C. Is depriving of facts, such as a reference to incorrect information.
D. Related subjects, intention, and contents which are treated as considered "insincere."

Step-3: Data Preparation: It is necessary to filter the meta data in order to educe the dimension of the dataset (Fig. 2).

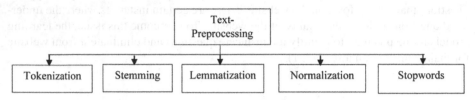

Fig. 2. Various text- preprocessing techniques

1. **Tokenization**
   A well-known Python module known as "regular expressions" is used to break the text into tokens [6]. Here the words also includes special characters, commas and the punctuation marks that increases the efficiency of the handling a sentence.
2. **Stemming**
   Stemming is a method of minimizing derived words to their root form. It enables us to determine the possible alternates of the base words using two methods such as: Porter Stemmer and Lancaster Stemmer.
3. **Lemmatization**
   It is a technique that switches any kind of a word to its base root mode. Python Natural Language Tool Kit (NLTK) contains a WordNet Lemmatizer that explores the WordNet Database for Lemmas.
4. **Normalization**
   It is the process of decreasing the number of distinct tokens in a text. It transforms the text into one canonical form that were not done earlier. Text normalization requires being conscious of the type of text is to be normalized and the way it's to be processed later on there's no specific procedure for normalization procedure.
5. **Stopwords removal**
   It refers to the repeatedly applied tokens in the document that have less importance. The elimination of these terms improves the efficiency of text readability and at the same time reduces the dimension of the dataset to a greater extent.

Step-4: Modeling

1. **Multinomial Naive Bayes**

   Multinomial Naive Bayes is a supervised learning classification method that analyses the explicit data. This technique is based on Bayes' theorem where it is assumed that the features are all independent.

$$P(X \mid y_k) = \prod_{i=1}^{n} P(x_i|y_k) \tag{1}$$

where $X = (x_1, x_2 \ldots \ldots \ldots x_n)$ are the feature vectors.
y_k is the class variable among K classes in the training data.

2. Logistic Regression + Naive Bayes

It is an ensemble method in which the coefficients of Bayes and learned coefficients of Logistic Regression are hybridized to improve the accuracy of the model. It extracts the good features of the two methods to reduce the complexity of the model.

$$\text{Logit(p)} = \log \frac{p}{1-p} \tag{2}$$

where ρ is the conditional probability.applied on the input vectors. If it is nearer to 1 then patterns are expected to be present otherwise it is 0.

3. **SVM**
   Support Vector Machine (SVM) is a supervised learning algorithm used for dividing data into classes using a separation boundary so that there is more distance between the different classes of data and the boundary.

4. **Nearest Centroid**
   This method classifies the features into the class where the mean is closest to it. There are 2 centroids for a binary classification. The centroid may be chosen randomly or k-means algorithm can be applied [7], followed by evaluation of Euclidean distance to determine the similar set of elements is two.

5. **Extreme Gradient Boosting**
   Extreme Gradient Boosting (Xgboost) is an ensemble supervised learning algorithm that comprises of a group of classification and regression trees. A score is allocated to each terminal node of the tree. It takes the form of a fitness function with a set of constraints and finds the best solution using the second order derivative [8]. Xgboost has the potential to enhance the training time and handling missing values by performing parallel processing.

6. **Decision Tree**
   This model is a supervised learning technique that draws conclusion based on a set of outcomes. The target variable can take a discrete set of values at a given instance of time. In our work, we have implemented this model to reach a valid conclusion regarding the type of question shared in the Quora site (sincere/insincere).

7. **Random Forest**
   Random forests is an ensemble mechanism in which each individual decision trees generates a predictive class and the class with the highest number of votes becomes the model prediction. During the simulation of the training set, a multiple number of decision trees are developed [11]. We have mapped various multiple trees with the different combinations of words posted in the website.

Step-5: Evaluation
The level of heterogeneity in the dataset makes it very cumbersome to evaluate the accuracy. So we have emphasized more on other matrices like F1 score, Area Under Curve, Precision and Recall.

Step-6: Deployment
At this stage the work process model needs to be deployed and the output generated has to be reviewed.

Step-7: Monitoring

A well defined maintenance strategy is formulated to keep track of the variations in languages or words etc.

4 Experimental and Results

In this paper, we have collected the dataset from a public website called Kaggle [10]. The dataset is available at the link: https://www.kaggle.com/competitions/quora-insincere-questions-classification. It consists of 3 parameters such has Q_ID, Question Text and Target variable. There are approximately 13,16,122 instances, out of which 12,35,312 are sincere questions and 80,810 instances of insincere questions within the dataset. Table 1 described training dataset is used for this work.

Table 1. Training dataset sample

```
In [3]: dataset

Out[3]:
```

	qid	question_text	target
0	00002165364db923c7e6	How did Quebec nationalists see their province...	0
1	000032939017120e6e44	Do you have an adopted dog, how would you enco...	0
2	0000412ca8e4628ce2cf	Why does velocity affect time? Does velocity a...	0
3	000042bf85aa498cd78e	How did Otto von Guericke used the Magdeburg h...	0
4	0000455dfa3e01eae3af	Can I convert montra helicon D to a mountain b...	0
5	00004f9a462a357c33be	Is Gaza slowly becoming Auschwitz, Dachau or T...	0
6	00005059a06ee19e11ad	Why does Quora automatically ban conservative ...	0
7	0000559f875832745e2e	Is it crazy if I wash or wipe my groceries off...	0
8	00005bd3426b2d0c8305	Is there such a thing as dressing moderately, ...	0
9	00006e6928c5df60eacb	Is it just me or have you ever been in this ph...	0

The performance measures of all the methods are evaluated in Table 2. It is observed that the ensemble methods like Logistic Regression and Naive Bayes, Extreme Gradient Boosting, Random Forest have better accuracy as compared to other methods [12]. Random Forest has yielded an accuracy of 96% which is the highest among all other methods. Even though Logistic Regression + Naive Bayes method have 95% accuracy which is same as Extreme Gradient Boosting and Decision tree but there is variation in the other parameters such as precision, recall and F1_Score. Figure-3 demonstrates the graph plotted with X-axis representing the performance metrics and Y-axis with the list of methods employed. All the parameters like accuracy, precision, recall etc. are easily distinguishable with different colours (Table 2 and Fig. 3).

Table 2. Performance Measures

SL_no	Methods applied	Accuracy	Precision	Recall	F1_Score
1	Multinomial naive bayes	0.93	0.55	0.53	0.58
2	Logistic Regression + Naive bayes	0.95	0.64	0.62	0.63
3	SVM	0.93	0.45	0.42	0.43
4	Nearest centroid	0.92	0.59	0.61	0.62
5	Extreme gradient boosting	0.95	0.54	0.58	0.63
6	Decision tree	0.95	0.67	0.64	0.68
7	Random forest	0.96	0.75	0.76	0.71

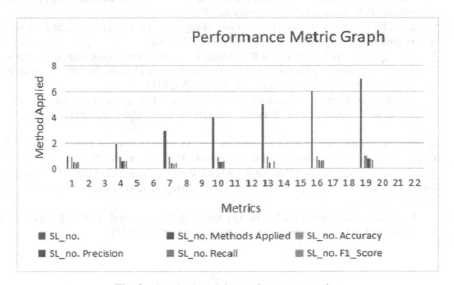

Fig. 3. Graph plotted for performance metrics

5 Conclusions and Future Work

From our experiment we have inferred that for various methods the performance metrics have different computational values, even though the dataset is same for all methods. In the future, many more hybridized methods can be experimented on multiple records. Deep learning models can be implemented for training the samples with enhanced accuracy.But one of the biggest limitation lies in the data imbalance factor where the ratio of the sincere and insincere questions need to be at par.

References

1. Luo, X.: Efficient English text classification using selected machine learning techniques. Alexandria Eng. J. **60**, 3401–3409 (2021)

2. Endalie, D., Getamesay, H.: Automated amharic news categorization using deep learning models. Comput. Intell. Neurosci. **2021** (2021)
3. Hasan, A., Tripti, S., Azizuddin, K., Mohammed Hasan, A.A.: analysing hate speech against migrants and women through tweets using ensembled deep learning model. Comput. Intell. Neurosci. **2022** (2022)
4. Zhou, Y.: A review of text classification based on deep learning. In: Proceedings of the 2020 3rd International Conference on Geoinformatics and Data Analysis (2020)
5. Kaddoura, S., Chandrasekaran, G., Elena Popescu, D., Duraisamy, J.H.: A systematic literature review on spam content detection and classification. PeerJ. Comput. Sci. **8**, e830 (2022). https://doi.org/10.7717/peerj-cs.830
6. Muneer, A., Suliman, M.F.: A comparative analysis of machine learning techniques for cyberbullying detection on Twitter. Future Internet **12**, 187 (2020)
7. Liu, P., Yu, X.T., Lan, C.: Research on archives text classification based on naive bayes. In: 2017 IEEE 2nd Information Technology, Networking, Electronic and Automation Control Conference (ITNEC), pp. 187–190, December 2017
8. Onan, A., Korukoglu, S., Bulut, H.: Ensemble of keyword extraction methods and classifiers in text classification. Expert Syst. Appl. **57**, 232–247 (2016)
9. Taiwanese, H., Yusril, M., Awangga, R., Efendi, S.: Comparison of multinomial naive bayes algorithm and logistic regression for intent classification in chatbot. In: 2018 International Conference on Applied Engineering (ICAE), pp. 1–5 (2018)
10. Zhuang, X., Zhu, Y., Peng, Q., Khurshid, F.: Using deep belief network to demote web spam. Future Gener. Comput. Syst. **118**(1), 94–106 (2021). https://doi.org/10.1016/j.future.2020.12.023
11. Abishek, K., Hariharan, B.R., Valliyammai, C.: An Enhanced Deep Learning Model for Duplicate Question Pairs Recognition. In: Nayak, J., Abraham, A., Krishna, B., Chandra Sekhar, G., Das, A. (eds.) Soft Computing in Data Analytics . Advances in Intelligent Systems and Computing, vol. 758, pp. 769–777. Springer, Singapore (2019). https://doi.org/10.1007/978-981-13-0514-6_73
12. Yu, J., Zhiliang, Q., Liansheng, L., Yu, Q., Yingying, L.: Temporal feature aggregation for text classification based on ensembled deep-learning models (2021)

Conventional Feature Engineering and Deep Learning Approaches to Facial Expression Recognition: A Brief Overview

Shubh Lakshmi Agrwal[1,2]([✉]), Sudheer Kumar Sharma[2], and Vibhor Kant[3]

[1] Manipal University Jaipur, Jaipur, India
shubhu.agarwal@gmail.com
[2] LNM Institute of Information Technology, Jaipur, India
[3] RGSC, Banaras Hindu University, Varanasi, India

Abstract. Facial expression recognition (FER) is vital in pattern recognition, artificial intelligence, and computer vision. It has diverse applications, including operator fatigue detection, automated tutoring systems, music for mood, mental state identification, and security. Image data collection, feature engineering, and classification are vital stages of FER. A comprehensive critical review of benchmarking datasets and feature engineering techniques used for FER is presented in this paper. Further, this paper critically analyzes the various conventional learning and deep learning methods for FER. It provides a baseline to other researchers about future aspects with the pros and cons of techniques developed so far.

Keywords: Facial expression recognition · Feature engineering · Conventional learning · Deep learning · Face expression dataset

1 Introduction

Facial expressions are crucial for social communication. Verbal and nonverbal communication are standard. Facial expressions communicate non-verbally. Mehrabian [40] revealed that 55% of information passes between people through facial expressions, 38% via voice, and 7%via language [66]. Facial expression recognition has evolved into an outstanding and demanding field of computer vision. Disgust, anger, happiness, fear, surprise, and sadness are fundamental emotions [13]. Humans are highly skilled at identifying a person's emotional state; a computer would have difficulty doing so. It is caused by a variation in occlusion, head postures, changes in lighting, and computing complexity. FER applications include operator tiredness detection, [77], automobile, healthcare, automated tutoring systems [67], mental state recognition [39], security [6], music for mood [12], and rating products or services in banks, malls, and showrooms. With the help of a FER, users can also study how well students interact in a classroom or talk with teachers. [56]. FER inbuilt mobile applications can help visually impaired persons (VIPs) to communicate daily. FER systems can detect the driver's fatigue

I. Woungang et al. (Eds.): ANTIC 2022, CCIS 1798, pp. 577–591, 2023.
https://doi.org/10.1007/978-3-031-28183-9_41

state and stress level to make better decisions about driving safely. Facial image acquisition, pre-processing, feature engineering, training, and classification are typical FER stages. The Fig. 1 depicts face expression recognition steps. Pre-processing is used to remove noise. Feature engineering extracts distinct visual characteristics. The popular feature engineering techniques are, Histogram of Gradient(HOG) [10], Local Directional Pattern (LDP) [23], Gabor filters [61], Local Binary Patterns (LBP) [52], Principal Component Analysis (PCA) [2], Independent Component Analysis (ICA), and Linear Discriminant Analysis(LDA) [5]. Extracted features are utilized for training a classifier using expression class labels. FER approaches are deep learning and conventional learning based on feature engineering. In deep learning huge number of examples and images are used to learn and tune feature extraction parameters, while conventional learning uses algorithms to extract hand-crafted features. Deep learning classifiers contain a sigmoid or softmax layer on the classification stage with Fully connected layers. K-nearest neighbor (KNN)and support vector machine(SVM)are well-known classifiers in conventional learning. The FER system's accuracy depends on captured data variability, feature extraction, classification, and fine-tuning. Model inference time depends on camera resolution, feature engineering, classifier, and hardware computation capabilities.

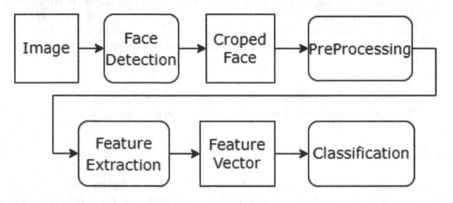

Fig. 1. Different steps of facial expression recognition system

This work primarily concerns various FER approaches, with three primary processes: pre-processing, feature engineering, and classification. This paper also demonstrates the benefits of different FER methods and a performance analysis of various FER methods. Only image-based FER approaches are used in this work for the literature review; video-based FER techniques are not used. FER systems often deal with illumination fluctuations, skin tone variations, lighting variations, occlusion, and position variations. This work also provides a vital research suggestion for future FER research. The remaining research paper is organized into five 6 sections, including an introduction. Section 2 represents the related research work, including state-of-the-art for FER. Section 3 lists the most often used benchmarking datasets for FER. Section 4 provides an overview of FER feature engineering. Section 5 compares the performance of different FER systems. Finally, Sect. 6 offers a conclusion.

2   Related Work

FER has a wide range of applications in computer vision. Because of differences in position, illumination, scale, and orientation, recognizing facial expressions can be difficult. The primary goal of feature engineering is to find robust features that can improve the robustness of expression recognition. The feature extraction and classification stages are critical in FER. There are two kinds of feature extraction: geometric and appearance-based. Geometrically-based feature extraction includes the eye, mouth, nose, brow, ear, and other facial components, whereas appearance-based feature extraction includes the exact region of the face [66].

Abdullah et al. [1] reduced the face picture into a small feature set called eigenface and utilized PCA to extract facial features like eigenfaces into a class of finite feature descriptions. Yadav et al. [70] extracted facial features using Gabor filters and two-dimensional PCA. ICA is used to identify characteristics from statistically independent local faces [59]. Lee et al. [30] used ICA to extract statistically autonomous features from local face parts in various facial expressions. Mehta and Jadhav [41] classified human emotions using the Gabor filter. Islam et al. [22] used HOG and LBP to extract local characteristics. LBP features are easy to compute. ICA is less tolerant of illumination fluctuations than LBP. Edge pixels are needed to extract face features from an image. Local Directional Pattern (LDP) shows visual gradients. In FER, LDP represents gradient-based properties of the local face in the pixel's eight prime directions [23].

In classic LDP features, the highest edge strengths determine binary values, which vary by experiment. LDP ignores a pixel's direction strength sign, differentiating edge pixels with comparable strengths but opposite signs. Uddin et al. [60] overcame this LDP problem by grouping pixels' major edge strengths in decreasing order and using their signs to build stable features. Many recent attempts have been made to recognize facial expressions from videos or images using deep learning. To learn appearance features from video frames and geometric features from raw face landmarks, Jung et al. [24] merged two deep learning-based models. Then, a joint learning method was used to connect the two models' outputs. Zeng et al. [75] improved the performance by incorporating hand-picked features into the deep network training. Recently several deep learning methods have been developed for FER and applied in real-time images. Wang et al. [63] introduced Region Attention Network (RAN) for pose variant and occluded face FER. In this paper, region-biased loss and region attention mechanisms are employed to capture the importance of pose variant and occluded facial images. Wang et al. [62] proposed a ResNet-18 CNN model in which uncertainties caused by low-quality images are suppressed by CNN architecture Self-Cure Network (SCN). Li et al. [32] proposed a model that includes an attention mechanism in CNN to recognize expression from a partially occluded face.

3   Review Analysis of Facial Expression Dataset

This section describes FER benchmark datasets. The summary of these datasets, i.e., collection condition, environment challenges, expression distribution, and the number of images and subjects, is shown in Table 1. In the CK+ dataset, training, testing, and validation sets are not specified. Due to non-uniform expressive representation, MMI contains substantial interpersonal discrepancy. The JAFFE dataset has fewer samples per subject expression. AFEW is a multi-model, temporal dataset containing environmental conditions. CMU Multi-PIE and BU-3DFE examine multi-view face expressions.

Table 1. Benchmarking datasets for facial expression recognition

Dataset	Images, subjects	Expression	Environment challenges	Collection
JAFFE [25]	213, 10	6 basic exp + neutral	Pos	Lab
CK+ [37]	593, 123	6 basic exp, Natural, contempt	Sp, Pos	Lab
SFEW [11]	1766, 95	6 basic exp	Sp, Pos	Movie
MMI [48]	740, 25	6 basic exp	Pos	Lab
CMU-MultiPIE [17]	755370, 337	Neutral, disgust, smile surprised, scream, squint	Pos	Lab
FER 2013 [8]	35887	6 basic exp	Sp, Pos	Web
RAF-DB [31]	29672	6 basic, 12 compound exp	Sp, Pos	Internet
EmotioNet [14]	1,000,000	6 basic, 17 compound exp	Sp, Pos	Internet
AffectNet [43]	450, 000	6 basic exp	Sp, Pos	Internet
ExpW [78]	91, 793	6 basic exp	Sp, Pos	Internet
RaFD [29]	1608,67	6 basic, 12 compound exp	Pos	Lab
BU3DFE [73]	2500, 100	6 basic exp + neutral	Pos	Lab
TFD [55]	112234	6 basic exp + neutral	Pos	Lab

4   Review of Feature Engineering Technique

FER accuracy depends on feature engineering. Feature engineering can be hand-picked or deep-learned. Single-task learning (STL) includes hand-picked features, whereas deep learning techniques are iterative. FER's traditional feature engineering methodologies are as follows:

4.1   Gaussian Mixture Model

Gaussian Mixture Model groups data into a cluster that is distinct from each other. A distribution models data points within a cluster. A weighted total of Gaussian functions can approximate many probability distributions. A Gaussian mixture model is the sum of k component Gaussian densities for vector x, as shown in Eq. 1.

$$p(x) = \sum_{j=1}^{k} w_j p(x|j) \tag{1}$$

where x is a data vector of D dimension; $w_j = 1, 2 \ldots k$, are the weights of the mixture; $p(x|j) =$ Gaussian Density Model for j^{th} Component,

Gaussian one-dimensional probability density function is represented in Eq. 2.

$$G(X|\mu, \sigma) = \frac{1}{\sigma\sqrt{2\pi}} e^{-(x-\mu)^2/2\sigma^2} \tag{2}$$

Here μ represents the mean, and σ^2 represents the distribution variance.

Multivariate Gaussian distribution probability density function is given by Eq. 3 [19].

$$G(X|\mu, \Sigma) = \frac{1}{\sqrt{2\pi^d|\Sigma|}} exp(-\frac{1}{2}(x-\mu)^T \Sigma^{-1}(X-\mu)) \tag{3}$$

where μ is a d dimensional vector denoting the mean of the distribution and Σ is the $d \times d$ covariance matrix. The Expectation-Maximization (EM) method estimates model parameters.

4.2   Local Binary Pattern (LBP) Based Features

LBP captures local spatial patterns and the contrast in the facial image. LBP labels image pixels by thresholding the nearby pixel and gives a binary number [47]. LBP is computed in four steps as follows:

- For each pixel (x, y) in an image I, P neighboring pixels are chosen at a radius R.
- Intensity difference of the P adjacent pixels is determined.
- Positive intensity differences are assigned one (1) and negative intensity differences are assigned zero (0).
- Convert the P-bit vector to decimal. LBP descriptor is shown in Eq. 4.

LBP operator $LBP_{P,R}$, here subscript represents the operator used in (P, R) neighborhood.

$$LBP(P, R) = \sum_{p=0}^{p-1} f(i_p - i_c) 2^p \tag{4}$$

where P denotes the number of neighboring pixels chosen at a radius R. i_c and i_p represent the intensity of the center and neighboring pixel, respectively. Thresholding function f is as follows:

$$f(x) = \begin{cases} 0 & x < 0 \\ 1 & x \geq 0 \end{cases} \tag{5}$$

The LBP histogram is defined as:

$$H_j = \sum_{x,y} I\{f_I(x,y) = j, \qquad j = 0, \ldots, n-1 \tag{6}$$

where n is the number of labels created by the LBP operator.

$$I(M) = \begin{cases} 1, & \text{if M is true} \\ 0, & \text{if M is false} \end{cases} \tag{7}$$

Different-sized image patches are normalized using Eq. 8.

$$N_j = \frac{H_j}{\sum_{k=0}^{n-1} H_k} \tag{8}$$

4.3   Gabor Filter Feature Extraction Technique

Edges and texture are essential features in the face image. The convolution of the face image and Gabor filter kernel creates these features. Gabor is an illumination-invariant Gaussian sinusoidal. Gabor filter kernel [65] is defined in Eq. 11. The Gabor filter components are the following: ϕ (Phase), λ (Wavelength), θ (Orientation) specify the number of cycles, angle of the normal to the sinusoidal plane, and offset of a sinusoidal. The frequency bandwidth of Gabor is:

$$b = \log_2 \frac{(\sigma/\lambda)\pi + \sqrt{\log 2/2}}{(\sigma/\lambda)\pi - \sqrt{\log 2/2}} \tag{9}$$

$$\frac{\sigma}{\lambda} = (1/\pi)\sqrt{\log 2/2} \frac{2^b + 1}{2^b - 1} \tag{10}$$

The bandwidth b affects σ value. Convolution of Face image $I(x,y)$ with Gabor kernel $\Psi(\theta, \lambda, \gamma, \phi)$ produces Gabor texture-edge features, shown in Eq. 13 [18]. Gabor kernel $\Psi(\theta, \lambda, \gamma, \phi)$ is composite number as shown in Eq. 14. Gabor real (GI_R) and imaginary (GI_{Im}) components are created by convolution between Gabor kernel Ψ and image $I(x,y)$ for real $R(\Psi)$ and imaginary $Im(\Psi)$ as shown in Eq. 15 and 16. Equation 17 shows amplitude features $G(x,y)$ of the Gabor kernel. Gabor filter has the problem of redundant features and high dimensions; PCA and ICA can fix this issue.

$$\Psi_{\theta,\lambda,\gamma,\phi}(x,y) = \exp\left(-\frac{a'^2 + \gamma^2 b'^2}{2\sigma^2}\right) e^{j\frac{2\pi a'}{\lambda}} \tag{11}$$

Here, a', b' are direction coefficients and θ represents projection angle.

$$a' = a\cos\theta + b\sin\theta \quad \text{and} \quad b' = a\cos\theta + b\sin\theta \tag{12}$$

$$GI = I(x,y) * \Psi(\theta, \lambda, \gamma, \phi) \tag{13}$$

$$\Psi(\theta, \lambda, \gamma, \phi) = R(\Psi(\theta, \lambda, \gamma, \phi) + Im(\Psi(\theta, \lambda, \gamma, \phi) \tag{14}$$

$$GI_R(\theta, \lambda, \gamma, \phi) = I(x, y)) * R(\Psi(\theta, \lambda, \gamma, \phi) \tag{15}$$

$$GI_{Im}(\theta, \lambda, \gamma, \phi) = I(x, y) * Im(\Psi(\theta, \lambda, \gamma, \phi)) \tag{16}$$

$$GF(\theta, \lambda) = (GI_R(\theta, \lambda, \gamma, \phi)^2 + (GI_{Im}(\theta, \lambda, \gamma, \phi)^2)^{1/2} \tag{17}$$

4.4   SIFT-Scale Invariant Feature Transform

SIFT Features are invariant to the scale of the image. The steps for calculating SIFT features are following.

1. Scale-space extrema detection: Gaussian difference finds scale- and rotation-invariant nearest points. Scale and image location are computed.
2. Key point localization: Only solid and fascinating points are selected based on intensity.
3. Orientation assignment: Key points are formed based on the gradient's direction.
4. Key point descriptor: SIFT descriptions around important points are used to describe the local appearance of key points.
5. Keypoint matching: Two images' nearest neighbors are matched.

4.5   Histogram of Oriented Gradient (HOG) Feature Extraction

Facial characteristics vary. A woman's face is rounder than a man's, which helps distinguish gender. HOG extracts picture curvature direction. Edge directions define the shape and local appearance [10]. The image is divided into blocks, and HOG features are computed for each block. All HOG features are integrated into one vector. HOG computation process: Calculate image gradient. For a face image F,

$$F_x = F(r, c + 1) - F(r, c - 1), \qquad F_y = F(r - 1, c) - F(r + 1, c) \tag{18}$$

here r and c represent rows and columns, respectively.

The magnitude (G) and orientation (θ) of the gradient is computed by

$$\mid G \mid = \sqrt{F_x{}^2 + F_y{}^2} \quad \text{and} \quad \theta = \tan^{-1}\frac{F_y}{F_x} \tag{19}$$

Orientation range (0–360°) for signed gradients and (0–180°) for unsigned gradients. After determining the size and orientation of each cell's pixel, the histogram is normalized using a block pattern. Combining HOG features creates a feature vector.

4.6 Discrete Wavelet Transform (DWT)

DWT can be computed by first evaluating 1D-DWT on rows of the 2D image matrix, then on the column of evaluated 1D-DWT. LL(low frequency), LH, HL, and HH (high frequency) represent approximation, horizontal, vertical, and diagonal frequency blocks, respectively, in DWT. LL block approximates low-resolution images by deleting extraneous details. Low-frequency band (LL) smooths input image while high frequency creates edge patterns [54]. Iteratively utilizing 2D-DWT on the LL band helps to reduce feature size.

4.7 Principle Component Analysis (PCA)

PCA finds correlations across attributes and uses a strong variance pattern to reduce data dimensions. In PCA, the given image is subtracted from the mean; the covariance matrix is calculated using FM^T, then eigenvalues and eigenvectors are calculated. Eigenvectors that match up with certain high-magnitude eigenvalues at a certain significant level are essential information about the image's variance. Equation 20 is used to figure out the PCA significance level.

$$\varepsilon = \frac{\sum_{i=1}^{m} \lambda_i}{\sum_{i=1}^{n} \lambda_i} \quad m \leq n \quad and \quad 0 \leq \varepsilon \geq 1 \tag{20}$$

here λ_i depicts the eigen value of ith order in order of amplitude and $m \leq n$.

4.8 Deep-Learning Feature Engineering

Recent research has emphasized deep learning. Deep learning features are extracted using a convolution neural network (CNN). A DNN was proposed to retrieve patterns from high-dimensional data [27]. DNNs train slowly and overfit. Deep Belief Network [35]is used to tackle DNN challenges, with Restricted Boltzmann Machine (RBM) for training features [42]. A joint learning algorithm is used to combine geometry and appearance features [24].

5   Performance Analysis of Different FER Systems

The performance analysis of this review is based on the pre-processing, recognition accuracy on various datasets, feature extraction methods, contribution, and advantages of different FER techniques. Table 2 shows a comparative analysis of facial expression recognition techniques to better understand how complicated and accurate the method is.

5.1 Conventional Learning-Based FER Analysis

LBP feature extraction and paired classification outperformed JAFFE with 99.05 accuracy [9]. Pairwise classifiers select features by class pair. Feature extraction is more dependable because it doesn't rely on manually or automatically assigned

Table 2. Performance comparison based on different hand-picked feature engineering (conventional learning) and deep learning approaches for facial expression recognition.

	Authors	Feature extraction, classification	Dataset	Accuracy (%)
Conventional learning	Islam et al. [22]	HOG+LBP, ANN	JAFFE	93.51
			CK+	99.67
	Kumar et al. [28]	WPLBP, SVM	JAFFE	98.15
	Cossetin et al. [9]	LBP, Pairwise Classifier	JAFFE	99.05
	Mehta and Jadhav [41]	Log Gabor-+PCA-CNN	JAFFE	93.57
	Mollahosseini et al. [42]	Intra Face DNN	FER-2013	66.4
	Xu and Zhao [69]	LBP-CNN	FER-2013	94.73
	Aghamaleki et al. [3]	LBP+Sobel-multistream CNN	CK+	98.18
	Shan et al. [53]	Haar like features, CNN	JAFFE	76.74
	Nazir et al. [44]	HOG+DCT, KNN	MMI	99.4
	Kar et al. [26]	HOG+PCA+LDA	CK+	99.2
	Liu et al. [36]	LBP+HOG	CK+	99.6
	Tsai and Chang [57]	DCT+Gabor Filter, SVM	JAFFE	97.10
	Ryu et al. [50]	LDTP, SVM	JAFFE	94.8
			MMI	99.8
	Nigam et al. [46]	DWT+HOG, SVM	JAFFE	71.43
Deep learning	Alam et al. [4]	Sparse deep recurrent model (S-DSRN)	CK+	99.23
	Liu et al. [35]	Boosted deep belief network (BDBN)	CK+	96.70
			JAFFE	93
	Liu et al. [33]	3D CNN with deformable action parts (3D-CNN-DAP)	CK+	92.40
	Liu et al. [34]	CNN +SVM	CK+	93.50
	Zhang et al. [76]	Deep spatial-temporal networks	CK+	98.5
	Kim et al. [27]	Hierarchical DNN	JAFFE	91.27
			CK+	96.46
	Happy et al. [21]	Salient Facial Patches	CK+	94.09
	Xie and Hu [68]	DCMA-CNN	CK+	93.46
	Yang et al. [72]	De-expression Residue Learning (DeRL)	CK+	97.3
	Yu et al. [74]	Deeper Cascaded Peak- piloted Network (DCPN)	CK+	99.6
	Pramerdorfer et al. [49]	CNN	FER-2013	75.2
	Wang et al. [64]	Pose generative-adversarial network (PGAN)	FER-2013	71.1
			JAFFE	95.7
	Mahmoudi et al. [38]	CNN based bilinear model	FER 2013	77.81
	Saurav et al. [51]	Dual integrated convolution neural network (DICNN)	FER 2013	72.77
			CK+	96.68
	Liu et al. [35]	Boosted DeepBelief Net (BDBN)	JAFFE	93
			CK+	96.7
	Turan et al. [58]	Soft Locality Preserving Map (SLPM)	CK+	96.10
			JAFFE	91.8
	Hamester et al. [20]	Multi-channel Convolutional Neural Network (MCCNN)	JAFFE	95.8
	Gonzalez [16]	CNN+SVM linear	JAFFE	92
	Ng et al. [45]	CNN	SFEW	55.6
	Cai et al. [7]	CNN	SFEW	59.41
	Zhao et al. [79]	Global multi-scale and local attention network (MA-Net)	SFEW	59.4
	Fan et al. [15]	Fusion of RNN and 3D CNN	AFEW	59.02
	Yan et al. [71]	CNN and bidirectional RNN	AFEW	56.66

fiducial points. Islam et al. [22] used HOG, LBP features, artificial neural network(ANN) classifier to get 99.67% accuracy on CK+ dataset. Feature fusion gives promising results, and ANN employs the limited memory (L-BFGS) technique for weight optimization but the dimension increases. Principle Component Analysis(PCA) is used to reduce dimension. Ryu et al. [50] extracted features via Local Directional Ternary Pattern(LDTP), used classifier as Support vector machine (SVM) and got accuracy 99.8% on MMI dataset.

5.2 Deep Learning-Based FER Analysis

Deeper Cascaded Peak-piloted Network (DCPN) [74] is achieved best accuracy 99.6% on the CK+ dataset, which is greater than other approaches in Table 2. Mahmoudi et al. [38] developed a CNN-based bilinear model and outperformed on FER-2013 dataset (unconstrained dataset) with 77.81% accuracy.

6 Conclusions

This paper present review of different features engineering techniques and provides detailed analysis including pros and cons of each techniques and comparative study of benchmarking dtaset. The techniques are categorized into conventional learning and deep-learning. Conventional learning including LBP, PCA, Gabor filter, HOG, DCT, DWT etc. feature extraction techniques while deep learning includes convolution neural networks and its variant for facial expression recognition. FER systems based on conventional learning and deep learning are presented with the help of bench-marking datasets based accuracy. Hybrid features provide a better recognition rate as compared to single features. This paper analyzed the different FER techniques according to pre-processing, feature engineering, classification, recognition accuracy, and critical contributions. The success of the FER approach depends on pre-processing of the facial images due to illumination and prominent feature engineering. Deep learning model performance is significantly better than conventional learning for real-time datasets but needs a huge amount of datasets and variability of images. The performance of these algorithms improves with the amount of the dataset. JAFFE and CK+ datasets are most frequently used in FER systems, but they do not contain all variability of real-time images. Although much research has been done on FER, Identifying facial expressions in real life is difficult due to frequent movements of the head and subtle facial deformations, and other real-time variability that motivate researchers to provide their efforts to find a possible solution.

References

1. Abdullah, M., Wazzan, M., Bo-Saeed, S.: Optimizing face recognition using PCA. arXiv preprint arXiv:1206.1515 (2012)
2. Abdulrahman, M., Gwadabe, T.R., Abdu, F.J., Eleyan, A.: Gabor wavelet transform based facial expression recognition using PCA and LBP. In: 2014 22nd Signal Processing and Communications Applications Conference (SIU), pp. 2265–2268. IEEE (2014)

3. Aghamaleki, J.A., Chenarlogh, V.A.: Multi-stream CNN for facial expression recognition in limited training data. Multimedia Tools Appl. **78**(16), 22,861–22,882 (2019)
4. Alam, M., Vidyaratne, L.S., Iftekharuddin, K.M.: Sparse simultaneous recurrent deep learning for robust facial expression recognition. IEEE Trans. Neural Netw. Learn. Syst. **29**(10), 4905–4916 (2018)
5. Belhumeur, P.N., Hespanha, J.P., Kriegman, D.J.: Eigenfaces vs. fisherfaces: recognition using class specific linear projection. IEEE Trans. Pattern Anal. Mach. Intell. **19**(7), 711–720 (1997)
6. Butalia, M.A., Ingle, M., Kulkarni, P.: Facial expression recognition for security. Int. J. Mod. Eng. Res. **2**(4), 1449–1453 (2012)
7. Cai, J., Meng, Z., Khan, A.S., Li, Z., O'Reilly, J., Tong, Y.: Island loss for learning discriminative features in facial expression recognition. In: 2018 13th IEEE International Conference on Automatic Face & Gesture Recognition (FG 2018), pp. 302–309. IEEE (2018)
8. Carrier, P.L., Courville, A., Goodfellow, I.J., Mirza, M., Bengio, Y.: FER-2013 face database. Universit de Montral (2013)
9. Cossetin, M.J., Nievola, J.C., Koerich, A.L.: Facial expression recognition using a pairwise feature selection and classification approach. In: 2016 International Joint Conference on Neural Networks (IJCNN), pp. 5149–5155. IEEE (2016)
10. Dalal, N., Triggs, B.: Histograms of oriented gradients for human detection. In: 2005 IEEE Computer Society Conference on Computer Vision and Pattern Recognition (CVPR 2005), vol. 1, pp. 886–893. IEEE (2005)
11. Dhall, A., Goecke, R., Lucey, S., Gedeon, T.: Static facial expressions in tough conditions: data, evaluation protocol and benchmark. In: 1st IEEE International Workshop on Benchmarking Facial Image Analysis Technologies BeFIT, ICCV2011 (2011)
12. Dureha, A.: An accurate algorithm for generating a music playlist based on facial expressions. Int. J. Comput. Appl. **100**(9), 33–39 (2014)
13. Ekman, P., Friesen, W.V.: Constants across cultures in the face and emotion. J. Pers. Soc. Psychol. **17**(2), 124 (1971)
14. Benitez-Quiroz, C.F., Srinivasan, R., Martinez, A.M.: EmotioNet: an accurate, real-time algorithm for the automatic annotation of a million facial expressions in the wild. In: Proceedings of the IEEE Conference on Computer Vision and Pattern Recognition, pp. 5562–5570 (2016)
15. Fan, Y., Lu, X., Li, D., Liu, Y.: Video-based emotion recognition using CNN-RNN and C3D hybrid networks. In: Proceedings of the 18th ACM International Conference on Multimodal Interaction, pp. 445–450 (2016)
16. González-Lozoya, S.M., de la Calleja, J., Pellegrin, L., Escalante, H.J., Medina, M.A., Benitez-Ruiz, A.: Recognition of facial expressions based on CNN features. Multimedia Tools Appl. **79**(19), 13,987–14,007 (2020)
17. Gross, R., Matthews, I., Cohn, J., Kanade, T., Baker, S.: Multi-PIE. Image Vis. Comput. **28**(5), 807–813 (2010)
18. Gupta, S.K., Nain, N.: Gabor filter meanPCA feature extraction for gender recognition. In: Chaudhuri, B.B., Kankanhalli, M.S., Raman, B. (eds.) Proceedings of 2nd International Conference on Computer Vision & Image Processing. AISC, vol. 704, pp. 79–88. Springer, Singapore (2018). https://doi.org/10.1007/978-981-10-7898-9_7
19. Gupta, S.K., Agrwal, S., Meena, Y.K., Nain, N.: A hybrid method of feature extraction for facial expression recognition. In: 2011 Seventh International Conference on Signal Image Technology & Internet-Based Systems, pp. 422–425. IEEE (2011)

20. Hamester, D., Barros, P., Wermter, S.: Face expression recognition with a 2-channel convolutional neural network. In: 2015 International Joint Conference on Neural Networks (IJCNN), pp. 1–8. IEEE (2015)

21. Happy, S., Routray, A.: Automatic facial expression recognition using features of salient facial patches. IEEE Trans. Affect. Comput. **6**(1), 1–12 (2014)

22. Islam, B., Mahmud, F., Hossain, A., Goala, P.B., Mia, M.S.: A facial region segmentation based approach to recognize human emotion using fusion of hog & LBP features and artificial neural network. In: 2018 4th International Conference on Electrical Engineering and Information & Communication Technology (iCEEiCT), pp. 642–646. IEEE (2018)

23. Jabid, T., Kabir, M.H., Chae, O.: Facial expression recognition using local directional pattern (LDP). In: 2010 IEEE International Conference on Image Processing, pp. 1605–1608. IEEE (2010)

24. Jung, H., Lee, S., Yim, J., Park, S., Kim, J.: Joint fine-tuning in deep neural networks for facial expression recognition. In: Proceedings of the IEEE International Conference on Computer Vision, pp. 2983–2991 (2015)

25. Kamachi, M., Lyons, M., Gyoba, J.: The Japanese female facial expression (JAFFE) database (1998). http://www.kasrl.org/jaffe.html. 21:32

26. Kar, N.B., Babu, K.S., Jena, S.K.: Face expression recognition using histograms of oriented gradients with reduced features. In: Raman, B., Kumar, S., Roy, P.P., Sen, D. (eds.) Proceedings of International Conference on Computer Vision and Image Processing. AISC, vol. 460, pp. 209–219. Springer, Singapore (2017). https://doi.org/10.1007/978-981-10-2107-7_19

27. Kim, J.H., Kim, B.G., Roy, P.P., Jeong, D.M.: Efficient facial expression recognition algorithm based on hierarchical deep neural network structure. IEEE Access **7**, 41,273–41,285 (2019)

28. Kumar, S., Bhuyan, M.K., Chakraborty, B.K.: Extraction of informative regions of a face for facial expression recognition. IET Comput. Vision **10**(6), 567–576 (2016)

29. Langner, O., Dotsch, R., Bijlstra, G., Wigboldus, D.H., Hawk, S.T., Van Knippenberg, A.: Presentation and validation of the Radboud faces database. Cogn. Emot. **24**(8), 1377–1388 (2010)

30. Lee, J., Uddin, M.Z., Kim, T.S.: Spatiotemporal human facial expression recognition using fisher independent component analysis and hidden Markov model. In: 2008 30th Annual International Conference of the IEEE Engineering in Medicine and Biology Society, pp. 2546–2549. IEEE (2008)

31. Li, S., Deng, W.: Reliable crowdsourcing and deep locality-preserving learning for unconstrained facial expression recognition. IEEE Trans. Image Process. **28**(1), 356–370 (2018)

32. Li, Y., Zeng, J., Shan, S., Chen, X.: Occlusion aware facial expression recognition using CNN with attention mechanism. IEEE Trans. Image Process. **28**(5), 2439–2450 (2018)

33. Liu, M., Li, S., Shan, S., Wang, R., Chen, X.: Deeply learning deformable facial action parts model for dynamic expression analysis. In: Cremers, D., Reid, I., Saito, H., Yang, M.-H. (eds.) ACCV 2014. LNCS, vol. 9006, pp. 143–157. Springer, Cham (2015). https://doi.org/10.1007/978-3-319-16817-3_10

34. Liu, M., Li, S., Shan, S., Chen, X.: Au-inspired deep networks for facial expression feature learning. Neurocomputing **159**, 126–136 (2015)

35. Liu, P., Han, S., Meng, Z., Tong, Y.: Facial expression recognition via a boosted deep belief network. In: Proceedings of the IEEE Conference on Computer Vision and Pattern Recognition, pp. 1805–1812 (2014)

36. Liu, Y., Li, Y., Ma, X., Song, R.: Facial expression recognition with fusion features extracted from salient facial areas. Sensors **17**(4), 712 (2017)
37. Lucey, P., Cohn, J.F., Kanade, T., Saragih, J., Ambadar, Z., Matthews, I.: The extended Cohn-Kanade dataset (CK+): a complete dataset for action unit and emotion-specified expression. In: 2010 IEEE Computer Society Conference on Computer Vision and Pattern Recognition-Workshops, pp. 94–101. IEEE (2010)
38. Mahmoudi, M.A., Chetouani, A., Boufera, F., Tabia, H.: Improved bilinear model for facial expression recognition. In: Djeddi, C., Kessentini, Y., Siddiqi, I., Jmaiel, M. (eds.) MedPRAI 2020. CCIS, vol. 1322, pp. 47–59. Springer, Cham (2021). https://doi.org/10.1007/978-3-030-71804-6_4
39. Mandal, M.K., Pandey, R., Prasad, A.B.: Facial expressions of emotions and schizophrenia: a review. Schizophr. Bull. **24**(3), 399–412 (1998)
40. Mehrabian, A.: Communication without words. In: Communication Theory, pp. 193–200. Routledge (2017)
41. Mehta, N., Jadhav, S.: Facial emotion recognition using log Gabor filter and PCA. In: 2016 International Conference on Computing Communication Control and automation (ICCUBEA), pp. 1–5. IEEE (2016)
42. Mollahosseini, A., Chan, D., Mahoor, M.H.: Going deeper in facial expression recognition using deep neural networks. In: 2016 IEEE Winter Conference on Applications of Computer Vision (WACV), pp. 1–10. IEEE (2016)
43. Mollahosseini, A., Hasani, B., Mahoor, M.H.: AffectNet: a database for facial expression, valence, and arousal computing in the wild. IEEE Trans. Affect. Comput. **10**(1), 18–31 (2017)
44. Nazir, M., Jan, Z., Sajjad, M.: Facial expression recognition using histogram of oriented gradients based transformed features. Clust. Comput. **21**(1), 539–548 (2018)
45. Ng, H.W., Nguyen, V.D., Vonikakis, V., Winkler, S.: Deep learning for emotion recognition on small datasets using transfer learning. In: Proceedings of the 2015 ACM on International Conference on Multimodal Interaction, pp. 443–449 (2015)
46. Nigam, S., Singh, R., Misra, A.: Efficient facial expression recognition using histogram of oriented gradients in wavelet domain. Multimedia Tools Appl. **77**(21), 28,725–28,747 (2018)
47. Ojala, T., Pietikainen, M., Maenpaa, T.: Multiresolution gray-scale and rotation invariant texture classification with local binary patterns. IEEE Trans. Pattern Anal. Mach. Intell. **24**(7), 971–987 (2002)
48. Pantic, M., Valstar, M., Rademaker, R., Maat, L.: Web-based database for facial expression analysis. In: 2005 IEEE International Conference on Multimedia and Expo, p. 5. IEEE (2005)
49. Pramerdorfer, C., Kampel, M.: Facial expression recognition using convolutional neural networks: state of the art. arXiv preprint arXiv:1612.02903 (2016)
50. Ryu, B., Rivera, A.R., Kim, J., Chae, O.: Local directional ternary pattern for facial expression recognition. IEEE Trans. Image Process. **26**(12), 6006–6018 (2017)
51. Saurav, S., Gidde, P., Saini, R., Singh, S.: Dual integrated convolutional neural network for real-time facial expression recognition in the wild. Vis. Comput. **38**(3), 1083–1096 (2022)
52. Shan, C., Gong, S., McOwan, P.W.: Facial expression recognition based on local binary patterns: a comprehensive study. Image Vis. Comput. **27**(6), 803–816 (2009)
53. Shan, K., Guo, J., You, W., Lu, D., Bie, R.: Automatic facial expression recognition based on a deep convolutional-neural-network structure. In: 2017 IEEE 15th International Conference on Software Engineering Research, pp. 123–128. Management and Applications (SERA). IEEE (2017)

54. Soni, K., Gupta, S.K., Kumar, U., Agrwal, S.L.: A new Gabor wavelet transform feature extraction technique for ear biometric recognition. In: 2014 6th IEEE Power India International Conference (PIICON), pp. 1–3. IEEE (2014)
55. Susskind, J.M., Anderson, A.K., Hinton, G.E.: The Toronto face database. Technical Report, Department of Computer Science, University of Toronto, Toronto, Canada 3 (2010)
56. Ts, A., Guddeti, R.M.R.: Automatic detection of students' affective states in classroom environment using hybrid convolutional neural networks. Educ. Inf. Technol. 25(2), 1387–1415 (2020)
57. Tsai, H.H., Chang, Y.C.: Facial expression recognition using a combination of multiple facial features and support vector machine. Soft. Comput. 22(13), 4389–4405 (2018)
58. Turan, C., Lam, K.M., He, X.: Soft locality preserving map (SLPM) for facial expression recognition (2018). arXiv preprint arXiv:1801.03754
59. Uddin, M.Z., Lee, J., Kim, T.S.: An enhanced independent component-based human facial expression recognition from video. IEEE Trans. Consum. Electron. 55(4), 2216–2224 (2009)
60. Uddin, M.Z., Hassan, M.M., Almogren, A., Zuair, M., Fortino, G., Torresen, J.: A facial expression recognition system using robust face features from depth videos and deep learning. Comput. Electric. Eng. 63, 114–125 (2017)
61. Verma, K., Khunteta, A.: Facial expression recognition using Gabor filter and multi-layer artificial neural network. In: 2017 International Conference on Information, Communication, Instrumentation and Control (ICICIC), pp. 1–5. IEEE (2017)
62. Wang, K., Peng, X., Yang, J., Lu, S., Qiao, Y.: Suppressing uncertainties for large-scale facial expression recognition. In: Proceedings of the IEEE/CVF Conference on Computer Vision and Pattern Recognition, pp. 6897–6906 (2020)
63. Wang, K., Peng, X., Yang, J., Meng, D., Qiao, Y.: Region attention networks for pose and occlusion robust facial expression recognition. IEEE Trans. Image Process. 29, 4057–4069 (2020)
64. Wang, W., et al.: A fine-grained facial expression database for end-to-end multi-pose facial expression recognition (2019). arXiv preprint arXiv:1907.10838
65. Weldon, T.P., Higgins, W.E., Dunn, D.F.: Efficient Gabor filter design for texture segmentation. Pattern Recogn. 29(12), 2005–2015 (1996)
66. Wen, G., Chang, T., Li, H., Jiang, L.: Dynamic objectives learning for facial expression recognition. IEEE Trans. Multimedia 22(11), 2914–2925 (2020)
67. Wu, Y., Liu, W., Wang, J.: Application of emotional recognition in intelligent tutoring system. In: First International Workshop on Knowledge Discovery and Data Mining (WKDD 2008), pp. 449–452. IEEE (2008)
68. Xie, S., Hu, H.: Facial expression recognition using hierarchical features with deep comprehensive multipatches aggregation convolutional neural networks. IEEE Trans. Multimedia 21(1), 211–220 (2018)
69. Xu, Q., Zhao, N.: A facial expression recognition algorithm based on CNN and LBP feature. In: 2020 IEEE 4th Information Technology, Networking, Electronic and Automation Control Conference (ITNEC), vol. 1, pp. 2304–2308. IEEE (2020)
70. Yadav, P., Poonia, A., Gupta, S.K., Agrwal, S.: Performance analysis of Gabor 2D PCA feature extraction for gender identification using face. In: 2017 2nd International Conference on Telecommunication and Networks (TEL-NET), pp. 1–5. IEEE (2017)
71. Yan, J., Zheng, W., Cui, Z., Tang, C., Zhang, T., Zong, Y.: Multi-cue fusion for emotion recognition in the wild. Neurocomputing 309, 27–35 (2018)

72. Yang, H., Ciftci, U., Yin, L.: Facial expression recognition by de-expression residue learning. In: Proceedings of the IEEE Conference on Computer Vision and Pattern Recognition, pp. 2168–2177 (2018)
73. Yin, L., Wei, X., Sun, Y., Wang, J., Rosato, M.J.: A 3D facial expression database for facial behavior research. In: 7th International Conference on Automatic Face and Gesture Recognition (FGR06), pp. 211–216. IEEE (2006)
74. Yu, Z., Liu, Q., Liu, G.: Deeper cascaded peak-piloted network for weak expression recognition. Vis. Comput. **34**(12), 1691–1699 (2018)
75. Zeng, G., Zhou, J., Jia, X., Xie, W., Shen, L.: Hand-crafted feature guided deep learning for facial expression recognition. In: 2018 13th IEEE International Conference on Automatic Face & Gesture Recognition (FG 2018), pp. 423–430. IEEE (2018)
76. Zhang, K., Huang, Y., Du, Y., Wang, L.: Facial expression recognition based on deep evolutional spatial-temporal networks. IEEE Trans. Image Process. **26**(9), 4193–4203 (2017)
77. Zhang, Z., Zhang, J.: A new real-time eye tracking for driver fatigue detection. In: 2006 6th International Conference on ITS Telecommunications, pp. 8–11. IEEE (2006)
78. Zhang, Z., Luo, P., Loy, C.C., Tang, X.: From facial expression recognition to interpersonal relation prediction. Int. J. Comput. Vision **126**(5), 550–569 (2018)
79. Zhao, Z., Liu, Q., Wang, S.: Learning deep global multi-scale and local attention features for facial expression recognition in the wild. IEEE Trans. Image Process. **30**, 6544–6556 (2021)

Forecasting of Rainfall Using Neural Network and Traditional Almanac Models

R. Ragunath, S. Dhamodharavadhani, and R. Rathipriya[✉]

Department of Computer Science, Periyar university, Salem, Tamilnadu, India
rathi_priyar@periyaruniversity.acin

Abstract. The Indian meteorological department provides only short term forecasts of weather, but long term forecasting is required for effective planning of agro production related activities. Generally, long term rainfall forecasting can be achieved by two approaches, traditional almanac forecasting (TAF), and scientific weather forecasting (SWF). TAF is based on observations and experience using a combination of meteorological and astronomical indicators, activities of animals, insects, and plants, and almanacs (also called as panchangams). SWF is based on past records of climate in a particular region using mathematical models. The main objective of this study is to recommend crops based on forecasted rainfall in Tamilnadu, India using TAF and SWF models. In this work, a hybrid non-linear autoregression Neural Network is used as SWF and saint Kaikkadar Rainfall Prediction Methodology is used as TAF. An empirical study is conducted to compare the performance of TAF and SWF models It is clear that the hybrid AF NARNN model outperformed the baseline AF NARNN model in terms of RMSE value. The hybrid AF NARNN model improved forecast accuracy by 4.0%, 3.3%, 5.4%, 5.1%, 6.9%, 0.3%, 5.3%, 2.6%, 1.0%, 6.0, and 6.0, respectively, with the exception of October. The prediction of TAF model is more than 65% similar to SWF. As a result, the TAF model can be utilised as a tool for long-term forecasting of activities related to agriculture.

Keywords: Almanac · Panchangam · Rainfall prediction · Neural Network · NAR · Hybrid NARNN · Crop recommendation

1 Introduction

Panchangam or almanac is a Hindu calendar and almanac that follows the traditional units of Hindu timekeeping and predicts celestial events such as solar eclipses, weather (rainy, dry seasons) and more mundane events. Since 5,000 years ago, panchangam has been used in India. It is a cherished repository of priceless meteorological rainfall forecasts. Indians have been using these panchangam techniques to predict and forecast the weather since ancient times. These techniques include nature observation, the study of omens and prognostics, wind analysis, cloud pattern analysis, planetary placements and conjunctions, nakshatra (star) influences, and other astrological concepts [1, 2].

The word 'Panchang' has its roots in two Sanskrit words, viz., 'panch' and 'ang', which means 'five' and 'body part/limb' respectively. These parts are

© The Author(s), under exclusive license to Springer Nature Switzerland AG 2023
I. Woungang et al. (Eds.): ANTIC 2022, CCIS 1798, pp. 592–608, 2023.
https://doi.org/10.1007/978-3-031-28183-9_42

- Tithi (or) Lunar day - Total of thirty tithis in a lunar month, fifteen in each fortnight.
- Vara of week day - seven varas, namely Ravivara (Sunday), Somavara (Monday), Mangalavara (Tuesday), Budhavara (Wednesday), Guruvara (Thursday), Shukravara (Friday) and Shanivara (Saturday)
- Nakshatra (or) asterism (or) constellation - Total of twenty seven nakshtras named according to the yagataras (or) identifying stars of each of the twenty seven equal parts of the ecliptic (or) solar path.
- Yoga (or) time during which the joint motion of the sun and the moon covers the space of the nakshatra (there are twenty seven yogas).
- Karana (or) half of a lunar day (or) half-tithi [2–4].

Estimating rainfall is the most crucial determining element in meteorology, particularly in a nation like India where agriculture is the only source of income for roughly 70% of the people and where agricultural productivity is entirely dependent on the monsoon. So, for optimal agricultural production, precise and intelligent forecasts are necessary [5], and these forecasts become even more crucial to prevent losses in agroforestry resources during unfavourable weather and natural disasters in many regions of the world [6].

Forecasting Models for Time-Series Data is categorised into two groups. They are: Traditional almanac forecasting (TAF) Models (includesTamil and Telugu Panchangam. Kaikkadar Panchangam) and Scientific weather forecasting (SWF) Models using Neural Network (includes NAR-Extraneous (NARX), NAR, etc.,). Table 1 summarizes the different forecasting models which are used for predictions. Table 2 outlines the pseudocode of hybrid prediction algorithm namely AF_HNARNN:

Table 1. Summary of forecasting models for prediction

Year	References	Forecasting models-type	Methods/Model/Methodology	Task
2020	[1]	TAF	Panchangam	Weather Prediction
2022	[2]	TAF	Astronomy	Weather Prediction
2008	[3]	TAF	Traditional almanac	Rainfall Prediction
2012	[4]	TAF	Traditional Hindu almanac	Weather Prediction
2011	[5]	TAF	Traditional	Weather Forecast
2009	[6]	TAF	Traditional Weather forecasting Model	Weather Prediction
2014	[7]	SWF	ANN - NARNN	Disease Forecasting
2020	[8]	SWF	ANN - NAR. Activation Function	Rainfall Prediction
2019	[9]	SWF	ANN - NARX	Wind Speed Forecasting
2022	[10]	SWF	NAR, ARIMA	Rainfall Prediction
2020	[11]	SWF	Hybrid SSA-ARIMA-ANN model	Daily Rainfall Prediction
2019	[12]	SWF	Neural Network Model	Rainfall Prediction
2022	[13]	SWF	SARIMA	Weather Prediction

Table 2. Hybrid NARNN-GRNN algorithm

Pseudocode: AF_HNARNN: Hybrid NARNN and GRNN Algorithm
Step 1: Pre-process the raw rainfall time series dataset.
Step 2: Initialize model parameters for AF_NARNN with different activation function and optimal training algorithms.
Step 3: Input dataset into the AF_ NARNN model, and predict (Prednew) for 'n' time period ahead or for given set of dataset.
Step 4: Validate the performance of AF_NARNN using RMSE value.
Step 5: Calculate the error or residual of AF_NARNN model
Step 6: Initialize model parameters for GRNN model.
Step 7: Input these residuals of AF_NARNN model into GRNN time series forecasting model
Step 8: Forecast the residual values (F_Error) for forecasted values (F_rainfall)of AF_NARNN model.
Step 9: Optimized forecasted rainfall Opt_rainfall=F_rainfall+F_Error
Step 10: Return Opt_rainfall as optimized output

The goal is to research and develop a reliable rainfall forecasting system that allows users to track the predicted rainfall of their locations in Tamilnadu, India, using insights from Panchangam or almanac data and artificial intelligence to assist our farmers in forecasting rainfall. Therefore, in this work, a hybrid non-linear autoregression Neural Network is used as Scientific Weather Forecasting (SWF) model and saint Kaikkadar Rainfall Prediction Methodology is used as Traditional almanac forecasting (TAF) model. Aimed to conduct an empirical study to compare the performance of TAF and SWF models to find out the extent to which almanac forecasting and artificial intelligence-based rainfall forecasts are accurate. The primary contributions of this work are:

- First, the creation of a SWF model for predicting rainfall using a NAR-neural network. To enhance the NAR neural network model's performance, a hybrid strategy is suggested.
- Second, the long-period average (LPA) rainfall value is used to categorise the predicted rainfall results.
- Third, a comparison study between SWF and TAF-based rainfall categorization models is conducted to assess the reliability of traditional almanac-based rainfall forecasting.

The following is the planned format for this paper: The NARNN model is briefly explained in Sect. 2. Section 3 details the suggested methodology. The outcomes of SWF and TAF models are thoroughly discussed in Sect. 4. The final section elaborates summary of this research's findings along with a possible future work.

2 NARNN Model

NARNN is a model for predicting futuristic values of an input variable using a time series NN. It is mainly used for nonlinear datasets and predicts future values via a refeeding method. The projected value may be utilised as an input for forward-looking point-based future predictions [7]. The NARNN framework is constructed by defining network design variables like "feedback delays, the number of neurons in the hidden layer, training methods, and activation functions". These factors are domain-specific like open/closed loops, and determining their optimum values are a difficult job. The feedback network is fed a new projected value.

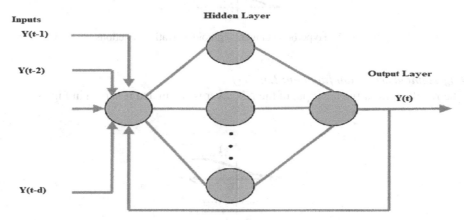

Fig. 1. NARNN network architecture

Figure 1 illustrates the design of the NARNN network. It is made up of an input layer with n time points, an output layer, and a hidden layer with a predefined number enhance its accuracy. It has a minimum error rate and superior predictive accuracy.

Equation (1) depicts the numerical form of NARNN by designating the new estimated values as time series and past observation values.

$$\text{Ypredicted} = \text{fn}(y(t-1) + y(t-2) + \cdots + y(t-d)) + \varepsilon(t) \qquad (1)$$

where fn is an arbitrary nonlinear function that can be estimated by feedforward neural networks during training; Ypredicted is the predicted value of the y at a discrete time step t; d represents past values of the series; and ε (t) is the approximation error of the y at 't'.

2.1 Activation Functions

A key part of the NN is the activation function. It decides whether a neuron should be activated by computing the weighted total and adding additional partialities to it. The objective is to induce nonlinearity in the neuron output and let it learn and execute the complicated tasks in a single activation function [8].

Hyperbolic tangent sigmoid activation function: Tansig()
It is a neural transfer function and a layer's output is calculated by its net input is shown in Fig. 2 [8].

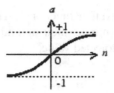

Fig. 2. Hyperbolic tangent sigmoid activation functions

Log-sigmoid activation function: Logsig()
The resultant from the net input of the NN layer is calculated is shown in Fig. 3.

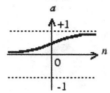

Fig. 3. Log-sigmoid activation functions

Elliot symmetric sigmoid activation function: elliotsig()
In this, the net input of the NN layer is translated to the net output. Figure 4 shows the Elliot symmetric sigmoid activation function [8].

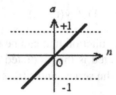

Fig. 4. Elliot symmetric sigmoid activation function

Linear activation function: Purelin()
It's a function of neural transfer and the output of a layer is determined from its net input. Figure 5 shows the linear activation functions [8].

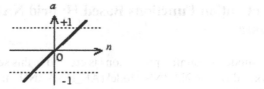

Fig. 5. Linear activation functions

General regression neural networks (GRNN)

GRNN model [14] comprises of two networks that are combined into a single architecture to handle various target variable types. The GRNN model delivers accurate predicted target probability scores by emulating Bayes optimum classification and is typically faster to train, more accurate, and reasonably insensitive to outliers. Figure 6 illustrates the four layers of the GRNN: input layer: $\{x1,x2,\ldots xn\}$, pattern layer: $\{p1,p2,\ldots,pm\}$, summation layer: $\{s1,s2,\ldots,sd\}$, and output layer: $\{y1,y2,\ldots,yk\}$.

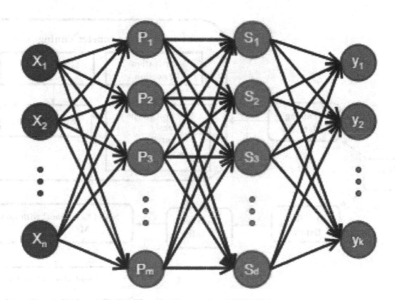

Fig. 6. Structure of GRNN

3 Activation Functions Based Hybrid NARNN Model for Rainfall Data

A new model for rainfall predictions is created in this section using the Activation Functions based Hybrid NARNN Model (AF_HNARNN) model. The proposed methodology includes different activation functions in the hidden layer and the linear activation function for the resultant layer. This proposed hybrid neural network model recognises the historical rainfall patterns from the time series rainfall data and forecasts future monthly rainfall values. The effectiveness of the proposed methodology is evaluated by changing the hyperparameters of NN design such as "activation functions, number of hidden neurons (H) and initial weight (IW)". This reduces the issue of overfitting and enhances the precision of the forecast. The AF_HNARNN model is assessed using benchmark performance measures such as RMSE and R-value. The value of RMSE is used as the selection criterion for identifying the best prediction model for forecasting the rainfall. The graphical abstract of this work is shown in Fig. 7.

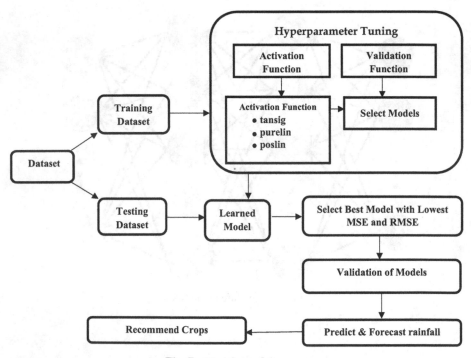

Fig. 7. Workflow of the paper

Generally, predictive or regression models suffer from predictive error or residuals. Similarly, the proposed activation function-based NARNN model has some problems. To address this issue, this research suggested a hybrid methodology that incorporates a GRNN time series prediction model with the NARNN model in order to produce a greater accuracy predictive model. The GRNN time series predictions model thus identifies and anticipates trends in the predictive error of the NARNN model's prediction. The combined output of these models surely offers increased predictive accuracy.

4 Result and Discussion

This section discusses the results obtained using the proposed hybrid methodology for the rainfall datasets. Table 3 showed NARNN and GRNN model parameter setup. It included training algorithms, activation function, and hyperparameters.

Table 3. Neural Network Model parameters setup

Model parameters	Base Model: NARNN	Hybrid Model: GRNN
Hidden Layer (HL)	Fixed Architecture	Fixed Architecture
Number of Neurons in HL	5–20	20
Training algorithm	Bayesian Regularization	Bayesian Regularization
Hyper parameter	Number of hidden neurons, Number of feedback, Activation functions	Nil
Activation function	tansig, logsig, elloitsig, purelin, radbsn	Tansig
Performance	RMSE	RMSE

Table 4. Best parameter setting of activation function: logsig for rainfall dataset

Month	Training function	Hidden layer	Delay	RMSE
January	trainbr	19	2	13.7
February	trainbr	19	4	10.99
March	trainlm	12	1	13.61
April	trainscg	15	3	10.36
May	trainlm	7	3	18.23
June	trainscg	8	2	35.18
July	trainbr	16	1	35.06
August	trainbr	20	2	32.11
September	trainbr	13	4	37.30
October	trainbr	15	1	29.61
November	trainbr	16	2	18.80
December	traincgf	5	1	16.31

The essential network parameters of the NARNN model are shown in Table 4 along with their various functions and logsig activation functions for each month. Between the months of February and April, the RMSE value was at its lowest. In the months of June and July, the RMSE value was at its highest. This is due to the scale dependent nature of the RMSE value.

Table 5. Best parameter setting of purelin activation function: for rainfall dataset

Month	Training function	Hidden layer	Delay	RMSE
January	Traincgf	8	2	9.1
February	Trainlm	8	3	10.82
March	Trainscg	8	1	11.67
April	Traincgf	13	3	9.69
May	Trainscg	7	1	15.46
June	Trainlm	18	3	34.39
July	Trainscg	7	2	39.51
August	Trainscg	5	3	33.43
September	Trainlm	19	4	35.27
October	Trainscg	12	1	27.13
November	Trainbr	14	1	16.29
December	Trainlm	7	2	8.83

The NARNN model's primary network hyperparameters employing purelin activation functions are shown in Table 5 for each month. It has the optimal hyperparameter values for the training function, activation function, number of neurons in the hidden layer, and feedback delay.

The important network hyperparameters of the NARNN model utilising the Radbasn activation function are shown in Table 6 for each month. The best learning algorithm to increase prediction accuracy for rainfall datasets using a radbasn-based NARNN model is traincgf.

The NARNN model using the tansig activation function's main network hyperparameters for each month are shown in Table 7. Trainbr is the best learning algorithm for increasing the prediction accuracy of a Tansig-based NARNN model for datasets relating to rainfall.

For the monthly rainfall datasets, Table 8 lists the top activation functions and training methods. For the dataset of monthly rainfall, it is found that trainbr is a great learning algorithm. This is because the NARNN model's optimal activation and learning functions for the short and non-linear dataset are elliotsig and trainbr.

The best model performance metrics for the Rainfall dataset utilising the standard and hybrid NARNN models are displayed in Table 9 respectively. When comparing monthly rainfall predictions, the hybrid model's RMSE value for various months is the lowest. Farmers will nevertheless benefit from this research because it will provide them with essential knowledge regarding the hybrid NARNN model's ability to predict rainfall accurately.

Table 6. Best parameter setting of activation function: radbasn for rainfall dataset

Month	Training function	Hidden layer	Delay	RMSE
January	Traincgf	5	4	38.8
February	Traincgf	5	4	29.81
March	Traincgf	5	2	37.42
April	Traincgf	5	4	31.84
May	Traincgf	5	3	52.66
June	Traincgf	5	3	109.71
July	Traincgf	5	4	94.16
August	Traincgf	5	4	80.76
September	Traincgf	5	1	111.39
October	Traincgf	5	2	89.39
November	Traincgf	5	4	48.93
December	Traincgf	5	1	41.89

Table 7. Best Parameter Setting of Activation Function: tansig for rainfall dataset

Month	Training function	Hidden layer	Delay	RMSE
January	Trainbr	20	2	7.6
February	Trainbr	18	1	9.72
March	Trainbr	20	1	9.82
April	Trainbr	20	3	8.10
May	Trainbr	20	4	13.48
June	Trainbr	20	2	28.76
July	Trainbr	18	1	34.14
August	Trainbr	15	2	29.29
September	Trainbr	18	4	31.69
October	Trainbr	17	1	22.41
November	Trainbr	19	2	13.94
December	Trainbr	19	2	8.21

The forecasts for monthly rainfall produced by the hybrid AF_NARNN for the years 2021 to 2030 are displayed in Table 10. The graphical comparison of the RMSE value of the hybrid and standard AF_NARNN models for the monthly rainfall datasets is shown in Fig. 8. In terms of RMSE value, it is evident that the hybrid AF_NARNN model outperformed the standard AF_NARNN model. With the exception of October,

Table 8. Characteristics of best model for monthly rainfall dataset

Months	Activation function	Training algorithm	No of neurons in hidden layer	Delay	RMSE	R
January	elliotsig	trainbr	20	2	7.49	0.58
February	elliotsig	trainbr	20	4	9.10	0.55
March	elliotsig	trainbr	18	1	9.33	0.60
April	elliotsig	trainbr	16	3	7.94	0.58
May	elliotsig	trainbr	18	4	13.03	0.56
June	elliotsig	trainbr	16	2	29.02	0.56
July	elliotsig	trainbr	19	1	31.94	0.60
August	elliotsig	trainbr	20	2	27.39	0.59
September	elliotsig	trainbr	20	4	30.17	0.53
October	elliotsig	trainbr	19	1	21.46	0.62
November	elliotsig	trainbr	17	2	13.44	0.57
December	elliotsig	trainbr	19	1	6.74	0.66

Table 9. Performance metrics of standard NARNN Model for Rainfall Dataset

	Jan	Feb	Mar	Apr	May	Jun	Jul	Aug	Sep	Oct	Nov	Dec
Standard NARNN Model												
RMSE	7.5	9.1	9.3	7.9	13.0	28.8	31.9	27.4	30.2	21.5	13.4	6.7
R-value	0.5	0.5	0.5	0.6	0.5	0.6	0.5	0.5	0.5	0.6	0.5	0.4
Hybrid NARNN Model												
RMSE	7.2	8.8	8.8	7.5	12.1	28.7	30.2	26.7	29.9	21.5	12.6	6.3
R-Value	0.3	0.3	0.3	0.3	0.4	0.1	0.3	0.3	0.2	0.1	0.4	0.3

the hybrid AF_NARNN model increased forecast accuracy by 4.0%, 3.3%, 5.4%, 5.1%, 6.9%, 0.3%, 5.3%, 2.6%, 1.0%, 6.0, and 6.0, respectively.

Table 11 expounds the rainfall categorization starts from very low rainfall to extremely heavy rainfall. These data will be very useful to classify the forecast rainfall for the coming years. Table 12 lists the actual annual rainfall amounts for the years 1950 to 2000, rainfall classification based on LPA and traditional almanac, and whether or not the two rainfall classification methods are similar. It was found that 66% of predictions obtained using LPA and traditional almanac based rainfall classification are similar. Figure 9 depicts the similarity of rainfall predictions by two models. Therefore, it is concluded that traditional almanac based rainfall forecasting method is suitable for rainfall forecasting.

Table 10. Predicted value using hybrid model (10 years in mm)

Month	2021	2022	2023	2024	2025	2026	2027	2028	2029	2030
Jan	25.6	26.9	30.8	29.7	20.3	24.9	25.5	17.1	27.2	23.7
Feb	39.7	26.2	26.5	33.1	33.0	34.1	35.0	25.1	26.5	26.2
Mar	30.3	30.9	31.4	32.0	32.4	32.9	33.4	33.8	34.2	34.6
Apr	45.0	34.8	36.7	40.7	40.4	40.4	37.7	37.8	37.9	41.4
May	75.5	63.1	68.1	69.1	91.6	80.4	80.0	80.5	74.2	94.1
Jun	206.1	161.4	153.9	196.3	183.4	169.7	181.9	195.0	178.4	184.4
Jul	278.9	258.2	285.6	269.7	262.7	271.9	258.8	277.3	255.3	283.8
Aug	277.9	289.7	259.7	287.7	246.5	285.1	209.1	282.5	276.6	280.5
Sep	155.3	121.9	153.7	145.7	171.5	163.9	170.6	113.9	164.0	146.5
Oct	78.6	95.4	64.3	91.4	85.8	66.8	60.1	114.2	91.3	88.0
Nov	27.0	17.3	24.0	40.0	25.2	15.4	23.0	38.6	24.8	17.0
Dec	10.2	11.1	8.4	12.2	10.4	11.9	9.2	12.6	10.8	12.4

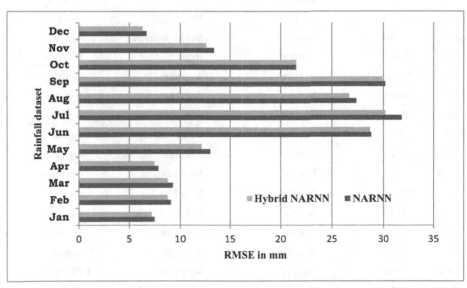

Fig. 8. RMSE based Comparison of Standard NARNN and Hybrid NARNN model for rainfall dataset

Table 13 presents the annual rainfall for 2021–2030 and their classification using LPA and traditional almanac-based rainfall classification. More than 50% of almanac-based rainfall predictions are correctly aligned with science-based rainfall forecasting methods. Table 14 shows the crops recommendation for India using Rainfall categorization.

Table 11. Categorization of rainfall (in millimetres)

S.No	Category	Rainfall Range (%)
1.	Normal	+ 19 to -19
2.	Deficient	-20 to -59
3.	Large deficient	-60 to -99
4.	No rain	-100
5.	Excess	20% to 59%
6.	Large excess	≥ 60%

Table 12. Comparison of yearly actual rainfall with LPA and traditional almanac based rainfall classification

Year	Actual Rainfall	LPA based rainfall classification	Traditional almanac based rainfall classification	Similarity of Predictions
1950	747.5	Low	Very high	Disagree
1951	855.1	Normal	Very high	Disagree
1952	716.4	Low	Below average	Agree
1953	968.0	Normal	High	Disagree
1954	1016.2	Normal	Average	Agree
1955	1060.6	Normal	Average	Agree
1956	989.7	Normal	Average	Agree
1957	866.9	Normal	Below average	Agree
1958	852.5	Normal	Average	Agree
1959	894.3	Normal	Very low	Disagree
1960	1013.9	Normal	Very low	Disagree
1961	910.7	Normal	Below average	Agree
1962	941.6	Normal	Very low	Disagree
1963	1072.8	Normal	Average	Agree
1964	910.6	Normal	Very low	Disagree
1965	926.9	Normal	High	Disagree
1966	1166.9	Normal	Average	Agree
1967	899.1	Normal	Average	Agree
1968	789.4	Normal	High	Disagree
1969	961.8	Normal	Average	Agree

(*continued*)

Table 12. (*continued*)

Year	Actual Rainfall	LPA based rainfall classification	Traditional almanac based rainfall classification	Similarity of Predictions
1970	942.1	Normal	High	Disagree
1971	1047.6	Normal	High	Disagree
1972	1093.4	Normal	Below average	Agree
1973	858.5	Normal	Very high	Disagree
1974	652.8	Low	Very high	Disagree
1975	923.6	Normal	Below average	Agree
1976	858.9	Normal	Very low	Disagree
1977	1246.0	Normal	Very low	Disagree
1978	998.8	Normal	Above average	Agree
1979	1103.4	Normal	Below average	Agree
1980	709.1	Low	Below average	Agree
1981	1045.9	Normal	Low	Disagree
1982	678.6	Low	Average	Disagree
1983	1007.7	Normal	Average	Agree
1984	1023.8	Normal	High	Disagree
1985	1063.5	Normal	Above average	Agree
1986	953.0	Normal	Average	Agree
1987	967.4	Normal	Above average to heavy	Agree
1988	837.2	Normal	Above average to heavy	Agree
1989	858.2	Normal	Above average	Agree
1990	912.1	Normal	Below average	Agree
1991	956.3	Normal	Heavy	Agree
1992	918.7	Normal	Heavy	Agree
1993	1082.3	Normal	Average	Agree
1994	905.9	Normal	Above average	Agree
1995	845.0	Normal	Above average	Agree
1996	1070.3	Normal	Average	Agree
1997	950.5	Normal	Above average	Agree
1998	1079.7	Normal	Average	Agree
1999	922.6	Normal	Below average	Agree
2000	972.0	Normal	Below average	Agree

Table 13. Classification of forecasted rainfall

Year	Forecasted Rainfall using Hybrid AF_NARNN	LPA based Rainfall Classification	Traditional Almanac based Rainfall Classification
2021	1250.1	High	Very Low
2022	1136.9	Normal	Normal
2023	1143.1	Normal	Very Low
2024	1247.6	Normal	Normal
2025	1203.2	Normal	Very Low
2026	1197.4	Normal	High
2027	1124.3	Normal	Normal
2028	1228.4	Normal	Normal
2029	1201.2	Normal	High
2030	1232.6	Normal	Normal

Table 14. Rainfall based crop recommendations

Rainfall categorization	Suggested crops for cultivation in India
Very low	Vegetable, oil seed
Low	Sugarcane, Millets, Cotton, Maize
Normal	Sugarcane, Paddy, Millets, Cotton, Maize, Millet
High, Very High	Sugarcane, Paddy, Millets, Cotton, Maize, Jute

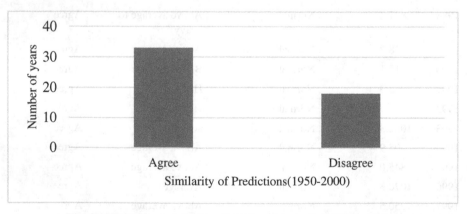

Fig. 9. Comparison of SWF and TWF models for Rainfall Prediction

Some researchers consider TAF to be completely vague and completely impossible to measure forecast. However, this study showed that TAF has an accuracy greater than 65%, which is a significant prediction accuracy for real-time rainfall forecasting. Similarly, SWF fails to accurately predict rainfall as it depends on many factors such as meteorological parameters, planetary motion, cyclones etc. The reason is that while developing their forecasting models, most SWFs only take a portion of these elements into account. From this study, it is clear that traditional almanac based weather forecasting model is very useful for rural farmers who do not have access to technology to plan their agricultural activities.

5 Conclusion

With multiple activation functions, a variable number of neurons in the hidden layer, and various feedback delays for neural network parameters, the accuracy of the SWF model known as NARNN is examined for the rainfall dataset in this study. Next, to lower the forecast error for rainfall forecasting, the GRNN was hybridised with the NARNN model that had the best hyperparameter value. Using performance metrics like RMSE and R-value, the output of both the standard and hybrid NARNN models were assessed. According to these findings, the best learning algorithm for rainfall prediction is Bayesian regulation, and the best activation function is elliotsig. Using the LPA value, these predicted rainfall for the years 1950 to 2000 were categorised. The findings of this SWF-based rainfall classification were compared with those obtained using an ancient almanac. Over 65% of rainfall forecasts are equivalent. This is a key finding of this research work.

Though most of the predictions in Panchangam are qualitative and usually generalized over a given area, say a state, an in-depth study and analysis of the propositions enshrined in the almanac, in conjunction with the modern sophisticated meteorological science will result in the evolution of a more accurate, reliable and accountable weather forecasting in the near future. Our ancient Indians did not have the luxury of sophisticated and automated weather mapping devices. Yet, they were able to develop astonishingly erudite and pertinent theories and principles often without even looking at the sky, which significantly coincided with the modern findings of late.

References

1. Yeole, S.: Panchang and its forgotten values and wisdom in perspective of Agriculture, Medium, 24-Sep-2020. https://medium.com/@snehal.yeole2112/panchang-and-its-forgotten-values-and-wisdom-in-perspective-of-agriculture-fbc6ff1d6937. Accessed 22 Oct 2022
2. Mahindrra, T.: Astronomy - Prediction of Monsoon Rains; Parashara, Varamihira, Panchanga in comparison to modern methods, Panjangam Inteligence. https://www.techmahindra.com/en-in/agtech/panchang-intelligence/. Accessed 25 Aug 2022
3. Sivaprakasam, S., Kanakasabai, V.: Traditional almanac rainfall prediction a case study (2008)
4. Vanadeep, K., Sada Siva Murty, R., Krishnaiah, M.: Meteorological predictions preserved in the Panchangam versus real-time observations – a case study over Tirupati region – a semi-arid tropical site in India. Indian J. Sci. Technol. (2012)

5. Acharya, S.: Prediction of rainfall variation through flowering phenology of night ...," Prediction of rainfall variation through flowering phenology of night-flowering jasmine (Nyctanthes arbor-tristis L.; Verbenaceae) in Tripura, 2011. https://www.researchgate.net/publication/292 009604_Prediction_of_rainfall_variation_through_flowering_phenology_of_night-flower ing_jasmine_Nyctanthes_arbor-tristis_L_Verbenaceae_in_Tripura. Accessed 21 Oct 2022

6. Galacgac, E.S., Balisacan, C.M.: Traditional weather forecasting for sustainable agroforestry practices in Ilocos Norte Province, Philippines. For. Ecol. Manage. **257**(10), 2044–2053 (2009)

7. Yu, L., et al.: Application of a new hybrid model with seasonal Auto-Regressive Integrated Moving Average (ARIMA) and Nonlinear Auto-Regressive Neural Network (NARNN) in forecasting incidence cases of HFMD in Shenzhen, China. PLoS ONE, **9**(6) (2014)

8. Kaleeswaran, V., Dhamodharavadhani, S., Rathipriya, R.: A comparative study of activation functions and Training Algorithm of NAR neural network for crop prediction. In: Sarkar, R., Julai, S., Hossain, S., Chong, W.T., Rahman, M. (eds.) 2020 4th International Conference on Electronics, Communication and Aerospace Technology (ICECA), Mathematical Problems in Engineering, vol. 2019, pp. 1–14 (2019)

9. Rawat, D., Mishra, P., Ray, S., et al.: Modeling of rainfall time series using NAR and ARIMA model over western Himalaya. India. Arab J Geosci **15**, 1696 (2022)

10. Unnikrishnan, P., Jothiprakash, V.: Hybrid SSA-ARIMA-ANN model for forecasting daily rainfall. Water Resour. Manage **34**(11), 3609–3623 (2020). https://doi.org/10.1007/s11269-020-02638-w

11. Tran Anh, D., Duc, D.T., Pham, V.S.: Improved rainfall prediction using combined preprocessing methods and feed-forward neural networks. J **2**(1), 65–83 (2019). https://doi.org/10.3390/j2010006

12. Ray, S., Das, S.S., Mishra, P., Al Khatib, A.M.G.: Time series sarima modelling and forecasting of monthly rainfall and temperature in the south Asian countries. Earth Syst. Environ. **5**(3), 531–546 (2021). https://doi.org/10.1007/s41748-021-00205-w

13. Ravi Shankar, K.R., Maraty, P., Murthy, V.R.K., Ramakrishna, Y.S.: Indigenous rain forecasting in Andhra Pradesh. In: Central Research Institute for Dryland Agriculture, Santoshnagar, Saidabad P.O., Hyderabad, pp. 59–67 (2008)

14. Martínez, F., Charte, F., Frías, M.P., Martínez-Rodríguez, A.M.: Strategies for time series forecasting with generalized regression neural networks. Neurocomputing, **491**, 509–521 (2022). https://doi.org/10.1016/j.neucom.2021.12.028

Retinal Blood Vessel Segmentation Based on Modified CNN and Analyze the Perceptional Quality of Segmented Images

Swapnil V. Deshmukh[✉] and Apash Roy

Department of Computer Science and Engineering, Lovely Professional University (LPU), Jalandhar, Punjab, India
jaykantdeshmukh@gmail.com, apash.23550@lpu.co.in

Abstract. Diabetic retinopathy is a major issue faced all over the world peoples that causes permanent blindness. With the onset of symptoms of diabetic retinopathy and the illness advances to an extreme level, it is difficult to recognize diabetic retinopathy at an earlier level. This paper presents the automatic detection of blood vessel segmentation based on U-net architecture. First, the retina blood vessels were segmented using a U-Net Architecture with the encoder/decoder module of multiple convolutional neural networks. For segmentation, binary conversion techniques are used. For the classification, deep learning models were proposed, namely ResNet50, Inception V3, VGG-16, and modified CNN. The final results are measured on a standard benchmark DRIVE dataset that contains 2865 retinal blood vessel images. For image classification, the proposed modified CNN performed better for DRIVE datasets with an accuracy score of 98%. Precision of 98%, Recall is 94.5% and F1-score is 95%. This paper evaluates the perceptional quality of segmented retinal images using SSIM. In this study pixel intensity was measured using RMSE, and PSNR to assess the quality of the retinal vessel segmented image.

Keywords: Diabetic Retinopathy · Convolutional Neural Network · Segmentation · Blood vessel · Fundus images

1 Introduction

Analyzing retinal fundus images has become more important in diabetic retinopathy detection, obtaining essential information underlying the condition of eyes in diabetic patients and early diagnosis of specific illnesses such as cataracts and diabetic retinopathy [1]. The human eye is one of the most important and delicate parts of the human system. The fundus, which contains the retina, optic disc, macula, and fovea, is the area of the upper eyelid facing the lens. When in an eye test, it can be noticed by peering through the retina. The principal structural components apparent from color fundus imaging are the retinal blood vessels [2]. Color fundus imaging can reveal hemorrhages in the retina arteries, fundus hemorrhage, edema, and other disorders. Medical experts rely on

© The Author(s), under exclusive license to Springer Nature Switzerland AG 2023
I. Woungang et al. (Eds.): ANTIC 2022, CCIS 1798, pp. 609–625, 2023.
https://doi.org/10.1007/978-3-031-28183-9_43

these foundations to recognize and effectively treat disorders. They form the foundation on which eye doctors identify and treat disorders. Early detection, early diagnosis, and treatments of diabetic retinopathy illnesses all require precise segmented retinal blood vessel images. Manually segmentation is a time-consuming process, difficult, and needs advanced skills. When various specialists segment identical blood vessel images in medical practice, the outcomes are inconsistent, resulting in inaccuracies in vessel segmentation [3]. The retinal vascular segmentation technique can ease eye specialist diagnosis stress and efficiently handle the concerns of unskilled medical experts. As a result, automated retinal vascular segmentation is critical for the medical detection and treatment of ocular illnesses.

There are various difficulties in segmenting retinal blood vessels is exacerbated by the extremely complicated design of retinal blood vessels, poor contrast between both the retinal targeted artery and the foreground image, and noise contamination when obtaining retinal images. Though there are numerous obstacles to achieving correct retinal vascular segmentation, it is critical for early detection of DR and therapy [4].

The main contribution of the paper is given below.

- We use preprocessing methods such as image augmentation to increase the number of images and to enhance the number of training instances and data normalizing to denoising to accurately forecast classifications to create the best massive retinal datasets for training the proposed model.
- We proposed the U-net architecture for retinal blood vessel segmentation of detecting the DR at early
- Measuring the perceptual quality of segmented images to improve the accuracy of detecting DR at an early stage after vessel segmentation.
- We train the proposed CNN model (Resnet50, InceptionV3, and VGG16) to distinguish the minor variations among retinal images for diabetic retinopathy detection.

2   Related Work

By detecting and recognizing diabetic retinopathy using a segmentation strategy, several investigators have contributed to a considerable increase in detection and diagnosis approaches. The method for optical disc segmentation based on the histogram matching approach were suggested in [5]. In this approach, portions of the retinal fundus images were utilized to generate a framework, and then the mean of histograms for every colored element was determined to locate the optical disc's center. The association between several RGB elements of the source image and the framework is also calculated, and the location with the highest significance level is chosen as the optical disc center. The author in [6] suggested the model for automatic retinal Hard Exudates recognition using the fuzzy c-mean clustering approach and SVM classifier to classify the retinal images. The proposed model was trained using ophtha EX and tested on the DIARETDB1 dataset. The cross-validation were performed using 10 folds. In [7] author suggested the automatic Diabetic Retinopathy Diagnosis Method analyzed fundus images of a comparable level as angiograms to improve the visibility of abnormalities. The optical disc is segmented utilizing fast powerful features, and blood vessels are extracted utilizing morphological image processing methods. For automated optical disc recognition, the researchers in [8] used a clustering technique with a unique correction mechanism and vessel transformation. The suggested approach were used scale-space analysis to detect the optical disc's borders. In [9] suggested the hybrid approach for optical disc segmentation based on the vessel vector phase portrait analysis approach and used the modified clustering analysis for vessel transformation. In [10], another tree-based graph cut approach were suggested for retinal blood vessel and optic disc segmentation and achieve a better performance of the suggested model. The graph cut approach were suggested in [11-12] for extracting the retinal vascular tree and blood vessel information was used to recognize the location of the disc which is useful for training the neural network. In [13], several image processing methods were used for detecting the blood vessel and optical disc. The morphological operation and thresholding techniques were utilized for effective performance. In [14], suggested another model for blood vessel segmentation based on adaptive histogram and distance transformation. The adaptive histogram was used for preprocessing and distance transformation was used for segmentation. In [15], suggested the convolutional model with number of augmented retinal images and then preprocessed using normalization, transformation for blood vessel segmentation. In the work [16] presented the deep neural network model for segmentation of retinal blood vessel images and resolve the problem of cross modality. In [17], suggested the deep learning for classification of diabetic retinopathy based on inception-v3 architecture. Extract the retinal features using local binary pattern and classify the retinal images using convolutional neural network [18-27]. Another work on retinal images classification used TLBO [19] approach for binary and multiclass classification. In [20], suggested the hybrid approach of vessel segmentation and morphological operations for extraction of vessels. Several models were suggested based on hybrid approach [21-23]. After examination of some of previous studies, it was discovered that poor luminance and resolution of retinal dataset images make it impossible to examine it using image processing methods. As a result, image pre-processing approaches are critical for improving clarity and brightness for subsequent image analysis and interpretation such as Optical disc classification and segmentation, Optical disc elimination, and retinal blood vessel identification. As a result, the investigators of this study devised a method for optical disc, and retinal blood vessel segmentation to aid optometrists in the accurate identification of retinal illnesses utilizing retinal fundus image processing. In this paper, implemented and classify the grade of retinal images critically analysed segmentation methods and proposed a Mathematical Morphology based efficient extraction of blood vessels. This paper uses the U-Net architecture for retinal funds images segmentation and then use mathematical model to extract a feature based on Gaussian filters. Because extracting just relevant blood vessels, segmentation enables a more accurate examination of structural information of vessels, which is one of its main ad-vantages. Funds images obtained from the standard publicly available DRIVE database.

3   Material and Methods

Dataset: In this study used the publically available benchmark retinal DRVIE [23] datasets that contains2865 retinal blood vessel images which are extracted from the Kaggle website.

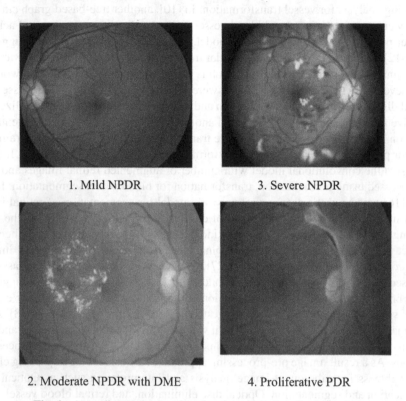

1. Mild NPDR   3. Severe NPDR

2. Moderate NPDR with DME   4. Proliferative PDR

Fig. 1. According to the severity of various diabetic retinopathy images

The Fig. 1 shows the labels are assigned according to the rank 0, 1, 2, 3, 4 of DR images for recognizing the diabetic retinopathy. Each labels have special meaning Mild NPDR, Moderate, Severse NPDR, and Proliferative PDR.

Figure 2 shows the classification of DR severity in dataset. it shows the percentage of various severity of various diabetic retinopathy images.

3.1   Preprocessing and Image Augmentation

The original dataset of retinal images could not provide the necessary resolution for a thorough study of retinal blood vessel segmentation because of noise is present in images. By overcoming the unclear edges of blood vessels in image, the retinal layers can be used augmenting approaches. The original retinal images have large noise and low SNR value. Figure 3 shows the schematic block diagram of proposed model with several steps. Some preprocesing step of proposed model.

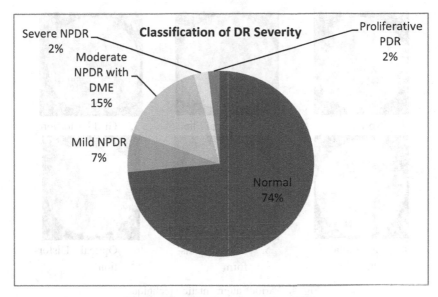

Fig. 2. Classification of severity of DR

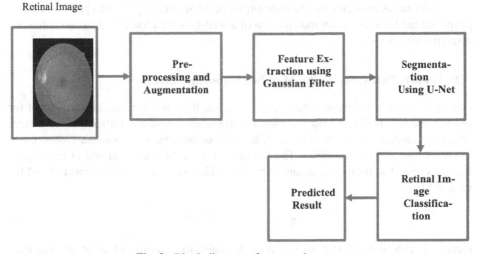

Fig. 3. Block diagram of proposed system

1. Removal of noise from retinal image.
2. Retinal image flattening for contour adjustment on morphological diversity of blood vessel image scanning.
3. Binary transformation to detect the lower and upper boundaries of vessels and extract the detected boundary of vessels.
4. Resize retinal images and provide input to the U-Net architecture.

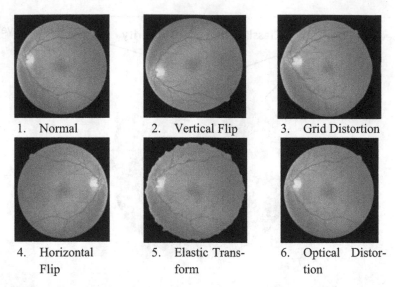

1. Normal 2. Vertical Flip 3. Grid Distortion

4. Horizontal 5. Elastic Trans- 6. Optical Distor-
Flip form tion

Fig. 4. Various augmentation techniques

Figure 4 shows the various augmentation techniques used for increasing the number of retinal images to overcome the over-fitting problem and improve the performance of proposed model. it assists in the creation of a well-balanced training data and enhanced effectiveness of model.

3.2 Feature Extraction Using Modified Gaussian Filter

Because retinal blood vessels have great contrast, the Gaussian functional concept for retinal imaging is derived on the uses a comprehensive of the retinal fundus image. Several examples of the vessel shape, as well as the adjusted Gaussian curves using the least square error condition. The features of the vessel segment and fit curve have been reversed for clarity. Equation 1 shows the Gaussian function that was utilized for matching.

$$g(x) = Ae^{-(x-z)^2/2w^2} \tag{1}$$

Here x is indeed the linear vector, A is the intensity, z is the place of the profiling peaks, and w is a Gaussian functional variable that determines the width. Fitted relative residual errors are smaller than 4 Gy - level on average. The formula for calculating error is $\{\sum |(m_i - v_i)|\}/n$. Here, m_i and v_i are the framework data and real data's profiles scores, accordingly, and n represents total pixels present in blood vessel image.

Equation 2 describes the revised Gaussian filter with values between 0 for vessel identification.

$$f(x) = \frac{1}{\sqrt{2\pi\sigma^5}}\left(x^2 - \sigma^2\right)e^{-x^2/2\sigma^2} \tag{2}$$

Here σ is a Gaussian filter functional variable that regulates the size of filter, such as the w. Equation 3 shows how to update the functions $f(x)$.

$$f(x) = \left(x^2 - \sigma^2\right)e^{-x^2/2\sigma^2} \tag{3}$$

If element is adjusted furthermore to reasonable levels, as illustrated in Eq. 4, the σ amplitude value of element is altered to 3.

$$f(x) = \frac{1}{\sqrt{2\pi\sigma^3}}\left(x^2 - \sigma^2\right)e^{-x^2/2\sigma^2} \tag{4}$$

It means that for a certain vessel, this filter might provide the best reaction. As a result, using a modified Gaussian filter, it is better to improve the vessel. When both the peak values such as Gaussian vessel and Gaussian filter are overlap, get the maximum convolution. Equation 5 depicts the maximum convergence peak.

$$h(t) = \int_{-\infty}^{+\infty} \frac{1}{\sqrt{2\pi\sigma^t}}\left(x^2 - \sigma^2\right)e^{-x^2/2(\omega^2+\sigma^2)/\omega^2\sigma^2)}dx \tag{5}$$

here, t is amplitude parameter of filter to assign the power of second order filter. 1 is assigned to vessel for evaluation. Equation 6 can be rearranged by substituting the exponentially ordering element by $1/S2$.

$$h(t) = \int_{-\infty}^{+\infty} \frac{1}{\sqrt{2\pi\sigma^t}}\left(\left(x^2 - s^2\right)e^{-x^2/2s^2} + (s^2 - \sigma^2)e^{-x^2/2s^2}\right)dx \tag{6}$$

The 2nd order generalized Gaussian functional value is first element in the integrant, as well as its integral value is equals zero. Used this association as a tool.

$$\int_{-\infty}^{+\infty} e^{-2}dx = \sqrt{\pi} \tag{7}$$

$$\frac{1}{\sqrt{2\pi\sigma^t}}\cdot\sqrt{2\pi}\left(s^2 - \sigma^2\right)s = \frac{\omega\sigma^{5-t}}{(\omega^2 - \sigma^2)^{1.5}} \tag{8}$$

The convolutional peak intensity of a blood vessel segmentation associated with factor and 2nd order Gaussian filter related with factor are given in Eq. 8. Equation 9 shows how when variable t varies, the value in the previous equation modifies as well.

$$h = \frac{\omega\sigma^{1.5}}{(\omega^2 - \sigma^2)^{1.5}} \tag{9}$$

It is simple to determine that convolutional peak value reaches its highest. Further situations' maximum value conditions can also be determined. The conditions are maximal when t is $5, 4, 3,$ and 2, for example. Consequently, when the modified Gaussian filters with parameters $t = 4$ and $t = 3$ have been employed, the related filters yield the highest convolutional peaks. Processing is performed with a proposed revised Gaussian filter.

3.3 Segmentation Using U-Net Architecture

Figure 5 shows the U-net architecture used for retinal blood vessel segmentation. It consists of encoder and decoder blocks with four convolutional layers (Channel). Each layer of encoder block mapped (Copy & Crop) with each layer decoder block. Initial value of channel is 64. The channel changes from 64- > 512, as convolutional process

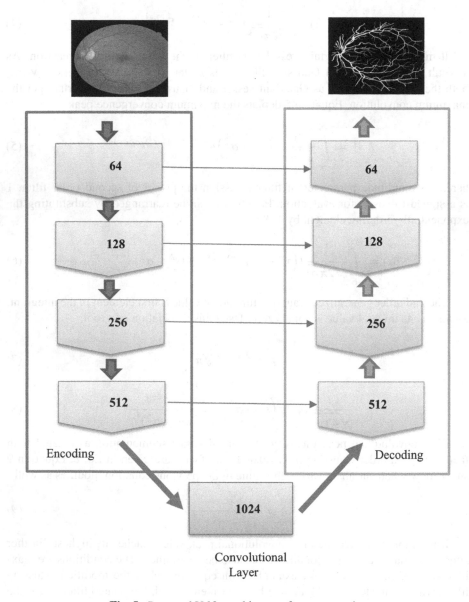

Fig. 5. Proposed U-Net architecture for segmentation

is increased step by step in downward direction. The arrow shows the max-pooling operation.

In decoding phase, convolutional process are decreased by step by step in upward direction called as up sampling approach that increases the size of retinal images. The arrow indicates the padding operation. The last layer of U-net architecture uses a filter for vessel segmentation.

After converting the all the retinal image to grayscale. For the linear motion used motion filter for approximation. The difference between the initial image and filtered image is calculated, yielding the final image. The final output image is obtained by taking the differences between the images bit by bit.

Let, P is the initial image, and M is the represents the motion filter , D is difference of final image and initial image $D = M - P$.

Image Adjustment: The retinal images were enhanced via image alterations. Numerous factors such as image levels of intensity, luminance, and contrast adjustment were modified. The modifications increased the image quality, which leads to greater feature extracted. Color casts were removed using image intensity levels. Simple brightness and contrast adjustments were rapidly change the quality of an image. Color balance were enables for colors changes to rectify white balance issues.

Binary Conversion: To transform the basic pre-processed image to binary sequence in that step. B binary image is a computer image in which each pixel has just two distinct values. A binary image is often made up of two color: black and white, however the certain color may be utilized. The image intensity determines whether the pixel is black or white, and a threshold is determined appropriately.

Condition Check: To determine the blood vessels, the conditions is examined. The criterion is that a pixel in the image normalized differential image should be white, while the identical pixel in the binary transformed image should be black. If a pixel meets both of these criteria, it is chosen and sent for subsequent analysis, which involves the morphology encoding procedure. The little portions under a predefined threshold are deleted after erosion is complete, and the other pixels were collected.

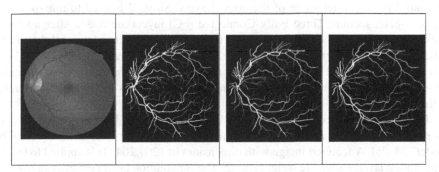

Fig. 6. Segmented blood vessel retinal image

Figure 6 depicts the retinal image final appearance following post-processing. Figure 6 (b) has less noise than Fig. 6 (a), the image taken before post-processing, and the vessels' widths are closer to the actual value.

3.4 Classification

ResNet50: Featured pictures are fed into the input layer of the ResNet50 architecture, which is subsequently fed into convolution block-1, which contains conv2d, batch normalisation, relu activation, and max pooling processes. These techniques are used to map and filter images in order to detect context similarity. ResNet50 is made up of 50 weighted layers, each of which is connected to the next block in the same way that block-1 is connected to the next block. It changes the dimensions of 32, 64, 128, 256, 512, 1024, and 2048 forms internally. To reduce overfitting in the model, two dense layers with dropout layers have been included. Relu activation, L2 kernal regularisation with penalty value 0.01, and dropout value 0.5 are all present in the dense layer. Finally, a sigmoid activation function is applied to the output layer. Hyper-parameters such as the Adam optimizer with a learning rate of 0.0001 and the binary cross-entropy loss function are used to compile the model. Model is tested on batch sizes of 32 and 40 epochs, but at epoch 10, the model becomes stagnant and overfits.

InceptionV3: The InceptionV3 architecture uses convolutions, average pooling, max pooling, concatenations, dropouts, and fully connected layers to feed featured images from the input layer to the model, which is built up of symmetric and asymmetric building blocks. The activation inputs are batch normalized, and batch normalization is employed extensively throughout the model. This structure is made up of 42 weighted layers in which blocks are connected in a sequential manner. Two dense layers with dropout layers are also added to this model to reduce overfitting. Relu activation, L2 kernal regularization with penalty value 0.01, and dropout value 0.5 are all present in the dense layer.

VGG-16: The VGG-16 design takes featured images in the input layer and feeds them to the cov1 layer, which is 264×264 pixels in size. The image is loaded into a convolutional layer stack, where filers are used to capture the smallest image in the left/right, up/down, and centre positions. The convolution stride is set to 1 pixel, and the spatial padding of convolution layer input is set to 1 pixel for 3×3 convolution layers in order to maintain spatial resolution after convolution. Five max-pooling layers do spatial pooling after some of the conv. Layers. Stride 2 is used to max-pool over a 2×2-pixel section. Three Fully-Connected (FC) layers are added after a stack of convolutional layers, the first two of which each have 4096 channels, and the third of which conducts 1000-way classification and so has 1000 channels. Two thick layers with dropout layers are also added to this model to reduce overfitting. Relu activation, L2 kernal regularization with penalty value 0.01, and dropout value 0.5 are all present in the dense layer.

Proposed CNN Architecture: Conv2D, MaxPooling2D, Relu activation, Dropout operations, and a fully linked layer are among the eight layers that make up the CNN model [24, 25]. A featured image with dimensions of (264,264, 3) is applied to the first convolution layer, with node weights of 32. The convolution layer performs striding and padding to ensure that the output image has the same dimensions as the input image. The pooling layer receives the output of the convolution layer, which is used to lower the size of the convolved feature map and hence the computational expenses. This is accomplished by reducing the connections between layers and operating independently on each feature map. The MaxPooling2D operation with pool size (2, 2) is utilized to pool the largest element from the feature map in this study. Following pooling, a dropout player is introduced to reduce overfitting, with a dropout value of (0.5), implying that 50% of neurons are dropped throughout the training phase. At the convolution layer, the Relu activation is used. The same procedure is used with the other 7 CNN layers, which have varied node weights of 64, 128, 256, 128, 64, 32, and 16. After flattening the vector, one dense layer with relu activation and node weight 16 is employed, and this layer is represented as a fully linked layer. The model is tested with batch sizes of 16 and 100 epochs, but it becomes stagnant and overfits around epoch 25.

4 Performance Metrics

Accuracy, sensitivity, and specificity are the performance evaluation parameters used to measure the effectiveness of different deep learning classifiers. Accuracy is defined as the proportion of overall accuracy of the models.

$$Acc. = \frac{(TN + TN)}{(TP + TN + FP + FN)} \tag{10}$$

$$Precision = \frac{TP}{(TP + FP)} \tag{11}$$

$$Recall = \frac{TP}{(TP + FN)} \tag{12}$$

$$F1 - Score = \frac{2TP}{(2TP + FP + FN)} \tag{13}$$

$$RMSE = \frac{1}{3MN} \sum \sum \sum_{1}^{3} (OutputImage - InputImage)^2 \tag{14}$$

$$PSNR = 10\log 10 \left[\frac{maxvalue^2}{\frac{1}{3MN} \sum \sum \sum_{1}^{3} (OutputImage - InputImage)^2} \right] \tag{15}$$

$$SSIM(x, y) = \frac{(2\mu_x\mu_y + c_1)(2\sigma_{xy} + c_2)}{\left(\mu_x^2 + \mu_y^2 + c_1\right)(\sigma_x^2 + \sigma_y^2 + c_2)} \tag{16}$$

where $\mu x, \mu y, \sigma x, \sigma y, and \sigma xy$ are the local means, standard deviations, and cross-covariance for the input image x, and output image y. SSIM values greater than 0.95 indicate the high perceptual quality in the objective evaluation.

5 Result Analysis

Table 1 and Fig. 8, 9, 10 shows the performance evaluation of proposed U-net architecture for retinal blood vessel segmentation. The total area of segmented image was calculated. In Table 2 measured the RSME, PSNR, and SSIM and total execution time. The SSIM shows the perceptional quality of segmented retinal image with the range 0 to 1. The 0.8781 is the maximum achieved values. In this study pixels intensity measured using RMSE, and PSNR to assess the quality of retinal vessel segmented image. The effectiveness of all the vessel segmented images in the Dataset is evaluated only for the 9 retinal segmented image.

Table 1. Classification results of various classifiers

Classification models	Accuracy	Precision	Recall	F-Score
ResNet50	75.5	56.7	75.4	64.6
InceptionV3	75.6	72.6	75.2	73.6
VGG16	64.4	69.4	64.5	66.8
Modified CNN	98	98.2	94.5	95

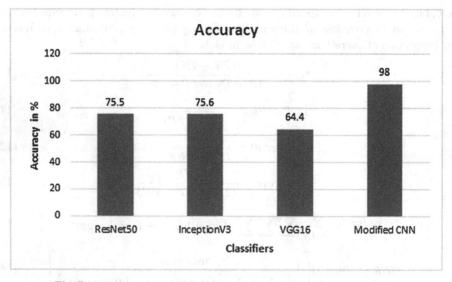

Fig. 7. Bar chart represent the Accuracy score of Deep learning models

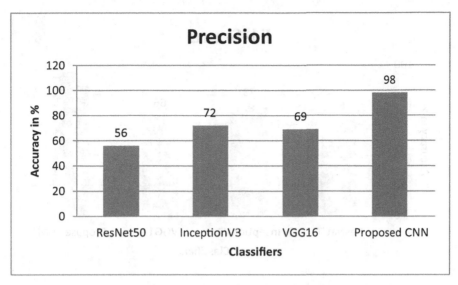

Fig. 8. Bar chart represent the Precision score of Deep learning models

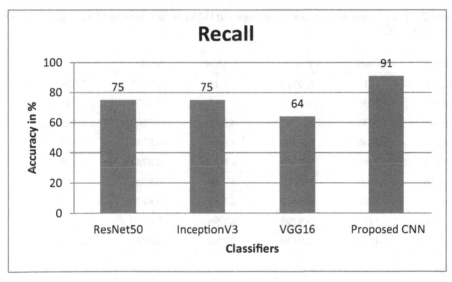

Fig. 9. Bar chart represent the Recall score of Deep learning models

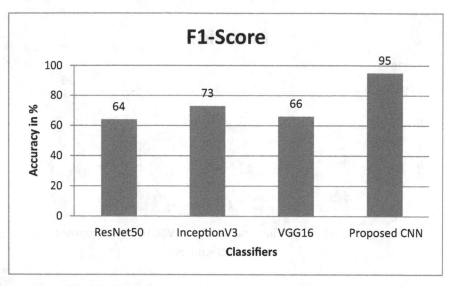

Fig. 10. Bar chart represent the F1-Score of Deep learning models

Table 2. The performance evaluation of proposed U-Net architecture for blood vessel segmentation on DRVIE

Image	Pixel	RMSE	PSNR	SSIM	Time (Sec)
Imag1	2013	0.9519	47.45	0.8707	2.678
Imag2	2030	0.9438	47.53	0.8739	2.045
Imag3	2034	0.9565	47.41	0.8689	2.125
Imag4	2040	0.9303	47.65	0.8781	2.745
Imag5	2060	0.9406	47.55	0.8744	3.065
Imag6	3020	0.9473	47.49	0.8721	2.023
Imag7	3294	0.9447	47.52	0.8736	2.853
Imag8	3945	0.9398	47.56	0.8750	3.256
Imag9	4528	0.9470	47.50	0.8725	3.145

6   Comparative Analysis

Table 3 indicate that the proposed strategy is more accurate in segmentation phases. This approach also shows that it can get a good performance whiteout the use of a training stage.

Table 3. Comparison results with related works for vessel segmentation

Methods	DRIVE			
	accuracy	Precision	Recall	F1-Score
Primitivo Díaz et. al. 2019 [29]	94.41	–	–	94.93
Ambaji S. Jadhav et. al. 2020 [28]	93.185	86.36	–	86.36
Muhammad Mateen et al., 2020 [27]	97	96	94	95
Proposed CNN	98	98	94.5	95

Table 4. Comparative analysis of perceptional quality of segmented image of proposed model with previous methods

Sr. No	Method	RMSE	PSNR
1	Adaptive median filter	10305	8.00
2	CLAHE	129	27.00
3	Mathematical Morphology [30]	0.96	48.53
4	Proposed CNN	0.95	50.01

Table 4 shows the Comparative analysis of perceptional quality of segmented image of proposed model with previous methods. It is observed that proposed model gives the smaller the value of RMSE for better the segmentation performance of retinal segmented image as compare to the previous methods. The proposed model gives the better values of PSNR.

7 Conclusion and Future Scope

This paper presents the segmentation techniques for blood vessel retinal images segmentation. The modified CNN approach is proposed based on the U-net architecture of deep learning by applying the binary conversion mechanism for segmentation. The experimental results were carried on all the images of DRIVE dataset obtained from Kaggle. It is found that proposed approach is effective for detecting the blood vessel used for early diagnosis of DR. For the major analysis part of this study is to measure the perceptional quality of segmented retinal image using SSIM. In this study pixels intensity measured using RMSE, and PSNR to assess the quality of retinal vessel segmented image. The final results are measured on standard benchmark DRIVE dataset that contains 2865 retinal blood vessel images. For image classification, proposed modified CNN performed better for DRIVE datasets with the accuracy score 98%. Precision of 98%, Recall is 94.5% and F1-score is 95%. The future work of this study is to compare the retinal blood vessel analysis for feature selection and extraction, and classification to recognise the optical disc, excluded, HEMs etc. for the other various standards benchmark datasets for early detection diabetic retinopathy.

References

1. Ashraf, M.N., Habib, Z., Hussain, M.: Texture feature analysis of digital fundus images for early detection of diabetic retinopathy. In: 2014 11th International Conference on Computer Graphics, Imaging and Visualization, pp. 57–62 (2014). https://doi.org/10.1109/CGiV.201 4.29
2. Kar, S.S., Maity, S.P.: Automatic detection of retinal lesions for screening of diabetic retinopathy. IEEE Trans. Biomed. Eng. **65**(3), 608–618 (2018)
3. Bai, C., Huang, L., Pan, X., Zheng, J., Chen, S.: Optimization of deep convolutional neural network for large scale image retrieval. Neurocomputing **303**(16), 60–67 (2018)
4. Kar, S.S., Maity, S.P.: Automatic detection of retinal lesions for screening of diabetic retinopathy. IEEE Trans. Biomed. Eng. **65**(3), 608–618 (2016)
5. Dehghani, A., Moghaddam, H., Moin, M.: Optic disc localization in retinal images using histogram matching. EURASIP J. Image Video Process. (1) (2012). https://doi.org/10.1186/1687-5281-2012-19
6. Wang, S., Yin, Y., Cao, G., Wei, B., Zheng, Y., Yang, G.: Hierarchical retinal blood vessel segmentation based on feature and ensemble learning. Neurocomputing **149**, 708–717 (2015)
7. Manjiri, P., Ramesh, M., Yogesh, R., Manoj, S., Neha, D.: Automated localization of optic disk, detection of microaneurysms and extraction of blood vessels to bypass angiography. In: Satapathy, S.C., Biswal, B.N., Udgata, S.K., Mandal, J.K. (eds.) Proceedings of the 3rd International Conference on Frontiers of Intelligent Computing: Theory and Applications (FICTA) 2014. AISC, vol. 327, pp. 579–587. Springer, Cham (2015). https://doi.org/10.1007/978-3-319-11933-5_65
8. Muangnak, N., Aimmanee, P., Makhanov, S., Uyyanonvara, B.: Vessel transforms for automatic optic disk detection in retinal images. IET Image Proc. **9**(9), 743–750 (2015). https://doi.org/10.1049/iet-ipr.2015.0030
9. Sreng, S., Maneerat, N., Hamamoto, K., Win, K.Y.: Deep learning for optic disc segmentation and glaucoma diagnosis on retinal images. Appl. Sci. **10**(14), 4916 (2020). https://doi.org/10.3390/app10144916
10. Muangnak, N., Aimmanee, P., Makhanov, S.: Automatic optic disk detection in retinal images using hybrid vessel phase portrait analysis. Med. Biol. Eng. Compu. **56**(4), 583–598 (2017). https://doi.org/10.1007/s11517-017-1705-z
11. Gonzalez, A.S., Kaba, D., Li, Y., Liu, X.: Segmentation of the blood vessels and optic disc in retinal images. IEEE J. Biomed. Health Inform. **18**(6), 1874–1886 (2014)
12. Jestin, V.K.: Extraction of blood vessels and optic disc segmentation for retinal disease classification. In: Recent Advances in Computer Science, pp. 440–444 (2015)
13. Phyo, O., Khaing, A.S.: Automatic detection of optical disc and blood vessels from retinal images using image processing techniques. Int. J. Res. Eng. Technol. **3**(3), 300–307 (2014)
14. Prakash, R.S., Aditya, R., Sameer, Y., Parameswari, S., Kumar, G.S.: Retinal blood vessel extraction and optical disc removal. Int. J. Res. Eng. Technol. **4**(04), 80–83 (2015)
15. Oliveira, A.F.M., Pereira, S.R.M., Silva, C.A.B.: Retinal vessel segmentation based on fully convolutional neural networks. Expert Syst. Appl. (2018). https://doi.org/10.1016/j.eswa.2018.06.034
16. Liskowski, P., Krawiec, K.: Segmenting retinal blood vessels with deep neural networks. IEEE Trans. Med. Imaging **35**(11), 2369–2380 (2016). https://doi.org/10.1109/TMI.2016.2546227
17. Fu, H., Xu, Y., Wong, D.W.K., Liu, J.: Retinal vessel segmentation via deep learning network and fully-connected conditional random ELDS. In: 2016 IEEE 13th International Symposium on Biomedical Imaging (ISBI), vol. 698, p. 701 (2016). https://doi.org/10.1109/ISBI.2016.7493362

18. de la Calleja, J., Tecuapetla, L., Auxilio Medina, M., Bárcenas, E., Urbina Nájera, A.B.: LBP and machine learning for diabetic retinopathy detection. In: Corchado, E., Lozano, J.A., Quintián, H., Yin, H. (eds.) IDEAL 2014. LNCS, vol. 8669, pp. 110–117. Springer, Cham (2014). https://doi.org/10.1007/978-3-319-10840-7_14

19. Sidibé, D., Sadek, I., Mériaudeau, F.: Discrimination of retinal images containing bright lesions using sparse coded features and SVM. Comput. Biol. Med. **62**, 175–184 (2015). https://doi.org/10.1016/j.compbiomed.2015.04.026

20. Li, Y.-H., Yeh, N.-N., Chen, S.-J., Chung, Y.-C.: Computer-assisted diagnosis for diabetic retinopathy based on fundus images using deep convolutional neural network. Mob. Inf. Syst. (2019)

21. Jiang, X., Mojon, D.: Adaptive local thresholding by verification-based multithreshold probing with application to vessel detection in retinal images. IEEE Trans. Pattern Anal. Mach. Intell. **25**(1), 131–137 (2003)

22. Lam, B., Yan, H.: A novel vessel segmentation algorithm for pathological retina images based on the divergence of vector fields. IEEE Trans. Med. Imaging **27**(2), 237-246 (2008)

23. Ghoshal, R., Saha, A., Das, S.: An improved vessel extraction scheme from retinal fundus images. Multimedia Tools Appl. **78**(18), 25221–25239 (2019). https://doi.org/10.1007/s11042-019-7719-9

24. Staal, J.J., Abramoff, M.D., Niemeijer, M., Viergever, M.A., Ginneken, B.V.: Ridge based vessel segmentation in color images of the retina. IEEE Trans. Med. Imaging **23**, 501–509 (2004)

25. Zhexin, J., Zhang, H., Wang, Y., Ko, S.-B.: Retinal blood vessel segmentation using fully convolutional network with transfer learning, CDATA. Comput. Med. Imaging Graph. (2018). https://doi.org/10.1016/j.compmedimag.2018.04.005

26. Gadekallu, T.R., Khare, N., Bhattacharya, S., Singh, S., Maddikunta, P.K., Srivastava, G.: Deep neural networks to predict diabetic retinopathy. J. Ambient Intell. Human. Comput. (2020).https://doi.org/10.1007/s12652-020-01963-7

27. Muhammad, M., Wen, J., Nasrullah, N., Sun, S., Hayat, S.: Exudate detection for diabetic retinopathy using pretrained convolutional neural networks. Complexity, **11** (2020). https://doi.org/10.1155/2020/5801870

28. Jadhav, A.S., Patil, P.B., Biradar, S.: Optimal feature selection-based diabetic retinopathy detection using improved rider optimization algorithm enabled with deep learning. Evol. Intel. **14**(4), 1431–1448 (2020). https://doi.org/10.1007/s12065-020-00400-0

29. Primitivo, D., et al.: A hybrid method for blood vessel segmentation in images. Biocybern. Biomed. Eng. **39**(3), 814–824 (2019). https://doi.org/10.1016/j.bbe.2019.06.009

30. Bhardwaj, C., Jain, S., Sood, M.: Automated optical disc segmentation and blood vessel extraction for fundus images using ophthalmic image processing. In: Luhach, A.K., Singh, D., Hsiung, P.-A., Hawari, K.B.G., Lingras, P., Singh, P.K. (eds.) ICAICR 2018. CCIS, vol. 955, pp. 182–194. Springer, Singapore (2019). https://doi.org/10.1007/978-981-13-3140-4_17

Heuristics for K-Independent Total Traveling Salesperson Problem

Sebanti Majumder and Alok Singh[(✉)]

School of Computer and Information Sciences, University of Hyderabad,
Hyderabad 500046, India
alokcs@uohyd.ernet.in

Abstract. This paper is concerned with K-independent total traveling salesperson problem (KITTSP) which is a variant of the famous traveling salesperson problem (TSP). KITTSP seeks K mutually independent Hamiltonian tours such that the total cost of these K tours is minimized. KITTSP is an $\mathcal{NP}$-hard problem since it is a generalisation of TSP. KITTSP is a recently introduced problem, and, so far no solution approach exists in the literature for this problem. We have proposed six constructive heuristics to solve KITTSP which are the first approaches for this problem. We have evaluated the performance of these heuristics on an extensive range of TSPLIB instances and presented a detailed comparative study of their performance.

Keywords: Combinatorial optimization · Traveling salesperson problem · K-independent total traveling salesperson problem · Heuristic

1 Introduction

In the domain of combinatorial optimization problems, traveling salesperson problem (TSP) stands out to be one among the most famous one with a variety of applications [3–5]. In TSP, for a given set of cities and edges connecting the cities, with their corresponding weights, the shortest Hamiltonian tour needs to be found. Since the problems in reality are more complicated than TSP, different variants of TSP have surfaced to model various real world applications. One such recent variant is K-independent total traveling salesperson problem (KITTSP) proposed by Iwasaki and Hasebe in [2]. In this paper, they have proposed another problem, called K-independent average TSP and solved it using Ant colony optimization. However, they have only proposed KITTSP, but no solution to this problem has been proposed. In KITTSP, the objective is to build K mutually independent Hamiltonian tours such that the total cost of these K tours is minimized. KITTSP can find its application in vehicle routing and job scheduling. In a transportation company's delivery plan, though a shortest tour is already available to them, there may arise a situation when there are obstructions in that tour. In this situation we have to use an alternative tour. Thus having K independent tours, provide a certain minimum level of fault tolerance.

I. Woungang et al. (Eds.): ANTIC 2022, CCIS 1798, pp. 626–635, 2023.
https://doi.org/10.1007/978-3-031-28183-9_44

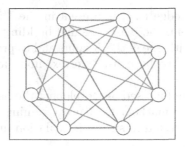

Fig. 1. An example of K-Independent tours (with $K = 3$) on a complete graph with 8 nodes.

An example of K independent tours has been shown in Fig. 1. Here we have taken a complete graph with $N = 8$ nodes and has designed $K = 3$ tours which are marked in three different colours.

TSP is an $\mathcal{NP}$-hard problem [1]. In TSP, the objective is to find a single Hamiltonian tour with minimum cost. On the other hand, in KITTSP, K independent Hamiltonian tours needs to be found such that the total cost of these tours is minimised. Clearly, TSP is a special case of KITTSP with $K = 1$. Hence, KITTSP is also an $\mathcal{NP}$-hard problem.

In the literature, no solution approach exists for KITTSP. As we have already mentioned, Iwasaki and Hasebe [2] only formulated the KITTSP without proposing any solution approach for it. This unexplored nature of KITTSP has motivate us to develop heuristic approaches to solve this problem. In this paper, we have presented six different constructive heuristics to solve KITTSP along with their comparative analysis.

The remainder of this paper is organized as follows: In Sect. 2, KITTSP has been formally defined. Section 3 describes the proposed heuristics in detail. Section 4 presents the computational results, and finally, in Sect. 5, we have concluded the paper listing our contributions and some directions for future work.

2 Problem Definition

Let us consider a complete undirected graph $G = \{V, E\}$, where $V = \{0, 1, ..., n-1\}$ is the set of vertices and E is the set of edges. Each edge $(i, j) \in E$ is associated with a weight w_{ij} which represents the cost or distance between the vertices i and j. The objective is to find K mutually independent Hamiltonian tours in G such that the total cost of these K tours is minimized. The tours must be built in such a way that no edge is common among these tours. The objective function of KITTSP can be expressed mathematically as follows:

$$\min \quad \sum_{i \in V} \sum_{j \in V} \sum_{k \in K} w_{ij} x_{ijk} \tag{1}$$

$$\text{s.t.} \quad x_{ijk} \in \{0, 1\}$$

x_{ijk} is equal to 1 if the edge (i,j) is present in the kth tour and is equal to 0 otherwise. In this problem, the reason behind building K tours is to substitute the present faulty tour with one of the K tours and to provide a certain minimum level of fault tolerance. We have used vertex, node and city interchangeably throughout the paper.

In this paper, we have focussed on developing the heuristics for KITTSP. So we are not providing any mathematical programming formulation of KITTSP here. Those who are interested in such a formulation may refer to [2].

3   Proposed Heuristics for KITTSP

Being formulated only in 2021 [2], KITTSP is a very recent problem. In [2], Iwasaki and Hasebe formulated two problems, namely KITTSP and K-Independent Average TSP, but solved only latter problem via an ant colony optimization approach. So no approach exists in the literature for KITTSP. Further, it has been observed that heuristic and metaheuristic approaches work well for $\mathcal{NP}$-hard combinatorial optimization problems. These facts have motivated us to develop six different problem specific heuristics which have been named as H1, H2, H3, H4, H5 and H6. The heuristics that we have developed make use of the concept of nearest neighbour.

Nearest neighbour heuristic is very famous for solving TSP based problems. It is a very simple approach. The tour is constructed by starting from a node and then iteratively selecting the nearest node from the set of unvisited nodes till a complete tour is formed. The six heuristics that we have developed for solving KITTSP can be considered as modifications of nearest neighbour heuristic for TSP. In all these heuristics, ties are broken arbitrarily. It is pertinent to mention that none of these heuristics is guaranteed to return K independent tours always. Depending on the value of K and the composition of the problem instance under consideration, some of these heuristics may not yield K independent tours. Further, a heuristic may return K independent tours in one run, but may not return K independent tours in another run depending on the random choices made regarding the starting cities. Our heuristics make multiple attempts to build K independent tours but if all attempts fail then an infeasible solution with less than K tours is returned. Subsequent subsections describe details of these six heuristics.

3.1   First Heuristic (H1)

This heuristic can be considered as a straightforward extension of nearest neighbour heuristic for TSP for solving KITTSP. In this heuristic, K independent tours are going to be generated one-by-one. For generating each of the K tours, the first node is to be selected at random. Each tour will then be built by selecting the nearest neighbour available. This heuristic uses greedy approach. To select the nearest neighbour the following constraints should be satisfied– The neighbour must not be visited before in that tour and the edge formed with the neighbour should not be present in any of the previously formed tours. While generating a tour if it is

Table 1. Results for $K = 3$ on small sized instances

Instance	Nodes	K=3											
		H1		H2		H3		H4		H5		H6	
		Avg	Time	Avg	Time	Avg	Time	Avg	Time	Avg	Time	Avg	Time
eil51	51	2298.6	0.0002	2887.2	0.0001	2355.9	0.001	2875.2	0.0016	2397.7	0.0016	2884	0.0025
berlin52	52	38696	0.0002	48743.9	0.0001	40542	0.0004	48460.2	0.0003	40593	0.0005	49184.1	0.0004
brazil58	58	130979.3	0.0002	170307.9	0.0001	137919	0.0005	178787.2	0.0001	139670.9	0.0008	176977.4	0.0004
st70	70	3810.1	0.0002	4765.5	0.0001	3977.5	0.0004	4976.4	0.0008	3940.5	0.0009	4839	0.0019
eil76	76	791.4	0.0007	3927.7	0.0004	3360.8	0.017	4008.3	0.0672	3304.1	0.0201	3994.2	0.0621
pr76	76	612601.3	0.0002	763528.9	0.0001	634220.6	0.0007	768732.1	0.0004	639889.4	0.0004	776515.5	0.0005
gr96	96	284557.7	0.0002	362862.9	0.0001	297845.4	0.0007	374067	0.0004	292871.1	0.0004	372515.6	0.0003
rat99	99	6708.3	0.0002	8526.9	0.0001	7028.2	0.0019	8698.9	0.0018	6996.1	0.0009	8618.8	0.0013
kroA100	100	116189.3	0.0002	154529.9	0.0001	120858.8	0.0004	155554	0.0002	121098.2	0.0006	154830.5	0.0005
kroB100	100	119925.3	0.0001	153743.1	0.0001	122399.9	0.0005	157525.5	0.0002	122970	0.0005	154767.6	0.0004
kroC100	100	114588.4	0.0002	151609.3	0.0001	117388.4	0.0004	155892.2	0.0003	117171.7	0.0007	151838.1	0.0003
kroD100	100	112451	0.0001	150838.6	0.0001	116412	0.0004	153289.3	0.0001	115580.5	0.0002	151984.9	0.0001
kroE100	100	119413.4	0.0001	156789.5	0.0001	121952.9	0.0004	156668.1	0.0004	124172.5	0.0002	157670.8	0.0003
rd100.	100	42633.4	0.0003	55603.6	0.0001	43896.7	0.0009	55247	0.0003	44438.6	0.0006	55326.2	0.0002
eil101	101	3630	0.0004	4294.9	0.0018	3733.2	0.2212	4503.1	39.9772	3778.7	0.1576	4500.4	24.9702
lin105	105	82029.5	0.0001	115600.1	0.0001	84396	0.0003	116093.1	0.0003	84751.6	0.0006	114308.1	0.0002
pr107	107	238615.6	0.0001	358784.7	0.0001	256282.8	0.0002	360163.2	0.0003	246661.5	0.0002	355567.4	0.0004
gr120	120	36374.7	0.0002	45764.8	0.0001	37237.4	0.0004	45847.8	0.0004	37749.6	0.0004	47350.3	0.0006
pr124	124	346104.8	0.0001	498674.5	0.0001	375149.2	0.001	505355.3	0.0003	384648.3	0.0008	503134.9	0.0004
bier127	127	604669.8	0.0007	777183.1	0.0002	622827.1	0.0007	783043.6	0.0003	628254.7	0.0006	795182.2	0.0004
ch130	130	33898	0.0002	43726.1	0.0002	35635.1	0.0008	44080.9	0.0007	35525.2	0.0009	43171	0.0006
pr136	136	479274.9	0.0001	632061.9	0.0001	493667.1	0.0002	641630.7	0.0006	497698.2	0.0005	636995.4	0.0005
gr137	137	401263.2	0.0002	513451.9	0.0002	411044	0.0003	521201.3	0.0003	415272.2	0.0006	527565.1	0.0002
pr144	144	387472.5	0.0002	537714	0.0002	399332.4	0.0003	536673.3	0.0003	393289.9	0.0008	542860	0.0005
ch150	150	34537	0.0002	45611.1	0.0002	36073.1	0.0004	46069	0.0003	35424.9	0.0007	46891	0.0005
kroA150	150	139881.9	0.0002	189246.3	0.0003	149564.8	0.0004	187599.9	0.0004	147456.8	0.0006	191455.1	0.0004
kroB150	150	138091	0.0002	185182.8	0.0003	145375.3	0.0003	184599.9	0.0005	144878.2	0.0005	185601.7	0.0002

not possible to add any more edges (due to all candidate edges being present in already built tours), then this heuristic starts over that particular tour again with a new depot selected at random. But if there is no new depot left, then it terminates and an infeasible solution with less than K tours is returned. Otherwise, a feasible solution with K independent tours is returned.

3.2 Second Heuristic (H2)

In this heuristic also, K tours are generated one-by-one. To generate each of the K tours, the first node is to be selected at random. To build each node, we need to select the nearest neighbour out of p nearest neighbours at random. This heuristic exploits the features of GRASP (greedy randomized adaptive search procedure) approach [6]. While selecting the nearest neighbour, it should be checked that the neighbour is not visited before in that tour and also the edge formed with the neighbour is not present in any of the previously formed tours. Clearly, with these conditions, sometimes less than p neighbors are available for selection. The termination condition for this heuristic is same as H1.

3.3 Third Heuristic (H3)

In this heuristic, K tours are generated in parallel. This heuristic implements a greedy approach. At first random nodes are selected for all of the K tours. The next node is then selected for each of the K tours one-by-one in the order

Table 2. Results for $K = 3$ on medium sized instances

Instance	Nodes	$K = 3$											
		H1		H2		H3		H4		H5		H6	
		Avg	Time	Avg	Time	Avg	Time	Avg	Time	Avg	Time	Avg	Time
pr152	152	**375977.3**	0.0002	581124.8	0.0002	385759.6	0.0018	582747.2	0.0002	386066.1	0.0004	580220.4	0.0003
u159	159	**257383.1**	0.0003	345196.3	0.0002	264454.2	0.0008	339851.8	0.0004	267117.6	0.0007	345561.5	0.0008
rat195	195	**12799.9**	0.0003	16311.1	0.0006	13427.2	0.0027	16565.3	0.0066	13282.3	0.0029	16576.4	0.0059
d198	198	**102636.7**	0.0002	125829.4	0.0004	101893.7	0.0033	130040.4	0.0011	102294.1	0.004	129242.3	0.0017
kroA200	200	**160292.2**	0.0003	214466.7	0.0004	169309.2	0.0005	214840.2	0.0003	166883.3	0.0007	215994.2	0.0005
kroB200	200	**157616.2**	0.0004	208996.4	0.0004	163700.1	0.0003	212655.4	0.0003	165458.8	0.0004	211943.9	0.0004
gr202	202	**205885.8**	0.0002	253741	0.0003	209497.1	0.0008	258554.5	0.0005	209758.5	0.0015	261139	0.0006
tsp225	225	**22674.4**	0.0003	28789.6	0.0005	23119.4	0.004	29439.3	0.0052	23522	0.0034	29564.2	0.0026
pr226	226	**600907.6**	0.0005	760442.6	0.0006	593366.5	0.0009	770920.8	0.0006	607024.5	0.0015	774302.5	0.0005
gr229	229	**681723.3**	0.0002	893194.7	0.0004	704728.9	0.0015	915228.1	0.0005	705105.5	0.0011	912696.9	0.0006
gil262	262	**14468.6**	0.0005	18541.2	0.0018	14644.6	0.0804	19023.8	0.9988	14635.4	0.1759	18994.7	1.0602
pr264	264	**463285.8**	0.0009	591539.5	0.0008	464294.3	0.0265	585773.7	0.01	460395.9	0.0185	604285.4	0.0103
pr299	299	**282682.4**	0.0006	374829.4	0.0005	290663.8	0.0013	381084.3	0.001	287426.6	0.001	382026	0.0014
lin318	318	**231251.9**	0.0004	313673.9	0.0005	240437.8	0.0011	316268.7	0.0011	240670.5	0.0012	318991.7	0.0009
rd400	400	**79271.2**	0.001	106468.1	0.0007	82577.9	0.0014	106995.8	0.0019	83417.8	0.003	109089.5	0.0029

Table 3. Results for $K = 3$ on large sized instances

Instance	Nodes	$K = 3$											
		H1		H2		H3		H4		H5		H6	
		Avg	Time	Avg	Time	Avg	Time	Avg	Time	Avg	Time	Avg	Time
fl417	417	**140292.1**	0.0139	147985.3	0.0093	–	–	–	–	–	–	–	–
gr431	431	**866281.7**	0.0006	1134181.3	0.0007	887369.3	0.0024	1148836.2	0.0012	884888.8	0.0026	1153040.9	0.0013
pr439	439	**628386.8**	0.0006	849501.2	0.0007	638717.3	0.0024	851855.3	0.0017	636542.1	0.0029	849994.1	0.0011
pcb442	442	**408472.2**	0.0082	483570.7	0.0088	420633.8	18.47	488084.8	45.6342	419186.1	29.7924	486532.8	67.5748
d493	493	**181981.5**	0.0013	232959.3	0.001	186012	0.001	235154.8	0.0025	187011.3	0.002	235083.4	0.0022
att532	532	**147799.1**	0.0009	195181.3	0.0011	152111.9	0.0035	198786.5	0.002	150526.4	0.003	198009.2	0.0022
u574	574	**209815.9**	0.0011	271726.1	0.0013	214498.8	0.0037	274672.4	0.0021	214349.9	0.0053	275370.8	0.0041
rat575	575	**37615.3**	0.0019	47007.6	0.0033	38777.1	0.2557	48602.6	0.8837	39063.7	0.2756	48301.1	1.1844
d657	657	**260559.6**	0.0013	342880.2	0.0016	269000.2	0.0037	340734.8	0.003	269571.2	0.0031	343853.4	0.0033
gr666	666	**1462073**	0.0013	1899826.9	0.0015	1488718.9	0.0026	1904805.8	0.002	1502019.4	0.0029	1929109.7	0.002
u724	724	**234350.6**	0.0018	305166.8	0.0019	238519.8	0.0102	313224.6	0.0061	241063.7	0.0125	314768.5	0.0067
rat783	783	**49911.6**	0.0032	64541.7	0.0092	51637	1.5866	65005.6	13.5277	52116.7	1.833	65074.2	19.8473
nrw1379	1379	**284607**	0.0062	367716	0.0059	290116.9	0.019	374000.3	0.0345	292320.7	0.0416	373471.1	0.0441
fl1577	1577	**250576.167(6)**	0.1234	327320	0.0235	254564.3	47.7413	334757.1	11.5846	259383.9	60.4724	329714.8	13.5053
d1655	1655	**453335.7**	0.0125	559813.8	0.01	463321.1	0.5626	564546	0.281	464435.1	0.8818	563532.7	0.1998
vm1748	1748	**1949507.6**	0.0096	2660536	0.009	2018381.3	0.0282	2684565.7	0.0263	2022707.2	0.019	2702154.7	0.0216
u1817	1817	**484902.4**	0.018	588580	0.0328	491172.2	28.2392	–	–	489435.3	11.9627	594676.7	66.7063
rl1889	1889	**1979237.6**	0.0118	2754359.6	0.0103	2040947.5	0.0582	2781041.4	0.0122	2029151.9	0.0243	2760865.9	0.0183

$k = 1, 2, ...K$ and this process is repeated till complete tours are built. The next node should be the nearest neighbour and should not be visited before in the tour currently being considered. Also the edges generated with the neighbours should not be present in any of the K partially formed tours. The reason for building tours in parallel is to provide all the tours more-or-less equal opportunity to utilize the best edges. When we constructs the tours one-by-one, initial tours have more opportunity to utilize the best edges in comparison to tours that are constructed latter. As in this heuristic K independent tours are formed in parallel and therefore, if in any of the K tours, if it is not possible to add any further edges (because all candidate edges are already present in other partial tours), then the tour building process will restart from scratch and all of the K paths will be built again. This heuristic terminates either when it has find a feasible solution or it has executed for 70 s without any success. Due to these

Table 4. Results for $K = 6$ on small sized instances

Instance	Nodes	$K = 6$											
		H1		H2		H3		H4		H5		H6	
		Avg	Time	Avg	Time	Avg	Time	avg	Time	Avg	Time	Avg	Time
eil51	51	5849.1	0.0002	6610	0.0004	6187.6	3.0459	6789	8.1577	6264.9	4.0053	6818	5.5035
berlin52	52	103054.4	0.0001	114857.6	0.0001	106345.7	0.0304	116655.2	0.0042	106790.4	0.0272	115882.2	0.0067
brazil58	58	349145.4	0.0002	416335.1	0.0002	–	–	424561.2	0.0173	–	–	428482	0.0426
st70	70	9951.4	0.0002	11229	0.0002	10293.4	0.1204	11678.2	0.1985	10382.4	0.287	11667.5	0.124
eil76	76	–	–	9008.625(8)	0.0013	–	–	–	–	–	–	–	–
pr76	76	1573569.9	0.0001	1757125.4	0.0002	1635159.6	0.0113	1800623.4	0.0012	1628726	0.0125	1809755	0.0013
gr96	96	754419.4	0.0001	858699.3	0.0002	782253.1	0.0025	896008.9	0.0015	772451.4	0.0054	888963.3	0.0009
rat99	99	17251.8	0.0002	19793.6	0.0004	18346.2	0.1108	20666.2	0.1607	17946.4	0.3284	20564	0.0723
kroA100	100	313058.1	0.0001	367996.1	0.0002	327718.4	0.0047	374223.9	0.0007	330215	0.0049	377752.7	0.0016
kroB100	100	312700.4	0.0001	361799.1	0.0002	324728.8	0.0018	369862.6	0.0006	329842.6	0.0067	375101.8	0.0012
kroC100	100	319771.3	0.0001	358121.3	0.0002	324070.2	0.0061	377053.6	0.001	322517.8	0.0079	370944.2	0.0017
kroD100	100	316951.1	0.0001	366491.5	0.0001	327257.1	0.0171	377600.7	0.0009	330300.6	0.0222	374190.9	0.0019
kroE100	100	315418.8	0.0001	366962.7	0.0003	322322.6	0.0041	374710.6	0.0007	322113.1	0.0026	375207.1	0.001
rd100	100	110946.1	0.0001	126470.3	0.0002	116746.1	0.0044	131956.2	0.0015	115377.7	0.0063	132094.2	0.0013
lin105	105	238382.5	0.0002	268230.2	0.0003	251273.5	0.0193	281848.1	0.0021	245060.2	0.0369	277245.2	0.0032
pr107	107	677123.4	0.0001	824894.9	0.0002	713526.3	0.0211	882284.3	0.0024	721557.4	0.0163	873164.6	0.002
gr120	120	93747.6	0.0002	107586.9	0.0002	96451.2	0.0141	110753.3	0.0034	95019.1	0.0247	110507.7	0.0029
pr124	124	964964.4	0.0001	1185013.7	0.0002	1009934.1	0.0076	1214822.4	0.0008	1003358.9	0.0084	1200005	0.0014
bier127	127	1586155.3	0.0003	1793275.9	0.0004	1642754.2	0.0292	1836703.9	0.0066	1654352.2	0.0455	1852380	0.0031
ch130	130	89566.5	0.0002	103213.2	0.0003	93596	0.0223	106111.9	0.004	93697.3	0.013	106738.2	0.0019
pr136	136	1261762.9	0.0002	1466240.7	0.0003	1295271.3	0.0041	1510266.4	0.0019	1300799.3	0.0064	1521795.3	0.0023
gr137	137	1057986	0.0004	1197390.2	0.0003	1076542.1	0.0255	1234429.8	0.0014	1080893.6	0.0225	1210608.2	0.0015
pr144	144	1142857.2	0.0003	1328879.5	0.0002	1158785.9	0.023	1354607.5	0.0009	1166405.9	0.0267	1366517	0.002
ch150	150	91608.2	0.0003	105461.3	0.0005	94371.5	0.0058	109407.8	0.0009	95049.4	0.0165	109791.9	0.003
kroA150	150	384552.1	0.0003	444346.4	0.0004	407712	0.0074	462058.1	0.0005	399255.9	0.0167	463901.3	0.0015
kroB150	150	370112.3	0.0002	426540.6	0.0003	377587.4	0.0046	443723.4	0.0011	378917.6	0.0037	438940.2	0.001
kroB150	150	138091	0.0002	185182.8	0.0003	145375.3	0.0003	184599.9	0.0005	144878.2	0.0005	185601.7	0.0002

restarts, the running time of this heuristic can vary a lot and can be considerably higher in comparison to H1 and H2. Further, its an all or nothing approach, i.e., either it returns a feasible solution with K tours or a null solution without any tour. Next three heuristics, viz. H4, H5 and H6 also have the same termination criteria, and hence, their execution times also vary a lot like H3

3.4   Fourth Heuristic (H4)

In this heuristic, K tours are generated in parallel like H3, but using a GRASP approach like H2. At first random nodes are selected for all of the K tours. The next node is then selected for all the K tours one-by-one in the order $k = 1, 2, ..., K$ and this process is repeated till complete tours are formed. The next node is selected at random from p nearest neighbours of the current node. While selecting the next node it is checked that the neighbour is not already visited in the kth tour. It should also be checked that the edges generated with the neighbours are not already present in any of the K partially formed tours.

3.5   Fifth Heuristic (H5)

This heuristic is similar to H3 except for the fact that tours are considered in random order rather than in their natural order for adding the nodes. Such an strategy provides most fair treatment to all the tours as far as their opportunities to utilize the best edges are concerned.

3.6   Sixth Heuristic (H6)

This heuristic is similar to H4 except for the fact that tours are considered in random order rather than in their natural order for addition of nodes.

4   Computational Results

The implementation of our heuristic approaches to solve KITTSP has been done in C. These six heuristics have been executed on Intel Core i5 processor with 8GB RAM running under Ubuntu 16.04 at 3.40 GHz. We have evaluated the performance of these heuristics on instances of different sizes ranging from small, to medium, to large sized instances. All the instances are standard TSPLIB instances. All the heuristics have been executed 10 independent times on each instance. Results are reported in terms of average solution quality and average

Table 5. Results for $K = 6$ on medium sized instances

Instance	Nodes	$K = 6$											
		H1		H2		H3		H4		H5		H6	
		Avg	Time	Avg	Time	Avg	Time	Avg	Time	Avg	Time	Avg	Time
pr152	152	1200294.1	0.0005	1471325.1	0.0004	1223288.1	0.0218	1511563.3	0.0013	1241246.5	0.0227	1514479.8	0.0026
u159	159	695389	0.0003	814813.9	0.0004	724330.5	0.0273	824609.7	0.0069	727437	0.0616	838096.5	0.0074
rat195	195	32227.4	0.0005	37307.7	0.0012	34503.5	0.6812	39046.7	2.4634	33976.7	1.0854	39160.6	1.7344
d198	198	260747.6	0.0006	298355.9	0.0009	269250.6	0.4977	302555.5	0.0722	263319.9	1.1686	304208.3	0.0652
kroA200	200	430517.5	0.0004	499694.6	0.0005	447419.6	0.0116	518324.9	0.001	445517.3	0.0103	512615.3	0.0018
kroB200	200	415554.3	0.0003	486075.8	0.0004	425965.3	0.0057	508241.9	0.0006	425651.3	0.006	500513.5	0.0017
gr202	202	503419	0.0006	580960.9	0.001	526085.2	0.3542	596615.9	0.0157	525348.4	0.3851	594742.7	0.0098
tsp225	225	57004.4	0.0006	67484	0.0008	60171.3	0.5946	70359.4	0.1672	59645.1	0.8822	70232	0.1864
pr226	226	1456420.3	0.0004	1782558.2	0.0007	1481832	0.0109	1828709.9	0.0016	1492958.6	0.032	1828444.3	0.0024
gr229	229	1831958.8	0.0006	2081351	0.0006	1931306.2	0.182	2147430.4	0.0038	1909189.1	0.1899	2141005.4	0.0087
gil262	262	37375.6	0.0013	43708.6	0.0053	–		–		–		–	
pr264	264	979137.7	0.0011	1215987.7	0.0011	968016.3	0.9818	1205283.2	0.1395	964237.6	1.0184	1209516.5	0.2314
pr299	299	734485.2	0.0004	866845	0.0007	762505.8	0.0225	899000.4	0.0025	763642.8	0.0183	905015.9	0.0044
lin318	318	640605.8	0.0006	745983.7	0.0008	657031.1	0.0496	759738.9	0.0042	656362.9	0.0399	764123.1	0.0054
rd400	400	209155	0.0007	249153	0.0011	218712.3	0.0421	255445.5	0.0127	217697.9	0.0533	256036.3	0.0174

Table 6. Results for $K= 6$ on large sized instances

Instance	Nodes	$K = 6$											
		H1		H2		H3		H4		H5		H6	
		Avg	Time	Avg	Time	Avg	Time	Avg	Time	Avg	Time	Avg	Time
fl417	417	–	–	344350.25(8)	0.0351	–		–		–		–	
gr431	431	2262781	0.001	2613661.4	0.0013	2369317.8	0.1918	2669554.5	0.0102	2360492.7	0.4055	2683262.1	0.0191
pr439	439	1699074.9	0.0011	1988557.4	0.0012	1778925.8	0.4902	2053043.2	0.0212	1765609.6	0.727	2039218.2	0.0176
pcb442	442	990273.667(3)	0.0182	1107396.33(3)	0.0404	–		–		–		–	
d493	493	462773.1	0.001	534937	0.0014	480243.2	0.0113	548886.7	0.0091	482039.2	0.0086	550001.9	0.0089
att532	532	383199.1	0.0011	448082.8	0.0016	396331.9	0.0299	462185	0.0154	393032.8	0.0622	458681.7	0.0137
u574	574	544654.8	0.0015	626253.5	0.0018	564575.6	0.23	644626.8	0.0155	558867.4	0.4032	643874.4	0.0153
rat575	575	93954.1	0.0038	109233.5	0.0111	–		–		–		–	
d657	657	674849.6	0.0015	788556.3	0.0022	697306.8	0.0342	806821.3	0.0125	695744.2	0.0339	806969.4	0.0089
gr666	666	3748578	0.0015	4372212.2	0.0022	3849067	0.0109	4457296.3	0.0049	3855260.2	0.0291	4462271.4	0.0092
u724	724	592795	0.0019	701107.6	0.0028	615013.8	0.0638	720088.4	0.0336	614286.5	0.0689	723395.9	0.0339
rat783	783	127307.8	0.0085	147007.2	0.0333	–		–		–		–	
nrw1379	1379	713936.3	0.0055	841073.6	0.0083	744403.7	1.4106	865998.8	0.3776	742640.8	1.1392	865546.1	0.7278
fl1577	1577	639665.75(8)	0.1058	758186.2	0.0516	–		–		–		–	
d1655	1655	1113553.4	0.014	1282000.1	0.0155	–		1297562.1	57.8335	–		1297315.9	34.1999
vm1748	1748	5064539.6	0.0078	6127367.8	0.011	5197507.6	0.1143	6229118.4	0.036	5231302.3	0.1161	6277334.3	0.0527
u1817	1817	1168643.6	0.022	1351842.7	0.1164	–		–		–		–	
rl1889	1889	5436735.1	0.0106	6524090.7	0.0125	5605520.9	1.4554	6632282.9	0.0476	5626927.1	1.3315	6666666.2	0.0487

Table 7. Results for $K = 9$ on small sized instances

Instance	Nodes	H1 Avg	Time	H2 Avg	Time	H3 Avg	Time	H4 Avg	Time	H5 Avg	Time	H6 Avg	Time
eil51	51	–	–	11169(4)	0.0006	–	–	–	–	–	–	–	–
berlin52	52	177859 (8)	0.0004	194643.3	0.0005	–	–	–	–	–	–	–	–
brazil58	58	655756.333 (9)	0.0004	722710.2	0.0004	–	–	752229.4	41.4204	–	–	752416.3	63.2121
st70	70	17755	0.0003	19292.2	0.0006	–	–	–	–	–	–	–	–
pr76	76	2757656.8	0.0003	2957319.3	0.0003	2854524.6	19.3116	3052889.8	0.0911	2865626.6	44.7031	3054252.2	0.1137
gr96	96	1336619.5	0.0002	1470384.7	0.0003	1402486.6	0.2509	1545703.3	0.0065	1404892.1	0.6914	1541440.8	0.0139
rat99	99	30791.3	0.0005	33583.3	0.001	–	–	–	–	–	–	–	–
kroA100	100	565054.5	0.0002	637171.6	0.0005	593766.6	0.2716	653618.7	0.0146	582075.9	0.3059	661546.1	0.0068
kroB100	100	563236.8	0.0002	617885.7	0.0003	592986.7	0.3275	653192	0.0077	585850.6	0.2761	648391.1	0.0097
kroC100	100	563655	0.0002	621007.3	0.0005	589420.6	0.2868	645603.4	0.0092	585017.2	0.165	641008.6	0.0035
kroD100	100	588077.1	0.0003	641431.5	0.0004	613414.9	4.2436	661622.4	0.03	613011.6	3.1268	663830.5	0.0345
kroE100	100	579661.2	0.0004	627784.9	0.0005	592294.9	0.2345	657836.3	0.0125	591816	0.7867	655494.7	0.0084
rd100	100	198254.4	0.0002	217513.1	0.0003	207012.9	0.2798	227469	0.0133	206732.1	0.5951	227902.9	0.0165
lin105	105	431617.7	0.0006	467559.5	0.0004	450579.2	13.5174	483472.5	0.161	449603.9	26.6	482942.9	0.2111
pr107	107	1315117.3	0.0003	1505039.8	0.0005	1376105.6	14.3426	1587950.8	0.0511	1365247.8	14.8772	1583985.6	0.2018
gr120	120	166199.6	0.0004	183092.2	0.0005	171995.1	2.2548	187825.3	0.1032	170472.9	5.5024	187903	0.1868
pr124	124	1861421.7	0.0003	2103341.8	0.0005	1915090.3	0.7516	2181208.5	0.0329	1920821.4	1.3438	2183996.7	0.0146
bier127	127	2819777.6	0.0007	3026077.5	0.0009	2890580.1	38.6157	3123395.8	0.5594	2912657.1	60.0069	3107291	0.8997
ch130	130	160811.6	0.0005	176249.6	0.0005	166007.9	2.2575	182164.1	0.1173	167627.3	3.4378	181727.6	0.1869
pr136	136	2277177	0.0004	2543554.8	0.0005	2357306.7	0.5314	2644436.2	0.0418	2339881.4	0.9182	2623117.6	0.0358
gr137	137	1838982.4	0.0006	2036012.6	0.0005	1916891.3	1.0395	2124695	0.0271	1913528.7	1.6167	2114789.9	0.0428
pr144	144	2142063.4	0.0003	2357076.7	0.0006	2173499.7	0.5616	2449083.5	0.0156	2154661.6	1.8793	2446594.9	0.0152
ch150	150	164150.1	0.0003	179760	0.0009	170312.6	0.6303	187997.3	0.0413	170420.4	1.0506	189177.3	0.0399
kroA150	150	698263.7	0.0004	769724.7	0.0007	724335	0.3472	802993.8	0.0142	720605.2	0.3837	796237.1	0.0048
kroB150	150	661051.9	0.0006	733953.2	0.0005	687131.8	0.1885	755565.8	0.0027	688327.1	0.1517	764913.2	0.0084

Table 8. Results for $K = 9$ on medium sized instances

Instance	Nodes	H1 Avg	Time	H2 Avg	Time	H3 Avg	Time	H4 Avg	Time	H5 Avg	Time	H6 Avg	Time
pr152	152	2402375.7	0.0005	2690192.1	0.0005	2482085.7	5.8734	2782234	0.0215	2473818	8.3333	2808923.5	0.0297
u159	159	1279003.3	0.0005	1418600.6	0.0007	1318779.6	11.8065	1455455.3	0.3978	1316061.5	9.6965	1470926.7	1.1782
rat195	195	57489.5	0.0014	63665	0.0026	–	–	–	–	–	–	–	–
d198	198	439362	0.0015	490547.2	0.0015	–	–	512166.4	6.1809	–	–	510666	10.8059
kroA200	200	776186	0.0005	856579.7	0.0009	804731.2	0.4314	887525.6	0.0046	807347.1	0.4765	894168.4	0.013
kroB200	200	739546.9	0.0007	838959.4	0.0006	777197.9	0.0972	883913.2	0.0039	781457.4	0.095	877707.7	0.0159
gr202	202	879209.8	0.0014	968775.4	0.0011	–	–	1000257.5	2.7726	–	–	1001783.6	4.4471
tsp225	225	102427.6	0.0017	116234.8	0.002	–	–	–	–	–	–	–	–
pr226	226	2870326.7	0.001	3216630.5	0.0012	2942511.1	15.8321	3333909.6	0.1718	2965611.8	47.6625	3280772.3	0.1278
gr229	229	3210004.6	0.0012	3523618.3	0.0009	–	–	3651647.5	0.39	–	–	3640641.6	0.7381
gil262	262	66610.1	0.0028	74589.9	0.0082	–	–	–	–	–	–	–	–
pr264	264	1562163.4	0.0008	1919041.3	0.0016	1554444.3	42.8976	1923416.5	4.0489	1538275.3	31.9304	1909074.4	4.0686
pr299	299	1318435.3	0.0008	1477824.6	0.001	1361994.2	0.2958	1535679.8	0.0281	1367204.6	0.5687	1545331.4	0.0139
lin318	318	1154392.4	0.0008	1268921.6	0.0012	1190495.6	1.3342	1308655.7	0.0389	1192875.7	2.5944	1302338.9	0.0385
rd400	400	376463.3	0.0012	424552.6	0.0018	393814.6	1.0381	438624.8	0.2423	393264.6	2.7334	439612.9	0.2554

execution times in seconds in those runs out of 10 where K independent tours can be found. We have taken $p = 3$ for H2, H4 and H6. We have reported the results in nine different tables. Tables 1, 2 and 3 report the results of heuristics H1, H2, H3, H4, H5 and H6 with $K = 3$ for small, medium and large sized instances respectively. Tables 4, 5 and 6 present the results of these six heuristics with $K = 6$ for small, medium and large sized instances respectively. Tables 7, 8 and 9 report the results of heuristics H1, H2, H3, H4, H5 and H6 when $K=9$ and for small, medium and large sized instances respectively. In these 9 tables, entries marked '–' are the ones where the concerned heuristic fails to find K independent tours in all the 10 runs. Entries with parenthesis ('()') are the ones where the concerned heuristic finds K independent tours in less than 10 runs and

Table 9. Results for $K = 9$ on large sized instances

Instance	Nodes	K = 9											
		H1		H2		H3		H4		H5		H6	
		Avg	Time	Avg	Time	Avg	Time	Avg	Time	Avg	Time	Avg	Time
gr431	431	**3975759.6**	0.0019	4382250	0.0021	4155207.3	43.0815	4544203.6	0.4374	4112188.8	58.987	4548409	0.7084
pr439	439	**3062419.6**	0.0018	3421755.4	0.0021	–	–	3532994.7	0.8773	–	–	3525005.9	0.7451
d493	493	**826907.5**	0.0028	909688.5	0.0025	861427.7	47.3183	937051.8	0.3706	859501.3	65.3211	936089.2	0.5188
att532	532	**677559.2**	0.0018	757430.2	0.0024	694222.6	0.9774	780143.4	0.1363	692186.1	0.6722	785422.3	0.076
u574	574	**961067.3**	0.0027	1067878.1	0.0025	1000854.5	15.7564	1099960.8	0.2004	995592.5	31.6188	1097160.3	0.1763
rat575	575	**165596.8**	0.0098	183700.4	0.0297	–	–	–	–	–	–	–	–
d657	657	**1199645.4**	0.0021	1336085.9	0.0029	1233672.1	0.6241	1379494.3	0.0731	1235963.4	1.1331	1380774.1	0.0614
gr666	666	**6663196.2**	0.0023	7376042.5	0.003	6824794.2	0.5838	7573964.6	0.0314	6820038.1	0.3508	7572414.1	0.0274
u724	724	**1057336.5**	0.0025	1186859.1	0.0042	1085828.3	1.3271	1218360.9	0.1991	1078359.5	0.4258	1222775.8	0.1995
rat783	783	**221394.9**	0.0307	246417.9	0.1025	–	–	–	–	–	–	–	–
nrw1379	1379	**1267829.9**	0.0073	1415032.2	0.0108	1310901.6	29.0039	1463223.4	10.7832	–	–	1466771.5	17.0534
fl1577	1577	**1115176.8(5)**	0.3297	1292629.7	0.1573	–	–	–	–	–	–	–	–
d1655	1655	**1913683**	0.0234	2131284.4	0.0229	–	–	–	–	–	–	–	–
vm1748	1748	**9076454.2**	0.0099	10366388.6	0.0137	9342000.9	1.0855	10662135.5	0.1158	9349660.9	1.4418	10652736.2	0.1852
u1817	1817	**2051521.8**	0.0464	2282584.3	0.3027	–	–	–	–	–	–	–	–
rl1889	1889	**10038729.9**	0.0153	11224445.9	0.0157	10306130.6	52.5283	11506710.2	0.1362	10360526.5	30.0319	11518476.9	0.2569

in such cases number inside the parenthesis provide the number of runs where K independent tours have been found. The results in bold font are the one where we have got the best results.

From these 9 tables, following observations can be made:

- H1 performed the best in terms of solution quality and running time both. Since in H1, the tours are build one-by-one in a greedy manner, and the objective as well is to minimize the total cost of all the tours, the tours will be built by selecting the best possible option in each step. This is the reason behind the best performance of H1. Also, while selecting the next edge immediately, the chances of availability of such an edge is more in comparison to those heuristics which build K tours in parallel. This in turn decreases the running time of this heuristic.
- H2 is able to build K independent tours for all the instances and for all the three values of K though for a few instances in less than 10 runs.
- GRASP based heuristics H2, H4 and H6 performed poorly in comparison to their respective pure greedy counterparts, namely H1, H3 and H5 respectively.
- Equal opportunity based heuristics H3 and H5 performed poorly in comparison to their non-equal opportunity counterpart H1. Likewise, equal opportunity based heuristics H4 and H6 performed poorly in comparison to their non-equal opportunity counterpart H2.
- Those heuristics which construct tours in parallel fail more often in finding K independent tours than those which constructs tours one-by-one.
- In Table 3, for the instance fl1577, 3 independent paths was obtained in only 6 runs.
- In some instances such as fl417, it has been observed that K independent paths were build in all the 10 runs while building one-by-one, but while building parallelly it did not yield any result. This might have happened because of not obtaining nearest neighbour from a particular node and having to start the entire route building process over and over again.

5   Conclusion and Future Work

KITTSP is a recently formulated problem for which no solution approach exists in the literature. In this paper, we have proposed six constructive heuristics, namely H1, H2, H3, H4, H5 and H6 for solving the KITTSP. We have evaluated the performance of these heuristics on a wide range of TSPLIB instances and presented a comparative analysis of their performance. It has been observed that H1 is giving better result for every case. As these heuristics are the maiden approaches for KITTSP, these heuristics will serve as baseline approaches for any approach developed in future to solve KITTSP.

As a future work, we would like to develop metaheuristic approaches for KITTSP. We also intend to develop a few local search based heuristics for this problem for use with our metaheuristic approaches. Performance of the constructive heuristics presented here can also be further improved by combining these heuristics with local search based heuristics.

References

1. Garey, M.R., Johnson, D.S.: Computers and Intractability: A Guide to the Theory of NP-Completeness. W. H. Freeman, San Francisco (1979)
2. Iwasaki, Y., Hasebe, K.: Ant colony optimization for K-independent average traveling salesman problem. In: Tan, Y., Shi, Y. (eds.) ICSI 2021. LNCS, vol. 12689, pp. 333–344. Springer, Cham (2021). https://doi.org/10.1007/978-3-030-78743-1_30
3. Lenstra, J.K., Kan, A.R.: Some simple applications of the travelling salesman problem. J. Oper. Res. Soc. **26**(4), 717–733 (1975)
4. Lin, S., Kernighan, B.W.: An effective heuristic algorithm for the traveling-salesman problem. Oper. Res. **21**(2), 498–516 (1973)
5. Matai, R., Singh, S.P., Mittal, M.L.: Traveling salesman problem: An overview of applications, formulations, and solution approaches. In: Traveling Salesman Problem, Theory and Applications. InTechOpen, London (2010)
6. Resende, Mauricio G. C., Ribeiro, Celso C.: Optimization by GRASP. Springer, New York (2016). https://doi.org/10.1007/978-1-4939-6530-4

A Comparative Study and Analysis of Time Series Forecasting Techniques for Indian Summer Monsoon Rainfall (ISMR)

Vikas Bajpai$^{(\boxtimes)}$ ⓘ, Tanvin Kalra, and Anukriti Bansal ⓘ

The LNM Institute of Information Technology, Jaipur, Rajasthan, India
vikas.bajpai87@gmail.com, anukriti1107@gmail.com

Abstract. The importance of monsoon rains cannot be looked over, as it has an impact on activities all year round, from agricultural to industrial. In the domains of water resource management and agriculture, accurate rainfall estimation and forecast is extremely useful in making crucial decisions. This study presents various deep learning approaches such as Multi-layer Perceptron, Convolutional Neutral Network, Long Short-Term Memory Networks, and Wide Deep Neural Networks to forecast the Indian summer monsoon rainfall (ISMR) (June–September) based on seasonal and monthly time scales. For modeling purposes, the ISMR time series data sets are divided into two categories: (1) training data (1871–1960) and (2) testing data (1961–2016). Statistical analyses reveal ISMR's dynamic nature, which couldn't be predicted accurately by statistical and mathematical models. Therefore, this study provides a comparative analysis that demonstrates the effectiveness of various algorithms to forecast ISMR. Moreover, it also weighs the result with established existing models.

Keywords: Rainfall prediction · Indian summer monsoon rainfall. · Deep learning · Multi-layer perceptron · 1D Convolutional Neural Networks · Stacked LSTM · Deep & wide monsoon rainfall prediction model

1 Introduction

India is an agriculture-based country with a heavy reliance on agricultural products in its economy. Indian farmers usually depend on the summer monsoon (June-September) rains for a better agricultural output. As a result, the amount of summer monsoon rainfall impacts the agricultural industry. The summer monsoon (June-September) rainfall affects around 65 percent of India's total cultivated land [1]. As a result, knowing the amount of rainfall expected during

---

V. Bajpai, T. Kalra and A. Bansal—The authors have contributed equally.

the summer monsoon (June - September) might assist Indian farmers in taking advantage of it. This knowledge will also aid them in preventing crop damage during periods of low rainfall. As a result, forecasting the amount of rainfall during the summer monsoon (June-September) is a key challenge in monsoon meteorology.

A number of authors have proposed several models for forecasting ISMR using time series data. Singh [2] for example, found that ISMR may be predicted using a time series data collection. Clark et al. [3] found that monsoon rainfall variability is mainly determined by sea surface temperature (SST). As a result, Chattopadhyay [4] used a feed-forward neural network (FFNN) to forecast the ISMR utilising SST anomalies and tropical rainfall indices as predictors. Using time series data, Chattopadhyay and Chattopadhyay (2008) [13] discovered a non-linear approach for forecasting the ISMR. To forecast the ISMR over India, Chattopadhyay and Chattopadhyay (2010) [14] developed a statistically based univariate model.

ISMR forecasting has been going on for over a century. Various statistical and mathematically based methods for ISMR forecasting are available in the literature (Barnston et al., 2010, Sinha et al., 2013). However, because of its nonlinear character and reliance on global factors or predictors (Singh et al., 2012), its predicting accuracy failed to meet expectations. The failure of these numerical models could be explained by the droughts of 2002, 2004 and 2009, which were not forecasted by the Indian Meteorological Department (IMD). These hybridize-based models need a lot of complex computer resources. As a result, numerous academics have attempted to use artificial neural networks (ANN) to forecast ISMR. Several types of neural networks can be found in the literature. However, in most ISMR forecasting applications, only feed-forward neural networks (FFNN) and back-propagation neural networks (BPNN) are used [5].

On a daily basis, several data repository centres throughout the world gather a massive amount of meteorological data. Our processing capacity was not as high a few years ago, and classic statistical methods, like spatial statistics, were also affected by significant computational weights. As a result, the raw data also wasn't thoroughly examined. However, in recent years, our capabilities have improved significantly, allowing us to analyse terabytes of spatio-temporal data on a vast scale.

This paper uses advanced deep learning models to solve the challenge of predicting ISMR employing monthly time series data in this work. For this, we applied various deep-learning based models like Multi-layer Perceptron, Convolutional Neutral Network, Long Short-Term Memory Networks and Wide Deep Neural Networks and compared their results with each other. ISMR data sets are used in this study for simulation and modelling.

The rest of the paper is organized as follows. Section 2, contains the details of the dataset used in this paper. Section 3 briefly explains time-series-based forecasting methods and the challenges associated with them. Architecture of various deep learning models used in this paper is explained in Sect. 4. Section 5 provides details of the experimental setup. Results are presented in Sect. 6. Finally, we conclude the paper in Sect. 7.

2 Data-Set Description and Statistical Analysis

ISMR runs from June to September in India. The primary goal of this study is to forecast rainfall levels for four months, namely June, July, August, and September, as well as seasonal. Because India is such a huge country with so many climate variations, large variations in monsoon rainfall amounts can be seen in different parts of the country. During the monsoon season, it is common to find certain locations with excessive rainfall and some areas with little rain in this country. As a result, storing all of these monsoon season fluctuations in a single time series data store is extremely time consuming. To tackle this problem, Mooley and Parthasarathy (1984) suggested using the arithmetic mean of all rainfall values from all meteorological stations in the area. As a result, Parthasarathy et al. (1992) and Pathasarathy et al. (1994) created a historical time series data set of rainfall amount in India by averaging all-India rainfall values and weighting each sub-divisional rain-fall area (306 well-distributed rain-gauges). For the period 1871–2014, this historical monthly time series data can be found in Pathasarathy et al. (1994) [6] (1871–1994) and IITM (2017) (1995–2014) for every month and seasonal.

Time series-based prediction models are based on the idea that the present value of a time series is always dependent on the values of preceding time series. Consequently, we use the previous months' rainfall quantity to forecast the current month's rainfall amount in this study. In this paper we experimented with the number of months utilised to forecast rainfall for the present month. For example, if the parameter's value is set to five, the preceding five months' (January to May of 1961) rainfall amounts of the corresponding year to predict rainfall amounts for the month of June 1961. For the period 1871–2014, all of these monthly and seasonal ISMR data sets were acquired from Pathasarathy et al. (1994) [6] (1871–1994) and the website (IITM, 2017) [7] (1995–2016).

To investigate the variability in the ISMR time series data, we conducted two statistical studies, namely mean and standard deviation (SD), spanning over the period of a year (January to December, 1871–2016). Table 1 shows the statistical values for these two analyses. The SD and mean values for this time period (1871 - 2016) are also presented in a bar chart for March to October which is shown in Fig. 1. The graph also shows that the most significant changes occur throughout the primary four months of the ISMR, namely June-September.

Table 1. Analyses of the ISMR time series data set for the years 1871–2016 using mean and standard deviation.

Statistics	Mar	Apr	May	Jun	Jul	Aug	Sep	Oct
Mean	15.23	26.44	52.73	163.06	272.53	242.23	170.34	77.53
SD	9.33	9.1	15.93	36.27	37.35	37.57	36.59	28.62

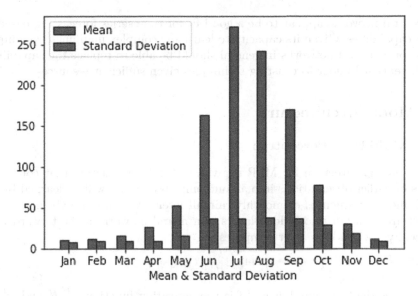

Fig. 1. Analyses of the ISMR time series data set for the years 1871–2016 using mean and standard deviation.

3   Time Series Based Forecasting of ISMR with Deep Learning

ISMR Forecasting based on time series data is a challenging task. Time series problems add the complication of order or temporal dependence between observations, in contrast to the more straightforward classification and regression issues. This might be challenging because the data must be handled carefully while fitting and assessing models. This temporal structure can help with modelling as well, offering extra structure like trends and seasonality that can be used to increase the performance of the model.

Time series forecasting using classical methods such as ARIMA suffer from some limitations, which are listed below:

- Incomplete data poses problems for the efficient functioning of classical methods.
- Classical methods often assume a linear relationship which excludes the possibility of identifying more complex joint distributions.

Deep learning neural networks can effectively learn arbitrary intricate mappings from inputs to outputs in addition to accommodating numerous inputs and output. Particularly on issues with complex-nonlinear relationships and multi-step forecasting, neural networks offer strong characteristics that demonstrate a lot of potential for time series forecasting. Moreover, Convolutional Neural Networks (CNNs) provide automatic feature learning which could hold enormous promise for the task of forecasting ISMR.

Neural networks appear to be a good fit for time series forecasting based on their capabilities. Given its capacity to learn any complex mappings from inputs to outputs, neural networks in general should be able to replace the capabilities of conventional linear forecasting techniques given sufficient resources.

4   Model Architecture

4.1   Multi-layer Perceptron

The model architecture for MLP is given in Fig. 2. A function that converts a series of earlier observations into an outcome observation will be learned by the MLP model. Sequences of monthly rainfall intensity values are given as input, which are then fed into hidden layers of a neural network in the forward pass. Typically, each hidden layer computes:

$$a^{(l+1)} = f(w^l.a^l + b^l) \tag{1}$$

where, l is the layer number and f is the activation function, a^l, b^l and w^l are the activations, bias and model weights at l^{th} layer [8].

The model consists of 2 hidden layers with 32 and 128 units of neurons respectively. Both of the layers use rectified linear units (ReLUs) as their activation function. We have also added Dropout layers in between the hidden layers to avoid over fitting. The sliding window that we have taken for our model is 60 months.

4.2   Convolutional Neural Networks

The model architecture selected for CNN is shown in Fig. 3. Sequences of monthly rainfall intensity values are given as input, which are then fed in the convolution layer. The output of one-dimensional convolutional layer with input size N_l is:

$$a_k^{(l+1)} = b_k^{(l+1)} + conv1D(w_{i,k}^l + a_i^l) \tag{2}$$

where, l is the layer number, $w_{(i,k)}^l$ is the kernel from the ith neuron at layer $l - 1$ to the kth neuron at layer l, a^l, b^l activations, bias at k^{th} layer [8]. A pooling layer is used to provide shift invariance by lowering the resolution of the feature maps after the convolutional layer. The model consists of two 1D convolution layers with 32 and 64 filter sizes of 1X3. Both of the layers use rectified linear units (ReLUs) as their activation function. Each CNN layer is followed by a MaxPooling layer with pool size of 2. The model also includes Dropout layers are inter - leaved between the convolution layers to avoid over fitting. The sliding window that we have taken for our model is 60 months.

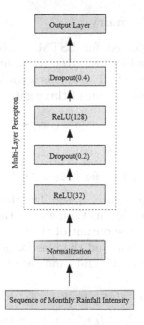

Fig. 2. Architecture of multi-layer perceptron (MLP) model

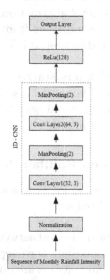

Fig. 3. Architecture of convolutional neural network (CNN) model

4.3 Long Short Term Memory

The model architecture selected for LSTM is given in Fig. 4. Sequences of monthly rainfall intensity values are given as input, which are then fed in the LSTM unit.The output of one LSTM unit is a combination of results produced by its components, where the output of three gates is as follows:

$$i_t = \sigma(w_i[h_{t-1}, x_t] + b_i) \tag{3}$$

$$f_t = \sigma(w_f[h_{t-1}, x_t] + b_f) \tag{4}$$

$$o_t = \sigma(w_o[h_{t-1}, x_t] + b_o) \tag{5}$$

where, o_t signifies the output gate, f_t signifies the forget gate, i_t signifies the input gate, σ represents sigmoid function. w_x are the weights for respective gate (x) neurons, h_{t-1} represents the output of the previous LSTM block. x_t and b_x denote the input at current step and the bias for gates (x) respectively.

The cell state at timestep t, C_t and candidate for cell state D_t are computed by:

$$C_t = tanh(w_c[h_{t-1}, x_t] + b_c) \tag{6}$$

$$D_t = f_t * C_{t-1} + i_t * D_t \tag{7}$$

To forecast ISMR, we have adopted a stacked LSTM architecture. This design is made up of several LSTM layers stacked one on top of the other.By increasing the depth of the model, new high-level abstraction representations can be created while integrating the learnt representations from earlier layers. This has led to the development of a more reliable method for solving challenging sequence prediction issues.

The setup contains 2 LSTM layers stacked on top of another with 16 and 32 units of neurons respectively. The model also includes Dropout layers inter - leaved between the LSTM units to avoid over fitting. The sliding window that we have taken for our model is 24 months.

4.4 Deep and Wide Monsoon Rainfall Prediction Model(DWRPM)

DWRPM, proposed by Bajpai et al [8] is a neural network consisting of two components which are described below:

Deep Component: A feed-forward neural network, specifically a multilayer per- ceptron (discussed in Sect. 3.1), makes up the deep component. In contrast to the wide component, high-dimensional features are obtained utilising this section.

Wide Component: Low-dimensional characteristics are extracted using the wide network. Convolutional networks (discussed in Sect. 3.2) are used as wide components in this work.

Joint training method is used to train the model, which simultaneously opti- mises all parameters by considering the weighted total of both components.

Figure 5 shows the network architecture chosen for DWRPM. We have chosen a 24-month sliding timeframe as our input length. A 1-D convolutional layer with

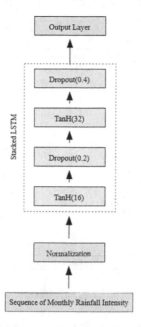

Fig. 4. Architecture of stacked LSTM model

100 1X12 filter sizes makes up the wide component. A layer using average pooling follows it. A feed-forward neural network with ReLU layers that have 36 and 64 units of neurons respectively, makes up the deep component.

5   Experimental Setup

5.1   Data Preprocessing

In order to make time-series prediction problem simpler to learn, it is a good idea to scale the target variable, particularly in the case of neural network models [9]. The learning process may become unstable as a result of a target variable with a wide range of values producing significant error gradient values that cause weight values to drastically shift.To solve this problem, we normalise all rainfall intensity values to numbers between 0 and 1, using the min-max approach. The min-max normalisation equation is represented as follows:

$$x_n = \frac{x - x_{min}}{x_{max} - x_{min}} \tag{8}$$

where, x_t represents the normalized value, signifies the actual value, x_{min} and x_{max} are the minimum and maximum values, respectively [10] (Fig. 6).

5.2   Implementation Details

The TensorFlow framework's Keras API [11] is used to program all of the different deep learning algorithms. The system arrangement features an Intel i7-8750H

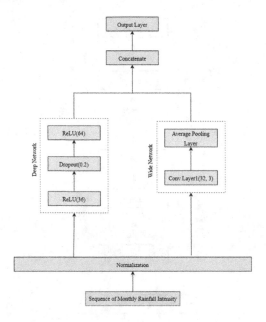

Fig. 5. Network architecture of DWRPM

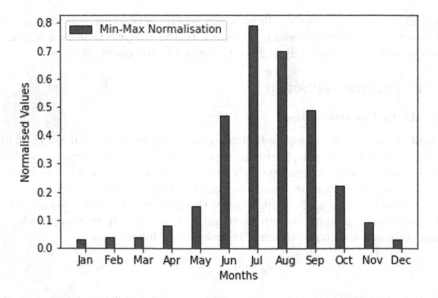

Fig. 6. Graphical visualization of min-max normalization.

computer processor paired with 16 GB of RAM and a GeForce GTX 1050 Ti GPU. The designing and execution setup of the suggested algorithms, followed by the results attained, are described in the following subsections.

We take into account various training windows with lengths ranging from 24 months to 120 months for the prediction of monthly rainfall during the monsoon season. In order to get the best accurate forecast results for the monsoon months of June, July, August, and September, we found that varying the training window from 24 to 60 months is essential.

5.3 Training and Test Sets

We performed the challenge of forecasting rainfall using the ISMR dataset. For the purposes of modelling and simulation, these data sets are separated into two components: (1) training data set from 1871 to 1960, and (2) testing data set from 1961 to 2016. The training set contains predictions from 1871 to 1960, while the testing set contains predictions from 1961 to 2016. Based on the time series values of the previous months, this study forecasts the time series values of the four primary months of ISMR-June, July, August, and September.

5.4 Evaluation Metrics

We employ mean absolute error (MAE) as the fundamental evaluation metrics to assess the overall accuracy of forecasts. Better prediction accuracy is indicated by low MAE values for the model.

$$MAE = \frac{1}{N} \sum_{i=1}^{N} |x_i - y_i| \tag{9}$$

where, N denotes the number of samples, x_t represents the actual rainfall of the i_{th} sample and y_t represents the corresponding prediction.

5.5 Model Training

Multi-layer Perceptron. Figure 2 depicts the MLP network configuration used in our experiments. As the input, the model receives sequences of normalised monthly rainfall intensity values. Two hidden layers with 32 and 128 units of neurons each make up the arrangement. ReLU serve as the activation function for both layers. In order to avoid the model being overfit, drop - out layers are inter - leaved between the hidden layers. We train using the Adam optimizer MSE loss function, which was explained in Sect. 4.4. Model is trained using a 16-batch size over 100 training iterations. In our experiments, we also used the trial-and-error method to optimise a variety of hyperparameters, including the batch size, number of neurons in hidden layers, number of epochs, and dropout rates.

Convolutional Neural Networks. The CNN network configuration used in our tests is shown in Fig. 3. Sequences of normalised monthly rainfall intensity values are provided to the model as input. The model has two 1D convolution layers with 1×3 filters in sizes 32 and 64. Rectified linear units (ReLUs) serve as the activation function for both layers. MaxPooling layer with a pool size of two follows each CNN layer. The Adam optimizer and MSE loss function is used for our training. Model is trained during 100 training iterations with a 32-batch size. In our trials, we additionally optimised the batch size, number of epochs, number of convolution layers, type of pooling layers, and dropout rates using the trial-and-error method.

Long Short Term Memory. Figure 4 depicts the LSTM network design we employed for our studies. The model receives a series of normalised monthly rainfall intensity values as input. Two LSTM layers, having 16 and 32 units of neurons respectively, are placed on top of one another in the model. To prevent over-fitting, dropout layers are interspersed between the LSTM units of the model. We have chosen a 24-month sliding timeframe for our concept.TanH operate as our model's activation function. For our training, we employ the MSE loss function and the Adam optimizer. With a 16-batch size, the model is trained across 100 training iterations. We also optimized the batch size, number of epochs, lstm units, number of neurons, and other factors during our trials.

Deep and Wide Monsoon Rainfall Prediction Model. Figure 5 depicts the DWRPM network configuration we employed for our tests. The model receives a series of normalised monthly rainfall intensity values as input. A 1D convolutional layer with 100 1 × 12 filter sizes makes up the wide component. A layer using average pooling follows it. A feed-forward neural network with ReLU layers that have 36 and 64 units of neurons respectively makes up the deep component. 500 training iterations with an 32-batch size are used to train the model. Adam optimizer and MSE loss function is used for our training. During our tests, we also used the trial-and-error method to optimize the batch size, number of epochs, number of neurons in the deep section, type of polling layer (Global and Average), number of filters in convolution layers, and dropout rates.

6   Results

The experimental study and comparison of the various deep learning methods discussed in the previous section are discussed as follows:

6.1   Multi-layer Perceptron

The prediction results for the monsoon months of June, July, August, and September are tabulated in Table 2. The visualizations for the same are also given in Fig. 7.

Table 2. Prediction results of MLP for the monsoon months.

Month	MAE
June	40.16
July	38.75
August	35.29
September	32.57
Overall	24.90

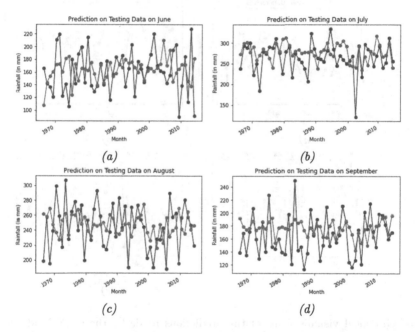

(a)   *(b)*

(c)   *(d)*

Fig. 7. Graphical visualizations of the predictions made by the MLP Model for the monsoon months. Blue line graph signifies the actual observations while the red line graph signifies the predicted results. (Color figure online)

6.2   Convolutional Neural Networks

Table 3 lists the forecast results for the monsoon months of June, July, August, and September. Figure 8 includes the visual representations for the same.

Table 3. Prediction results of CNN for the monsoon months.

Month	MAE
June	37.96
July	39.09
August	34.78
September	38.12
Overall	25.76

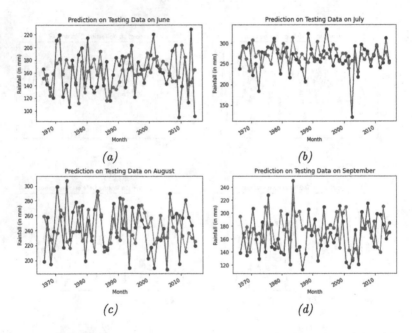

Fig. 8. Graphical visualisations of the predictions made by the CNN Model for the monsoon months. Blue line graph signifies the actual observations while the red line graph signifies the predicted results. (Color figure online)

6.3   Long Short Term Memory

The results for the monsoon months of June, July, August, and September are shown in Table 4. The same is visually represented in Fig. 9, as well.

Table 4. Prediction results of LSTM for the monsoon months.

Month	MAE
June	38.88
July	37.75
August	34.20
September	31.21
Overall	23.94

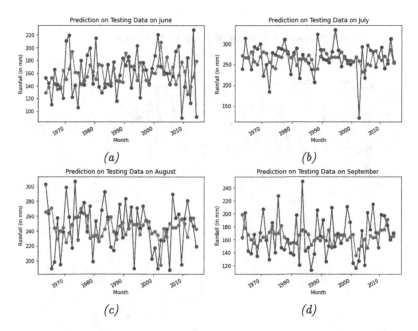

(a)   *(b)*

(c)   *(d)*

Fig. 9. Graphical visualizations of the predictions made by the LSTM Model for the monsoon months. Blue line graph signifies the actual observations while the red line graph signifies the predicted results. (Color figure online)

6.4 Deep and Wide Monsoon Rainfall Prediction Model

Table 5 displays the predictions for the monsoon months of June, July, August, and September.

Table 5. Results of the DWRPM's monsoon season predictions..

Month	MAE
June	44.67
July	53.27
August	40.09
September	35.28
Overall	30.13

Figure 10 shows a graphic representation of the same.

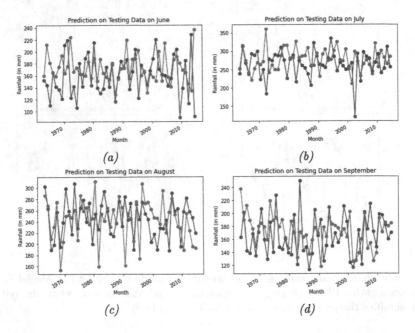

(a)   *(b)*

(c)   *(d)*

Fig. 10. Graphical visualizations of the predictions made by the DWRPM Model for the monsoon months. Blue line graph signifies the actual observations while the red line graph signifies the predicted results. (Color figure online)

7 Conclusion and Future Work

This study compares various time series forecasting deep-learning algorithms for the prediction of rainfall during the Indian Summer Monsoon (ISMR). We have used four algorithms for the task of rainfall prediction, namely: Multi-layer Perceptron, Convolutional Neural Network, Long Short Term Memory, and Deep & Wide Rainfall Prediction Model. The predicted and actual means for each algorithm for the monsoon months are shown in the tables below.

Table 6. Results of the MLP model where: (a) shows the results for the training data-set. (b) shows the results for the testing data-set.

(a)			(b)		
Month	Predicted mean	Observed mean	Month	Predicted mean	Observed mean
Jun.	163.46	164.42	Jun.	163.18	160.54
Jul.	285.09	276.30	Jul.	277.15	263.91
Aug.	247.63	242.64	Aug.	246.91	244.26
Sep.	172.78	171.64	Sep.	176.06	164.73

Table 7. Results of the CNN model where: (a) shows the results for the training data-set. (b) shows the results for the testing data-set.

(a)			(b)		
Month	Predicted mean	Observed mean	Month	Predicted mean	Observed mean
Jun.	161.10	164.42	Jun.	160.77	160.54
Jul.	271.86	276.30	Jul.	269.89	263.91
Aug.	242.99	242.64	Aug.	241.68	244.26
Sep.	169.32	171.64	Sep.	173.30	164.73

Table 8. Results of the LSTM model where: (a) shows the results for the training data-set. (b) shows the results for the testing data-set.

(b)			(b)		
Month	Predicted mean	Observed mean	Month	Predicted mean	Observed mean
Jun.	161.56	164.87	Jun.	158.71	159.10
Jul.	268.25	276.88	Jul.	263.73	264.44
Aug.	244.33	241.94	Aug.	245.09	245.70
Sep.	163.02	172.41	Sep.	164.25	164.99

From the observations made by the Tables 6, 7, 8 and 9, we can conclude the stacked LSTM implementation predicted the rainfall intensity for the testing data most efficiently. In addition to this, as Table 10 shows Stacked LSTM

Table 9. Results of the DWRPM model where: (a) shows the results for the training data-set. (b) shows the results for the testing data-set.

(a)			(a)		
Month	Predicted mean	Observed mean	Month	Predicted mean	Observed mean
Jun.	167.86	164.87	Jun.	171.57	159.10
Jul.	280.49	276.88	Jul.	276.61	264.44
Aug.	244.59	241.94	Aug.	242.68	245.70
Sep.	173.81	172.41	Sep.	171.27	164.99

Table 10. Comparison of Actual Mean(mm) with Forecasted Mean (mm) made by different deep learning algorithms and existing models for testing data

Month	Actual mean (mm)	MLP	CNN	LSTM	DWRPM	Singh and Borah [5]
Jun.	159.1	163.18	160.77	158.71	167.42	158.03
Jul.	264.45	277.15	269.89	263.735	273.98	261.06
Aug.	244.7	246.91	241.68	245.09	235.96	240.02
Sep.	164.99	176.06	173.301	164.25	163.75	164.2

architecture also out-performs the model proposed by Singh and Borah [5]. Although, the accuracy of DWRPM was less than the MLP and CNN models, we can't conclude that DWRPM model doesn't perform well for time series forecasting. This is due to the fact the DWRPM overfitted to the training data-set. This is signified by the RMSE for the DWRPM for the training data - set which is *5.31*.

7.1   Scope of Further Work

To further improve forecast accuracy, we intend to integrate more rainfall parameters in the future. In addition, we also intend to fine-tune models to prevent over-fitting, as was the case with DWRPM. We would also broaden the hunt for deep-learning techniques that can be applied to time-series forecasting applications such as transformers [12].

References

1. Swaminathan, M.S., Koteswaram, P.: First memorial lecture-23rd March 1998, climate and sustainable food security. Vayu Mandal **28**, 3–10 (1998)
2. Singh, C.V.: Long term estimation of monsoon rainfall using stochastic models. Int. J. Climatol. **18**(14), 1611–1624 (1998)
3. Clark, C.O., Cole, J.E., Webster, P.J.: Indian ocean SST and Indian summer rainfall: predictive relationships and their decadal variability. J. Clim. **13**(14), 2503–2519 (2000)

4. Chattopadhyay, S.: Feed forward artificial neural network model to predict the average summer-monsoon rainfall in India. Acta Geophys. **55**, 369–382 (2007). https://doi.org/10.2478/s11600-007-0020-8
5. Singh, P., Borah, B.: Indian summer monsoon rainfall prediction using artificial neural network. Stoch. Environ. Res. Risk Assess **27**, 1585–1599 (2013). https://doi.org/10.1007/s00477-013-0695-0
6. Pathasarathy, B., Munot, A.A., Kothawale, D.R.: All India monthly and seasonal rainfall series: 1871–1993. Theor. Appl. Climatol. **49**, 217–224 (1994)
7. ITM, Homogeneous Indian Monthly Rainfall Data Sets (2017). http://www.tropmet.res.in/
8. Bajpai, V., Bansal, A.: A Deep and Wide Neural Network-based Model for Rajasthan Summer Monsoon Rainfall (RSMR) Prediction (2021). https://doi.org/10.48550/arXiv.2103.02157
9. Shanker, M., Hu, M.Y., Hung, M.S.: Effect of data standardization on neural network training. Omega **24**(4), 385–397 (1996)
10. Gopal Krishna Patro, S., Sahu, K.K.: Normalization: a preprocessing Stage (2015). https://doi.org/10.48550/arXiv.1503.06462
11. Chollet, F., et al.: Keras (2015). https://github.com/fchollet/keras
12. Vaswani, A., et al.: Attention is all you need. arxiv.org/abs/1706.03762 (2017)
13. Chattopadhyay, S., Chattopadhyay, G.: Comparative study among different neural net learning algorithms applied to rainfall time series. Met. Apps. **15**, 273–280 (2008). https://doi.org/10.1002/met.71
14. Chattopadhyay, S., Chattopadhyay, G.: Univariate modelling of summer-monsoon rainfall time series: comparison between ARIMA and ARNN. Comptes Rendus Geosci. **342**(2), 100–107 (2010). https://doi.org/10.1016/j.crte.2009.10.016

YOLOv4 Vs YOLOv5: Object Detection on Surveillance Videos

Nikita Mohod[1,2](✉) [ID], Prateek Agrawal[1] [ID], and Vishu Madaan[1] [ID]

[1] School of Computer Science and Engineering, Lovely Professional University, Phagwara, Punjab, India
nikita.mohod@gmail.com, dr.agrawal.prateek@gmail.com,
prateek.agrawal@lpu.co.in
[2] SIPNA College of Engineering and Technology, Amravati, Maharashtra, India

Abstract. Now-a-days, Object detection algorithms becomes more popular because of their significant contribution to the field of computer vision. Object detection algorithms are divided into two approaches i) region-based approach and ii) region-free approach. In this paper, we implemented YOLOv4 and YOLOv5 techniques of region-free approach due to their high detection speed and accuracy. The objective of this paper is to identify the relevant and non-relevant parts of surveillance videos as watching entire video footage is a time-consuming process. The use case for this research work is ATM surveillance footage, where the dataset is publicly not available, to train the network we developed our data set and then train and compare the proposed models. After experimental results, it is observed that YOLOv5 archives 84% accuracy and give better results than YOLOv4 which achieve 56% accuracy only.

Keywords: Video surveillance · Object detection · YOLO · DarkNet · Pytorch

1 Introduction

Over the past few decades, the use of Video surveillance popularly known as CCTV (closed circuit television) increases rapidly. For the purpose of safety and security in indoor and outdoor environments, surveillance cameras becomes an essential component of daily life. The benefits of video surveillance include effective monitoring, fewer resource requirements, affordable monitoring abilities, and the flexibility to implement new security protocols. Many sectors such as banks, ATM-machine, shops and multiplexes, city roads and highways, government offices, classrooms and universities, etc. used surveillance system for monitoring purposes.

In this paper, we used ATM surveillance footage as a use case to detect the objects in a video and then determine the relevant and non-relevant frames of videos. The surveillance cameras present in an ATM room produced unusually long videos. As CCTV present in the ATM room captured 24*7 surveillance

I. Woungang et al. (Eds.): ANTIC 2022, CCIS 1798, pp. 654–665, 2023.
https://doi.org/10.1007/978-3-031-28183-9_46

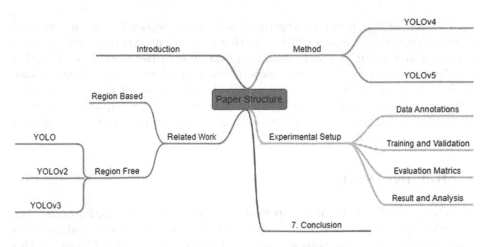

Fig. 1. Diagrammatic representation of the paper

footage, it is noted that just a small portion of the transaction activity took place in an ATM room during those hours, and the remaining surveillance only showed the constant object (i.e. ATM Machine). Hence, there is a need to detect relevant and non-relevant parts of surveillance videos, so that time required to monitor the entire surveillance video may be reduced. Relevant frames of video are those frames where some activity is performed for example withdrawing money from an ATM or robbery etc. while non-relevant frames mean where only a steady object ATM machine is visible(no activity seen). To identify the relevant and non-relevant parts of surveillance videos object detection plays a vital role. Object detection (OD) is a technique in computer vision that is used to detect the object in videos.

From the last decades, deep learning (DL) based OD techniques achieved remarkable success. OD algorithms using neural network techniques give promising results as compared to traditional methods. A good detection algorithm must have ability to determine semantic cues as well as spatial information in the image. Currently, DL based OD algorithms are categorized into two parts: 1) region-based methods and 2) region-free methods. RCNN [4], Fast-RCNN [3], Faster-RCNN [16], Mask RCNN [5] are the popular algorithms region-based method while You only look once (YOLO) and its variant [11,13,14] are examples of region free method. The main contributions of our paper are listed as follows:

i) We propose a DL-based approach to determine the relevant and non-relevant parts in surveillance videos.
ii) We present a comparison of region-free approaches YOLOv4 and Yolov5 on surveillance videos in terms of evaluation metrics.

The rest of the paper is structured as follows. Section 2 gives a review of object detection techniques which is further divided into two parts region-based approach and region-free approach. Section 3 explain the working of YOLOv4 and YOLOv5 models, to detect relevant and non-relevant part of surveillance videos. Section 4 gives information about the generation of data-set (labeling and annotation) and gives a broader comparison of the used approach in terms of evaluation metrics and Sect. 5 concludes our research work. Figure 1 gives a diagrammatic review of our paper.

2   Related Work

Detecting objects is the first step in many computer vision applications. Face detection, pedestrian detection, logo detection, video detection, vehicle detection, and medical image detection are vital applications of OD. Currently, DL-based object detection algorithms are categorized into two parts: 1) region-based methods and 2) region-free methods. Region-free algorithms are substantially more time-efficient and have greater applicability to real-time object detection, while region-based methods achieve better detection efficiency and surpass state-of-the-art results on public benchmarks.

2.1   Region-Based Approach

The region-based approach is divided into two parts: i) region proposal generation and ii) making a prediction of the proposed region. Hence, this approach is also termed a two-stage detector. In the first phase, the detector determines the region containing the object using a bounding box while in the second phase detector identifies the object with a categorization label using a neural network approach. This section gives a review of the most successful region-based approach.

In 2014 Girschik proposed R-CNN [4] which outperformed traditional approaches significantly and achieves 53.7% mAP. The architecture of RCNN is divided into three steps i) region proposal- generate sparse set proposal using selective search ii) feature extraction- extract fixed length feature vector from each proposal and iii) region classification- set of support vector machine (SVM) classifier. However, R-CNN faces two major limitations related to being extremely time-consuming for training and testing and relying on selective search to generate high-quality proposals. He et al. proposed SPP-net [6] which stepped up the concept of R-CNN by removing the cropping and warping part. This model computes the feature from the entire image with the help of a deep convolutional network (CNN) and extracts fixed-length feature vectors on the feature map by spatial pyramid pooling (SPP). These extracted features are fed into the SVM classifier and bounding box regression., SPP-net performs better as compared to R-CNN but due to multistage training, unable to optimize a region-free approach. Girschik and his team present Fast-RCNN [3] which overcomes the limitations of R-CNN and SPP net in terms of training and testing time, and detection accuracy. Faster R-CNN [16] introduces the concept of RoIPool to extract features from each bounding box, followed by classification. With the concept of "less channels with more layers" Hong et al. [9] revised the feature extraction part in Faster R-CNN.

To enable object detection in feature maps at different scales, Lin et al. [10] proposed feature pyramid networks (FPN). FPN uses a top-down architecture with lateral connections and made considerable progress in detecting multi-scale objects. In 2017 He et al. [5] introduces the concept of Mask R-CNN which performs three task simultaneously for a very first time. Mask R-CNN extends the spirit of Faster R-CNN by adding a branch for predicting segmentation masks on each Region of Interest, in parallel with the existing branch of classification and bounding box regression. To locates objects by predicting grid points at the pixel level, Lu et al. [12] proposed grid R-CNN which is a better alternative for regression based localization methods. Yang et al. [20] introduced a novel algorithm called Mask-Track R-CNN which jointly performs the detection, segmentation and tracking tasks simultaneously. In addition, proposed new approach which combines single-frame instance segmentation and object tracking, with the goal of providing some preliminary research into this issue.

Chen et al. [2] proposed a model Mask Lab: which produces three outputs: box detection, semantic segmentation, and direction prediction. MaskLab performs foreground/background segmentation within each region of interest by integrating semantic and path prediction. Wang et al. [18] proposed a novel technique called the moving-object proposals generation and prediction framework (MPGP) to reduce the searching space and produce some reliable proposals which minimized the computation cost. In addition, explore the relationship between moving regions in feature maps of various layers and predict candidates based on the results of previous frames. MPNET shows superior performance in average precision.

2.2   Region-Free Approach

As compared to region-based algorithms, region-free algorithms do not have a distinct step for proposal generation. However, they attempt to categorize each area of the region as either background or a target object depending on every point on the image that is often thought of as a possible object. YOLO and its variants are examples of region-free approaches which are summarized in detail in this section.

YOLO. [13] speed up the detection process and improves object detection efficiency. YOLO treated object detection as a regression problem, by dividing the entire image into a fixed number of grid cells and predicting locations based on these grids. YOLO could predict at 45 frames per second and hit 155 frames per second. On the other hand, YOLO suffers from some limitations: i) it identifies only two items at a time, making small objects and crowded objects difficult to detect. ii) only the last function map was used for prediction, which was insufficient for predicting objects at various scales and aspect ratios.

YOLOv2. [14] is a real-time process that integrates detection and classification to identify over 9000 object categories in real-time. Yolov2 performs better than YOLO as it accelerates network convergence and increases the capacity for network generalization using batch normalization techniques. Develops high-resolution classifiers to handle images with more resolution. To address the YOLO objects poor generalization capacity for multiple aspect ratios. In YOLOv2, the concept of an anchor is added, and each grid cell can forecast three scales and three aspect ratios. Researcher jana and his team [7] used YOLOv2 to detect and classify objects of recorded videos to enhance processing and computation speed.

YOLOv3. [15] inherits the principle of YOLO and YOLOv2 enhances their flaws in order to maintain a balance between speed and accuracy. The authors modify YOLO to YOLOV3 by combining the residual block, FPN, and binary cross entropy loss which also enhances the predicted probability. For feature extraction, YOLOv3 uses the Darknet-53 network, which employs 53 convolutional layers. Instead of using a softmax classifier, YOLOv3 uses logistic regression to predict the object class for each bounding box. Saturation, hue, exposure, blur, cropping, and aspect ratio data augmentation techniques can be used with YOLOv3 models. Several researchers changed the original models by changing the number and type of convolution layers. YOLOv3 can identify boxes at various scales with the help of three separate YOLO classifier layers. The Darknet-19 architecture, which utilizes 19 CNN, is the backbone of YOLOv3-tiny. YOLOv3-tiny uses two YOLO classifier layers to predict boxes at two distinct scales. Many researchers used YOLOv3 architecture to perform object detection, Tian et.al. [17] used to detect apples in the orchard at different growth stages while Wu et.al [19] used to detect helmets of workers at the construction site.

3   Methods

3.1   YOLOv4

YOLOv4 [1] published in April 2020 with a number of improvements in YOLOv3 and used cross-stage partial connections (CSP) Darknet-53 as a baseline. Bag-of-freebies and bag-of-specials methods used for detector training added a star to the performance of YOLOv4 as compared to YOLOv3. Bag-of-freebies methods are used in both the backbone and head part but as the task of both are different so the techniques are also varied. For backbone, cut mix and cutout, mosaic data augmentation (combination of four different training images in some ratio), drop block regularization and class label smoothing were used and for backbone, it uses mish activation, CSP and multi-input weight residual connection. The input data is divided into two categories using CSP: the first set is processed by the convolutional layer (DenseNet), and the other set bypasses CNN and is used as input for the next layer. Used of DenseNet architecture solves the problem of vanishing gradient and also improves the learning capacity of CNN.

Spatial pyramid pooling (SPP) is used in the neck part of YOLOv4 while the head is composed of various YOLO layers. In order to optimize central point distance, overlap area and aspect ratio of predicted bounding box concept of complete IoU loss function used in YOLOv4 (Table 1).

Table 1. Comparison of YOLO architecture

	YOLOv3	YOLOv4	YOLOv5
Backbone	Darknet53	CSPDarknet53	CSPDarknet53
Head	YOLO Layer	YOLO Layer	YOLO Layer
Neck	FPN	SPP and PANet	PANet
Loss function	MSE	CIoU	GIoU

3.2 YOLOv5

YOLOv5 [8] is unique from earlier editions. Rather than Darknet, it uses the PyTorch framework and then CSPDarknet53 as a backend. This backend eliminates the issue of redundant gradient information seen in large backbones and incorporates gradient change into feature maps, which speeds up inference, improves accuracy, and minimizes the size of the model by reducing the number of parameters. It enhances the information flow using the path aggregation network (PANet) as a neck. PANet uses the concept of FPN which enhances model propagation for low-level features. Furthermore, YOLOv5 uses the same head as YOLOv4 and YOLOv3, which results in three distinct feature map outputs for multi-scale prediction. Additionally, it improves the model's ability to predict small objects effectively. Initially, for feature extraction input is given to CSP-Darknet53 and then to PANet for feature fusion at last yolo layer generates the desired output. YOLOv5 uses SPP as a pooling layer to free the network from its fixed size constraint.

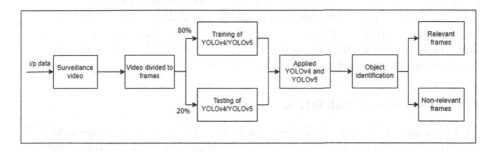

Fig. 2. Flowchart of implemented method

Figure 2 gives pictorial representation of implemented method. Here, surveillance video is taken as input and then it is divided into the frames, 80% of the frames used for training while 20% used for testing purpose. YOLOv4 and YOLOv5 methods were implemented on prepare dataset and then depending on the object identified in the frames, they are further divide into relevant and non-relevant frames.

4   Experimental-Setup

As the use case for this research work is ATM surveillance, and the data set is not publicly available. For developing the data set initially, the surveillance videos are divided into frames and then labeling and annotation of frames were done which are explained further. Pytorch was utilized for YOLOv5 training, whereas the Darknet framework was used for YOLOv4 training. For further processing and comparison on evaluation Google Colaboratory (Colab) was used (Table 2).

Table 2. Experimental requirement

Requirements	Details
Operating system	windows11
Programming language	Python3.7
GPU	NVIDIA GeForce
Architecture	DarkNet and pytorch

4.1   Data Annotations

An essential part of deep learning is data annotation (labeling) which directly influences the model's ability to train itself. Annotation of data frames was done using the makesense.ai which is open-source software that supports multiple label types. We have 3160 frames which are divided into two sets:- train and validation, 80% of the data frames are used for training and the remaining 20% for validation purposes. Figure 3 represents how the annotation of the frame is done. Here we define three classes person, chair and ATM machine to determine the relevant and non-relevant frames of the video.

4.2   Training and Validation

YOLOv4 and YOLOv5 both the models were trained using mentioned ATM surveillance dataset. The pre-trained weights provided by the YOLO developers were used for the training operations. YOLOv4 were trained for 5000 epochs while YOLOv5 was trained for 60 epochs as different models need different iteration. Training hyperparameters were calibrated individually for each model and to optimize performance during training, hyperparameters can be modified

Fig. 3. Annoation of the frame using makesense.ai

in the YOLO config file. The config file contains information about the batch size as well as the size of the re-sampled images used during training. A batch size of 64 images was used to train the YOLOv4 detector while a batch size of 3 was selected for YOLOv5 due to the model's increased complexity (Figs. 4 and 5).

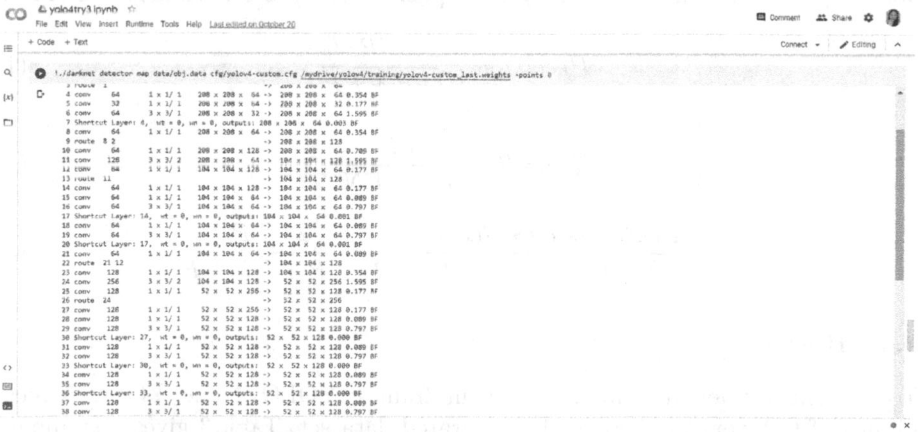

Fig. 4. Code snippet of YOOLOv4 representing the training of model

4.3 Evaluation Metrics

Evaluation metrics for YOLO and its variant is F1 score and mAP (mean average precision). Precision and recall values are used to determine the F1 score and mAP. The F1 score has a maximum value of 1, which denotes perfect precision

Fig. 5. Code snippet of YOOLOv5 representing the training of model

and recall, and a minimum value is 0, which denotes either zero precision or zero recall. Additionally, mAP is determined by taking the mean of the average precision (AP) for all classes. By calculating the mean of AP, one can then determine mAP. Precision defines the accuracy of prediction while recall measure how well your model determines all the positives. To determine precision and recall we have to determine the confusion matrix which is the combination of true positive (TP), true negative (TN), false positive (FP) and false negative (FN).

$$Precision = \frac{TP}{TP + FP} \tag{1}$$

$$Recall = \frac{TP}{TP + FN} \tag{2}$$

$$F1 = \frac{2 * Precision * Recall}{Precision + Recall} = \frac{2 * TP}{2 * TP + FP + FN} \tag{3}$$

4.4 Results

To determine relevant and non-relevant frames, YOLOv4 and YOLOv5 techniques of OD were applied to the generated data set. Table 3 gives a summary of the comparison of both approaches on surveillance data-set. It is observed that Yolov5 performs better and has good computation time on surveillance data as compared to Yolov4. We train YOLOv5 in the PyTorch framework and YOLOv4 in the Darknet framework. As both the models use SPPNet, they generated the fixed data output image, YOLOv4 generates 512×512 and YOLOv5 generates 384×640. The training time for YOLOv4 is maximum as compared to YOLOv5. Figure 5 gives output YOLOv5 in the form of a graph on the generated dataset (Fig. 6).

Table 3. Comparison of YOLOv4 Vs YOLOv5

YOLOv4	Vs	YOLOv5
Precision	0.567	0.849
Recall	0.779	0.996
F1	0.655	0.915
mAP	0.782	0.994

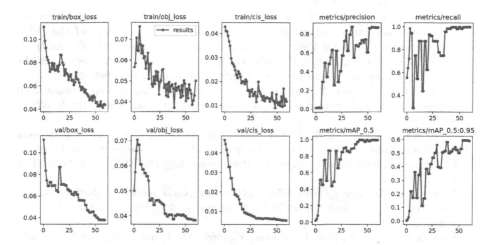

Fig. 6. Result of YOLOv5 on ATM surveillance

5   Conclusion and Future Scope

For safety, security and monitoring the demand for surveillance cameras increases rapidly. Hence, there is a need to identify relevant and non-relevant parts of surveillance videos using the object detection technique of computer vision to save time. We used ATM surveillance videos as a dataset to implement the two novel methods of the YOLO variant i.e. YOLOv4 and YOLOv5. ATM surveillance footage contains very less amount of transaction activity, so there is a need to separate the relevant and non-relevant parts of videos. In this paper, we implement object detection techniques to save time of monitoring by watching only relevant parts of videos. Because of high accuracy and good detection speed, YOLOv4 and YOLOv5 models gives promising results. After an extensive experiment, it is observed that YOLOv5 gives a promising result as compared to YOLOv4.

In the future, we study and deal with the difference between the accuracies of YOLOv4 and YOLOv5. We also consider the issue of an imbalance between negative and positive samples when the majority of samples are negative and then compared the work with state-of-the-art works in terms of computational time and space.

References

1. Bochkovskiy, A., Wang, C.Y., Liao, H.Y.M.: Yolov4: optimal speed and accuracy of object detection. arXiv preprint arXiv:2004.10934 (2020)
2. Chen, L.C., et al.: Masklab: instance segmentation by refining object detection with semantic and direction features. In: Proceedings of the IEEE Conference on Computer Vision and Pattern Recognition, pp. 4013–4022 (2018)
3. Girshick, R.: Fast r-cnn. In: Proceedings of the IEEE International Conference on Computer Vision, pp. 1440–1448 (2015)
4. Girshick, R., Donahue, J., Darrell, T., Malik, J.: Rich feature hierarchies for accurate object detection and semantic segmentation. In: Proceedings of the IEEE Conference on Computer Vision and Pattern Recognition, pp. 580–587 (2014)
5. He, K., Gkioxari, G., Dollár, P., Girshick, R.: Mask r-cnn. In: Proceedings of the IEEE International Conference on Computer Vision, pp. 2961–2969 (2017)
6. He, K., Zhang, X., Ren, S., Sun, J.: Spatial pyramid pooling in deep convolutional networks for visual recognition. IEEE Trans. Pattern Anal. Mach. Intell. **37**(9), 1904–1916 (2015)
7. Jana, A.P., Biswas, A., et al.: Yolo based detection and classification of objects in video records. In: 2018 3rd IEEE International Conference on Recent Trends in Electronics, Information & Communication Technology (RTEICT), pp. 2448–2452. IEEE (2018)
8. Jocher, G.: ultralytics/yolov5: v6.0 - YOLOv5n 'Nano' models, Roboflow integration, TensorFlow export, OpenCV DNN support (2021). https://doi.org/10.5281/zenodo.5563715
9. Kim, K.H., Hong, S., Roh, B., Cheon, Y., Park, M.: Pvanet: deep but lightweight neural networks for real-time object detection. arXiv preprint arXiv:1608.08021 (2016)
10. Lin, T.Y., Dollár, P., Girshick, R., He, K., Hariharan, B., Belongie, S.: Feature pyramid networks for object detection. In: Proceedings of the IEEE Conference on Computer Vision and Pattern Recognition, pp. 2117–2125 (2017)
11. Liu, W., et al.: SSD: single shot multibox detector. In: Leibe, B., Matas, J., Sebe, N., Welling, M. (eds.) ECCV 2016. LNCS, vol. 9905, pp. 21–37. Springer, Cham (2016). https://doi.org/10.1007/978-3-319-46448-0_2
12. Lu, X., Li, B., Yue, Y., Li, Q., Yan, J.: Grid r-cnn. In: Proceedings of the IEEE/CVF Conference on Computer Vision and Pattern Recognition, pp. 7363–7372 (2019)
13. Redmon, J., Divvala, S., Girshick, R., Farhadi, A.: You only look once: unified, real-time object detection. In: Proceedings of the IEEE Conference on Computer Vision and Pattern Recognition, pp. 779–788 (2016)
14. Redmon, J., Farhadi, A.: Yolo9000: better, faster, stronger. In: Proceedings of the IEEE Conference on Computer Vision and Pattern Recognition, pp. 7263–7271 (2017)
15. Redmon, J., Farhadi, A.: Yolov3: An incremental improvement. arXiv preprint arXiv:1804.02767 (2018)
16. Ren, S., He, K., Girshick, R., Sun, J.: Faster r-cnn: towards real-time object detection with region proposal networks. Adv. Neural Inf. Process. Syst. **28** (2015)
17. Tian, Y., Yang, G., Wang, Z., Wang, H., Li, E., Liang, Z.: Apple detection during different growth stages in orchards using the improved yolo-v3 model. Comput. Electron. Agric. **157**, 417–426 (2019)

18. Wang, H., Wang, P., Qian, X.: MPNET: an end-to-end deep neural network for object detection in surveillance video. IEEE Access **6**, 30296–30308 (2018)
19. Wu, F., Jin, G., Gao, M., Zhiwei, H., Yang, Y.: Helmet detection based on improved yolo v3 deep model. In: 2019 IEEE 16th International Conference on Networking, Sensing and Control (ICNSC), pp. 363–368. IEEE (2019)
20. Yang, L., Fan, Y., Xu, N.: Video instance segmentation. In: Proceedings of the IEEE/CVF International Conference on Computer Vision, pp. 5188–5197 (2019)

Author Index

Printed in the United States
by Baker & Taylor Publisher Services